CONTENTS

PART ONE: THE ECONOMIC PROBLEM

PART TWO: MARKETS

PART THREE: FACTOR MARKETS

PART FOUR: EFFICIENCY, MARKET FAILURE AND GOVERNMENT INTERVENTION

PART FIVE: THE NATIONAL AND INTERNATIONAL ECONOMY

PART SIX: FIRMS AND THEIR OBJECTIVES

PART SEVEN: MARKET PERFORMANCE

PART EIGHT: INTERNATIONAL TRADE

PART NINE: MACROECONOMIC PROBLEMS AND POLICIES

PART TEN: TOPICS IN ECONOMICS

PREFACE TO THE SEVENTH EDITION

George Stanlake's *Introductory Economics* has proved to be deservedly popular with students for its comprehensive coverage, clarity of language and real world examples. In this new edition I have sought to retain these features whilst taking into account the philosophy and coverage of the new A level specifications and developments in the economy, government policy and economic theory. This has involved editing chapters, writing some new chapters, rearranging some of the material, updating tables, facts and figures and including some new topics.

A major new feature of this edition is the inclusion of a variety of types of question — short, multiple choice, data response, case study and essay — at the end of each chapter. These questions can be used to assess understanding and to practise applying economic concepts and theories to problems and real world issues.

As with the previous editions, the aim is to cover the specifications of all examining boards and to assist students to develop a clear and critical understanding of economic concepts, theories, how the economy works and current economic issues.

My work on this edition has been greatly assisted by the patience and very useful suggestions of Andrew Thraves and by the support of Sheila Stanlake.

S.J.G.
June 1999

PART ONE: THE ECONOMIC PROBLEM

I THE NATURE, SCOPE AND METHODS OF ECONOMICS

THE INDIVIDUAL AND SOCIETY

Most introductory textbooks of Economics begin by asking the question 'What is Economics about?' Although Economics is a vast subject and precise definitions are usually complex and controversial, it is not a difficult matter to give a simple and sensible answer to this basic question. Economics is essentially a study of the ways in which people provide for their well-being. Economists are concerned with the study of 'human behaviour as a relationship between ends and scarce means which have alternative uses' (Lionel Robbins).

MICRO AND MACROECONOMICS

Economics can be divided into microeconomics and macroeconomics. Microeconomics is the study of individual markets. (A market is an arrangement which links buyers and sellers.) For instance, an economist may study the market for compact discs. This will involve looking at the decisions and behaviour of people who buy compact discs, the firms that sell the compact discs and any other groups which influence the price and availability of compact discs, such as the government. While macroeconomics is the study of the whole economy. It includes, for example, the study of the nature, causes, consequences of unemployment, inflation, economic growth and international trade and government policy.

WANTS AND NEEDS

Economics, both macro- and microeconomics, is about the satisfaction of wants. It is necessary to be quite clear about this; it is people's wants rather than their needs which provide the motive for economic activity. People go to work in order to obtain an income which will buy them the things they want rather than the things they need. It is not possible to define 'need' in terms of any particular quantity of a product, because this would imply that a certain level of consumption is 'right' for an individual. Economists tend to avoid this kind of value judgement which tries to specify how much people ought to consume. It is assumed that individuals wish to enjoy as much well-being as possible, and if their consumption of food, clothing, entertainment and other goods and services is less than the amount required to give them complete satisfaction they will want more of them.

SCARCITY

Resources are scarce when they are insufficient to satisfy people's wants. Scarcity is a relative concept. It relates the extent of people's wants to their ability to satisfy those wants. Neither people's wants nor their ability to produce goods and services are constant. Most countries' productive potential is increasing but so is the appetite of their citizens for goods and services. When a certain living standard is reached, people strive for even better living conditions. A good example of this is health care. As medical science and technology advances, people expect more ailments to be treated. So scarcity is a feature of all societies from the poorest to the most affluent.

CHOICE

The resources available to satisfy people's wants are, at any time, limited in supply. As most people cannot have all the goods and services they want, they have to make choices. With no rise in income, if someone wants to buy, for instance, a new coat they may have to spend less on eating out for a while. Similarly with limited resources, if a country wishes to devote more resources to health care it will have to reduce the resources it devotes to, for example, education.

OPPORTUNITY COST

In considering scarcity and choice economists make use of opportunity cost. This is a very important concept in economics. It makes clear the true resource cost of any economic decision. For instance, building a new hospital may mean that the construction of a stretch of motorway has to be postponed. So opportunity cost is the cost in terms of the best alternative forgone. For example, if a person buys a watch it may cost £50 but what is more significant is what has to be given up to make the purchase. This may be the opportunity to purchase a pair of shoes or the opportunity to have extra leisure instead of working to earn the £50.

ECONOMIC AND FREE GOODS

In the case of the vast majority of goods and services, resources have to be used in order to produce them. For example, to provide health care requires the use of labour in the form of doctors and nurses, land on which the hospital is built and capital in the form of beds, operating tables, dialysis machines and other equipment. So the production of most goods and services involves an opportunity cost — the resources employed could be put to other uses. These products are called economic goods. However there are a few goods which do not involve an opportunity cost, for example sea water and sunshine. This is because they do not require resources to produce them — they are in existence naturally. These products are known as free goods.

ECONOMICS AS A SOCIAL SCIENCE

NORMATIVE AND POSITIVE STATEMENTS

In studying economics and a range of other subjects it is useful to distinguish between positive and normative statements. An understanding of the difference between the two types of statement helps people to appreciate the scope and limitations of economics.

Positive statements are those that deal only with facts. 'Hong Kong is now part of China', 'General Motors employs x number of workers', and 'Jane Smith obtained a grade A in Economics', are all positive statements. If a disagreement arises over a positive statement it can be settled by looking at the facts and seeing whether or not they support the statement. Positive statements must be either true or false, where the word 'true' is taken to mean 'consistent with facts'.

Normative statements usually include or imply the words 'ought' or 'should'. They reflect people's moral attitudes and are expressions of what some individual or group thinks ought to be done. 'Britain should join the single currency', 'more aid should be given to developing countries' and 'income should be distributed more equally', are all normative statements. These statements are based on value judgements and express views of what is 'good' or 'bad', 'right' or 'wrong'. Unlike positive statements, normative statements cannot be verified by looking at the facts. Disagreements about such statements are usually settled by voting on them.

SCIENTIFIC ENQUIRY

Scientific enquiry, as the term is generally understood, is confined to positive questions. It deals with those questions which can be verified or falsified by actual observations of the real world (i.e. by checking the facts).

One major objective of science is to develop theories. These are general statements or principles which describe and explain the relationships between things observed in the world. Theories are developed in an attempt to answer the question 'Why?'. Tides rise and fall at regular intervals of time, a city is afflicted by smog at certain times of the year, the price of strawberries falls sharply during the summer months. When some definite regular pattern is observed in the relationships between two or more things, and someone asks why this should be so, the search for a theory has begun.

SCIENTIFIC METHOD

In trying to produce an explanation of observed phenomena, scientific enquiry makes use of procedures which are common to all sciences. These procedures are called the scientific method.

The first step is to define the concepts to be used in such a way that they can be measured. This is necessary if a theory is to be tested against the facts. If the task is to discover a relationship between 'income' and 'consumption', these terms must be defined in a clearly understood manner.

The next step is to formulate a hypothesis. This is an untested statement which attempts to explain how one thing is related to another. For example, an economist asked to say why prices vary over time might offer the hypothesis that changes in prices are caused by changes in the quantity of money. Hypotheses will be based on observation and upon certain assumptions about the way the world behaves. These assumptions may themselves be based upon existing theories which have proved to have a high degree of reliability. In economics, for example, many theories are based upon the assumptions that people will behave in such a manner as to maximise their material welfare. Using observed facts and making use of certain assumptions, a process of logical reasoning leads to the formation of a hypothesis. This must be framed in a manner which enables scientists to test its validity.

It is now necessary to think about what would happen if the hypothesis is correct. In other words, the hypothesis is used to make predictions (or the hypothesis itself may be framed as a prediction). If the hypothesis is correct, then if certain things are done, certain other things will happen. If the general level of prices is causally related to the supply of money, it may be deduced that an expansion of bank deposits would be followed by an increase in prices.

The hypothesis must now be tested — are the predictions of the hypothesis supported by the facts? In the natural sciences the testing of hypotheses can be carried out by controlled experiments in the laboratory, but this, as explained below, is not possible for the social scientist. If the hypothesis is supported by the factual evidence it becomes a theory which can be used to explain and predict behaviour and relationships. It must be noted, however, that, since the number of tests which can be carried out is limited, it is never possible to say that a theory is true for all times and in all places. A successful theory is one which up to now has not been proved false. If, at some future time facts emerge which prove the theory and its predictions unreliable, it will be discarded and a search for a better theory will begin. A successful theory is extremely useful because it helps economists predict with a high degree of probability the outcome of certain events.

THE NATURE OF ECONOMICS

Economics is defined as a social science. A social science is a subject which is concerned with human behaviour. Social sciences, which include, for instance, politics and sociology as well as economics, differ from the natural sciences in a number of ways.

The most obvious limitation experienced by the social scientist is that she or he cannot test her or his hypothesis by laboratory experiment. Her or his laboratory is human society; s/he cannot put a group of human beings into a controlled situation and then see what happens. The predictions of economic theory must be tested against developments in the real world. Economic activities must be observed and recorded and the mass of resulting data subjected to statistical analysis. Modern statistical and information technology techniques help the economist determine the probability that certain events had certain causes. S/he can assess from recorded data, for example, the probability that some given increase in consumption was caused by an increase in income.

The fact that 'all people are different' is not such a handicap to the social scientist as might appear at first sight. The economist is interested in group behaviour. S/he is concerned with, for example, the total demand for butter rather than the amount purchased by any one individual. While the behaviour of any one person may be unpredictable, this is not necessarily true of the whole group. When Manchester United score a goal at Old Trafford it is possible to predict with a high degree of certainty that there will be a roar from the crowd, although we cannot forecast how this or that individual will react. The economist is able to make generalisations about economic groups (consumers, workers, shareholders) which are quite dependable guides to their expected behaviour.

Another problem facing economists is the complexity of the world they are studying — so many things are changing simultaneously. Natural scientists in their laboratories can 'hold other things constant', while they study the effects which changes in X have on Y. Economists cannot do this. They cannot vary the quantity of money in the economy, hold everything else constant, and then see what happens. What they have to do is to assume that other things remain constant. Many propositions in economics begin with the phrase 'If other things remain equal' (or the Latin equivalent *ceteris paribus*).

ECONOMIC MODELS

From the vast array of facts observed, economists (and other scientists) must isolate those things which are important and study them in isolation. They have to abstract from reality in order to build a simplified model of a small part of the real world which will help them to see how things are related to one another. In fact the influences surrounding real-life situations are so many and so varied that they cannot all be taken into account. All that economists can do is to try to get close to the real world by extending their model to include more and more 'other influences' — but no one can construct or understand a model which includes everything.

Indeed economic models vary from very simple models of economic reality to more and more sophisticated ones which include more data. These models are constructed by governments, by central banks, by international organisations and by groups of economists working in universities and for financial and other companies. It is also possible for students to develop their own computerised models of how the economy works.

Economic models are used to help understand how the economy works and to make forecasts. For instance, economists will use models to predict how a change in the rate of income tax will affect inflation and the balance of payments.

WHY ECONOMISTS DISAGREE

It is often said that economics cannot be a science because no two economists agree on any economic problem. This is an exaggeration, but it is certainly true that economists disagree. Disputes among economists often arise from problems of definition and from the inadequacy of statistical data. For example there are debates about who should be classified as unemployed and although statistical information on economic affairs is now available to a far greater extent than ever before, there are still many deficiencies. Such information often takes a long time to become available in processed form, and often it is too late to be used in current analysis. It may often be presented in a form which is not very convenient for analysis. These deficiencies therefore leave room for disagreement among economists.

Economics is a relatively young science, and although economic analysis has made great strides in recent years there is still a great deal about the workings of the economic system that is imperfectly understood. There are many aspects of existing theories which have not yet been tested, either because insufficient time has elapsed to provide adequate data, or because no one has found a satisfactory way of testing them. Technical, cultural and economic changes also bring about changes in economic behaviour so that assumptions about human behaviour which served as useful bases for predictions at one period of time may become increasingly unreliable as the social and economic environment changes. Economists, then, will be in dispute over the adequacy of certain existing theories — but it is these very disputes which lead to improvements in existing theories and the development of new ones.

The main area of disagreement among economists is on matters of economic policy. This is exactly what one would expect because policy recommendations are influenced by both economic and political analysis and are affected by value judgements.

PROFILE

NAME: John Kenneth Galbraith
Academic, journalist, and government adviser

BORN: 15 October, 1908 in Ontario, Canada

NATIONALITY: Canadian

EDUCATED: Ontario Agricultural College, University of California, University of Cambridge

KEY POSTS HELD: Professor of Economics at Harvard and Princeton Universities

BOOKS PUBLISHED INCLUDE:

American Capitalism: The Concept of Countervailing Power (1952)
The Great Crash 1929 (1954)
The Affluent Society (1958)
The New Industrial State (1967)
Economics and the Public Purpose (1973)
The Nature of Mass Poverty (1979)

1976: Hosted a twelve part series for the BBC entitled 'The Age of Uncertainty' which was shown in the UK and the USA

MAIN AREA OF WORK: Wide ranging including development of Keynesian economics and the influence of big business

QUOTES ABOUT GALBRAITH:
'… he may well be the most widely read economist of this or any other time.'
  ('The Academic Scribblers' by William Briet and Roger Ransom)

THE SKILLS OF AN ECONOMIST

The famous British economist, John Maynard Keynes wrote

> ...the master economist must possess a rare combination of gifts. He must reach a high standard in several different directions and must combine talents not often found together. He must be mathematician, historian, statesman, philosopher — in some degree. He must understand symbols and speak in words. He must contemplate the particular in terms of the general, and touch abstract and concrete in the same flight of thought. He must study the present in the light of the past for the purposes of the future. No part of man's nature or his institutions must lie entirely outside his regard.[1]

[1] 'Essays in Biography', *The Collected Writings of John Maynard Keynes*, Vol. X, Royal Economic Society. Published by Macmillan Press Ltd 1972.

This is an ambitious list. Economists need to know what has happened in the past, have a keen interest in and knowledge of current affairs, understand human behaviour and appreciate the role of the key economic institutions including the central banks, the World Trade Organisation and the International Monetary Fund. They must be able to think logically, write clearly and be able to use and interpret statistics, basic algebra, diagrams and graphs.

You will develop these skills gradually. They are worth acquiring. They will enable you to analyse current problems and to consider how the quality of people's lives can be improved.

QUESTIONS

SHORT QUESTIONS

1. Explain the relevance of the concept of opportunity cost in a person's decision to go to the cinema.
2. What is meant by a positive statement?
3. Why is Economics a social science?
4. Explain why the phrase 'If other things remain equal' (*ceteris paribus*) is important for economists.

MULTIPLE CHOICE

1. Which of the following is a normative statement?

   A Attendance at university increases a person's potential earnings.

   B Student grants should be increased and student loans should be phased out.

   C Additional funding for university education could be provided by switching expenditure from other programmes.

   D More students from higher income groups undertake degree courses than those from lower income groups.

2. What is an economic good? One which:

   A is sold at a profit

   B has an opportunity cost

   C is supplied by the private sector

   D is produced under conditions of increasing efficiency.

3. What does the existence of scarcity imply?

   A All goods are economic goods.

   B Economic agents have to make choices.

   C It is not possible to increase the quantity of resources.

   D Productive potential is decreasing.

4. A person buys a raffle ticket for £2. She then wins the second prize which offers the choice of a holiday to Paris, which would cost £300, or £250 in cash. If she selects the holiday what is the opportunity cost of her choice?

   A £2   B £50   C £250   D £300

DATA RESPONSE

In all societies people want more than they are capable of producing. At any given moment in time the supply of economic resources is limited so that more of one thing usually can be produced only if less of something else is produced. Likewise incomes are limited and in spending our incomes we have to choose between alternatives. Economists use the term 'opportunity cost' to describe the idea of measuring cost in terms of the alternatives forgone. This is a very important concept. We have to make choices all the time. We have to decide how we spend our time, how we spend our incomes and what employment we undertake. For example in choosing to visit the cinema I may be forgoing the opportunity to play badminton. In buying one model of car I am forgoing the opportunity to buy another model and in working as a teacher I am unable to work as a civil servant.

Producers and governments also have to make choices. A producer must decide what goods to produce and which resources to employ. For example, a farmer opting to use an area of land for growing corn has chosen not to use it for another purpose, e.g. keeping sheep. In growing the corn he has the choice of using labour intensive or capital intensive methods. Governments also have to consider the opportunity cost of any decision they make. The real cost of building an NHS hospital is not the cost in terms of money but the cost in terms of the alternative uses of the resources, i.e. the opportunity cost.

a] What is meant by economic resources? **(3)**

b] Explain the link between scarcity, choice and opportunity cost. **(5)**

c] Why do consumers, producers and governments have to make choices? **(4)**

d] What factors influence which products firms choose to produce? **(6)**

e] Give two examples of the possible opportunity cost of a government building a new hospital. **(4)**

f] Is it likely that wants will ever be satisfied? **(3)**

CASE STUDY

The following is a job advertisement which appeared in *The Economist* magazine on 12 June 1999.

Europe Economics

Microeconomics Consultancy

European Economic Research Ltd (Europe Economics) specialises in the application of economics to utility regulation, competition policy and business issues.

Our clients include government, regulators, the European Commission, law firms and private-sector companies. Our approach aims to combine the client-based professionalism of leading management consultancies and law firms with the theoretical rigour of academic research.

Due to expansion of our business, we wish to recruit up to another 12 microeconomists who are interested in consultancy, at all levels of seniority. Candidates will usually have a high quality post-graduate degree in economics, and must possess excellent written and verbal communication skills. Familiarity with quantitative techniques and/or fluency in European languages would be a further advantage for some posts.

For at least one post, candidates should have experience in the application of economics of competition policy. Another post is likely to be offered to someone who is a qualified accountant as well as a first-class economist.

We offer a friendly but intellectually demanding working environment, competitive remuneration, and prospects for rapid professional growth.

Please send a short CV no later than 30 June to:
Chairman, Europe Economics

a] Explain what is meant by 'competitive remuneration'. **(4)**

b] What is the role of an economist? **(6)**

c] Which groups use the services of economists? **(6)**

d] Explain what is meant by microeconomics. **(6)**

e] i Explain what is meant by quantitative techniques and why familiarity with them is desirable for an economist. **(6)**

  ii What other skills of an economist are mentioned in the advertisement? **(4)**

  iii Discuss three skills not mentioned in the advertisement. **(9)**

f] Discuss three reasons why someone may choose to become an economist. **(9)**

STRUCTURED ESSAY

a] Explain how economists develop theories. **(12)**

b] Discuss why economists may disagree. **(13)**

PRODUCTION POSSIBILITIES AND OPPORTUNITY COST

Scarcity, choice and opportunity cost can be examined by considering what a country can produce with its existing resources of land, labour, capital and technical knowledge.

The quantity and quality of its resources limits the maximum amount of goods and services an economy is capable of producing at any particular time. It will, however, have a wide range of choices as to what to produce.

EXAMPLE

Most countries are capable of producing thousands of different types of goods and services. However, to explain the basic concept of production possibilities the situation can be simplified by assuming that the economy can produce two types of good, for example, agricultural products and manufactured products. Table 2.1 illustrates this situation.

TABLE 2.1 PRODUCTION POSSIBILITIES

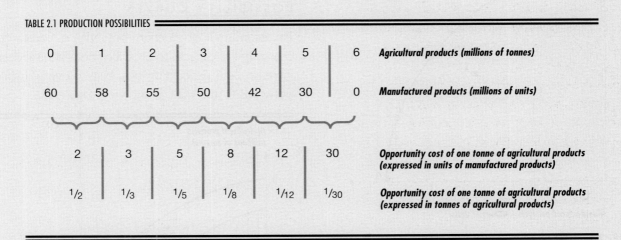

0	1	2	3	4	5	6	**Agricultural products (millions of tonnes)**
60	58	55	50	42	30	0	**Manufactured products (millions of units)**
	2	3	5	8	12	30	**Opportunity cost of one tonne of agricultural products (expressed in units of manufactured products)**
	1/2	1/3	1/5	1/8	1/12	1/30	**Opportunity cost of one tonne of agricultural products (expressed in tonnes of agricultural products)**

The extreme possibilities are that the economy devotes all its resources to agriculture and produces 6m tonnes of food and no manufactured goods or all the resources are used in the manufacturing industry. These are unlikely choices. It is more probable that the economy will choose some combination of the two goods.

The third and fourth columns illustrate the important point mentioned in Chapter 1 that the production of one thing involves the sacrifice of another thing: it has an opportunity cost. The third column shows the opportunity cost of producing one more tonne of agricultural produce measured in terms of manufactured products forgone. For example, if this economy increases its food production from 3m to 4m tonnes, the opportunity cost of the additional output is 8m units of manufactured products. The fourth column shows the opportunity cost of manufactured products measured in terms of the output of agricultural products which have to be forgone when more resources are allocated to manufacturing.

PRODUCTION POSSIBILITY CURVES

The combination of goods that an economy, or other economic unit such as a firm, is capable of producing can be illustrated by a production possibility curve. This can also be referred to as an opportunity cost curve, a transformation curve, a production possibility frontier or a production possibility boundary. Figure 2.1 is based on the information contained in Table 2.1.

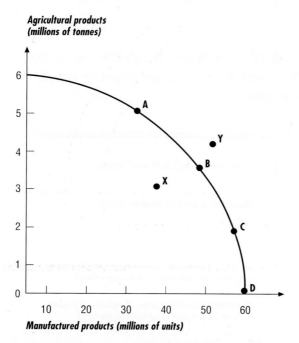

FIG. 2.1

The production possibility curve shows that as the production of food increases, so does the opportunity cost of the food. This is because some resources will be more suited to agriculture and some more suited to manufacturing. As food production increases, the resources being moved into the industry will be less and less suited to agriculture. So each extra resource used in agriculture will result in a smaller increase in agricultural output. Diminishing returns will occur (see Chapter 13).

POINTS AND THE CURVE

Points on the production possibility curve such as A, B and C show the maximum possible combined outputs of the two goods. Point D shows the maximum amount of manufactured products which can be produced if all resources are devoted to manufactured products.

The economy can produce any combination inside the curve, but this would mean that some resources are unemployed or that inefficient methods of production are being used. Point X illustrates this type of situation. In this case the economy could produce more of both goods by moving to a point such as B. Points outside the production possibility, such as Y, are not attainable with the economy's present productive capacity.

SHIFTS IN PRODUCTION POSSIBILITY CURVES

An economy's production potential is constantly changing. If its capacity to produce goods and services increases, the production possibility curve will shift outwards to the right as shown in Figure 2.2.

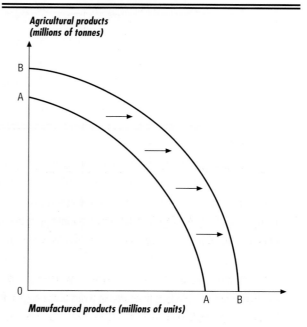

FIG. 2.2

An economy will be able to produce more goods and services if the quantity and/or quality of its resources increases. So among the causes of a rightward shift are an increase in the labour force, an increase in the stock of capital goods (offices, factories, transport networks, power stations, machinery, etc.), an increase in technical knowledge and an improvement in training.

The production possibility curve can also shift inwards to the left as shown in Figure 2.3 if an economy's production potential declines. This could occur due to a war or a natural disaster which reduces a country's resources.

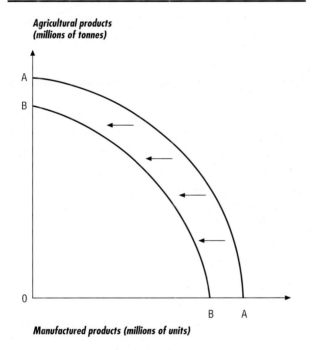

Agricultural products (millions of tonnes)

Manufactured products (millions of units)

FIG. 2.3 ════════════════

A CHANGE IN THE SLOPE OF THE PRODUCTION POSSIBILITY CURVE

If there is a change in the quantity or quality of resources which are specific to the production of one type of good, the slope of the curve will change. For example, an invention may improve production

techniques in manufacturing. This will increase the potential output of manufactured products and cause the production possibility curve to change its slope as shown in Figure 2.4.

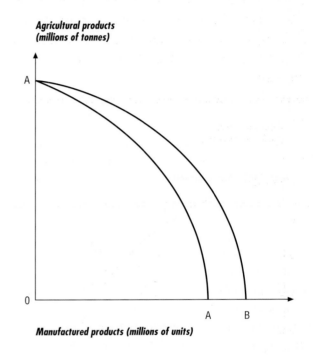

Agricultural products (millions of tonnes)

Manufactured products (millions of units)

FIG. 2.4 ════════════════

THE SHAPE OF THE PRODUCTION POSSIBILITY CURVE

Figures 2.1, 2.2, 2.3 and 2.4 show the usual shape of the production possibility curve. They show that as more of one good is produced the opportunity cost rises. The curves are concave to the origin of the graph, that is they are bowed outwards.

However there is the chance that if two products use similar methods of production there may be a constant opportunity cost. In this case the production possibility curve will be a straight line as illustrated in Figure 2.5.

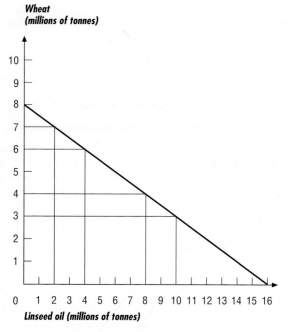

FIG. 2.5

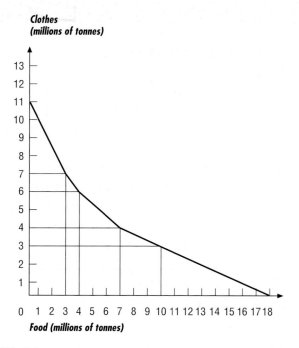

FIG. 2.6

Here, resources are able to switch easily from producing wheat to producing linseed oil and are equally good at producing each crop. To move from producing 3m tonnes of wheat to 4m tonnes of wheat, 2m tonnes of linseed oil have to be forgone. The opportunity cost of 2m tonnes of linseed oil remains the same when the output of wheat is raised from 6m tonnes to 7m tonnes, and at any other level of production.

If a decreasing opportunity cost is experienced the production possibility curve will be bowed inwards (convex to the origin of the graph) as shown in Figure 2.6.

To increase the output of clothes from 3m units to 4m units, 3m tonnes of food have to be forgone. Whereas to increase the output of clothes from 6m to 7m units, the opportunity cost falls to 1m units of food. This may because resources initially being used to produce food are more suited to producing clothes. This situation can be referred to as increasing returns since as more resources are devoted to producing clothes their output increases by larger quantities. It is, however, a very unusual case as it is more logical to use the best resources first.

QUESTIONS

SHORT QUESTIONS

1. Give two other names for a production possibility curve.

2. What is the most common shape of a production possibility curve? Explain why this is so.

3. What are the basic economic concepts illustrated by a production possibility curve?

4. Explain the effect an increase in the retirement age would have on a country's production possibility curve.

MULTIPLE CHOICE

1. XY in Figure 2.7 is a production possibility curve. Which points are attainable?

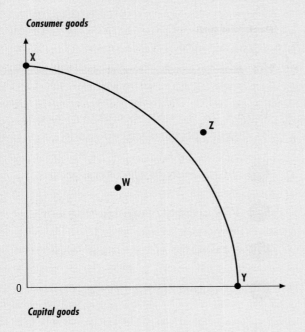

Consumer goods

Capital goods

FIG. 2.7

A. W B. X and Y C. W, X and Y

D. W, X, Y and Z

2. What is implied by the shape of the production possibility frontier shown in Figure 2.8?

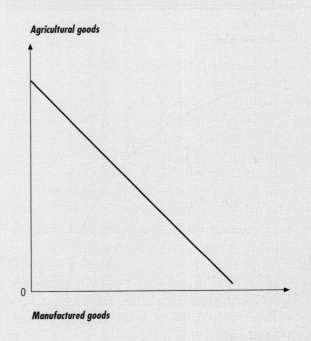

Agricultural goods

Manufactured goods

FIG. 2.8

A. The economy will operate at full employment.

B. The output of manufactured goods will be greater than the output of agricultural goods.

C. There is a constant rate of opportunity cost involved in transferring resources from the production of agricultural goods to manufactured goods.

D. Resources are not equally good at producing both manufactured and agricultural goods.

3   WX and YZ in Figure 2.9 are two production possibility curves. Which of the following could explain the movement from point R to point S?

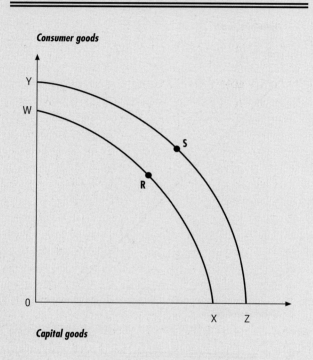

FIG. 2.9

A   a reduction in unemployment

B   an increase in the price of both consumer and capital goods

C   improvements in technology affecting both consumer and capital goods

D   a more efficient allocation of resources between consumer and capital goods.

4   Figure 2.10 shows a production possibility frontier, XZ.

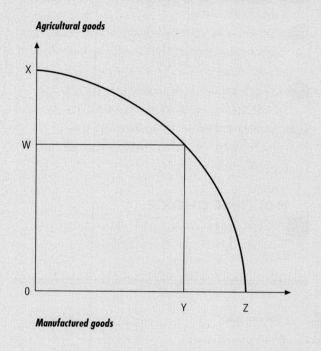

FIG. 2.10

What is the opportunity cost of producing 0Y quantity of manufactured goods?

A   0W quantity of agricultural goods

B   WX quantity of agricultural goods

C   0X quantity of agricultural goods

D   YZ quantity of manufactured goods.

DATA RESPONSE

Six weeks after the Ganges and other rivers flowing into Bangladesh burst their banks, the government is grappling with a disaster whose size it failed to acknowledge until the homes, livestock and crops of millions of people had been swept away. So far, over 700 Bangladeshi have been killed. More than 22m have been made homeless or left marooned by the deluge, which now covers two-thirds of the country. Health officials fear that disease, spread by increasingly foul water, will greatly increase the number of victims.

It took a month for the authorities to overcome their reluctance to call for outside help. Then, in August, the government appealed for $880m, a huge amount for Bangladesh, which is one of the world's poorest countries.

The finance minister says much of the money is needed not for emergency aid but for reconstruction. In many places roads, bridges and electricity lines have been damaged or destroyed.

Relief agencies say hunger and water-borne diseases are spreading among the poor, many of whom are ill fed at the best of times. At least half of the seedlings for the next rice crop have been washed away, leaving millions of Bangladeshis dependent on imports or food aid for months.

Source: Page 79, The Economist, 12/9/98.

a] Which resources were reduced by the flood? **(6)**

b] Using a production possibility curve, illustrate the effect of the flood. **(6)**

c] What does the extract imply is the opportunity cost of using foreign aid for reconstruction? **(2)**

d] How would a poor country's production possibility curve be likely to compare with that of an industrial country's? **(5)**

e] What could cause the production possibility curve of Bangladesh to shift to the right? **(6)**

CASE STUDY

A university cannot provide tuition in all courses to an unlimited number of students. This is because it has limited resources. So it has to make choices as to which courses to offer and which students to accept.

To illustrate this, the choices facing a fictionalised university, the University of the Windrush Valley, can be considered in a simplified example. It may, for instance, be able to use its resources of lecturing staff, buildings, libraries, computers, etc. to provide degree courses in English literature and/or media studies. The production possibility curve shown in Figure 2.11 illustrates the initial options facing the university.

The university's courses are initially under-subscribed and its production point is at X. When its reputation increases its production point moves to Y. Building on its increased reputation the university seeks sponsorship from a local TV company to build an all purpose media studio and appoint two new lecturers in media studies. Its long term aim is to take over a nearby further education college, which currently offers HND and A level courses in both English and media studies.

a] What is the opportunity cost of the university moving from point X to point Y? **(6)**

b] If the university is producing at point Y what would be the opportunity cost of increasing the number of English literature students taught from 2500 to 3000? **(4)**

c] i What is the maximum number of English literature students who can be taught? **(3)**

   ii Why do you think the maximum number of English literature students who can be taught is greater than the maximum number of media studies students? **(7)**

d] i Explain why the production possibility curve illustrated is bowed outwards. **(7)**

   ii Discuss why if the two degree courses being considered were English literature and medicine the curve would be bowed out even more than the one illustrated. **(7)**

e] Explain and illustrate on a production possibility curve the success of:
   i the sponsorship bid **(8)**
   ii the take over bid. **(8)**

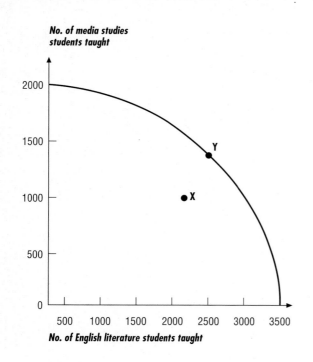

FIG. 2.11

STRUCTURED ESSAY

a] Explain what is meant by a production possibility curve. **(7)**

b] What effect will the following have:
   i   a movement from inside to on the curve **(6)**
   ii a movement along the curve **(6)**
   iii a movement from one curve to another curve further to the right. **(6)**

3 ECONOMIC SYSTEMS

There are a variety of economic systems operating in the world. These can be categorised into planned economies, market economies and a combination of the two, mixed economies. Two key features distinguish economic systems; who owns the land and capital, and who decides what is produced.

THE QUESTIONS FACING ALL ECONOMIES

All societies face three fundamental questions and how these are answered will depend on the type of economic system being operated. These questions are as follows.

WHICH GOODS AND SERVICES SHALL BE PRODUCED AND IN WHAT QUANTITIES?

This problem concerns the composition of total output. The community must decide which goods and services it is going to produce and hence which goods and services it is not going to produce. Having decided the range of goods and services to be produced, the society must then decide how much of each good and service should be produced. In reality the choices open to a society are rarely of the 'all or nothing' variety. They usually take the form of more of one thing and less of another. The first and major function of any economic system is to determine in some way the actual quantities and varieties of goods and services that will best meet the wants of its citizens.

HOW SHOULD THE VARIOUS GOODS AND SERVICES BE PRODUCED?

Most goods and services can be produced by a variety of methods. Wheat can be grown by making use of much labour and little capital, or by using large amounts of capital and very little labour. Electrical appliances can be made by using large and complex machines operated by relatively few semi- or un-skilled workers. Alternatively they might be produced in hosts of small workshops by highly skilled technicians using relatively little machinery. Different methods of production can be distinguished from one another by the differences in the quantities of resources used in producing them. Economists use the terms capital-intensive and labour-intensive to describe the alternative methods just outlined. The total output of the society depends not only on the total supply of resources available but also on the ways in which these resources are combined. A society must make decisions on the methods of production to be adopted.

HOW SHOULD THE GOODS AND SERVICES BE DISTRIBUTED?

This is the third question which an economic system has to answer. The total output has to be shared out among the members of the society. The economic system has to determine the relative sizes of the shares going to each household. Should everyone be given an equal share? Should the division depend upon the individual's contribution to production? Should the output be shared out in accordance with people's ability to pay for the price, or should the shares be decided according to tradition and custom?

PLANNED ECONOMIES

A planned economy is one in which the government makes the decisions on what to produce, how to produce it, and who gets it. The communist regimes in Cuba and North Korea can be described as planned economies, although this type of economic system is not just found in communist countries. It is applicable wherever the economic resources of a nation are directly controlled by some centralised authority. The UK became a planned economy during the years of the Second World War when the government took control of all important economic affairs.

Planned economies can also be referred to as command or collectivist economies.

OWNERSHIP AND CONTROL OF RESOURCES

Although economic planning may be employed in societies where property is privately owned, it seems realistic to assume that a fully planned economy means one in which all the important means of production are publicly owned. In communist and socialist societies (which are the most important examples of planned economies) all land, housing, factories, offices, power stations, transport systems, and so on are usually owned by the state.

The logic of public ownership in these societies is based upon the desire for a fairer distribution of income and wealth. Private ownership of property leads to great inequalities of wealth, and this, in turn, means that the wealthier groups are able to exercise great economic power. Such a situation implies great inequalities of opportunity. The better-off members of society are able to use their greater wealth to obtain superior education, better health services, more effective training and better business opportunities. The elimination, or severe limitation, of private ownership is seen, therefore, as the most effective way of removing these inequalities of opportunity. It is also argued by the supporters of the planned economy that only the direct ownership of the means of production can give the state the full control that it needs in order to carry out its economic plan.

FORMS OF COLLECTIVE CONTROL

In planned economies land and capital may be owned collectively rather than individually but this does not mean that control of these resources has to be centralised. In some planned economies the state keeps a tight control on the use of economic resources and all important economic decisions are taken by powerful central committees. They decide what should be produced, how and where production should take place, and how the output should be shared among the people. This is described as bureaucratic organisation, because the running of such an economy will require large numbers of planners and administrators to draw up and operate the national plan.

Alternatively, although the ultimate ownership of resources may be in the hands of the state, the control and day-to-day running of the farms, factories, offices and shops may be handed over to co-operative groups of workers and consumers. These organisations are usually described as workers collectives, as opposed to the state enterprises which are controlled directly by the government.

One important feature of a society in which property is publicly owned is that there will be no form of personal income which is derived from the ownership of property. In the market system incomes take the form of wages, interest, rent and profits — the last three of which arise from the ownership of various types of property.

PRODUCTION DECISIONS

The administrators in a planned society face a most complex task. They must begin by making a survey of the productive potential of the economy. This involves looking at the resources of workers, machines, factories, offices, etc., the country has and what can be produced with them. First, assessments must be prepared showing the outputs which might be produced by the mines, farms, factories, etc., together with estimates of the capacities of the transport networks and the capacities of the other service industries. Decisions on the quantities and varieties of goods and service to be produced must then be made and each unit of production (e.g. each farm or factory) will be given a target output for the period of the plan — normally five years. The next task is to allocate the necessary supplies of materials, equipment, and labour to the various units of production.

A modern economic system is exceedingly complex. The output of any one factory is dependent upon supplies from many different sources. The fitting together of all these planned outputs into one huge national plan is a formidable task. In fact it is virtually impossible for central planners to fix targets and resource allocation for every single farm, factory, office and shop. The planners are more likely to give directives (orders) to whole industries. Whilst the ways in which the targets set down in these orders may be left to local decisions at the industry and factory levels, it is most probable that the allocations to various industries of the more vital resources (e.g. new capital) will be centrally controlled.

In order to co-ordinate resources and output for each industry planners usually employ input-output analysis. This involves estimating what inputs, i.e. resources, firms need in the form of materials, labour, machinery, etc. and what output they are capable of producing. Then the planners check where the inputs can come from and where the output can go — either to other firms or to consumers and that the inputs and output match. A flow chart of inputs and output is drawn up.

DISTRIBUTION DECISIONS

While it is possible, although very difficult, to subject the outputs of goods and services to complete control by planners, it is much more difficult to use these methods in the markets for labour and consumer goods and services. In respect of industrial investment (i.e. capital goods), defence requirements, and social investment (e.g. schools, hospitals, housing) the necessary allocations of resources can be directly controlled and the outputs firmly determined. In the case of consumer goods and services, however, there are restraints on the planners' ability to use direct controls.

Ideally, the complete planning of production should be accompanied by the complete planning of distribution. What is produced can then be allocated to consumers by some kind of physical rationing scheme. Workers could be paid in kind, receiving vouchers which entitle them to various quantities of different goods and services. In this manner the pattern and volume of consumption could be matched exactly to the planned output. Such a system might operate perfectly well in a poor country where all resources are committed to the bare necessities of life. In a more developed economy, however, consumers are likely to demand a large measure of freedom of choice in how they spend their income. Allowing for freedom of choice in the consumers' market makes the planners' problems much more difficult. It is very unlikely that the spending plans of consumers will exactly match the production targets of the planners. This does not mean that direct planning will not work; it means the plan must contain some flexibility so that production can respond to the various surpluses and shortages as they appear in the consumer markets.

ASSESSING CONSUMER DEMAND

There are various ways in which planners can test consumer demand — assuming, that is, that they wish to respond to it. They might conduct a continuous poll or carry out surveys of public attitudes and preferences. Alternatively they could allow the goods and services to be sold in free markets. Goods and services which are in short supply will rise in price whilst those in surplus will fall in price. These price movements could then be used as indicators to producers as to which industries should expand their outputs and which should contract output. Planners may, however, regard such price movements as an inequitable means of testing the market (e.g. a shortage of bread might cause its price to rise beyond the means of the poor). The state may, therefore, fix prices, and where shortages arise the good or service may be physically rationed. In this case it would be the movements in retail stocks (the shortages and the surpluses) which act as indicators to the planners.

LABOUR MARKET DECISIONS

There are similar problems to be dealt with in the market for labour. Whilst iron ore, machines, lorries and so on can be distributed directly to the different industries, workers will not usually continue to accept such direction. They will demand some degree of freedom in choosing their jobs and the part of the country in which they wish to work. Getting the right amounts of labour in the right places to meet the production targets cannot normally be achieved by the direction of labour; it must be done by inducement. As is the case with consumer goods and services, it means that some limited use must be made of the price mechanism.

Firms which are short of labour will have to be given permission to offer higher wages in order to attract labour from other sources. In the longer run the state can influence the supplies of the different types of labour by providing more and better training facilities for those skills which are in short supply and reducing the intake of trainees for occupations where demand is declining.

MARKET ECONOMIES

A society may attempt to deal with the basic economic problems by allowing free play to what are known as market forces. The state plays little or no part in economic activity. Most of the people in the world now earn and spend in economies in which market forces play a significant role.

The market system of economic organisation is also commonly known as a free enterprise, or *laissez-faire*, or capitalist system. Strictly speaking the pure market or *laissez-faire* system has never existed. Whenever there has been some form of political organisation, the political authority has exercised some economic functions (e.g. controlling prices or levying taxation). It is useful, however, to consider the way in which a true market system would operate because it provides us with a simplified model, and by making modifications to the model it is possible to approach more realistic situations. The framework of a market system contains six essential features:

- private property
- freedom of enterprise and choice
- self-interest as the dominating motive
- competition
- a reliance on the price system
- a very limited role for the government.

PRIVATE PROPERTY

The institution of private property is a major feature of a market economy. It means that individuals have the right to own, control, and dispose of land, buildings, machinery, and other natural and man-made resources. Man-made aids to production such as machines, factories, docks, oil refineries and road networks are known as capital.

Private property not only confers the right to own and dispose of real assets, it provides the owners of property with the right to the income from that property in the form of rent, interest, and profits.

Although all non-human resources can be privately owned, labour cannot be bought and sold in the same way. Except in slave societies, labourers own themselves, whilst land, buildings, and machinery are owned by others. Owners of land and capital purchase the services of labour in order to operate their factories, offices, farms, shops and so on.

FREEDOM OF ENTERPRISE AND CHOICE

Freedom of enterprise means that individuals are free to buy and hire economic resources, to organise these resources for production, and to sell their products in markets of their own choice. Persons who undertake these activities are known as entrepreneurs. These people are risk takers and such people are free to enter and leave any industry.

Freedom of choice means that owners of land and capital may use these resources as they see fit. It also means that workers are free to enter (and leave) any occupations for which they are qualified, although this is a rather meaningless freedom when there is a high level of unemployment. Finally it means that consumers are free to spend their incomes in any way they wish. This freedom of consumer choice is usually held to be the most important of these economic 'freedoms'. The consumer is regarded as being sovereign since it is the way in which s/he chooses to spend his income which determines the ways in which society uses its economic resources. In the model of a market system, producers respond to consumers' preferences — they produce what consumers demand.

SELF-INTEREST

Since a market system is based on the principle that individuals should be free to do as they wish, it is not surprising to find that the motive for economic activity is self-interest. Each unit in the economy attempts to do what is best for itself. Firms will act in ways which, they believe, will lead to maximum profits (or minimum losses). Owners of land and capital will employ these assets so as to obtain the highest possible rewards. Workers will tend to move to those occupations and locations which offer the highest wages. Consumers will spend their incomes on those things which yield the maximum satisfaction.

Advocates of the market system such as Adam Smith argue that the individual pursuit of self-interest leads to the maximum public good. 'By pursuing his own interest he (the individual) frequently promotes that of society more effectually than when he really intends to promote it.'[1]

COMPETITION

Economic rivalry, or competition, is another essential feature of a free enterprise economy. Competition, as economists see it, is essentially price competition. The model of the market economy envisages a situation where, in the market for each commodity, there are large numbers of buyers and sellers. Each buyer and seller accounts for an insignificant share of the business transacted and hence has no influence on the market demand or market supply. It is the forces of total demand and total supply which determine the market price, and participants, whether buyers or sellers, must take this price as given since it is beyond their influence or control. In theory at least, competition is the regulatory mechanism of the market system. It limits the use of economic power since no single firm or individual is large enough or strong enough to control a market and exploit the other buyers and sellers.

MARKETS AND PRICES

Perhaps the most basic feature of the market economy is the use of the price mechanism for

[1] Adam Smith, *The Wealth of Nations* (see Chapter 6).

allocating resources to various uses. The price system is an elaborate system of communications in which innumerable free choices are totalled and balanced against each other. The decisions of producers determine the supply of a product; the decisions of buyers determine the demand. The interactions of demand and supply cause changes in market prices and it is these movements in market prices which bring about the changes in the ways in which society uses its resources.

A simple example can illustrate this. A particular product proves to be increasingly popular with consumers. Increasing demand outstrips supply at the existing price, a shortage develops and price increases. This rise in price makes production more profitable, so that existing firms will tend to expand their outputs and new firms will be attracted to this industry. More and more resources will move into the industry because the greater profitability will enable firms to offer higher rewards in order to bid labour and capital away from other uses. The opposite process will apply when the demand for a product is declining. Price movements act as indicators and provide an essential link between consumers' preferences and producers' profit-seeking decisions.

In a market economy, price has another important function — it acts as a rationing device. Price serves to ration scarce goods and services among the people who are demanding them. Where the supply of a good or service is insufficient to meet the demands of prospective buyers at the existing price, the market price will rise and continue to rise until the quantity demanded is just equal to the existing supply. Those unable to pay the higher prices will be eliminated from the market. Price rations scarce goods to those who can afford to pay the price. If supply exceeds demand, the price will fall, bringing in more buyers (and expanding the purchases of existing buyers) until a price is established which equates the quantities being demanded and supplied. Note that price rations goods and services, not on any basis of need or want, but on the basis of the ability to pay the price.

The price mechanism allocates resources to different uses on the basis of consumer 'votes'. The act of purchasing a product is, in effect, a vote for the production of that product. Under this system those with the greater purchasing power have more votes. This might be regarded as an inequitable system especially where there is great inequality in the distribution of income.

MIXED ECONOMIES

As noted above, there is some use of the market mechanism in planned economies. Likewise there is some measure of state control in market economies. Indeed, there are no pure planned or pure market economies in the world. Where there is both a public (i.e. a state) sector and a private sector (where non-government firms and individuals decide what is produced), the economy is called a mixed economy. It has features of both a command and a market economy.

As discussed in the next chapter many economies are moving towards greater reliance on the market system. Nevertheless, all economies have some degree of state intervention and are essentially mixed economies.

QUESTIONS

SHORT QUESTIONS

1. What are the three fundamental questions that all economies face?

2. What type of economic system did the UK operate between 1940 and 1945? Explain your answer.

3. How may planners seek to assess consumer demand in a planned economy?

4. What are the essential features of a market economy?

MULTIPLE CHOICE

1. What is the main difference between a planned and a market economy? In a market economy:

   A most of the economy is state owned

   B government officials are the ultimate decision takers

   C production is planned on the basis of input-output analysis

   D the price mechanism is the main mechanism for allocating resources.

2. What is meant by consumer sovereignty?

   A Products are sold at low prices.

   B Consumers are able to satisfy all their wants.

   C The preferences of consumers influence the pattern of production.

   D Output decisions are taken on the basis of the needs of consumers.

3. Which is the most likely reason why some industries in a planned economy may fail to reach their output targets?

   A A lack of demand.

   B A change in consumer preferences.

   C An increase in the general price level.

   D Problems of co-ordination between industries.

4. How is the economic problem of what shall be produced determined in a pure planned economy?

   A Consumers and the state.

   B Direction by the government.

   C The pattern of consumers' spending.

   D The independent decisions of entrepreneurs.

DATA RESPONSE

In a pure market economy the state would play no part in deciding what is to be produced, how it is to be produced and who is to receive it when it has been produced. Consumers would decide what they want, vote with their purchases, and producers would respond by increasing the output of goods and services which are in increasing demand and reducing the output of goods and services which are declining in popularity. The price mechanism would facilitate this process. It would signal changes in demand to producers by raising the price of popular products and lowering the price of less popular products. It also restricts the demand for scarce products to their available supply.

However in practice even societies which are described as market economies have some government intervention. This is because of the limitations of the market mechanism. Even Adam Smith, who was a strong advocate of *laissez-faire*, acknowledged the need of the state to intervene to protect children and to protect consumers from monopolies (firms which dominate a market). Governments intervene in the running of the economy in order, for example, to help weak members of society (including the poor, elderly and disabled), to create greater economic stability, to reduce pollution, to encourage the consumption of certain goods and services and to finance those goods and services which would not be produced by the private sector because it is not possible to charge people for the amount they consume e.g. the police force and street lighting.

The level of government intervention varies between countries and over time. In the 1990s a number of planned economies started to move towards market systems. They were seeking to gain the advantages of a market system.

a] Who determines the allocation of resources in a market economy? **(2)**

b] What encourages producers to switch production from unpopular to popular products? **(6)**

c] What are the functions of the price mechanism in a market economy? **(4)**

d] Explain what is meant by *laissez-faire*. **(3)**

e] Why might the weak members of society suffer in a market economy? **(6)**

f] Explain two reasons why a government may intervene in an economy. **(4)**

CASE STUDY

STATISTICS FOR NORTH AND SOUTH KOREA (1997)		
	SOUTH KOREA	NORTH KOREA
Area, sq. km 000	99	123
Population, m	46	23
Income per head, $	9350	741
Life expectancy, males	69	61
Life expectancy, females	76	65
Armed forces, 000	672	923

Source: *The Economist*, 10/7/99.

In the late 1990s the countries of South Korea and North Korea, which operate very different economic systems, experienced economic problems.

The collectivist economy of North Korea experienced a famine in the mid 1990s. Its economic system has been criticised for being 'incapable of giving out the normal economic signals'. Its factories use out of date machinery and methods and produce goods which are of poor quality. Despite its low income it maintains the fifth largest army in the world.

South Korea, which had been regarded as an Asian tiger, developed rapidly from the 1960s to the late 1990s. Its companies, including Hyundai, Daewoo and Samsung, became well-known for their innovation and price competitiveness. However, even before the Asian crisis the performance of South Korean firms began to deteriorate. Large wage rises, low labour productivity and inappropriate diversification reduced South Korea's firms' competitiveness. When the Asian crisis struck some of the country's best-known companies went bankrupt.

a] i What is another name for a collectivist economy? **(2)**

   ii Give two other examples of collectivist economies. **(4)**

b] What type of economic system operates in South Korea? Explain your answer. **(6)**

c] Using the Table compare the economic performance of South Korea and North Korea. **(8)**

d] Explain why a collectivist economy may be 'incapable of giving out the normal economic signals.' **(8)**

e] Why might firms which produce low quality goods survive in a collectivist economy but not a market economy? **(8)**

f] Explain what is meant by innovation and why this would be encouraged in the type of economic system which operates in South Korea. **(8)**

g] Explain what caused some of South Korea's well-known companies to go bankrupt. **(6)**

STRUCTURED ESSAY

a] Explain how resources are allocated in a market and in a planned economy. **(10)**

b] Discuss the advantages and disadvantages of planned and market economies. **(15)**

4 THE MOVE TO MARKET ECONOMIES

1989 witnessed the collapse of the communist regime in Poland. Solidarity, the trade union movement, pressured the government into holding free elections and won most of the seats. This was the start of the change in the political and economic systems in a number of East European countries, including Hungary, East Germany, Romania and, probably the most famous, the former Soviet Union. The role of the price mechanism in allocating resources has also increased in many African and Asian countries. China, whilst still a communist country, has undertaken a number of economic reforms including introducing a stock market.

REASONS FOR THE MOVE TOWARDS MARKET ECONOMIES

Increased information about living standards in Western Europe and the USA increased the dissatisfaction felt by people in Eastern Europe with the goods and services on offer to them. They were unhappy about the poor quality of many goods and services, including housing and clothing, and the lack of other goods and services including cars, telephones and CDs. Shortages and rationing also meant that people wasted much of their time standing in queues.

The shortages and poor quality arose largely due to problems of planning and co-ordination. Information proved difficult and expensive to obtain and it often quickly became out of date. The large quantity of information and its inadequacies posed serious problems for the complex process of input-output analysis.

It was also found to be easier to set targets for and monitor quantity rather than quality. Indeed, there grew up something of a target mentality with producers often sacrificing quality and environmental concerns in order to meet quantity targets. High levels of pollution occurred in all the Eastern European countries. For instance, more than 90% of rivers in Poland were heavily polluted.

The absence of the profit motive meant that inefficient firms continued in production while efficient firms did not always expand. Additionally, it was also usually not possible for new, non-government, firms to set up to meet expanding consumer demand. Producers of state-run industries, unable to benefit from profits were not encouraged to introduce new techniques and products.

Although there were differences in wages, there was a lack of incentives for workers since wage differences were nevertheless limited and many workers had almost complete job security. So those workers who were most skilled often earned little more than those who were unskilled and those who did not work as hard. The desire to maintain full employment also lead to overmanning and, in some cases with workers being in inappropriate jobs, low productivity.

In the 1970s and 1980s Eastern Europe experienced problems in exporting goods and services. This was largely due to increased competition from the newly industrialised countries including Singapore and South Korea. To make up for the fall in export revenue Bulgaria, Hungary, Romania and other Eastern European countries borrowed heavily from the West. Paying off the debt meant that these countries had less to spend on improving living standards within their own countries. In the early 1990s there was also a breakdown in the trade between the East European countries.

THE TRANSITIONAL ECONOMIES

The countries of Eastern Europe which are developing market economies are often referred to as transitional economies. They are usually divided into two groups. One is the Central and East European countries (CEE) which includes countries previously closely connected with the former Soviet Union, e.g. Poland, Hungary, Bulgaria, the Czech Republic, Croatia and Romania. The other is the Commonwealth of Independent States (CIS) group which includes countries which emerged from the former Soviet Union e.g. Armenia, Belarus, Georgia, Moldova, Russia and Ukraine.

In general the CEE countries have been experiencing fewer problems in their transition than the CIS countries where output is still below the levels experienced during the last years of operating planned economies. This is due, in part, to the fact that some of the CEE countries, e.g. Poland and the Czech Republic, started economic reforms earlier and so have been able to make the change to a different system more gradually and more smoothly.

PROBLEMS OF TRANSITION

INFLATION

Price levels rose, and in some cases continue to rise, at high rates when the transition started. There were a number of reasons why this occurred. One is that planned economies usually keep prices below those charged by private sector producers. So when price controls were removed price levels rose. The early stages of transition also saw output falling. Governments trying to avoid high levels of unemployment gave subsidies to loss making firms to ensure their survival and financed these losses by printing money. So there was more money to spend on fewer goods and services and again price levels

rose. Russia, in particular, experienced very high rates of inflation.

INDUSTRIAL UNREST

Workers pressed for wage rises to enable them to pay the higher prices and to maintain job security. In the 1990s a number of strikes occurred in key Russian industries, including mining.

CHANGING PATTERN OF INTERNATIONAL TRADE

International trade between the Soviet Union and its communist partners was organised through a trade bloc known as Comecon (The Council for Mutual Economic Assistance) which was established in 1949. This co-ordinated energy policies, organised loans between members, operated a central payments system, based on trade roubles, between member countries and discouraged trade with non-members by a system of export and import taxes. It was dissolved in 1991. The former members then had to build up trading relationships with other countries. They sought in particular to trade more with the European Union (EU).

CHANGING PATTERN OF EMPLOYMENT

There was, and continues to be, significant structural change with some industries expanding, some contracting and some going out of business. This has required workers to move from one job to another. A number have found this difficult, indeed many were unaccustomed to changing jobs or retraining.

FALL IN LIVING STANDARDS

The early stages of transition saw output falling as some of the previous state-run enterprises failed to survive when exposed to market forces, and there was insufficient time, experience and skills to set up new firms.

LACK OF WELFARE SYSTEMS

In many of the transitional economies provision for education, health care and housing had been provided for their employees by state-run enterprises. There was also no official unemployment and so no social security system. So when economic systems started to change the appropriate welfare systems were not in place and some vulnerable groups suffered as a result.

LACK OF MARKETS

These economies also lacked functioning markets for goods and services, labour and capital. So there was a need for microeconomic reform in each country including privatising former state run enterprises, developing a commercial banking sector, building up a financial capital market, and the establishment of a legal framework for the enforcement of property rights, valuation and transfer of assets.

MACROECONOMIC REFORM

As well as reforming markets there has been the need to change macroeconomic policy. For example the role of central banks has had to change, the tax base has had to be built up and new trade relationships established.

RELATIONSHIPS WITH THE EU

It is particularly the CEE countries which are developing closer links with the EU although CIS countries are also seeking to build up their trade links and are accepting assistance from the EU.

TACIS

This is Technical Assistance to the CIS countries provided by the EU to help transition. Aid is provided to help reform social services, education, public administration, to improve nuclear safety and carry out environmental projects.

EBRD

The European Bank for Reconstruction and Development (EBRD), based in London, was founded in 1991 in order to help East European countries achieve transition from planned to market economies. Its funds come from the EU and from a number of countries outside the EU. It lends for private sector commercial investment and for infrastructure investment projects.

THE PHARE PROGRAMME

The Phare programme (Pologne, Hungarie, assistance pour la reconstruction economique) was established in 1989. It got its name from its original intention to help the transition of Poland and Hungary by giving grants for improving infrastructure. However it now applies to all the CEE countries.

ASSOCIATION AGREEMENTS

These were started in 1991. They are intended to help CEE countries prepare for full membership of the EU. They involve reducing trade restrictions, providing technical assistance and developing closer economic and political links.

FUTURE MEMBERSHIP OF THE EU

Ten CEE countries have applied to join the EU. These are Bulgaria, the Czech Republic, Estonia, Hungary, Latvia, Lithuania, Poland, Romania, Slovakia and Slovenia. It may be some time before they are all allowed to join. This is because at the moment their incomes are lower than those of the other EU members which would mean they would qualify for large grants under the EU's regional and social funds while their workers, given the free movement of labour in the EU, may migrate in large numbers to the West. Also the Common Agricultural Policy (CAP) would have to be reformed first. This is because with more than approximately a quarter of the CEE countries' labour force employed in agriculture the cost of running CAP, should these countries join the EU, would be too high.

ADVANTAGES OF A MOVE TO A MARKET ECONOMY

It is possible that a number of advantages may be gained from moving from a planned to a market economy. These include:

- Consumers can influence what goods and services are produced directly by their purchases, i.e., they can exercise consumer sovereignty and greater use of the price mechanism will provide an automatic and quick way to signal to producers what consumers want.
- The market system provides incentives to entrepreneurs in the form of profits and to workers in the form of higher wages. This should encourage entrepreneurs to produce high-quality products and to innovate, and workers to work hard.
- Consumers will have a greater choice of producers. Instead of having to buy from one government firm they may have a choice of a number of private-sector producers. This increased competition may increase the quality of products since rival producers will seek to attract new customers by improving the standard of their goods and services.
- Foreign investment may be encouraged since overseas producers may expect a higher return

on their investment and be less fearful of government intervention.
- Efficiency may increase since those firms which do not produce what people want at low cost (and hence low prices) may go out of business.

DISADVANTAGES OF A MOVE TO A MARKET ECONOMY

There are also potential disadvantages of making greater use of market forces:

- Private-sector firms may try to reduce their costs by, for example, dumping waste materials in rivers. As private-sector firms are concerned primarily with profits they may not take into account the effects their production has on the environment.
- Some people will not be able to earn adequate incomes. These people include the sick, the elderly, and those with skills that are not in high demand. These people may fall into poverty.
- Those with the highest purchasing power will have the most influence on what is produced and some goods and services wanted by the poor may be under-produced.
- Goods and services that are difficult to make consumers pay for directly may not be produced, e.g., defence.
- Whilst people may buy less of some products, such as seat belts for example, than is desirable they may buy more of other products, e.g. cigarettes and alcohol, than is beneficial. The first type of product is called merit goods and the second type is referred to as demerit goods.
- One feature of the market economy, especially in more recent times, is that firms tend to increase in size and power. Modern technology has made it possible for large-scale producers to obtain great advantages in the form of lower production costs. This tendency towards market domination by giant firms reduces, or removes, the limiting role of competition and gives the

large firm the power to exploit the consumer by charging prices well above costs.

- Advertising may persuade people to want products they would not otherwise have chosen. In this case it will be producers rather than consumers who will determine what is produced.
- There is no guarantee that everyone who wants a job will be able to find one.

THE ROLE OF GOVERNMENT

Even in market economies governments have a role to play. They must seek to offset the problems outlined above by implementing various measures.

CREATING A LEGAL FRAMEWORK

Most of the rules and regulations under this heading are designed to see that there is 'fair play' in the competition between producers and in the relations between producers and consumers. Most of the regulations are necessary if the freedom to compete is not to be abused. There are laws which protect property rights, and which enforce contractual obligations (e.g. people are legally obliged to pay their debts). The public is protected from fraud by regulations such as those which oblige firms to publish adequate financial information so that investors will not be misled, and which prevent the dishonest labelling of products. Regulations which insist on adequate standards of hygiene and on minimum safety standards in manufacture protect the public from unnecessary dangers and health hazards. To ensure a reasonable degree of competition the state may pass laws forbidding restrictive trade agreements between producers (e.g. agreements between firms to limit output so as to maintain high prices). Workers are protected by regulations which govern the conditions of work in factories, offices and shops. In most modern economies, industrial and commercial behaviour is closely regulated by the state.

SUPPLEMENTING AND MODIFYING THE PRICE SYSTEM

It has long been recognised that certain goods and services regarded as essential to civilised existence will not be provided by private enterprise, or, if provided, will not be made available on a scale or at a price which society thinks desirable. Such things as defence, internal law and order, education, roads, and health services, are typical of the kind of service which some argue should, to differing degrees, be financed by the state. The government may also influence the pattern of production by making use of taxes and subsidies. The output of goods and services subject to taxation is likely to fall, while subsidies generally lead to an increase in output.

REDISTRIBUTING INCOME

Governments may aim to promote the general economic welfare of the population by creating a more equitable distribution of income and wealth. They may aim to achieve this by a system of taxation which bears more heavily on the richer members of society, combined with the provision of benefits for needier groups. These benefits may take the form of money grants such as child benefit but in other cases the government may attempt to ensure greater equality by providing the services directly at zero market prices. In a number of countries, education and health services are examples of essential services financed from taxation.

STABILISING THE ECONOMY

Governments have a large number of macro-economic policy instruments which they use to influence, e.g. the level of spending, the amount of investment, level of employment, rate of inflation and international trade position. Their aim is to ensure a steady rise in output and improvements in living standards.

QUESTIONS

SHORT QUESTIONS

1. Why is a country that is changing its economic system from a planned to a market economy likely to experience inflation?
2. Which markets have to be developed if a planned economy is to make a successful transition to a market economy?
3. Name three CIS and three CEE countries.
4. What is the Phare programme?

MULTIPLE CHOICE

1. Which is an advantage of a planned economy?

   A. The existence of incentives.

   B. The encouragement of competition.

   C. The full employment of resources.

   D. Quick response to changes in consumer demand.

2. What is the fundamental economic problem which faces all societies?

   A. The redistribution of income.

   B. The elimination of pollution.

   C. The reduction of inflation.

   D. What, how and for whom to produce.

3. An essential feature of a pure market economy is that:

   A. there is state ownership of the means of production

   B. there is control of profits in the private sector

   C. there is free working of the price mechanism

   D. directives are the main mechanism for allocating resources.

4. A mixed economy is one in which:

   A. there is both a state and private sector

   B. some industries are declining and some are expanding

   C. both goods and services are produced in large quantities

   D. there is planning at both the central and local levels.

DATA RESPONSE

CEE AND CIS COUNTRIES % ANNUAL CHANGE IN OUTPUT								
	1991	1992	1993	1994	1995	1996	1997	1998
CEE countries								
Bulgaria	−12	−7	−2	2	3	−11	−7	3
Estonia	−11	−14	−9	−3	3	4	10	6
Hungary	−12	−3	−1	3	2	1	4	5
Poland	−7	3	4	5	7	6	7	6
CIS countries								
Armenia	−11	−52	−15	5	7	6	3	6
Azerbaijan	−1	−23	−23	−21	−8	1	5	7
Russia	−13	−15	−9	−13	−4	−5	0	2
Turkmenistan	−5	−5	−10	−20	−10	−8	−25	12

Source: Table 29.2, *Applied Economics*, 8th edition, edited by A. Griffiths and S. Wall, Longman, 1999.

a] Which countries' output recovered most quickly from the transition towards a market economy? **(2)**

b] Which countries' output recovered most slowly from the transition? **(2)**

c] Compare the performance of the CEE and CIS countries. **(8)**

d] Explain why output fell during the transition period. **(5)**

e] Discuss two reasons why the countries have sought to make the transition. **(8)**

CASE STUDY

According to the central deduction of economic theory, under certain conditions markets allocate resources efficiently. 'Efficiency' has a special meaning in this context. The theory says that markets will produce an outcome such that, given the economy's scarce resources, it is impossible to make anybody better-off without making somebody else worse-off.

Economic theory, in other words, offers a proof of Adam Smith's big idea: in a market economy, if certain conditions are met, an invisible hand guides countless apparently unco-ordinated individuals to a result that is, in one plausible sense, the best that can be done.

In rich countries, markets are too familiar to attract attention. Yet a certain awe is appropriate. When Soviet planners visited a vegetable market in London during the early days of perestroika, they were impressed to find no queues, shortages, or mountains of spoiled and unwanted vegetables. They took their hosts aside and said: 'We understand, you have to say it's all done by supply and demand. But can't you tell us what's really going on? Where are your planners, and what are their methods?'

Source: 'State and market', Schools Brief, The Economist, 17/2/96.

a] Explain what is meant by:
   i   efficiency **(6)**
   ii a market economy. **(6)**

b] Comment on two conditions which have to be met for a market economy to work efficiently. **(8)**

c] What evidence of markets clearing did the Soviet planners find on their visit to London? **(8)**

d] Explain what is meant, in the context of the extract, by 'it's all done by supply and demand'. **(12)**

e] What was the role of Soviet planners in the former Soviet Union? **(10)**

STRUCTURED ESSAY

a] What are the main criteria for distinguishing between different types of economic systems? **(8)**

b] Discuss the economic problems which transitional economies have and are experiencing. **(17)**

5 ECONOMIC RESOURCES

THE MEANING OF PRODUCTION

Production consists of all those activities which provide goods and services to satisfy wants. The complete cycle of production in a modern society can be a complex process which is not complete until the product is in the hands of the final consumer. For example the production of a shirt may begin in the cotton fields of Alabama, but it will not be complete until a consumer makes a purchase in a retail store. The making of a shirt will engage the efforts of workers in fields, factories, offices, ships, docks, railways, road transport, banks, insurance companies, warehouses, and shops. In the UK more than three quarters of the labour force is now engaged in producing services.

OUTPUT

Economic activity results in the output of an enormous variety of goods and services. The composition of total output can be classified into consumer goods, capital goods and services.

- *Consumer goods* are products which satisfy people's wants directly — people want them for their own sake. This group of products can be divided into non-durable and durable consumer goods. *Non-durable consumer goods* are items such as food, heating, lighting, cigarettes, etc. They are consumed or destroyed in the very act of being used. Some of them are good only for a single use while others, such as soap, can be used up a bit at a time. *Durable consumer goods* include such things as books, furniture, television sets, motor cars, and domestic electrical appliances. Such goods produce a steady stream of satisfaction while their value diminishes relatively slowly through age and use.

- *Capital goods*, which can also be called producer goods, do not satisfy wants directly. They are used to produce other goods and services (both consumer and capital products). Lathes, lorries, bulldozers, cranes, factory buildings, and blast furnaces are examples of capital goods.
- *Services* are intangible products, i.e. products which cannot be touched such as banking, dentistry, accountancy and education.

THE STRUCTURE OF INDUSTRY

The many different activities which lead to the production of goods and services can be grouped into three broad categories.

- *Primary production.* This is carried out by what are generally known as the extractive industries because they extract natural resources from the earth's surface, from beneath the earth's surface and from the oceans. Primary industries, therefore, include farming, mining, oil extraction, forestry and fishing.
- *Secondary production.* This includes those industries which process the basic materials into semi-finished and finished products. They are generally described as manufacturing and construction industries. They include examples such as engineering and building, car manufacturing, furniture, clothing and chemicals.
- *Tertiary production.* Industries in the tertiary sector do not produce goods, they produce services. These services are supplied to firms in all types of industry and directly to consumers. Examples of tertiary industries include banking, insurance, law, administration, transport and communication.

- Some economists identify a fourth sector which they call the *quaternary sector*. It consists of those services which are concerned with the collection, processing and transmission of information (e.g. microtechnology), with research and development (e.g. higher education) and with administration and financial management (e.g. accountancy).

ECONOMIC RESOURCES

Production cannot take place unless the necessary resources are available. These resources include factories, railways, farms, mines, human skills, offices and shops. Resources can also be called factors of production or inputs and can be divided into four main types, land, labour, capital and the entrepreneur. Land is the term used for natural resources; labour represents all human resources; capital is the term used for all man-made resources; the entrepreneur is a special form of labour.

This classification is not completely satisfactory because it is sometimes difficult to allocate the real-world resources into these neat categories. For example, land which has been fertilised, drained and fenced is really a combination of land and capital.

LAND (NATURAL RESOURCES)

The term 'land' is used to describe all those natural resources which are used in production. It therefore includes farming and building land, forests, mineral deposits, fisheries, rivers, and lakes.

The supply of land is limited. Although reclamation work has tended to increase the supply in some areas, this is offset by erosion of various kinds so that changes in the total area are probably relatively insignificant.

Land is also geographically immobile: it cannot move from one area of the country to another. No matter how high the price may rise for city centre sites the supply of land in the centre cannot be increased. However land is occupationally mobile. This means that it can change its use. For example, the amount of land used for growing wheat can be increased by growing less of some other crop (e.g. barley). The supply of building land can be increased at the expense of farmland, while the area of cultivated land may be increased by drainage, irrigation and the use of fertilisers.

LABOUR

Labour is human effort — physical and mental — which is directed to the production of goods and services. But labour is not only a factor of production, it is also the reason why economic activity takes place. The people who take part in production are also consumers, the sum of whose individual demands provides the business person with the incentive to undertake production. So labour has to be given special consideration. There are social and political problems which have to be taken into account. For example, the question of how many hours per day a machine should be operated will be judged solely in terms of efficiency, output and costs. The same question applied to labour would raise additional considerations of the need for leisure time.

It must also be borne in mind that it is the services of labour which are bought and sold, and not labour itself. Firms cannot buy and own labour in the same way that capital and land can be bought and owned.

CAPITAL

Capital is a man-made resource. It is used in the production of other goods and services. For example, machines, offices, factories and delivery vans. Capital can be divided into working and fixed capital.

Working capital

This is capital which is used up in the course of production. It consists of the stocks of raw materials, partly finished goods and stocks of unsold goods. This kind of capital is also sometimes called circulating capital as it keeps moving and changing.

Fixed capital

This is not used up in the course of production. It consists of equipment such as buildings, machinery, railways etc. This type of capital does not change its form in the course of production and move from one stage to the next — it is 'fixed'. A significant part of a nation's stock of capital, particularly its fixed capital, consists of houses, schools, hospitals, libraries, and other types of property which are not directly concerned with the production of products. The term social capital is used to describe this type of asset. Such property is part of the capital stock because it assists people in the production of goods and services, but it does so only indirectly. For example schools improve the knowledge and skills of future workers.

Sunk capital

This is a form of fixed capital. It consists of capital equipment which has a specific purpose. It cannot be used for any other purpose other than the current one and has no resale value. An example of this is the tunnelling equipment which was used in the construction of the Channel Tunnel.

Capital accumulation

People use capital not to satisfy any personal craving, but to produce goods and services with less output and lower costs than would have been the case if labour were unassisted by capital. But in order to use capital goods, people must first produce them

and this usually calls for a sacrifice. While it is producing capital goods, labour cannot also be producing consumer goods. The opportunity cost of the capital goods is the potential output of consumer goods which has to be forgone in order to produce that capital.

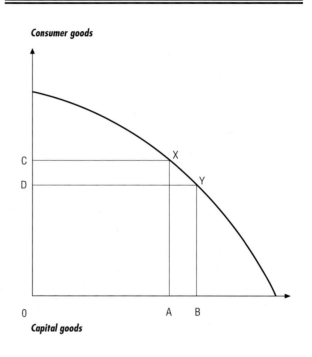

FIG. 5.1

Figure 5.1 shows an economy making full use of its resources, producing at point X initially. To increase output of capital goods from A to B and produce at point Y, CD amount of consumer goods have to be forgone. So unless there are appropriate unemployed resources the creation of capital goods means forgoing some present consumption for the prospect of a higher level of future consumption. People are prepared to make this sacrifice because the use of capital equipment greatly increases labour's productivity.

Two things make possible the creation of capital: saving and a diversion of resources. Saving is the act of forgoing consumption. It means that a claim on the resources required to produce consumer goods and services is not being exercised. By choosing not to buy consumer goods and services with some part of their income, people do not buy the services of the resources required to make the products. The resources might, therefore, remain unemployed. However the savings might be borrowed (by entrepreneurs) and used to finance the production of capital goods. This is the second step — the diversion of resources from the production of consumer goods and services to the production of capital goods. Saving makes possible capital accumulation — it does not cause it.

Gross and net investment

Industrial economies produce a large output of capital goods each year. However not all of this adds to the national stock of capital. This is because some of the capital goods produced are used as replacements for capital goods which have either physically worn out or have become obsolete because of advances in technology. The value of replacement capital is known as depreciation or capital consumption. The total output of capital goods is called gross investment, and any additions to the capital stock is called net investment. So:

Gross investment − depreciation = net investment

It could happen that the rate of depreciation exceeds the total output of capital so that there is negative net investment. In this case some of the capital goods which are wearing out or becoming obsolete are not being replaced. In this case the productive capacity of the country will decline and the production possibility curve move inwards.

THE ENTREPRENEUR

Some economists identify a fourth economic resource — enterprise. Entrepreneurs organise the other factors of production, decide what to produce (i.e. the type of good or service and the quantity), how to produce it (i.e. the methods of production) and where to produce it (the location of the enterprise).

Whoever takes these decisions, and the consequent risks, is known as the entrepreneur. There is no really suitable alternative way of describing such a person though 'enterpriser' may come close. The entrepreneur is the person who undertakes production with a view to profit. In a market economy, production would not take place unless someone was prepared to buy and organise economic resources for production on the basis of expected profits.

The entrepreneur is a risk-bearer. This is the key, defining role of the entrepreneur.

Most production is undertaken in anticipation of demand: firms will produce only those products which they believe will yield a profit — they do not know that they will do so, because the future is unknown. Entrepreneurs must therefore bear the costs involved during the time that elapses between the decision to produce and the eventual marketing of the product. They must pay rent for their land, interest on the money borrowed, wages to labour and meet the costs of materials. These payments must be made without any certainty that such costs will be covered by receipts. If the sales revenue entrepreneurs receive exceeds their expenses, they will make a profit — if not, they must bear the loss. The risks borne by entrepreneurs arise from uncertainty. Economic conditions are always changing and past experience is not necessarily a good guide to future prospects.

Some economists do not accept that the functions just described represent those of a factor of production which is clearly distinguishable from labour. They argue that the entrepreneurial function is no more than a particular and specialised form of labour. They point out that risk-bearing is not peculiar to the entrepreneur. Many types of labour take risks — the steeplejack and the miner run the risk of personal injury — while most forms of labour cannot avoid the risk of unemployment.

INTRAPRENEURS

Some economists now distinguish between entrepreneurs and intrapreneurs. Entrepreneurs are people who start their own business whilst intrapreneurs are people who work their way to the top of existing companies. In a 1994 study into 'Business Elites' conducted by Cary Cooper, professor of organisational psychology, entrepreneurs were found to be loners, innovative and keen to take risks but also people who found the growth of their companies difficult to handle because it brought with it the need for more structure and greater decentralisation. In contrast, intrapreneurs were found to be less original but better at handling detail, more methodical and more efficient.

PRODUCTION AND PRODUCTIVITY

Production is the output of economic resources. The production of a firm, for example, is the total output of the firm over a given time period. Whereas productivity is the output of a unit of a factor of production in a given period. For example labour productivity is the output per worker hour.

Production and productivity often move in the same direction. Indeed a rise in productivity increases a country's productive potential. If all an economy's workers are employed a rise in productivity will increase a country's production. However if unemployment is increasing a rise in productivity may be accompanied by a fall in production.

QUESTIONS

SHORT QUESTIONS

1. What is meant by durable consumer goods?

2. What is unique about land as a factor of production?

3. What is the difference between working and fixed capital?

4. Giving examples, explain the types of risk entrepreneurs bear.

MULTIPLE CHOICE

1 Which worker is employed in the secondary sector?

- A A banker.

- B A doctor.

- C A farmer.

- D A printer.

2 Which of the following is a capital good?

- A A fishing area.

- B A motor car used for leisure purposes.

- C A bank loan to a newly established company.

- D A photocopying machine used in an accountancy firm.

3 A company buys ten machines costing £6000 each. Six of the machines are purchased to replace worn out machines and four to expand production. What is the value of the net investment?

- A £12000
- B £24000
- C £36000
- D £60000

4 What is the defining function of an entrepreneur?

- A To bear uncertain risks.

- B To set up new companies.

- C To employ the other factors of production.

- D To organise the other factors of production.

DATA RESPONSE

Members of the golden-grey club, third age entrepreneurs, call them what you like, but the number of people over 50 starting a business is growing and their success and lifestyle is enough to make entrepreneurs half their age envious.

Overall there are 50 000 small businesses starting up each year by people over 50 — around 10% of all start-ups.

They tend to survive — 70% will still be trading after five years compared with the average survival rate for all small businesses of only 28% after five years — and 38% are still going after 11 years.

When it comes to technology third age entrepreneurs are not dilatory. Nearly two-thirds have a computer or word processor, half have a fax and a quarter use the internet and email. Less than half of average small businesses have a computer.

Motivations for over-50s starting up businesses:

Made redundant/retired	26%
To make money	25%
Job satisfaction	19%
Turn hobby into money	18%
Wanted freedom	9%
Had time to fill	5%

'In many ways it is easier for the over-50s to start businesses,' says Alastair Camp, head of small business banking at Barclays. 'At the older end of the spectrum business owners have the experience of life behind them — and the cash. So they start with a number of advantages.' 'What they lack in drive, they make up for in experience, knowledge and confidence,' he says.

Extracts from: 'Age is no bar to success'
by John Dunn, the Guardian, 27/4/99.

a] What is meant by third age entrepreneurs? **(2)**

b] How risky is setting up a new business? **(4)**

c] What skills do older entrepreneurs have? **(6)**

d] i Discuss the reasons why older entrepreneurs start up new companies. **(6)**

ii What do you think are the reasons why younger entrepreneurs start up new companies? **(7)**

CASE STUDY

Fiona Cannon is in ground-breaking mode. 'Most business are set up on the basis that people work nine to five, begin their career at 21 and work right through to 65. But life isn't like that any more. Nothing is like that now,' says the head of equal opportunities at Lloyds TSB.

The bank has embarked on an experiment designed to increase productivity and reduce costs. At its heart is a generous offer to employees; you choose how, when and where you work, and we'll accommodate it.

Applications have roared in from all over the organisation. Even branch managers have requested reduced hours and job shares. Teleworking and variable working hours are also up for grabs.

The scheme aims to accommodate the conflicting obligations on staff of work and family and, by doing so, should boost staff loyalty and reduce turnover costs. At the same time, the bank may be better placed to offer service outside usual working hours.

The move is one example of how flexible working patterns, and the rapid growth of part-time work in particular, are influencing the economy. Official figures show that the proportion of people working traditional hours is declining: part-time jobs grew twice as fast as the number of full-time jobs between 1993 and 1998.

Rapid growth in services and the steady stream of women into employment has helped bring about this shift.

Cambridge Econometrics, an economics consultancy, says part-time jobs will account for all the employment growth of the next decade. At present, there are 6.8m part-timers, a quarter of the 27.4m in employment. Many work in the retailing and catering industries. Financial services also account for a large proportion. By 2010, the report says, nearly a third of all jobs will be part-time, up from fewer than a fifth in 1980.

In theory, part-time working and other flexible work practices should make the economy fitter by enabling employers to respond more smoothly to swings in demand and consumer spending habits. Many companies have been forced to extend their opening hours in order to compete effectively and have recruited staff to meet these requirements.

Source: 'Business wakes up to the end of working nine to five', by Christopher Adams, Financial Times, 26/5/99.

a] Describe the experiment that Lloyds TSB were undertaking. **(6)**

b] What is meant by teleworking? **(4)**

c] What benefits may employees and companies gain from part-time and flexible working? **(16)**

d] Why has part-time employment increased? **(6)**

e] Why is it predicted that part-time employment will continue to increase in the future? **(3)**

f] In which industries is part-time working already significant? **(3)**

g] In which sector, primary, secondary or tertiary are these industries? **(3)**

h] Discuss three possible disadvantages of working part-time. **(9)**

STRUCTURED ESSAY

a] Describe the characteristics of the factors of production. **(12)**

b] Explain the opportunity cost of capital accumulation and the benefits of capital accumulation. **(13)**

6 SPECIALISATION

In developed economies most workers specialise in performing particular tasks in the production of a good or service. Very few workers make a complete product. Firms, areas and countries may also specialise. For example Cornwall and Devon, in the UK, concentrate on tourism and agriculture.

THE DIVISION OF LABOUR

The division of labour is the splitting of the production process into a number of individual operations and making each operation the special task of one worker. So it involves workers specialising. For example, in a hotel some workers will be employed as cleaners, some as receptionists, some as waiters and waitresses, some as cooks and some in a management capacity.

THE DEVELOPMENT OF THE DIVISION OF LABOUR

At a very early stage in human development, people realised the gains to be obtained by applying this principle. The earliest people must have attempted to provide all their daily wants by their own efforts. They would have been obliged to provide food, clothing, shelter, and protection for themselves. In doing so they could have produced little more than the barest essentials for survival. By living in communities where some degree of specialisation was practised they learned that the total output of any group was much greater than the sum of the individual outputs of independent producers. One person might specialise in hunting, another in making tools, and so on. Each would exchange his or her surplus for the products made by other specialists. From these earliest times the principle of the division of labour has been progressively extended. The process is still going on in both developed and developing economies. A visit to most modern factories and offices gives a vivid picture of the extent to which production is now specialised. However, as noted below, some companies in developed countries are now moving away from too much specialisation.

ADAM SMITH AND SPECIALISATION

Adam Smith, writing in the latter part of the eighteenth century, provided what has now become the most famous account of specialisation. On a visit to a factory engaged in making pins he observed: 'One man draws out the wire, another straightens it, a third cuts it, a fourth points it, a fifth grinds the top to receive the head; to make the head requires two or three distinct operations; to put it on is a peculiar business; to whiten it is another; it is even a trade in itself to put them into paper. The important business of making pins is, in this manner, divided into 18 distinct operations.'

He estimated that production in this factory was about 5000 pins per person employed. If the whole operation had been carried out from start to finish by each employee, Smith estimated that he would have been able to make only a few dozen each day.

ADVANTAGES OF THE DIVISION OF LABOUR

A number of reasons put forward as to why the division of labour may increase productivity and hence lower average (unit) costs of production. These include:

- A person who spends his or her time performing one relatively simple task becomes very efficient at that particular operation — 'practice makes perfect'.
- No time is wasted in moving from one job to another.
- A saving of equipment. If workers specialise they will not need to have a full set of tools or other equipment.
- There is a saving of time in training of operatives. A man or woman can be trained very quickly for the performance of a single operation.
- There is a saving of skill. Specialisation means that many different occupations are created, each one of which calls for some particular aptitude. It is possible, therefore for each worker to specialise in the job for which he or she is best suited.
- It makes possible a greater degree of mechanisation. When a complex process has been broken down into a series of separate, simple processes it is possible to devise machinery to carry out each individual operation. With advances in technology it is becoming possible to mechanise more areas of production.

EXAMPLE

It might be thought that if a person is more efficient in all tasks than another person specialisation will not be beneficial. However it can be shown that specialisation of labour might still be advantageous. A simple arithmetical example will make this point clear. Suppose there are two leather workers, A and B, each producing shoes and handbags.

In 1 week A can make either 10 pairs of shoes, or 10 handbags

In 1 week B can make either 8 pairs of shoes, or 4 handbags

In the absence of any specialisation it is supposed that each week:

A makes 5 pairs of shoes and 5 handbags
B makes 4 pairs of shoes and 2 handbags
Total: 9 pairs of shoes and 7 handbags

A is more efficient in both activities, but the fact that he is relatively more efficient in producing handbags (10:4) than in producing shoes (10:8) means that specialisation will result in a greater total output.

It can be assumed that B specialises completely in shoes while A partially specialises in handbags. So each week:

A makes 2 pairs of shoes and 8 handbags
B makes 8 pairs of shoes and 0 handbags
Total: 10 pairs of shoes and 8 handbags

This is a simplified example of the principle of comparative advantage which is discussed in detail in Chapter 47.

DISADVANTAGES OF THE DIVISION OF LABOUR

There are a number of reasons why workers specialising may not result in a rise in productivity. These include:

- *Loss of flexibility*. If workers specialise too much it may be difficult for them to switch to performing other tasks when there is a need to cover for sick colleagues on training courses or when demand changes.
- *Monotony*. Workers can get bored performing the same tasks each day. This may result in them making mistakes and may result in higher sickness rates and higher labour turnover.
- *Loss of skills*. Some claim that by breaking production into a series of separate, simple and often mechanised tasks, workers are not challenged and are not able to gain sufficient job satisfaction.
- *Increased risk of unemployment*. Specialisation means that workers may not have a wide range of skills. When demand or supply conditions change their particular skills may no longer be needed. However some argue that the division of labour, by simplifying tasks, makes jobs in one

industry very similar to those in another. Since the tasks are easy to learn, retraining is easily and quickly accomplished and workers can, without great difficulty, move from one job to another.

- *Interdependence.* A specialised system of production increases the extent to which different sectors of the economy depend upon one another. It is not simply a question of workers specialising, factories, firms and even whole industries specialise. A problem in production in one company may cause hold-ups throughout the industry and related industries. For example a break-down in temperature control in a food processing company may disrupt supplies to a number of supermarket chains and other retailers.

MOVES AWAY FROM SPECIALISATION

Modern technology allied to the extensive use of the division of labour has made enormous increases in the output of goods and services possible. It has transformed the living standards of millions of people, removed much of the back-breaking toil from people's daily labour and made possible an increase in leisure time.

However, the loss of job satisfaction, particularly in manufacturing industries, is causing some firms to consider various projects aimed at achieving job enrichment by enlarging the role and responsibilities of the workers.

For example, Volvo moved away from specialisation in order to increase the quantity and quality of output. Allowing workers to undertake a number of different tasks may increase workers' enjoyment of their jobs, identify their strengths, increase their ability to make suggestions for improving production methods and the product, enable workers to cover for colleagues who are sick or undertaking training and increase labour flexibility.

SPECIALISATION AND EXCHANGE

A system of specialised production, no matter how simple, cannot exist without exchange. When people become specialists they are dependent upon some system of exchange to provide them with the variety of goods and services required to satisfy their wants. For example, without some means of exchange, farmers would have too much corn for their personal needs, but would have no coal, oil, electricity, or machinery. There must be some means whereby the outputs of specialist producers can be exchanged. In most economies the use of money enables people to exchange labour for a wage which in turn is exchanged for a wide variety of goods and services.

SPECIALISATION AND THE SIZE OF THE MARKET

The principle of the division of labour can also only be applied extensively when there is a large market for a standardised product. For workers to specialise, output must be high enough for there to be a large enough labour force for each worker to carry out specialised tasks. For example, within the car industry there is considerable specialisation, and the application of technically advanced machinery, in the production of standardised popular models which are produced in large quantities. However there is less scope for the division of labour in the production of racing cars which are produced in much smaller quantities and to individual designs. The size of the market, and hence the opportunity to apply the division of labour, also depends on the existence of a good transport system which facilitates the distribution of products.

SPECIALISATION AND THE APPLICATION OF MACHINERY

As briefly mentioned above the application of large-scale machinery is only worth while if there is a market (i.e. a potential demand) large enough to keep the equipment fully employed. However, as micro technology becomes cheaper, it becomes possible for firms to cater for smaller markets. For example, desk-top publishing means that now even relatively narrow interests, such as parrot-keeping, can have specialist magazines produced for them.

SPECIALISATION AND ECONOMIC CHANGE

When labour and other resources become very specialised it can become difficult to adapt quickly and smoothly to changes in methods of production and changes in demand. For example, a chemist might find it hard to switch to being an accountant if demand for chemists falls whilst demand for accountants increases, and a petrol tanker cannot easily be used to carry coal. Indeed, much is designed for a specific task and cannot be used for other purposes.

Q U E S T I O N S

SHORT QUESTIONS

1. When is division of labour uneconomic?

2. To what extent can car manufacturers take advantage of division of labour?

3. Explain two advantages of the division of labour for the worker.

4. Explain two disadvantages of the division of labour for a firm.

MULTIPLE CHOICE

1 Which economist described a pin factory engaging in the division of labour?

A. Milton Friedman.

B. John Kenneth Galbraith.

C. John Maynard Keynes.

D. Adam Smith.

2 Which would reduce the benefits to be gained from the division of labour?

A. An improved transport system.

B. An improved monetary system.

C. A decrease in international trade restrictions.

D. A decrease in demand for standardised products.

3 What is the main benefit claimed for division of labour?

A. An improvement in the quality of the goods and services produced.

B. An improvement in the job satisfaction of the workers involved.

C. A decrease in the average cost of production.

D. A decrease in the use of machinery.

4 Which does not occur as a result of the introduction of the division of labour?

A. An increase in productivity.

B. The use of more specialised machinery.

C. A reduction in the training period of workers.

D. The development of a wider range of skills by workers.

DATA RESPONSE

This great increase in the quantity of work which, in consequence of the division of labour, the same number of people are capable of performing is owing to three different circumstances; first, to increase the dexterity in every particular worker; secondly, to the saving of the time which is commonly lost in passing from one species of work to another; and lastly, to the invention of a great number of machines which facilitate and abridge labour, and enable one man to do the work of many.

First, the improvement of the dexterity of the workman necessarily increases the quantity of the work he can perform; and the division of labour, by reducing every man's business to some one simple operation, and by making this operation the sole employment of his life, necessarily increases very much the dexterity of the workman. Secondly, the advantage which is gained by saving the time commonly lost in passing from one sort of work to another is much greater than we should at first view to be apt to imagine it. Thirdly and lastly, everybody must be sensible how much labour is facilitated and abridged by the application of proper machinery.

Source: The Wealth of Nations, Adam Smith.

a] The extract mentions three advantages of the division of labour. Explain two other advantages. **(6)**

b] Does reducing the number of tasks a worker has to do necessarily result in improvements in the quantity and quality of output? **(7)**

c] Is the saving of time 'lost in passing from one sort of work to another' more significant in the tertiary or secondary sector? **(6)**

d] Explain how the division of labour facilitates the introduction of machinery. **(7)**

CASE STUDY

Tomkins, the diversified engineering and food conglomerate, yesterday confirmed plans to de-merge its food manufacturing division in a move which signals the end of Britain's last remaining major conglomerate built up during the Eighties.

Following similar moves by Hanson, Williams Holdings and BTR in recent years, Tomkins is to slim itself down and concentrate on a narrower spectrum of businesses.

Greg Hutchings, Tomkins chairman said: 'Business is a dynamic thing. You've got to change with the times. We always follow industry developments and have decided that the time is right to focus on our industrial businesses.'

Announcing flat pre-exceptional annual profits of £496m, Mr Hutchings said Tomkins will spin off its Rank Hovis McDougall food business into a separately quoted company early next year.

RHM, which includes brands such as Hovis, Mothers Pride, Bisto gravy and Robertson's jams, is expected to be valued at as much as £2bn. Another major division, which includes lawnmower and bicycles is to be sold.

The deals will leave Tomkins focused on two divisions: automative parts such as windscreen wipers and fuel caps and construction which includes businesses making baths, axles and plastic panels.

It was all so different in the Seventies and Eighties as conglomerates like Hanson and Williams Holdings and their respective leaders Lord Hanson and Nigel Rudd were lionised in business circles. The maxim chanted by Lord Hanson was that it didn't matter what business a company was in, a good management team ought to be able to get the best out of it.

Source: 'End of guns-to-buns group sounds the last post for the big conglomerates' by Nigel Cope, the Independent, 13/7/99.

a] Explain what is meant by:
   i   a conglomerate **(3)**
   ii a de-merger **(3)**
   iii diversified. **(3)**

b] What type of products did Tomkins produce? **(4)**

c] What are the advantages and disadvantages of a company deciding to concentrate on a narrower range of products? **(14)**

d] To what extent do you think that the process of the division of labour can be applied to the production of:
   i   processed food **(5)**
   ii lawnmowers **(5)**
   iii baths. **(5)**

e] Do you think it is as easy to manage a business which makes a wide range of products as one which makes a narrower range? **(8)**

STRUCTURED ESSAY

a] Explain how the application of the division of labour depends on (i) the size of the market, (ii) money and (iii) an efficient transport system. **(10)**

b] Discuss whether the advantages of division of labour are mainly economic, whilst the disadvantages are mainly personal and social. **(15)**

7 MONEY

Money is any item which is generally acceptable in exchange for goods and services. Money enables the exchange of goods and services to take place more easily and so (as discussed in Chapter 6) encourages specialisation. For example, a person could concentrate on producing jewellery, then exchange the jewellery for money and use the money for whatever goods and services s/he requires. Without money, exchange has to take the form of barter.

BARTER

Barter is the direct exchange of goods and services. This system can work if people produce for themselves most of the goods and services they need and rely on market exchanges for only a small number of items. However, barter has a number of significant disadvantages for economies which specialise. People wanting to save and those who are prepared to accept payment later may be uncertain as to what items will be in demand in the future. It will also be difficult to make comparisons of the value of different items. However, the main disadvantage of barter is that it depends upon a 'double coincidence of wants.'

For example, a hunter who wants to exchange his skins for corn must find, not merely a person who wants skins, but someone who wants skins and has a surplus of corn for disposal. The alternative is to exchange his skins for some other article and then carry out a series of similar exchanges until he finally gets his corn. Time and energy which could be devoted to production is devoted to a time-consuming system of exchange. Most economies adopt money to overcome these problems.

THE FUNCTIONS OF MONEY

The functions which money carries out makes it easier for people to buy and sell goods and services, make comparisons of the value of different items, save, borrow and lend. These functions are described as:

- *A medium of exchange.* Money enables people to exchange their labour for wages which in turn they can use to buy goods and services. This function makes possible a great extension of the principle of specialisation.
- *A measure of value.* The first step in the use of money was probably the adoption of some item as a unit of account or measure of value. Money, most likely, came into use within the barter system as a means whereby the values of different goods and services could be compared. The direct exchange of goods and services for other goods and services would raise all sorts of problems regarding valuation. For example how may bushels of corn are equal in value to one sheep, if twenty sheep exchange for three cows and one cow exchanges for ten bushels of corn? This problem of exchange rates is easily solved when all other commodities are valued in terms of a single commodity which then acts as a measure of value. Money now serves as such a measure, making it possible to know, immediately, the value of one product in terms of any other product.
- *A store of value.* Once an item becomes universally acceptable in exchange for goods and services, it is possible to store wealth by holding a stock of this item. It is a great convenience to hold wealth in the form of money. Consider the problems of holding wealth in the form of some other item,

for example wheat. It may deteriorate, it is costly to store, it must be insured, and there will be significant handling costs in accumulating and distributing it. In addition, its money value may fall while it is being stored. However whilst money does not physically deteriorate and is not costly to store it can fall in value if inflation occurs.

- *A standard for deferred payments.* An important function of money in the modern world, where so much business is conducted on the basis of credit, is to serve as a means of deferred payment. When goods and services are supplied on credit, the buyer has immediate use of them but does not have to make an immediate payment. Sellers would be unlikely to accept promises to pay in the future which were expressed in terms of products other than money. They would have no idea how much of the products they would need in the future and, if they do not want them, they face the trouble and risks involved in selling them. Sellers will accept promises to pay, expressed in terms of money, because they know that they can use the money to buy the goods and services they require. So money makes it easier to borrow and lend as it is a convenient way of measuring debt and repaying debt.

THE FUNCTIONS OF MONEY AND INFLATION

Inflation, especially if it is at a high and accelerating level, affects the ability of money to carry out its functions. If the general price level is rising rapidly people may become reluctant to keep their savings in the form of money, for example current accounts (sight deposits), as this will be losing its value in terms of purchasing power. People may, instead, seek to hold assets which rise in value by more than the rate of inflation, e.g. antiques and property.

When there is hyperinflation people may also become reluctant to accept money in settlement of debts. For example in Germany in the 1920s when inflation reached 7 000 000 000 000 % people asked to be paid in cigarettes and other items which they believed would be more acceptable when they came to make their own payments.

THE CHARACTERISTICS OF MONEY

To serve as money and to carry out its functions efficiently an item must possess certain characteristics.

The essential characteristic of money is that it must be generally acceptable. As noted above unless the medium of exchange is freely acceptable by everyone, no producer is going to take the risk of accepting it in exchange for his products. He must have confidence that the 'money' will, in turn, be accepted by the sellers of the things s/he wishes to buy.

An efficient medium of exchange must be portable by having a high ratio of value to bulk and weight. It would be inconvenient to use large, heavy, and bulky items as money.

The item used as money must also be divisible, that is, capable of subdivision into smaller units without any loss in value. Suppose hides are being used as money and two sheep are worth one hide. How does one buy one sheep? When the hide is cut into two equal parts, the value of the two halves is less than the value of the whole hide.

Another important characteristic of whatever is to serve as money is durability. People will not accept anything which is subject to rapid deterioration and hence loses its value while it is in their possession. Nor will they want to save the item.

The item must also be limited in supply. Unless there is some limitation on its supply, either natural or artificial, people will have no confidence in the value of the item.

FORMS OF MONEY

PRECIOUS METALS

Over time a variety of items have acted as money. These have included the precious metals gold and silver. Gold and silver are portable since they have a very high commodity value and it is very easy to use them to produce items of uniform fineness. These metals are divisible without loss in value and they are easily recognisable. They can be stored without risk of deterioration and, most important, they are limited in supply. Gold especially is difficult and costly to extract. Since the annual additions to the existing world stocks of gold and silver are relatively very small there is virtually no risk of a large increase in supply destroying the value of gold. However, there is an opportunity cost involved in using gold and silver as money. These precious metals have other uses including for jewellery and in industry.

COINS

The precious metals were first used as money on the basis of weight. However, the inconvenience of weighing out the metals each time a transaction took place led to the introduction of coins. It was appreciated that exchange would be greatly facilitated if the pieces of metal to be used as money carried some clear indication of their weight and fineness. Coins are shaped pieces of metal bearing some authoritative imprint which certifies their money value. Their money value exceeds their intrinsic value.

BANK NOTES

Bank notes first came into existence as people began to use claims to precious metal as money instead of the metal itself. The dangers of theft and lack of security in the average home meant that gold and silver were deposited in goldsmiths' vaults — the depositors receiving some written acknowledge-ment of their ownership. These receipts developed into the bank notes we know today, with the promise on them to pay the bearer (i.e. anyone) instead of a named person. This promise originally meant that people could convert the notes into gold (or silver). However, nowadays bank notes are not backed by gold or silver.

MAIN FORMS OF MONEY TODAY

The main forms of money used now are bank notes, coins and money placed in bank and building society accounts which are also known as deposits. As already noted, coins and bank notes no longer have any intrinsic value but they are universally acceptable. Nevertheless the most important component of the money supply in developed economies is now bank and building society deposits. In the UK these deposits account for more than 90% of the money in circulation.

MEASURES OF THE MONEY SUPPLY

Currently, the two measures of the money supply which receive the most attention are the M0 and M4 measures. M0 includes notes, coins and the operational balances of commercial banks held at the Bank of England. M4 consists of notes and coins in circulation and, in the UK, sight and time deposits (current accounts and deposit accounts) held in UK banks and building societies.

M0 is known as a narrow measure of the money supply and it is concerned with forms of money used as a medium of exchange. Conversely, M4 is a broad measure since it includes forms of money which are used both as a medium of exchange and as a store of value.

LEGAL TENDER

Not all money used in the UK is legal tender. Legal tender is defined as any form of money that must by law be accepted in settlement of a debt. All UK bank notes and £1 coins are full legal tender, and coins up to certain values. For instance, 10p coins are legal tender up to £5 but people have the right to refuse to accept amounts above that as payment.

NEAR MONEY

This can also be referred to as quasi-money. It consists of financial assets such as postal orders which are held mainly as a store of value rather than as a medium of exchange. Near money items fulfil some but not all the functions of money and usually have to be converted into true money before they can be spent. However, they are close to true money as they can usually be converted into cash quickly and at little or no cost.

QUESTIONS

SHORT QUESTIONS

1 What is money?

2 Explain the disadvantages of barter.

3 Are bank deposits:
i money
ii legal tender?

4 Distinguish between the M0 and M4 measures of the money supply.

MULTIPLE CHOICE

1 In choosing an item to serve as money which of the following is the most important characteristic? It must be:

A divisible

B issued by the state

C easily recognisable

D generally acceptable.

2 Which function of money is the ability to assess costs, and choose between competing projects, most dependent on?

A Medium of exchange.

B Unit of account.

C Store of value.

D Standard for deferred payments.

3 Which is the most common form of money, measured by value, in a developed country?

A Coins.

B Bank notes.

C Bank deposits.

D Cheques.

4 Which of the following items is included in the UK M4 measure of the money supply but not the M0 measure?

A Current accounts (sight deposits) in commercial banks.

B Commercial banks' operational balances at the Bank of England.

C Notes and coins in circulation outside the commercial banks.

D Notes and coins held in tills by the commercial banks.

DATA RESPONSE

Trade originally involved people swapping goods. This direct exchange of goods is known as barter. However, there are a number of disadvantages. These include the double coincidence of wants. This means the need to find someone who wants a good or service you have to exchange and who has an item you want. Barter within most countries is not now very common. The smooth operation of complex economies, with workers specialising in producing particular products, is dependent on money.

Money is defined as any item which is generally acceptable in exchange for goods and services. It carries out four main functions including acting as a medium of exchange. This involves money being used to buy goods and services.

Many items have been used as money including stamps, salt, grain, shells and strips of fur. The main forms of money in the UK now include notes, coins and bank deposits.

Coins were first used in India between 1000 and 800 BC. A number of metals have been used including gold, silver, copper and nickel. Most modern coins are made from cheap, base metals and their face value, based on acceptability, exceeds their intrinsic value.

Paper money originated in China in the T'ang Dynasty between 650 and 800 AD. It was first used in the UK in the seventeenth century and developed from receipts issued by goldsmiths. Now the Bank of England is the only note issuing institution in England and Wales.

Sight deposits (current accounts) are used mainly as a medium of exchange. Writing a cheque is one way of transferring money. The cheque is not money itself but merely an instruction to move money from one deposit to another. Time deposits (deposit accounts) are kept mainly as a store of value.

a] Explain one disadvantage of barter not mentioned in the passage. **(3)**

b] Discuss the three functions of money not mentioned in the passage. **(6)**

c] What characteristics of money do stamps and salt possess? **(8)**

d] Explain why the face value of modern coins exceeds their intrinsic value. **(3)**

e] Why are bank deposits the main form of money in most economies? **(5)**

CASE STUDY

In what some will view as a wildly optimistic move, the European Central Bank today starts the presses rolling on the first batch of 13bn euro banknotes, due to enter cash registers on January 1, 2002. With the euro dwindling in value by the hour, one wonders whether 13bn will be enough. Another 18 months, and it will be the Weimar Republic all over.

But, however grim its prospects, the euro's hard currency debut is being anticipated with excitement in more than just the hallowed quarters of Brussels. When the day dawns, Europe, overnight, will find itself flooded with billions in crisp, freshly printed, totally unfamiliar banknotes — a recipe, many believe, for one of the biggest outbreaks of opportunist crime ever seen.

Police and banking authorities fear that criminal elements will take advantage of the confusion to dump hundreds of millions in counterfeit notes on to an unsuspecting public. Few will know what the euro looks like, let alone know what security measures to look for, and the result could be a criminal bonanza on a scale never seen before.

It is an open secret that the Mafia and others have been stockpiling forged euros in anticipation of the great day. Euroland's 11 member states have until the end of 2000 to produce 13bn euro banknotes, yet the printing process has already fallen behind schedule.

National currencies such as the franc and mark will remain legal tender alongside the euro until June 2002, doubling the number of bills in circulation to 26bn, at its peak, and adding to the chaos. There are some in Germany who are calling for the mark to be retained indefinitely as a parallel currency, keeping the options open.

An added problem with the euro is that it is being produced in denominations of up to €500 notes (about £325).

Source: 'Euro counterfeiters will forge ahead' by Jon Ashworth, 15/7/99, The Times.

a] Explain what is meant by counterfeit notes. **(4)**

b] Why is it suggested that the introduction of euro banknotes will result in a rise in counterfeiting? **(8)**

c] What effect do you think advances in colour photocopiers and PC-based desk-top publishing packages have had on counterfeiting? **(4)**

d] Why may high denominations of banknotes encourage more bank robberies? **(6)**

e] What qualities of money may euro banknotes lack in the early years of their use? **(10)**

f] Explain what is meant by a parallel currency. **(4)**

g] Discuss whether you think it would be a good idea to keep the German mark as a parallel currency. **(14)**

STRUCTURED ESSAY

a] Explain why bank and building society deposits possess the characteristics needed to act as money. **(13)**

b] Outline the functions of money. **(12)**

PART TWO: MARKETS

8 DEMAND

Economists study demand in order to understand consumer behaviour and the determination of price levels. In the absence of government intervention, prices are determined by the forces of demand and supply. Buyers and sellers are brought into contact with one another in a market. A market does not have to be an actual location. For example, part of the book market now exists on the Internet.

DEFINITION

In economics demand is not the same thing as desire, or need, or want. This is because the strength of the desire for something will not, in itself, have any influence on the price of the item. Only when desire is supported by the ability and willingness to pay the price does it become an effective demand and have an influence on the market. Demand, in economics, means effective demand and may be defined as 'the quantity of the commodity which will be demanded at any given price over some given period of time.'

INDIVIDUAL AND MARKET DEMAND

For the great majority of goods and services, experience shows that the quantity demanded will increase as the price falls. Economists have found this out by studying markets.

It is possible to study individual demand which is the relationship between the quantity demanded of a good or service by a single individual and the price of that good or service.

It is also possible to study market demand. This is the total demand for the good or service. It is found by adding the quantities demanded by each individual buyer at each price. For example one person's demand for crisps at the current price may be four a week and the total demand may be 30 000.

Market demand will depend on how the market is defined. For example, the total demand for all brands of crisps may be studied, or the total demand for one particular brand or the total demand for snacks (of which crisps are a part). It is also possible to examine the demand for crisps at different levels. For example, the demand for crisps from one particular supermarket or in one particular area might be studied.

DEMAND SCHEDULES AND CURVES

Individual and market demand information can be expressed in the form of demand schedules and demand curves. A demand schedule is a table giving the quantities demanded at a range of prices.

TABLE 8.1 DEMAND SCHEDULE

Price £	Quantity demand (per week)
5	50
4	80
3	130
2	190
1	300

A demand curve can be drawn which plots this information on a graph with price on the vertical axis and quantity demanded at a range of prices. This is shown on Figure 8.1.

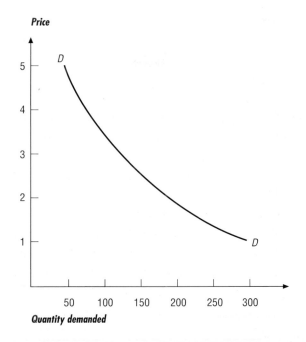

Price

FIG. 8.1

beginning, that the demand curve shows what happens to quantity demanded when price changes and there is no change in any of the other factors influencing demand (e.g. income, taste, fashion and so on).

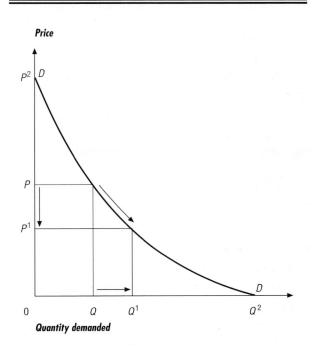

FIG. 8.2

A market demand schedule and a corresponding market demand curve, can be calculated by adding up the amounts each individual demands at different prices. This is sometimes referred to as the horizontal summation of all the individual demand curves.

TABLE 8.2 QUANTITY DEMANDED PER WEEK

Price £	Individual demand schedules						Market demand
	A	B	C	D	E	F	
5	50	20	40	25	30	70	235
4	80	50	80	50	62	140	462
3	130	90	130	86	96	230	762
2	190	140	200	140	135	340	1145
1	300	200	280	200	210	500	1690

THE DEMAND CURVE

The demand curve shows what quantities would be demanded at any given price, if other things do not change. These other things are discussed later in this chapter but it is important to realise, right at the

Figure 8.2 shows a typical demand curve. It can be seen that at a price of P the quantity demanded would be Q. If price fell to P^1 quantity demanded would rise to Q^1. Alternatively, the demand curve can be used to find the maximum price consumers are willing to pay for a given quantity. For example the maximum consumers are willing to pay for Q^1 amount is P^1.

In this case the demand curve also shows the price at which the good or service would be priced out of the market. At P^2 none of the good or service would be demanded. If the good or service were to be provided free, Q^2 quantity would be demanded. The areas of the rectangles under the demand curve represent the total revenues/total expenditures which would occur at different prices, since they are equal to price × quantity.

EXTENSIONS AND CONTRACTIONS IN DEMAND

Movements along a demand curve can be referred to as extensions and contractions in demand or changes in quantity demanded. Figure 8.3 shows an extension in demand from Q to Q^1 as a result of a fall in price from P to P^1. This can also be referred to as an increase in the quantity demanded.

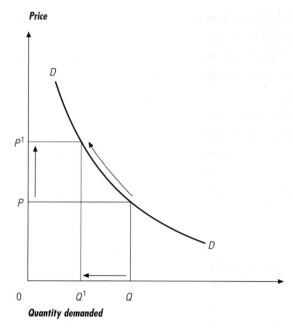

FIG. 8.4

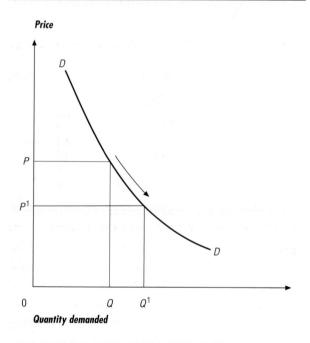

FIG. 8.3

Figure 8.4 shows a contraction in demand (decrease in quantity demanded) from Q to Q^1 caused by a rise in price from P to P^1. It would be misleading to refer to this as a change in demand since this term is usually applied to movements of the whole demand curve (discussed below).

REASONS WHY DEMAND CURVES SLOPE DOWN FROM LEFT TO RIGHT

For most products demand extends as price falls. To explain this inverse relationship economists discuss income and substitution effects and diminishing marginal utility.

INCOME AND SUBSTITUTION EFFECTS

When the price of a product changes, the real income of the consumer changes. The purchasing power of money income rises when the price of a product falls, it will be less when the price rises. When the price of a product falls the tendency will be for consumers to buy more because they can afford to buy more. Existing buyers will probably increase their purchases and new buyers, who did not purchase at the higher price, will tend to enter the market. This is referred to as the *income effect*.

A fall in the price of a product also makes it relatively cheaper when compared with competing products. There will probably be some 'switching' of purchases away from the now relatively dearer substitutes towards the product which has fallen in price. This is the *substitution effect*.

Both the income and substitution effects cause consumers to buy more of a product when it becomes cheaper. Consumers become more able and more willing to buy the product. The opposite effects will apply when the price of a product rises. Consumers' purchasing power will fall, reducing their ability to buy the product, and they are likely to switch to substitute products which have become relatively cheaper.

DIMINISHING MARGINAL UTILITY

The shape of the typical demand curve may also be explained by the action of diminishing marginal utility. Economists define utility as the satisfaction someone gains from the consumption of a good or service. A person buys a product because it provides satisfaction. The more a person buys, the greater the total utility he or she will receive. However, total utility may not rise in line with the quantity purchased.

The additional utility gained from the last unit purchased is defined as the *marginal utility* of the product. For most goods and services, marginal utility diminishes as consumption increases. For example,

the first cup of tea in the morning may provide someone with a high level of satisfaction. A second cup might also be very welcome but it is unlikely to yield as much utility as the first, while a third cup will provide an even lower level of satisfaction. If that person continued to consume more cups of tea on the same day a stage would be reached where drinking tea became positively distasteful. Marginal utility would become negative. Of course a rational person would stop consumption before that point is reached.

Table 8.3 shows that total utility rises until six cups of tea are drunk. Disutility would occur after six cups, as marginal utility becomes negative and total utility falls. The information can also be plotted on a graph (see Figure 8.5).

TABLE 8.3 UTILITY OF TEA DRINKING

No. of cups of tea	Total utility	Marginal utility
1	80	80
2	150	70
3	210	60
4	250	40
5	275	25
6	280	5
7	278	−2

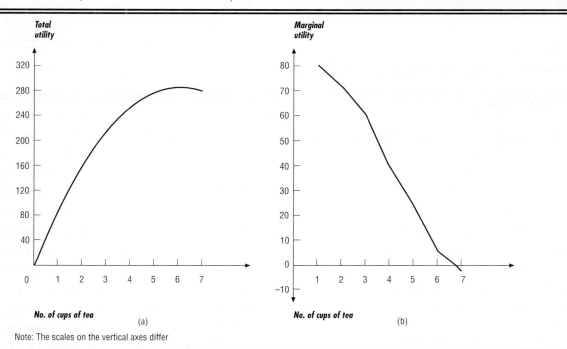

(a)

(b)

Note: The scales on the vertical axes differ

FIG. 8.5

MARGINAL UTILITY AND THE DEMAND CURVE

As rational consumers would not consume the product when marginal utility falls to zero, the marginal utility curve would therefore in practice be as shown in Figure 8.6. This curve may look familiar. It is the basis of the demand curve. Indeed, the demand curve for a product is the same as its marginal utility curve, measured in money terms.

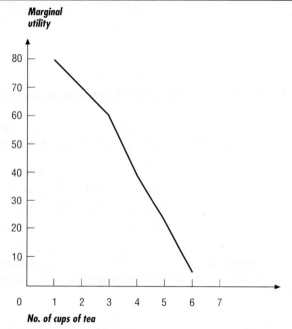

FIG. 8.6

Whilst utility is a subjective matter and so is difficult to measure, it can be estimated. One way of doing this is to look at what a person is prepared to sacrifice in order to obtain a product. Price measures this sacrifice in the sense that it indicates what other things might have been obtained with the money. Since marginal utility diminishes, consumers will be tempted to buy more of a good only if its price is lowered.

By assuming that the sacrifices a person is prepared to make in order to obtain something gives an indication of the utility derived from that good, it is possible to obtain the demand curve.

Of course different individuals will derive different levels of satisfaction and so will have different individual demand curves. As mentioned earlier, the market demand curve is found by adding together the amount each person will demand at the different prices. Figure 8.7 shows how the market demand curve is calculated in a simplified market which consists of only three consumers: A, B and C.

MAXIMISING SATISFACTION

It is assumed that people will try to maximise their total utility (satisfaction). This is achieved when they equate the marginal utility per penny (or any other unit of money) they spend on the goods they buy:

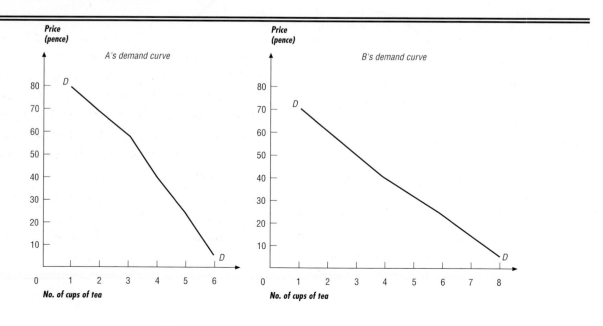

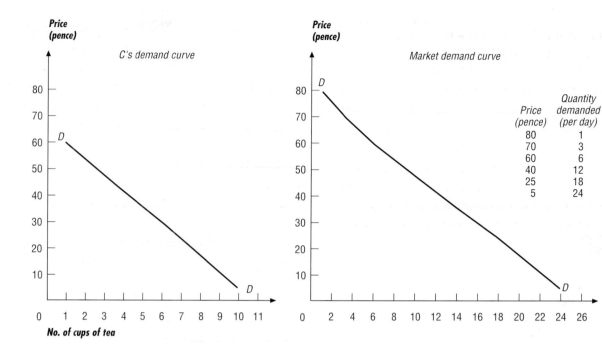

FIG. 8.7

marginal utility of good A / price of good A = marginal utility of good B / price of good B = marginal utility of good C / price of good C

$$\frac{\text{marginal utility of good A}}{\text{price of good A}} = \frac{\text{marginal utility of good B}}{\text{price of good B}} = \frac{\text{marginal utility of good C}}{\text{price of good C}}$$

This is logical. If a person could obtain more satisfaction per penny spent from good A than from good B he or she would buy more of good A and less of good B. For example, suppose a woman gains more satisfaction from spending money on apples than on chocolate, taking into account their respective prices, she will probably buy more apples and less chocolate. As she does so, the marginal utility she obtains from apples will fall whilst the marginal utility she gains from chocolate will rise. She is likely to continue to alter her purchases until the marginal utilities per penny spent are equal.

MARGINAL UTILITY AND CHANGES IN PRICE

Marginal utility explains why a change in price will cause a change in a person's spending patterns.

Assume originally that a person divides his expenditure between steak and trout and that he buys six steaks and four trout. Further assume that steaks cost £6 each and trout £4 each and that he gains 12 units of marginal utility from steak and eight units from trout so that:

$$\frac{\text{marginal utility of steak}}{\text{price of steak}} = \frac{12}{6} = \frac{\text{marginal utility of trout}}{\text{price of trout}} = \frac{8}{4}$$

Now if the price of steak rises to £8 each, the marginal utility per £ spent on steak will fall and will be less than the marginal utility per £ spent on trout. The consumer will then buy more trout and less steak. As he does so the marginal utility derived from steak will rise (as he has less he will appreciate each unit more) and the marginal utility from trout will fall until:

$$\frac{\text{marginal utility of steak}}{\text{price of steak}} = \frac{14}{8} = \frac{\text{marginal utility of trout}}{\text{price of trout}} = \frac{7}{4}$$

CONSUMER SURPLUS

Consumer surplus occurs when people pay less for a product than they were willing to pay (i.e. less than the value they place on the product based on their marginal utilities). Figure 8.8 shows an individual's demand curve for wine.

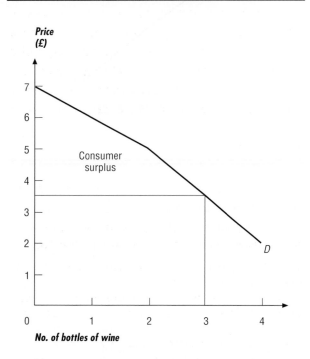

Price (£)

Consumer surplus

D

No. of bottles of wine

FIG. 8.8

The person would have been prepared to pay £6 for the first bottle, £5 for the second bottle, £3.50 for the third bottle, and £2 for the fourth. If the actual price charged is £3.50, the person will buy three bottles receiving consumer surplus of £2.50 on the first bottle, £1.50 on the second and no consumer surplus on the third bottle. So the total consumer surplus received is £4. The area of consumer surplus is the area under the demand curve and above the price line.

EXCEPTIONAL DEMAND CURVES

As has been seen, most demand curves slope downwards from left to right. They obey the general law that more will be demanded at lower than at higher prices. There are, however, some unusual demand curves which show more being demanded as price rises. This relationship is shown in Figure 8.9 where a fall in price from P to P^1 causes a contraction in demand from Q to Q^1.

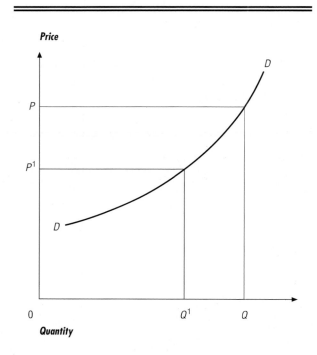

Price

P

P^1

D

D

0   Q^1 Q

Quantity

FIG. 8.9

One type of good for which demand is exceptional is *Veblen goods*, named after the American economist Thorstein Veblen who coined the phrase *conspicuous consumption*, i.e. people buying expensive goods and services to prove how rich they are. These can also be called goods with 'snob value' or ostentatious goods. They are bought in order to impress people. Examples may include designer label clothes and expensive watches. A fall in their price might cause them to lose some of their appeal and the quantities demanded might fall. They will not be so effective as a means of displaying wealth.

Another category of good with exceptional demand is *Giffen goods*. These are named after the Scottish economist Robert Giffen who first described the inverse relationship which may exist between price and quantity demanded of staple foodstuffs such as potatoes, bread, rice and corn in countries where living standards are very low. In these countries most of people's income is spent on basic foodstuffs. In such circumstances, an increase in the price of the staple food could well lead to an extension in demand. This is because if consumers' income and the prices of other goods remained unchanged, people would be obliged to buy at least the same quantity of potatoes, or rice,

as before and they would have less to spend on other things. The amount of money remaining for the purchase of those 'extras' to the staple diet may now buy such negligibly small amounts of them that consumers may well decide that they would get much better value by using the remaining income to buy more of the staple foods.

This direct relationship can also be explained by the income and substitution effects. In the case of a Giffen good the effects work in opposite directions with the income effect being the dominant one. If the price of a Giffen good falls there may be a tendency to switch towards it from more expensive substitutes but the rise in purchasing power will mean that people can now afford to buy better quality food and demand will contract.

NAME: Charles Dunstone
Entrepreneur

BORN: 1965

NATIONALITY: British

EDUCATED: Uppingham School, turned down a place at Liverpool University to read Business Studies

KEY POSTS HELD: Sales manager with NEC, the electronics company
1989, seeing a gap in the mobile phone market for small traders seeking impartial advice, he set up Carphone Warehouse
1999 he purchased 270 Tandy Computer Stores
In 1999 he had personal wealth of £130m and was placed 170th in the *Sunday Times* richest 1000 people in Britain list.

Charles Dunstone on developments in the mobile phone industry, including videophones and internet-connected mobiles: 'People call people, not places. The market is going to be very exciting. I can't think of one I'd rather be in.'

CHANGES IN DEMAND

A change in demand means that one or more of the factors which determine demand (other than the price of the product) have changed. It means that the whole demand curve will move.

An increase in demand means that more is now demanded at each and every price. Figure 8.10 illustrates an increase in demand. An increased quantity is now demanded at any given price. At the price P the quantity demanded has increased from Q to Q^1; at the price P^1 the quantity demanded has increased from Q^2 to Q^3.

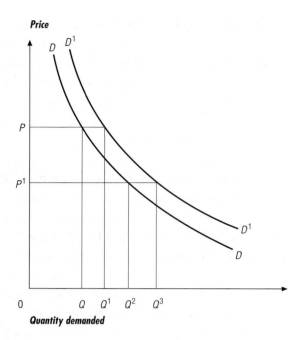

FIG. 8.10

Figure 8.11 shows a decrease in demand. At any given price less is demanded. For example at the price of P demand falls from Q to Q^1 and at a price of P^1 demand decreases from Q^2 to Q^3.

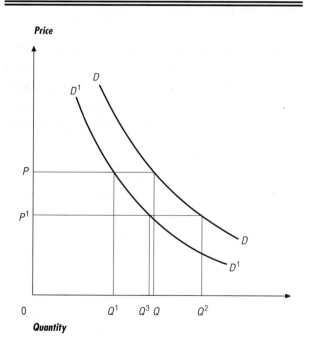

FIG. 8.11

CAUSES OF CHANGES IN DEMAND

CHANGES IN DISPOSABLE INCOME

For most commodities a very important influence is the level of incomes, in particular the level of real, disposable incomes. Disposable income is income after direct taxes have been deducted and state benefits have been added. Real income is actual money (nominal) income adjusted for inflation. For example if money incomes rise by 5%, but over the same time period prices rise by 10%, real income will have fallen and this means that people's ability to buy things is reduced.

Demand for most goods and services increases as real, disposable incomes rise. However, for a few goods and services demand may fall as incomes rise. These are called *inferior goods* and include, for example, cheaper basic foodstuffs, cheaper clothing and bus travel.

CHANGES IN THE DISTRIBUTION OF INCOME

If income becomes more unevenly distributed, demand for luxury goods will increase whilst demand for basic necessities, for example, heating and bread will decrease.

CHANGES IN THE PRICES OF RELATED GOODS AND SERVICES

Many goods and services have substitutes. People are influenced in their purchases by the relative prices of competing goods and services. For example, if the price of butter fell, the demand for margarine is likely to decrease. An increase in the fares on public transport might increase the demand for private transport. So a change in the price of a substitute will move the demand curves for competing goods and services.

The demand for some goods and services will be affected by changes in the prices of complementary goods and services. Products are complementary when they are jointly demanded — the use of one requiring the use of the other. The demand for videos is linked to the demand for video recorders; the demand for petrol is associated directly with the demand for motor cars. Thus a sharp increase in the price of motor cars might cause the demand for petrol to fall.

CHANGES IN TASTE AND FASHION

The demands for some goods and services are very susceptible to changes in taste and fashion. Particularly affected are the clothing trades, but industries producing furniture, processed foods and beverages are also subject to movements in taste and fashion. Peer group pressure can influence demand for products. For example, many youngsters influenced by their friends, buy, or have bought for them, mountain bikes rather than ordinary bikes.

ADVERTISING

Advertising is a powerful instrument affecting demand in many markets. Its aim, quite clearly, is to move the product's demand curve to the right and at the same time move the demand curves for competing products to the left.

THE AVAILABILITY OF CREDIT

If it becomes easier or cheaper to borrow, demand for a range of goods and services will increase, for example, houses, furniture and cars.

CHANGES IN POPULATION SIZE

An increase in population will increase demand for most goods and services.

CHANGES IN THE AGE STRUCTURE OF POPULATION

The UK, most of Europe, Japan, the USA and a number of other countries are currently experiencing the development of an ageing population. They have more elderly people in their populations and those elderly people are living longer. This results in an increase in demand for health care, residential care and holidays specifically designed for the elderly.

WEATHER

Changes in weather conditions can affect demand for some goods and services. For example, a period of hot and dry weather may increase demand for suntan lotion, barbecues, ice creams and lager whereas it may cause a decrease in demand for heating, umbrellas and hot drinks.

QUESTIONS

SHORT QUESTIONS

1. Define effective demand.

2. Explain what may cause an extension in demand for a product.

3. Distinguish between the income and substitution effects of a fall in the price of a product.

4. Give three reasons for an increase in demand for apples.

MULTIPLE CHOICE

1. Which of the following would cause the demand curve for a good to shift to the left?

   A. A rise in the price of the good.

   B. An increase in the supply of the good.

   C. A decrease in the price of a substitute good.

   D. A decrease in the tax imposed by the government on the good.

2. The following table shows the total utility gained by an individual from the consumption of three goods.

Units		Total utility	
consumed	cabbages	carrots	peas
1	10	7	9
2	18	14	16
3	25	21	21
4	30	28	23
5	32	35	22

Which of the goods are subject to diminishing marginal utility?

   A. Peas only.

   B. Cabbages and peas.

   C. Cabbages and carrots.

   D. Cabbages, carrots and peas.

3. Figure 8.12 shows the marginal utility a person gains from the consumption of successive units of good Z.

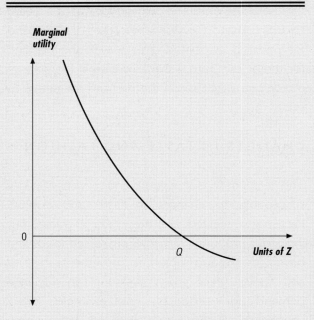

FIG. 8.12

If the person is consuming Q units, what can be concluded?

   A. Total utility is at a maximum.

   B. The person is gaining no satisfaction from consumption of the good.

   C. The person is in equilibrium with her purchases of Z.

   D. Disutility is experienced.

4. 'A rise in price results in an extension in demand'. This is true of which types of goods?

   A. Inferior.   B. Superior.

   C. Giffen.   D. Scarce.

DATA RESPONSE

Chocoholic Britons have forced a sweet firm to introduce rationing. Nestlé is limiting the number of KitKat Chunky bars it sends to shops because it can't meet public demand.

Last night the firm admitted that the shortage could last several weeks. Sales director Peter Basham said: 'Demand has outstripped our most ambitious forecasts. Inevitably it will take us time to catch up.' He added: 'We are victims of our own success. We're looking at ways of increasing our capacity soon.' Chunky sales, launched seven weeks ago, have already hit 54m — one for every person in Britain. The new bar is aimed at teenagers and people in a hurry who don't want to fiddle with tinfoil.

Unlike the much-loved four-fingered KitKat, it is just one chocolate-covered biscuit four-and-a-half inches long, three-quarters of an inch thick and an inch wide.

Britain's confectionery market is huge. We munch through far more sweets than any other country in Europe. Last year we gorged more than half-a-million tons of confectionery. This was almost half as much again as second placed Germany. Britons spent £3.6bn on chocolate alone — £62.63 each. KitKat, started in 1937, has been the nation's favourite chocolate bar for the past 13 years.

Nestlé spent £150m launching Chunky. They correctly gambled that it wouldn't affect sales of their four-fingered bars.

'Chunkaholics!', Robert Hutton, the Mirror, 1/6/99.

a] Explain what is meant by:
i rationing **(2)**
ii the confectionery market. **(2)**

b] How does demand for chocolate in Britain compare with that of demand in other EU countries? **(2)**

c] Explain what Nestlé would expect to happen to demand for KitKat Chunky bars if it lowered their price. Illustrate your answer with a diagram. **(5)**

d] Discuss, on the basis of the evidence in the article, whether the KitKat Chunky bar was originally under, over or appropriately priced? **(4)**

e] Explain whether the article suggests the KitKat Chunky bar is a substitute for the traditional four-fingered KitKat. **(4)**

f] Discuss three reasons why demand for chocolate has increased in Britain in recent years. **(6)**

CASE STUDY

The Office for National Statistics said there had been a sharp upward trend since December in the number of mobiles being made, reflecting surging demand for what has become the latest fashion accessory.

Companies such as Motorola and Ericsson manufacture mobile phone handsets in the UK, partly for the export market. The number of subscribers in Britain has rocketed from about 12m before Christmas to 15.5m last month and is growing by nearly 4% a month, according to the Federation of Communications Services. The introduction of pre-paid handsets before Christmas fuelled the boom.

Source: 'Mobile phones "mania" revives stagnant economy' by Diane Coyle, the Independent, 10/6/99.

On display in Asprey & Garrad showrooms, discerning buyers will find a calfskin leather-covered bow with a golden clasp whose doors open to reveal six mechanical wrists that rotate just often enough to keep the mechanical wristwatches stored upon them up and running. Its price? Only £3500.

Sales trends in the wristwatch industry are just like those in virtually every other product category. Thus, while total car sales have been essentially static in recent years, sales of luxury cars have been growing at record rates; and whereas overall wine sales are down slightly, sales of ultra-premium wines have risen sharply.

The luxury boom has not been confined to the wealthy. In the United States, for example, the average size of a house built last year was 2200 sq ft, up from 1500 sq ft in 1970, and the average price of a new car has risen more than 75% in the past decade.

At one level, the recent up-grades in what we buy might seem a benign symptom of the fact that we are more productive, and hence richer, than

ever before. But there is a dark side to our current spending patterns: whereas those at the top of the economic heap have done spectacularly well, those in the middle have gained virtually no ground at all during the past two decades, and the earnings of the least well-off have declined. Middle- and low-income families have had to finance their higher spending by lower savings and sharply rising debt.

Even for those who can easily afford today's luxury offerings, however there has been a price to pay. All of us, rich and poor alike, are spending more time at the office and taking shorter holidays.

Source: 'The big spenders who make all of us poorer' by Robert Frank, the Observer, 16/5/99.

a] What happened to the demand for mobile phones from December 1998 to May 1999? **(4)**

b] What do you think may have caused this alteration in demand? **(8)**

c] Does the extract from the *Observer* suggest that luxury cars are normal or inferior goods? Explain your answer. **(6)**

d] What factors influence demand for cars? **(9)**

e] What do you think may have caused 'total car sales to have been essentially static in recent years'? **(7)**

f] The second extract mentions that top income earners are better off and the earnings of the least well-off have declined. Discuss the effect this will have on the pattern of demand. **(10)**

g] What does the second extract suggest is the opportunity cost of purchasing luxuries? **(6)**

STRUCTURED ESSAY

a] Distinguish between a contraction and a
   decrease in demand. **(10)**

b] Discuss the possible causes of a decrease in
   demand for Volvo cars. **(15)**

9 ELASTICITIES OF DEMAND

MEANING OF ELASTICITY

Elasticity is concerned with the extent to which one variable, for example, demand, responds to a change in another variable, for example, price. The three types of elasticity of demand measure how the quantity demanded responds to changes in the key influences on demand; price, price of related products and income. With elasticity of demand, economists are concerned not only with the direction of the change in demand but also the size of the change.

PRICE ELASTICITY OF DEMAND

Price elasticity of demand refers to the responsiveness of quantity demanded to a change in price. Where quantity demanded is very responsive to price changes — a small change in price leading to a relatively large change in quantity demanded — demand is said to be elastic. Whereas when quantity demanded is relatively unresponsive to price changes, demand is inelastic. To be more precise, elasticity of demand is the relationship between the proportionate change in price and the proportionate change in quantity demanded.

MEASURING PRICE ELASTICITY OF DEMAND

The concept of elasticity is concerned with proportionate changes in price and quantity and not absolute changes. Price elasticity of demand can be given a numerical value by using the following formula:

$$\text{Price elasticity of demand} = \frac{\text{percentage change in quantity demanded}}{\text{percentage change in price}}$$

This can also be abbreviated to: $\text{PED} = \dfrac{\%\Delta QD}{\%\Delta P}$

For example if the price of a product rises from £20 to £24 and demand falls from 400 to 300 the coefficient will be $\dfrac{-25\%}{+20\%} = -1.25$

Price elasticity of demand is usually negative since for most products price and demand are inversely related.

DEGREES OF PRICE ELASTICITY OF DEMAND

Demand for most products is either elastic or inelastic. Products with elastic demand have a coefficient greater than one and less than infinity. In this case a given percentage change in price will cause a greater percentage change in demand. Demand tends to be elastic for goods and services which have close substitutes, take up a large portion of consumers' income, are perceived as luxuries and whose purchase can be postponed.

When a given change in price causes a smaller percentage change in demand, the product has inelastic demand. Basic necessities, goods and services which take up a small portion of consumers' incomes, addictive goods and services, goods and services with no substitutes and those which have a number of different uses have inelastic demand.

The other three degrees of price elasticity of demand are less common and may, with certain products, occur over a limited price range.

Unit price elasticity of demand occurs when a percentage change in price results in an equal percentage change in demand. In this case the coefficient will be 1.

Perfectly inelastic demand is when a change in price causes no change in the quantity demanded. For instance, a person with a serious illness might be prepared to buy the same quantity of a medicine when its price rises and may not find it beneficial to increase the quantity they take when its price falls. However there are few products with perfectly inelastic demand just as there are few products with perfectly elastic demand.

When demand is perfectly elastic a change in price will cause an infinite change in the quantity of demand. The coefficient is infinity. For example, suppose there are a number of people selling CDs of a pop group at one of their concerts; if one lowered his/her price below those of his/her competitors s/he may capture all the customers at the concert.

THE DETERMINANTS OF PRICE ELASTICITY OF DEMAND

As indicated above there are some key determinants of price elasticity of demand.

- The major influence on price elasticity of demand is the availability of close substitutes. When a close substitute is available in the relevant price range, demand will be elastic. If the supplier of such a product were to raise its price, many buyers would switch to the close substitute. If the supplier were to lower his/her price s/he would attract many customers away from the substitutes. For example, the demands for a particular brand of cigarettes or paint will be elastic because there are several other brands which are close substitutes. The total demands for cigarettes and paint, however, will be inelastic as there are no close substitutes for these products.
- The more widely defined a good or service is the less elastic demand will be. This is because there will be fewer substitutes. Whereas the narrower the definition the more substitutes there

are likely to be and hence the more elastic demand will tend to be. For instance the demand for meat will be less elastic than demand for beef which in turn will be less elastic than demand for rump steak.

- Some products are habit forming, e.g. cigarettes, whisky and chocolate, and the demands for such products will tend to be inelastic.
- If it is possible to postpone the purchase of a product, for example a dishwasher, demand will tend to be elastic.
- Demand tends to be more elastic in the long run than in the short run. This is because it takes consumers time to adjust to price changes. For instance, if the price of electricity rises people may try to reduce their consumption by economising on heating in the short run. However, in the long run, the consumption of electricity will fall to a greater extent as people replace electric cookers and heating systems with gas. Figure 9.1 shows that the long-run demand curve for electricity is more elastic than the short-run demand curve.

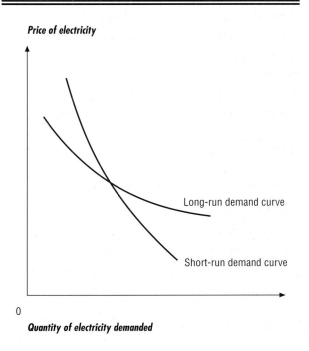

Price of electricity

Long-run demand curve

Short-run demand curve

0

Quantity of electricity demanded

FIG. 9.1

PRICE ELASTICITY OF DEMAND AND TOTAL REVENUE (EXPENDITURE)

The degree of price elasticity of demand a product possesses can be judged by what happens to total revenue (which is usually equivalent to total expenditure) when price changes. When demand is elastic, price and total revenue will move in opposite directions. So that a rise in price will cause a fall in total revenue, and a fall in price will cause a rise in total revenue.

Figure 9.2 shows a product with elastic demand over the given price range. When price is £4 total revenue is £120 (£4 × 30). A fall in price to £3 causes a larger percentage rise in quantity demanded and total revenue to rise to £180 (£3 × 60). Price elasticity of demand is 4.

When demand is inelastic, price and total revenue will move in the same direction. So in the case of inelastic demand, a rise in price will cause a rise in revenue and a fall in price will cause a fall in total revenue. When price is £4 total revenue is £80 (£4 × 20). This time when price falls to £3, demand changes by a smaller percentage to 24 and total revenue falls to £72 (£3 × 24). Elasticity of demand is 0.8. Figure 9.3 illustrates this.

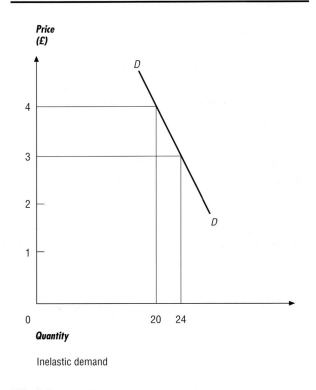

Inelastic demand

FIG. 9.3

Total revenue does not change when price elasticity of demand is unity. This is because a given percentage in price will cause an equal percentage change in demand, leaving total revenue unchanged.

PRICE ELASTICITY OF DEMAND ALONG A DEMAND CURVE

Price elasticity of demand on most demand curves becomes more inelastic as price falls. A straight line

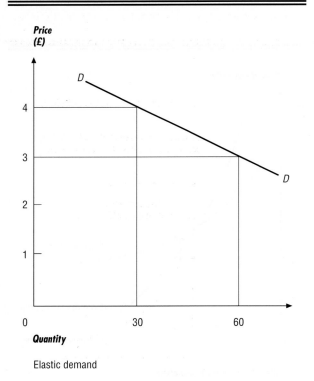

Elastic demand

FIG. 9.2

demand curve can be used to illustrate this point. On Figure 9.4 price changes by 2p each time and quantity by 20 units, but the elasticities of demand are not equal. For example:

When price changes from 20p to 18p

$$PED = \frac{33\frac{1}{3}\%}{-10\%} = -3.33$$

Whereas when price changes from 10p to 8p

$$PED = \frac{12\frac{1}{2}\%}{-10\%} = -0.625$$

Price elasticity of demand is a relationship between proportionate and not absolute changes in price and quantity demanded. As price falls people become less sensitive to price changes.

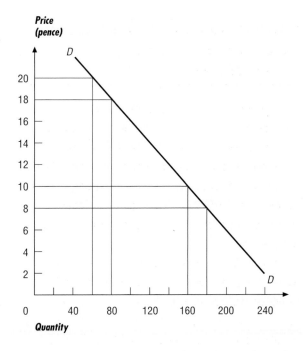

FIG. 9.4

The three exceptional cases where price elasticity of demand is constant along a demand curve are shown in Figure 9.5.

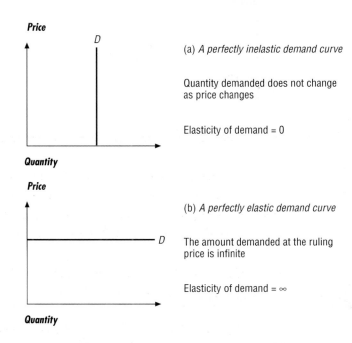

(a) *A perfectly inelastic demand curve*

Quantity demanded does not change as price changes

Elasticity of demand = 0

(b) *A perfectly elastic demand curve*

The amount demanded at the ruling price is infinite

Elasticity of demand = ∞

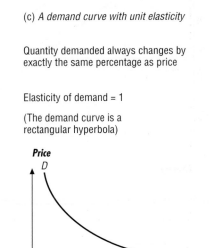

(c) *A demand curve with unit elasticity*

Quantity demanded always changes by exactly the same percentage as price

Elasticity of demand = 1

(The demand curve is a rectangular hyperbola)

FIG. 9.5

SHIFTS IN THE DEMAND CURVE

A shift in the demand curve will alter the price elasticity of demand at any given price. An increase in demand will make demand more inelastic. At higher levels of demand people will be less sensitive to price changes. This is illustrated in Figure 9.6. Initially a fall in price from £10 to £8 causes demand to extend from 100 to 160, so price elasticity of demand is 3. When demand increases to D^1D^1, a change in price from £10 to £8 causes demand to extend from 200 to 260 giving a price elasticity of demand of 1.5. A decrease in demand will make demand more elastic as people become more sensitive to price changes.

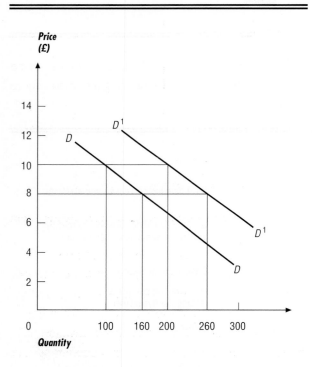

FIG. 9.6

CROSS ELASTICITY OF DEMAND

The relationship between changes in the price of one product and the resulting changes in the quantity demanded of another product is described as the cross elasticity of demand. This concept is useful as a means of assessing the extent to which products are close substitutes or closely related complements. This form of elasticity is measured as:

$$\text{cross elasticity of demand} = \frac{\text{percentage change in quantity demanded of Good A}}{\text{percentage change in price of Good B}}$$

$$XED = \frac{\%\Delta QD \text{ of Good A}}{\%\Delta P \text{ of Good B}}$$

In the case of substitute products, cross elasticity of demand will be positive; an increase in the price of B will lead to an increase in demand for A (and vice versa).

Figure 9.7 shows the relationships between a change in the price of apples and a change in the demand for pears.

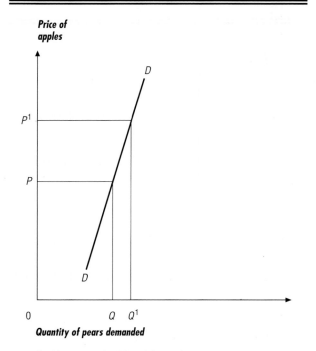

Positive cross elasticity of demand

FIG. 9.7

As the price of apples rises the demand for pears increases. Apples and pears are not very close substitutes and so do not have a high positive cross elasticity of demand. Whereas if the two products are very close substitutes, cross elasticity of demand will have a high positive value. Thus, if an increase of 10% in the price of one brand of petrol leads to a rise of 40% in the sales of another brand, the cross elasticity of demand is + 4.

In the case of complementary products, the cross elasticity of demand will be negative; an increase in the price of B will lead to a decrease in demand for A (and vice versa).

Figure 9.8 shows the negative cross elasticity of demand relationship which exists between gin and tonic.

When two products are closely related complements, the cross elasticity of demand will have a high negative value.

Products which are unrelated have zero cross elasticity of demand. For instance, a rise in the price of watercress is unlikely to have any effect on the demand for jeans. Figure 9.9 shows this relationship. Products with zero cross elasticity of demand are referred to as independent products.

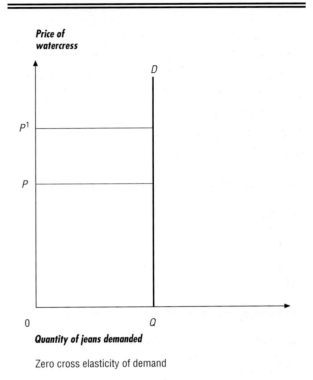

Zero cross elasticity of demand

FIG. 9.9

In practice, a change in the price of one product may affect demand for what appear to be unrelated products. This is because a change in the price of a product will affect people's purchasing power. Obviously, the larger the price change and the greater the proportion of income spent on the product, the larger the effect will be.

INCOME ELASTICITY OF DEMAND

Income elasticity of demand is concerned with the relationship between changes in income and changes in demand. This relationship is known as the income

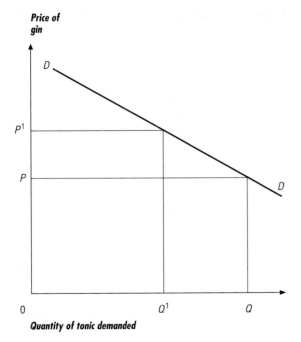

Negative cross elasticity of demand

FIG. 9.8

elasticity of demand. It is measured by the following formula:

$$\text{Income elasticity of demand} = \frac{\text{percentage change in quantity demanded}}{\text{percentage change in income}}$$

$$\text{YED} = \frac{\%\Delta QD}{\%\Delta Y}$$

As with cross elasticity of demand, economists are concerned with both the sign and the size of the coefficient of YED.

Most products have positive income elasticity of demand. This means that in most cases income and demand will move in the same direction — an increase in income will lead to an increase in quantity demanded and a decrease in income will cause a decrease in demand. So that income elasticity of demand will be positive. For example, if a 5% increase in income leads to a 10% increase in the demand for motor cars

$$\text{YED} = \frac{10\%}{5\%} = 2$$

Figure 9.10 shows the positive income elasticity of demand which exists in the case of wine.

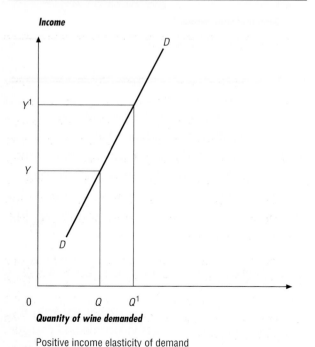

Quantity of wine demanded

Positive income elasticity of demand

FIG. 9.10

Products which have positive income elasticity of demand are called normal goods. Those normal goods which have positive income elasticity of demand greater than one are sometimes referred to as superior goods.

In the case of inferior goods increases in income will lead to decreases in demand so that income elasticity of demand will be negative. Here income and demand move in opposite directions. Figure 9.11 shows negative income elasticity of demand.

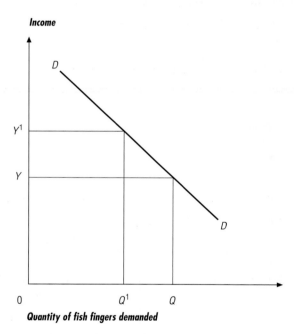

Quantity of fish fingers demanded

Negative income elasticity of demand

FIG. 9.11

When demand does not change as income changes, income elasticity of demand is zero; Figure 9.12 illustrates zero income elasticity of demand.

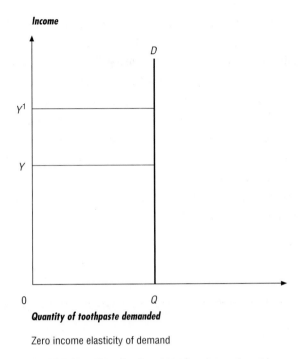

Zero income elasticity of demand

FIG. 9.12

and then falling as people become richer and replace blankets with duvets.

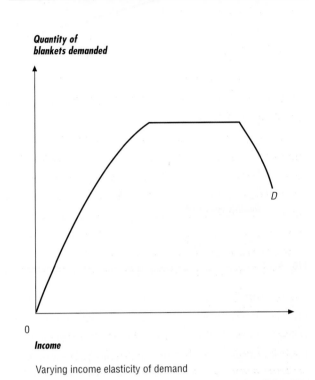

Varying income elasticity of demand

FIG. 9.13

For any particular product, income elasticity of demand depends on the current standard of living. In developed countries cars and foreign holidays, for example, have a positive income elasticity of demand whereas the demands for some staple foodstuffs (e.g. potatoes), poor quality clothing and public transport have negative income elasticities of demand. In developing countries some of these products have positive income elasticity of demand.

Income elasticity of demand can also vary over time. Figure 9.13 shows demand for blankets increasing as a country becomes richer, then demand remaining constant when a certain standard of living is reached,

Economists are concerned not only with the direction of the change in demand when income changes but also the extent to which demand changes. Products may have income elastic demand. This will mean that a given percentage change in income will cause a greater change in demand. Foreign travel and double glazing are two examples of products with income elastic demand.

Products with both negative and positive income elasticity of demand can have income elastic demand. Figure 9.14 shows income elastic demand in the case of (a) an inferior good and (b) a normal good.

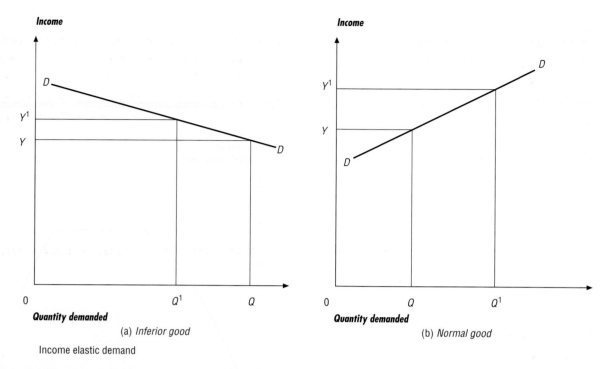

(a) Inferior good

(b) Normal good

Income elastic demand

FIG. 9.14

Income inelastic demand means that a given change in income will cause a smaller percentage change in demand. Potatoes, beer and postage stamps have income inelastic demand. Again, products with both negative and positive income elasticity of demand can have income inelastic demand. Figure 9.15 shows income inelastic demand in the case of (a) an inferior good and (b) a normal good.

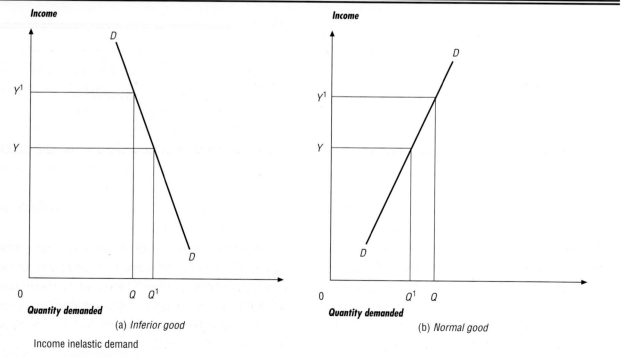

(a) Inferior good

(b) Normal good

Income inelastic demand

FIG. 9.15

DIFFERENT TYPES OF GOOD

Having discussed price, cross and income elasticity of demand, the differences between normal, inferior, Giffen and Veblen goods can be reviewed.

Normal goods have negative price elasticity of demand. In this case both the income and substi-tution effects of a price change will work in the same directions and reinforce each other. Normal goods have positive income elasticity of demand. The price and income elasticities of demand for normal goods are shown in Figure 9.16.

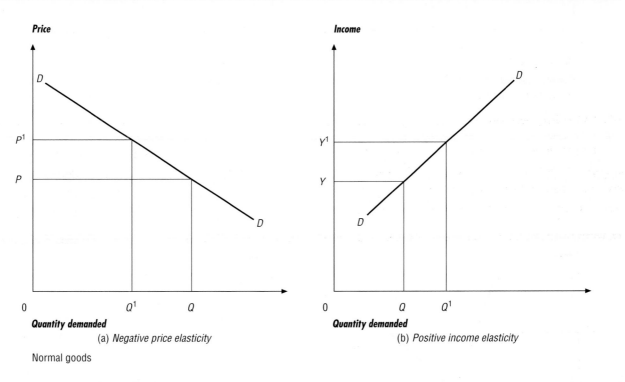

(a) *Negative price elasticity*

Normal goods

(b) *Positive income elasticity*

FIG. 9.16

Inferior goods have negative income elasticity of demand. Most have negative price elasticity of demand. The income and substitution effects of a price change work in opposite directions with the substitution effect being stronger. So whilst a rise in price, by lowering people's purchasing power, may stimulate them to purchase more of the product, this is more than offset by the tendency to switch to a rival product. Therefore with inferior goods a rise in price will cause a contraction in demand. The price and income elasticities of demand for inferior goods are illustrated in Figure 9.17.

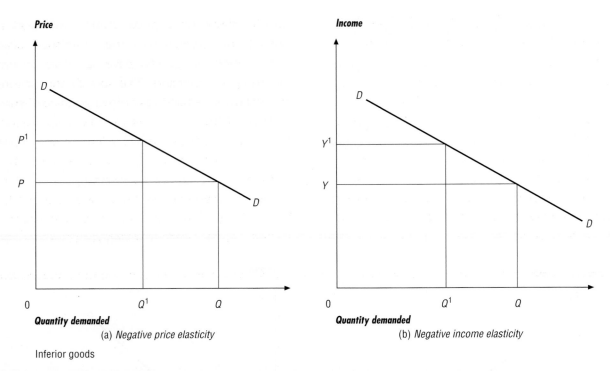

(a) *Negative price elasticity*

(b) *Negative income elasticity*

Inferior goods

FIG. 9.17

Giffen goods are a special type of inferior good. They have negative income elasticity of demand but positive price elasticity of demand. As with inferior goods the income and substitution effects work in opposite directions but this time the income effect will be stronger so that a rise in price will cause an extension in demand. Figure 9.18 shows the price and income elasticities of demand for Giffen goods.

(a) *Positive price elasticity*

(b) *Negative income elasticity*

Giffen good

FIG. 9.18

It is interesting to note that whilst all Giffen goods are inferior goods, not all inferior goods are Giffen goods. For instance bus travel is an inferior good but not a Giffen good. So that whilst a rise in income will be likely to lead to a fall in demand for bus travel, as people switch to alternative means of transport, a rise in the price of bus travel is unlikely to cause people to make more journeys by bus.

Veblen goods have both positive price elasticity of demand and positive income elasticity of demand. People buy more of a Veblen good as its price rises because they associate quality with price. So in this case the income and substitution effects work in opposite directions but the 'perverse' substitution effect will be stronger. As a product rises in price people's purchasing power falls but this time as the product becomes more expensive, people switch to it and away from cheaper substitutes. Veblen goods also have increasing rather than diminishing marginal utility. As people have more of a Veblen good, their satisfaction from extra units increases because they are able to impress other people with their wealth. Figure 9.19 illustrates the price and income elasticities of demand for Veblen goods.

(a) *Positive price elasticity*

Veblen good

(b) *Positive income elasticity*

FIG. 9.19

QUESTIONS

SHORT QUESTIONS

1. What type of goods have:
   i   negative price elasticity of demand
   ii negative cross elasticity of demand
   iii negative income elasticity of demand?
2. Giving reasons, explain what size of price elasticity of demand cigarettes have.
3. Explain what is meant by superior goods.
4. What are the main determinants of price elasticity of demand?

MULTIPLE CHOICE

1. A good has unit price elasticity of demand. What will decrease as a result of an increase in the price of the good?

   A Quantity demanded.

   B Quantity supplied.

   C Expenditure on substitutes.

   D Expenditure on the good.

2. Which of the diagrams in Figure 9.20 illustrates negative cross elasticity of demand?

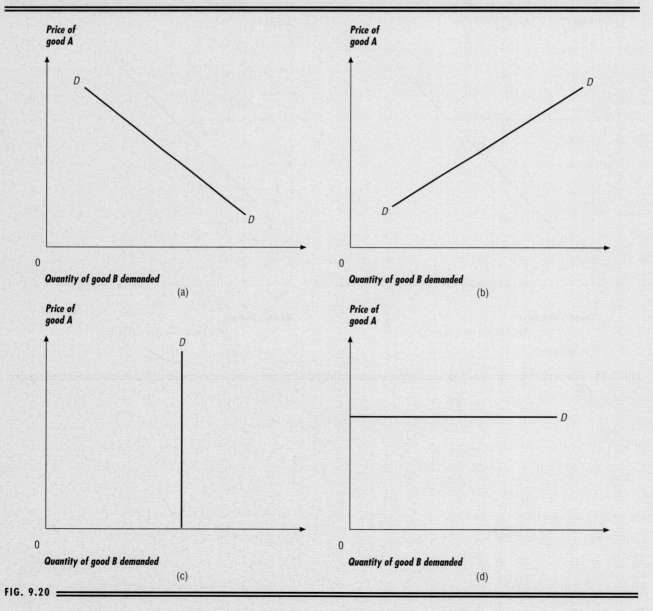

(a)

(b)

(c)

(d)

FIG. 9.20

3 A person's real income rises from £600 per week to £630 per week. As a result she increases her spending on wine from £20 per week to £22 per week. What is her income elasticity of demand for wine?

A 0.5

B 0.67

C 1.0

D 2.0

DATA RESPONSE

Price (£)	Quantity demanded
10	2
9	5
8	10
7	16
6	22
5	30
4	40
3	52

4 Independent goods have:

A zero cross elasticity of demand

B zero income elasticity of demand

C zero price elasticity of demand

D zero cross, income and price elasticity of demand.

a] When price falls from £8 to £7 demand rises from 10 to 16. What is the technical term for this change in the quantity demanded? **(3)**

b] At which price is total expenditure (revenue) maximised? **(5)**

c] What is the price elasticity of demand when price falls from £8 to £7? **(4)**

d] Between which two prices is price elasticity of demand 1.67? **(6)**

e] Explain what usually happens to price elasticity of demand as price falls. **(7)**

CASE STUDY

A married couple run two businesses in a town in Wales. One is a taxi firm and the other is a launderette. To help their review of their future business strategy they hired a local economist to research the markets. Extracts from her report provide the following information.

The taxi firm

There are eight other companies operating in the town charging similar prices. The elasticities of demand facing the firm are:

PED −1.5
YED 2.0
XED 1.6

New firms are due to move into the town over the next few years. It is also expected that the government will raise the tax on petrol in its next budget.

The launderette

There are three other launderettes operating in the town, all of which charge lower prices. Two years ago there had been six launderettes. The elasticities of demand in this case are:

PED −2.0
YED −1.8
XED 2.5

Ownership of washing machines is increasing and it is predicted that within three years 90% of the town's households will have a washing machine.

a] Comment on the elasticities of demand facing the taxi firm. **(6)**

b] If the couple want to raise the revenue they receive from the taxi firm should they raise or lower the price they charge? Explain your answer. **(4)**

c] Comment on the elasticities of demand facing the launderette. **(6)**

d] Distinguish between normal and inferior goods. **(4)**

e] From the information given decide whether
   i   the taxi service is a normal or inferior good. Explain your answer. **(2)**
   ii the launderette service is a normal or inferior good. Explain your answer. **(2)**

f] Discuss whether the couple should expand or close down
   i   the taxi firm **(10)**
   ii the launderette. **(10)**

g] Discuss three measures the taxi company could take to increase demand for its service. **(6)**

STRUCTURED ESSAY

a] Define and explain price elasticity of demand, cross elasticity of demand and income elasticity of demand. **(12)**

b] How may knowledge of these concepts be used by a coach firm seeking to increase its revenue? **(13)**

10 SUPPLY

Supply is the willingness and ability to sell a good or service. It is not the same thing as the 'existing stock' or 'amount available'. For example, the supply of housing in a town consists of the number of houses, bungalows and flats, etc. which are up for sale and not the total number of houses, bungalows and flats, etc. in the town. In the spring the supply of housing tends to increase as more properties come onto the market.

THE SUPPLY CURVE

In most cases the more is supplied the higher the price. So supply curves slope upwards from left to right. Figure 10.1 shows a supply curve based on the supply schedule in Table 10.1.

TABLE 10.1

Price pence	Quantity supplied (week)
50	250
40	220
30	180
20	120
10	50

To supply larger quantities firms need higher prices in order to cover their higher costs.

MOVEMENTS ALONG A SUPPLY CURVE

Movements along the supply curve are referred to as extensions and contractions or as changes in the quantity supplied. Figure 10.2 shows an extension in supply. A rise in price from P to P^1 causes an increase in the quantity supplied from Q to Q^1.

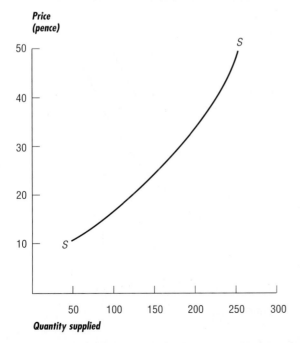

Price (pence)

FIG. 10.1

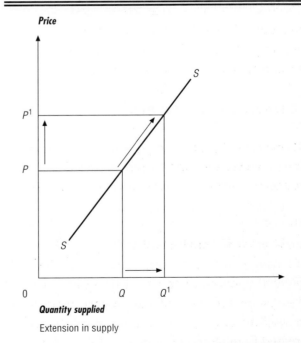

Price

Extension in supply

FIG. 10.2

Figure 10.3 shows a contraction in supply. A fall in price from P to P¹ causes a decrease in the quantity supplied from Q to Q¹.

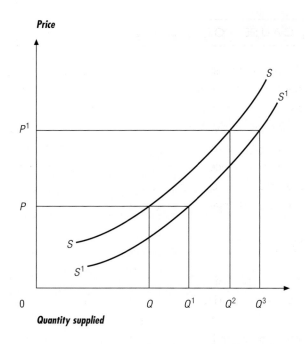

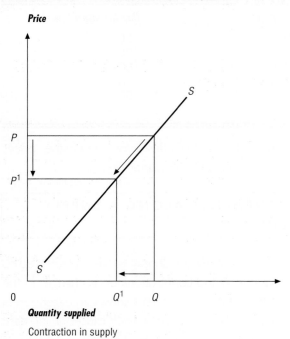

Contraction in supply

FIG. 10.3

CHANGES IN SUPPLY

An increase in supply means that more is supplied at each and every price. A decrease in supply means that less is supplied at each and every price. Figure 10.4 illustrates an increase in supply from SS to S¹S¹. This leads to an increase in the quantity supplied at any given price. For example, at the price P suppliers are now prepared to offer quantity Q¹ whereas under the original supply conditions, at this price, they were only prepared to supply quantity Q. Similarly at price P¹ the quantity supplied has increased from Q² to Q³.

FIG. 10.4

Figure 10.5 illustrates a decrease in supply. The supply curve shifts to the left from SS to S¹S¹. The effect will be to reduce the quantities supplied at all prices.

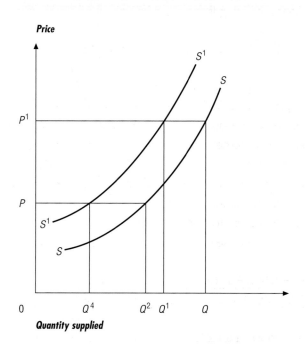

FIG. 10.5

CAUSES OF CHANGES IN SUPPLY

A shift in the supply curve indicates that there has been a change in the conditions governing supply. For example, if producers are prepared to supply greater quantities at given prices, shown by a movement of the supply curve to the right, it may indicate that they have experienced reductions in their labour costs, material costs or capital costs. Among the possible causes of changes in supply are:

WEATHER

The supply of agricultural products is seriously affected by variations in weather conditions. A bad harvest means that the supply curve moves to the left; a bumper harvest is represented by a shift of the supply curve to the right.

DISEASE

The output of agricultural products can also be affected by disease affecting crops and disease and illness affecting livestock.

TECHNOLOGICAL PROGRESS

Technological progress is a term which covers improvements in the performance of capital goods and labour, in the quality of raw materials, in organisation and management, in factory and office layouts, in communications, in methods of production, and so on. It is the main source of improvements in productivity and these increases in output per hour will move the supply curve to the right, because, if other things remain unchanged, average costs of production will fall.

CHANGES IN THE PRICES OF FACTORS OF PRODUCTION

An important determinant of changes in supply is changes in the prices of factors of production. In-creases in wages, the prices of raw materials, fuel and power, interest rates, rent and other factors prices will cause supply to decrease, unless offset by a rise in the productivity of the factors of production. For example, if wage rates rise by 10% but labour productivity also increases by 10%, then labour costs per unit have not changed.

CHANGES IN THE PRICES OF OTHER COMMODITIES

Changes in the prices of other goods and services may affect the supply of a product whose price is not changing. If, because of increases in demand, the prices of other goods and services increase, the production of these goods and services will become more profitable, and resources would tend to move towards the industries making these more profitable products. The production of goods and services, with prices unchanged, would now be less attractive to suppliers.

In the case of products which are substitutes in supply (in competitive supply), a rise in the price of one product will cause the supply of that product to extend and the other product/products to decrease. However some products are in joint supply, for instance, petrol and paraffin. So if there is a rise in the price of petrol this will cause the supply of petrol to extend and the supply of paraffin to increase.

INDIRECT TAXATION AND SUBSIDIES

The imposition of indirect taxes will add an extra cost to producers who are now responsible for passing a specific amount or a percentage of the price of the product onto the government. So indirect taxes cause a decrease in supply. Subsidies to producers have the opposite effect. They increase the incentive and reward for producers and cause supply to increase.

CHANGES IN THE NUMBER OF PRODUCERS

Supply will increase if new firms enter the market. For instance, in the 1990s the number and range of magazines for sale increased with the rise in the number of producers, many using desk-top publishing.

UNEXPECTED EVENTS

The Gulf War (1990–91) decreased the supply of oil. Natural disasters, for example may reduce the supply of a range of products.

PRICE ELASTICITY OF SUPPLY

Price elasticity of supply is a relationship between the proportionate changes in price and the pro-portionate changes in quantity supplied. The formula used to measure elasticity of supply is:

$$\text{Price elasticity of supply} = \frac{\text{percentage change in quantity supplied}}{\text{percentage change in price}}$$

$$PES = \frac{\%\Delta QS}{\%\Delta P}$$

Most products have either elastic or inelastic supply. Elastic supply is when a percentage change in price causes a greater percentage change in supply. Whereas inelastic supply is when a given percentage change in price causes a smaller percentage change in supply. Figure 10.6 illustrates these two degrees of elasticity of supply ((a) and (b)) plus the three less common types ((c), (d) and (e)).

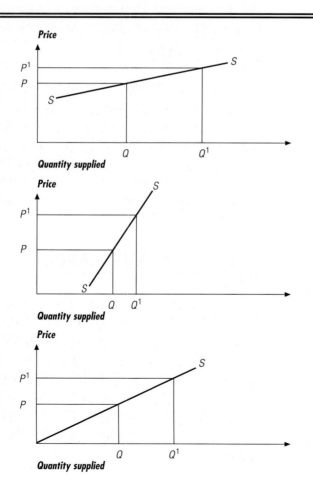

(a) *Supply is elastic in price range illustrated.*

Percentage change in *Q* > percentage change in *P*

PES = > 1 < ∞

(b) *Supply is inelastic in price range illustrated.*

Percentage change in *Q* < percentage change in *P*

PES = > 0 < 1

(c) *Elasticity of supply is unity.*

Percentage change in *Q* = percentage change in *P* for all price changes

PES = 1

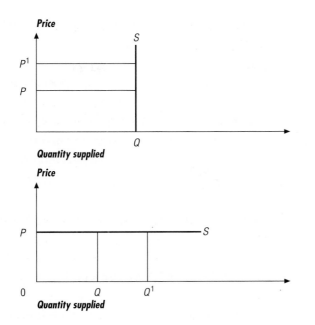

FIG. 10.6

Note that any straight line passing through the origin will have unit price elasticity of supply. The proportionate changes in supply will be equal to the proportionate changes in price.

THE DETERMINANTS OF THE DEGREE OF PRICE ELASTICITY OF SUPPLY

The extent to which supply is elastic depends upon the flexibility and mobility of the factors of production. If production can be expanded easily and quickly and/or products can easily be brought out of storage in response to an increase in demand and the resulting rise in price, supply will be elastic; if not, supply will be inelastic. Similarly, when demand and price fall, supply will be elastic if production can be cut back quickly and easily and/or the products can be taken off the market and stored. Among the influences on the degree of elasticity of supply of a product are the following:

THE LEVEL OF SPARE CAPACITY IN THE INDUSTRY

Where an industry is operating below full capacity and so there are unemployed resources, supply is elastic. The industry will be able to expand production fairly easily by using more variable factors and bringing into use its previously idle fixed assets.

THE LEVEL OF EMPLOYMENT

This is linked to the point above. In a situation of full employment, the supply of most goods and services will be inelastic. Supply may be increased by improved productivity, but in the short run no significant increases in output will be possible. Supply in the domestic market may still be elastic if it is possible to obtain supplies from other countries, but this may lead to balance of payments difficulties.

THE ABILITY TO STORE THE PRODUCT

Supply will be elastic if the product can be stored. If price rises, the quantity offered for sale can be increased quickly and easily by drawing on stocks. If price falls, supply can be reduced by adding to stocks.

WHETHER THE PRODUCTS ARE AGRICULTURAL OR MANUFACTURED ONES

In the case of agricultural products, supply in the short run is inelastic because the quantity supplied in any one year is governed by the acreage planted in the sowing season. Some commodities such as natural rubber, coffee, and cocoa will be inelastic in supply over fairly long periods of time since it takes several years for newly planted trees to reach maturity. So, in the short run, an increase in demand will lead to a sharp increase in price. The supplies of products such as beef and milk will also be inelastic because it takes a considerable time to increase the size of the herds of cattle. The supply of manufactured products tends to be more elastic as the production process is usually shorter, although of course it varies. It takes a few moments, given spare capacity, to raise the output of paper clips whilst it takes years to increase the output of passenger jets.

THE TIME IT TAKES TO INCREASE CAPACITY

In some industries the expansion of capacity takes a long time. Once such industries are operating at full capacity, therefore, supply will be inelastic (as far as expansion is concerned) for several years. This is true of mining industries because the sinking of new mines and the extension of existing ones is a lengthy procedure. Thus, the supply of most minerals tends to be inelastic.

PRICE ELASTICITY OF SUPPLY AND TIME

As indicated above time is an important influence on the elasticity of supply. In most cases while changes in demand can take place in the short run, especially in markets subject to changes in fashion or where advertising is very effective, changes in supply, because of technical problems and the immobilities of the factors of production, take much longer. It is usual to distinguish three time periods in supply and demand analysis.

THE MOMENTARY PERIOD

This is defined as the period of time during which supply is restricted to the quantities actually available in the market. Supply is fixed (i.e. perfectly inelastic) in the momentary period, and the supply curve will be a straight line parallel to the price axis. Normally, this period will be a very short one. In the case of perishable products such as fish, fruit, and vegetables, the supply for the day, in local markets, is limited to the quantities delivered in the morning.

THE SHORT PERIOD

The short period (or short run) is the interval which must elapse before more can be supplied with the existing capacity. There will be at least one fixed factor of production. More fish can be supplied by trawlermen fishing longer hours or further afield. More fruit can be supplied by speeding up the harvesting or by using up existing stocks more quickly. More shoes can be produced by taking on more labour or by working overtime. The short period in some industries (e.g. the jeans industry) may be only a matter of a few days, but in others (e.g. housebuilding) it may be many months. The short period, then, is the period of time which allows for changes to take place in the quantities of the variable factors employed. Changes in supply in this period are shown as movements along the supply curve — extensions and contractions.

THE LONG PERIOD

The long period (or the long run) is the time interval which is long enough to change the quantity of all factors of production employed, i.e. the whole scale of operation. In other words, in the long period the quantities of both fixed and variable factors of production may be changed. Existing firms may increase or reduce their capacity; they may extend their factories, install more machines, adopt new methods and so on. New firms may enter (or existing firms leave) the industry. The fishing industry may expand by bringing new boats into use; the supply of fruit may be increased by planting more trees; and the output of the steel industry may be increased by building new plants.

The long run may be a matter of months in the case of some manufacturing and service industries, or several years in the case of mining, steel production, electricity generating, or fruit growing. The long run period changes in supply represent changes in the conditions of supply (the capacity of the industry has changed) and these changes involve a series of shifts in the short run supply curves. Each short run supply curve describes the supply situation for a given capacity.

ILLUSTRATING THE THREE TIME PERIODS

The relationships described above are illustrated in Figure 10.7 which shows the effects of an increase in demand in the momentary period, the short period and the long period. $S^{(m)}$ is the momentary period supply curve and S^1 the original short period supply curve.

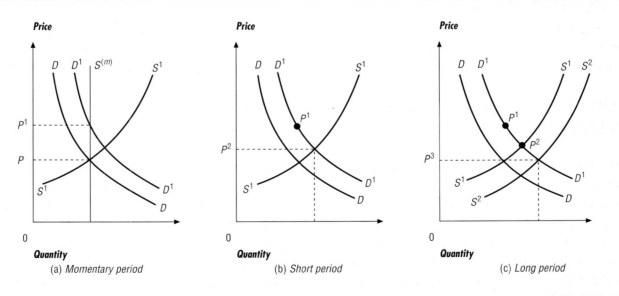

(a) *Momentary period*   (b) *Short period*   (c) *Long period*

FIG. 10.7

In Figure 10.7 (a) the situation following an increase in demand in the momentary period is shown. Supply is perfectly inelastic and price rises from P to P^1, that is, by the full extent of the change in demand.

Figure 10.7 (b) shows the situation after sufficient time has elapsed for the industry to react to the increase in demand. The higher price has stimulated a rise in the output of the existing firms and is represented by a movement along the existing short run supply curve. Price falls from P^1 to P^2.

In Figure 10.7 (c) the long run position is shown. This is the time period over which it is possible for new firms to enter the industry and for there to be an increase in the scale of production. The supply curve shifts to the right causing price to fall and demand to extend. The price P^3 may be higher or lower than the original price, P, depending on the extent to which the expansion of the industry has yielded economies of scale or diseconomies of scale.

QUESTIONS

SHORT QUESTIONS

1. Give three reasons for a decrease in the supply of cabbages.
2. Explain why price elasticity of supply is usually positive.
3. Discuss three determinants of the elasticity of supply of televisions.
4. Explain why supply tends to be more elastic in the long run than in the short run.

MULTIPLE CHOICE

1. Which would cause a shift in the supply curve of wheat to the right?

   A   A rise in incomes.

   B   A subsidy given to wheat producers.

   C   A rise in the price of wheat.

   D   A rise in the price of barley.

2. The price elasticity of supply for a firm's product is 0.8. At a price of £40 the quantity supplied by the firm is 600 units. Then the price rises to £50. What is the firm's revenue after this rise in price?

   A   £24 000   B   £30 000

   C   £32 400   D   £36 000

3. Which of the following diagrams in Figure 10.8 illustrates unit price elasticity of supply?

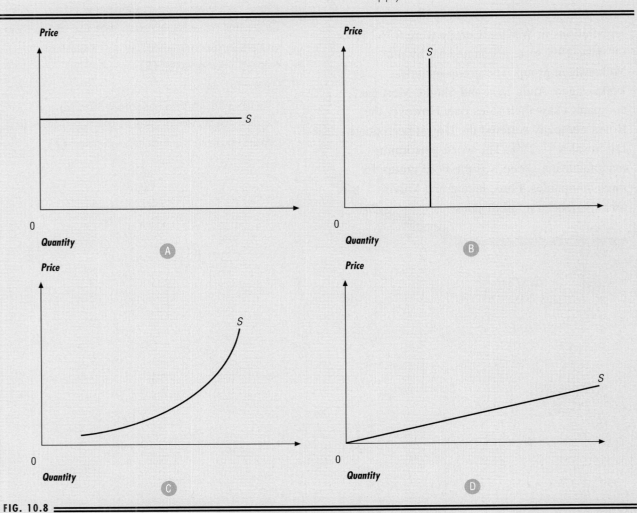

FIG. 10.8

4 Which of the following will make supply of a product more elastic?

(A) An increase in the period of time over which the product can be stored.

(B) An increase in the production period of the product.

(C) A decrease in the level of unemployment in the industry.

(D) A decrease in the mobility of the labour force in the industry.

DATA RESPONSE

In May 1999 car sales in Western Europe rose by more than had been anticipated. Sales rose particularly rapidly in Spain where, following a reduction in income tax, new car sales increased by 25% on the previous year. Germany, which is Western Europe's largest single market, saw a 5.1% rise in car registrations.

From January to May 1999 new car registrations in Western Europe were 6 762 169. Of these 19% were accounted for by the Volkswagen group. The group includes Volkswagen, Audi, Seat and Skoda. Most car companies saw their sales rise. However the Rover company suffered the largest percentage fall in sales — 21%. The worst performing manufacturing group was the Ford group. Its three companies, Ford, Jaguar and Volvo, all experienced a fall in sales.

a] Discuss the relative performance of the car companies mentioned in the extract. **(3)**

b] Does the extract suggest the supply of cars in Spain in May 1999 was elastic or inelastic? **(4)**

c] What factors influence the price elasticity of supply of cars? **(6)**

d] More cars were sold in Germany in May 1999. Does this necessarily mean that the production of cars in Germany in May 1999 increased. Explain your answer. **(5)**

e] Discuss why some car companies may experience a rise in sales at the same time that others experience a decline in sales. **(7)**

CASE STUDY

Commodities include raw materials, minerals and foodstuffs. In the 1970s the price of one commodity, oil, increased fourfold when oil producers cut sales to the West. Fears of shortages also led to a rapid rise in the price of sugar.

However the late 1990s saw a significant fall in a wide range of commodity prices compared to their mid 1990s level as shown in the table below.

PRICES IN 1999 COMPARED TO THE MID 1990s	
	%
Coffee	−54
Cotton	−51
Wheat	−41
Sugar	−51
Rubber	−65
Aluminium	−39
Copper	−52
Nickel	−60
Lead	−41

These price falls hit the developing world hard. In sub-Saharan Africa, for example, commodities account for three quarters of export earnings.

Commodity prices have always been subject to large price changes. For example the production of foodstuffs can be affected by weather conditions and diseases and demand is influenced by changes in tastes and, occasionally, medical reports and health scares. The market for raw materials and minerals is affected by new discoveries, development of substitutes, changes in technology and levels of activity.

However the falls in price in the 1990s, caused in part by low growth and economic crisis in Asia, Russia and Brazil, shocked commodity dealers and led to concerns about future supplies of commodities.

a] Which commodity witnessed the largest and which the smallest price reduction from the mid 1990s to 1999? **(2)**

b] Using a supply diagram, illustrate and explain the effect on the supply of oil of oil producers withholding sales of oil. **(5)**

c] Using a demand diagram, illustrate and explain the effect on the demand for sugar of a fear of a future shortage of sugar. **(5)**

d] Explain what effect falling commodity prices would have had on demand for food and housing in sub-Saharan Africa. **(8)**

e] Why is the supply of commodities volatile? **(6)**

f] Explain the effect on the future supply of aluminium of the development of substitutes to aluminium. **(6)**

g] Why would a fall in world output reduce demand for commodities? **(8)**

h] Explain the effect of a fall in the price of commodities on the supply of commodities
   i   in the short run **(4)**
   ii in the long run. **(6)**

STRUCTURED ESSAY

a] What factors may cause an increase in the supply of potatoes? **(12)**

b] Discuss whether the supply of potatoes is elastic or inelastic. **(13)**

11 MARKET PRICE

MARKETS

Markets exist for the vast majority of goods and services. Markets can be defined broadly or narrowly. For example there are the consumer goods, capital goods, commodities, financial and labour markets. Each of these broad categories can be broken down into more specific markets. For example within the financial market there are markets for foreign exchange and for long term loans, within the commodities market there are the markets for corn and copper and within the consumer goods market there are the markets for clothes and cars. Prices usually play an important role in these markets.

EQUILIBRIUM PRICE AND OUTPUT

In the absence of government intervention, price is determined by demand and supply. The equilibrium price is where demand and supply are equal. At this point there are no forces causing the price to change. The quantity which consumers want to buy will equal the quantity which producers want to sell at the current price.

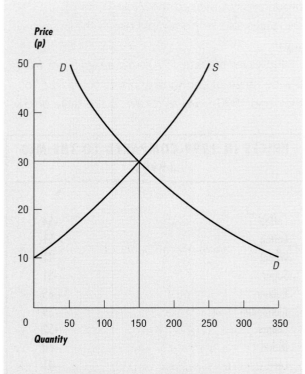

FIG. 11.1

EXAMPLE
In Figure 11.1 the equilibrium price is 30p as at this price demand equals supply.

Price	Quantity demanded	Quantity supplied
50p	50	250
40p	90	200
30p	150	150
20p	220	80
10p	350	0

At prices higher than the equilibrium price the quantity supplied will be greater than the quantity demanded and the excess supply would oblige sellers to lower their prices in order to dispose of their output. For example, if price is 40p supply would exceed demand by 110. This situation, illustrated in Figure 11.2, where supply exceeds demand and there is downward pressure on price is sometimes described as a buyers' market.

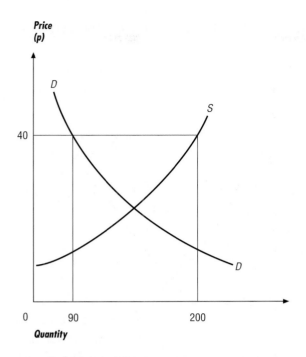

Price
(p)

D

S

40

D

0   90   200

Quantity

FIG. 11.2

The equilibrium or market price is 30p, because at any other price there are market forces at work which tend to change the price.

CHANGES IN EQUILIBRIUM PRICE

As market prices are determined in free markets by the interaction of demand and supply, changes in market prices are due to changes in demand or supply, or both.

At prices lower than the market price, e.g. 20p, the quantity demanded will exceed the quantity supplied, giving rise to a condition known as a sellers' market. This is illustrated in Figure 11.3.

THE EFFECTS OF SHIFTS IN DEMAND

The effects of changes in demand may be stated in terms of economic predictions.

- In the short run, other things being equal, an increase in demand will raise the price and this, in turn, will cause an extension in supply.
- In the short run, other things being equal, a decrease in demand will lower the price and cause a contraction in supply.

Figure 11.4 illustrates the effects of an increase in demand. *DD* is the original demand curve so that the equilibrium price is *P* and quantity *Q* is demanded and supplied. If demand increases from *DD* to D^1D^1 the immediate effect is to cause a shortage (shown by the dotted line) at the ruling price *P*. This shortage will cause the price to be bid upwards and supply to extend until a new equilibrium price is established at P^1. The quantity demanded and supplied is now Q^1.

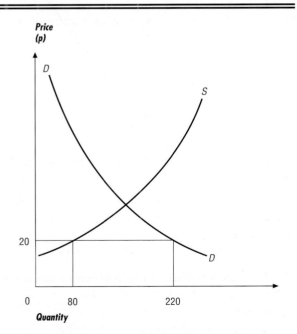

Price
(p)

D

S

20

D

0   80   220

Quantity

FIG. 11.3

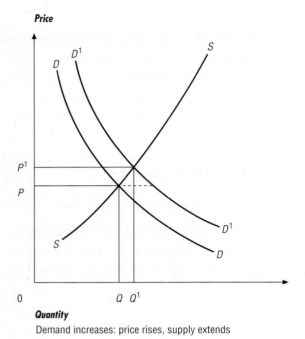

Quantity
Demand increases: price rises, supply extends

FIG. 11.4

Figure 11.5 shows a decrease in demand. The demand curve shifts to the left (D^1D^1). There is a surplus at price P (equal to the horizontal distance between the demand curves). Suppliers will be obliged to lower prices to P^1 in order to clear their stocks. This fall in price will cause a contraction in supply.

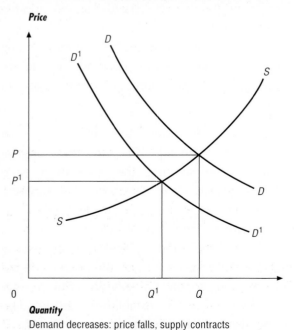

Quantity
Demand decreases: price falls, supply contracts

FIG. 11.5

THE EFFECTS OF SHIFTS IN SUPPLY

The effects of changes in supply may also be summarised in the form of two economic predictions:

- in the short run, other things being equal, an increase in supply will lower the price and this in turn will cause an extension in demand;
- in the short run, other things being equal, a decrease in supply will raise the price and cause a contraction in demand.

Figure 11.6 demonstrates the effects of an increase in supply. The supply curve moves from SS to S^1S^1. The immediate effect is a surplus (shown by the dotted line) at the ruling price P. This surplus will force price downwards to P^1 and the lower price will result in an extension in demand. The quantity demanded and supplied will be Q^1.

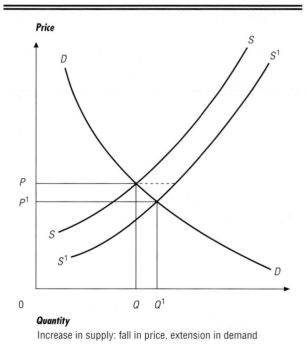

Quantity
Increase in supply: fall in price, extension in demand

FIG. 11.6

Figure 11.7 shows a decrease in supply. When supply falls from SS to S^1S^1 there will be excess demand at price P (equal to the horizontal distance between the supply curves). This will cause the price to rise to a new equilibrium price of P^1. This higher price results in a contraction in demand.

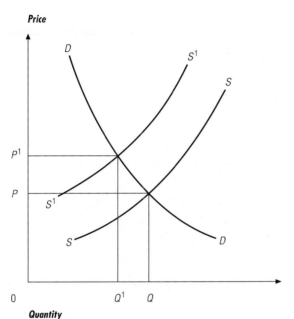

Decrease in supply: rise in price, contraction in demand

FIG. 11.7

THE DISTINCTION BETWEEN MOVEMENTS ALONG AND SHIFTS IN DEMAND AND SUPPLY

In analysing changes in market prices it is important to consider what has caused the change in price. For example if there has been an increase in demand, higher demand will be associated with a higher price. Whereas if the cause of the price rise is a decrease in supply, lower demand will be associated with a higher price. So it is very important to recognise the cause of the change in price and the order of events.

PRICE ELASTICITIES OF DEMAND AND SUPPLY

As well as knowing the direction of changes in prices, it is also important to know the extent of such changes. Knowledge of price elasticity of demand and price elasticity of supply enable economists to calculate the extent to which changes in demand affect prices and the quantity supplied and the extent to which changes in supply affect prices and quantity demanded.

For example, if demand is elastic, an increase in supply will cause a relatively small fall in price and a greater percentage change in quantity demanded. In this case total revenue will rise. Figure 11.8 shows the effect of an increase in supply when demand is elastic.

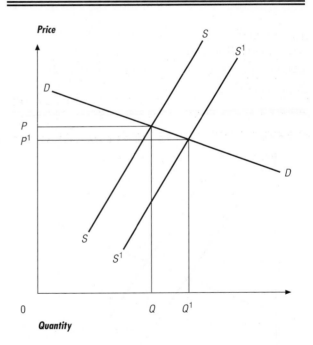

FIG. 11.8

If demand is inelastic an increase in supply will cause a relatively large fall in price and a smaller percentage change in quantity demanded. In this case total revenue will fall. Figure 11.9 shows the effect of an increase in supply in a market where demand is inelastic.

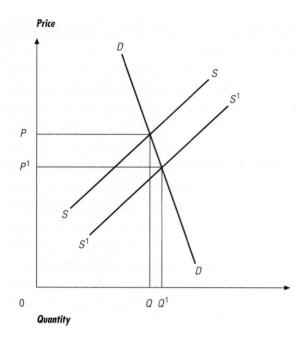

FIG. 11.9

If supply is elastic an increase in demand will cause a relatively small rise in price and a greater percentage change in quantity supplied as shown in Figure 11.10.

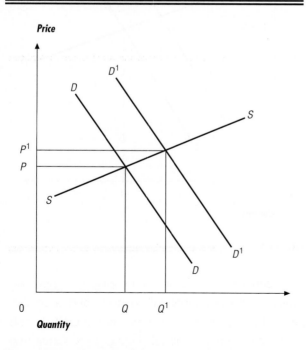

FIG. 11.10

On the other hand if supply is inelastic an increase in demand will cause a relatively large rise in price and a smaller percentage in the quantity supplied. This is shown in Figure 11.11.

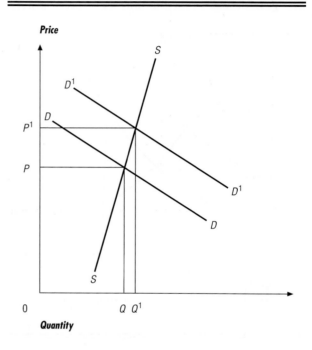

FIG. 11.11

In markets where both demand and supply are inelastic, as occurs in the markets of many agricultural products, a shift in demand and/or supply will have a significant effect on price. This is illustrated in Figure 11.12 which shows the effect of a decrease in supply.

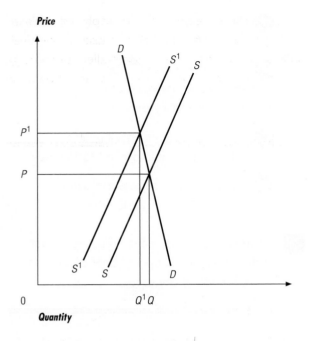

FIG. 11.12

In markets where both demand and supply are elastic, a change in demand and/or supply will have a significant impact on the quantity bought and sold but only a small impact on the equilibrium price. Figure 11.13 shows the effect of decrease in supply in such a market.

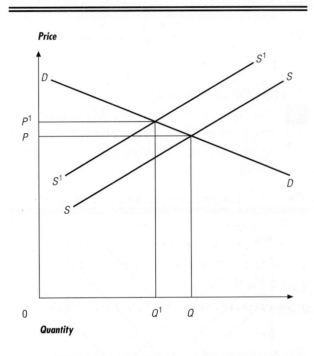

FIG. 11.13

QUESTIONS

SHORT QUESTIONS

1. Explain what is meant by equilibrium price.

2. What will be the outcome if price is set above the equilibrium?

3. What effect will an increase in supply have on price and demand?

4. What effect will a decrease in demand have on price and supply?

MULTIPLE CHOICE

1. The Figure 11.14 shows the demand and supply curves for a consumer good. The initial equilibrium price is *P*. Which of the following would explain a fall in price to *P*¹?

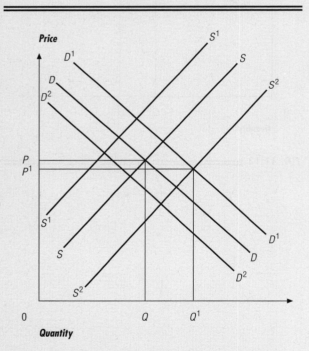

Price

Quantity

FIG. 11.14

A. An increase in real incomes and a fall in raw material costs.

B. A subsidy granted to producers and an increase in the price of a complementary product.

C. An increase in income tax and the introduction of improved technology.

D. An increase in population and an increase in value added tax.

2. What would be the effect in a free market on the price and supply of beef of a change in preference of chicken?

TABLE

	Price	Supply
A	rise	fall
B	rise	rise
C	fall	fall
D	fall	rise

3. In a free market a reduction in costs of production increases supply by 10% at all prices. At the same time a rise in incomes causes consumer demand to rise by 10% at all prices. What will be the outcome?

A. A 10% increase in both prices and sales level.

B. A 10% higher price with unchanged sales level.

C. An unchanged price with 10% higher sales level.

D. Unchanged price and unchanged sales level.

4 TABLE

	Consumers' expenditure in market prices (£2000m)	
	1992	2002
Food	43 000	49 000
Clothing & footwear	22 500	33 000
Housing	50 000	82 000
Transport & communications	60 500	81 000
Tobacco	7 900	6 200
Total consumers' expenditure	345 000	460 000

It can be deduced from the data that:

A expenditure on transport and communications rose by a greater percentage than expenditure on clothing and footwear

B expenditure on food formed a smaller percentage of total expenditure in 2002 than in 1992

C the price of cigarettes and other tobacco products fell over the period 1992 to 2002

D the supply of housing increased by a greater percentage than the demand for housing between 1992 and 2002.

DATA RESPONSE

The table below shows the demand and supply schedules for ice cream in a holiday resort.

DEMAND AND SUPPLY SCHEDULES (ICE CREAM)

Price (pence per cone)	Quantity demanded 000 per week	Quantity supplied 000 per week
120	4	80
100	20	50
90	40	40
80	65	18
70	95	4

a] What is the equilibrium price? Explain your answer. **(3)**

b] What would be the unsold surplus if price is set at 120 pence? **(2)**

c] At what price will there be a shortage of 47 000? **(3)**

d] If supply decreased by 300 000 at each price what would be the new equilibrium price? **(4)**

e] Why may the price of ice cream rise during peak holiday periods? **(5)**

f] Explain what effect a fall in the price of chocolate may have on the equilibrium price and output of ice cream. **(8)**

CASE STUDY

The housing market

Since the beginning of the year, property transactions have increased sharply, house prices have risen, mortgage approvals have jumped and net mortgage lending has accelerated.

Estate agents normally have a stock of unsold houses on the books, in part because of differences between sellers' asking prices and buyers' offers. As a result, the first sign of an upturn usually comes in transaction data — as buyers' price offers move up towards sellers' asking prices and houses already on the market sell more quickly. This appears to be the case this year.

As the stock of houses for sale is exhausted, turnover may slow, despite the upturn in demand. The second stage sees upward movement of prices driven by growing shortages of property for sale. But in some areas, notably London, the market appears to have been in this stage for some time.

The upward movement of prices may eventually lead to more houses being offered for sale, which raises turnover but stems price inflation. There is little evidence of this yet. But to understand where the market may go from here, we need to examine what is driving the upturn. Three interrelated factors stand out: a recovery in personal income growth; falling interest rates; and rising consumer confidence.

Alongside changes in the overall level of housing demand, the nature of that demand is likely to shift. A large rise is projected in single person households over the next ten years, which accounts for three quarters of the projected growth in total households. Those under retirement age account for most of the growth of single person households. These are the type of households most likely to rent, and in many cases, with lowest resources.

Source: 'No boom for housing' by Patrick Foley, Lloyds TSB Economic Bulletin, July 1999.

a] Does the extract suggest that the housing market is normally in equilibrium, in a situation of surplus or shortage? Explain your answer. **(4)**

b] Why is the supply of houses lower than the stock of houses? **(6)**

c] What causes the price of houses to rise? **(4)**

d] What does the extract suggest will be the effect of a rise in house prices on the supply of houses? Illustrate your answer. **(5)**

e] What factors does the extract suggest will cause a shift to the right of the demand curve for houses? **(6)**

f] Discuss two other factors which could cause an increase in demand for houses. **(8)**

g] As a result of changes in the housing market discussed in the extract what may happen to the size of houses built in the future? **(5)**

h] Discuss the effects of a rise in the price of houses on the market for rented accommodation. **(12)**

STRUCTURED ESSAY

a] Explain how and why price in a free market moves towards equilibrium. **(10)**

b] Discuss the effects on the market for bicycles of
   i   an increase in incomes **(5)**
   ii a rise in the price of petrol **(5)**
   iii an improvement in the technology of bicycle production. **(5)**

RELATIVE PRICES

The price paid for a product is its nominal or absolute price. However, economists are concerned mainly with relative prices. This is because when people consider what to buy they look at the price of a product in comparison to the price of other products.

For example if the price of electricity rises and other prices do not change, electricity will have become relatively more expensive.

However, if all, or most, prices are changing at the same time (as occurs when there is inflation), it becomes more difficult to work out changes in relative prices. In this case electricity will experience a rise in its relative price, if its price rises faster than the average of all other prices.

DEMAND RELATIONSHIPS

JOINT DEMAND

Some products are jointly demanded. This means that they are complementary in the sense that the use of one implies the use of the other. This relationship gives rise to their name of complements. For example the demand for petrol is associated with the demand for motor cars and the demand for tennis balls is linked to the demand for tennis racquets.

Where products are complementary a change in the price of one of them will cause a change in the demand for the other one. For example, technological progress might lead to a reduction in the costs of producing cameras and so make them available at lower prices. As a result of cameras being cheaper, demand for films is likely to increase as shown in Figure 12.1.

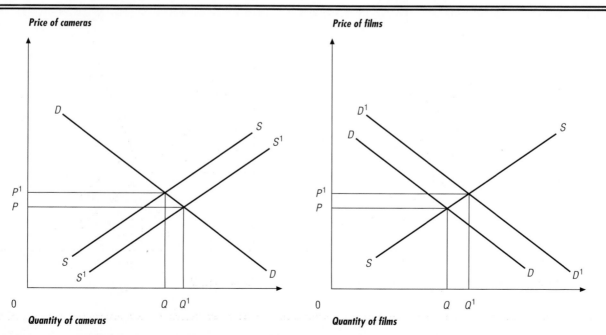

FIG. 12.1

This relationship can also be shown on a cross elasticity of demand curve as Figure 12.2 illustrates. As explained in Chapter 9 complements (complementary products) have negative cross elasticity of demand.

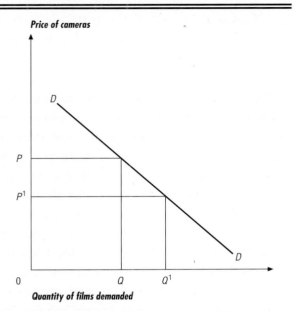

FIG. 12.2

COMPETITIVE DEMAND

Products which are close substitutes for one another are said to be in competitive demand. Other things being equal, the demand for a product will tend to vary directly with the price of its substitute. Figure 12.3 explains this relationship between products in competitive demand. It shows in (a) how a decrease in the supply of beef has raised the price and reduced the quantity demanded. This has caused an increase in demand for pork, an increase in its price, and an extension in supply as shown in (b).

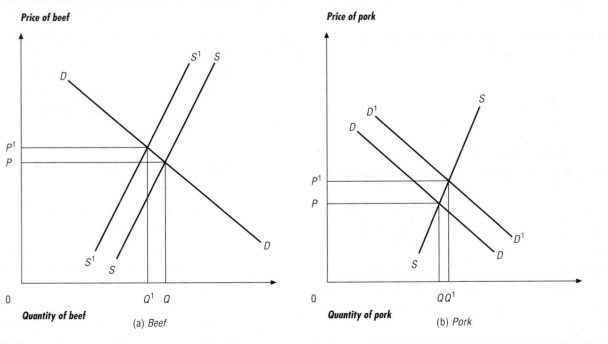

FIG. 12.3

This information can also be shown on a cross elasticity of demand diagram. This time, as Figure 12.4 illustrates, the cross elasticity of demand is positive.

COMPOSITE DEMAND

A product is said to be in composite demand when it is demanded for several different uses. The demands for such products are the totals of the demands of the various users. For example wool will be demanded by the textile industry, carpet manufacturers, blanket manufacturers, the hosiery industry and many others. An increase in the demand for wool by any one industry will raise the price and affect the prices of all the other products made

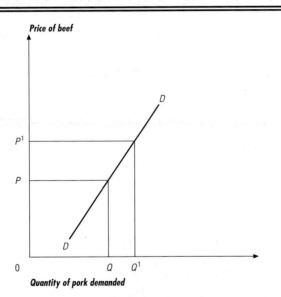

FIG. 12.4

from wool. Copper, nylon and rubber provide good examples of basic commodities widely used in many different industries. So a large increase in the demand for central heating (copper pipes) might increase prices in the electrical components industries (printed circuits and cables).

SUPPLY RELATIONSHIPS

JOINT SUPPLY

Joint supply occurs where the production of one product automatically leads to an output of another. Lead and zinc are found in the same ore so that the extraction of one leads to the extraction of the other. The production of beef also results in the production of hides and the production of mutton leads to a supply of wool. An oil refinery produces many different fuels from crude oil and an increased output of any one product, say petrol, will automatically increase the output of the others (benzine, diesel oil, etc.).

One very important, but not so obvious, example of this relationship is to be found in the transport industry. Haulage contractors, bus companies, and the railways cannot normally supply an outward journey without supplying an inward journey. This gives rise to the very costly problems of 'empty running'.

Where products are in joint supply an increase in the demand for one of them will cause a fall in the price of the other. This is demonstrated in Figure 12.5. In Figure 12.5 (a) the demand for beef increases, causing the price of beef to rise from P to P^1 and an extension in supply. This also increases the supply of hides as shown in Figure 12.5 (b).

COMPETITIVE SUPPLY

Most products are in competitive supply. As noted in Chapter 2, if a country operating on its production possibility curve decides to produce more of one type of product, it will have to reduce its output of the other type of product.

Similarly, if one firm wishes to expand its output of one product it produces, perhaps because of a

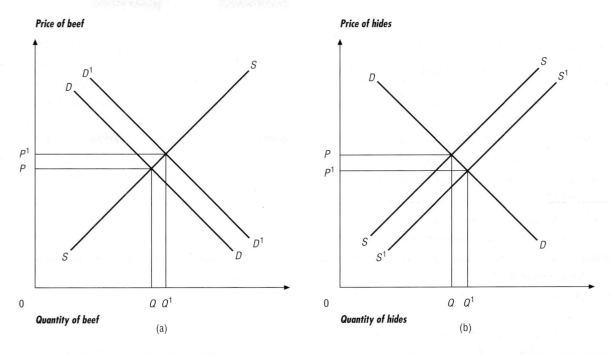

FIG. 12.5

rise in its profitability, it may have to shift resources away from making other products, thereby reducing their supply. Figure 12.6 (a) shows that an increase in demand for Star Wars

toys causes their price to rise and their supply to extend. Figure 12.6 (b) shows the supply of model cars produced by the same firm decreasing.

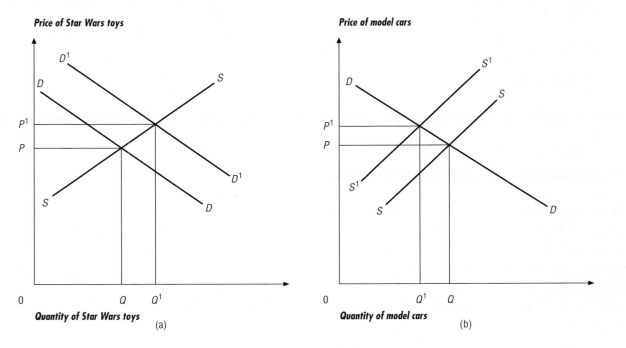

FIG. 12.6

RELATIONSHIPS BETWEEN PRODUCT AND FACTOR MARKETS

A change in demand and/or supply of product will affect not only the market for that product but also the factor markets involved (the markets for the resources that produce the product). Similarly changes in the factor markets will have repercussions in the product markets.

These relationships can be examined by looking at two examples. If in a country there is a move away from eating meat towards vegetarianism, the price of vegetables will increase and the price of meat will fall. Figure 12.7 shows how an increase in demand for vegetables causes their price to rise and supply to extend, whilst the decrease in demand for meat causes its price to fall and its supply to contract.

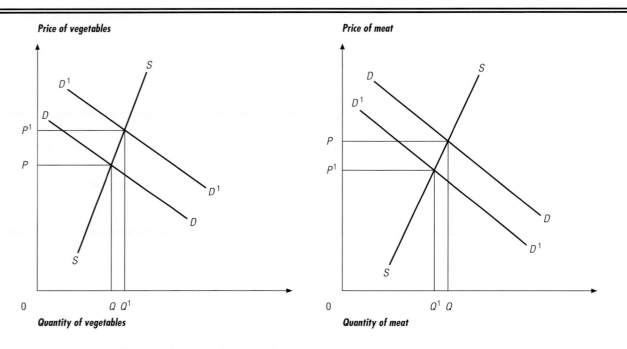

FIG. 12.7

If the rise in the price of vegetables leads to an increase in the profitability of growing vegetables, the demand for greenhouses, for workers in the vegetable industry, for vegetable-processing equipment and for vegetarian restaurants, etc. will increase. On the other hand, if the profitability of meat production falls, the demand for land to graze cattle, for lorries to transport animals, for hot-dog stalls and for abattoirs, etc., will decrease. Figure 12.8

shows the likely effect of this on the market for butchers.

Changes in factor markets also affect product markets. For example, if actors at the Royal Shakespeare Company, based in Stratford-on-Avon, receive a rise in real pay, then the cost of producing plays will rise. This in turn is likely to raise the price of theatre tickets.

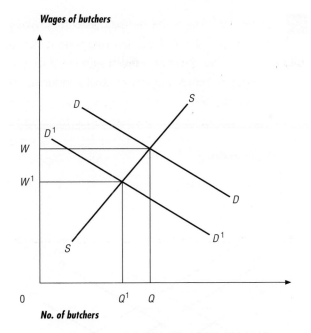

FIG. 12.8

QUESTIONS

SHORT QUESTIONS

1. Giving examples, explain which type of goods are:
   i in joint demand
   ii in joint supply.

2. What effect is a rise in demand for duvets likely to have on the market for blanket workers?

3. Explain what is meant by composite demand.

4. What effect has the rise in the average age of the population of many countries had on demand for health care and the wages of nurses?

MULTIPLE CHOICE

1. Which of the following goods are in joint demand?

   A Tea and coffee.

   B Gas and electricity.

   C Wool and lamb.

   D Strawberries and cream.

2. X is a complement to Y and a substitute to Z. What will be the effect on the price and supply of Y and Z of a rise in the price of X?

	Y		Z	
	price	supply	price	supply
A	rise	rise	fall	fall
B	fall	fall	rise	rise
C	fall	rise	rise	fall
D	rise	fall	fall	rise

3. Figure 12.9 shows the demand and supply of televisions. The initial equilibrium price is X. What will be the new equilibrium price if incomes increase and the cost of producing televisions falls?

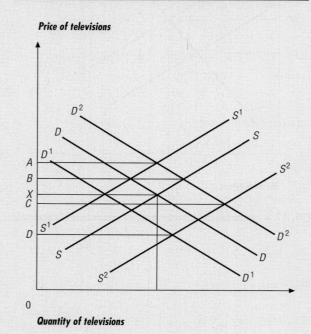

Price of televisions

Quantity of televisions

FIG. 12.9

4. Which change in the market for perfume would be likely to lead to an increase in the wages for chemists working on developing new perfumes?

   A A fall in incomes.

   B The imposition of a tax on perfume.

   C A successful advertising campaign for perfume.

   D An increase in the cost of producing perfume.

DATA RESPONSE

The record growth of the organic food market over the past year means supermarkets are struggling to keep pace with demand, leading to fears that standards could be diluted.

Supermarkets have doubled their sales of organic products — topping the £1 million-a-week mark at Sainsbury's as pressure from health conscious customers beats the hefty price premium on most 'naturally produced' goods.

But supermarkets can barely keep up with demand, and some rogue market traders and butchers are known to be exploiting the rapidly growing market by selling as 'organic' produce grown with pesticides or antibiotics.

'The rate of growth is something that would astonish even the most bullish forecasters,' Dino Adriano, chief executive of Sainsbury's, will tell the meeting at the Royal Agricultural College in Cirencester. 'What were once niche products are now part of the supermarkets' main product range.' The store's high profiling of organic foods has been matched at Tesco, which will report a 100% increase in organic sales, and at Waitrose, which has 600 organic lines and has seen organic babyfoods take 40% of sales.

The supermarket will tell the conference that growth is expected to continue for at least five further years of rising demand, with the sector expanding at an estimated 2.5% annually overall.

Supermarkets are being obliged to import most of their organic food from abroad because not enough is grown in Britain.

Source: 'Organic food outgrows its image with huge rise in demand — and worries over dirty deals' by John Vidal and Martin Wainwright, the Guardian, 8/1/99.

a] Why are supermarkets able to charge high prices ('hefty price premium') for organic food? **(4)**

b] Explain and illustrate the effect on the supply of organic food of the change in the market for organic food discussed in the extract. **(5)**

c] How have supermarkets responded to the change in demand for organic foods? **(4)**

d] Discuss two possible causes of the change in demand for organic food. **(6)**

e] What effect will the change in demand for organic food have on the market for organic butchers? **(6)**

CASE STUDY

One US industry expert said: 'New entrants, or revamped competitors, throw away the history books and create new ways of doing things. The business environment is sometimes transformed in a matter of two or three years and the winners in the old order will never be the first to recognise that the world has changed.'

Computer giant IBM ruled the planet until the Eighties when, convinced that mainframes were the only serious game in town, it got left behind in the personal computer revolution.

Rivals such as Compaq and Apple got ahead and, later, newcomers such as Dell turned the traditional method of selling computers in the shops on its head by selling everything over the telephone.

Microsoft, whose Windows program is the software used in more British personal computers than any other, very nearly lost the plot when it decided in the early Nineties that the world wide web would never catch on.

A rash of start-up Internet providers disagreed — and if Microsoft had not realised its mistake and started including Internet facilities in its software three years ago it would have been eclipsed.

Of course, size is not necessarily an advantage. Many commentators complain that once a company has reached a certain volume it can suffer from bureaucratic inertia, so that it either fails to notice rivals or fails to react quickly and radically enough when threat manifests itself.

One UK strategy consultant said: 'Marks & Spencer became resistant to change and moved away from its actual customers in the market place. A number of competitors in both food and clothing have damaged M&S but I doubt it even picked them up on its radar screen until it was too late.'

In the steel business, giants like the American USX, British Steel and Germany's Thyssen paid little heed to Indian entrepreneur Lakshmi Mittal until his steel company Ispat rose from virtually nothing in the mid-Nineties to become the fourth largest producer in the world.

Source: 'The harder they fall' by Joanna Walters, the Observer, 16/5/99.

a] What happened to the number of computer manufacturers in the 1980s and 1990s? What effect would this have on the supply of computers? **(5)**

b] Explain the relationship between computers and software. **(3)**

c] Explain the relationship between food and clothing sold in Marks & Spencer and food and clothing sold in other supermarkets. **(3)**

d] Discuss two factors which may have caused a fall in the demand for Marks & Spencer goods. **(6)**

e] i What effect would the entry of new companies into the steel industry be likely to have on the price of steel? Illustrate your answer with a diagram. **(6)**

   ii What effect will an increase in the number of competitors be likely to have on the price elasticity of demand for the product of the original companies? **(6)**

f] Explain the role of the entrepreneur. **(4)**

g] What does the extract suggest is the main cause of the difficulties faced by the companies mentioned? **(5)**

h] Discuss how Marks & Spencer could increase the demand for its products. **(12)**

STRUCTURED ESSAY

a] What factors influence the demand and supply
for lamb? **(10)**

b] What effect will an increase in the price of
lamb have on the markets for:
  i   mint sauce **(5)**
  ii beef **(5)**
  iii shepherds. **(5)**

13 COSTS OF PRODUCTION

OPPORTUNITY COST

Costs are usually measured in monetary terms and include such items as wages, rent, interest and the amounts paid for raw materials, fuel, power, transport, and so on. However it is also important to bear in mind the 'true' or 'real' costs of committing resources to a particular use as the output they might have produced had they been put to another use. This is the idea of opportunity cost which was explained in Chapter 1.

Opportunity cost is important because 'money' costs may not provide a true measure of the sacrifices incurred in producing a product. If the production of a product leads to pollution of the atmosphere or water supplies, the opportunity costs of production would include the clean air or clear water forgone by society as well as the costs of the factors employed in production.

OUTPUT AND COSTS

In dealing with the relationship between output and costs there are two circumstances to consider. First, short-run changes which cover periods when it is only possible to adjust the amount of the variable factors of production being used and when there is at least one fixed factor. For example, in the short run it may be possible to change the amount of labour and raw material used but there is not sufficient time to change the size of the factory. Secondly, long-run changes which apply to periods of time which are sufficiently long for all the factors of production to be changed.

SHORT RUN COSTS

FIXED COSTS

These are costs which do not vary as output varies. They are obviously the costs associated with the fixed factors of production, and include such items as rent, rates, insurance, interest on loans, and depreciation.

Fixed costs (sometimes called overheads or indirect costs) are not influenced by changes in output. Whether a firm is working at full capacity or half capacity these costs will be unaffected. Indeed, fixed costs are the costs which have to be paid even when output is zero. For example when a super-tanker is lying empty in port, or a chartered plane is standing in the hangar or a building society is closed over the Christmas period, costs are still being incurred.

VARIABLE COSTS

These are the costs which are related directly to output and so change when output changes. The most obvious items of variable costs are the wages of labour, the costs of raw materials, and fuel and power. Variable costs are sometimes referred to as direct or prime costs. Variable costs are not incurred when output is zero.

TOTAL COSTS

Short-run total costs represent the sum of fixed and variable costs. When output is zero, total costs will be equal to fixed costs since variable costs will be zero. When production commences, total costs will begin to rise as variable costs start to increase.

Total costs will continue to rise as production increases, because there must be some increase in variable costs as output expands and more raw materials and labour are used. What is important, however, is the rate at which total costs increase; if they are rising at a slower rate than output, average costs must be falling. Figure 13.1 shows how total cost is composed of both fixed and variable costs.

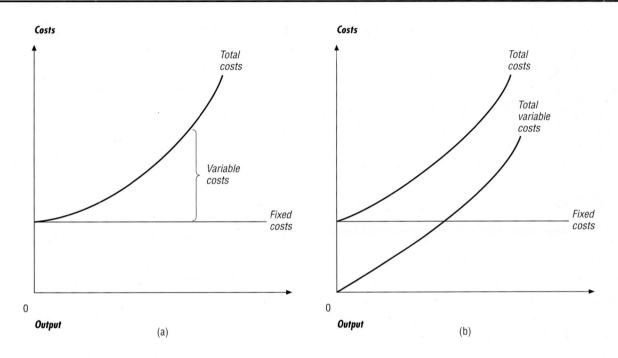

FIG. 13.1

AVERAGE COST

Average cost (or cost per unit or unit cost) is total costs divided by output. It can also be called average total cost. When output is small, average cost will be high because fixed costs will be spread over a small number of units of output. As output increases, average cost will tend to fall as each unit is 'carrying' a smaller element of fixed cost. Average cost will also fall because, for a time, as more resources are employed they can be used more efficiently and more specialised methods adopted. However, as output continues to increase average costs may start to rise. This is because the wrong combination of resources may be being used — for example,

there may not have been enough time to enlarge the size of the factory. Management problems may increase; less efficient stand-by equipment may be pressed into use; less efficient labour may have to be recruited; it may be necessary to work overtime at higher wage rates; and increasing demand may cause the price of materials to rise.

So it may be expected that, for the individual firm with a fixed capacity, average cost will at first decline but as output increases there will come a point where it will rise. In which case the average cost curve will be U-shaped. When the firm is producing at its minimum average cost it is said to have reached its optimum output. Figure 13.2 shows the short-run average cost curve.

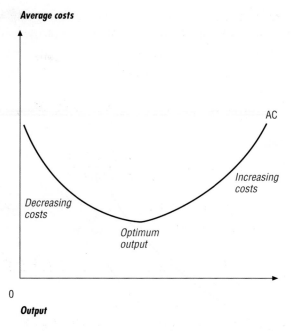

FIG. 13.2

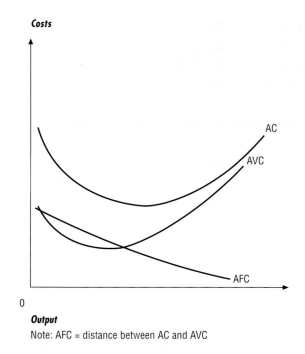

Note: AFC = distance between AC and AVC

FIG. 13.3

AVERAGE VARIABLE COST

Average variable cost is total variable cost divided by output. The average variable cost curve is U-shaped.

AVERAGE FIXED COST

Average fixed cost is total fixed cost divided by output. As total fixed cost is constant, average fixed cost must fall with output. The fixed cost is spread over a greater and greater output. Figure 13.3 shows the three average cost curves: average cost (AC), average variable cost (AVC) and average fixed cost (AFC).

MARGINAL COST

Economists are interested in marginal quantities because most economic decisions involve changes in some existing situation. Marginal cost is what happens to total costs when output is varied by some small output. More precisely, marginal cost is the change in total costs when output is changed by one unit.

Marginal cost = total cost of n units − total cost of (n−1) units

Since marginal cost is a measurement of changes in total cost it is obviously influenced by variable costs but not by fixed costs. Marginal fixed cost is zero as fixed costs do not change with output. So marginal cost is equal to marginal variable cost (i.e. the change in total variable cost when output is changed by one unit).

When firms expand their output, marginal costs usually fall at first as the firms' variable resources work more efficiently (increasing their returns) but later, as a result of their fixed capacity and the problems noted above, output rises less slowly than the variable resources (diminishing returns) and marginal costs rise. So, as shown in Figure 13.4 the marginal cost curve is usually U-shaped.

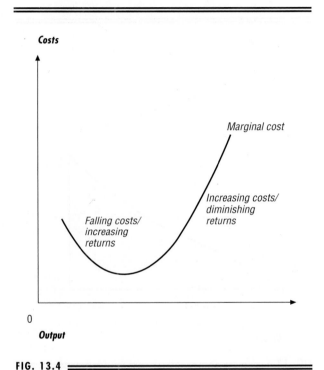

FIG. 13.4

SUMMARY

1. Total cost = fixed costs + variable costs

2. Average cost = $\dfrac{\text{total cost}}{\text{total output}}$

3. Average variable cost = $\dfrac{\text{total variable cost}}{\text{total output}}$

4. Average fixed cost = $\dfrac{\text{total fixed cost}}{\text{total output}}$

5. Marginal cost = change in total cost when output is changed by one unit

SHORT RUN COST SCHEDULES AND COST CURVES

Table 13.1 is designed to illustrate the relationship between the different categories of short run cost.

Column 4 shows total cost at different levels of output and is the result of adding together the figures in columns 2 and 3. Average cost in column 5 is the result of dividing the figures in column 4 by those in column 1. Average fixed cost in column 7 is total fixed cost in column 2 divided by output. Average variable cost in column 8 is found by dividing total variable cost in column 3 by output in column 3 and by output in column 1. Marginal cost in column 6 is obtained from column 4 by calculating the increases in total cost for each unit increase in output.

TABLE 13.1 COSTS OF PRODUCTION (£)

(1) Units of output	(2) Fixed costs	(3) Variable costs	(4) Total cost	(5) Average cost	(6) Marginal cost	(7) Average fixed cost	(8) Average variable cost
0	18	0	18	Infinity	—	—	—
1	18	15.2	33.2	33.2	15.2	18	15.2
2	18	28.4	46.4	23.2	13.2	9	14.2
3	18	40.0	58.0	19.3	11.6	6	13.3
4	18	50.4	68.4	17.1	10.4	4.5	12.6
5	18	60.0	78.0	15.6	9.6	3.6	12
6	18	70.0	88.0	14.7	10.0	3	11.7
7	18	81.2	99.2	14.2	11.2	2.6	11.6
8	18	94.8	112.8	14.1	13.6	2.3	11.9
9	18	112.4	130.4	14.5	17.6	2	12.5
10	18	134.4	152.4	15.2	22.0	1.8	13.4

Notice that as output increases, the marginal cost, average cost and variable cost begin to fall, reach a minimum and then begin to rise. The relationship between average and marginal costs is an important one and it is shown in Figure 13.5, a graphical representation of the information in Table 13.1. Both the average cost (AC) and the marginal cost (MC) curves fall and then rise. Note that when MC is below AC, AC is falling; when MC is above AC, AC is rising. Marginal cost is equal to average cost when average cost is at its minimum value.

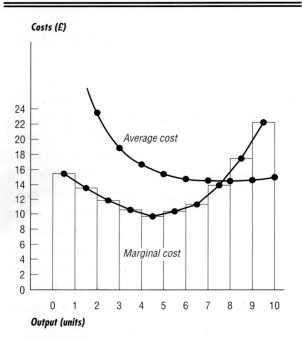

Costs (£)

Output (units)

FIG. 13.5

THE RELATIONSHIP BETWEEN MARGINAL AND AVERAGE COSTS

The relationship between marginal and average cost can be proved mathematically, but it can also be easily understood on a common-sense basis.

Consider a cricketer's batting average. If, in his/her next innings, his/her score (i.e. his/her marginal score) is less than his/her existing average, then his/her average score must fall. If, in his/her next innings, s/he scores more than his/her existing average, his/her average score must increase. So if the marginal quantity is less than the average quantity, the average must be falling; if the marginal quantity is greater than the average quantity, the average must be rising. Figure 13.6 presents another view of the relationship between costs. It shows how the different kinds of cost can be derived from the total cost curve.

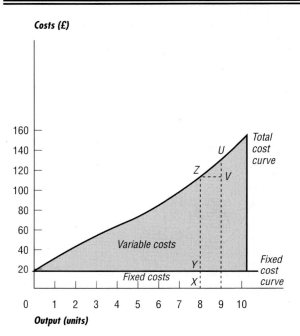

Costs (£)

Output (units)

FIG. 13.6

When output is X (i.e. 8 units), total costs = XZ, and this is made up of fixed costs (XY) and variable costs (YZ). At this output average cost = XZ/X and marginal cost = UV.

LONG-RUN COSTS

The long run is defined as the period of time in which it is possible to change the quantity of all factors of production employed. So it is the time period when not only more workers and more machines can be employed but also when the size of the factory, office or farm can be altered. As the whole scale of operation can be changed there are no fixed costs. For example, if a firm expands it will use more land and capital and so will pay more rent and interest and if it contracts its scale of operation it is likely not to replace some plant and machinery as they wear out and may sell some of its assets. So in the long run, all costs are variable costs.

THE RELATIONSHIP BETWEEN SHORT-RUN AND LONG-RUN COSTS

Figure 13.7 helps to explain the changing cost structure of a firm as it changes its scale of production. When it starts its operations as a small business, its original short-run average cost curve is represented by SAC (1). If this firm is successful and increases its size, a new short-run average cost curve becomes effective for each particular scale of production. These short-run average cost curves are represented by SAC (2), SAC (3), SAC (4) and SAC (5). Each of these curves represents a different stock of capital and other fixed factors.

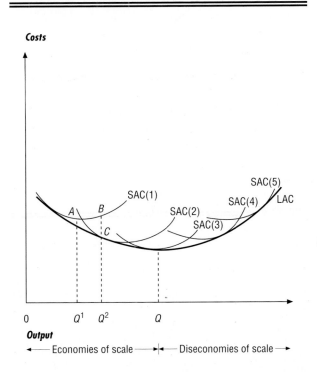

FIG. 13.7

Assuming that a firm will always choose the size of plant (i.e. factory, farm, office or other business unit) and equipment which minimises the cost of producing any given output, it can be seen why it will tend to increase its scale of production as the demand for its product increases. Assume that it is initially operating on cost curve SAC (1) producing an output of Q^1 at an average cost of AQ^1. Now in order to meet an increased demand, its output increases to Q^2. With its existing resources, this change in output would raise average cost to BQ^2. But by increasing the size of the firm and moving to cost curve SAC (2), an output of Q^2 can be produced at an average cost of CQ^2. This same reasoning can be applied to explain movements to cost curves SAC (3), SAC (4) and SAC (5). Instead of moving up an existing cost curve, lower costs of production can be obtained by moving on to a cost curve of a firm with greater capacity.

The long-run average cost curve therefore consists of a series of points on five different short-run cost curves. These points represent the lowest costs attainable for the production of any given output. If it is assumed that there are many such short-run curves, the long-run cost curve will assume a shape similar to LAC in Figure 13.7. The LAC curve is described as an 'envelope curve' to the series of SAC curves.

THE SHAPE OF THE LONG-RUN AVERAGE COST CURVE

Long-run average cost curves are often drawn as U-shaped. When a firm expands its capacity it is likely that it will experience economies of scale. These are the cost advantages of operating on a large scale. For example, larger firms tend to find it easier and cheaper to raise finance, can buy in bulk and can make use of larger, more efficient machines. Economies of scale are discussed in more detail in Chapter 39.

Figure 13.7 shows a firm experiencing economies of scale until it reaches output Q on SAC (3). This is the optimum size of the firm since any further increase in the scale of production leads to rising average cost. In the long run, average cost will rise as a result of the firm experiencing diseconomies of scale. These are the disadvantages which arise when a firm grows too large. For example, it may take longer for decisions to be made and industrial relations may deteriorate. Diseconomies of scale are discussed in more detail in Chapter 39.

DIFFERENT SHAPED LONG-RUN AVERAGE COST CURVES

As mentioned before, the conventional average cost curve is U-shaped. It may also be drawn with a flat bottom, showing that over a given level of output average cost does not change — this is referred to as constant returns to scale. This shape is shown in Figure 13.8.

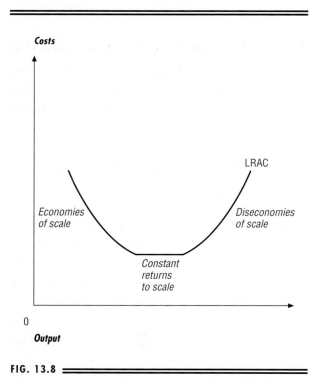

FIG. 13.8

However, most economists do not now think this is the most common shape for most businesses. The practical experience of firms in such industries as aircraft production, motor cars, chemicals, oil, and the manufacture of television tubes appears to contradict the idea that increasing the size of the firm in such industries is disadvantageous because the technical economies of scale are so great that they more than offset any managerial and administrative diseconomies of scale. In this case, the long-run average cost curve will slope down from left to right as shown in Figure 13.9.

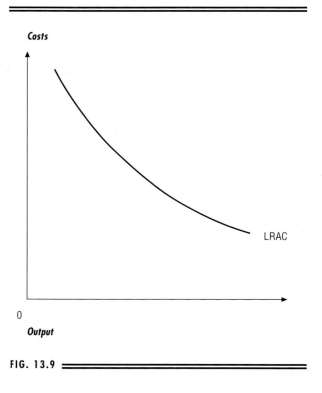

FIG. 13.9

In other industries empirical evidence seems to indicate that the average cost falls as the scale of production increases but then levels out. Constant returns to scale may apply over very large ranges of output. In this case the curve will be L-shaped as shown in Figure 13.10.

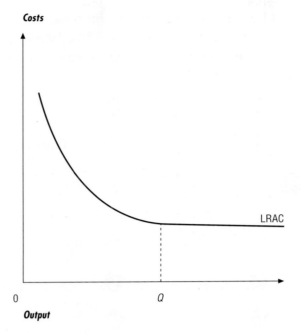

FIG. 13.10

In this figure, *Q* represents the minimum efficient scale. This is the lowest level of output at which a firm can produce and, by gaining all available economies of scale, minimise average cost.

LONG-RUN MARGINAL COST

The conventional long-run marginal cost curve is U-shaped as is the short-run marginal cost curve.

This time, however, it will fall because of economies of scale and rise due to diseconomies of scale. The long-run marginal cost curve cuts the long-run average cost curve at its lowest point as shown in Figure 13.11.

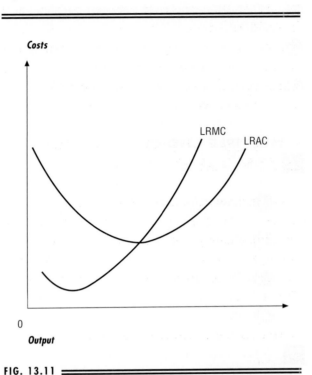

FIG. 13.11

The long-run marginal cost curve initially pushes down the long-run average cost curve as output increases and then pulls up the long-run average cost curve.

QUESTIONS

SHORT QUESTIONS

1. Distinguish, with examples, between a firm's fixed and variable costs.
2. What is the difference between the short run and long run?
3. Explain why a long-run average cost curve may be U-shaped.
4. Explain what is meant by the minimum efficient scale.

MULTIPLE CHOICE

1. Which is a fixed cost?

   (A) Raw materials.

   (B) Rent.

   (C) Transport.

   (D) Wages.

2. A firm initially produces 20 conservatories at an average total cost of £8000 each. It then increases production to 21 conservatories. The production of the additional conservatory reduces the average total cost to £7900. What is the marginal cost of this additional conservatory?

   (A) £100

   (B) £376.19

   (C) £5900

   (D) £7900

3. This table shows the total cost of different levels of a firm's output.

Output (units)	Total cost (£)
0	15 000
10	20 000
20	23 000
30	24 000
40	27 000
50	35 000

   The firm's average variable cost curve is U-shaped. Within which one of the following ranges of output will average variable cost be minimised?

   (A) 10–20 units   (B) 20–30 units

   (C) 30–40 units   (D) 40–50 units

4. Figure 13.12 shows a firm's short-run total cost curve.

   At output Q average variable cost is:

   (A) XQ (B) YZ

   (C) $\dfrac{XZ}{Q}$ (D) $\dfrac{XQ}{Q}$

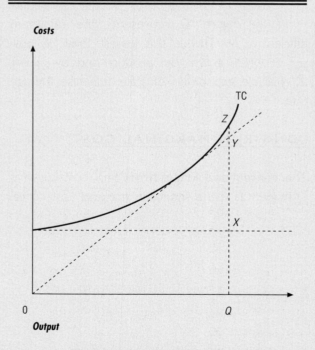

FIG. 13.12

DATA RESPONSE

Output	Total cost
0	10
1	18
2	24
3	27
4	32
5	40

a] Calculate fixed cost and explain what is meant by fixed cost. **(5)**

b] Calculate average fixed cost at four units of output and explain what must happen to average fixed cost as output increases. **(5)**

c] Explain what is meant by marginal cost and calculate the marginal cost of the third unit. **(5)**

d] Explain why marginal cost must equal marginal variable cost. **(5)**

e] Discuss the shape of this firm's average variable cost curve and its total cost curve. **(5)**

CASE STUDY

In 1999 Japan's largest tyre maker, Bridgestone, decided to manufacture tyres for trucks and buses in China through a joint venture with a local company, Shengang Santai Tyre, based in Liaoning Province, north east of Beijing. This made it the second Japanese tyre maker to set up in China. Four years before Toyo Tyre and Rubber had started a joint venture with a local group. Joint ventures have also been set up in China by Michelin and Goodyear.

The plant which Bridgestone took a stake in, produced 140 000 tyres in 1998. Bridgestone's aim was to raise its production to the plant's full capacity of 200 000 tyres by the end of 1999. Although it was planned to limit production initially to truck and bus tyres it was hoped to expand this later to passenger cars.

The main motive behind the move was to gain access to China's large and growing market.

a] Explain what is meant by:
   i   joint venture **(3)**
   ii fixed capacity. **(3)**

b] What are the fixed costs of tyre production? **(5)**

c] Give examples of costs which would increase when the company expanded its production. **(5)**

d] What effect would diversification into passenger car tyres be likely to have on the firm's average costs? **(8)**

e] Explain what shape you think the firm's long-run average cost curve would be. **(8)**

f] Discuss the potential benefits of producing tyres in China. **(12)**

g] Discuss the likely nature and degree of cross elasticity of demand between tyres produced by the different tyre companies. **(6)**

STRUCTURED ESSAY

a] Explain what is meant by total, average and marginal cost and the relationship between them. **(15)**

b] Discuss the effect that a rise in output may have on total, average and marginal cost. **(10)**

PART THREE: FACTOR MARKETS

14 PROFIT

Profit is usually defined as a reward for bearing uncertain risks. There are many risks involved in running a business. Some of these, such as the risk of loss due to flood, fire or burglary, or injuries to employees, are insurable because the laws of probability can be applied to such events and insurance companies can calculate the degree of risk involved. But no statistician can calculate the numerical probability that a firm, or group of firms, will make profits or losses in the future. Economic conditions are changing all the time and the success or failure of a particular enterprise in the past is not a good guide as to the likely success or failure of a similar enterprise in the future. So profits are the reward for taking non-insurable risks.

PURE PROFIT

It is very difficult to isolate the return described as profit from the other factor incomes — wages, interest and rent. This may be especially true in the case of businesses owned by one person.

For example, a person owning and working in his or her own business may declare a £60 000 profit during the year. This figure is gross profit and is obtained by deducting costs from revenue. To obtain pure profit the owner should deduct as costs an implicit figure for wages. This could be based on how much he or she could have earned as an employee in a similar concern, i.e. the opportunity cost of working in the business. An amount should also be deducted for implicit interest and rent for the financial capital and any premises the owner has put into the business. These could be calculated by examining the interest forgone on savings and rent which could have been earned by letting out the premises.

DISTINGUISHING BETWEEN PROFIT AND INTEREST

A major problem is to distinguish between interest and profit because these terms are sometimes used as though they are synonymous. Both are payments to the providers of capital. If the funds for investment are supplied by creditors of the company in the form of loans, the returns to capital are described as interest. When the money is provided by shareholders, who by purchasing shares become owners of the business, the returns to capital are described as *profit*. Again, the opportunity cost principle should be applied to shareholders' profits. Shareholders have forgone the interest their funds might have earned if they had been used to buy, e.g., government bonds. A deduction equal to this implicit interest should be made from their dividends in order to arrive at the company's true profit. However, in practice it is very difficult to identify pure profit.

FEATURES OF PROFIT

Profit differs from the other factor payments in three main ways.

- *It may be negative.* A firm may make losses, a negative figure, whereas wages, interest and rent are unlikely to be negative items.
- *It is more volatile.* Rent, interest and wages tend to change only relatively steadily, and usually increase. In contrast, profits can fluctuate by large amounts and may move from positive to negative and back again in a short time.

- *It is residual*. Profit is what remains of revenue after all other costs have been met. Whereas wages, interest and rent are usually fixed in advance of the performance of the services for which they are payments, the amount of profit which will be earned by a company cannot be known for certainty in advance.

FUNCTIONS OF PROFIT

Profit fulfils a number of functions in a market economy and in the market sector of a mixed economy. These are as follows.

- It provides a reward for bearing the uncertainty associated with running a business.
- It stimulates innovation. The introduction of a new product, a new method of production or an attempt to enter a new market carry a high risk; profit provides an incentive for entrepreneurs to take these risks.
- It creates a source of funds for investment and expansion. Retained profits provide an important source of investment finance.
- It indicates the need for expansion (supernormal profits) and the need for contraction (losses). Indeed, profit plays an important part in the allocation of resources. If a product becomes more popular, the firms producing it will earn more profits. These higher profits will provide the firms with the incentive and finance to expand. They may also encourage other firms to try to enter the industry to increase supply.

PROFILE

NAME: James Dyson
Inventor and entrepreneur

BORN: 1949

NATIONALITY: British

EDUCATED: Industrial design student at the Royal College of Art

EMPLOYMENT: Worked at the inventor Jeremy Fry's engineering firm, Rotork

INVENTIONS INCLUDE: Amphibious sea truck — a multi-terrain vehicle
Ballbarrow
Dyson bagless, dual cyclone vacuum cyclone
Superfast washing machine

COMPANIES: Dyson Appliances (manufactures products)
Dyson Research (develops and licences products)

QUOTES ON DYSON:
'James is like one of the Great Victorian ironmasters. He is a one-man attempt to revive British manufacturing industry through design.' (Professor Christopher Frayling, rector of the Royal College of Art)

QUOTES FROM DYSON:
'It would give me a thrill to know that when I'm dead people will talk of giving the room a Dyson.'

TYPES OF PROFIT

There are three main types of profit, although a fourth can be identified.

SUPERNORMAL PROFIT

This can also be referred to as *abnormal* profit. It is earned where average revenue (price) exceeds average cost. As mentioned above, this will encourage other firms to seek to enter the industry. This will be possible when there are no obstacles to new firms starting to produce the product. However, when there are barriers to entry and exit to an industry, e.g. patents and economies of scale, existing firms may be able to protect their supernormal profits in the long run.

NORMAL PROFIT

Normal profit is included in average cost. It is earned where average revenue equals average cost. It is also called the *supply price of entrepreneurship* or the *opportunity cost of capital* as it is the minimum which the entrepreneur or entrepreneurs have to receive to provide their services and for their firms to stay in the industry in the long run.

The amount of normal profits will vary from industry to industry according to the degree of risk involved. For example, the minimum expected rate of profit required to persuade a firm to carry on prospecting for oil will be much greater than that needed to keep a firm in the brewing industry.

LOSS

This is negative profit and is experienced where average cost exceeds average revenue. Those firms which cannot cover their variable costs and/or which do not believe their position will improve in the future will leave the industry and seek positive profit levels elsewhere or go out of business.

SUBNORMAL PROFIT

This occurs where a firm is covering all its other costs and is making some profit but not at a level sufficient to keep the firm in the industry in the long run. In other words, normal profit is not achieved. A firm with a significant market share may deliberately lower its profit below the normal profit level in the short run in order to drive some of its rivals out of business — predatory pricing.

QUESTIONS

SHORT QUESTIONS

1. Explain the meaning of pure profit.

2. How does profit differ from the other three rewards to factors of production?

3. How does a rise in profits encourage an increase in output?

4. Name two industries which are likely to have high normal profits.

MULTIPLE CHOICE

1. Normal profit is earned by a firm when:

   A. marginal cost is equal to marginal revenue

   B. marginal cost is equal to average cost

   C. marginal cost is equal to average revenue

   D. average cost is equal to average revenue.

2. What is the share of profits which shareholders receive called?

   A. Dividends.
   B. Interest.
   C. Capital gain.
   D. Retained profit.

3. Supernormal profit is defined as:

   A. profit above the average level earned over a number of years

   B. the level of profit achieved where marginal revenue equals marginal cost

   C. the level of profit above that needed to keep a firm in the industry in the long run

   D. the level of profit above variable costs in the short run.

4. Which statement about profit is correct?

   A. It is always a positive figure.

   B. It encourages innovation.

   C. It is a reward for bearing insurable risks.

   D. It is not essential to the working of the price system.

DATA RESPONSE

Vijay Patel is the sort of businessman Tony Blair says he wants to encourage. Starting from a single chemist's shop, Mr Patel's Waymade HealthCare now employs 350 people and turns over more than £130m.

This is the kind of entrepreneurial spirit the prime minister is keen to foster in a country where many people prefer the safer working life of being an employee to the risks and rewards of starting their own business.

But Mr Patel is an example of the problems that face UK entrepreneurs. No bank manager would lend him a penny when he started out, and he feels even now that what he has achieved is far from widely appreciated.

Mr Blair is keen to encourage the efforts of people like Mr Patel because there is abundant evidence of the importance of entrepreneurs to the economy. Not only can such individuals become rich but they can provide employment.

Fast growing firms — known as 'gazelles' — matter most of all because they create the most jobs. Several studies have found they account for 80% of job growth in both the US and Britain.

The lack of an innate entrepreneurial spirit in the British is an age-old concern. But it has become more pressing as the established companies in manufacturing and other traditional industries provide fewer and fewer jobs. Paul Reynolds, professor of entrepreneurial studies at Babson College in Boston, says the key point seems to be that three times as many people in the US are actively engaged at any time in trying to start a business.

Studies show that this willingness to take risks is also apparent in Israel and Canada. All three countries says Mr Reynolds, are immigrant societies where government is seen as a facilitator of people's desires to run their own lives.

Kumar Bhattacharyya, professor of management systems at Warwick University, points out that a disproportionate number of entrepreneurs are Asian immigrants, some of whom have built huge fortunes in a couple of decades.

Source: 'From cowboy to hero' by Kevin Brown, Financial Times, 21/5/99.

a] Explain the meaning of:
   i   entrepreneurial spirit **(3)**
   ii gazelle companies. **(2)**

b] Why was the Prime Minister, Tony Blair, keen to encourage entrepreneurs? **(3)**

c] How are the average costs of new companies likely to compare with those of more established ones? **(6)**

d] Why may countries with significant immigrant populations have more 'entrepreneurial spirit'? **(4)**

e] Discuss the risks and rewards of running a business. **(7)**

CASE STUDY

In July 1999 J. Sainsbury, the UK's second largest supermarket retailer, announced disappointing sales figures. In the first quarter its sales fell and it was expected that sales would not rise by the end of the first half. The announcement caused the company's share prices to fall.

Dino Adriano, Sainsbury's Chief Executive, blamed the poor performance of its core supermarket business on a poor advertising campaign and on the disruption caused by the reorganisation of its supermarkets.

Not all its parts performed badly. Sales at the Homebase DIY division and Shaw's US food chain experienced an increase in sales.

To reverse the decline in sales Dino Adriano announced plans to open 200 convenience stores in the next three years, and a little later a further 800, selling about 2000 products including fresh ready meals, salads and sandwiches. These are to be called Sainsbury's Local and will be located in suburbs, small towns and railway stations and will be opened from 6am to midnight seven days a week. With the exception of 40 high demand lines, goods will cost more than in a regular supermarket but mark up will not be more than 10p.

The company also plans to revise its product range in its existing supermarkets, a new advertising campaign and an increase in product development and marketing strategy of Sainsbury Banking, focusing on personal loans.

a] What caused the difficulties experienced by the Sainsbury chain at the start of 1999? **(6)**

b] Explain what is likely to have happened to Sainsbury's profits in this period. **(4)**

c] What effect would the difficulties have had on Sainsbury's ability to raise finance? **(5)**

d] What effect would a successful advertising campaign have on the level and elasticity of demand for Sainsbury's products? **(7)**

e] Discuss how the average and total costs of the Sainsbury's Local Shops will be likely to compare with those of the Sainsbury's supermarkets. **(8)**

f] What are the implications of different costs for the prices to be charged in the different types of outlets? **(5)**

g] As the Sainsbury company wanted to expand Sainsbury Bank what does this suggest about the level of profit being experienced by the UK banking industry? Explain your answer. **(6)**

h] Discuss why one supermarket chain might perform well in one country whilst another supermarket chain, owned by the same company might perform less well in another country. **(9)**

STRUCTURED ESSAY

a] Explain the meaning of normal and supernormal profit. **(10)**

b] Discuss the role of profit in bringing about a re-allocation of resources in a market economy. **(15)**

15 ECONOMIC RENT

THE DISTINCTION BETWEEN RENT AND ECONOMIC RENT

Everyone is familiar with the procedure of renting. Land, houses, machines, offices, cars, television sets, videos: almost any durable good can be rented. Rent simply means the payment which is made for the use of a particular asset. It is a contractual payment fixed in terms of money arranged on a periodic, and, in business, on an annual, basis.

Economic rent has a more specific meaning and can be applied to all factors of production. It is a payment above the minimum necessary to keep the relevant factor in its present usage. This minimum amount may be called the *supply price* or more commonly *transfer earnings*.

ECONOMIC RENT AND TRANSFER EARNINGS

As noted above, the transfer earnings of a factor of production is the minimum payment required to keep the factor in its present occupation. This also means that it is the minimum payment needed to prevent the factor transferring to another employer or another occupation. It is determined by what that factor could earn in its next best paid employment. So transfer earnings may be regarded as the opportunity cost of keeping a factor of production in its present use. For example, suppose the minimum weekly wage which would persuade someone to work as a lorry driver is £400, but he actually receives a wage (as a lorry driver) of £450 per week. His transfer earnings amount to £400 per week and he is receiving £50 per week in the form of economic rent.

So economic rent may be defined as any payment made to a factor of production which is in excess of its transfer earnings.

HOW ECONOMIC RENT IS CREATED

Economic rent arises when demand increases and the supply cannot fully respond to the increased demand. Factors of production already employed will experience an increase in income. This means that they will earn more than their supply price (transfer earnings).

Figure 15.1 shows the demand and supply curves for a factor of production.

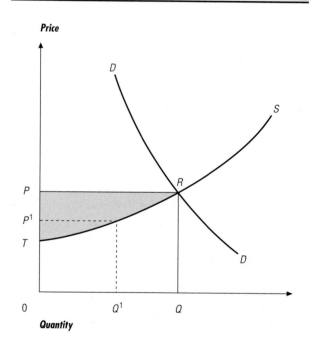

FIG. 15.1

The equilibrium price is P and Q units of the factor are employed. Total earnings are equal to the area OPRQ, and all the units of the factor receive the same reward, P. It will be the wage rate if the factor is labour. But all units of this factor, except the last one taken into employment, were prepared to offer their services at prices less than P. For example Q^1 units would be available to firms at a price of P^1.

The shaded area PRT, which lies above the supply curve and below the payment line, is the economic element in the total earnings. The area OTRQ represents the total transfer earnings. Only the last unit of the factor to be employed earns no economic rent, because the price P is the supply price of this particular unit.

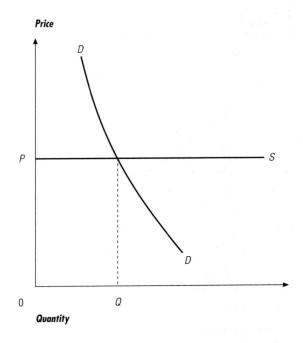

FIG. 15.2

ECONOMIC RENT AND ELASTICITY OF SUPPLY

The proportion of earnings which is economic rent is determined principally by the elasticity of supply. The more inelastic supply is the greater the proportion of earnings will be economic rent. And the more elastic supply is the smaller the proportion of the earnings will be economic rent.

Figure 15.2 shows a situation where the supply of the factor is perfectly elastic. This might be the case where there is perfect competition in the factor market. A firm could obtain any amount of the factor at the ruling price P. At prices less than P there will be no supplies available to the firm. The whole of the factor earnings represent transfer earnings, and, in this case, an increase in demand will not give rise to any economic rent. The price P is the minimum payment which will prevent the factor leaving the firm.

ECONOMIC RENT AND LABOUR

The amount of economic rent in the return to labour obviously depends upon the elasticity of supply and the level of demand. The greater the occupational mobility of labour, the smaller will be the element of economic rent. If labour is very mobile, quite small changes in the wage rate will cause large movements of labour, into the industry when wages rise, and out of the industry when wages fall.

Highly specialised labour is in very inelastic supply. This is true of specialists such as surgeons and highly qualified architects and those with other special skills such as international football players. Figure 15.3 shows that when supply is inelastic, a high proportion of earnings consists of economic rent.

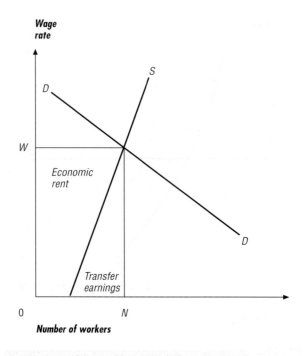

FIG. 15.3

A most frequently quoted example of earnings which contain a large proportion of economic rent are those of top entertainers, and particularly those of pop stars. Each one has, it seems, some unique characteristic and the supply of his or her particular talent is perfectly inelastic. The earnings of pop stars can reach amazing figures in a very short time period. Transfer earnings make up only a small percentage of their incomes. This is because many of them would earn considerably less in their next best paid jobs.

ECONOMIC RENT AND CAPITAL

Much of the nation's capital consists of very specialised equipment. It is designed for a particular purpose and cannot be transferred to another use. Once the equipment (e.g. a blast furnace) has been installed it could be argued that any income greater than the variable costs is economic rent. No matter how low this net revenue falls, the equipment cannot be transferred to another use and any net return (i.e. any return greater than operating costs) is better

than no return at all. It will only be beneficial to leave the equipment idle when the revenue falls below the running costs. This view is correct if a short run view is taken. Looking at the situation over the life of the existing equipment its transfer earnings are the current operating costs — if it does not cover these expenses it will leave the industry (i.e. go out of use). But if a longer view is taken, there will come a time when the capital equipment will be worn out. It will not be replaced if its earnings have not been sufficient to cover both the variable costs and the fixed costs it has accumulated such as depreciation. If it does not earn this minimum return the supply of capital to this particular use will cease. So over the longer period the transfer earnings of capital will be total costs.

ECONOMIC RENT AND LAND

In the case of land which has only one use (i.e. it is completely specific) the whole of its income is economic rent, as shown in Figure 15.4.

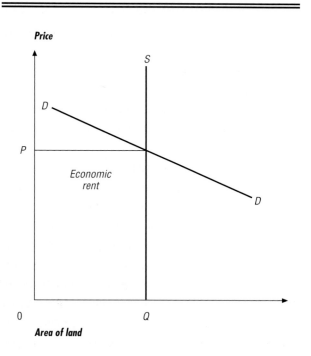

FIG. 15.4

The land cannot transfer to another use and it will remain in that use indefinitely even when its earnings are zero. Most land, however, has alternative uses and whenever this is the case a particular piece of land will be earning economic rent only to the extent that its income in its present use exceeds what it could earn in its next most remunerative use.

Suppose some land is being used for growing wheat and farmers are paying a rent of £300 per acre for it. Its next most profitable use would be for growing barley, but farmers are only prepared to pay £260 per acre for barley land. Payments for the land in its present use therefore contain an element of economic rent equal to £40 per acre. Any price greater than £260 per acre would lead to land being transferred from barley to wheat. So why do farmers pay as much as £300 per acre to grow wheat? The explanation lies in the strength of demand relative to supply. If wheat is a very profitable crop, farmers will bid against each other for suitable and available land and this could lead to prices rising well above the land's transfer earnings.

The land values which attract considerable attention are those in city centres. The number of sites available in city centres is strictly limited. No matter what price is paid, there is no way of increasing the land available for building offices, shops, restaurants and cinemas etc. The high price paid for such sites is explained by the inelasticity of supply and a rapidly increasing demand.

Since these sites have many alternative uses the economic rent element in the price paid for any one use may be quite small, although the price itself may be very high. Figure 15.5 illustrates the situation. D^1, D^2 and D^3 represent different demands for a particular site where D^1 is the demand from companies building cinemas, D^2 is the demand from supermarket developers and D^3 the demand from developers of office blocks. The highest bids come from people wishing to build office blocks and the market price is P^3. Of the total revenue only the shaded area represents economic rent.

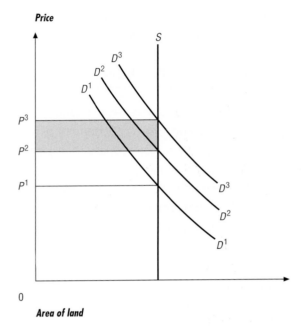

FIG. 15.5

TAXING ECONOMIC RENT

Some economists argue that economic rent should be taxed as a surplus. Two main reasons are put forward. One is that such a tax, provided it does not take all the surplus, is unlikely to alter the allocation of resources. For example, if a commodities dealer is earning £3000 a week and could earn only £400 a week as an advertising agent in her next best paid job, taking, for example, 40% of her economic rent in tax is unlikely to make her change her job.

Another argument is that at least part of the economic rent may have arisen as a result of government expenditure. Workers and entrepreneurs who receive high salaries may have benefited from state education (including university education). Capital equipment may have been developed in part by government expenditure on research and development. Part of the economic rent earned by land may have arisen from government expenditure on infrastructure.

However, in practice it is difficult to identify and measure economic rent. This is because it may be difficult, or impossible, to estimate what a factor could earn in its next best paid employment.

QUASI ECONOMIC RENT

Quasi economic rent is short-run economic rent which in the long run turns into transfer earnings. Where the supply of a factor is less than perfectly elastic an increase in demand will lead to some units of the factor receiving economic rent. This economic rent may be of a temporary nature, however, because the higher price may lead to an increase in supply which will, in turn, lower the price. For example, increased earnings in an occupation may persuade more people to undertake the necessary training and thereby increase supply.

Also, as noted above, the earnings above variable costs of machinery with a specific use can be regarded as economic rent in the short run, i.e. as quasi economic rent. As supernormal profits experienced by perfectly competitive and monopolistically competitive firms will be competed away in the long run they are another example of quasi economic rent.

QUESTIONS

SHORT QUESTIONS

1. Discuss what could cause an increase in the economic rent earned by bakers.

2. Explain whether it is possible for economic rent to be negative.

3. In what circumstances will all of a factor of production's earnings consist of transfer earnings?

4. Both premier league football players and barristers receive high salaries. Explain which group's pay is likely to consist of the higher proportion of economic rent.

MULTIPLE CHOICE

1. The supply of a factor of production is completely inelastic. Its earnings will consist:

   A entirely of economic rent

   B mostly of transfer earnings

   C equally of economic rent and transfer earnings

   D entirely of transfer earnings.

2. Which of the following is a definition of transfer earnings?

   A Payments made to workers during periods of training.

   B Payments made to the unemployed and pensioners by the state.

   C That part of the earnings of a factor of production which consist of economic rent.

   D The minimum payment necessary to keep a factor of production in its current employment.

3. Figure 15.6 shows the market for a factor of production.

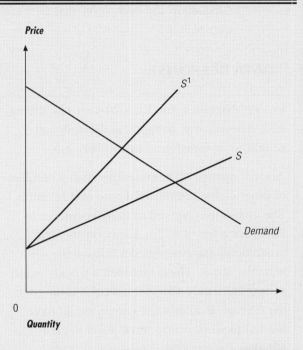

FIG. 15.6

What is the effect on the proportion of economic rent and transfer earnings earned of a change in the supply curve from S to S^1?

	Economic rent	Transfer earnings
A	rises	rise
B	rises	fall
C	falls	rise
D	falls	fall

4 What is meant by quasi economic rent?

A Rent on property which is held below the equilibrium level by means of government controls.

B The payment which a factor of production can earn in its next best paid occupation.

C The 'rent of ability' earned by any factor of production in the long run.

D A surplus in the short run which becomes a transfer earning in the long run.

DATA RESPONSE

In 1999 Nicholas Anelka, a 20-year-old striker with Arsenal, was unhappy at the club and sought to be transferred to another club.

Arsenal opened up negotiations with a number of other clubs, principally Lazio and Juventus. The club finally agreed to transfer Anelka to Lazio for a fee of £22m. However the deal broke down because Anelka refused the personal terms. These included a weekly salary of approximately £56 000 a week. At the time the average British wage earner would have needed to work nearly three years to earn £56 000.

Many of the top players in the Premier league were earning £20 000 or more a week although pay for players in lower divisions was considerably lower. Pay rates in most other sports in the UK, even for top names, was also lower.

However top golfers, formula one racing drivers and top boxers were earning even higher salaries. For example in 1999 Damian Hill, the formula one racing driver, earned £5m from his driving contract.

As well as their earnings from their sporting activities, top sportsmen and women, earned large, and in some cases larger, sums from, e.g., appearing in advertisements, product endorsements and personal appearances.

a] For what economic reason may Nicholas Anelka have turned down the deal to Lazio? **(2)**

b] What is the economic argument for paying talented and popular football players high wages? **(5)**

c] A top footballer loses some of his skill or fitness and is transferred to a lower division club. Explain what is likely to happen to:
  i   his wage rate **(1)**
  ii the proportion of his wage rate accounted for by economic rent **(3)**
  iii the proportion of his wage rate accounted for by transfer earnings. **(3)**

d] If the number of people capable and willing to play golf at the top level increased, explain what would happen to:
  i   the wage rate of top golfers **(1)**
  ii the proportion of their wage rate accounted for by economic rent **(3)**
  iii the proportion of their wage rate accounted for by transfer earnings. **(3)**

e] Why are companies prepared to pay top sports people large sums to endorse their products? **(4)**

CASE STUDY

Top directors in Britain's biggest companies gave themselves pay rises of more than 26% last year — five times the growth in average earnings and 10 times the rate of inflation, according to a special *Guardian* survey published today.

And it is not only the highest paid director in each company who is benefiting from the good times. The study reveals that the average increase for all executive members of the boardroom was 22% last year.

There were more than 30 executives whose basic pay and bonus topped £1m. The average remuneration picked up by Britain's best paid executives was £960 000. An average employee in one of their companies would have to work for nearly 50 years to earn the same.

The increases, which dramatically outstripped the improvement in company profits, came even though senior industrialists knew the government had boardroom pay in its sights and despite calls for restraint from the Chancellor, Gordon Brown.

Stephen Byers, the trade and industry secretary, will today set out the government's determination that large pay awards for directors must reflect similar improvements in corporate performance.

But the *Guardian Index of Top Executive Pay*, compiled in association with remuneration consultants Inbucon, shows that the UK's top companies last year managed to increase their average trading profits by just 6.9%. This follows years in which directors' earnings have dramatically outstripped the growth in their companies performance. Of the 13 companies which gave their boards rises of more than 30% last year, only six recorded an increase in trading profit.

The fourth best paid executive, Robert Mendelsohn, the boss of insurer Royal and Sun Alliance, hit the headlines this year when he e-mailed his workforce to defend his 67% increase in salary to £2.4m. As thousands of his staff faced loss of their jobs, he told them that redundancies were now just a fact of life.

The US-born Mr Mendelsohn is one of an influx of top executives recruited by UK firms. The huge salaries which now characterise British boardrooms underline the extent to which these executives are importing the pay packages they are used to.

THE HIGHEST PAID DIRECTORS				
RANKING	COMPANY	NAME	TITLE	TOTAL REMUNERATION £m
1	Royal Bank of Scotland	Larry Fish	Director	3.30
2	Amvescorp	Charles Brady	Chairman	2.77
3	Royal and Sun Alliance	Bob Mendelsohn	Chief Executive	2.37
4	EMI	Ken Berry	Chief Executive	2.06
5	EMI	Martin Bandier	Director	2.05
6	SmithKline Beecham	Jan Leschly	Chief Executive	1.92
7	Glaxo Wellcome	Sir Richard Sykes	Chairman	1.86
8	Cadbury Schweppes	John Brock	Director	1.65

Source: 'Top pay rises by 26%' by Lisa Buckingham and Julia Finch, the Guardian, 19/7/99.

a] How did the pay rise which top directors received in 1998 compare with:
 i   the rate of inflation **(1)**
 ii   average earnings **(1)**
 iii all executive boardroom members? **(1)**

b] What would be the likely proportion of economic rent in the earnings received by a director whose previous job was:
 i   a director in another company **(5)**
 ii   an average employee in the same company? **(5)**

c] What are the functions of profits? **(4)**

d] Why would an increase in profits be expected to lead to a rise in the pay of top executives? **(8)**

e] Using the remuneration data given and assuming that Bob Mendelsohn's next best paid job was as Chief Executive of SmithKline Beecham estimate:
 i   his economic rent **(2)**
 ii   his transfer earnings. **(2)**

f] Discuss whether top directors should be paid high salaries. **(14)**

g] Evaluate the arguments for taxing economic rent. **(15)**

STRUCTURED ESSAY

a] Distinguish between economic rent and transfer earnings. **(10)**

b] Why are shop assistants likely to earn less economic rent than North Sea divers? **(15)**

16 INTEREST

Interest rates can be influenced by demand and supply and government intervention. In a free market it is the forces of demand and supply which set interest rates. Changes in interest rates can have a wide ranging effect on the economy and so government bodies often influence the rate of interest.

DEFINITION

Interest can be regarded as the price which has to be paid for the services of capital. If firms borrow money to buy, e.g. machines, it is the direct cost of capital. If, as they more commonly do, they use their own funds, it is the opportunity cost. This is because if these funds were not used to purchase capital goods they could be placed in, e.g., a bank or building society where they could earn interest.

However as loans are demanded for more purposes than just the purchase of capital, the rate of interest can be described as the payment for the use of money. In order to create a supply of loans, people with the necessary financial resources have to be persuaded to lend them. In normal circumstances, loans can only be obtained when lenders are offered some reward for the sacrifices, risks, and trouble involved. This reward is the rate of interest and it contains several elements.

- A payment for the sacrifice of current spending power. The lender forgoes the opportunity to spend and consume now.
- A payment for the risks involved. The future is always uncertain and circumstances are always changing. All lenders run the risk that the borrower may default.
- A payment to compensate, if only partially, for any fall in the value of money. In recent years most countries have experienced some degree of inflation and lenders have come to expect some payment to make up for the loss in the purchasing power of the money loaned.

THEORIES OF INTEREST RATE DETERMINATION

There are two main theories which attempt to explain how the rate of interest is determined in terms of demand and supply. One is the *loanable funds theory* and the other is the *liquidity preference theory*.

THE LOANABLE FUNDS THEORY

This is the older theory. According to this theory the rate of interest is determined by the interaction of the demand for loanable funds and the supply of these funds as shown in Figure 16.1.

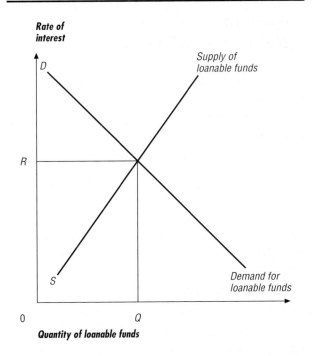

FIG. 16.1

THE DEMAND FOR LOANABLE FUNDS

In early versions of the theory, the demand for loanable funds was assumed to come entirely from firms seeking investment funds. Firms invest (i.e. buy capital goods) because they expect to earn profits. They anticipate that this newly created capital will yield a series of returns during its lifetime which will exceed the costs incurred in its purchase and maintenance. The firm undertaking investment will estimate the net additional profits to be derived from the increased output it hopes to achieve; these expected net annual receipts can then be expressed in the form of a percentage annual return on the initial outlay. This percentage yield is the productivity of capital. If additional investment in the chemical industry is expected to yield a return of 20% per annum, while an addition to the stock of capital in the footwear industry is expected to earn 15% per annum, capital will tend to flow to the chemical industry rather than the footwear industry.

OTHER SOURCES OF DEMAND FOR LOANABLE FUNDS

Present-day supporters of the loanable funds theory include more than the business sector when they consider the demand for loanable funds. Households also borrow. They borrow by means of a variety of credit arrangements and loans in order to purchase new houses and durable consumer goods. People also need to take out loans in order to buy assets (e.g. shares and securities). The government is also a large-scale borrower of loanable funds. Whilst the government's demand for loanable funds is not likely to be significantly affected by changes in the prevailing rate of interest, the demand from both households and firms will be expected to move in the opposite direction to changes in the rate of interest. This gives a downward sloping demand curve for loanable funds.

THE SUPPLY OF LOANABLE FUNDS

According to the loanable funds theory the main determinant of the supply of funds for loans is the current rate of saving. However to convert savings into loanable funds, savers have to be willing to lend their savings. To be prepared to forgo the use of their savings for a given time period, people will have to be compensated with interest. The payment of interest will enable them to enjoy a higher level of consumption in the future. The higher the rate of interest, the more they are likely to be willing to lend and so the supply curve of loanable funds slopes up from left to right.

THE LIQUIDITY PREFERENCE THEORY

The UK economist John Maynard Keynes stated that the rate of interest is determined not by the demand and supply of loanable funds but by the demand and supply of money. He defined the demand for money as the demand for money to hold. In everyday speech the expression 'a demand for money' is usually taken to mean a demand for money to spend; but this is not a demand for money as such, but a demand for the things money will buy. By contrast, the liquidity preference theory refers to the demand for money as a desire to hold wealth in the form of money.

LIQUIDITY

This preference for money over other kinds of assets is known as *liquidity preference*. Liquidity describes the readiness with which an asset can be converted into cash without any significant loss in value. Wealth held in the form of money provides people with the maximum freedom of action, because it is readily convertible into any other type of asset; money, by definition, has a constant money value. If people exchange money for, e.g., shares, the money value of their wealth becomes uncertain, but they do have an income-earning asset. Money has the disadvantage that it does not earn an income. The great advantages of holding money are that it is the most liquid of all assets and its money value is certain. However, during inflation its exchange value falls.

Money, therefore, is one way in which an individual may choose to hold his or her wealth, but it is only one of many ways. Wealth may be held in the form of land, buildings, works of art, jewellery, government securities (bonds), shares and so on. Households and firms hold wealth in all these forms and they adjust the proportions held in each form according to their means, desires, and the circumstances prevailing. It will be assumed that decisions to change the amount of money they hold will cause households and firms to hold more, or less, fixed-interest government securities (bonds). A decision to hold less money will give rise to an increased demand for bonds, and a desire to hold more money will lead to a greater willingness to sell bonds. There are three motives for holding money.

THE TRANSACTIONS MOTIVE

This is the desire to hold money in order to make purchases of goods and services. The amount of money held depends upon the level of income, the movements in prices and the frequency with which income payments are made. If income rises, people tend to buy more and better goods and services and so hold larger transactions balances. If prices rise, people hold more money in order to pay the higher prices. The frequency with which income is paid also has an important influence on the size of the average transaction balance. If a person receives a weekly wage of £320 and spends the whole of it evenly during the week, the average amount held over the week will be £160. If s/he is now paid at the same rate but receives her/his remuneration monthly (i.e. £1280 per month) and s/he maintains the same spending pattern, her/his average daily holding of money will be £640.

THE PRECAUTIONARY MOTIVE

In addition to the money balances needed to finance their regular day-to-day expenditures most people hold additional balances to deal with emergencies or to take advantage of some unexpected bargain. They may have to make an unplanned journey; unexpected visitors may involve people in unplanned spending on entertainment; something in a shop window or on the internet may catch their eye; or some domestic appliance may need repair.

The transactions and precautionary motives are equally applicable to firms. A firm will hold a 'working balance' to meet payments during periods when the flow of income is less than the flow of expenditures. It will also need money balances to meet unexpected deviations in the pattern of trade (e.g. an unexpected rise in costs).

Money held for transactions and precautionary motives is likely to be spent in the near future and so is referred to as demand for active balances. The amount held for these motives is not significantly influenced by the rate of interest — the motives are interest inelastic.

THE SPECULATIVE MOTIVE

Households and firms hold money in excess of the amounts needed for transactions and precautionary purposes when they are convinced that, for the time being, it is more rewarding to hold money than financial, or real, income-earning assets. One of these assets is a *government security (bond)*. This is a loan to the government which earns interest. The interest is guaranteed as the government will not go out of business. However there is a risk of making a capital loss. People will prefer to hold money rather than securities when they believe that the price of securities is about to fall.

EXAMPLE

An undated government security has a face value of £100 and carries a fixed rate of interest of $2\frac{1}{2}\%$. The holder of such a security will receive £2.50 per annum. Its current market price is £30. This means that purchasing 100 such securities will cost £300 and bring in an annual income of $100 \times £2.50 = £250$. This income represents a yield of $8\frac{1}{3}\%$ on the outlay of £3000.

Now suppose a prospective purchaser believes that over the coming year security prices will fall and decides to hold on to his/her money. In the event s/he is proved correct and at the end of the year the price of this particular security has dropped to £15. £3000 will now purchase 200 such securities giving an annual return of £500 (i.e. $16\frac{2}{3}\%$).

By waiting for one year the investor has sacrificed £250 in the form of income forgone, but he will enjoy a net gain of £250 per annum as long as s/he holds these securities.

When people expect the price of securities to fall, there will be a strong preference for holding money rather than securities. When security prices are expected to rise, there will be a much weaker liquidity preference; people will be anxious to buy securities before the expected price increase.

THE PRICES OF SECURITIES AND THE RATE OF INTEREST

When the prices of fixed interest securities change, the rate of interest changes. The market rate of interest is the current yield on undated government securities. Government securities are described as 'gilt-edged' because there is no risk of default. A simple example may make the relationship between security prices and the rate of interest clearer.

EXAMPLE

A   An undated 5% security, nominal value £100 (i.e. owner receives £5 per annum), stands at £80.

$$\text{Yield} = \frac{5}{80} \times 100 = 6\frac{1}{4}\% = \text{current rate of interest}$$

B   The price of the security now falls to £60

$$\text{Yield} = \frac{5}{60} \times 100 = 8\frac{1}{3}\% = \text{current rate of interest}$$

C   The price of the security rises to £120

$$\text{Yield} = \frac{5}{120} \times 100 = 4\frac{1}{6}\% = \text{current rate of interest}$$

Thus the rate of interest varies inversely as the market prices of fixed interest securities. If the market price of securities rises the rate of interest will fall and vice versa.

LIQUIDITY PREFERENCE AND THE RATE OF INTEREST

The demand for active balances (the transactions and precautionary motives) is, as noted earlier, interest inelastic as shown by curve *La* in Figure 16.2.

Whereas the demand for idle balances (the speculative motive) is interest elastic. This is shown by curve *Li* in Figure 16.2. At high rates of interest very little money is demanded for speculative purposes whereas at low rates of interest, large amounts of money are demanded. Note that the curve becomes horizontal at a positive rate of interest. This is because it is believed that some minimum reward (approximately 2%) is required to persuade people to forgo the advantages of holding money.

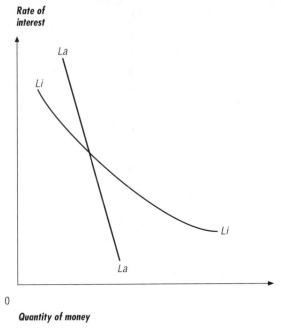

FIG. 16.2

The speculative demand for money is influenced by expected changes in the price of government securities. When security prices are expected to fall, speculators will be anxious to sell securities and hold money balances in order to avoid capital losses and also because they can increase their income by buying securities at a later date when security prices are lower. Expectations of falling prices will be very strong when security prices are high — the next movement is likely to be downwards. So when interest rates are low, liquidity preference will be high. There is the further point that the opportunity cost of holding money balances will be low when interest rates are low (the amount of interest forgone is relatively small).

When speculative prices are low (and interest rates are high), speculators will expect the next movement in prices to be upwards. They will want to buy securities now, before prices rise, either in anticipation of re-selling them at the expected higher price, or to secure the high yield which low-priced securities now offer (i.e. before rising prices reduce

this yield). Speculators will, therefore, be anxious to exchange their money balances for securities. Thus, when interest rates are high, liquidity preference will be relatively low.

If the demand for active balances (*La*) is added to the demand for speculative balances (*Li*) the total demand for money (*LL*) is obtained as is shown in Figure 16.3. This curve, the liquidity preference curve, shows how the quantity of money demanded varies as the rate of interest varies.

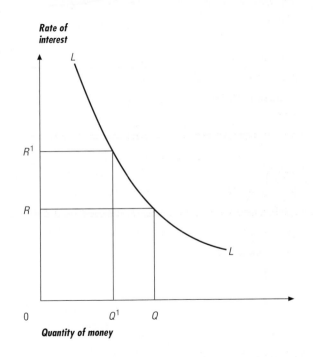

FIG. 16.3

THE RATE OF INTEREST DETERMINED

If the supply of money is determined by the monetary authorities (e.g. in the UK the Treasury and the Bank of England) it can be taken as fixed in the short run. It is identified as the vertical line *MM* in Figure 16.4. The rate of interest is now determined by the intersection of the demand curve for money (*LL*) and the supply curve (*MM*). It is equal to *R*.

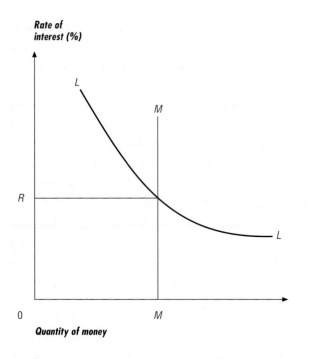

Rate of interest (%)

R

Quantity of money

FIG. 16.4

Figure 16.5 shows the effects of changes in the demand for money and the supply of money.

An increase in liquidity preference (i.e. a stronger desire or capacity to hold money) brought about by an increase in income, or an increase in prices, or a widely held conviction that prices in general are about to fall, will raise the liquidity preference curve from *LL* to *L¹L¹* as in Figure 16.5 (a). This causes the rate of interest to rise from *R* to *R¹*. What happens is that the increased preference for money balances leads to an increased desire to sell securities. The increased supply of securities in the market depresses their prices. As a result, the rate of interest rises. In contrast a fall in liquidity preference will lower the rate of interest as the demand for securities rises.

The effect of a change in the supply of money is illustrated in Figure 16.5 (b). When the supply of money increases from *MM* to *M¹M¹*, the increase in the supply of money must leave some groups holding excess money balances (assuming no change in liquidity preference). They will be holding a greater proportion of their wealth

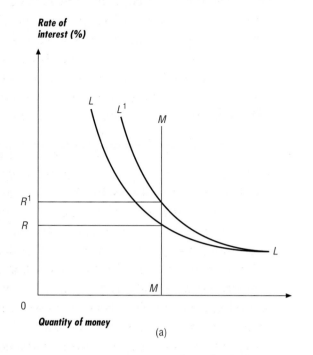

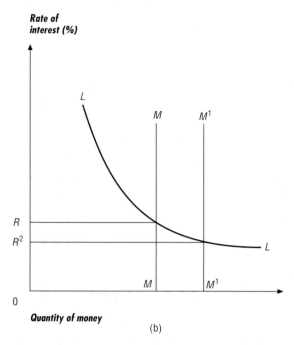

(a)

(b)

FIG. 16.5

in the form of money than they wish to hold at current rates of interest. In trying to adjust the distribution of their wealth among the different types of asset, these people will try to buy more bonds. The increased demand for bonds increases their price and therefore lowers the rate of interest. An increase in the supply of money when the *LL* curve is horizontal will have no effect on the rate of interest. This horizontal part of the *LL* curve is known as the liquidity trap as it is not possible to lower the rate of interest by increasing the money supply. This is because all the extra money will be held in idle balances, in the expectation that the price of bonds will fall in the near future.

A fall in the supply of money will leave the economy with less money than it wishes to hold at current interest rates. People will try to increase their money balances by selling securities. In doing so they will raise the rate of interest.

THE STRUCTURE OF INTEREST RATES

So far the rate of interest referred to has been the rate earned on government securities. However there is a wide variety of interest rates operating in most economies. For example the National Savings Bank may pay 6% on deposits, building societies may pay 7% on time deposits and banks may charge 8% on mortgages. Whilst one individual rate may change relative to another, interest rates tend to move in the same direction.

There are a number of reasons why there are so many different rates of interest existing at the same time including the following.

- *The duration of the loan.* The longer the period for which the money is borrowed, the greater the risk of default by the borrower. The future is uncertain and the longer the period of the loan, the greater is the uncertainty. Short-term loans, therefore, will normally carry lower rates of interest than long-term loans. Lenders will accept lower prices because they feel more capable of estimating the course of events over the next few weeks than over the next few years, and, of course, they are postponing their ability to consume for a much shorter period.

- *The credit-worthiness of the borrower.* Lending is a risky business and the degree of risk varies according to the evidence of the borrower's ability to repay. The risk of default by the government is negligible. Borrowers with a credit standing almost as high as governments are the great industrial and commercial companies, often referred to as blue chip companies. Lenders will demand relatively low rates of interest from borrowers such as these. Individuals and firms with low credit ratings (probably because they are unknown quantities) will be charged much higher rates of interest.

- *The purpose of the loan.* Firms and individuals who are borrowing money for purposes which will generate future income, or create a rise in the value of an asset, e.g. for the building of an extra garage, are likely to be charged a lower rate of interest than those borrowing for reasons which will not generate higher income or rise in the value of assets, e.g. for a holiday.

- *The marketability of the IOU.* Most government securities are marketable and may be bought and sold on the stock exchange. Where the ownership of the claim can be transferred very easily, the lender has a liquid asset. S/he can, if s/he wishes, 'change his/her mind' about lending his/her money and recover his/her money. If s/he does decide to sell his security s/he cannot be sure of recovering the full amount of his/her loan, because the market prices of securities are always changing; s/he may get more than s/he loaned, s/he may get less. Where the acknowledgement of the loan is in the form of a marketable security, the loan will attract lower rates of interest, because the loan is a liquid asset.

FIXED AND VARIABLE INTEREST RATES

Traditionally, households and firms in the UK have borrowed at variable interest rates. This means that the rate of interest they are charged can alter as interest rates change. For example, when a person takes out a mortgage on a house s/he may initially be charged 8% interest. However if interest rates rise their mortgage interest rate may be increased to, e.g., 10%.

Recently, more UK households and firms have been taking out loans on fixed interest rate terms. The interest rate charged on fixed interest rate loans does not change when general interest rates change. Fixed interest rate loans are popular in a number of countries, e.g. France and Germany.

Households and firms who take out loans on fixed interest rates will benefit if the rate of interest rises. However, if they take out a loan on a fixed interest of, e.g., 6% and the rate of interest falls to 3% they will lose out.

EFFECTS OF INTEREST RATE CHANGES

Interest rate changes may have a number of effects. A rise in the rate of interest may:

- *increase savings.* A rise in interest rates increases people's incentive to save. However, target savers, those saving to reach a particular sum to buy a car for example, may save less.
- *discourage spending.* A higher rate of interest will, by making saving more attractive, reduce spending (people can either spend or save their income). It will also mean that those people who have borrowed, perhaps to buy a house, on variable interest rate terms will have less money to spend. Net savers will have more money but they tend to spend a smaller proportion of their income than net borrowers so the overall effect is likely to be a reduction in spending.
- *discourage borrowing.* Higher interest rates will make borrowing more expensive. So demand for mortgages and loans to purchase, e.g., cars and consumer durables is likely to fall.
- *reduce investment.* Firms are likely to reduce their expenditure on capital goods as the cost of borrowing rises, as the opportunity cost of using their own funds increases and as they will expect demand for their products to fall.
- *raise firms' costs.* Firms which have borrowed before on variable interest rate terms and those which have to borrow in the future will be faced with higher costs.
- *raise the exchange rate.* A rise in the rate of interest may raise the country's exchange rate which will cause its export prices to rise and its import prices to fall (this is explained in Chapter 51).

GOVERNMENT INTERVENTION

In the UK in May 1997 the Government passed responsibility for interest rate changes to the Bank of England. It set the Bank of England the targets of achieving price stability and, subject to that, supporting its policy objectives including employment and growth. The Government has defined price stability as an inflation target of 2.5% with a 1% point margin either side.

If the Bank of England believes that prices will rise by more than 3.5% it is likely to raise its rate of interest, which is likely to be followed by rises in other interest rates, to discourage spending and encourage saving.

To decide on the approximate rate of interest the Bank of England set up the Monetary Policy Committee. This is made up of Bank of England representatives and Government appointments. In

August 1999 the nine members were:

Eddie George	The Governor of the Bank of England
Mervyn King	Deputy Governor of the Bank of England
David Clementi	Deputy Governor of the Bank of England
Ian Plenderleith	Bank of England Officer
John Vickers	Bank of England Officer
Willem Buiter	Cambridge University
Charles Goodhart	London School of Economics
DeAnne Julius	Formerly Chief Economist at British Airways
Sushil Wadhwani	Formerly Head of Research at hedge fund Tudor Proprietory Trading

In the Euro Area (the members of the EU which have adopted the single currency) the rate of interest is set by the European Central Bank.

QUESTIONS

SHORT QUESTIONS

1 In what sense is the rate of interest the opportunity cost of capital?
2 Distinguish between the transactions, precautionary and speculative motives.
3 Explain why a fall in the price of government securities is associated with a rise in the rate of interest.
4 Why do people have to be paid interest to lend money?

MULTIPLE CHOICE

1 Which of the following influences the speculative demand for money?

A The value of current transactions.

B The productivity of capital.

C The expected level of interest rates.

D The frequency with which income payments are made.

2 What is meant by liquidity preference?

A The desire to hold wealth in the form of money.

B The demand for loans by firms wishing to expand.

C The wish to earn a high rate of return on financial assets.

D The preference of financial institutions to hold government securities.

3 A rise in the price of government fixed-interest securities indicates that the:

A market rate of interest has fallen

B the supply of money has decreased

C liquidity preference has increased

D the supply of fixed-interest securities has increased.

4 Which of the following, other things being equal, will cause interest rates to rise?

A An increase in the precautionary demand for money.

B The expectation that the price of government securities will rise.

C An increase in the supply of loanable funds.

D A reduction in the demand for overdrafts by households and firms.

DATA RESPONSE

| Year | UK | | Japan | |
	Interest rate %	Savings ratio[1]	Interest rate %	Savings ratio[1]
1995	6.6	10.3	1.2	11.9
1996	6.0	9.5	0.6	12.2
1997	6.9	9.5	0.6	11.3
1998	7.2	7.0	0.7	11.8
1999[2]	5.4	7.8	0.2	11.3
2000[2]	5.3	8.4	0.3	11.2

NOTES [1]Savings ratio = the percentage of disposable income saved.
[2]1999 and 2000 figures are estimates.

a] Discuss the relationship between changes in the rate of interest and savings in:

  i the UK **(2)**

  ii Japan. **(2)**

b] Are the relationships you found the ones you would have expected to find? **(6)**

c] What factors determine interest rates? **(3)**

d] What may account for differences in UK and Japanese interest rates? **(6)**

e] Explain how two economic variables, other than savings, may be affected by changes in the rate of interest. **(6)**

CASE STUDY

The mortgage question is difficult. If low inflation is the norm, should you have a variable or a fixed-rate one? The Council of Mortgage Lenders says that in recent months, 60% of borrowers have opted for variable-rate mortgages, the rest fixed. There are two reasons. One is the expectation that mortgage rates have further to fall, so why fix now? The other is that, at these levels, fees and lock-in periods for fixed-rate mortgages make them unattractive.

Last week, however, I spoke to some building society executives who were unanimous in saying that, even if the MPC cut rates further — as I expect it to — they would not cut mortgage rates. It was time, they said, to start looking after savers.

This interested me. With the base rate at 5%, one of the lowest variable mortgage rates on offer is the Nationwide's 6.45%. More typically rates are 6.85%. If that is the floor for mortgage rates, does it not make sense to fix if lower rates than this are available? And does it not also mean that the MPC might as well leave the base rate at 5% because there will be little pass-through from further cuts to personal borrowers?

I think the answer is no on both counts. Despite my building society executives' sincerity, the market will lead a move to lower mortgage rates, a point made by Willem Buiter of the MPC when I put this to him. The competition driving down product prices will also drive down mortgage rates; when base rate was 5% in 1960

the mortgage rate averaged 5.89%, when the base rate was 4.5% in 1955 mortgage rates were just 4.66%. Times have changed but mortgage-rate cuts have not yet ended.

Source: 'History points to stable prices' by David Smith, the Sunday Times, 11/7/99.

a] Explain the difference between variable and fixed interest rates. **(6)**

b] Why in mid 1999 were most people opting for variable mortgages? **(6)**

c] What is the MPC? **(5)**

d] Why were building societies reluctant to cut interest rates? **(5)**

e] Why did the writer expect mortgage rates to fall? **(5)**

f] What is the demand relationship between houses and mortgages? **(3)**

g] Explain the effect of a rise in interest rates on the market for houses. Illustrate your answer with a diagram. **(10)**

h] Discuss the effects of a fall in the rate of interest on consumption, borrowing and investment. **(10)**

STRUCTURED ESSAY

a] Explain what is meant by liquidity preference. **(10)**

b] Discuss the causes and the consequences of an increase in liquidity preference. **(15)**

17 LABOUR MARKETS

DIFFERENT LABOUR MARKETS

When economists discuss the labour market they are often examining the total (aggregate) demand for labour and total (aggregate) supply of labour. They also, however, study individual labour markets.

Labour markets can be classified according to the demand and supply of labour in a particular industry, in a particular firm, in a particular occupation and in a particular region.

DERIVED DEMAND

The demand for labour is a *derived demand*. This means that labour is not required for itself, but for what it will produce. The demand for labour derives directly from the demand for the product of labour. The greater the demand for the product, the greater the demand for labour. No matter how skilful workers are, no matter how long their period of training, if what they produce is no longer in demand, their services will no longer be required.

INFLUENCES ON THE LEVEL OF DEMAND

The aggregate demand for labour is influenced by the level of economic activity. If the economy is expanding, more labour will be demanded either in terms of more hours from existing workers (overtime) or in terms of more workers.

The demand for labour in individual labour markets will be determined by the output per worker hour, how much the output can be sold for, the wage rate and the price of other factors of production. Demand will increase if there is a rise in the price of the product being produced (which will raise marginal revenue), an increase in the pro-

ductivity of labour, a rise in the price of a substitute factor of production, or a fall in the price of a complementary factor of production. A fall in the wage rate will result in an extension in demand for labour.

In recent years the increased interest in gardening has resulted in a rise in the number of people employed in garden centres whilst the increased application of technology in banking has reduced demand for bank staff.

ELASTICITY OF DEMAND FOR LABOUR

Demand for labour will be elastic if a given percentage change in wages causes a greater percentage change in demand. Figure 17.1 shows that the rise in the hourly wage rate from £10 to £12 results in a greater percentage fall in demand for workers from 400 to 300.

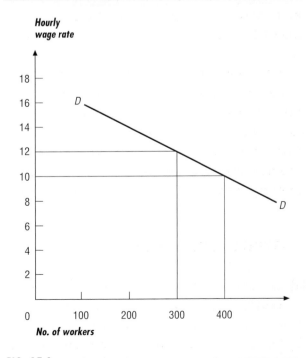

FIG. 17.1

Demand for labour is inelastic if demand changes by a smaller percentage than the change in the wage rate. There are four main influences on the elasticity of demand for labour in an industry.

THE ELASTICITY OF DEMAND FOR THE PRODUCT

If labour is producing a commodity which has a very inelastic demand, an increase in wages will have a relatively small effect on the demand for labour. Even if the whole of the increase in wages is passed on in the form of higher prices, the fall in the quantity demanded of the product will be relatively small. So there will be a correspondingly small reduction in the demand for labour. If, however, the demand for the product of labour is very elastic, a small increase in price will lead to a relatively large reduction in the quantity demanded. Under these circumstances an increase in wages which is passed on in the form of higher prices will cause a relatively large reduction in the demand for labour.

THE PROPORTION OF TOTAL COSTS ACCOUNTED FOR BY LABOUR COSTS

Where wages account for only a small proportion of total costs, the demand for labour will tend to be inelastic. Some industries such as house building, are labour intensive and labour costs make up a large part of the total costs of production. Other industries are capital intensive, e.g. chemicals and oil refining, and in these industries the cost of labour accounts for a relatively small part of the cost of the product.

For example suppose wages increase generally by 10% while productivity remains unchanged. In a labour-intensive industry, labour costs might account for, say, 60% of average total cost. The effect of the increase in wages will be to raise unit cost by 6%. In contrast in a capital-intensive industry where labour costs are, say, 20% of average total cost, the increase in wages will raise unit cost by only 2%. If these increased costs are passed on in the form of higher prices, the effects on the demand for labour are likely to be much greater in the case of the labour-intensive industry.

THE DEGREE TO WHICH LABOUR CAN BE SUBSTITUTED BY OTHER FACTORS OF PRODUCTION

Other things being equal, an increase in wage rates will increase the cost of labour relative to the costs of the other factors. Where possible, therefore, entrepreneurs will tend to substitute other factors for the now relatively dearer labour. As wages increase, the substitution of labour-saving machinery becomes more and more attractive. Labour-intensive methods are more common in countries with low wages, e.g. Pakistan, whilst countries with relatively high wages rates such as the USA make the most use of capital-intensive methods. Where it is fairly easy to substitute capital for labour, the demand for labour will become more and more elastic as wage rates rise relative to other factor prices.

THE PERIOD OF TIME

Demand for labour will be more elastic in the long run. This is because it will take time for firms to change their methods of production and replace some workers by machines. Labour may also have fixed contracts and periods of notice may have to be given.

THE AGGREGATE (TOTAL) SUPPLY OF LABOUR

The supply of labour available to an economy is not the same thing as the number of people in that community. The labour supply is a measure of the number of hours of work which is offered at given wage rates over some given period of time. It is determined, therefore, by the number of workers and the average number of hours each worker is prepared to offer. Both of these features are subject to change and, at any moment of time, they will depend upon a number of things.

THE SIZE OF THE TOTAL POPULATION

This is obviously very important because the size of the total population sets an upper limit to the supply of labour.

THE AGE COMPOSITION OF THE POPULATION

The age composition of a population takes account of the proportions in the different age groups. Two countries might have the same total populations but very different age compositions and hence very different numbers in the working age group.

THE LABOUR FORCE

In many countries the minimum age at which a person may engage in full-time employment is legally controlled. In the UK this is now 16 years and the normal age for retirement is 65 years. The age range 16 to 65 covers the working age group, but this does not mean that the total working population embraces all the people in that age group. Many people now continue in full-time education well beyond the age of 16. Another large group which must be excluded consists of people who do not engage in paid employment outside the home — homemakers. A number of people also retire early. Those groups who do not participate in the labour force are referred to as economically inactive.

Those of working age who are eligible for work and offer themselves for employment are called the labour force. They are referred to as economically active. As a proportion of the total population the labour force differs from country to country. For example in countries where it is considered unacceptable for married women to work the size of the labour force is correspondingly lower.

THE WORKING WEEK AND HOLIDAYS

The number of people who work (or are available for work) is an important determinant of the supply of labour, but so is the average number of hours each person works. The supply of labour provided by 20 people working for 40 hours is the same as that provided by 40 people working for 20 hours. The number of hours worked per week varies from country to country. The UK has higher working hours than most EU countries. Over time, working hours have been reduced and annual holiday periods increased. This reduces the supply of labour. However, sometimes when people work fewer hours the quantity and quality of their output increases.

PAY

Usually when wage rates are relatively low, increases in the wage rate will tend to lead to an increase in the supply of labour. However, there may come a point when higher incomes make leisure more attractive (see below).

THE SUPPLY OF LABOUR TO A GIVEN OCCUPATION

The main influences on supply are the wage rate offered, the non-monetary aspects of the job, the qualifications and skills demanded and the extent of unemployment. The higher the wage rate offered the more workers will be attracted. However, workers will also take into account more than financial reward. They also consider working conditions, promotion chances, job security, number of days holidays, working hours, etc. The more attractive these are, the more inclined people will be to work in the occupation. For instance, most actors do not earn high wages but the possibility of high earnings and the fame and glamour attached to the job causes many people to train as actors. The general level of education and training in a country will influence the relative supply of skilled and unskilled labour. If education and training standards are low, a high-skill industry such as the chemical industry will find it difficult to recruit staff. Supply of potential workers to a particular industry, in contrast, will be high if there is sufficient unemployment among suitably qualified people.

THE INDIVIDUAL'S SUPPLY OF LABOUR

In many occupations individual workers cannot freely choose the number of hours they work. Self-employed people such as taxi-drivers, shop-keepers and builders can vary the hours they work and some employed people can exercise some choice over whether they work over-time and how many hours of over-time they do. For many other people the working hours are settled by negotiation between trade unions or professional bodies and employers. However in recent years there has been an increase in flexibility in terms of the number of hours people work and when they work them (see below).

THE BACKWARD SLOPING SUPPLY CURVE

The supply curve of labour for the individual worker may be of the normal shape for only part of its length. A higher wage rate may result in an extension of supply up to a certain wage level. Beyond this point a higher wage may lead to a reduced

amount of labour being offered. As real income increases people can buy a much wider range of goods and services and they will demand more leisure in order to enjoy the consumption of these commodities. One only has to think of such activities as motoring, sailing, golf and foreign travel to appreciate the increasing preference given to leisure as income rises. As the hourly wage rate rises, there will come a point at which the individual's or group of individuals' supply curve of labour will bend backwards. This is illustrated in Figure 17.2.

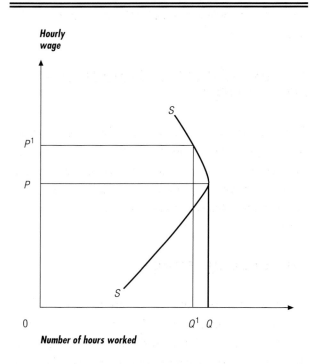

Number of hours worked

FIG. 17.2

As the hourly wage rate increases up to the level *P*, the worker is tempted to work longer hours. As the wage rate rises above *P*, the worker reduces the number of hours he is prepared to work. This does not mean that he is reducing his weekly income. For example, he might be prepared to work a 40 hour week when the wage rate is £8.00 per hour, giving him a wage of £320. If the hourly wage rate increases to £10.00 he might offer 36 hours work giving him a wage of £360 per week.

Up to the wage rate of *P* the substitution effect is more powerful than the income effect. Leisure is becoming more costly in terms of income forgone. At wage rates higher than *P*, however, the income effect predominates. Alternatively, in terms of utility analysis, at wage rates above *P* the marginal utility of leisure exceeds the marginal utility of income. This is true of the labour supplied by an individual; it will not be true of the supply of labour to an industry. The supply curve of labour to an industry will be of the normal shape because higher wages will attract more workers to that industry.

THE ELASTICITY OF THE SUPPLY OF LABOUR

The supply of labour is elastic when a given percentage change in the wage rate causes a greater percentage change in the supply of labour. The supply of labour is inelastic when a percentage change in the wage rate causes a smaller percentage change in the supply of labour. This is shown in Figure 17.3.

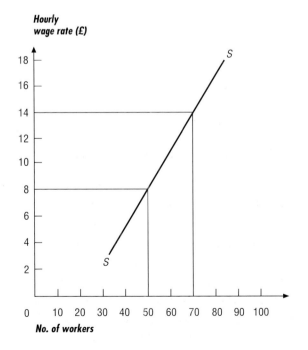

FIG. 17.3

The main determinants of the elasticity of supply in an industry are:

- *The level of employment.* If there is high unemployment the supply of labour will be relatively elastic. A small rise in the wage rate is likely to attract a high number of job applicants.
- *The mobility of labour.* The more occupationally and geographically mobile labour is, the more elastic the supply of labour will be.
- *The length of training.* The longer it takes to train a worker, the more inelastic supply will tend to be. For instance, it takes approximately seven years to train a surgeon. So a rise in wages of surgeons will take some time before it is reflected in a rise in the number of surgeons.
- *The qualifications and skills required.* The higher the level of qualifications and skills needed, the fewer potential workers there will be to draw on and hence the more inelastic supply will be. So surgeons are in inelastic supply not only because they have to undergo a long period of training but also because they have to possess high academic qualifications before they start their medical training.

CHANGES IN THE NATURE OF THE LABOUR FORCE

The last few years have seen significant changes in the nature of the labour force. These include the following.

- *A rise in part-time employment.* Women constitute four-fifths of the part-time labour force and part-time workers in the service sector account for 35% of the labour force whereas they account for 8% in the manufacturing sector. However, part-time working is now increasing most rapidly in manufacturing and among male workers. Employers are attracted to the increased flexibility part-time working offers them. However there is a management cost involved in changing work rotas and keeping part-timers informed and involved.

- *A rise in temporary employment.* More workers are being offered temporary contracts. This enables employers to adjust their labour forces more cheaply and quickly but it also creates uncertainty among workers about job security.

- *A rise in the participation of women in the labour force.* In 1944, 68% of the labour force was male. There were 14.9m men in work and 7.1m women in work. In 1999, 56% of the labour force were male and hence 44% were female. Also whilst the number of women in work increased to 12.1m the number of men fell to 14.1m. There

are a number of reasons why more women are working. These include the increase in part-time employment, changing social attitudes to women working, the invention of labour-saving household appliances, higher educational standards achieved by women and the expansion of the tertiary sector where a high proportion of married women are employed.

- *A change in the pattern of employment.* A smaller number of people and a smaller proportion of the labour force work in the primary and secondary sectors. Employment in the tertiary and, in particular, the quaternary sectors are increasing. The IT related industries are experiencing particularly fast growth.

QUESTIONS

SHORT QUESTIONS

1. Explain why the demand for labour is a derived demand.
2. What factors determine the aggregate supply of labour?
3. In what circumstances will an increase in wages not result in an increase in a firm's total wage bill?
4. Explain why firms pay over-time rates which are usually higher than nominal wage rates.

MULTIPLE CHOICE

1. Which of the following would reduce the elasticity of demand for labour in a particular labour market?

   A   An increase in the proportion of labour costs in total costs.

   B   An increase in the ease of substituting capital for labour.

   C   A reduction in the elasticity of demand for the final product.

   D   A reduction in the national level of employment.

2. Figure 17.4 shows a worker's labour supply curve.

   What could explain the change in the supply curve from W to W^1?

   A   The firm substituting capital for labour.

   B   The worker substituting leisure for work.

   C   Consumers switching to another firm's products.

   D   The government imposing an indirect tax on the good the worker produces.

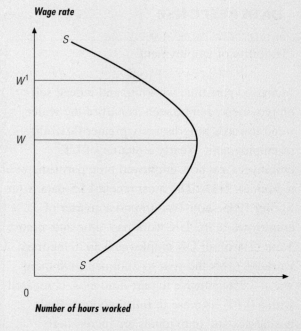

Wage rate

Number of hours worked

FIG. 17.4

3. Which of the following will influence the elasticity of supply of a specific type of labour?

   A   The elasticity of supply for the final product.

   B   The productivity of the workers.

   C   The qualifications required to undertake the job.

   D   The ease with which labour can be substituted for capital.

4. Which of the following could cause a firm's demand for labour curve to shift to the right?

   A   An increase in the wage rate.

   B   A rise in the price of the final product.

   C   A decrease in labour productivity.

   D   A decrease in the supply of labour.

DATA RESPONSE

Flexibility of employment

Increased part-time working, and indeed self-employment, can be seen as part of the wider trend towards progressively greater flexibility of employment. Nearly a quarter of UK employees are now employed on a part-time or temporary basis. The most recent LFS data from Spring 1996 show that around a quarter of employees in the UK work part-time and almost 1.6m (7% of all UK employees) are temporary workers. Over the year to Summer 1996 there was a 3.2% increase in part-time jobs, compared with a 0.1% increase in full-time jobs. Both businesses and individuals are increasingly looking at, and using, alternatives to full-time permanent employment.

For employers, flexibility aids competitiveness by adjusting the amount of labour used more quickly and closely to prevailing market conditions. They say the main benefits are cost effectiveness, efficiency and response to customer demands. Because companies increasingly operate in an uncertain environment, they need to be able to respond quickly to new circumstances, so labour flexibility and adaptability are vital.

Many employees find positive advantages in working on a part-time or temporary basis. For instance there can be increased employment opportunities and it allows work to be balanced with other commitments, such as family. 27% of employers adopt flexible working methods in response to employees' demands and 81% of women working part-time do not want a full-time job.

The term 'flexibility' is widely used but there is no one clear definition of what it means. There are a variety of types of flexibility found in the labour market. Part-time working is one of the most common and, as has been discussed, increasing flexibilities in the UK labour market. Varying the hours or days worked by employees is often termed Temporal Flexibility. There has also been a growth in flexible working patterns that apply to full-time staff, such as annual hours contracts and flexitime (worked by 4% and 10% of all employees in Spring 1996), over-time or short-time working.

Source: Labour Market and Skill Trends 1997/98, Department for Education and Employment.

a] Briefly define flexibility of employment. **(3)**

b] Explain how a more flexible labour force may increase 'effectiveness, efficiency and response to customer demands'. **(5)**

c] Discuss why some people work part-time. **(4)**

d] Identify and explain three disadvantages employees may find in working on a part-time or temporary basis. **(6)**

e] Temporal flexibility is one type of labour market flexibility. Explain two other forms of flexibility. **(8)**

CASE STUDY

The activity rates for women from different ethnic groups vary considerably. In 1997 these ranged from around three-quarters for Black-Caribbean women down to one-fifth for Bangladeshi women.

The level of qualifications obtained also influences the labour market participation of women. A higher proportion of women without dependent children have no formal qualifications (22%) than those with children (19%). The proportion also increases with the age of the youngest child under 16; some 15% of women with a youngest child aged under five have no qualifications compared with 20% of those with children aged 11–15. These differences may, however, be entirely age-related and result from the increasing qualification levels of the population over the decades. The percentage of women with no qualifications has fallen from 46% in 1984 to 21% in 1998. Over the same period the percentage for men fell from 36% to 15%.

The highest economic activity rates are for women with higher qualifications (i.e. above A-level or equivalent). In Spring 1998, 86% of highly qualified women were active, compared with 50% of those without qualifications. This is a similar but more marked effect to that among men, where the economic activity rate falls from 92% of those with higher qualifications to 66% for unqualified men. While the average economic activity rate for women has risen slightly, for those with higher qualifications it has risen eight percentage points from 78% in 1984, but for women with no qualifications it is now nearly nine percentage points lower, down from 59%. Activity rates for men in general were lower in 1998 than 1984, but qualifications have a similar effect. Among men with higher qualifications the rate is only slightly lower, while for men with no qualifications the rate has fallen from 84% in 1984 to 66% in 1998.

The effect of qualifications is most marked among women with pre-school-age children, where only 27% of unqualified women were economically active compared with 76% of highly qualified women. Well-qualified women also have higher employment rates and lower unemployment rates than the unqualified, as do their male counterparts.

Source: 'Women in the labour market: results from the Spring 1998 LFS' by Tim Thair and Andrew Risdon, March 1999, Labour Market Trends.

a] Explain what is meant by the activity rate of a particular group. **(4)**

b] Give two reasons why the activity rate of Black Caribbean women is higher than that of Bangladeshi women. **(6)**

c] Explain the likely effect of a rise in the qualification levels of the population on the productivity of the labour force. **(4)**

d] Give two reasons why people may be economically inactive. **(4)**

e] Why are highly qualified women with pre-school-age children more willing and able to enter the labour force than unqualified women with pre-school-age children? **(6)**

f] What may be the opportunity cost of not gaining high qualifications? **(4)**

g] Explain why both the demand for and supply of highly qualified workers is more inelastic than the demand for and supply of unqualified workers. **(10)**

h] Explain why the participation rate of women, particularly married women, in the labour force has increased in recent years. **(12)**

STRUCTURED ESSAY

a] Explain the meaning of the elasticity of supply
of labour and describe the factors that
influence the elasticity of supply. **(12)**

b] Using income and substitution effects, explain
how an individual worker may react to a rise in
the wage rate. **(13)**

18 WAGE DETERMINATION

Wages are the price of labour. As with any price they are influenced by demand and supply and can be affected by institutional factors.

WAGE DIFFERENTIALS AND DIFFERENT LABOUR MARKETS

Wages differ between countries, areas, industries and occupations. This would not occur if labour was all the same (homogeneous). However in practice there are differences in the skills and abilities of, and in the demands for, different types of worker. This gives rise not to one labour market but many different labour markets each with its own supply and demand conditions.

CONTINUANCE OF WAGE DIFFERENTIALS

It might be expected that there would be a large-scale movement of workers from low-paid to high-paid jobs. Such a movement would tend to equalise wages as the movements out of the lower-paid jobs would reduce the supply of this type of labour and raise its price. At the same time the movements into the more highly paid jobs would increase the supply and tend to lower the price. However in practice this does not occur to any great extent. This is because workers take into account non-monetary advantages and disadvantages of jobs and more significantly because there are barriers to entry into different labour markets. For example, it might be expected that the supply of barristers would be high, attracted by the current high salaries and the interesting nature of the occupation. This would be expected to reduce the wage rate. In contrast, as a result of low pay, sometimes unsociable hours and perhaps lack of job satisfaction, it can be anticipated

that the supply of cleaners would be low and the wage rate high. However, it is barristers who are highly paid because the need for high qualifications and completion of a long period of training restricts supply and keeps the wage rate high. Not many people want to be cleaners but because they do not need academic qualifications to do so the number of people who have to try to undertake this type of unskilled work is relatively high.

DEMAND AND SUPPLY INFLUENCES

Demand and supply conditions are important influences on wage rates. Wage rates are likely to be high in labour markets where demand is high and inelastic and where supply is low and inelastic.

The demand for labour depends on the physical productivity of labour and the price of the product. These two factors determine the return from employing labour and hence the shape of the demand curve. As noted in the previous chapter the elasticity of demand for labour in any market depends on the elasticity of demand for the product, the extent to which labour can be substituted by other factors of production and the proportion of labour costs in total costs.

The supply of labour to a particular market will be influenced by the skills and qualifications required, the ability of trade unions and professional associations to influence recruitment, relative pay and the non-monetary advantages of the job such as length and timing of working hours, working conditions and promotion chances.

Figure 18.1 compares the markets for skilled (a) and unskilled workers (b). The demand for skilled workers is high and, because of their importance in the production process, relatively inelastic. Because skilled workers need training and qualifications, their supply is low and inelastic. In contrast, the demand for unskilled workers is both low (and in most developed countries falling) and elastic, as it is often possible to replace them with machinery if their wages rise too high. The supply of unskilled workers is high and elastic because the level of training and qualifications they need is low. As a result of the differences in the levels and elasticities of demand and supply in the markets for skilled and unskilled workers, the wages of skilled workers are likely to be higher than those for unskilled workers as shown in Figure 18.1.

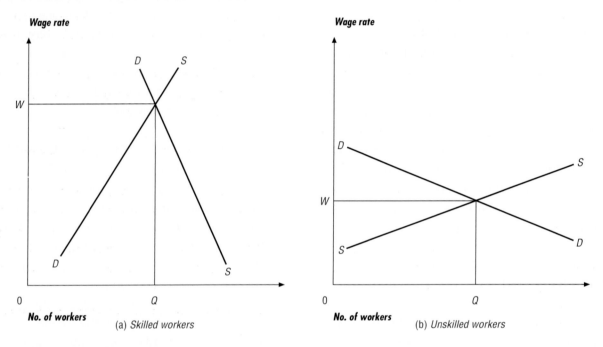

(a) Skilled workers (b) Unskilled workers

FIG. 18.1

TRADE UNIONS AND COLLECTIVE BARGAINING

A number of workers have their wages and salaries influenced by some kind of collective bargaining procedure. The individual worker is in a weak bargaining position in relation to his/her employer; the main purpose of a trade union is to remove this weakness by forcing the employer/s to negotiate with representatives of the whole, or a proportion of, the labour force. Unions also provide a channel of communication between workers and employer/s.

In the 1980s and 1990s trade union membership in the UK fell because of the rise in unemployment, the weakening of the power of trade unions as a result of government legislation and changing social attitudes. From 1989 to 1997 membership fell from 39% of all employees to 30% in 1997. The decline was particularly significant among male employees, manual employees and those in production industries. These are all areas where membership has traditionally been higher. After 1997 membership began to increase again.

THE BASES OF WAGE CLAIMS

Trade union demands for higher wages are usually based on one or more of the following four grounds.

- *A rise in the cost of living.* The argument here is that inflation reduces the real income of workers and they need a pay rise in order to restore their real wages. However, there is the risk that wage demands can allow a wage price spiral to develop. Here, a rise in prices generates a rise in wages which, if not matched by a rise in productivity, will increase costs of production and so raise prices further, increasing wage demands.

- *The differential argument.* One group of workers may claim a wage rise on the grounds that they are paid less than workers in similar occupations. However, it may be difficult to establish comparability. For example, what job is similar to that of a teacher? There is also the risk of a wage-wage spiral developing. A wage settlement in one market may cause wage demands in other markets intended to restore differentials, which then provoke further wage claims. It may also not be desirable for wage differentials to remain un-changed if labour market conditions are changing. If one labour market is expanding and one contracting, a widening of the wage differential between the two will facilitate the movement from the latter to the former market.

- *The profitability argument.* Unions may argue that increased profits in a particular industry justify a higher return to labour since the efforts of the workers have contributed to the rise in the profits.

- *The productivity argument.* Improvements in labour productivity are widely accepted as justifiable reasons for increases in wages. There are, how-ever, some problems involved. Most increases in productivity arise from improvements in the quality and performance of the capital equipment on which the labour is employed. Many would regard it as unfair that workers who happen to be employed in industries where there is a rapid rate of technical progress should obtain all the benefits from the resulting increases in productivity. However, where increases in productivity result from the workers' acceptance of new methods

of production which impose greater strain, or responsibility, or call for retraining, claims for higher rewards are justified since the return from employing labour will have increased. Another problem is that a large number of workers are employed in occupations where it is difficult to measure productivity or where circumstances beyond the control of workers may reduce their productivity. For example, increased traffic congestion reduces the productivity of bus drivers.

WAYS TRADE UNIONS AND PROFESSIONAL ORGANISATIONS CAN RAISE WAGES

To raise their members' wages, trade unions and professional organisations may support measures designed to restrict the supply of labour into a particular occupation or industry. For example, unions and professional bodies could insist on a longer period of training or higher qualifications. This will shift the supply curve to the left and raise the wage rate as shown in Figure 18.2 below.

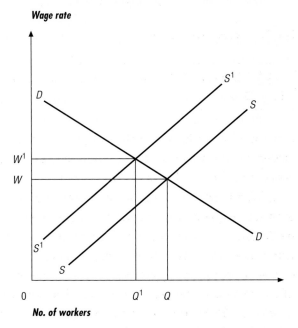

FIG. 18.2

Unions and professional bodies may also be able to raise wage levels by supporting measures intended to increase demand for the good or service provided. For example, participating in an advertising campaign for the product will be likely to raise demand for the product and hence the return from employing labour, the demand for labour and the wage rate.

Unions can also increase the return from employing labour by participating in schemes which will raise productivity — in particular training. In addition, they can increase productivity by acting as a collective voice for their members. Enabling grievances to be avoided and/or settled quickly raises productivity, lowers labour turnover and, by negotiating on a collective basis, reduces firms' costs below the level of that which would result if they had to negotiate on an individual basis.

Workers' representatives negotiate with employers to raise wage rates and improve working conditions. They do not want to drive the wage rate so high that a significant number of their members lose their jobs. So their power is limited by the need to protect their members' jobs.

Their power is also influenced by their bargaining strength relative to that of the employers. They will have to judge the strength of the employers and their ability to pay higher wages. They will be in a stronger position if the employers are enjoying high profits, if there is low unemployment and hence a scarcity of labour, if demand for the product is inelastic, if it is difficult to substitute capital for labour and if wages form a small proportion of total costs.

Workers can be in a powerful position to drive up wages without causing unemployment if they are negotiating with a *monopsonistic* (sole) employer or *oligopsonistic* (a small number of large) employers. Figure 18.3 shows that before negotiation the wage rate is W and the number of workers employed is Q. After negotiation a wage rate of W^1 is set and employment actually rises to Q^1.

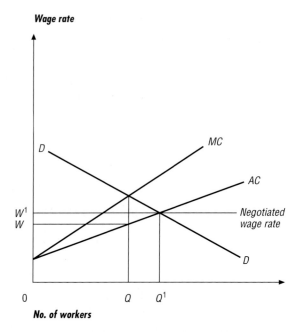

FIG. 18.3

The wage rate negotiated by the union/professional body becomes the new marginal cost (MC) which now equals the average cost (AC). The employer cannot force down the wage rate by employing fewer workers and taking on more workers will not raise the wage rate.

INDUSTRIAL ACTION

Unions may undertake a range of industrial actions. These include go-slows, work-to-rules (workers only carry out the tasks specifically mentioned in their job descriptions) and strikes. Strikes tend to be the action of last resort and may have limited effect on the national economy, though they may be very damaging to the companies involved. For example, in the UK the number of working days lost through strike action has been very low in recent years. Even in the 1970s when these figures were much higher, the days lost from strike action were still significantly below those lost through illness. In addition to measuring the number of working days lost through strikes, The Office for National Statistics also measures the number of stoppages, which indicate the number of separate disputes, and the number of workers involved, which gives an indication of the support that the disputes have.

EMPLOYER ORGANISATIONS

Employer organisations can influence wages directly in their bargaining with labour on a national scale for their industry and indirectly in the influence they can seek to exert on government policy. Examples of employer organisations include the National Farmers Union, The Engineering Employers Federation and the Newspaper Society. Most employers belong to the Confederation of British Industry (CBI).

GOVERNMENT POLICY

The government is the largest employer in the UK so its approach to the pay of its own workers has a significant impact on the determination of wage levels. The government can also influence pay in both the private and public sectors by passing legislation such as the 1995 Disability Act and the 1999 National Minimum Wage Act, and by introducing incomes policies which may themselves have statutory power.

Government policy on trade union reform will affect the bargaining power of workers and thereby influence wage rates. Similarly, government policy on education, training and housing and unemployment-related benefits will affect the mobility and supply of labour. Changes in government spending, taxation, the rate of interest and the exchange rate will alter the level of aggregate demand and may thereby affect the demand for labour.

SOCIAL CONVENTION

Public opinion can also influence wage claims and settlements. Occupations in which the workers are mainly middle class, male and white may be more highly regarded than those which have a high proportion of lower class, female and ethnic minority workers.

TABLE 18.1 HIGHEST AND LOWEST PAID OCCUPATIONS; GREAT BRITAIN; APRIL 1998

Full-time employees on adult rates whose pay for the survey period was unaffected by absence	Average gross weekly pay (£)
Highest paid	
1 General administrators; national government	1 116.9
2 Treasurers and company financial managers	976.5
3 Medical practitioners	901.2
4 Underwriters, claims assessors, brokers, investment	794.3
5 Organisation and methods and work study managers	743.4
6 Police officers (inspector and above)	720.1
7 Advertising and public relations managers	716.6
8 Marketing and sales managers	686.9
9 Education officers, school inspectors	685.6
10 Computer systems and data processing managers	683.2
Lowest paid	
1 Kitchen porters, hands	166.8
2 Bar staff	175.7
3 Hairdressers, barbers	175.9
4 Retail cash desk and check-out operators	176.2
5 Petrol pump forecourt attendants	178.9
6 Waiters, waitresses	182.0
7 Counterhands, catering assistants	185.0
8 Launderers, dry cleaners, pressers	187.1
9 Other childcare and related occupations n.e.c.	190.9
10 Sewing machinists, menders, darners and embroiders	195.2

Source: New Earnings Survey 1996, Office for National Statistics

QUESTIONS

SHORT QUESTIONS

1. Discuss three arguments a trade union could advance in support of a pay claim for its members.
2. What economic effects may trade unions have on the wages of non-unionised labour?
3. Apart from pay, what factors influence a person's choice of job?
4. Use demand and supply analysis to explain the effect of an increase in the resources devoted to training teachers on the market for teachers.

MULTIPLE CHOICE

1. In order to increase his/her labour force from 20 to 21 workers, an employer is obliged to raise the weekly wage rate from £510 to £530. What is the marginal cost of employing the 21st worker?

   A £420   B £530

   C £930   D £1590

2. Which of the following would make the supply of lawyers more elastic?

   A A fall in the wage rate.

   B A fall in unemployment.

   C A rise in educational provision and performance.

   D An increase in the qualifications needed to be a lawyer.

3. Which is a barrier to entry into the market for vets?

   A The payment of high wages.

   B High regard for the profession.

   C The existence of job satisfaction.

   D A long period of training.

4. Which of the following would increase a trade union's ability to gain a wage rise for its members?

   A A high level of national unemployment.

   B Inelastic demand for the product the workers produce.

   C A low level of membership among workers.

   D A fall in the profit level earned by the employer/s.

DATA RESPONSE

Year	Trade Union membership (millions)	Working days lost in all stoppages in progress (millions)	UK unemployment % ILO measure
1989	8.96	4.13	7.3
1990	8.85	1.90	6.9
1991	8.63	0.76	8.4
1992	8.00	0.53	9.9
1993	7.81	0.65	10.5
1994	7.55	0.28	9.8
1995	7.28	0.42	8.8
1996	7.22	1.30	8.3
1997	7.12[1]	0.23	7.2
1998	7.11	0.28	6.3

NOTE [1] estimate
Sources: Labour Market Trends, May 1996 and April 1999 and the Annual Abstract of Statistics 1998, Office for National Statistics.

a] Identify and briefly comment on two other measures of labour disputes. **(4)**

b] Comment on the change in trade union membership over the period shown. **(4)**

c] Analyse the relationship between UK unemployment and working days lost in stoppages. **(5)**

d] Do your findings in (c) accord with what you would expect from economic theory? **(6)**

e] Discuss three other influences on the number of working days lost in any one year. **(6)**

CASE STUDY

Average pay for full-time workers has passed the £20 000 a year mark — a salary level earned only by the 'fat cats' of the day a generation ago — according to a report today.

An analysis of government figures published last autumn, updated with the current rate of earnings increase of 3.6%, shows that the average full-time gross salary is now £20 770, compared with the male equivalent 25 years ago of £2480.

However, 'around three quarters of British workers earn less than the new £20 000 plus land-mark figure,' the research group Incomes Data Services estimates, because a relatively small group of very high earners skews the mean average upwards, and because around 6m part-timers, who mostly get paid less than £100 a week, are not included.

More than 60% of full-time workers earn less than the £20 770 average and the bulk of the difference with the earnings levels of the early 1970s is accounted for by inflation. The proportion of national income accounted for by wages has fallen back over the period.

The lowest paid have meanwhile benefited least from the real increases in earnings that there have been over the last 25 years, at the same time as very steep rises for the already well-paid — boosted by income tax cuts — have pushed up the average. The largest group of full-timers now earn between £9000 (£173 a week) and £18 500 (£356 a week).

Source: 'Average full-time pay passes £20,000 mark' by Seumas Milne, the Guardian, 5/7/99.

One in four QCs earns more than £266 200 a year after expenses, or more than £346 000 gross, according to the first authoritative survey of barristers' income.

The Bar's chairman, Daniel Brennan QC, said the survey showed it was not a 'fat cat' profession, and that most were in the reasonable range. The rest were at the top of the profession earning fees commensurate with their skills.

Source: 'One in 4 QCs earn over £1/4m' by Clare Dyer, the Guardian, 5/7/99.

a] Why are there more people with wages below than above the average wage rate? **(5)**

b] How does the weekly wage of part-timers compare with the weekly wage of full-timers? **(5)**

c] Why do some people work part-time? **(6)**

d] The first article states that 'the proportion of income accounted for by wages has fallen'. What are the payments to the other three factors of production? **(3)**

e] How does the pay of top barristers compare with the average pay? **(4)**

f] Discuss three reasons why a group of workers may be paid considerably less than the average rate. **(9)**

g] Explain how the proportion of economic rent earned by barristers is likely to compare with the proportion of economic rent earned by part-time workers? **(6)**

h] Discuss why barristers are so highly paid. **(12)**

STRUCTURED ESSAY

a] Why are university lecturers paid more than bus drivers? **(12)**

b] Discuss the factors which could cause the wage differential between university lecturers and bus drivers to narrow. **(13)**

PART FOUR: EFFICIENCY, MARKET FAILURE AND GOVERNMENT INTERVENTION

19 THE OPERATION OF MARKETS

Markets perform differently. The markets for some products and some factors of production adjust quickly and smoothly to changes in demand whilst in other markets there are shortages or surpluses or other problems.

THE EFFICIENT OPERATION OF MARKETS

Markets operate efficiently when resources are fully employed, the quantity of goods and services produced reflect consumers' preferences and are produced at lowest possible average cost.

PRODUCTIVE AND ALLOCATIVE EFFICIENCY

Production possibility curves can be used to illustrate the difference between productive and allocative efficiency. In terms of the whole economy productive efficiency is achieved when it is not possible to increase the output of one type of good or service without reducing the output of another. This means that all resources are fully employed and the economy is operating on its production possibility curve. In Figure 19.1, production at point *A* is not efficient since more of both types of product (i.e. both health care services and other goods and services) could be produced with existing resources. Point *B*, in contrast, is productively efficient. All resources are being employed and it is not possible to increase the output of both types of product.

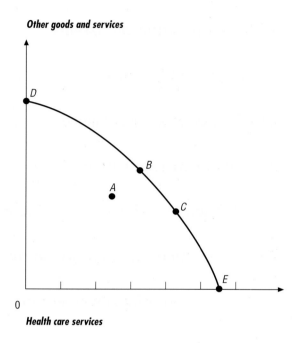

Other goods and services

Health care services

FIG. 19.1

Whilst productive efficiency is concerned with the quantity of goods and services produced, allocative efficiency is concerned with the combination of goods and services produced. Allocative efficiency is achieved when the product mix reflects consumers' tastes and so resources are allocated in the right proportions to producing the different goods and services. In Figure 19.1, if people value health care highly point *C* may be allocatively efficient. It is unlikely that points *D* and *E* will be allocatively efficient as most economies will not want to devote all their resources to producing one type of good or service.

PARETO EFFICIENCY

This type of efficiency is named after the Italian economist, Vilfredo Pareto. He described efficiency as occurring when it is not possible to change the existing allocation of resources in such a way that someone is made better off without making someone else worse off. So Pareto efficiency (which can also be called Pareto optimality) is achieved when productive and allocative efficiency coincide.

INFLUENCES ON THE PERFORMANCE OF MARKETS

Traditionally, economists have argued that for markets to work efficiently there has to be a high level of competition between firms. Essentially, the argument is that if firms are competing for customers they will produce what customers want at low prices.

However, some economists question this view and argue that, in some circumstances, firms which face less competition may benefit customers more.

In markets where the forces of demand and supply are allowed to operate freely but do not produce the desired output or quality, or in which prices are unduly high, there are arguments for government intervention.

MARKET STRUCTURE

Market structure describes the different levels and forms of competition in which firms in different industries can operate. Economists identify four main forms of market structure. These are perfect competition, monopoly, monopolistic competition, and oligopoly. The highest level of competition occurs under perfect competition and the lowest level under monopoly.

PERFECT COMPETITION

In perfect competition, many firms sell to many buyers. The products produced by the firms are all the same (homogeneous). This makes them perfect substitutes and means that individual firms cannot charge more than the market price. If they did they would lose all their customers to their rivals. In this type of market structure consumers decide what is produced and there is no advertising to distort their choice.

Both firms and consumers are assumed to have perfect knowledge of prices and what is going on in the market. In the long run only normal profits are earned. This is because if supernormal profits are earned in the short run new firms are encouraged to enter the market. There is nothing to stop these new firms from producing the product. The resulting increase in supply lowers prices and profits.

In practice very few industries come close to the model of perfect competition. However economists have traditionally argued that this market structure will respond quickly to changes in consumer tastes, will produce in the long run at lowest average cost and will always allocate resources efficiently. Figure 19.2 shows how a perfectly competitive market reacts to a change in demand.

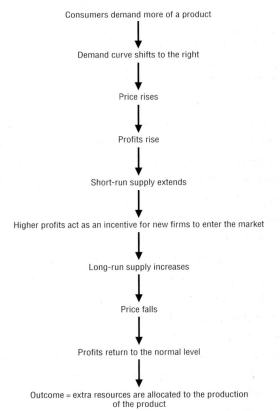

FIG. 19.2

MONOPOLY

A pure monopoly is a single supplier of a product. This means that the firm has no direct competitor. Monopolies can arise for a number of reasons. For example, a government may grant monopoly powers to a firm making it illegal for other firms to enter the industry, a firm may take out a patent giving it the sole right to sell a product, firms may merge together to form one large firm or the market may be able to support only one firm. New firms wishing to start producing the product will usually encounter obstacles. These are referred to as *barriers to entry* and include, e.g., economies of scale.

The lack of competition means that a monopolist has considerable market power. Some economists believe that a monopolist firm is encouraged to exploit its power by charging prices well above the average cost of production. This will mean that the firm will earn supernormal profits. However, to raise its prices it may have to restrict output below the level desired by consumers and so allocative efficiency will not be achieved.

The absence of direct competition may also mean that the firm will not seek to keep its costs low (and so fail to achieve productive efficiency) and that it may not be concerned to improve the quality of its product. It may not, for example, introduce new, more cost efficient methods of production. Consumers will not have a choice of producers and the firm may have more say in what is produced than the consumers.

However monopolies do have some supporters. Some economists argue that whilst monopolies may be forced by the pressure of competition to be dynamically efficient and to develop and introduce new methods of production and products, there are other, perhaps more important, reasons why they may be more likely to invent and innovate than perfectly competitive firms. These are greater financial resources and the knowledge that any financial gains will not have to be shared with rivals. Monopolies

are likely to earn supernormal profits and some of these can be spent on research and development. If this spending eventually results in greater demand for the product it is unlikely new firms will be able to enter the market to reduce profit levels.

A monopoly market structure may also benefit consumers more than a perfectly competitive one in a situation where economies of scale are very significant. Indeed in some cases average costs may fall over a range of output. So the minimum efficient scale of production may mean that for full advantage to be taken of the available economies of scale and for the market to operate efficiently there can only be one firm. This is referred to as a natural monopoly.

MONOPOLISTIC COMPETITION

This is the second most competitive market structure. It is one in which there are a large number of firms producing a similar, but not homogeneous, product. Firms compete in terms of price but also in terms of non-price competition e.g. with low scale advertising and brand names. There are no, or only low, barriers to market entry and as a result only normal profits are earned in the long run.

OLIGOPOLY

This market structure is less competitive than monopolistic competition but more competitive than monopoly. It is a market structure in which a few firms dominate the market in terms of sales. For example an industry may consist of two hundred firms but 80% of sales may be accounted for by the four largest firms.

Oligopolists may adopt a number of strategies. They may get together to set a price or they may decide to compete either in terms of price or, more commonly, in terms of non-price competition including large scale advertising, free gifts, competitions, brand names, after-sales service, and packaging. There are barriers to entry in oligopolistic markets and firms usually earn supernormal profits in the long run.

EXAMPLES OF MARKETS

The operation of markets is complex but interesting. Looking at two important markets, the market for sport and leisure and the market for housing, will show how they work.

SPORT AND LEISURE

This is a fast growing market in many countries. This is because the demand for watching and playing sport and other leisure activities is income elastic. As countries' income rises their citizens may have more leisure time and are likely to spend more on leisure activities. The amount of time which people have to spend on leisure activities is influenced by how many hours they work but also on the hours they spend on maintenance time, e.g. sleeping, washing and cooking. Of course some maintenance activities such as cooking may also be considered, by some people, to be leisure activities. Table 19.1 describes how adults spend their day.

It shows that most people spend approximately a third of each day sleeping and that how they spend the rest of their time is influenced by, among other things, their economic status and gender.

The most popular home based leisure activity for UK adults is watching television, followed by visiting/entertaining, listening to the radio, listening to CDs/tapes, reading books, DIY, and gardening. The most common leisure activity outside the home for UK adults is visiting a public house. This is true of all social groups but some leisure activities are more popular with some social groups than others. For example a visit to the library is more popular with non-manual social groups than manual groups whereas the reverse is the case for visiting a betting shop.

SPORT

There are two main markets within sport. These are the market for playing sport and the market for watching sport.

Playing sport

Sport is played more by the young. Governments frequently promote participation in sport as it is considered to be beneficial for health. Sporting injuries impose a cost on health services but overall it is thought that the rise in fitness which results from playing sport reduces health care costs. Participating in sport is also thought to develop character. Governments promote playing sport in a number of ways. For example, they can make it compulsory in schools and can subsidise sports centres.

Watching sport

Far more adults watch sport than participate in it. They watch it live, e.g. at a football ground, and on the television. In terms of watching live sport the supply of seats in a sports stadium or the number of people who can enter e.g. a race course is fixed in the short run. This can lead to shortages. For instance, the Wimbledon Tennis Final is often sold out with a large number of people willing to pay the pre-set prices unable to buy a ticket. This often results in a black market with those who have been able to purchase tickets selling them illegally at a price above the official price.

Firms and organisations which run sporting events and clubs often operate a sophisticated pricing system. For example, a football club is likely to charge different prices for seats in different parts of the ground and many in the UK now charge different prices for games involving different teams. This recognises that demand for matches featuring a visit

TABLE 19.1   TIME USE: BY ECONOMIC ACTIVITY STATUS AND GENDER, MAY 1995[1]

Great Britain   *Hours and minutes per day*

| | Working age[2] | | | | Retired | | |
| | Working | | Not working | | | | All |
	Males	Females	Males	Females	Males	Females	adults
Sleep	8:10	8:22	8:56	9:01	9:51	9:22	8:42
TV and radio	2:04	1:49	3:12	2:47	3:58	3:22	2:33
Cooking, routine housework	0:32	2:02	0:58	2:45	1:01	2:46	1:35
Eating at home	0:47	0:50	1:04	1:07	1:28	1:28	1:01
Personal care	0:40	0:48	0:36	0:41	0:39	0:51	0:44
Gardening and DIY	0:37	0:19	1:20	0:31	1:22	0:31	0:39
Care of children and adults	0:19	0:36	0:18	1:23	0:02	0:09	0:27
Other home leisure[3]	0:50	0:40	1:52	1:06	1:51	1:34	1:08
Paid work	5:51	4:14	0:17	0:16	0:17	0:19	3:01
Travel	1:02	0:56	0:35	0:32	0:26	0:26	0:46
Socialising[4]	0:48	1:05	1:19	1:30	0:57	1:09	1:03
Shopping	0:20	0:37	0:34	0:55	0:38	0:55	0:36
Eating or drinking out	0:41	0:35	0:43	0:13	0:22	0:13	0:31
Other out-of-home leisure[5]	1:11	0:51	2:02	1:00	0:27	0:43	1:03

Notes   [1] *Components do not add to 24 hours due to rounding and activities not stated.*
[2] *Males aged 16 to 64, females aged 16 to 59.*
[3] *Includes study at home.*
[4] *Includes telephone conversations.*
[5] *Includes education, voluntary work and various other leisure activities.*
Source: *Social Trends 28, 1998, Office for National Statistics*

by a top club will be higher and more inelastic and so a higher price can be charged. Sport stadiums also provide different quality accommodation for customers. For example, a number of football clubs have executive boxes while company hospitality tents are found at cricket matches and rowing events. Firms and organisations running sporting events and clubs earn money not only from ticket sales but also from the merchandise which they sell. For some this is a major source of revenue.

THE EFFECTS OF A MAJOR SPORTS EVENT

Hosting a major sports event such as the World Athletics Championship, a Grand Prix or the Olympic Games, can bring advantages and disadvantages to an area. It can bring income into the area or country from visitors, some of whom may stay on after the event as tourists. It also publicises the area and can promote it as a place for tourists to visit, while special facilities built for the event can be used by the local population afterwards. However there are also potential costs. The event itself may be run at a loss and may incur environmental costs. For example, staging a Grand Prix is likely to cause road congestion nearby as people seek to attend the event and to generate a significant amount of noise.

THE HOUSING MARKET

This is a very significant market. A buoyant housing market is likely to stimulate economic activity. When house prices are rising and there is a high level of activity in the housing market people feel confident. Consumer spending (consumption) is likely to be high due to this confidence, to the rise in the value of people's main asset and to the fact that people tend to buy a range of consumer durables when they move home.

FORMS OF TENURE

In Western Europe there are three main forms of tenure:

- owner occupation
- private rented accommodation
- social rented housing, including council rented and housing associated dwellings.

Table 19.2 shows the tenure of dwellings in some of the EU countries. In the UK, owner occupation has increased significantly in recent years particularly after the Housing Act 1980 which gave local authority tenants the right to purchase their properties at discounted rates. The number of dwellings rented from housing associations has increased. There have been large scale transfers of tenancy agreements from the council sector to housing associations. Although the number of dwellings rented from the council sector by tenants has declined the council sector still dominates the rented sector.

DEMAND FOR OWNER OCCUPIED HOUSING

There are a number of factors which influence demand for owner occupied housing including the following.

- *Income.* Demand for houses is very income elastic. When incomes rise people tend to trade up in the housing market.

TABLE 19.2 TENURE OF DWELLINGS: EU COMPARISON, 1994

					Percentages
	Owned outright	Owned with mortgage	Rented from social sector[1]	Rented privately	All tenures (=100%) (millions)
Greece	69	8	5	18	3.7
Spain	62	17	8	13	12.0
Italy	57	13	14	15	20.4
Portugal	49	11	15	24	3.2
Irish Republic	42	38	13	6	1.1
Belgium	37	29	11	22	4.0
Luxembourg	34	32	7	28	0.2
France	29	25	21	23	22.8
United Kingdom	24	42	24	10	24.3
Germany	22	19	17	41	36.0
Netherlands	8	39	46	7	6.4
Denmark	7	45	27	20	2.5
EU average[2]	34	24	19	22	136.7

NOTES [1] Includes rent-free accommodation.
[2] Average of the 12 member states. Data are not available for Austria, Finland and Sweden.
Source: European Community Household Panel Survey, Eurostat

- *Population trends.* Increases in population size and a rise in single households will increase demand for houses.
- *The price and availability of substitutes.* Demand for houses will increase if the price of rented accommodation rises and/or it becomes more difficult to obtain.
- *The price of complements.* The main complement to a house is a mortgage. Most people cannot afford to buy a house out of their income and most, especially first time buyers, have to take out a mortgage (a loan on the purchase of a house) instead. The greater the ease of obtaining a mortgage and the lower the rate of interest the higher the demand for housing is likely to be.
- *Changes in the price of houses.* A house is sometimes seen as both a consumption and an investment good. A house provides the service of accommodation and, if it rises in price by more than the general rise in the price level, can provide a capital gain. However, as the late 1980s in the UK showed, house prices can also fall. When they do, some people can be caught in a negative equity trap — the value of their house becomes worth less than the mortgage which has been taken out on it. If this occurs it can be difficult or impossible for people to move as they cannot afford to sell their home.
- *Social attitudes.* In some countries such as Germany, renting from the private sector is a popular option whereas in the UK most people seek to own their own home.
- *Government policy.* Past UK governments have encouraged home ownership by selling off council houses and, until recently, providing tax rebates on mortgage interest payments.

THE SUPPLY OF OWNER OCCUPIED HOUSING

The stock of housing is the number of houses in existence. This tends to be added to slowly. The supply of owner occupied housing consists of those houses up for sale at a particular time. The supply is influenced by many factors including the following.

- *Price.* If the price of owner occupied housing is rising this will encourage a rise in the supply of housing in a number of ways. More people will be willing to put their house up for sale — anticipating a good price and a quick selling. Building firms will be encouraged to start new projects and landlords of rented accommodation may become tempted to sell their properties.
- *Planning permission.* The easier it is to gain planning permission the more houses are likely to be built.
- *Weather.* Housing projects can be held up by prolonged periods of bad weather.
- *Changes in the prices of the factors of production.* House building is a labour intensive industry so a rise in wages is likely to increase costs and reduce supply.
- *Government policy.* Subsidies to building companies or a reduction in taxes on companies would cause an increase in the supply of houses.

RENT CONTROLS

A government may impose limits on how much rent the private sector can charge. Its motive for doing this may be to help the poor. A home can be regarded as a merit good. Warm, uncrowded and secure accommodation helps promote good health, makes it easier for children to do their homework and, being able to give a settled address, helps adults when applying for a job.

However imposing rent controls may actually harm the poor. Figure 19.3 shows that imposing a rent of *P* which is below the equilibrium rent causes a contraction in supply and a shortage of rented accommodation. Not only may some landlords pull out of the market — selling off their property for owner occupation but those who stay in the market may seek to operate a black market or to cut back on, e.g., the maintenance of their property.

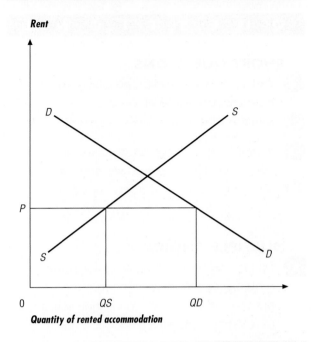

FIG. 19.3

QUESTIONS

SHORT QUESTIONS

1 Explain how production possibility curves can illustrate productive efficiency.

2 What is meant by market structure?

3 In which type of market structure do consumers have most power and why?

4 Why might a local authority subsidise a sports centre?

MULTIPLE CHOICE

1 Figure 19.4 shows the market for private rented accommodation. The free market price was *P*. The government then sets a rent of *R*. What is the effect?

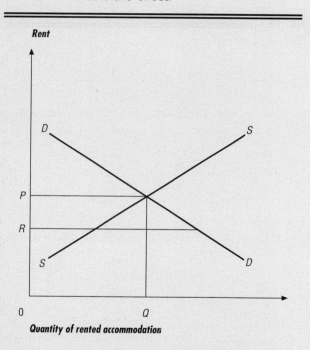

Rent

Quantity of rented accommodation

FIG. 19.4

A An over supply of rented accommodation.

B An extension in the supply of rented accommodation.

C A reduction in the number of rooms available to rent.

D A contraction in demand for rented accommodation.

2 In which market structure do individual firms have no power to influence price?

A Perfect competition.

B Monopolistic competition.

C Oligopoly.

D Monopoly.

3 Which of the following leisure activities has negative income elasticity of demand?

A Driving for pleasure.

B Eating out.

C Playing bingo.

D Visiting a museum.

4 Figure 19.5 shows the market for a tennis tournament held in a stadium with a fixed seating capacity of 5000. It is anticipated that demand will be represented by curve *DD*. Price is fixed at *P*. What will be the effect if demand is actually reflected by curve D^1D^1?

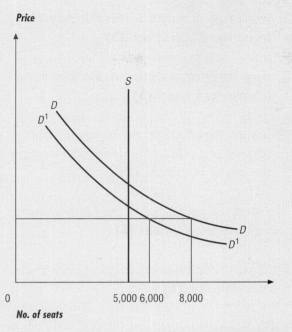

Price

No. of seats

FIG. 19.5

A Supply will contract.

B Market equilibrium will be restored.

C The shortage of seats will fall to 1000.

D A surplus of 3000 seats will develop.

DATA RESPONSE

You know the club, but are you ready for the Manchester United lifestyle? There you sit in your Man Utd sweater, watching the Man Utd-dedicated cable TV channel, perhaps dialling the Internet on your Manufree.net connection. The baby gurgles happily in its Man Utd babygro, while you sip tea from Man Utd mugs. Upstairs, the kids are curled up beneath duvet covers adorned with the face of star striker Ryan Giggs. But don't think you are anything special — a fellow fan will be doing the same in China, if the club's business strategists have their way.

When Manchester United kicks off the new domestic football season in Sunday's Charity Shield against Arsenal at Wembley, to an uneducated eye the team may just look like 11 grown men on a pitch. But the match will once again focus attention on the club that has turned itself into one of the most marketable commodities in sport. The Man Utd brand has become a moneymaking

machine in red shirts and Adidas boots, a wannabe global megabrand. With international expansion now a major part of the game plan, its business horizons extend far beyond the gates of Old Trafford.

Crucial to United's financial success — which has seen sales double in five years and profits before transfer fees almost treble — has been its expansion on several fronts. Only £30m of United's £87m turnover last year came from the traditional area of gate receipts and programme sales. Revenue from TV rights soared by a third to £16m and merchandise sales topped £24m.

On the pitch, the Old Trafford stadium is being expanded to take 65 000, an increase of 10 000 and the Theatre of Dreams museum and Red Café are being constantly upgraded. Off the pitch the launch of Manchester United International two years ago is a key plank in taking the United brand worldwide.

United has signed franchise deals to open United shops and Red Cafés in places such as Singapore and Dubai.

The club's recent tour of East Asia was designed to boost local interest in the club and lay the foundations for taking United to the Chinese masses. The club has already said it will tour the Far East once every two years to maintain support.

That is a bold aim. The size of the Chinese market is certainly a mouth-watering prospect for the Old Trafford accountants. With a population of 1.2 billion and a booming interest in football it is a market ripe for exploitation. But critics say United will struggle against the persistent problem of branded goods counterfeiting in Asia. Others say interest in football may be transient and most Chinese people do not have the money to buy replica kits at £30-plus.

Source: 'United all over the world' by Nigel Cope, the Independent, 28/7/99.

a] What type of products does the Man Utd brand name help to sell? **(3)**

b] How significant are merchandise sales for Manchester United? **(3)**

c] Discuss the effects on the company's costs, revenue and profit of its decision to increase the size of its stadium. **(7)**

d] Assess the significance of the Chinese market for Manchester United. **(6)**

e] Discuss what could cause Manchester United's revenue to fall. **(6)**

CASE STUDY

It has all the echoes of the mid-Eighties, with house prices in some parts of the country more than doubling in a little over three years.

But while property values are generally rising faster than for a decade, experts insist that this time there is no sign that boom will be followed by bust.

The slump of the late Eighties and early Nineties left tens of thousands of families in negative equity — having a bigger mortgage than their home was worth. The nature of the market and general economic conditions are very different now, experts say.

Adrian Cooper, managing director of Oxford Economic Forecasting said: 'The conditions are coming into place for potentially a really rather strong housing market boom. There are two important ingredients in that we have seen interest rates fall sharply while the economic downturn during the winter did not produce a rise in unemployment. So people are confident to buy.'

A report from financial adviser Ernst & Young's ITEM Club is similarly upbeat, predicting an 8% national average rise next year as well.

However, closer analysis of the latest figures confirms what many people suspect — the trend conceals 'hot spots' where prices are rising even faster, and 'cold spots' where prices are actually falling.

The surge in prices has been fuelled by low cost of borrowing and availability of mortgages.

This has been underpinned, in the South particularly, by increased job security and a stable economy. But the collapse of traditional industries and an exodus of young people have hit prices in the North.

The location of good schools — now readily identifiable since the publication of exam league tables — also appears to be having a major impact on property values, so in some cases the 'hot spots' and 'cold spots' may be in neighbouring districts.

Source: 'House prices: is this the 80s again?' by Sean Poulter, Daily Mail, 4/8/99.

a] Explain what is meant by a housing bust. **(6)**

b] What is negative equity? **(2)**

c] What effect would negative equity have on labour mobility? **(5)**

d] Explain the connection between mortgage loans and house prices. **(6)**

e] Why were house prices rising in 1999? **(7)**

f] Discuss the differences in house price movements in different regions of the UK. **(6)**

g] What effect would a doubling in house prices be likely to have on the demand for and supply of rented accommodation? **(8)**

h] Discuss the factors which influence the supply of housing. **(10)**

STRUCTURED ESSAY

a] Explain the factors which influence demand for housing. **(12)**

b] Discuss the effect of a housing boom on the economy. **(13)**

20 COSTS AND BENEFITS

Market failure occurs when the free market forces of demand and supply fail to produce the quantities of goods and services people want at prices which reflect their marginal utilities. One cause of market failure is the difference which can occur between private costs and benefits and social costs and benefits.

PRIVATE COSTS

Private costs (which can also be called internal costs) are the costs incurred by those who buy products and by those who produce products. For example, if a person buys a bottle of whisky the cost (in the form of the price charged) may be £20, and if a firm produces a car the cost (in terms of wages, parts, overheads etc.) may be £15 000.

PRIVATE BENEFITS

Private benefits (which can also be called internal benefits) are the benefits received by those who buy products and by those who produce products. So continuing the examples given above the private benefit from buying a bottle of whisky is the enjoyment received from drinking the whisky as reflected in the marginal utility gained. The private benefit to the car company of selling the car is the revenue it receives.

EXTERNALITIES

Private costs and benefits go through the market mechanism and have a price attached to them. Whereas externalities (which can also be called *spill-over effects*) do not go through the price mechanism and so do not have a price attached to them. An externality is a cost or benefit to third parties, i.e. to those not directly involved in the production or consumption of the product. As discussed below, externalities are the differences between social costs and benefits and private costs and benefits.

NEGATIVE EXTERNALITIES

Negative externalities (which can also be called external costs) are the costs imposed on third parties of the economic activity of others. For instance, if someone buys and drinks a bottle of whisky over a short time span, this may have a number of adverse effects on others. They could become drunk and cause a nuisance in a public place. They could also make mistakes at work or become ill, thereby placing a burden on the health service.

As well as consumption having the potential to impose costs on third parties so can production. The production of cars may, for instance, cause noise, air and visual pollution in the area where the factory is located.

POSITIVE EXTERNALITIES

There can also be benefits to third parties (which can be called either positive externalities or external benefits) from the consumption and production of others. Drinking some whisky may actually make someone more sociable, and friends and colleagues can benefit from the person's more cheerful manner. If someone spends more time and money on their front garden, neighbours may take pleasure in this without paying anything for the enjoyment they derive. Similarly, if a firm spends money on training staff who leave on completion of the training, it is rival firms which gain the benefit and which are unlikely to compensate the firm which undertook the training.

Production can also lead to positive externalities. The production of cars in an area, through creating employment, will benefit the shops, places of entertainment, etc., in which the car workers spend their money; whereas the provision of rail services will reduce congestion, accidents and pollution on roads.

SOCIAL COST

Social cost is the total cost to society of an economic activity. It is the full opportunity cost, i.e. what the individual consumers and producers forgo (in terms of the price paid or expenditure on factors of production) plus what third parties forgo (e.g., clean air, safety). To summarise, social cost is private costs plus negative externalities (external costs).

It is often the case that the costs to society as a whole are greater than the costs to the individuals who buy and produce goods and services. Indeed social cost will equal private costs only when there are no negative externalities.

An example often used to illustrate social cost is smoking. The social cost of people smoking is the price they pay for the cigarettes (private cost) plus the passive smoking and the air pollution they cause and the burden they impose on the health service (negative externalities).

Figure 20.1 shows negative externalities (external costs) arising in (a) the production of a product and (b) the consumption of a product.

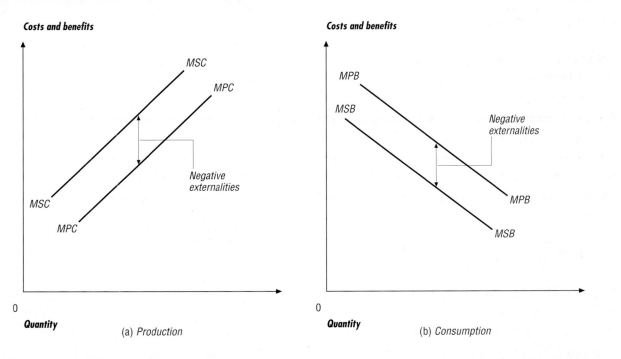

FIG. 20.1

SOCIAL BENEFIT

Social benefit is the total benefit to society from an economic activity. It consists of private benefits plus positive externalities (external benefits). Social benefit will equal private benefit only if there are no positive externalities. However, where the benefit to society as a whole from the consumption or production of a good or service is greater than the benefits to the individual consumers or producers, there are positive externalities. This is illustrated in Figure 20.2 showing positive externalities (external benefits) arising in (a) the production of a product and (b) the consumption of a product.

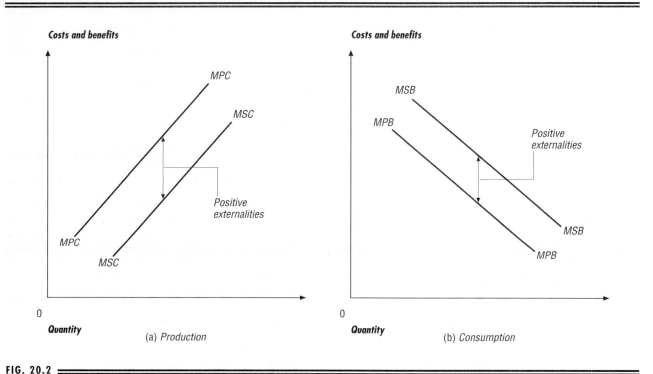

FIG. 20.2

Education is often used to illustrate how social benefit can exceed private benefits. People undertaking education receive consumption and investment benefits. Most will enjoy the education and it may stimulate lifetime interests (consumption benefit) and will increase their future earning power (investment benefit). In addition to these private benefits, third parties will gain from having a more educated, inventive labour force and a more informed population (positive externalities).

SOCIALLY EFFICIENT (OPTIMUM) OUTPUT

Profit maximising firms will produce where marginal private cost (MPC) equals marginal private revenue or benefit (MPB). However the socially efficient (optimum) output (which can also be called the allocatively efficient output) is achieved where the marginal social cost (MSC) equals the marginal social benefit (MSB) as shown in Figure 20.3.

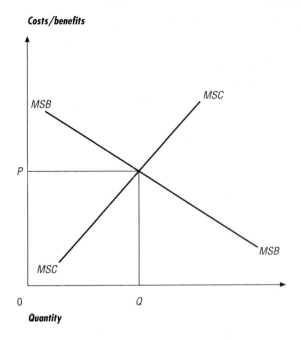

FIG. 20.3

Where marginal social cost equals marginal social benefit the value the consumers place on the last unit produced will be equal to the full cost of producing that last unit. Pareto optimality is achieved when MSC equals MSB in all industries. In this situation it is not possible to make one person better off without making someone else worse off.

WELFARE LOSS

If output is undertaken where MSC exceeds MSB there will be a socially inefficient allocation of resources and hence a welfare loss. This is shown in Figure 20.4. Welfare loss arises because the value that consumers place on the extra unit of the output at Q is less than the marginal social cost (i.e. what a society has to forgo as a result of producing that unit). Output is too high and a reduction in output to QX would increase the welfare of consumers.

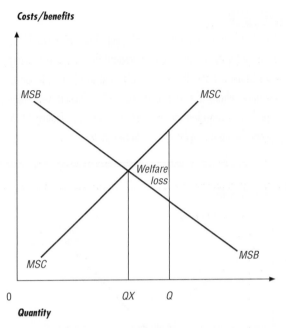

FIG. 20.4

A welfare loss will also arise if MSB exceeds MSC. Figure 20.5 shows the welfare loss which will result if output is at Q. In this case consumers value the product more than the marginal social cost of producing the product at Q. The product is under produced and society would benefit from an increase in output to QX.

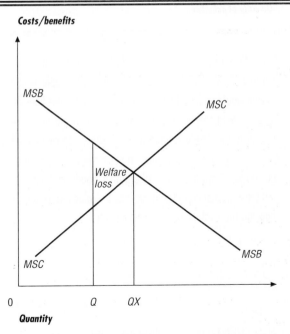

FIG. 20.5

EXAMPLE

People often think that the ideal level of pollution would be zero. But they fail to take into account the cost of achieving that Utopian state. The socially efficient level of pollution is actually where the marginal cost of pollution reduction equals the marginal social cost of pollution. Figure 20.6 shows the optimum level of pollution is Q.

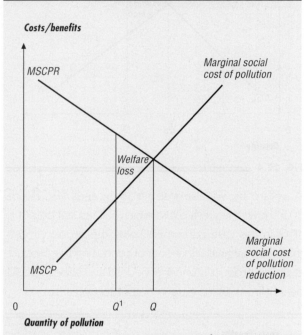

Costs/benefits

MSCPR

Marginal social cost of pollution

Welfare loss

MSCP

Marginal social cost of pollution reduction

0   Q^1 Q

Quantity of pollution

FIG. 20.6

The welfare of the community would be reduced by lowering pollution to Q^1. This is because the benefit people would receive would be less than the cost of achieving that benefit. People would receive more benefit if the resources were used in alternative occupations. For instance, to remove all litter from a town centre might require the employment of one hundred workers. The alternative goods and services that these workers could produce may be valued more highly than the removal of all crisp packets, etc.

COST BENEFIT ANALYSIS

Cost benefit analysis is a method of assessing investment projects by considering their social costs in relation to the social benefits they bring. It is usually applied to those projects where it is expected there will be a significant difference between private and social costs and benefits. The project will usually go ahead if the social benefits exceed the social costs.

Cost benefit analysis ensures that policy makers consider the effect of their actions on the wider community but there are a number of difficulties involved in the process. The private costs involved can be identified relatively easily. For instance, in the case of a city overhead railway the private cost of construction would include the cost of labour involved, materials used, land purchased for stations, etc. Private benefit could also be calculated as it will be the fares received. Negative and positive externalities (external costs and benefits) are not so easy to measure since by definition they do not have a price attached to them.

The possible negative externalities arising from an overhead railway may include visual pollution, congestion near the stations and some noise pollution. The positive externalities are likely to be greater and may include less pollution, less overall road congestion, fewer road accidents (thereby reducing the burden on police, health services, etc.), and savings in travel time.

Economists often use 'shadow prices' to estimate these. Shadow prices are imputed prices based on opportunity cost. For example, to estimate the value to passengers of the time they save by using the railway it would be necessary to measure the national average hourly wage rates. An additional problem is that the costs and particularly the benefits occur over a period of time. This means that the costs and benefits have to be discounted to present values. For instance £100 earned in three years is worth less than £100 earned now since the £100 received now can be e.g. placed in a time deposit and earn interest. So the £100 to be received in three years time will have to be adjusted downwards.

QUESTIONS

SHORT QUESTIONS

1 When will the private cost of producing a product equal the social cost of production?

2 What is the socially optimum output?

3 What are the social costs associated with people smoking?

4 What are the external benefits of education?

MULTIPLE CHOICE

1 Which of the following is a private, as opposed to external, cost of building a new car manufacturing factory?

A Visual pollution.

B Purchase of the land on which the factory is built.

C Increased traffic congestion in the vicinity of the factory.

D Damage to the natural environment of the land on which the factory is built.

2 What type of costs and benefits are considered in a cost benefit analysis?

A Financial.

B Private.

C External.

D Social.

3 In Figure 20.7, if a firm decides to produce an output of Q which area represents the welfare loss?

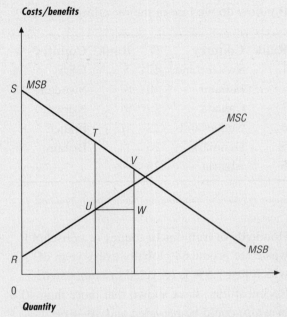

Costs/benefits

Quantity

FIG. 20.7

A RSV

B UTV

C UVW

D ORVX

4 Pareto optimality is achieved where:

A private costs equal private benefits

B external benefits exceed external costs

C marginal social benefits exceed marginal social costs

D marginal social benefits equal marginal social costs.

DATA RESPONSE

British households are being encouraged to recycle waste as part of a government environmental campaign launched this week. But how do we fare in the recycling league?

Rank	Country	%	Rank	Country	%
1	Switzerland	42	7	USA	24
2	Finland	30	8	Sweden	18
3	Canada	29	9	Norway	14
4	Netherlands	28	10	France	8
5	Denmark	26	11	Britain	5
6	Austria	25			

Source: Friends of the Earth Recycling Network Report, June 1998.

Hundreds of millions of tonnes of household waste are produced globally every year, of which just 7.5% is recycled or composted. Recent studies have shown that more than 40% of waste could be recycled and 30–40% composted.

In the past 25 years, there has been a growing awareness of the need to conserve resources and of the environmental damage caused by incineration and waste dumping, particularly in northern Europe and north America. This partly explains why recycling levels have increased dramatically in these regions.

High targets for the amount of household waste recycled, especially paper and glass have been set in Canada, Switzerland and parts of Scandinavia. Governments in these countries have installed structures making it easy for people to recycle waste, such as regular door to door collections, and are involved in ensuring there is a market for recycled materials.

Britain lags behind most developed nations in increasing its recycling levels. In 1990 a government target was set to increase the proportion of recycled waste from 4% to 25% by the year 2000 — the current figure stands at 5%. The proportion is about the same in Japan and Belgium, which last year recycled just 3%.

Source: 'Who recycles the most waste?' by Divya Kohli, the Guardian, 20/5/99.

a] How did Britain's recycling record compare with:
  i Finland **(2)**
  ii Japan? **(2)**

b] Discuss the external benefits of recycling. **(5)**

c] Explain why government intervention is needed to achieve the optimum level of recycling waste. **(4)**

d] Explain three measures a government could take to encourage households and firms to recycle waste materials. **(6**)

e] Discuss how a CBA could be carried out on a local authority's recycling scheme. **(6)**

CASE STUDY

Factories are polluting rivers with tonnes of chemicals that can change the sex of fish, according to official data.

The chemicals, known as alkylphenols, could be banned within five years as parts of efforts by European governments to move to a 'pristine environment'. But at present the top discharge sites in Britain are pouring more than 18 tonnes of the chemicals into rivers such as the Tees, Humber and Aire every year.

Almost half of that comes from a single site, ICI Chemicals factory in Wilton, Cleveland, which last year discharged 8.1 tonnes into the Tees estuary, as measured by the Environment Agency.

Alkylphenols are toxic, killing larve and shrimps at concentrations as low as 10 millionths of a gram per litre. They also mimic the female hormone oestrogen, disrupting the development of young male fish.

Studies in Canada have found that wild roach and Atlantic salmon are particularly affected by the chemicals, a by-product from the manufacture of industrial-strength detergents. Other fish affected include rainbow trout, shrimp and flounder.

Geoff Brighty, the environmental toxicology manager of the Environment Agency, said: 'There is experimental data to show that the alkylphenols and derivatives can partly sex-reverse fish: young male fish will grow up to be "intersex" and that applies to any fish. They also make male fish produce an egg protein that only female fish should make. However, we are actually more concerned about the toxic effects, which affect invertebrates like fly larvae at concentrations where the oestrogen-like effects are only beginning to be seen.'

The knock-on effects further up the food chain could lead to larger animals starving or being forced to move for nutrition.

Source: 'Named: the factories that pollute rivers' by Charles Arthur, the Independent 22/6/99.

a] What external costs are created by firms discharging chemicals into rivers? **(6)**

b] Why do firms pollute rivers? **(5)**

c] What shape of long-run average cost curves are chemical companies likely to have? **(5)**

d] What effect would a ban on firms discharging chemicals into rivers have on:
 i private costs **(3)**
 ii external costs **(3)**
 iii social costs of production? **(4)**

e] The article discusses water pollution. Identify two other main forms of pollution. **(4)**

f] Explain what effect publicity about a firm creating pollution would be likely to have on:
 i demand for its products **(2)**
 ii profit levels. **(2)**

g] Discuss whether a 'pristine environment' would be one in which there is no pollution. **(10)**

h] What external benefits may be created by chemical companies? **(6)**

STRUCTURED ESSAY

a] Explain and give examples of:
 i private and external costs **(6)**
 ii private and external benefits. **(6)**

b] Explain why the optimum level of pollution is unlikely to be zero. **(13)**

21 CAUSES OF MARKET FAILURE

As already noted, a market system would achieve allocative efficiency if it were to produce the products people want, in the quantities they desire and at prices which reflect their marginal utilities.

In a market system the price mechanism is used to transmit information from consumers to producers. If consumers demand more of a product, the price will rise and in the short run supply will extend. In the long run supply will increase as new firms, seeing higher profits being made from producing the product, move into the industry. In theory resources should move towards making those products which are increasing in demand.

For this to occur a number of conditions have to be met. Producers must be willing and able to respond to changes in demand, there must be no barriers to entry and exit, perfect mobility of factors of production and costs and prices must reflect social costs and benefits.

EXTERNALITIES

As discussed in Chapter 20 market failure will occur when marginal social cost and marginal social benefit are not equal. As externalities in production and consumption often exist and output is usually based on private costs and benefits, this is a significant cause of market failure.

For example car use creates a number of negative externalities including air and noise pollution, accidents, congestion and damage to the road network.

PUBLIC GOODS

Public (also called *collective*) goods are characterised by two important features, (a) non-rivalry in consumption and (b) non-excludability.

The first feature means that consumption by one person does not in any way reduce the consumption by another individual. The second feature (*non-excludability*) refers to the fact that consumption of a public good cannot be confined to those who have paid for it so there can be free riders. People can enjoy the product without paying for it.

Non-rivalry and non-excludability are the two key characteristics of public goods although there are a few other characteristics which most public goods share. They often have large external benefits relative to private benefits. Once provided, the marginal cost of supplying one more individual is zero. They may also be *non-rejectable*. This means that individuals may not be able to abstain from consuming them even if they want to.

Examples of public goods include national defence, the police service, lighthouses, flood-control schemes, street lighting, pavements and public drainage. Public goods will not be provided by the price mechanism because producers cannot withhold the goods for non-payment and, since there is no way of measuring how much a person consumes, there is no basis for establishing a market price.

As a result, the state must finance the provision of public goods by means of taxation (and sometimes borrowing). Some public goods such as the provision of defence by central government and street lighting by local authorities are provided directly by the state. Others, such as flood control, are provided by giving contracts to private sector firms.

Most goods and services are private goods. They have rivalry in consumption and excludability. This means that if one person consumes a piece of cake it prevents someone else consuming it, and that the enjoyment of the good can be made dependent on direct payment to the producer.

Some economists now identify a third category, *mixed goods*. These lie in between public and private goods, having some of the characteristics of both. The most widely quoted example is roads. Some economists claim that many miles of road are non-rival. However, with advances in technology, it is becoming increasingly possible to exclude non-payers.

MERIT GOODS

The state is concerned to increase the consumption of certain goods which it considers to be highly desirable for the welfare of the citizens. Such goods are described as *merit goods*. They are a special form of private goods. The best known examples are state health and education systems. Other examples include training, insurance, inoculation and seat belts.

In a pure market system, consumer spending on merit goods would be determined by the private benefits derived from them. Merit goods have positive externalities so that the social benefits derived from their consumption exceed the private benefits. In some cases, e.g. seat belts, consumers may fail to recognise their true private benefits.

Most economists argue that state intervention is necessary in the case of merit goods to ensure a greater provision of these products than would be supplied under the operation of the price mechanism in free markets.

To increase the provision of merit goods a number of measures can be used. They can be provided free by the state as occurs in the UK with state education and the National Health Service (NHS). Training can be encouraged by giving training vouchers to consumers while contracts for services such as refuse collection can be given to private-sector firms. The state can also encourage the consumption of merit goods by providing information about, for example, the benefits of inoculation and passing legislation requiring cars to take and pass MOT tests.

A few economists claim that merit goods do not exist because individuals are the best judges of what to consume and that the government is taking an over-paternalistic approach in promoting the consumption of these goods.

DEMERIT GOODS

Demerit goods include cigarettes, alcohol and non-prescribed drugs. These are over-consumed in a market system. Consumers may be unaware of the true cost of consuming them which includes negative externalities. In this case the government can ban their consumption or reduce it by taxation and by providing information about their harmful effects.

IMPERFECT COMPETITION

In practice power often lies to a greater extent with producers than with consumers. Most firms operate under conditions of imperfect competition with monopolists and oligopolists, as previously noted, able to restrict output, raise prices and produce where price exceeds marginal cost. They can also prevent new firms from entering the industry, thereby preventing full adjustment to changes in consumer demand occurring.

Advertising can be used to provide information to consumers but it can also be employed to promote producer sovereignty. Firms can encourage people to buy the products they want to sell by persuasive advertising. Firms will also delay the introduction of improved products and new products if it is in their financial interest to do so. For instance, firms had the technology to produce long-life light bulbs for some time before they went on the market. It is also debatable whether a cure for the common cold would find its way onto the market easily, as pharmaceutical companies currently earn a considerable amount from selling e.g. cough remedies and throat lozenges.

LACK OF INFORMATION

If consumers are to maximise their utility they need to have full information about the products they wish to buy and the producers selling them. Whilst advances in technology are increasing the amount of information to which people have access, they obviously do not have perfect information. As a result they may buy less of a product than they should if they are to maximise their welfare. They may also be operating on the basis of incorrect information, believing for example that a certain cream cures acne. This mistake may arise from a misunderstanding or from incorrect information provided by the producer.

Workers may also be unaware of job opportunities outside their current employment and may not fully appreciate all the advantages and disadvantages, including the health risks, of the jobs they currently have.

Entrepreneurs may also lack information about the costs, availability and productivity of factors of production and may be operating on the basis of incorrect information about the reliability and life span of the machines they use.

IMMOBILITY OF FACTORS OF PRODUCTION

Factors of production, particularly labour, can experience difficulty in moving occupationally and geographically to meet changes in consumer demand. This means that supply may adjust slowly and inadequately. During periods of high demand UK firms often experience problems in increasing their output because they cannot attract a sufficient number of skilled workers. Unskilled workers may be available but may not be able, willing, or have the time to gain the necessary skills. With greater technological change there is an increasing need for workers to be flexible, to be willing to update their skills throughout their working life, change employers, occupations and work patterns.

SHORT TERMISM

Private sector entrepreneurs are often criticised for pursuing short-term objectives at the expense of long-term planning. Short termism can result in the over production of consumer goods, the under production of capital goods and a failure to develop new methods of production and new products.

IMPERFECT DISTRIBUTION OF INCOME AND WEALTH

The market economy provides opportunities for people to earn an income and acquire wealth. But the opportunities for earning an income are not equally distributed. People do not have equal opportunities in education. Some are also limited in their capacity to learn or they may have acquired a skill only to find the demand for that skill is declining. Discrimination distorts earnings and can result in women, people from ethnic minorities and the disabled earning less for the same work as able-bodied, white male employees. In addition people are subject to illness and incapacity. The market system does not guarantee that everyone will have the same opportunity to accumulate wealth and once an inequality in the distribution of wealth arises it tends to be self-perpetuating because wealth can be inherited.

QUESTIONS

SHORT QUESTIONS

1. Explain what is meant by market failure.

2. What are the characteristics of a private good?

3. Explain why education is a merit and not a public good.

4. What is short termism and what problems can it cause?

MULTIPLE CHOICE

1 What is a demerit good? A good

A. that is both non-rival and non-excludable

B. where the average revenue obtained from selling it is exceeded by the average costs of production

C. where the private costs of consuming the good exceed its social costs

D. that the government believes consumers will buy too much of if it is provided by the private sector at market prices.

2 Which of the following is a public good?

A. Health care.

B. Public libraries.

C. Seat belts.

D. Street lighting.

3 What is the economic argument for charging higher prices for the use of congested than uncongested roads?

A. The demand for the use of congested roads is more elastic than demand for the use of uncongested roads.

B. The use of uncongested roads does not create any negative externalities.

C. The marginal social cost of using congested roads is greater than that of uncongested roads.

D. The supply of congested roads is more responsive to price changes than the supply of uncongested roads.

4 A public good is one which is supplied:

A. by the state

B. by public limited companies

C. to all taxpayers

D. to all consumers.

DATA RESPONSE

Public transport is the flavour of the moment as buses, trains and even trams are given a new priority but Tower Hamlets is going one better with the introduction of bicycle rickshaws to London's East End.

Next month the London borough will be introducing a fleet of trishaws (three-wheeled rickshaws) in an attempt to reduce motorised traffic by a third, and encourage visitors to the deprived inner-city area.

'We're home to the Tower of London, which attracts thousands of visitors a year. But once they've been there, they leave the borough,' says Andrew Bramidge, director of Cityside Regeneration, which is funding the six-month pilot project. 'We wanted to find a way of attracting people to other parts of Tower Hamlets, such as the regenerated Spitalfields market, and the Bangladeshi restaurants in Brick Lane, without increasing the amount of traffic.'

Riders and maintenance staff will be recruited locally and trained and Bramidge hopes that the scheme will develop into a full community taxi service for local schools, day centres, offices and restaurants. Additional funding will be sought through sponsorship and advertising by local and nearby city companies, whose support will be vital in ensuring the project's long term sustainability.

Although councils have new responsibilities and incentives to promote green transport — the Road Traffic Act of 1997 obliges councils to propose by July their transport plans for the next five years, on which future funding will depend — some operators proposing emissions-free options are facing barriers which could affect the viability of future schemes. Successful projects are running throughout the West, in places such as America, Canada, France, Holland and Ireland, but Britain is the only place, according to Steinhauer, where plans can be blocked at a local level.

Source: 'Car trouble' by Sue Flook, the Guardian, 21/5/99.

a] What positive externalities may be provided by rickshaws? **(7)**

b] Explain whether rickshaws are a private, merit, demerit or public good. **(5)**

c] How can the provision of a rickshaw service be financed? **(4)**

d] What is meant by green transport? **(3)**

e] Discuss three other forms of transport which would reduce emissions.

CASE STUDY

The biggest adjustment anyone from the private sector has to make when confronted with the National Health Service is to understand how different the economics of the NHS are compared with those of normal business life. At its most basic it means that a service that is free at the point of delivery defies the economic logic that drives virtually all commercial organisations.

This was explained to me in very blunt terms early on in my wanderings around the NHS by one doctor who asked me what I was hoping to achieve with the report I was producing. I told him the hope was to come up with some recommendations which, if implemented, would improve the experience for the patient. 'Why do you want to do that?' he replied. 'If you improve the experience we just get more patients, and we can't cope with any more.'

This doctor was not being entirely serious, but his point was an important one. Most commercial organisations have an economic incentive to improve the speed and efficiency of the service they deliver to their customers. But often in the health service the opposite applies. This doesn't mean that people working in the NHS do not strive to improve the quality of the service they deliver — they do all the time — but at times they are doing it despite the economic effects, not because of them. Improving the quality and efficiency of the service in most market based organisations usually leads to an increase in revenue which more than pays for the cost of introducing the changes. Even when they do not, the organisation has little choice if its competitors are striving to make themselves more efficient.

I found the same economic conundrum when looking at another major issue within the NHS: the failure of different parts of the organisation to exchange information about best practice and to learn from each other. Commercial organisations have an economic incentive to introduce best practice; if they do not and their competitors do, it makes them less competitive and potentially uneconomic. This is not true of the NHS, where the failure of different parts of the organisation to share best practice is legendary.

Source: 'Centre for best practice could straighten twisted economics' by Greg Dyke, The Times, 16/2/99.

a] Explain whether health care is a private, merit or public good. **(5)**

b] Is health care a free good? Explain your answer. **(6)**

c] Does the quote from the doctor suggest that the market for health care is in equilibrium? Again explain your answer. **(6)**

d] Compare the effects of an improvement in the quality of product provided by the NHS and that provided by a private health care company. **(7)**

e] Explain two meanings of the word 'efficiency'. **(8)**

f] What is likely to happen to private sector firms which are not efficient? **(5)**

g] In which market structure is information about best practice likely to be most freely available? **(4)**

h] Discuss the private and external benefits of health care. **(9)**

STRUCTURED ESSAY

a] Explain why market forces would generate the socially optimum output of merit, demerit and public goods. **(12)**

b] Discuss the other main causes of market failure. **(13)**

22 LABOUR MARKET FAILURE

THE NATURE OF MARKET FAILURE

In a perfect labour market all employers and all employees would be price takers, there would be perfect mobility of labour, no discrimination and perfect knowledge about job vacancies, wage rates and working conditions. Wage rates would adjust quickly and smoothly to reflect changes in demand and supply. Labour markets would clear, ensuring no shortages and no surpluses of labour — there would be full employment. These conditions obviously do not hold. In the real world labour markets often do not work in a perfect way — they fail to ensure, for example, that all workers are in jobs that they are most suited to, that shortages of skilled workers do not occur and that workers move easily from jobs in low demand to jobs in high demand.

The causes of labour market failure include immobility of labour, lack of information, discrimination, monopolies and monopsonies, attachment between workers and employers, and training.

IMMOBILITY OF LABOUR

There are two main types of immobility of labour: geographical and occupational.

GEOGRAPHICAL IMMOBILITY OF LABOUR

This occurs when workers find it difficult to move from one area to another in search of employment or better paid employment. There are various barriers to geographical mobility including the following.

- *Monetary cost.* Moving is expensive. In addition to the removal costs it can be expensive to sell and buy a house. The price of housing also varies from region to region and is usually higher in the high employment areas.
- *Availability of housing.* Workers may want to move but they may either not be able to find anyone to buy their property or may not be able to find suitable owner-occupier or rented accommodation in another area.
- *Social ties.* Some people may be reluctant to leave family and friends behind. It may be the case that one member of a couple is offered a job in another part of the country but turns it down because his or her partner has a well paid job that she or he is not prepared to leave.
- *Education.* Families may be immobile at certain stages of their children's education, for example, when their children are coming up to important examinations. They may also be concerned about differences in the standard and system of education in different parts of the country. The Scottish and English systems are not the same.

OCCUPATIONAL IMMOBILITY OF LABOUR

This occurs when workers find it difficult to move from one occupation to another. Again there are a number of causes, including the following.

- *Education and training.* The need for qualifications and training act as barriers to entry into and exit from a number of occupations. In this way they reduce the number of people who can enter particular labour markets and reduce competition in them. If the qualifications and period of training required for an occupation are appropriate for the tasks involved it can be claimed that the limitation in competition is justifiable in terms of ensuring quality. However, in some cases the level of qualifications and/or period of training required may be set artificially high in order to raise the wage rate.

- *Financial capital.* A certain amount of capital is required in order to enter some occupations. For example, in order to become established in a small business, as e.g., a hairdresser or builder, money is needed to purchase the necessary stock and equipment. To become an estate agent or solicitor it may be necessary to purchase a practice or partnership. These requirements will constitute a financial barrier to many prospective entrants.
- *Class.* Class may also restrict the occupational mobility of labour. In the UK some people believe that a particular type of social background with an education at one of the top public schools provides advantages in certain fields of employment.

LACK OF INFORMATION

Workers and employers may lack information about the labour markets in which they operate. Most workers are unaware of all the available vacancies. They are unlikely to know about the promotion chances, wage rates and working conditions in all the jobs they are capable of undertaking. This means they may stay in less well paid jobs. Employers may also be unaware of the wage rates being paid by rival firms and the number of people willing and able to undertake jobs in their companies.

Workers seeking jobs and employers seeking workers will incur search costs. Workers have to spend time, effort and money applying for jobs and employers may have to advertise jobs, produce shortlists and interview applicants. In seeking to cut down on these search costs, workers may not find the jobs to which they are most suited and employers may not find the most skilled employees.

DISCRIMINATION

Discrimination in labour markets occurs when a group of workers receives a different wage and/or is given different chances of employment and promotion from another group of workers performing the same jobs. Discrimination may be on the basis of gender, age, ethnic or social background and a number of other grounds such as height.

The effects of discrimination are shown in Figure 22.1 which shows that the demand for women workers is below their marginal revenue product (return from employing labour = marginal revenue × marginal product). This results in their wage (W) and the number being employed (Q) being lower than in a perfect market (WX and QX).

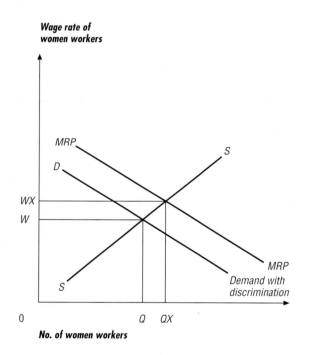

Wage rate of women workers

No. of women workers

FIG. 22.1

Discrimination in one labour market will have a knock-on effect on other labour markets. If women are discriminated against in one industry, their supply to industries which do not discriminate will increase. The effect of this higher supply will be to lower the wage rate they receive in these other industries. This is shown in Figure 22.2.

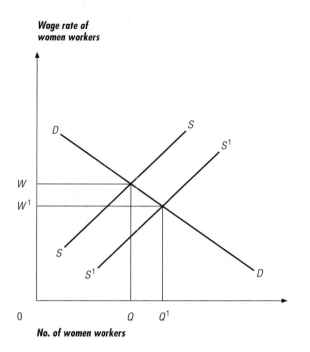

Wage rate of women workers

No. of women workers

FIG. 22.2

Discrimination by consumers may actually lower the return to employers from employing a particular group in comparison to other groups and thereby lower their wage rate. For instance, people prefer watching male track and field athletes and so the price which can be charged for events featuring male athletes is higher than that for all female meetings. So male athletes, on average, command higher appearance fees than female athletes.

Discrimination can also work the other way. For example many people appear to believe that food in Chinese restaurants served by waiters and waitresses of Chinese descent is better than that served by people from different ethnic groups. So Chinese people find it easy to obtain employment in such restaurants as waiters and waitresses. However as consumers are unaware of the ethnic background of the chefs this does not apply to their employment opportunities.

MONOPOLY TRADE UNIONS

Trade unions, by pushing the wage rate above the equilibrium level, may reduce employment. In Figure 22.3, the free market wage is W and at this wage the firm employs Q workers.

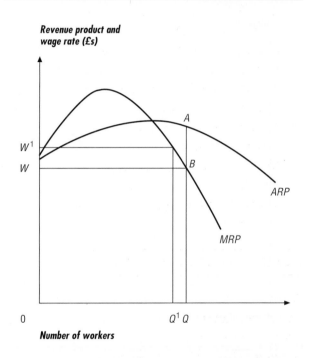

Revenue product and wage rate (£s)

Number of workers

FIG. 22.3

A union is formed and negotiates a wage of W^1 which it has the power to enforce on all firms in the industry. The effect of the union action may be to reduce employment to Q^1. However, unions have some power to control the supply of labour and may react to any reduction of employment by threatening strike action. The line AB shows the scope for bargaining between employer and union. AB represents the surplus earned on each worker employed when the wage rate is W and the numbers of workers employed is Q. It might well be that when the wage rate is raised to W^1 and employment remains at Q, the firm is still making profits in excess of normal profits. In this case the union might be able to raise wages and resist any cut in the numbers employed.

The position of the industry as a whole can also be considered. In Figure 22.4, DD and SS represent the free market demand and supply curves for a particular type of labour.

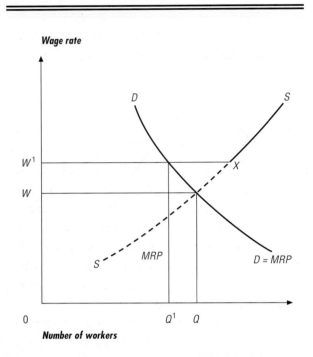

Wage rate

Number of workers

FIG. 22.4

A trade union negotiates a minimum wage of W^1. This means that the dotted part of the SS curve now has no relevance because, although some workers will be willing to work for less than W^1, they will not be allowed to do so. The supply of labour to this industry is now represented by the line W^1XS and the equilibrium position is where the demand crosses this line. At this point Q^1 workers will be employed. The result of the union action, according to this representation, has been to reduce employment by QQ^1 workers.

However this analysis assumes that other things remain unchanged and, in particular, that demand for labour remains unchanged. But an increase in wages might increase the motivation and productivity of workers. Productivity may also rise if, because they are paying them more, employers increase training in order to raise their return from labour. If productivity does rise, the MRP curve will move to the right. The demand for labour will increase and there may be no net reductions in the numbers employed.

Employment may also not fall if the increase in wages is part of a widespread increase in wages. In this case demand for most goods and services will rise and again the MRP curve will move to the right and offset the negative effect of the increased wages on employment.

MONOPSONY AND OLIGOPSONY EMPLOYERS

A monopsonist employer is the sole buyer, and an oligopsonist employer is one of only a few major buyers, of a certain type of labour. A local monopsonist would be the sole employer of a particular type of labour in a town or local area. Both monopsonists and oligopsonists are wage makers and may pay a wage rate below that which would operate in a perfect labour market.

As monopsonists and oligopsonists influence the wage rate their marginal cost of labour exceeds the average cost of labour. To employ an extra worker they have to pay a higher wage not just to the extra worker but to all the other workers as well. The number of workers employed will be determined by equating the marginal cost of labour with the marginal revenue product (Q). The wage rate paid is below the marginal revenue product. In a competitive labour market the wage rate would be higher (W^1) and the level of employment would also be higher (Q^1). This is shown in Figure 22.5.

BILATERAL MONOPOLY

It is possible that a monopsonist employer may face a monopolist trade union. This situation is referred to as a *bilateral monopoly*. In this case the level of

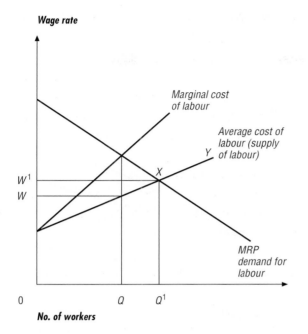

FIG. 22.5

wages and employment will depend on the relative bargaining strengths and skills of unions/professional organisations and employer representatives.

Unions may be able to raise both the wage rate and employment. Indeed it is likely that the wage rate and employment will be higher with a union presence than without. Referring back to Figure 22.5, if a union raises the wage rate to W^1 the supply curve becomes W^1XY. The marginal cost of labour now becomes W^1 up to Q^1 number of workers. The employer will hire the number of workers where $MRP = MC$ of labour. So now a higher number of workers, Q^1, is employed at a higher wage rate.

ATTACHMENT BETWEEN WORKERS AND EMPLOYERS

In a perfect market there would be no attachment between workers and employers so that a worker would feel free to move to a higher-paid job and an employer would feel free to dismiss existing workers if demand fell. However, a worker may in practice stay with an employer due to familiarity, a pleasant atmosphere and other non-monetary advantages. Employers may hoard labour during downturns, hoping that demand will pick up in the future and wishing to keep workers who have been trained in the ways of the firm. In practice, the attachments which exist between workers and employers reduce labour mobility.

LACK OF TRAINING

Training is a merit good providing positive externalities. A better trained labour force provides private benefits to those trained (higher lifetime earnings) and to firms which finance training (higher productivity and lower labour turnover). It also provides positive externalities in the form of higher national output arising from increased productivity and the overcoming of skill shortages.

If left to market forces, training may be under-consumed. Workers may be reluctant to finance their own training as they may not fully appreciate the benefits which may be gained. Firms may also be reluctant to spend much on training if the training is in general and transferable skills. This is because they recognise that the returns from their expenditure will be low if the workers leave the firm soon after they have been trained. It will then be other firms which will benefit from their expenditure.

QUESTIONS

SHORT QUESTIONS

1. Explain what is meant by the immobility of labour.

2. What is meant by a monopsonist?

3. Why does the marginal cost of labour exceed the average cost of labour in conditions of monopsony?

4. In November 1995 the Disability Act came into force. What major form of labour market discrimination is not covered by legislation in the UK? What impact do you think this omission has?

MULTIPLE CHOICE

1. Which of the following would increase the geographical mobility of labour?

    A   The use of national wage rates.

    B   Grants for workers transferring from areas of high unemployment.

    C   A reduction in the qualifications needed to enter the main professions.

    D   A decline in the size of the private rented sector in all parts of the country.

2. Figure 22.6 shows the demand for and supply of labour in a monopsonistic market.

    What will be the quantity of labour employed and the wage rate paid?

	Quantity of labour	Wage rate
A	Q^1	W^1
B	Q^1	W^3
C	Q^2	W^2
D	Q^2	W^4

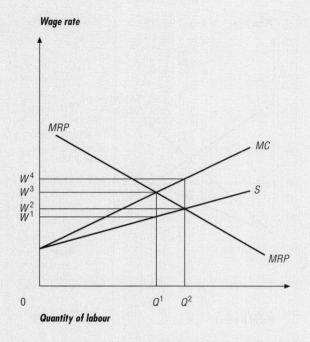

FIG. 22.6

3. Table 22.1 shows the average gross weekly earnings in different occupations in the UK in 1995.

TABLE 22.1

	Men £	Women £
Managers & administrators	537.0	367.8
Teaching professionals	482.9	400.6
Professional & technical occupations	442.9	333.3
Printing & related trades	343.6	235.3
Sales occupations	310.3	199.9
Receptionists, telephonists & related occupations	305.5	197.7
Plant & machine operatives	293.7	201.5
Catering occupations	209.5	158.8

Source: New Earnings Survey 1995, Office for National Statistics

What can be concluded from this data?

A The average gross weekly earnings in the printing and related trades was £289.45.

B Managers and administrators worked more overtime than those working in catering occupations.

C The gender differential, in percentage terms, was greatest in sales occupations.

D Women paid a higher percentage of their earnings in income tax than men.

4 Which is an example of an oligopsonist in a country's market for bus drivers?

A the only bus company operating in the country

B one of several bus companies operating in the country

C the trade union representing all bus drivers

D one of several trade unions representing bus drivers.

DATA RESPONSE

The legal definition of discrimination is disparate treatment of an individual on the basis of race, gender, age, religion or ethnic origin. The first economic attempt to understand such behaviour, developed by Gary Becker of the University of Chicago, suggested that prejudiced individuals with a 'taste for discrimination' must face additional costs if their prejudice is unfounded. A bigoted factory owner, for instance, will have to pay higher wages if he insists on hiring only white employees, and this will make his business less profitable than that of an unprejudiced competitor.

Since a price must be paid for prejudice, many economists have suggested (though Mr Becker's own model does not necessarily imply this) that in fully competitive markets discrimination should eventually disappear, because prejudiced firms will fail. Discrimination could persist only if entrepreneurs are willing to sacrifice part of their returns or if customers share — and are prepared to pay for — the employer's prejudice.

A second theory was developed by Kenneth Arrow and Edmund Phelps in the 1970s. This approach, called 'statistical discrimination', suggests that people use an individual's race or sex as a proxy for individual characteristics. Thus a mortgage company might be reluctant to lend to a black client because it believes blacks, in general, have higher default rates. Using a racial 'proxy' is cheaper for the mortgage company than examining the individual's own credit history.

Unfortunately, this theory also is hard to square with persistent discrimination. The reason is that even if such a proxy is generally correct for a large group, it will not be true for all individuals within the group. Those firms able to distinguish among, say, high-risk and low-risk borrowers on an individual basis will eventually win out over those who use crude — and discriminatory — proxies.

Source: 'Race, sex and dismal science', The Economist, 6/6/98.

a] Explain what is meant by labour market discrimination. **(3)**

b] Why, in economic terms, do consumers who discriminate against firms employing certain categories of workers lose out? **(4)**

c] Contrast the two explanations of discrimination given in the extract. **(6)**

d] Why is it suggested that market forces would eliminate discrimination? **(6)**

e] Discuss why labour market discrimination continues. **(6)**

CASE STUDY

British food and drink companies are 10% less efficient than overseas competitors because their employees lack adequate education and training, according to a report published yesterday by the industry's national training organisation.

British employees lack the training and education to deal with modern production equipment, the report says, forcing their employers to spend more than competitors on training at work.

Even so, the industry still lacks the multi-skilled machine operators needed to maximise output and minimise waste. 'In every UK company you visit, there is a shortage of skilled engineers and fitters capable of installing and maintaining computer operated equipment,' said Professor Mike Whieldon, the report's author.

The report is based on a benchmarking exercise by the Food and Drink Federation comparing UK factories with those in Japan, the US and the rest of the European Union.

It shows British companies have higher levels of down-time caused by machine faults and shortages than overseas competitors. And they take longer to change production lines between different product ranges.

UK employees are less likely to have vocational qualifications or basic educational qualifications than those in the rest of the EU, the US or Japan.

'One consequence of the shortage of skilled labour in the UK is that investment in new equipment often fails to make the expected returns,' said Terry Mills of Unigate Dairies who chaired the report's steering group. 'The companies that had the oldest plant had the least downtime and were the most competitive. This seemed to fly in the face of conventional wisdom until we realised the companies with the newest equipment had not trained their operators and maintenance staff at the commissioning stage.'

Another consequence is UK food and drink companies spend 3.9% of payroll costs on training. US and Japanese companies spend about 2% on training, while the rest of the EU spends 3.5%.

Source: 'Employees 'lack adequate training'' by John Willman, Financial Times, 16/6/99.

a] What type of product is training — a private, merit or public good? **(5)**

b] Why is training likely to be under-consumed if left to market forces? **(5)**

c] Why, in the UK, are companies using old machinery often more competitive than those using new machinery? **(4)**

d] What are the consequences, in the UK, of the shortage of skilled workers? **(6)**

e] Explain what effect improved education and training would have on:
   i   the productivity of labour **(3)**
   ii   firms' costs of production **(4)**
   iii firms' profit levels. **(3)**

f] Given the shortage of skilled workers in the UK what is likely to happen to their pay? Illustrate your answer with a diagram. **(6)**

g] Explain why supply of skilled workers is more inelastic than the supply of unskilled workers. **(6)**

h] Apart from a lack of people with appropriate education and training, what else may make it difficult for an industry to recruit more staff? **(8)**

STRUCTURED ESSAY

a] Explain the meaning and causes of labour market failure. **(15)**

b] Which groups may suffer as a result of discrimination? **(10)**

23 DISTRIBUTION OF WEALTH AND INCOME

Income is flow and wealth is a stock. Whilst income comes in each month, wealth is built up over time as stocks of assets are accumulated. There are three sources of income: earned income, unearned income (i.e. income earned from wealth in the form of, e.g., interest and dividends) and transfer payments (e.g. job seekers' allowance and state pensions). Income influences the wealth people can accumulate which in turn influences their earning capacity.

THE DISTRIBUTION OF WEALTH

Personal wealth is held in many forms, the most important of which is the ownership of dwellings. Other important forms of personal wealth are land, stocks and shares, consumer durable goods, deposits in banks and building societies, and other financial assets. It is now common to distinguish two kinds of personal wealth.

Marketable wealth consists of those assets which can be bought and sold, or which have an exchange value. It is composed of the types of item listed above. Non-marketable wealth consists primarily of pension rights. People contributing to pension schemes — both occupational schemes and the state retirement scheme — are building up rights to an income in the future.

Table 23.1 shows the distribution of marketable wealth amongst the top half of the population.

This distribution has not changed much since 1976 although the share of the richest 1% declined slightly between 1976 and 1991 and then increased again. Indeed the share of wealth earned by the top 50% increased from 1991 and 1994. When pension rights are included as part of personal wealth the inequality in the distribution is reduced.

TABLE 23.1 UK DISTRIBUTION OF WEALTH

Marketable wealth Percentage of wealth owned by:	1976	1981	1986	1991	1994
most wealthy 1%	21	18	18	17	19
most wealthy 5%	38	36	36	35	38
most wealthy 10%	50	50	50	47	51
most wealthy 25%	71	73	73	71	73
most wealthy 50%	92	92	90	92	93

Source: Social Trends 28, 1998, Office for National Statistics

Wealth is distributed unequally for a number of reasons. Two obvious reasons are the inequality in the distribution of income which affects people's ability to save and the fact that people have different propensities to save. Age too, is a factor. Older people generally hold more wealth than younger people because they have had more years to accumulate wealth. The fact that wealth can be inherited and earns income also helps to explain why, over a period of years, vast fortunes can be built up. Indeed the main source of large wealth is inheritance. Another source of wealth is private enterprise. A person who starts a business and builds it up to a successful enterprise not only increases his or her income but also creates a marketable asset (the firm itself), the value of which will be greater than the person's investment in the business. A few people become wealthy as a result of chance. A well known example of this is National Lottery winners.

THE DISTRIBUTION OF INCOME

The distribution of income can be examined in two main ways. One is by examining the distribution of income between factors of production. In this case wages account for the largest percentage but its share of income has fallen over recent years. Another way of examining the distribution of income is to examine how disposable income is distributed. Disposable income consists of the incomes derived from factor services together with various forms of cash benefits (e.g. social security payments) minus direct taxes (income taxes and national insurance contributions). Figure 23.1 shows that the proportion of people in the UK whose net household income is below half average rose from 59% in 1979 to 63% in 1994.

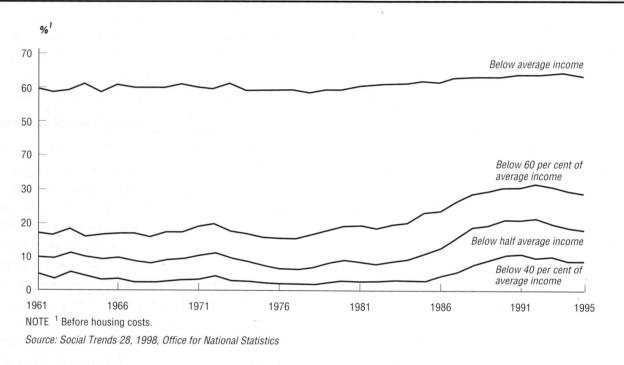

NOTE [1] Before housing costs.

Source: Social Trends 28, 1998, Office for National Statistics

FIG. 23.1

Whilst income is more evenly distributed than wealth there is still a marked inequality in its distribution. The income of a household depends to a large extent on the number of economically active people it contains. Households in the bottom fifth of the distribution contain very few people who are in employment, while those in the highest group contain an average of more than two. The aged, the sick and the disabled tend to be concentrated in the lowest group. This group also contains a large number of one-parent families, of families where the head of the household is unemployed, and of families with children where the wage earner is low paid.

Investment income and income from self-employment are important elements in the income of households in the top fifth of this distribution. The very unequal distribution of wealth is a major cause of the inequality in the distribution of income, since a fairly large percentage of the income of the highest income groups derives from the ownership of land, property, stocks and shares and other financial assets.

HOW MUCH INEQUALITY?

Gross inequalities in the distributions of income and wealth lead to feelings of 'unfairness' because, quite apart from creating inequalities in living standards, they lead to inequalities of opportunity. The wealthy can buy superior education and training for their children and there is no doubt that the possession of wealth confers certain social advantages. Inherited wealth provides the recipient with an income regardless of his/her abilities, aptitudes or efforts. In deciding what is an equitable distribution of income, the economist can offer no conclusive answers because it is a matter of personal judgement (i.e. a value judgement). On the assumption that the purpose of economic activity is to maximise the satisfaction of wants, it might be argued that an equal distribution of income would be the ideal. This conclusion is based on the notion that the law of diminishing marginal utility applies to income and that everyone derives the same utility from a given amount of income. For example, if satisfaction is measured in units called 'utils' then if, for each person, the satisfaction derived from the first £5 of income is 8 and this diminishes by 1 util for each additional £5 of income, then the total utility or satisfaction to be derived from £30 distributed among three people is maximised when each receives £10.

But incomes are also incentives to production. In order to get people to work harder, accept greater responsibility, develop new ideas, undertake long and difficult training or to carry out unpleasant tasks, it is claimed that it is necessary to offer higher rewards. Some economists argue that if these incentives are not forthcoming, the amount of real income available for distribution will probably be reduced. The problem is to weigh these considerations against each other. Equal distribution may give the highest level of satisfaction from any given income, but probably would cause total income to be less than it would be under an incentive system.

Purely economic arguments about the desirability of different patterns of income distribution may be inconclusive. In any case, the criterion of desirability (i.e. the satisfaction of wants) is only one of several possible ways of judging what is 'best'. There are people who think that rewards should be strictly related to effort, or risk or responsibility. Others believe that people's needs (e.g. family responsibilities) should be the deciding factor.

However, there is fairly general agreement that the distribution of income and wealth brought about by market forces is inequitable and most governments have policies for reducing these inequalities. The main instruments for doing this are a system of direct taxation which is progressive, and a distribution of cash benefits and benefits in kind to raise the incomes of those most in need.

REDISTRIBUTIVE EFFECTS OF TAXES AND BENEFITS

The Office for National Statistics carries out an annual study of the redistribution of income brought about by the effects of taxes and benefits. This analysis has three main stages.

The starting point is the original income. This is the income in cash and kind of all members of the household before the deduction of taxes or the addition of any state benefits. This first stage looks at the redistributive effects of cash benefits. There is a large number of benefits including retirement pensions, child benefit and job seekers' allowance. When cash benefits are added to original income the household's gross income is obtained.

Stage two deals with effect of direct taxes on the distribution of household income. As far as households are concerned the relevant direct taxes are income tax and the employee's and self-employed national insurance contributions. The deduction of direct taxes from gross income gives disposable income.

The third stage estimates the effects of indirect taxes and benefits in kind on household income. These indirect taxes include VAT, excise duties and council tax. The most important benefits in kind are health and education services. When disposable income is adjusted to take account of

TABLE 23.2 REDISTRIBUTION OF UK INCOME THROUGH TAXES AND BENEFITS, 1995–96 (£ PER YEAR)

Quintile group of households [1]

	Bottom fifth	Next fifth	Middle fifth	Next fifth	Top fifth	All house-holds
Average per household						
Wages and salaries	1390	4050	10390	17610	29810	12650
Imputed income from benefits in kind	30	30	100	290	890	270
Self-employment income	370	570	1250	1670	5050	1780
Occupational pensions, annuities	290	950	1310	1790	2410	1350
Investment income	200	340	580	830	2640	920
Other income	150	160	170	250	460	240
Total original income	2430	6090	13790	22450	41260	17200
plus Benefits in cash						
Contributory	1860	2280	1710	1180	770	1560
Non-contributory	3050	2380	1650	950	430	1690
Gross original income	7340	10750	17150	24580	42450	20450
less Income tax[2] and NIC[3]	540	930	2480	4470	9660	3610
less Local taxes[4] (gross)	590	690	650	710	820	670
Disposable income	6210	9230	14020	19400	31980	16170
less Indirect taxes	1930	2340	3290	4090	5090	3350
Post-tax income	4280	6890	10730	15310	26890	12820
plus Benefits in kind						
Education	1810	1300	1420	1070	830	1290
National Health Service	1890	1830	1730	1520	1330	1660
Housing subsidy	90	80	40	20	10	50
Travel subsides	50	70	60	60	140	70
School meals and welfare milk	100	30	10	–	–	30
Final income	8230	10200	13990	17980	29200	15920

Notes   [1] *Equivalised disposable income has been used for ranking the households.*
[2] *After tax relief at source on mortgage interest and life assurance premiums.*
[3] *Employees' national insurance contributions.*
[4] *Gross council tax, rates and water charges. Rates in Northern Ireland.*
Source: Social Trends 28, 1998, Office for National Statistics

indirect taxes and benefits in kind, final income is found.

EFFECTS OF BENEFITS AND TAXATION ON THE DISTRIBUTION OF INCOME

The most important measure in the policy for redistributing income appears to be the payment of cash benefits since these go largely to people who are not earning.

Direct taxes further increase the share of income going to the lower income groups but the net effect on distribution is much less than that arising from cash benefits.

The effects of indirect taxation are less clear. These taxes take a higher percentage of the disposable income of the middle-income households than households at the extremes of the range. This is due to the fact low-income households spend a large proportion of their income on food and rent (both of which are mainly exempt from indirect taxes) while high-income households tend to allocate more of their income to savings, mortgage interest and insurance premiums which attract little indirect tax.

The higher paid tend to receive more from benefits in kind than might be expected. They tend to keep their children in the education system for a relatively long period of time and are well informed about what the National Health Service can provide.

PROFILE

NAME: Amartya Sen
Academic and adviser to governments and international organisations

BORN: 3 November 1933 in Santiniketan, Bengal

NATIONALITY: Indian

EDUCATED: University of Calcutta, University of Cambridge

KEY POSTS HELD: Professor of Economics at Jadavpur University, Calcutta, Delhi University, London School of Economics, University of Oxford, Harvard University, Massachusetts Institute of Technology, University of Cambridge
Master of Trinity College, Cambridge
Chairman of the UN Expert Group on the role of Advanced Skill and Technology
President of the Development Studies Association
Resident advisor to the World Institute for Development Economics
Vice President of the Royal Economic Society

BOOKS PUBLISHED INCLUDE: Growth Economics (1970)
Collective Choice and Social Welfare (1971)
On Economic Inequality (1973)
Employment, Technology and Development (1975)
Poverty and Famines: An essay on entitlement and deprivation (1981)
Choice, Welfare and Measurement (1982)
Resources, Values and Development (1984)
Commodities and Capabilities (1985)
On Ethics and Economics (1987)
The Standard of Living (1987)
Hunger and Public Action (1989)
The Political Economy of Hunger (1990–91)
Inequality Re-examined (1992)

AWARDS: 1976: won the Indian Mahalanobis Prize
1998: won the Nobel Prize in Economics for his contributions to welfare economics 'in particular on social choice, welfare distribution and poverty.'

MAIN AREAS OF WORK: Welfare economics and development economics

QUOTES ON SEN:
'Areas that were once considered social science have become a crucial element of economics: he has forced people to put whole new chapters into the textbooks' (a Cambridge colleague).

POVERTY

Absolute poverty occurs when people are unable to purchase the basic necessities of life, whereas relative poverty occurs when people are poor in comparison to others in the society in which they live. It is possible for people to be able to afford more goods and services but to be relatively poor if the incomes of others have risen by even more.

There are a number of measures a government can take to reduce poverty. These include providing cash benefits and benefits in kind. However these tend to alleviate rather than solve poverty and more significant measures are raising employment levels and the longer-term measure of increasing the educational opportunities of the poor.

THE POVERTY TRAP

The poverty trap arises when people become worse off when they seek to improve their living standards by working more hours or gaining higher paid employment. Their disposable income falls because they pay more tax and lose benefits. Governments seek to avoid a poverty trap occurring.

QUESTIONS

SHORT QUESTIONS

1 Why is the distribution of wealth more unequal than the distribution of income?

2 Explain what is meant by marketable wealth.

3 Compare cash benefits and the direct provision of services as means of alleviating poverty.

4 What is the poverty trap?

MULTIPLE CHOICE

1 Which of the following government measures would make income more evenly distributed? A rise in:

A VAT

B cash benefits

C tax free allowances

D expenditure on higher education.

2 Which of the following assets is the most evenly distributed?

A Government securities.

B Pension rights.

C Property.

D Shares.

3 Which of the payments to factors of production account for the largest share of national income?

A Interest.

B Profit.

C Rent.

D Wages.

4 What is disposable income?

A Income minus direct taxes.

B Income plus state benefits minus direct taxes.

C Income plus state benefits minus direct taxes and mortgage interest payments.

D Income plus state benefits minus indirect taxes, mortgage interest payments and indirect taxes.

DATA RESPONSE

You are, by dint of reading this newspaper, information rich. You belong to the knowledge class, for the purchase of a paper such as this also implies you are more likely to have access, at home or work, to the internet with all its wealth of information.

But for those who haven't bought a broadsheet, the internet belongs to a distant world. They are the information poor, members of what is seen by some as a fast-developing underclass.

Its existence has been recognised at global level. The 1999 United Nations Development Programme human development report says that worldwide 30% of internet users have at least one university degree. The language of the internet is exclusive: 80% of it is English, spoken by less than a tenth of the world's population. The PC which costs only a month's salary in the United States is worth eight year's average income in Bangladesh. Parallel worlds are developing where 'those with income, education and — literally — connections have cheap and instantaneous access to information. The rest are left with uncertain, slow and costly access.'

The report continues: 'When people in these two worlds live and compete side by side, the advantage of being connected will overpower the marginal and impoverished, cutting off their voices and concerns from the global conversation.'

In America, putting computers in education can backfire. The college board, which oversees standards in American schools, suggests deprived and disadvantaged children may be getting left behind even further by clued-up classmates from better-off homes. 'Advantage magnifies advantage. While education is the great equaliser, technology appears to be a new engine of inequality.'

In Britain we speak the language of the internet and have a national telecommunications infrastructure capable of supporting widespread internet use. Two recent announcements point the way to opening up the net to British users from all backgounds. The first, from the telecommunications regulator Oftel, said British Telecom's monopoly on local telephone lines was to end, opening up the possibility of low-cost, but extremely powerful, lines into millions of homes, capable of delivering a wide range of information.

The second is the dramatic reduction in the cost of getting online. Dixons started the ball rolling and Tiny and Time are now offering free machines, linked to a telecoms rental deal costing, say, £9 a month over two years.

Source: 'The new poor' by Neil McIntosh, the Guardian, 22/7/99.

a] Who are the new underclass? **(5)**

b] Why is access to the internet more difficult for people in Bangladesh than for people in the USA? **(5)**

c] Why may access to the internet become more available in the future to poor groups in Britain? **(4)**

d] The article refers to information wealth. Identify three other forms of wealth. **(3)**

e] Discuss whether education is a 'great equaliser'. **(8)**

CASE STUDY

Successive generations of children are learning to be poor. New research has revealed that children growing up in low-income families learn from an early age to limit their expectations of what their parents can afford, leading them to reduce their hopes and aspirations.

The findings show that children who come from low income families or from lone parent families are more likely to want to do a job that requires fewer qualifications and training, are less likely to ask for expensive birthday presents, and are less likely to have a part-time job than other children.

A study by researchers at the Centre for Economic Performance, part of the London School of Economics found that the number of children living in poverty has increased dramatically in the past 30 years.

As many as one in three children, 4.3m, are living in households with less than half the average wage, compared with one in ten in 1968.

The findings show that the increase in inequality has a direct impact on the wellbeing of children as the spending by the poorest fifth of the population on children's clothing, fresh fruit, shoes and toys is no higher in real terms than it was 30 years ago.

The researchers also found poverty continued through the generations.

Children born in 1958 who had socially disadvantaged backgrounds were more likely to have lower earnings and had a higher risk of unemployment at the age of 33 compared with other children.

They are also more likely than other parents to have children who were performing poorly at school.

'Our study shows how the economic position of families strongly affects the present and future welfare of children,' says Stephen Machin, co-author of the report.

Source: 'Children learn lack of ambition as inequality triples in 30 years' by Cherry Norton, the Independent, 29/3/99.

a] What had happened to the number of children living in poverty? **(3)**

b] What disadvantages do the children of the poor suffer? **(6)**

c] Explain why poor performance at school is likely to reduce future earnings. **(6)**

d] Why do the children of the poor tend to suffer from poor health? **(7)**

e] Explain why poverty continues 'through the generations'. **(6)**

f] What evidence is there in the article of labour market failure? **(8)**

g] Explain why the wages of most low paid workers contain a high proportion of transfer earnings. **(5)**

h] Discuss three government policy measures which could make the distribution of income more equal. **(9)**

STRUCTURED ESSAY

a] Why is income unevenly distributed? **(12)**

b] Discuss whether taxation and benefits reduce the inequality of income. **(13)**

Governments intervene in markets in an attempt to correct market failure. Keynesian economists believe that there is a high risk of market failure in a free market and that government action can counter these risks, leading to a more socially efficient outcome.

METHODS OF INTERVENTION

There is a range of intervention measures which a government can use. This chapter will first consider the measures which can improve the markets for products and then look at measures which can improve the workings of the labour market.

INDIRECT TAXES

Taxes which are placed on goods and services are known as *indirect taxes* (or expenditure or outlay taxes) as opposed to direct taxes which are placed on income and wealth. When a tax such as VAT is levied on a product it has the same economic effects as an increase in the cost of production. The cost of bringing the product to the market is now increased by the amount of the tax. In terms of supply and demand analysis, therefore, the imposition of a tax may be seen as a fall in supply. This is shown in Table 24.1.

TABLE 24.1 THE EFFECTS OF IMPOSING A TAX OF 2p PER UNIT

Market price (p)	Quantity supplied (before tax)	Quantity supplied (after tax)	Quantity demanded
10	1100	900	100
9	1000	800	200
8	900	700	300
7	800	600	400
6	700	500	500
5	600	400	600
4	500	300	700

The second column in Table 24.1 shows the quantities supplied at different prices before the tax is imposed, and is represented by the supply curve SS in Figure 24.1. The third column shows the quantities supplied at different prices after the tax has been imposed. It is derived fairly easily from columns one and two. In the new situation a market price of 10p represents a supply price of 8p. Producers do not receive the full market price as 2p per unit is now taken by the government as tax. It is however, the supply price which determines how much suppliers are prepared to offer to the market. Thus when the market price is 10p, the market supply will now be 900 units. Similarly a market price of 9p will only give rise to a market supply of 800 units, and so on.

What has happened in fact is that supply has fallen: less is now supplied at each and every market price. Columns one and three make up the new supply schedule which is represented by the supply curve S¹S¹ in Figure 24.1.

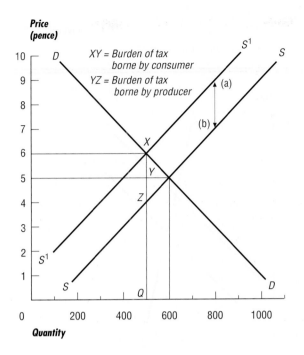

FIG. 24.1

Figure 24.1 represents the data shown in Table 24.1. The supply curve has shifted upwards by the amount of the tax (i.e. by 2p). At the original equilibrium price (5p), 600 units were demanded and supplied. The imposition of the tax reduces supply, price rises to 6p, and the quantity demanded falls to 500 units.

Note that the price has not risen by the full amount of the tax. The burden of the tax has been shared by producers and consumers. The amount of the tax per unit is equal to XZ. Of this, XY is borne by the consumers in the form of higher prices. However, YZ is the part of the tax borne by suppliers since they now receive Z per unit whereas before the tax they were receiving Y per unit.

In terms of the figures used in the table:

Original equilibrium price = 5p
New equilibrium price = 6p (consumers pay 1p per unit more)
New supply price = 4p (suppliers receive 1p per unit less)

Total revenue = 3000p (i.e. 500 × 6)
Tax yield = 1000p (i.e. 500 × 2p)
Suppliers' revenue = 2000p (i.e. 500 × 4p)

SPECIFIC AND *AD VALOREM* TAXES

The example used is a specific tax. A specific tax is a fixed-sum tax, in the example 2p per unit. The tax does not change with the price of the product. An example of a specific tax is the excise duty on whisky and other spirits. A specific tax causes a parallel shift to the left of the supply curve.

The second type of indirect tax is an *ad valorem* tax. This is a percentage tax, such as VAT. As it is a percentage tax the amount of tax paid will rise with the price of the product. An *ad valorem* tax causes a non-parallel shift of the supply curve to the left as shown in Figure 24.2.

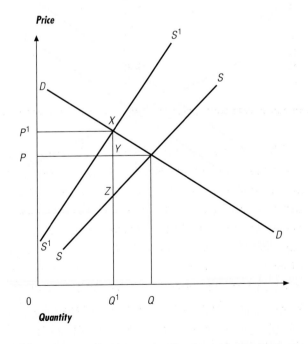

FIG. 24.2

THE INCIDENCE OF THE TAX BURDEN

In Figure 24.1 the burden of taxation was shared equally between buyers and sellers. How the burden of the tax is shared out depends upon the particular demand and supply conditions in the market. Whether the tax is borne largely by producers or whether they can pass the greater part of it on to consumers in the form of a higher price depends largely on the elasticities of demand and supply.

In Figure 24.3 the demand is elastic and producers experience a fall in supply price greater than the increase in market price experienced by the buyers (YZ>XY). The producers bear the main burden because they know that if they were to try to pass on most of the tax in the form of a higher price they would lose a large number of sales.

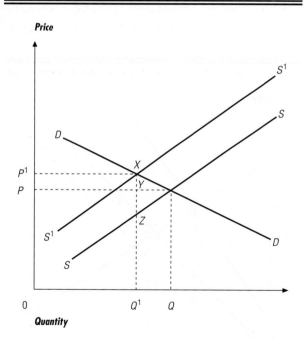

FIG. 24.3

In Figure 24.4 demand is inelastic. This time it is the consumers who bear most of the tax (XY>YZ). Producers can pass on a high proportion of the tax in the form of a price increase in the knowledge that they will not lose many sales.

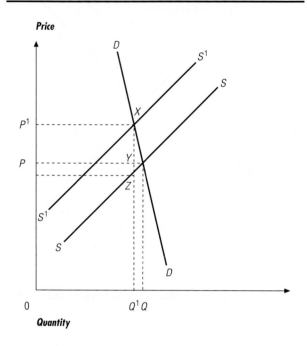

FIG. 24.4

When demand is perfectly inelastic producers can pass on the full amount of the tax and so consumers bear the whole burden of the tax. Whereas when demand is perfectly elastic the market price does not change. Producers bear all of the burden.

Price elasticity of supply is also relevant in determining the burden. The more inelastic supply is the greater the proportion of the tax borne by the producers. In general, if price elasticity of demand is greater than elasticity of supply, the producers bear the greater share of the tax burden; if price elasticity of demand is less than the elasticity of supply, the consumers bear the greater share.

REASONS FOR IMPOSING INDIRECT TAXES

The two main reasons for a government placing a tax on a good or service is to raise revenue and/or to discourage consumption and output. If the Chancellor of the Exchequer wished to raise large sums of money from indirect taxation s/he must concentrate heavily on those products for which demand is inelastic.

If the prime objective is to reduce the output and consumption of the product because of market failure, it is more advantageous if demand is elastic.

INDIRECT TAXES AND WELFARE

The market overproduces and undercharges for products with negative externalities. If the government is able to measure these negative externalities, it can impose an indirect tax equivalent to the marginal external cost. This will internalise the cost and reduce output to the socially optimum level. Figure 24.5 shows the market for a good, the production of which causes pollution. The market output is Q and the price charged is P. The socially optimum output is QX and the price is PX. So the tax should be YZ.

SUBSIDIES

Subsidies may be regarded as negative taxes. They normally take the form of payments by governments to producers and are particularly important in the case of agricultural products (wheat, milk, meat, etc.). The effect of a subsidy is to reduce the costs of supplying a product. In terms of demand and supply analysis this means that the supply curve moves downwards by the amount of the subsidy — more is now supplied at any given market price. Price will fall and the quantity demanded will expand. This is shown in Figure 24.6. Initially the equilibrium price was P and quantity Q was demanded and supplied. A subsidy to producers has moved the supply curve from SS to S^1S^1. Price has fallen to P^1 and demand has extended to Q^1.

The amount of subsidy is XZ. Consumers have benefited by a price fall equal to YZ. They now consume more at a lower price. Producers have benefited from an increase in the supply price from Y to X. They now supply more and receive a higher supply price.

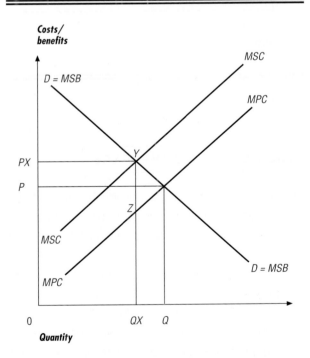

FIG. 24.5

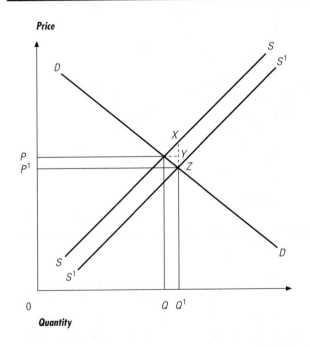

FIG. 24.6

If the demand is elastic, the granting of a subsidy would lead to a relatively small reduction in price, but a relatively large increase in consumption. If demand was inelastic, the movement of the supply curve would lead to a relatively large fall in price and a relative rise in demand.

SPECIFIC AND AD VALOREM SUBSIDIES

A subsidy can be either specific or *ad valorem*. A specific subsidy is a fixed sum payment. Figure 24.6 shows a specific subsidy. An *ad valorem* subsidy, in contrast, is a percentage payment. This causes a non-parallel shift in the supply curve as shown in Figure 24.7.

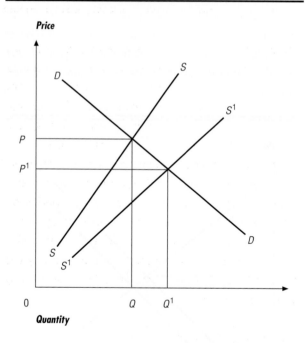

FIG. 24.7

REASONS FOR GIVING SUBSIDIES

A subsidy may be given to assist the poor, to help producers and/or to encourage the consumption

and output of goods and services with positive externalities. Subsidies can be given to consumers as well as to producers. Where a subsidy is given to consumers it will be the demand curve which will shift to the right as shown in Figure 24.8.

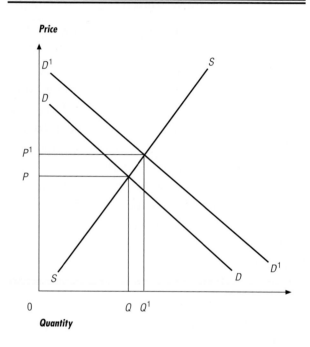

FIG. 24.8

SUBSIDIES AND WELFARE

The market under produces products with positive externalities. In this case to promote welfare, the government may subsidise the product. Figure 24.9 shows the market where the marginal social benefit exceeds the marginal private benefit. The market will produce an output Q. The socially optimum output is QX since this is where *MSC* and *MSB* are equal. To persuade people to consume, this quantity price will have to be lowered, via a subsidy, to *PX*.

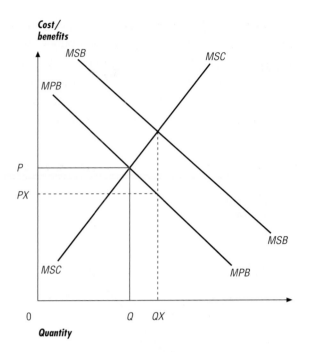

FIG. 24.9

FIG. 24.10

MAXIMUM PRICE

A government or another body may set a maximum price. This will only affect the market price if the maximum price is set below the equilibrium price. A government may introduce a maximum price in order to promote equity and enable poorer members of the community to purchase basic necessities like food, housing and public transport. Figure 24.10 shows the effect of introducing a maximum price. The initial market equilibrium price is *P* and the quantity bought and sold is *Q*. When the maximum price is imposed at *PX* the quantity demanded expands to *QD* but the quantity supplied contracts to *QS*. A shortage of *QD – QS* arises.

This is the major problem with a maximum price. Some method will have to be used to allocate the product to consumers. For example, allocation could be on the basis of first come, first served (queuing), or there could be rationing. However, whichever system is used, a black market is likely to develop.

For instance, the demand for tickets for the last night of the Proms exceeds the supply. The tickets are allocated in a number of ways including a lottery and queuing before the performance. The excess demand, however, also results in tickets being sold outside the Royal Albert Hall by ticket touts.

Maximum prices increase the welfare of those who are able to purchase the product. They are able to pay less for it than under free market conditions, and hence increase their consumer surplus. However others, some of whom would have been willing to pay the market price, would be unable to buy the product and so would not be able to enjoy any consumer surplus.

MINIMUM PRICE

A minimum price will only affect a market if it is set above the equilibrium price. A government or other body may impose a minimum price if it considers that the market price is too low. This may be because it wants to protect producers' incomes. Figure 24.11 shows the effect of introducing a minimum price. Pushing up the price to *PM* causes supply to extend, demand to contract and creates a surplus of *QS − QD*.

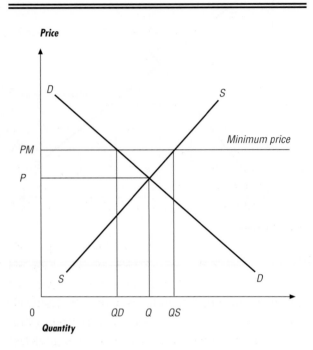

FIG. 24.11

To maintain the minimum price, the government or some other official body will have to buy up the surplus. Measures to cope with the surpluses in agricultural products arising from the Common Agricultural Policy (CAP) operated by the European Union have included storing the surpluses, destroying some products and selling some to East Europe and developing countries at reduced prices. The set aside scheme, introduced in 1988, seeks to reduce cereal production. It involves paying farmers a subsidy to convert arable land to an alternative use or to leave it fallow.

BUFFER STOCKS

A buffer stock makes use of a price band. It is a scheme operated by a central authority and its main aim is usually to stabilise prices and protect producers from sudden shifts in demand and supply. Figure 24.12 shows the effect of setting up a buffer stock for oil seed rape. If the market price is within the two boundaries set by the central authority no action is taken. However, if the market price starts to move outside, the buffer stock operators will intervene.

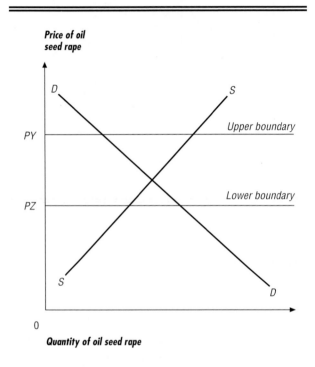

FIG. 24.12

Figure 24.13 shows the effect of a good harvest of oil seed rape. The supply curve shifts to the right. This puts downward pressure on the price at which point the operators step in to increase demand and to prevent the price falling below the lower boundary.

The quantity purchased will be put into storage, ready to be sold if there is a threat that price will rise above the upper boundary.

A buffer stock system, which can only be operated with products which can be stored, has often in practice proved to be unsuccessful. This is because the upper and lower boundaries which trigger action are often set too high. This means that buffer stock

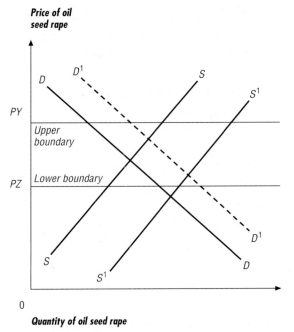

Price of oil seed rape

D¹

D

S

S¹

PY

Upper boundary

PZ

Lower boundary

S

S¹

D¹

D

0

Quantity of oil seed rape

FIG. 24.13

operators have to buy more often and in larger quantities than they sell, increasing storage and purchase costs, sometimes to the point where buffer stocks operators run out of money.

PUBLIC PROVISION OF GOODS AND SERVICES

The government may seek to overcome the problem of the non-provision of public goods and the under-provision, due to under-consumption, of merit goods by the private sector by producing the goods itself (e.g. through the National Health Service) or by giving a contract to a private sector company (e.g. for the building of a hospital).

In the case of public goods there is the problem of deciding on the quantity to produce since the price mechanism will not reveal consumers' demand. The socially optimum quantity will be, as with all products, where marginal social cost equals marginal social benefit. To estimate benefits people can be asked the maximum amount they would be willing to pay for an additional unit of the good. Then to find the economy's marginal benefit curve, the marginal benefit that each individual gains at each quantity of provision is added up.

In practice, of course, the level at which government chooses to provide a product is influenced by pressure groups, revenue constraints and the government's policy priorities.

PROVIDING INFORMATION

As noted before, consumers, workers and producers sometimes fail to make optimal decisions because of lack of information. A consumer may pay a high price for a product not knowing that there are cheaper alternatives while a producer may use inefficient production methods.

The government can seek to increase the quantity and quality of information available to economic agents in a variety of ways. The government can provide information directly. In the UK, the Office for National Statistics publishes detailed information about the country's economy and the government now provides a range of consumers of government services (such as students and NHS patients) with details about those services, including school league tables and hospital waiting lists. The government, by giving subsidies and grants to research institutions and universities, can promote the gathering and interpretation of information. For example, a number of studies have established the link between smoking and lung cancer, making people more aware of the true cost of smoking.

The government can also increase people's access to information and the quality of information by passing legislation. Producers of processed foods and patent medicines have to list their contents. The government also controls the information producers and retailers provide about their products.

PROPERTY RIGHTS

Market failure can arise because of a lack of property rights. Someone cannot dump rubbish in another person's garden because that person could take legal action. However, in many cases property rights are not seen to exist over air, water and some open ground. One solution is, therefore, to extend property rights to include, e.g., rivers, air and the sea. This would mean that a company wishing to pollute would have to negotiate with people in the area who could either prevent the pollution or charge the company. In theory this has the advantage of achieving an optimal level of pollution.

GOVERNMENT ACTION TO CORRECT LABOUR MARKET FAILURE

There are a number of measures a government can introduce in an attempt to improve labour market efficiency by removing or reducing the imperfections which occur in the labour market.

EDUCATION AND TRAINING

For labour markets to work effectively, workers have to be occupationally mobile and possess the skills in demand. To achieve this a certain level of education and training is required. The private sector will tend to under-provide both education and training, both of which are merit goods. A better-educated and better-trained workforce provides benefits (positive externalities) to society in the form of a more productive and adaptive workforce and higher national income. Firms tend to under-provide training, in part because they fail to appreciate all the long term benefits of training, but also because they expect that some of the benefits will go to other firms if workers leave the firm after a period of training. Parents and children may also take a short-term view of education, being more concerned with the current rather than the future earning potential of teenagers.

So governments promote education and training in a variety of ways including making attendance at school compulsory between certain ages, subsidising the provision of education and training so that it is free at the point of consumption.

PROVIDING LABOUR MARKET INFORMATION

Increasing information about job vacancies, wage rates and required skills should lower unemployment, increase the mobility of labour and create a more appropriate use of labour resources.

Government job centres provide information to the unemployed and to those who seek to change jobs. They also put employers in touch with potential employees.

TRADE UNION LEGISLATION

Governments can pass legislation to remove imperfections caused by unions' abuse of their power. For example, in the 1980s and 1990s the Conservative Governments in the UK implemented legislation which reduced trade unions' bargaining power and removed some of their legal immunities. This was done in the belief that the actions of trade unions raise the real wage rate above the competitive market level and lower productivity, thereby reducing domestic competitiveness and increasing unemployment. However, trade unions can provide benefits to society including acting as a counterbalance to the bargaining power of employers.

LEGISLATION AGAINST DISCRIMINATION

Discrimination against any group of workers can result in the wage rate and the employment level being below the efficient levels. In the UK legislation has been passed outlawing discrimination on the grounds of ethnic background, gender and disability.

NATIONAL MINIMUM WAGE

A national minimum wage may be introduced to help raise the living standards of poorly paid workers. In the UK a national minimum wage was introduced on 1st April 1999. It became illegal for any organisation to pay employees aged 22 and over less than £3.60 an hour and those aged 18 to 21 less than £3. However it does not apply to those aged under 18.

To have any effect a national minimum wage has to be set above the current level of pay given to low-paid workers. Opponents claim that whilst the introduction of such a national wage will cause the supply of labour to expand, demand for labour will contract and unemployment will increase. This is shown in Figure 24.14 where employment falls from Q to QD.

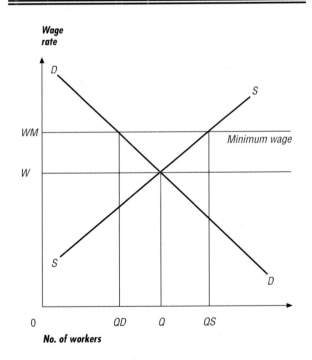

FIG. 24.14

Fewer workers may be employed because the cost of labour has risen. The workers who may be made redundant are likely to be from the most vulnerable groups including older workers, the disabled and the less skilled workers.

A national minimum wage may raise wages further by encouraging those who had previously earned near the minimum wage to press for a wage rise to retain their wage differentials. This may result in cost-push inflation, causing the country's goods and services to be less price competitive and thereby further raising unemployment.

However, supporters of a minimum wage claim that unemployment and inflation do not have to result from the introduction of a national minimum wage. In labour markets where there are monopsonist or oligopsonist employers a minimum wage may increase employment.

Even in markets where monopsony and oligopsony do not exist a minimum wage, they claim, may increase employment and output. The basis of their argument is that a minimum wage will raise incomes, thereby increasing demand. They also argue that a minimum wage may increase workers' morale, encourage employers to spend more on training and raise labour productivity.

LABOUR MARKET REFORMS

Governments may seek to increase the efficiency of labour markets by removing regulations and lowering the overhead costs of employing workers — although they have to be careful to avoid removing restrictions which offset other more serious labour market imperfections.

QUESTIONS

SHORT QUESTIONS

1. Explain the effect on the market for whisky of an increase in taxation on the product.

2. Explain how a buffer stock operates.

3. What are the arguments for introducing a minimum price?

4. When does a maximum price have no effect on the market?

MULTIPLE CHOICE

1. The table shows the demand and supply schedules for a product.

Price (£)	Quantity demanded	Quantity supplied
10	20	1280
9	60	1000
8	150	850
7	260	600
6	400	400
5	600	150
4	900	50

If a tax of £3 is imposed on the product, by how much will its price rise?

A £2   B £3

C £6   D £8

2. In Figure 24.15 demand is shown by the curve DD. The introduction of an expenditure tax shifts the supply curve from SS to S¹S¹.

What is the revenue received by the government as a result of the tax?

A £150   B £200

C £250   D £660

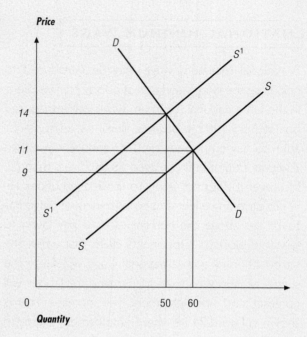

Price / Quantity

FIG. 24.15

3. In Figure 24.16 the initial supply is SS.

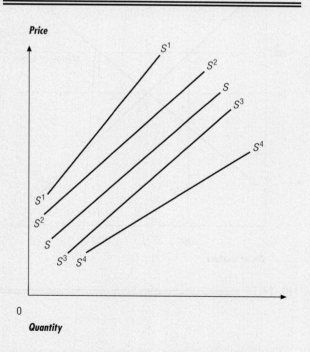

Price / Quantity

FIG. 24.16

Which curve shows the effect of the introduction of a specific subsidy?

A S^1S^1.

B S^2S^2.

C S^3S^3.

D S^4S^4.

4 Figure 24.17 shows the market for a product.

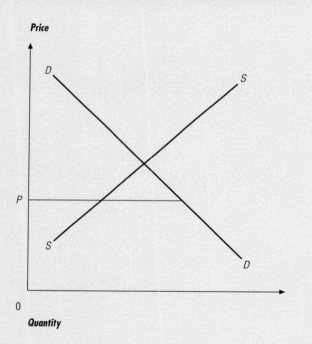

FIG. 24.17

What would be the effect of setting a minimum price of *P*?

A Supply will increase.

B It will have no effect.

C A shortage will develop.

D It will lead to a fall in the equilibrium price.

DATA RESPONSE

UK companies are calling for a shake-up in the nation's anti-discrimination laws in an effort to protect the rights of older workers. More than 100 companies have asked the government to establish a body to address discrimination in the work place, including racial, sexual, disability, and age-based.

Firms supporting the initiative include Tesco, British Aerospace, British Gas, ICI, BICC, ICL, Standard Life, Clydesdale Bank, Scottish Equitable, Midlands Electricity, Anglian Water and Peugeot.

'The fragmentation of commissions covering various aspects of equal opportunities is counter-productive and confusing,' said Mike Judge, personnel director at carmaker Peugeot.

According to a survey conducted by Carnegie Third Age Programme, a lobbying group, 70% of business executives and organisations favour a single commission to replace the three separate anti-discrimination bodies — the Equal Opportunities Commission for Racial Equality and the soon-to-be-established Disability Rights Commission.

Three-quarters of those surveyed believed that a unified equal working rights body should also address age discrimination.

Approximately 35% of Britons aged 50 to 64 are jobless and classified as 'economically inactive'. Nearly one-third of those — totalling well over one million possible workers — would prefer to be in paid employment.

Source: 'Firms fight ageism' by Laurie Laird, the Guardian, 4/5/99.

a] Why do the rights of older workers need protecting? **(5)**

b] Why do the firms mentioned in the article want the establishment of a new body to 'address discrimination in the work place'? **(6)**

c] What is meant by the term 'economically inactive'? **(4)**

d] Discuss the costs of discrimination against older workers. **(10)**

CASE STUDY

Gordon Brown stuck to a long-standing tradition and announced that excise duties on tobacco will increase by 5% above the rate of inflation, to help pay for a £3bn package of tax benefits for the elderly. The rise will add around 17.5p to a packet of cigarettes, pushing the cost of 20 Benson & Hedges to around £3.80. A pack of five small cigars will cost 7.5p more, while a 25g pack of pipe tobacco will go up by 9.5p.

Cigarette-makers and retailers reacted angrily to the decision to hike taxes, noting that taxes now account for nearly 80% of the retail price of cigarettes. John Carlisle of the Tobacco Association (ATM), which had called for a £1 cut in taxes said 'We are very cross. This is an ostrich-policy and a head-in-the-sand Budget. The Chancellor has totally ignored the problem of smuggling and the loss of tax revenues and the threat to the livelihood of retailers.'

The tobacco industry has attacked the Government's tax increases as a blueprint for smugglers. According to the TMA, the Exchequer loses £1.5bn in revenue a year to smuggling.

The TMA claims that UK taxes are almost £1.50 higher than the average of the rest of the European Union countries. The differential encourages smuggling and bootlegging. Over 15% of all cigarettes and over 75% of hand-rolling tobacco smoked in Britain comes from illegal imports, the TMA maintains.

Mr Brown acknowledged the problem of the black market in his speech to the House of Commons but added that smuggling 'will not be permitted to undo a policy on cigarettes which successive British governments have adopted for good and urgent health reasons.'

Anti-smoking pressure groups welcomed the decision to put the cigarette duties up. Clive Bates, director of Action on Smoking and Health (Ash) said: 'We are satisfied. When cigarette prices rise, tobacco consumption falls as smokers cut down, give up or never start in response to prices.'

Source: 'Surprise reprieve for drinkers but smokers pay a high price' by Francesco Guerrera, the Independent Budget Review, 10/3/99.

a] Discuss and illustrate the effect of an increase in excise duty on cigarettes. **(8)**

b] Explain why cigarettes are a good source of tax revenue. **(6)**

c] Why did the tobacco producers oppose the rise in excise duty on cigarettes? **(4)**

d] Explain what a black market is and why there was one in tobacco in the UK. **(6)**

e] To what extent do you think demand for cigarettes does fall when prices rise? **(6)**

f] How heavily taxed are cigarettes in the UK? **(3)**

g] Apart from taxes, discuss two other measures a government could use to reduce smoking. **(8)**

h] Discuss the arguments for taxing cigarettes. **(9)**

STRUCTURED ESSAY

a] Explain why stable grooms receive low pay. **(12)**

b] Assess the arguments for and against the use of a national minimum wage. **(13)**

25 ASSESSMENT OF GOVERNMENT INTERVENTION

DIFFERENT VIEWS

Keynesians, who base their work on the ideas of John Maynard Keynes, believe that market failure is a common occurrence. They also believe it causes serious problems. For example they think that the UK's economic growth rate is lower than its potential growth rate because of a failure of the private sector to undertake sufficient investment, spending on research and development and training. Whilst Keynesians favour government action to improve the workings of markets, a group of economists, called new classical economists, believe that government intervention should be kept to a minimum. They hold this *laissez-faire* attitude for two key reasons:

- they believe that markets usually work efficiently;
- they think that government intervention can make the situation worse.

New classical economists believe that the central role of the government should be to ensure that laws, regulations and institutions operate in such a way as to enable market forces to provide economic agents with sufficient information and incentives.

POSSIBLE PROBLEMS WITH GOVERNMENT INTERVENTION

There are a number of reasons why government action taken to offset market failure may result in markets working even less efficiently. These include the following.

- *A lack of information*. To set tax rates, subsidies, maximum and minimum prices a government has to possess accurate information about present and future market conditions. New classical

economists believe the market is more efficient at discovering and transmitting information about the most efficient ways of allocating and using information about the kinds of goods and services demanded by consumers and about the cheapest methods of production. They believe that as the economy is constantly changing governments cannot obtain the necessary relevant information at the right time.

- *A lack of continuity in government policy*. If government policy changes too frequently it will make it difficult for firms to plan ahead. For instance, if the level of subsidies is changed frequently firms may not have the confidence to proceed with investment projects.
- *Bureaucracy*. It may take time for a government to decide on a policy while implementing it may involve cumbersome procedures.
- *A reduction in incentives*. Government intervention distorts incentives which new classical economists argue are essential for the efficient working of markets as they provide the motivation for entrepreneurs, managers and workers to increase their effort. For example, some forms of government intervention, e.g. subsidies, may permit inefficient firms to survive. Here, a government may help a new firm to start up but there is a danger that the firm becomes reliant on government assistance and does not seek to improve its performance.
- *Self interest*. On occasion politicians and civil servants may pursue their own career interests rather than society's interest. For example a Minister who is hoping to gain employment as a director of a tobacco company when s/he retires may not support an increase in excise duty on tobacco. A government may also be pressured

by special interest groups to allocate resources to satisfy their own specific interests.

So government intervention carries risks as well as benefits.

ADVANTAGES AND DISADVANTAGES OF SOME PARTICULAR MEASURES

PRICE CONTROLS

Setting maximum and minimum prices in product markets is likely to result in shortages and surpluses. So these measures usually have to be accompanied by other measures.

THE PROVISION OF INFORMATION

This can help people to make better informed decisions. However, there is a danger that the information produced can be 'massaged' and the requirement to provide it may distort the actions of those producing the figures. For example, a school may not enter borderline students for examinations for fear of compromising its place in the schools league table and hospitals may treat uncomplicated, non-urgent cases before more urgent and time-consuming cases in order to reduce their waiting lists.

TAXES AND SUBSIDIES

These have the advantage of potentially moving prices closer to social cost and benefit levels. Taxes on pollution, for example, convert external costs into private costs while some of the tax revenue gained can be spent on pollution reduction measures.

However, it can be difficult to estimate external costs and benefits so taxes and subsidies may be set too high or too low. It is also administratively too difficult and expensive to set different rates for each individual firm or indeed each individual person and to change them every time that external costs and benefits change.

Indirect taxes are likely to fall more heavily on the poor and if only one country places a tax on the production of a certain product to, e.g., reduce air pollution the outcome may just be to shift the source of pollution from one country to another one as consumers buy more imports of the product.

PROPERTY RIGHTS

Extending property rights has the potential advantage of compensating victims directly and achieving the socially optimum level of output and prices. However, it would in practice be difficult to operate such a policy given the large number of households and firms involved. In addition, the introduction of new legislation implies litigation and so may favour the rich who will be in a stronger position to take legal action.

COMPULSION

A government can pass legislation banning certain actions, e.g. carrying hand guns, or making certain actions compulsory, e.g. the wearing of seat belts. These measures may have popular support in which case they can be relatively cheap to implement. However, where they do not have popular support they are expensive to implement.

REGULATIONS

For example, a government can pass legislation about the amount of acceptable pollution. This should reduce the supply of products creating negative externalities and is likely to be politically more popular with people than a tax. However, it would be difficult to determine, and monitor, the optimal level of pollution. Additional problems are that victims may not be directly compensated while regulations may not provide a sufficient incentive to reduce pollution below the prescribed limit.

TRADEABLE PERMITS

A government could set a level of pollution and then issue or sell permits or licences. This would give firms the right to pollute up to set limits. The firms could be allowed to trade these permits. This method has the advantage of giving firms a financial incentive to reduce pollution, since they could sell off some of their permits, and it enables a government to set precise levels of pollution. However, it may not lower the total amount of pollution but merely change its source. As with regulations, this method can also be expensive to monitor and does not directly compensate victims.

QUESTIONS

SHORT QUESTIONS

1. What are the main arguments for non-intervention in markets?

2. Explain what is meant by property rights.

3. Is it easy to set a socially efficient tax? Explain your answer.

4. Do public goods have to be supplied by the government?

MULTIPLE CHOICE

1. Why might government intervention to correct market failure make the situation worse?

   A. Private sector firms are more likely to take into account external costs and benefits than the government.

   B. Taxes, subsidies and regulations may distort price signals and incentives.

   C. Government action may reduce firms' market power.

   D. Government action may promote labour mobility.

2. In which of the following circumstances is there a strong argument for government intervention in a market?

   A. There are many buyers and sellers.

   B. There are significant negative externalities in production.

   C. Firms' main objective is profit maximisation.

   D. Significant economies of scale exist.

3. To help the poor, a government sets a maximum price on a basic commodity. Why might this make the situation worse for the poor?

   A. Price is likely to rise to the maximum price level.

   B. Fewer people will be able to purchase the product.

   C. The poor, having less access, to information sources, may be unaware of the price change.

   D. The maximum price will encourage the entry of new firms into the market.

4. A government places a tax on producers in the country which create pollution. Why might this not result in a reduction of world pollution?

   A. The producers pass all the tax on to consumers.

   B. The producers absorb all of the tax.

   C. Consumers switch to foreign producers.

   D. Consumers reduce demand for the product.

DATA RESPONSE

The demand for economists is rising. Public and private sector employers want more of them. Yet the supply of newly minted economics PhDs is so low that it is bringing British academic economics close to crisis point.

Top PhD programmes in this country are averaging less than two British people per year. At the London School of Economics, for example, none of the 27 PhD students taken on in October 1998 was British. Of course, nationality is not the issue. British people's reluctance is symptomatic of the fact most talented people irrespective of nationality no longer want to become academic economists.

Pay is probably the key factor. Salaries of university economists have fallen way behind those in the private sector. In addition, British universities pay much less than US universities.

Has economics as a discipline become less attractive? Probably not. According to a recent *Wall Street Journal* article, economics is the most popular undergraduate major in US Ivy League universities.

Neither is the problem that people do not want to study for undergraduate degrees. Masters courses remain popular. But people are increasingly stopping there and not going on to the PhD level. Only 6% of British MSc economics students want a university job and, in the longer term, without PhD economists to teach masters courses, it will not be possible to run them.

Source: 'Economists fail to meet demand' by Stephen Machin and Andrew Oswald, the Guardian, 5/7/99.

a] What would cause a rise in demand for economists? **(6)**

b] Why has the supply of British economists fallen? **(6)**

c] What would be the market solution to a shortage of academic economists? **(6)**

d] Why is economics more popular in American universities? **(3)**

e] What may happen to the quality of the teaching of economics in UK universities and why? **(5)**

CASE STUDY

The first national minimum wage in British history will be introduced today amid demands that it should be raised by more than 25%.

It is now illegal for any organisation to pay employees aged 22 and over less than £3.60 an hour, but the country's biggest union and the Labour Party's largest single financial backer are calling for a minimum wage of £5.

A rate of £3 applies to those aged 18 to 21 and the law does not apply to under-18s.

Rodney Bickerstaffe, general secretary of Unison, said his organisation would be pressing ahead with a 'Living Wage' rally in Newcastle on 10 April in protest at the £3.60 floor. He said the law would not cure the 'blight' of low pay.

The GMB general union pointed out that most employers were ignoring the differential pay rate for young people. Both McDonald's and Burger King, which have come under fire for allegedly exploiting youngsters, are paying the full adult rate to all employees.

The Labour Research Department has found few large firms that will pay younger staff less. Forte, the hotel group, is an exception, paying £3.30 for employees aged 18 to 21. Poundstretcher, the discount store, confirms that the under-22s will receive less than £3.60, the department said.

Official figures show that more than two million workers are likely to have pay increases because of the new law, but many employers have uprated wage rates well ahead of today.

Pub chains, charities, cinemas and manufacturing firms are among employers that have increased pay to comply with the legislation, according to Income Data Services (IDS) in a report published yesterday.

The research group believes there is little evidence that the wage requirement will hit employment. Jobs in the service sector, seen as most vulnerable, continue to increase, with 100 000 new positions in hotels and restaurants in the past year, IDS reports.

The findings conflict with the results of research conducted by Business Strategies, which predict that the minimum wage would cost more than 10 000 jobs in the South-east over the next two to three years. The study asserts that where employers are not already paying the minimum wage, its implementation and 'knock-on' effects would force firms to reduce profits or increase prices. Either option would eventually lead to the employment of fewer people.

Source: 'Today, two million will be better paid' by Barrie Clement, the Independent, 1/3/99.

a] Was it generally regarded that the minimum wage had been set too high or too low? **(4)**

b] Why might firms choose to pay young workers the full adult rate? **(6)**

c] Why might the introduction of the national minimum wage not have had much impact on firms' costs? **(6)**

d] Why were jobs in the service sector perceived as the most vulnerable? **(6)**

e] Why would either a reduction in profits or an increase in prices 'eventually lead to the employment of fewer people'? **(8)**

f] Explain why the introduction of a minimum wage may actually raise employment. **(8)**

g] When does a minimum wage have no effect on the labour market? **(4)**

h] Why might the introduction of the national minimum wage not reduce poverty? **(8)**

STRUCTURED ESSAY

A government seeks to promote the consumption of fruit.

a] Discuss the effects of introducing a subsidy on fruit production, setting a maximum price for fruit and lowering income tax on the amount of fruit purchased. **(12)**

b] Assess which of the measures is most likely to achieve the government's objective and discuss any drawbacks it may have. **(13)**

PART FIVE: THE NATIONAL AND INTERNATIONAL ECONOMY

The output of an economy has a significant influence on its inhabitants' living standards. The higher the output the more goods and services people can enjoy.

The level of output is influenced by the total level of demand for the country's goods and services. Some of the demand will come from foreign countries just as some of the goods and services produced will be sold to other countries.

THE CIRCULAR FLOW OF INCOME

The circular flow of income illustrates how the macroeconomy works. It shows how output generates income which is then spent and it shows the relationship between households, the government and the foreign trade sector.

A TWO SECTOR MODEL

A simple model of the economy in which there are only two sectors, firms and households, is illustrated in Figure 26.1.

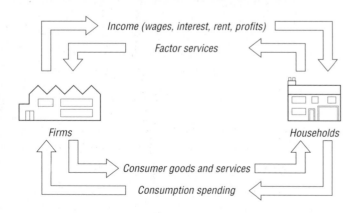

Firms   Households

Income (wages, interest, rent, profits)
Factor services
Consumer goods and services
Consumption spending

FIG. 26.1

Firms are the producing units which hire services provided by the people from the households. For these services firms pay wages (for labour), rent (for land), interest and dividends (for the services of capital). There is therefore, a flow of factor services from households to firms and a flow of income from firms to households. These flows are represented by the upper arrows in Figure 26.1.

In this model, households are also the purchasers of the national output. There is a flow of spending from households to firms and a flow of goods and services from firms to households. These flows are represented by the lower arrows in Figure 26.1. The costs of production represent the incomes paid to households.

LEAKAGES AND INJECTIONS

The simple model is very unrealistic because even in the simplest economy all the income received by households is not spent — some of it is saved. Saving represents a leakage (or withdrawal) from the circular flow of income because it is part of the income paid out by firms which is not returned to them through the spending of households. When saving takes place, firm's expenses will be greater than their receipts and some of their output will remain unsold. They will react by reducing output so that income and employment will fall. If households always save some fraction of their income and there are no other expenditures to offset this leakage, income must eventually fall to zero.

Fortunately there is an offsetting expenditure in the form of investment. The first model of the economy assumed that firms only produced consumer goods and services which were in turn bought by households. In fact, some firms produce capital goods for sale to other firms. This expenditure on capital goods adds to the circular flow of income; it has the opposite effect to a leakage and causes output and income to expand. Investment is an injection.

Figure 26.2 incorporates the saving leakage and the investment injection. The diagram concentrates on money flows; for purposes of simplification the real flows (i.e. goods and services) have been omitted.

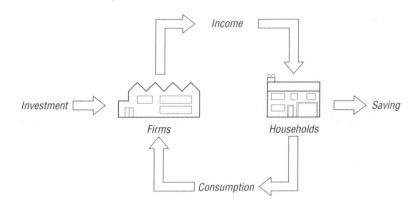

FIG. 26.2

A MORE REALISTIC MODEL

To make the model more realistic it is necessary to take into account the role that the government and the foreign trade sectors take in determining the level of economic activity.

FOREIGN TRADE

Some part of the expenditure of households does not flow back to domestic firms because households buy foreign products as well as home produced products. These imports are a leakage from the circular flow because they represent income paid by firms which does not flow back to them. Exports are an injection into the circular flow because this spending by foreigners on home produced output is an additional source of income which is not generated within the domestic system. If exports exceed imports there will be an expansionary effect on income while an import surplus will have a depressing effect on income.

GOVERNMENT

Government spending takes several forms. Government spending on goods and services is an injection because it adds to real output and creates employment. Transfer payments (e.g. state pensions and unemployment related benefits) do not, directly generate output and income — they transfer existing income from taxpayers to the recipients of the benefits.

Taxes are a leakage because they remove purchasing power from the system. The importance of government spending and taxation lies in the fact that they can be deliberately manipulated by government to influence the level of output and employment. A budget deficit (government spending exceeding taxation) will have an expansionary effect and a budget surplus (taxation exceeding government spending) a depressing effect on income.

Figure 26.3 shows a picture of the circular flow which takes into account all four sectors. It is, however, still simplified.

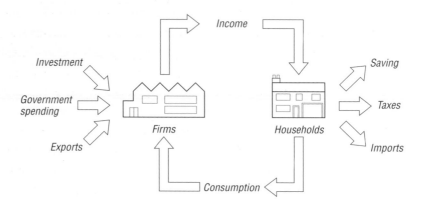

FIG. 26.3

According to Figure 26.3 all the leakages originate in the household sector. In the real world, of course, this is not the case, because the same leakages take place at different points in the circular flow. Firms pay taxes on their income, they save (i.e. they retain profits), and they buy foreign materials and machines. Taxes are levied on expenditures as well as incomes so that the tax leakage also applies to the streams of consumption and investment spending. Figure 26.3 would become very complicated if the locations of the injections and leakages were shown more accurately.

MEASURING NATIONAL INCOME

The main measure of national income now used is Gross Domestic Product (GDP). This is the total output of the resources located within the country.

There are three ways of measuring GDP. It can be measured as the total output from the domestically owned resources during the course of one year (the output approach).

Secondly, GDP may be measured in terms of the incomes earned by the factors of production engaged in producing the domestic output (the income approach).

Thirdly, GDP may be looked at from the point of view of its disposal. The country's output must either be bought for use or added to stocks. If it is assumed that net additions to stocks amount to 'expenditure' by the firm on its own output, national income can be measured by the amount spent on the country's output (the expenditure method). It should be apparent, therefore that:

National Output = National Income = National Expenditure

These totals should be equal as they are merely different ways of looking at the same thing. There are, however, a number of possible pitfalls in measuring the national income by these different methods.

THE OUTPUT METHOD

The most direct method of measuring the national output or income is to use the output figures of all the firms in the country. In the case of this method it is very important to avoid double counting.

Adding up the total outputs of all the firms in the economy will give a total many times greater than the true value of the national output. The problem of double counting arises because the outputs of some firms are the inputs of other firms. Suppose the annual output of the flour mills sells for £15m and the value of the output of the bakeries is £25m. Added together they give a total output of £40m, but the value of the flour has been counted twice. If the value of the wheat output from the farms, the flour output from the mills and the bread from the bakeries are added together the value of the wheat would be counted three times.

There are two possible ways of dealing with this problem. National output can be measured by adding the values of the final products, or by totalling the values added at each stage of production. In the example above the bakeries added £10m to the value of the flour they purchased from the mills — this is the true measure of their outputs. The total of the values added at each stage will be exactly the same as the total value of the final products. Table 26.1 shows the value added at each stage of the production of bread.

TABLE 26.1 VALUE ADDED IN BREAD PRODUCTION

	Value of output	Cost of intermediate goods	Value added
Farmers	10	0	10
Millers	15	10	5
Bakers	25	15	10
Retailers	30	25	5
			30

Intermediate goods and materials are the material inputs at the various stages of production — the goods each firm purchases from other producers. It can be seen that the value of the final product (which includes additions to stocks) is exactly the same as the total of the values added by the various production processes.

In addition if the general price level has changed it is necessary to make an adjustment for the purely monetary changes in the value of stocks. A rise in prices increases the value of existing stocks even when there is no change in their volume. In order to obtain an estimate of the real changes in stocks it is necessary to make a deduction equal to the 'inflationary' increase in value. This deduction is described as stock appreciation in the official tables.

THE INCOME METHOD

The main point to note here is the fact that all personal incomes are not included in the national income. Only incomes which have been earned for services rendered and for which there is some corresponding value of output are included. In many countries a sizeable proportion of total personal income is made up of *transfer payments*. These payments take the form of social security payments such as unemployment benefit, state pensions, child benefits, etc. They are not included because they are not payments for services rendered — there is no contribution to current real output by the recipients. The test of whether an income payment is a transfer payment or not is quite simple. The question to ask is: 'Is this a payment for services rendered during the period in which the income was received?' If the answer is 'No', then it is transfer payment.

THE EXPENDITURE METHOD

In estimating the value of the national output by the expenditure method it is important to record only final expenditures. All the expenditure on intermediate goods and services must be excluded. It is the usual practice to break down total expenditure into five large categories: consumption, government spending, investment, imports, and exports. This classification is extremely useful for purposes of analysis.

Care has to be taken to include only that part of government expenditure which represents payments for goods and services — government spending on transfer payments must be excluded.

REAL AND MONEY GDP

Using a monetary system of measurement gives rise to certain problems. Difficulties arise when comparisons are made if the value of money is changing. For example, output in one year may be the same as that of a previous year but if the price of goods and services has risen, then measuring GDP in current year prices will give the impression that output has increased.

To overcome this problem economists measure not only money GDP (i.e., GDP at current prices) but also real GDP. This is GDP adjusted for price changes so that actual changes in output can be identified. To achieve this economists measure GDP at constant prices, i.e. in the prices of a base year.

EXAMPLE

	Year 1	Year 2
GDP (£b)	100	120
Index of prices	100	105

GDP of Year 2 expressed in terms of the prices ruling in Year 1:

$$= 120 \times \frac{100}{105}$$

$$= £114.3b$$

The example shows that, although the GDP in monetary terms had increased by 20%, in real terms the increase was only about 14.3%.

USING THE INFORMATION

The measurement of the national income by official sources was first carried out in the UK in 1941 and the information is now published annually in the publication *United Kingdom National Accounts*, the 'blue book'.

National income figures are used for a number of purposes. Economic growth figures are based on changes in real GDP. Governments also use national income figures to compare changes in living standards over time and internationally.

THE STANDARD OF LIVING

Since income represents a flow of real output, movements in the national income are used to indicate changes in the standard of living. Care has to be taken, however, in using national income figures, including GDP, for this purpose.

As already mentioned it is important to use real GDP figures to assess changes in living standards. Account must also be taken of changes in the population because it is income per head which is relevant when living standards are being discussed. A 5% increase in real GDP which is accompanied by an 8% increase in the population probably means that the average standard of living has fallen. So economists often compare GDP per head figures.

It is also necessary to take note of the composition of total output. A large increase in total output which is due to an increased output of capital goods or defence equipment will not mean any immediate increase in economic welfare. Some goods and services, such as police services, are described as *regrettables*. If more police are recruited to tackle rising crime GDP will rise. However, people will feel worse off than they did before the rise in crime.

Indeed, GDP figures are a measure of the material standard of living rather than the quality of life. They measure the quantity of goods and services produced but the quality of life is affected by many factors. If increases in the quantity of goods and services produced are exactly offset by falls in their quality the standard of living will not have increased.

Higher GDP figures may also give a misleading indication of changes in economic welfare if they occurred at the same time that working hours have increased, working conditions declined and/or negative externalities have been created.

Externalities, both positive and negative are not taken into account in the calculations of the GDP. Pollution, noise, congestion and mental strain are possible by-products of an increasing GDP. If a nation spends, say, £10m on increasing the output of some product and then has to spend £1m on mitigating the nuisances associated with this output, it would be rather misleading to say that 'output' has increased by £11m.

Output may increase but if the distribution of income is very uneven only a few may experience a rise in their material living standards. It is also possible that official GDP figures may understate the quantity of goods and services which people enjoy. This is because some goods and services which are produced and sold are not recorded in the official figures. Their sale is not declared either because the activity involved is illegal or in order to avoid paying tax or losing benefits. The level of undeclared economic activity (known as the black economy) in a country is influenced by a number of factors including the marginal rate of tax, the chances of being found out, the penalties imposed and the range of activities which are declared to be illegal.

In addition a number of non-marketed services, for example child rearing and DIY, are not included in GDP figures, although they affect the quality of life.

INTERNATIONAL COMPARISONS

GDP per head is the most frequent indicator used to compare living standards in different countries. There are many reasons why such comparisons must be used with caution. The levels of accuracy in measurement may differ very widely. In countries where subsistence agriculture is the main activity there is a large element of guesswork in the final compilation.

There are great discrepancies in the patterns of income distribution in different countries. Two countries may have the same real GDP per head figures but the standards of living will be very different if in one country the income is very evenly distributed, while in the other income distribution is very unequal. The composition of total output may also be very different. For example, one country may devote a much greater proportion of its resources to defence than another country and yet the two countries may have similar figures for real GDP per head.

Externalities, the size of the black economy, working hours, working conditions and the quality of goods and services are also likely to differ between countries. Some differences arise from climate or geography. Inhabitants of cold countries have to spend a relatively large proportion of their incomes on keeping warm, while people living in sparsely populated countries will have to spend relatively more on communications and transport. It does not follow that living standards are lower where these expenditures are lower.

International comparisons also have to be undertaken in a common unit of measurement. For some time the most widely used unit has been the US dollar. The rate of exchange, however, may not be a good indicator of the relative domestic purchasing powers of the two currencies. For example if £1 = $2, it does not follow that $2 in the USA will purchase more or less of the same volume of goods and services as £1 in the UK. The official exchange rate only takes account of the products entering into international trade and these may represent a very small selection of the products traded within each nation. The exchange rate may also be held at an artificially high level by government action.

Since 1993 increasing use has been made by international organisations, including the United Nations, of purchasing power parity (PPP) exchange rates. These seek to measure the cost of a typical basket of goods and services in different countries, both internationally traded goods and services and non-internationally traded goods and services, for example, housing. If the typical basket of goods and services costs £7000 in the UK and $21 000 in the USA, the ratio is 1:3 and the effective exchange rate to be used to convert the national income figures would be £1 = $3.

ALTERNATIVE MEASURES OF LIVING STANDARDS

There are a number of other indicators of living standards which can be examined. These include, for example, the number of hospital beds and doctors per head of the population, the proportion of households which have a dishwasher, computer, two cars, and proportion of 16–18 year olds in further education.

A number of measures take into account a variety of indicators. These include the following.

- *Measurable economic welfare (MEW)*. In 1972, William Nordhaus and James Tobin developed MEW. This adjusts GDP by adding leisure, unpaid housework and the value of services given by consumer durables over the year. Deductions are made for 'regrettables' such as expenditure on commuting to work, defence, the police, negative externalities including pollution. This is an interesting approach which seeks to cover more of the aspects which affect economic welfare although it does not encounter the difficulty of having to attach a monetary value to non-marketed products.

- *Human Development Index (HDI)*. This also seeks to give a wider measure of economic welfare. It was introduced by the United Nations in 1990. The index is based on three sets of indicators. Real GDP (measured using PPP exchange rates) is one, adult literacy and average years of schooling is another and life expectancy is the third. The idea is that human development depends on the quantity of resources available to people in a country, their ability to use the goods and services produced and the time they have to use the goods and services.

QUESTIONS

SHORT QUESTIONS

1. Explain what is meant by the circular flow.

2. What is GDP?

3. Explain the difference between money and real GDP.

4. Why would it be misleading to calculate GDP by adding the values of the total outputs of all the firms in the economy?

MULTIPLE CHOICE

1. Which of the following is a leakage from the circular flow of income in an economy?

   A. Government spending on unemployment related benefits.

   B. The purchase of domestically produced products by foreign companies.

   C. The payment of sales tax on goods and services sold in the domestic market.

   D. Expenditure by domestic firms on capital goods.

2. In 1999 the gross domestic product of a country was £10 000m and the price index was 100. By the year 2003 the GDP has increased to £12 075m and the price index is 105. By what percentage has real GDP increased from 1999 to 2003?

   A. 5

   B. 14.71

   C. 15

   D. 20.75

3. Which of the following is not included in estimates of GDP?

   A. Rent paid by farmers.

   B. Wages paid to civil servants.

   C. State benefits paid to the disabled.

   D. Dividends paid by private sector companies.

4. A woman barrister earning £90 000 a year is made redundant. She finds a job as a legal advisor earning £36 000 a year. Her partner decides to stop being a home-maker and takes up a job as a journalist earning £26 000 a year. The couple hire a resident child carer to look after their two small children. They pay the child carer £9000 a year. What is the change in GDP, as measured by the income measure, which results from these changes?

   A. A fall of £19 000.

   B. A fall of £28 000.

   C. A rise of £9000.

   D. A rise of £35 000.

DATA RESPONSE

The underground economy has become one of the biggest money-spinners in the country, accounting for around a quarter of wealth generated every year, according to new research.

Contrary to earlier calculations that the 'black economy' soaked up around 10% of annual gross domestic product, a senior economist at Birmingham University now estimates it is over twice as much — the equivalent of about £10 000 for every person.

The findings John Burton prepared for the Social Market Foundation are underlined by a new report from a watchdog formed to clamp down on counterfeit goods. It estimates the market for fake products alone has risen to £3bn — probably a considerable underestimate.

Other areas, from drug-dealing to prostitution and poaching, are also worth billions. While many people dabble sometimes unknowingly, with the black market by moonlighting, or by employing moonlighters — from house cleaners to weekend tradesmen — the scale of the underground economy is alarming customs and excise, and the inland revenue, which is losing billions in lost taxes.

Researchers also say it is disguising the real level of unemployment by providing hundreds of thousands of people, mainly in the recession-hit north, with a small income.

Paul Covery of the pressure group the Unemployment Unit, said: 'There is a large pool of people in a twilight zone who find it impossible to live on the current level of benefits. On the one hand we have a flexible labour market encouraging casualised work, but on the other a very rigid benefits system … encouraging people to break the law.'

Source: 'Black economy booms as crooks eye a nice little earner' by Peter Hetherington, the Guardian, 5/7/99.

a] i Explain what is meant by the black economy. **(3)**

   ii According to the extract what is the size of the UK's black economy? **(2)**

b] What would be the benefits of a reduction in the size of the black economy? **(6)**

c] Discuss two possible disadvantages of a fall in the size of the black economy. **(6)**

d] Why has the size of the black economy grown? **(4)**

e] Explain what is meant by a flexible labour market. **(4)**

CASE STUDY

There is more money in Britain today, spread more liberally across the population, than at any previous time in history. The national income increased from about £2.5b in 1914 to nearly £800b in 1997: the amount of money generated by economic activity has increased sevenfold in real terms. Real disposable incomes, or what people have left to spend after inflation and taxes, have grown at slightly over 2% a year since the last war. Even at this stately pace, living standards double every 30 years or so.

As people earn more, they own more. In the 1950s, only one person in three owned a house; one in four a television set; one in 20 a fridge; one in six a washing machine; and one in seven a car. Central heating was the preserve of the rich. In the 1990s, two in three houses are owner-occupied; nine people out of 10 have central heating; four in five have a video recorder; nine out of 10 a washing machine; three in four have a car. Only one in 100 does not have a fridge. Forty years have passed since Harold Macmillan told a Conservative party rally: 'Most of our people have never had it so good.' Despite relative economic decline, militant trade unionism, two oil shocks and growing competition from abroad, most British people have carried on having it better since then.

When Macmillan spoke, the British people owned assets worth an estimated £66b. The Inland Revenue now estimates that they own 'marketable' assets (which can be sold or cashed in) worth £1955b. When the accrued value of occupational pension rights (£743b) and the notional value of the state pension scheme (£930b) are added, total personal wealth rises to £3628b. This is nearly £79000 for every person in the country — and it does not include consumer durables such as cars, televisions and washing machines.

These are not unimportant. Although they depreciate and have a low secondhand value, they are the means by which most people measure their standard of living — and they are not a bad proxy. Their price and the effort involved in their acquisition have both decreased dramatically and their quality has improved beyond recognition. A Ford Fiesta is more reliable, less uncomfortable and cheaper to run than a Ford Anglia of 30 years ago.

Yet people are miserable. One reason is that most people live to work rather than work to live. Significant minorities dislike their jobs so much that they skive off as often as they can, especially in the public sector. A Cabinet Office study reckons that the average public sector employee spends one third more time on sick leave (10–11 days) than his private sector counterpart (7–8 days). The Treasury estimated last year that absenteeism was costing the taxpayer £6b a year and the CBI thinks the figure for the private sector is £11b.

Source: 'Darling, we're rich so why is everybody so miserable?' by Dominic Hobson, the Sunday Times, 18/7/99.

a] Explain what is meant by national income in 'real terms'. **(4)**

b] What type of taxes are deducted in order to obtain disposable income? **(3)**

c] Distinguish between income and wealth. **(4)**

d] What effect will a rise in wealth have on consumption? **(5)**

e] What evidence is given in the extract that the material standard of living of British residents has increased? **(12)**

f] According to the extract how do most people judge whether their living standards have increased? **(4)**

g] Discuss three reasons, other than a dislike of their jobs, why some people may feel that the quality of their lives has declined. **(9)**

h] Explain three reasons why job dissatisfaction may raise firms' costs of production. **(9)**

STRUCTURED ESSAY

a] Explain three ways in which GDP can be measured. **(9)**

b] Discuss whether an increase in GDP necessarily means that living standards have risen. **(16)**

27 AGGREGATE DEMAND

AGGREGATE DEMAND AND AGGREGATE EXPENDITURE

Aggregate demand is total planned spending at a given price level. There are four main components of total spending on the country's goods and services. These are consumption (C), investment (I), government spending on goods and services (G), and net exports i.e. exports minus imports ($X–M$).

Total spending can also be considered in relation to income. It is then called aggregate expenditure and again consists of $C + I + G + (X–M)$. Whilst total spending falls as the price level rises, it rises as income rises. The largest component of total spending is consumption and the most volatile tends to be investment.

CONSUMPTION

Consumption (C) is the amount households spend on goods and services to satisfy their current wants. The proportion of their disposable income (Y), i.e. income after direct taxation plus any state benefits, which people spend is called the average propensity to consume (APC). $APC = C/Y$. For example, if a person spends £2000 out of a monthly disposable income of £3000 her APC will be £2000/£3000 = 0.67.

As income rises the total amount spent is likely to increase. However, the proportion spent tends to decline. For instance a person with a disposable income of £100 a week may have to spend all of her income to meet basic requirements (i.e., an APC of 1). Whereas a person with a disposable income

of £20 000 a week may spend £8000 (an APC of 0.4).

INFLUENCES ON CONSUMPTION

INCOME

The main influence on consumption is income. Economists agree on this but there is some debate as to which income is most significant. Keynesians argue that people's spending is based on their current income. Whereas the monetarist, Milton Friedman, argues that consumption is based on people's lifetime income. So that, for example, a medical student may spend extravagantly now in the expectation of a high future income. Duesenberry's *relative income hypothesis* suggests that people's spending decisions are influenced by how their current income compares with their previous income and, more significantly, by how much other people are spending (keeping up with the Joneses).

WEALTH

An increase in the value of people's assets is likely to encourage people to spend more (wealth effect). The main asset which most people own is their house. If house prices rise people feel able to spend more. They are able to borrow more on the strength of the value of their property. Rising house prices also tend to stimulate activity in the housing market and create a feel good factor. When people move house they tend to spend more on a range of goods and services including furniture, fittings and DIY equipment.

AVAILABILITY AND COST OF CREDIT

The easier and cheaper it is to borrow, the more people are likely to spend. When people spend more than they earn they are said to be dissaving.

DISTRIBUTION OF INCOME

A less even distribution may reduce spending. This is because the rich who receive higher incomes will not significantly increase their spending whereas middle- and lower-income groups experiencing reductions in their income will reduce their spending by quite large amounts.

AGE STRUCTURE

Middle-aged people tend to spend a lower proportion of their income than the young.

INFLATION

The effects of inflation are uncertain. People may be tempted to bring forward their purchases of cars, washing machines and other items if they expect their prices to continue to rise. However, this tendency may be more than offset by a desire to save more to maintain the real value of savings.

INDIRECT TAXES

A rise in indirect taxes will be likely to reduce consumption.

RANGE OF GOODS AND SERVICES

The greater the range of goods and services and the higher their quality the more people are likely to spend.

SAVING

Saving (S) is disposable income which is not spent. So it is expressed as $Y-C$. The proportion of disposable income which is saved is called the average propensity to save. $APS = S/Y$.

As income rises both the total amount saved and the proportion saved tend to increase. So a person with a disposable income of £1000 a month may save £100 ($APS = 0.1$), whereas a person with a disposable income of £4000 a month may save £1000 ($APS = 0.25$).

Figure 27.1 shows that as disposable income rises so does consumption. When disposable income is below Y people spend more than their income, i.e. there is dissaving. When disposable income rises above Y an increasing proportion of disposable income is saved.

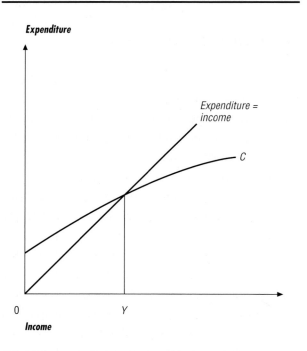

FIG. 27.1

INFLUENCES ON SAVINGS

INCOME

The most obvious requirement is the ability to save and this depends upon the level of income. No one can save until the level of income is sufficient to cover what are considered to be the necessities of life. As income rises beyond this level so does the ability to save. As already noted, as people earn more, the proportion of income which is devoted to consumption spending tends to fall. What is true of the individual is also true, in this case, of society as a whole. The rate of saving in rich countries is much higher than in poor countries.

SOCIAL ATTITUDES

The prevailing social attitude towards thrift (the careful management of money) influences the level of saving. Where thrift is regarded as a virtue, more will be saved. In some societies people place a higher value on leisure and consumption and there less is saved.

THE RANGE OF FINANCIAL INSTITUTIONS

In developed economies, all kinds of institutions for the safe deposit of savings are available. Savings banks, commercial banks, insurance companies, and building societies are all widely known, easily accessible, and usually have the confidence of the people. This range of opportunities not only stimulates savings but ensures that most of the potential saving is made available to borrowers. In some developing economies there is a lack of financial institutions or a lack of institutions which have the confidence of the public.

THE RATE OF INTEREST

In most cases a rise in the rate of interest will increase saving. However it may reduce the amount saved by target savers (see below).

INFLATION

Inflation tends to reduce the real value of money wealth. So people may save more when inflation rises in order to maintain the real value of their savings.

HABIT

People may get into the habit of saving, e.g. £50 a month. Changes in the rate of interest are not likely to affect this form of saving.

CONTRACTS

Contractual saving is carried out through insurance companies, pension funds, and building societies. The individual saver puts himself under a contractual agreement to pay a fixed annual sum (e.g. the insurance premium). Variations in the rate of interest will have little or no effect on existing contracts, although they might alter the nature of future contracts.

TARGETS

Many savers have a definite target such as the deposit for a new home, the purchase price of a motor cycle, or the cost of a holiday abroad. Saving in order to accumulate a fixed and known sum of money is not likely to be influenced greatly by changes in the rate of interest. In fact, an increase in the rate of interest might well reduce the level of such saving since, at the higher interest rate, the required sum will accumulate at a faster rate.

GOVERNMENT POLICIES

Governments encourage saving by, for example, allowing a certain amount to be saved in tax free saving schemes, e.g. ISAs.

CORPORATE SAVING

Companies save in order to build up reserves which will act as a cushion against future business fluctuations and provide funds for future expansion.

GOVERNMENT SAVING

A government saves when its income from tax revenue is greater than its expenditure. This may occur unexpectedly if the level of economic activity is higher than expected or it may result from deliberate government policy if the government raises tax rates and/or cuts government expenditure in order to reduce private sector demand.

INVESTMENT

There are a number of influences on private sector investment.

THE RATE OF INTEREST

Firms invest when the expected yield from investment exceeds the expected cost. The expected yield is sometimes referred to as the marginal efficiency of investment or the marginal efficiency of capital. Figure 27.2 shows the relationship between the marginal efficiency of capital and the rate of interest.

As the amount of capital increases the marginal efficiency of capital falls. This is because as, e.g., the number of machines increases the return from each extra machine declines as there may not be the ideal combination of resources (and so capital will be subject to diminishing returns) and the resulting higher output will reduce the price of the product.

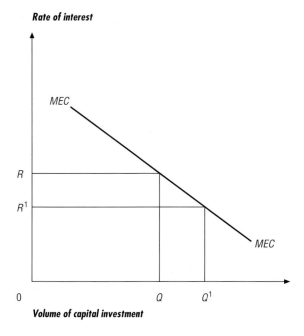

FIG. 27.2

The price of capital is taken to be the current rate of interest on the funds available to purchase capital equipment. A firm will employ capital up to the point where the marginal efficiency is just equal to its price.

In Figure 27.2 when the rate of interest is R, the firm will expand its capital stock to Q. Any further additions to the capital stock would only reduce the firm's profits because the cost incurred in acquiring the capital (i.e. the interest charges) would exceed the expected annual returns from the extra units of capital. If the rate of interest falls to R^1, the demand for capital increases to Q^1. Investment projects (QQ^1) which appeared unprofitable at the higher interest rate will now offer the prospect of profitable employment. Similarly an increase in the rate of interest will reduce the demand for capital goods. This analysis applies whether the firm is borrowing money or using its own savings. The rate of interest is the opportunity cost of investment in both cases. When the firm uses its own savings to purchase capital it sacrifices the interest it could have earned on those savings.

The marginal efficiency of capital indicates what quantity of capital will be demanded at any given price and it is, therefore, the demand curve for capital.

The marginal efficiency of capital will increase if either the productivity of capital increases or if the price of the product produced increases. The factors discussed below would all cause a shift in the marginal efficiency of capital (and hence the demand curve for capital).

CHANGES IN TECHNOLOGY

Advances in technology will make machines more productive and are likely to stimulate investment.

CHANGES IN COST OF CAPITAL

If capital becomes cheaper to buy and install more is likely to be purchased.

EXPECTATIONS

These can be referred to as 'animal spirits' and can have a significant influence. If entrepreneurs are optimistic about the future they are likely to invest more.

CORPORATION TAX

Corporation tax is a tax on the profits of firms. Lower corporation tax will increase post-tax returns and stimulate investment.

GOVERNMENT INCENTIVES

An increase in government grants and investment tax allowances will be likely to increase investment.

PROFIT LEVELS

Higher profit levels will encourage firms to invest and will provide them with the finance to do so.

RATE OF CHANGE OF INCOME

This is one of the main influences on investment and its significance is discussed below in the accelerator theory.

THE ACCELERATOR THEORY

The accelerator theory states that net investment is related to the rate of change of national income. For instance, if the growth of national income increases, consumption will rise and firms will seek to increase their productive capacity. According to the accelerator theory a change in the rate of growth of demand for consumer goods and services will cause a greater percentage change in demand for capital goods.

EXAMPLE

If in one year demand for consumer goods from one firm with eight machines rises from £80 000 to £90 000 (one machine makes £10 000 worth of output and there is no depreciation) the firm will order one machine. If then demand rises at a faster rate from £90 000 to £120 000 the firm will now order an extra three machines. So whilst in the second period demand for consumer goods rises by $33\frac{1}{3}\%$, demand for capital rises by 200%. The accelerator theory emphasises how volatile investment can be and how it can accentuate changes in national income, both increases and decreases.

However a change in the rate of growth of national income will not always cause a greater percentage change in demand for capital goods for a number of reasons.

- Entrepreneurs may not be convinced that the resulting change in demand will last and so will not adjust their productive capacity.
- Firms might initially have had spare capacity so they may be able to expand output, if demand is rising, without having to buy more machines and other capital equipment.

- In contrast, the capital goods industry may not have any spare capacity and so may not be able to supply more capital goods.
- A change in technology may mean that output can be increased with a smaller percentage rise in investment.

The accelerator theory concentrates on private sector investment. Whereas private sector investment will tend to increase as income rises, public sector investment may fall to offset possible inflationary effects.

GOVERNMENT SPENDING

The government spends money on both capital and consumer goods and services. The level of government spending is influenced by a number of factors including the level of economic activity, the age of the population and the level of provision of government financed or subsidised goods and services. (Government spending is discussed in more detail in Chapter 32.)

NET EXPORTS

The amount earned from exports and the amount spent on imports are again influenced by a range of factors including:

- the price of domestic goods and services relative to the price of foreign goods and services
- the quality of domestic goods and services relative to the quality of foreign goods and services
- exchange rates
- income levels at home and abroad
- the effectiveness of the marketing of domestic goods and services relative to the effectiveness of the marketing of foreign goods and services.

QUESTIONS

SHORT QUESTIONS

1. What are the main components of aggregate expenditure?
2. Explain what is meant by the average propensity to save.
3. What is the main influence on consumption and saving?
4. Explain what is meant by the marginal efficiency of capital.

MULTIPLE CHOICE

1. What is meant by the average propensity to consume?

   A. The proportion of total disposable income spent on consumption.

   B. The proportion of additional disposable income spent on consumption.

   C. The annual average consumption over the period of a year.

   D. The annual average amount spent on domestically produced goods and services.

2. Which of the following concepts explains how changes in the rate of growth of aggregate demand may bring about changes in new capital formation?

   A. The accelerator.

   B. The marginal efficiency of capital.

   C. Gross investment.

   D. The speculative demand for money.

3. Which of the following would cause an increase in the marginal efficiency of a new capital project?

   A. An increase in corporation tax.

   B. An increase in the rate of interest.

   C. A reduction in the purchase price of new machines.

   D. A reduction in government subsidies on investment.

4. A woman has a disposable income of £240 and spends £180. What is her average propensity to save?

   A. 0.25

   B. 0.50

   C. 0.75

   D. 0.80

DATA RESPONSE

Year	Real household disposable income	Consumption	Savings ratio
	£ billion, 1995 prices		
1995	494.6	443.7	10.3
1996	505.4	457.4	9.5
1997	525.7	457.7	9.5
1998	525.8	489.0	7.0
1999	546.2	504.7	7.6
2000	570.9	516.7	9.5
2001	583.9	529.6	9.3

Source: adapted from Table 3, Page 16, National Institute Economic Review, July 1999, NIESR.

a] Explain the meaning of 'disposable income'. **(3)**

b] Analyse the relationship between real disposable income and consumption in the period shown. **(9)**

c] Do your findings in (b) accord with what you would expect from economic theory? **(5)**

d] Explain the mean of the savings ratio. **(2)**

e] Identify and briefly comment on any three factors, other than income, which may influence the savings ratio. **(6)**

CASE STUDY

A 'persistent and widespread' fear of unemployment is stopping consumers from spending, according to a survey published yesterday.

The revival in confidence among British consumers has ground to a halt because of fears over job security, the European Commission's GfK survey said.

The survey found that 31% of consumers intended to reduce spending on major purchases over the next year; with only 27% planning to spend more, denting hopes of a retail-driven recovery. The reason for this was 'widespread and persistent fear of unemployment', said the survey.

Despite a gradual erosion of fears about joblessness, 42% still believed unemployment would increase over the next year. 'Spending intentions are likely to increase as the fear of unemployment recedes,' said GfK. 'However, at the current rate of improvement this promises to be a slow process.'

The fear of rising unemployment is counter to official figures, which have recorded drops in the number of benefit claimants for five consecutive months.

The GfK report supports the picture painted by surveys of sluggish high-street growth with consumers unwilling to accept any price rises. But GfK said the number expecting the overall economic situation to improve in the next year outweighed those expecting a deterioration for the first time since June last year.

Meanwhile Ian Plenderleith, a member of the Bank of England's Monetary Policy Committee, said the recent rise in house prices did not presage an unsustainable consumer boom.

He said the growth reflected an increase in home ownership rather than buyers seeing property as an investment opportunity.

Source: 'Job fears keep retail spending under control' by Philip Thornton, the Independent, 22/6/99.

a] Explain why fear of unemployment may reduce consumption. **(5)**

b] What is a consumer boom? **(5)**

c] In what sense may a house be an investment? **(5)**

d] Apart from unemployment, what other influence on consumption, is mentioned in the article? **(3)**

e] What effect would sluggish high-street growth be likely to have on investment? **(8)**

f] Discuss three factors, other than fears of unemployment and the one you have identified in (d), which can influence consumption. **(9)**

g] What effect may fears of unemployment have on pay claims? **(6)**

h] Discuss the effects of an increase in activity in the housing market on consumption. **(9)**

STRUCTURED ESSAY

a] Distinguish between saving and investment. **(8)**

b] Discuss the main influences on private sector investment. **(17)**

28 AGGREGATE DEMAND AND SUPPLY

AGGREGATE DEMAND

Aggregate demand is the amount which will be spent at different values of the price level. It is composed of consumption (C), investment (I), government spending (G) and net exports (X–M).

THE AGGREGATE DEMAND CURVE

The aggregate demand curve shows the quantity of goods and services which households, firms, overseas buyers and government are prepared to buy at different values of the general price level. It is drawn on the assumption that other things (e.g. the money supply, rates of taxation, the marginal propensity to consume) remain unchanged. Figure 28.1 shows an aggregate demand curve.

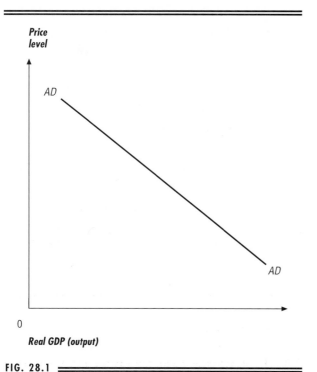

Price level

AD

AD

0

Real GDP (output)

FIG. 28.1

WHY THE *AD* CURVE SLOPES DOWN FROM LEFT TO RIGHT

There are three main reasons why there is an inverse relationship between the general price level and aggregate demand and hence why the AD curve slopes down from left to right.

- A rise in the price level reduces the real value of people's income and wealth and hence decreases their ability to consume.
- Higher prices increase people's and firms' demand to hold money for transactions purposes. This increase in the transactions demand for money is likely to raise the rate of interest and thereby reduce demand for consumer goods (consumption) and demand for capital goods (investment).
- An increase in the general price level will make domestic goods and services less competitive against foreign goods and services. This will reduce demand for domestic products from both domestic and foreign consumers.

MOVEMENTS ALONG THE DEMAND CURVE

As with a demand curve for a particular product, the cause of a movement along an aggregate demand curve will be a change in price, in this case a change in the general price level. A rise in the general price level will cause a contraction in aggregate demand and a fall in the general price level will cause an extension in aggregate demand. Figure 28.2 shows an extension in aggregate demand. If the general price level falls people's purchasing power will increase, the transactions demand for money will fall causing a reduction in interest rates and domestic goods and services will become more price competitive.

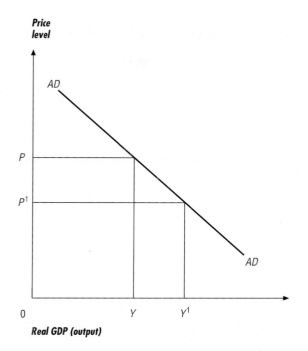

Price level

AD

P

P¹

AD

0   *Y*   *Y¹*

Real GDP (output)

FIG. 28.2

THE SHAPE OF THE AGGREGATE DEMAND CURVE

One group of economists, Keynesians, believe the aggregate demand curve is steep. This is because they think that a rise in the general price level will have only a small impact on the rate of interest and this in turn will have only a small impact on consumption and investment. They argue that the demand for money is dominated by the speculative motive. This is interest elastic so that an increase in demand for money will cause only a small rise in the rate of interest. In their view the main influence on both consumption and investment is income and not the rate of interest. The implication of the aggregate demand curve being steep is that a change in the general price level will not significantly alter aggregate demand.

In contrast new classical economists believe the aggregate demand curve is shallow. They think the main component of the demand for money is the transactions demand. This is interest inelastic so if a rise in the general price level leads to an increase in demand for money there may be a large rise in the rate of interest. Again, contrary to the Keynesian view, new classical economists believe a change in the rate of interest can have a significant impact on consumption and investment. So in their view, changes in the general price level can have a large effect on aggregate demand.

SHIFTS IN THE AGGREGATE DEMAND CURVE

The aggregate demand curve will shift to the right (an increase in aggregate demand) or shift to the left (a decrease in aggregate demand) if there is a change in an influence on aggregate demand other than a change in the general price level.

An increase in aggregate demand will cause more to be demanded at any given price level. An increase in aggregate demand is illustrated in Figure 28.3.

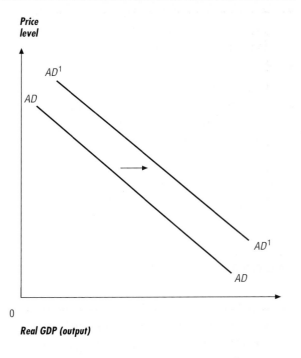

Price level

AD¹

AD

AD¹

AD

0

Real GDP (output)

FIG. 28.3

CAUSES OF SHIFTS IN AGGREGATE DEMAND

The aggregate demand curve will shift if households, firms, the government and/or foreigners alter the amount they wish to spend at any given price level. There are a number of factors which can cause a change in desired expenditure on consumption, investment, government spending and/or net exports. An increase in aggregate demand, for example, may be caused by any of the following.

- An increase in the money supply will increase demand directly as households and firms will have more money to spend and indirectly by lowering the rate of interest.
- A rise in optimism will increase both consumption and investment.
- A fall in the exchange rate will be likely to increase demand for net exports.
- Government policy resulting in a reduction in taxes and/or an increase in government expenditure will raise aggregate demand.
- An increase in the expected rate of inflation will be likely to increase consumption as people bring forward their spending plans.
- If income rises abroad, demand for exports will be likely to increase.
- A rise in population size will increase demand for a wide range of goods and services.
- A fall in the rate of interest will probably stimulate demand for consumer and capital goods.
- An increase in wealth is likely to lead to an increase in consumption.

AGGREGATE SUPPLY

Aggregate supply is the total output all firms are willing to supply at each given price level. Economists distinguish between short-run and long-run aggregate supply.

THE SHORT-RUN AGGREGATE SUPPLY CURVE

The short-run aggregate supply curve slopes up from left to right as illustrated in Figure 28.4.

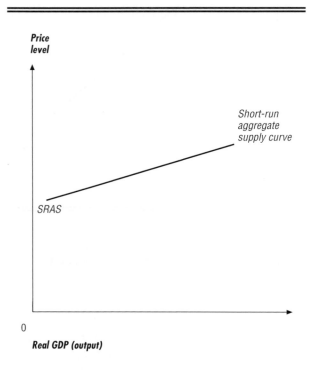

FIG. 28.4

In the short-run it is assumed that the prices of all factors of production are fixed. Nevertheless, an increase in output is likely to be associated with higher unit (average) costs. This is because overtime may have to be paid, less efficient machines may be used and less efficient methods of production may have to be employed. As higher output is associated with higher unit costs, firms will only supply more goods and services if they can be sold at higher prices, resulting in an upward sloping supply curve. Whilst unit costs do rise with output they rise by small amounts, making the short-run aggregate supply curve elastic.

SHIFTS IN THE SHORT-RUN AGGREGATE SUPPLY CURVE

The short-run supply curve will move to the right (an increase) and to the left (a decrease) as a result of a change in an influence other than a change in the general price level. Shifts in the short-run curve are often referred to as supply side shocks.

A decrease in the short-run aggregate supply curve will mean that firms will offer less for sale at any given general price level. Figure 28.5 illustrates a decrease in the short-run aggregate supply curve.

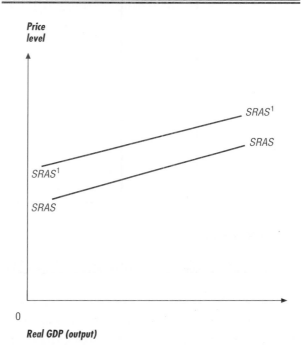

FIG. 28.5

Among the factors which can cause a decrease in short-run aggregate supply are:

- A rise in wage rates will increase firms' costs of production at any level of output, causing firms to reduce aggregate supply.
- A rise in raw material costs will again raise firms' costs of production, causing them to reduce their output.

- A rise in corporation tax will not only raise firms' costs of production but may also provide less of an incentive for entrepreneurs and reduce their willingness to produce.
- Unfavourable weather will affect agricultural production and construction work.
- Natural disasters, for instance, floods, may damage a number of firms' ability to produce.
- A decrease in the productivity of factors of production will raise costs and lower supply.

THE LONG-RUN AGGREGATE SUPPLY CURVE

The new classical view is that the long-run aggregate supply is vertical as shown in Figure 28.6.

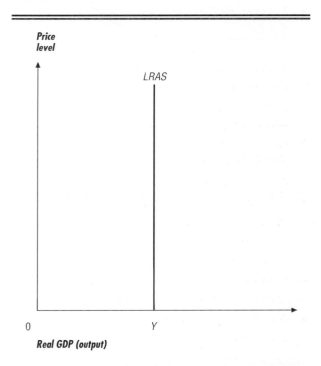

FIG. 28.6

This is because it is defined as the aggregate quantity of goods and services supplied when the economy is operating at full employment (as defined in terms of the natural rate of unemployment). It indicates the maximum potential output possible with given resources and given technology.

The Keynesian view is that even in the long run there can be unemployment so they think the long-run aggregate supply curve will have a different shape. Figure 28.7 illustrates this version.

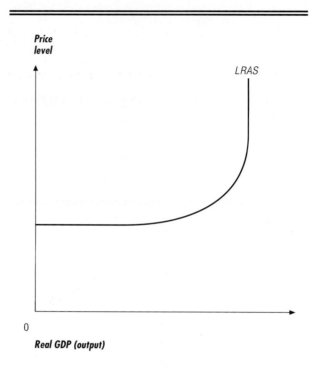

Price level

LRAS

0

Real GDP (output)

FIG. 28.7

At low levels of output the long-run aggregate supply curve is horizontal (perfectly elastic). This is because with a resulting high level of unemployment, output can be increased without a rise in costs. More workers can be recruited at the current wage rates and a rise in demand for raw materials and capital goods will not raise their price. Then at higher levels of output it starts to slope up as firms begin to experience rises in costs as they have to compete for increasingly scarce labour, raw materials and capital goods. At the full employment level the curve becomes vertical. Again this represents the maximum potential output.

SHIFTS IN THE LONG-RUN AGGREGATE SUPPLY CURVE

Over time, an economy's maximum potential output can change as a result of a change in the quantity and/ or quality of factors of production. An increase in the long-run aggregate supply curve is shown in Figure 28.8.

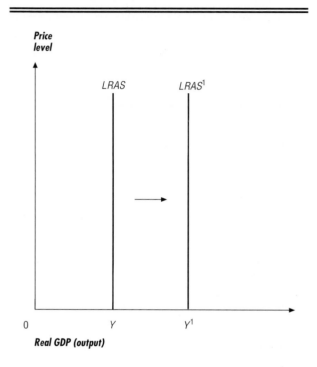

Price level

LRAS   LRAS¹

0   Y   Y¹

Real GDP (output)

FIG. 28.8

The specific causes of an increase in the curve include an increase in the supply of labour, an increase in human capital (resulting from, e.g., improved healthcare, training and/or education), increase in investment, technological progress, discovery of raw materials, and greater incentives to work.

SHORT-RUN EQUILIBRIUM OUTPUT AND PRICE LEVEL

In the short-run the *AD* curve is downward sloping and the *AS* curve is upward sloping. Where *AD* equals *AS* will determine the general price level and the level of output (real national income). In Figure

28.9 the equilibrium general price level is *P* and the equilibrium level of output is *Y*.

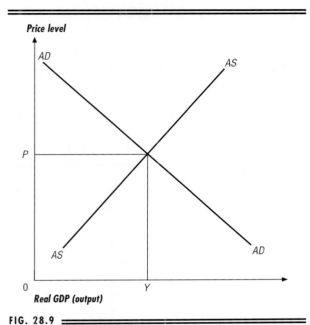

FIG. 28.9

EFFECTS OF SUPPLY-SIDE SHOCKS

Economists agree that a decrease in aggregate supply will increase the general price level and reduce output as shown in Figure 28.10.

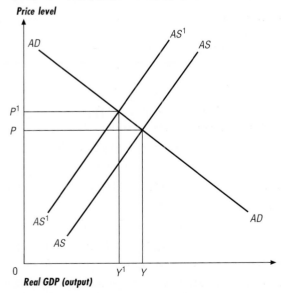

FIG. 28.10

LONG-RUN EQUILIBRIUM

New classical economists consider that free market forces result in an optimal allocation of resources. They believe that in the long-run the labour market will be in equilibrium and the economy will operate where aggregate demand equals aggregate supply at the full employment level. This is shown in Figure 28.11.

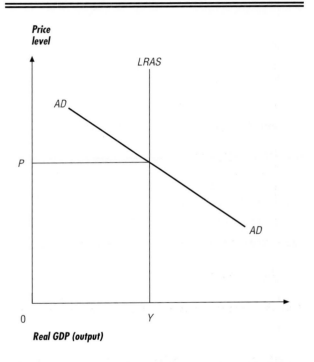

FIG. 28.11

Keynesians argue that the long-run equilibrium level of output can occur at any level of employment. Figure 28.12 shows the economy operating at less than full employment.

EFFECTS OF AN INCREASE IN AGGREGATE DEMAND

The different views on the long-run equilibrium level of output lead economists to different conclusions about the effects of an increase in aggregate demand. New classical economists believe an in-

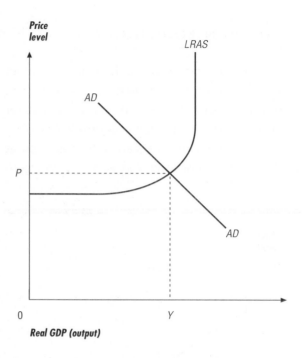

FIG. 28.12

crease in aggregate demand, without an increase in long-run aggregate supply, will result solely in a rise in the general price level. This is shown in Figure 28.13.

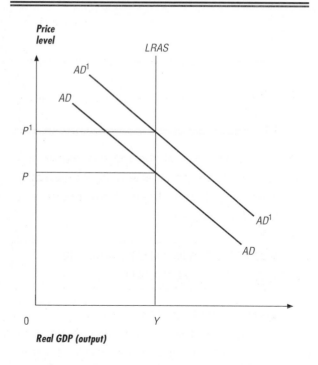

FIG. 28.13

Keynesians agree that an increase in aggregate demand will be purely inflationary if it occurs at the full employment level. However, they argue that it occurs at less than full employment but where shortages in resources are beginning to be experienced, both output and the general price level will rise or if it occurs at a low level of economic activity it will cause a rise solely in output. Figure 28.14 shows an increase in aggregate demand raising output but having no effect on the general price level.

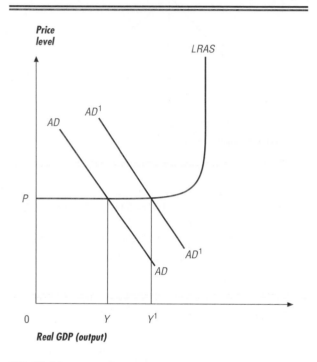

FIG. 28.14

THE IMPORTANCE OF INVESTMENT

Investment is a component of aggregate demand. So an increase in investment will shift the aggregate demand curve to the right which will stimulate economic activity.

Investment not only influences aggregate demand; it also affects long run aggregate supply. An increase in investment raises the productive potential of the economy. So investment generates demand and creates some of the resources to meet that demand.

QUESTIONS

SHORT QUESTIONS

1 Why does the aggregate demand curve slope down from left to right?

2 What can cause a movement along a short run aggregate supply curve?

3 In what circumstances would long run aggregate supply be perfectly elastic?

4 If the long run aggregate supply curve is vertical, what effect will an increase in demand for exports have on output and the general price level?

MULTIPLE CHOICE

1 What is aggregate demand?

A Total expenditure on domestically produced goods and services at a given income level.

B Total expenditure on domestically produced goods and services at a given price level.

C Total demand for consumer goods produced by domestic companies.

D Total of consumers' expenditure, government expenditure and investment.

2 Figure 28.15 shows the aggregate demand in an economy increasing from AD to AD¹.

What could have caused this increase?

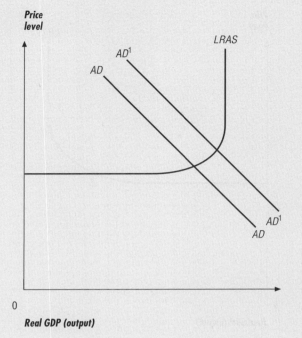

FIG. 28.15

A An improvement in training.

B An increase in the rate of interest.

C A reduction in the rate of exchange.

D A reduction in the general price level.

3 An economy is operating at point Z in Figure 28.16.

What effect will an increase in consumer spending have on output and the price level?

	Output	Price level
A	increase	reduce
B	reduce	increase
C	increase	increase
D	reduce	reduce

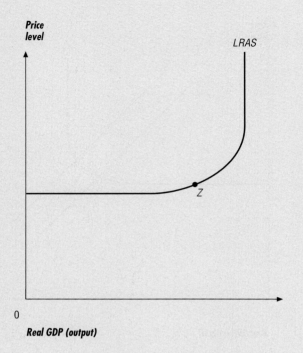

FIG. 28.16

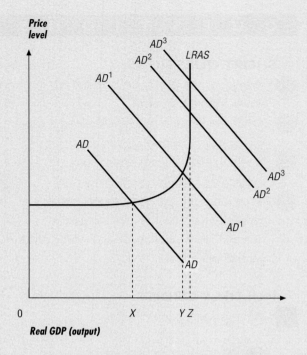

FIG. 28.17

4 Figure 28.17 shows an aggregate demand and an aggregate supply curve for an economy. Which of the following statements is correct?

A At real national income level X the economy is operating with spare capacity.

B The full employment level of real national income is Y.

C An increase in aggregate demand from AD^2 to AD^3 will cause a rise in output and the price level.

D A decrease in aggregate demand from AD^2 to AD^1 will reduce the price level and the rate of unemployment.

DATA RESPONSE

Up until 1995 the Colombian economy was performing well. For 25 years its growth rate, at an annual average of 4.7% a year, exceeded that of all other Latin American economies.

However since 1996 its average annual growth has fallen to just 1.8%. The economy has run into difficulties. Unemployment in 1999 reached 19.5% compared with 8% in 1994.

In July 1999 the Colombian central bank devalued its currency, the peso, to encourage a rise in demand for Colombian exports and a decrease in Colombian demand for imports.

The sharp decline in economic growth caused a rise in the government's budget deficit (the excess of government expenditure over tax revenue). To reduce this deficit the government cut its expenditure mainly on investment projects.

a] How did the performance of the Colombian economy in the second half of the 1990s compare with that in the first part of the 1990s? **(4)**

b] Use an aggregate demand and supply diagram to explain the possible effect on output and the price level of the change in unemployment which occurred between 1994 and 1999. **(7)**

c] What effect is devaluation likely to have on economic activity and the price level? Again use an aggregate demand and supply diagram to illustrate your answer. **(7)**

d] Use an aggregate demand and supply diagram to explain the possible effect on output and the price level of the change in government expenditure on investment projects. **(7)**

CASE STUDY

Economic activity was weak in Italy throughout last year, with GDP rising by only 1.4%.

Private consumption rose by only 1.9% in 1998, compared to 2.6% in 1997, with the slowdown in contrast to the acceleration apparent in most other Euro Area economies.

In 1998, domestic demand was mainly sustained by private investment. After two years of severe slowdown, investment started to pick up in the early part of the year, helped by the fall in interest rates, strong corporate profits and a high level of capacity utilisation. However, the progressive deterioration in the economic outlook, with the Asian crisis reducing external demand and the competitiveness of Italian firms in sectors such as textiles, led firms to be more cautious in their investment decisions.

Over 1998 as a whole, net external demand made a negative contribution to the growth in output. In 1998, the value of imports of goods and services rose by 6.1%. This reflects both the growth of imports from the Asian economies as well as the effects of public incentives for scrapping old cars. Weaker domestic demand has caused import growth to slow. The growth in exports of goods and services also slowed down in the second half of last year, partly because of the sharp slowdown in world trade. Italy is relatively specialised in sectors such as textiles, clothing and footwear which are highly exposed to competition from Asian producers. The weakening of demand in the other European countries intensified the slowdown in export growth.

Source: National Institute Economic Review, No.168, April 1999, National Institute of Economic and Social Research.

a] What is meant by GDP? **(3)**

b] Explain why private sector investment rose in Italy in 1998. **(7)**

c] Discuss two influences on private sector investment not mentioned in the extract. **(8)**

d] Why is investment so significant in influencing output? **(8)**

e] Explain what is meant by the statement 'net external demand made a negative contribution to the growth of output'. **(7)**

f] Which component of aggregate demand is not mentioned in the extract? **(3)**

g] Are exports a leakage or an injection into the circular flow of income? Explain your answer. **(5)**

h] What may cause an increase in aggregate demand? **(9)**

STRUCTURED ESSAY

a] What factors determine the level of aggregate supply in an economy? **(10)**

b] Compare the Keynesian and new classical views on the effect of an increase in aggregate demand on output, employment and the general price level. **(15)**

29 DETERMINATION OF OUTPUT, EMPLOYMENT AND PRICE

The level of economic activity in an economy is determined by aggregate demand and aggregate supply. There will no pressure for output, employment or price to change if aggregate demand = aggregate supply $(AD = AS)$ as shown in Figure 29.1. This relationship is discussed in Chapter 28.

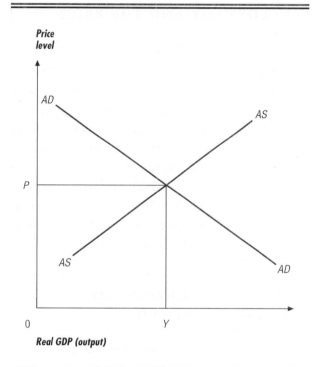

FIG. 29.1

Equilibrium output and the price level can also be stated to occur when total planned expenditure is just equal to the output that is actually produced i.e. $C + I + G + (X–M) = Y$. Figure 29.2 shows what is known as the 45° diagram. National income is measured on the horizontal axis and total planned expenditure, at different levels of GDP is measured on the vertical axis. GDP is in equilibrium at Y level of GDP. If all the output produced is sold there is no reason for producers to change their output.

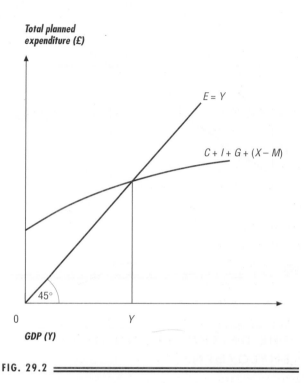

FIG. 29.2

LEAKAGES = INJECTIONS

Figure 29.3 can be used to derive another formula for the equilibrium condition. GDP will only be stable when the total planned injections are equal to the total planned leakages.

In a four sector economy with a government sector and a foreign trade sector, it is not a necessary condition for equilibrium that S should be equal to I, or that G be equal to T, or X be equal to M. The national output will be in equilibrium when:

Total planned injections = total planned leakages
$$I + G + X = S + T + M$$

Thus an excess of saving over investment may be offset by a budget deficit or an export surplus.

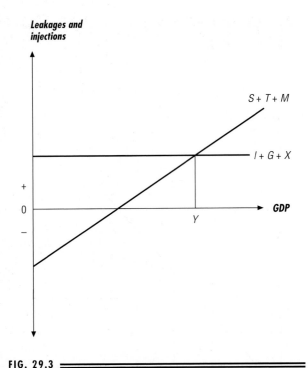

FIG. 29.3

THE DETERMINATION OF EMPLOYMENT

Employment is influenced by the level of economic activity. When output rises, employment is also likely to rise. More workers will be taken on to produce the higher level of output. However there may be a time lag between changes in output and employment. In the short run firms observing changes in demand may alter their output but may delay changing their employment levels until they are certain that the new level of demand will last. In the short run firms can raise their output by asking their existing workers to work overtime.

In the long run whilst output and employment are likely to be directly related they may not be proportionately related. For example a 6% rise in output may be achieved with a 2% rise in employment if productivity of labour rises.

FULL EMPLOYMENT

Once full employment is reached it is not possible to increase output in the short run. Any increases in planned expenditure will only cause a rise in the price level. Keynesian economists believe equilibrium GDP can occur at any level of employment. In contrast new classical economists believe that equilibrium GDP will occur at the full employment level.

CHANGES IN OUTPUT, EMPLOYMENT AND THE PRICE LEVEL

Changes in aggregate demand and supply (and hence leakages and injections) will alter output, employment and the price level. For example, if consumers become more optimistic they will start to spend more. This will raise consumption and hence aggregate demand. If there is spare capacity in the economy this will raise output which in turn is likely to increase employment. The effect on the price level will depend on whether firms can obtain more resources without bidding up their prices.

EFFECT OF A CHANGE IN AGGREGATE DEMAND

If consumption, or any of the other components of aggregate demand, increases by, for example, £30m the final effect on total spending will be greater. This is because, as already noted, income and spending circulates round the economy. People spend more money so firms receive high revenues. Profits, wages and other payments to the factors of production increase. Some of these payments will be spent and so there will be a secondary rise in spending. This knock-on effect will continue until again injections = leakages.

Changes in output, employment and the price level are discussed in more detail in Chapter 52.

QUESTIONS

SHORT QUESTIONS

1 Explain what is meant by the 45° diagram.

2 How may output rise without a rise in employment?

3 Explain what would cause producers to change their output.

4 Will the equilibrium level of national income ensure full employment?

MULTIPLE CHOICE

1 GDP is in equilibrium when:

A the balance of payments is in equilibrium

B the government achieves a balanced budget

C total planned expenditure is maximised

D there is no tendency for GDP to change.

2 In an open economy with a government sector, the equilibrium level of GDP will be that which results in the equality:

A $I = S$

B $I + G = S + T$

C $I + G + X = S + T + M$

D $I + G + T = S + X - M$.

3 Figure 29.4 shows the aggregate demand and aggregate supply curves of an economy.

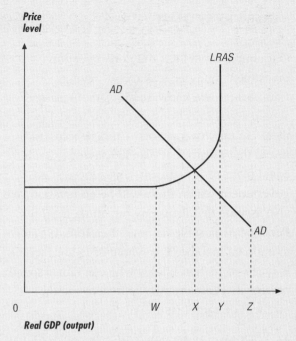

FIG. 29.4

What is the equilibrium level of GDP?

A W   B X   C Y   D Z

4 The table below shows figures for government spending (G), investment (I), imports (M), savings (S), taxation (T), exports (X) and GDP (Y) for an open economy.

	Y	G	I	M	S	T	X
				£m			
A	100	40	20	10	10	20	40
B	200	30	40	20	30	20	50
C	300	20	50	40	50	10	30
D	400	10	65	60	60	10	5

What is the equilibrium level of GDP?

A £100m   B £200m

C £300m   D £400m

DATA RESPONSE

Our simple model has only one injection — investment, and one leakage — savings. Equilibrium, we know, requires that leakages should equal injections and in our model (where there are only two sectors — households and firms) that means that planned savings should equal planned investment. Since there is no government sector, there will be no taxation. We also assume that firms pay out all their profits. Personal disposable income, therefore, is equal to national income. The whole of factor income is received by households who can either spend or save it. There are two approaches to the problem of equilibrium. We can ask:

1. What level of income will generate sufficient planned saving to equal planned investment? Or;

2. What level of income will generate sufficient planned consumption plus planned investment to buy the whole of current output?

Income is equal to output so that saving may be regarded as that part of output which consumers are prepared to forgo; that is, to leave for purposes other than consumption. If the amount of total output forgone by consumers is exactly equal to the demands by firms for capital formation (including additions to stocks) then planned saving is equal to planned investment, total demand is equal to total supply and equilibrium will exist. But if consumers plan to save more or less than firms plan to invest there will be a situation of disequilibrium.

Source: Macro-economics: an introduction, 4th edition by G.F. Stanlake, Longman.

a] What are the two injections not mentioned in the extract? **(2)**

b] What are the sectors in a four sector model? **(4)**

c] When income is in equilibrium what is the relationship between planned expenditure and output? Illustrate your answer with a diagram. **(6)**

d] Explain what will happen to output if consumers plan to save more than firms plan to invest. **(6)**

e] Discuss the factors that could cause an increase in savings. **(7)**

CASE STUDY

Britain's longest period of postwar economic expansion ground to a halt in the first three months of 1999 as last year's interest rate rises and the strength of the pound cut growth to zero, official figures showed yesterday.

It is the first time since the UK climbed out of the 1992 recession that quarterly growth has been stagnant. The slow-down has cut into corporate profits, which fell at their sharpest annual rate since the three-day-week hit British business in 1974.

Until the start of the year, the economy had been growing for 25 consecutive quarters, the longest expansion since the Office for National Statistics began keeping quarterly records in 1955. But growth has slowed rapidly since Labour came into power in 1997 and put the Bank of England in charge of setting interest rates. In an attempt to avoid inflation taking off, the Bank's monetary policy committee progressively raised rates to a peak of 7.5% in June last year.

Most of the slowdown has come in the manufacturing sector, where higher interest rates have boosted the pound and priced British goods out of overseas markets. Manufacturing output fell by 0.9% in the first three months of 1999, its third quarterly decline in a row.

The services sector, which has been propping up output, slowed sharply over the last three months, expanding by just 0.2%. Business services, which includes management consultants, insurance firms, advertising and recruitment, suffered a particularly sharp downturn, falling by 0.3% over the quarter, after recording growth of more than 1% a quarter for most of the last two years.

Source: 'Economy grinds to a halt' by Charlotte Denny, the Guardian, 25/5/99.

a] If national output is not changing what must be the relationship between injections and leakages? **(3)**

b] According to the extract what were the causes of the slowdown in the growth of output? **(5)**

c] Explain what effect a fall in corporate profits would have on investment. **(7)**

d] Why does the Office for National Statistics keep records of national income figures? **(6)**

e] What effect is a rise in output likely to have on living standards? **(10)**

f] Discuss the impact a rise in interest rates is likely to have on consumption. **(8)**

g] Distinguish between the manufacturing sector and the services sector. **(3)**

h] Why might advertising expenditure actually increase during an economic slowdown? **(8)**

STRUCTURED ESSAY

a] Explain what is meant by equilibrium GDP. **(8)**

b] Discuss the effects of a rise in aggregate demand on output and the general price level. **(17)**

30 GOVERNMENT MACROECONOMIC POLICY OBJECTIVES

THE OBJECTIVES OF GOVERNMENT POLICY

Government policies are designed to improve the workings of the economy. Governments will differ in the emphasis they give to particular objectives and the ways in which they try to achieve these. These differences will reflect the economic circumstances of the time, the extent to which the government believes it can influence the objective with the instruments it has and its priorities.

However despite these differences there seems to be broad agreement on the main aims. They are:

- a high level of employment
- a relatively stable price level
- a satisfactory balance of payments position
- a steady rate of economic growth.

EMPLOYMENT

High employment has a number of significant advantages. Most people receive higher incomes from employment than from state benefits. Indeed when employment is high, output and hence living standards are also usually high. Work also provides status and the opportunity to keep up with developments in technology and work practices.

In contrast unemployment imposes costs on the unemployed in particular and on the wider society. Those who are unemployed are likely to have lower incomes, are more prone to mental illness and miss out on training and promotion.

The whole economy suffers a loss of potential output and hence actual living standards are below potential living standards. There is also evidence of a direct link between the unemployment of young men and crime.

So high employment and low unemployment are generally considered to be desirable. However economists differ as to what level of employment they believe is possible and what measures may be taken to achieve it. Keynesians traditionally have discussed full employment. By this they do not mean zero unemployment since some people will always be in between jobs. Full employment has usually been defined as between 2% and 3% unemployment and occurs when the number of vacancies matches the number unemployed.

New classical economists refer to the non-accelerating inflation rate of unemployment (NAIRU). It can also be called the natural rate of unemployment. It is the rate of unemployment which exists when all those who want to work at the going wage rate and who have the appropriate skills can find a job. Whether it is e.g. 4% or 8% will depend on a number of factors. These include the gap between paid employment and state benefits, attitudes towards living on benefits, labour market information and skill levels. A government basing its policies on new classical theory would seek to reduce NAIRU by improving the workings of the labour market.

PRICE STABILITY

Governments usually aim not for complete price stability but for a low and stable rate of inflation. The Labour Government of the UK, elected in May 1997, set the Bank of England the target of achieving an underlying rate of inflation of 2.5% with a margin of one percentage point either way.

Complete price stability or zero inflation would mean that the general price level is not changing. In practice in a dynamic, growing economy the general price level is likely to rise by between 1% and 2%

per year. This rise will reflect the buoyant level of demand and the fact that the quality of goods tends to rise. For example a television purchased in 2005 may be 5% more expensive than one purchased in 2004 but it may also, for instance, have extra channels and give better reception.

If the rate of inflation is equal to or below rival countries, the country can at least maintain its international price competitiveness. If it is stable then firms do not have to encounter costs in estimating its future rate and workers do not have to guess what wage claims they need to make to maintain their real wages.

However, high and accelerating inflation is clearly undesirable. It can reduce a country's international price competitiveness, reduce the real income of some groups, create uncertainty, make it difficult for firms to plan and thereby may discourage investment. Very high levels of inflation, known as hyperinflation, can cause the economic and political system of a country to break down.

BALANCE OF PAYMENTS POSITION

The balance of payments records a country's transactions with other countries. It includes money which enters and leaves the country. Money can come into the country from abroad for a variety of reasons. These include selling goods abroad, providing services for foreigners, money being placed in UK financial institutions by people and companies from abroad, foreigners lending money to the country's citizens and companies, foreigners buying the country's shares and government bonds and foreign companies setting up in the country. Money leaves the country when imports and services are purchased from abroad and when the country's citizens and companies undertake financial and capital investment abroad.

A government will seek, over time, to earn as much from its sale of exports of goods and services abroad as it spends on imports of goods and foreign services. This will mean that its trade in goods and

trade in services will balance. It will not want to spend more than it earns because then the country will get into debt. It will also be unlikely to want a surplus since this will mean that the country is not purchasing all the goods and services it can afford and so living standards are not as high as possible.

When citizens and companies of the country invest abroad it involves money leaving the country. However, in the longer run it will generate an inflow of funds as profit, interest and dividends come into the country. So a country may not be concerned about the initial outflow unless domestic companies are setting up abroad when there is high unemployment at home.

Inward investment initially involves money coming into the country. It can also be beneficial as capital investment can generate employment in the home country. However in the longer run, money will leave the country in the form of profit, interest and dividends.

A government may seek to influence its capital account position if the investment flows have adverse effects on employment or the exchange rate.

ECONOMIC GROWTH

Economic growth is increases in output. It can occur if previously unemployed resources are employed, there are more resources or existing resources improve in quality.

If a country has unemployed resources it might be able to increase its output by a significant amount. In this case a government may seek e.g. a rate of economic growth of 6%. If, however, its resources are fully employed it will have to rely on increases in resources or more likely increases in the quality of resources. In the UK's case it is thought that potential output is likely to increase by approximately 2.25% per year as a result of improvements in technological and educational standards.

Governments prefer stable growth to periods of boom and recession as these create uncertainty and can be destabilising. So they prefer a situation where demand matches potential output and they increase steadily in line with each other.

Economic growth brings a number of advantages, in particular higher living standards. More goods and services will be available and these may be of a higher standard. However economic growth may also bring some disadvantages including pollution and the depletion of non renewable resources. Governments are becoming more aware of the need for sustainable development. This means increasing output in a way which does not damage the environment and which enables increases in output to continue.

OTHER OBJECTIVES

In addition to these four major economic objectives a government may have other objectives for the economy. These may include a more even distribution of income and wealth and a cleaner environment.

THE FRAMEWORK OF ECONOMIC POLICY

The first task is to determine the objectives. Then the target has to be selected. Targets are the variables through which the government attempts to achieve its objectives. The next task is to choose the instruments of policy to be used in pursuit of the objectives. These instruments are based upon some available range of measures.

For example, the government might decide that its objective is to reduce unemployment. For this purpose it may seek to influence (target) aggregate demand. To do this it might choose to use the instruments of taxation and government spending. The particular measures adopted might be a reduction in income tax and/or an increase in public spending on housing and roads.

The table below gives examples of government objectives and the instruments which can be used to achieve these.

Objective	Target	Policy	Instrument
reduction in unemployment	aggregate demand	fiscal	income tax
improvement in trade balance	price of exports & imports	exchange rate	devaluation
promotion of growth	investment	fiscal	corporation tax
lower inflation	bank lending	monetary	interest rate

QUESTIONS

SHORT QUESTIONS

1. What are the four main government macroeconomic objectives?

2. Explain what is meant by full employment.

3. What is meant by zero inflation?

4. What is the main advantage of economic growth?

MULTIPLE CHOICE

1. Which of the following is a macroeconomic policy objective?

   A. Privatisation.

   B. Low employment.

   C. Low inflation.

   D. The elimination of price discrimination.

2. What is the non-accelerating inflation rate of unemployment? The level of unemployment which will exist:

   A. when the labour market is in equilibrium

   B. after adjustment for seasonal variations

   C. when the rate of unemployment is falling

   D. when technological and frictional unemployment are excluded.

3. Which of the following could cause economic growth?

   A. Advances in technology.

   B. A reduction in the working population.

   C. Negative net investment.

   D. An increase in soil erosion.

4. The table shows unemployment figures expressed as a percentage of the total labour force.

	USA	Japan	Germany	UK	OECD average
1991	6.8	2.1	5.6	8.2	6.8
1992	7.5	2.2	7.8	9.9	7.4
1993	6.9	2.5	9.1	10.5	8.0
1994	6.1	2.9	9.6	9.5	7.9
1995	5.6	3.2	9.5	8.3	7.6
1996	5.4	3.3	10.5	7.6	7.5
1997	4.9	3.4	11.6	5.7	7.3

Source: Table 14, page 114, National Institute Economic Review, No.166, October 1998, National Institute of Economic and Social Research.

What can be concluded from the data shown?

A. Output fell in Japan throughout the period shown.

B. The number of people employed rose in both the USA and the UK from 1993 to 1997.

C. In the period 1992–1993, unemployment rose by the greatest percentage in Germany.

D. Japan and the USA had unemployment rates below the OECD average throughout the period shown.

DATA RESPONSE

		As at November 1998	
Country	Growth rate	Inflation rate	Trade balance ($bn)
China	7.6	−1.2	43.2
Hong Kong	−5.2	0.1	−12.4
Indonesia	−17.4	78.1	21.1
Malaysia	−8.6	5.6	11.9
Philippines	−0.1	11.2	−2.0
Singapore	−0.7	−1.7	6.2
South Korea	−6.8	6.8	38.3
Taiwan	4.7	3.9	6.1

Source: The Economist 19/12/98.

a] Explain what is meant by the trade balance. **(3)**

b] What is meant by negative growth? **(3)**

c] Which major macroeconomic objective is not covered by the data given? **(2)**

d] From the data given, and explaining your answers, state:

i   which country faced the most serious economic problems **(6)**

ii which country appeared to have the most successful economy. **(6)**

e] What do you think would have been the major economic objective of the Malaysian government in 1998? Explain your answer. **(5)**

CASE STUDY

The Asian crisis saw growth rates fall throughout the region with a number of previously successful economies experiencing negative growth. However despite this Australia reported, in early December 1998, a much higher than expected growth rate figure of 5%. This rate made Australia one of the fastest growing economies in the industrialised world.

Australian inflation also remained low and the unemployment rate fell from 8.4%, a year before, to 8.0%. Although the trade balance moved from a surplus of $1.8bn in 1998 to a deficit of $4.3bn, the Prime Minister, John Howard, was very optimistic about the state of the Australian economy. He said, 'We've got booming economic growth, the lowest interest rates in 30 years, and we have introduced a tax reform package that is going to build an even stronger Australian economy.'

Nevertheless some economists forecast that Australia would feel the main impact of the Asian crisis in 1999. They argued that Australian exports to Asian countries would decline and that its trade balance would be further hit by a continued decline in commodity prices. The reserve bank of Australia was also concerned about the future prospects for the Australian economy. As a result it cut the rate of interest to 4.75%, its lowest since 1993.

a] i What does a 5% growth rate mean? **(3)**

ii Why was this figure surprising for the Australian economy in December 1998? **(5)**

b] i What relationship would you expect to find between economic growth and unemployment, and why? **(6)**

ii Why might this relationship not hold? **(6)**

c] To what extent do you think the Australian government was achieving its macroeconomic objectives in December 1998? **(10)**

d] What was predicted to happen to the Australian economy in 1999 and why? **(5)**

e] How does your country's current economic performance compare to that of Australia's in December 1999? **(15)**

STRUCTURED ESSAY

a] Discuss the main government macroeconomic policy objectives. **(10)**

b] Assess the extent to which the government of your country is currently achieving its objectives. **(15)**

31 INDICATORS OF ECONOMIC PERFORMANCE

Economists and commentators make use of a range of indicators to assess how an economy is performing. Some of these are well known and correspond specifically to the main government macroeconomic policy objectives of a high level of employment, stable price level, satisfactory balance of payments position and a steady rate of economic growth. Other performance indicators are perhaps rather less well known and are rather more specific.

EMPLOYMENT

Countries measure a range of items connected with employment. The number of people employed is recorded as is the number of people who are unemployed. There are two main measures of unemployment. One is the *claimant count* which is based on the number of people receiving unemployment benefit (job seekers' allowance). The other is the *labour force survey measure* which, as its name suggests, is based on a survey of people of working age which asks if they are out of work and are seeking employment. The rate of unemployment is calculated by dividing the number of people unemployed by the number of people in the labour force (which includes both the employed and the unemployed). A healthy economy would obviously be expected to have a low rate of unemployment. However, as well as examining the percentage of potential workers who are unemployed it is also important to examine the length of time for which people are out of work. An unemployment rate of 6% with people out of work on average for three months is likely to be viewed as less serious than an unemployment rate of 4% with people out of work on average for two years.

In addition to these major measures economists and commentators also examine data on the number of vacancies and the type of jobs people are obtaining. A high level of job vacancies may indicate an expanding economy but it may also indicate a mismatch between the skills demanded and the skills of those unemployed.

The quality of jobs that people are obtaining can also provide an indication of how an economy is performing. If these jobs are mainly part-time, temporary and low-skilled this is likely to indicate that the country is experiencing economic problems.

OUTPUT

Economists assess the level of output and increases in output. The latter is referred to as an *economic growth*. In assessing output and changes in output economists use real GDP figures and if making comparisons over time and between countries they often use real GDP per capita. Chapter 26 discussed some of the problems involved in measuring and in interpreting GDP figures. These have to be taken into account when examining GDP figures.

In assessing a country's performance economists are increasingly making use of the concept of *sustainable economic growth*. This means increasing output in a way that does not endanger the prospect of future rises in output by damaging the environment and using up non-renewable resources.

BALANCE OF PAYMENTS

Economists examine sections of the balance of payments and trends within those sections. The current account records money earned from the sale of goods and services, citizens working abroad, and investment income (profits, interest and dividends) and money spent on goods and services from other countries, income earned by foreign residents working in the UK which they send home and profits, rent and interest earned in the UK and sent back to foreign countries. If, over time, there is a deficit (the country spends more than it earns) on this account it may indicate that the country is not producing the right mix of goods and services or that these are too expensive or of poor quality.

The financial account records direct investment (in, e.g., purchase of foreign land) and portfolio investment (e.g., the purchase of foreign shares) into and out of the country. If a country is regarded as having a strong economy it may be able to attract more foreign investment.

Economists also look at a number of other measures. These include relative export performance. This measures export volume and import volume relative to world trade. Export prices are also compared to world prices to gain an indication of international price competitiveness.

INFLATION

Countries aim for a stable and low level rate of inflation. There are various ways of measuring changes in the general price level.

THE RETAIL PRICE INDEX (RPI)

This is the best known measure of inflation and is often referred to as the *headline rate*. It is a weighted price index. It is calculated by first carrying out a family expenditure survey. This is a survey of a sample of 7000 households which asks them to record what they spend their money on. From the information obtained different weights are attached to a range of categories of goods and services. Greater weighting is given to items on which people allocate a high proportion of their expenditure than on items that they spend only a small proportion on. Changes in

prices of selected items are recorded from a range of retail outlets. Then the weights are multiplied by the price changes to obtain the weighted price index.

EXAMPLE

Category	Weight	Price change		Weighted price change
Food	$\frac{1}{2}$	× 10%	=	5%
Clothing	$\frac{1}{4}$	× 8%	=	2%
Housing	$\frac{1}{8}$	× 16%	=	2%
Leisure goods & services	$\frac{1}{8}$	× −8%	=	−1%
				———
				8%

In the RPI there are fourteen main categories of items and there are approximately 150 000 price quotations.

RPIX

This is RPI minus mortgage interest payments. It is sometimes known as the *underlying inflation rate*. This is because it measures price changes without taking into account changes in the rate of interest which may be raised by a government precisely in order to reduce inflation.

RPIY

This is also sometimes referred to as the underlying inflation rate or sometimes as the *core inflation rate*. It is RPIX minus indirect taxes (including local authority taxes). This measure shows the underlying inflation rate undistorted by changes in the government policy measures of interest rates and indirect taxes. For instance, if demand and wage and raw material costs are not rising but the government raises VAT and the rate of interest, RPIY will be constant whilst RPIX will rise and RPI will rise even more.

OTHER MEASURES OF INFLATION

These include the following.

- *The GDP deflator.* This is used to convert nominal national income figures into real figures — taking the effects of inflation out of the figures. The GDP deflator has a wide coverage. It measures changes in consumer goods and services and, unlike the RPI, changes in capital goods. Also, unlike the RPI, it measures changes in the price of exports but not the price of imports. So whilst the RPI is a measure of changes in the price of consumer goods and services purchased by people in the UK, the GDP deflator is a measure of changes in the price of capital goods and consumer goods and services produced in the UK.
- *The tax and price index (TPI).* This measures changes in real spending power. It takes into account not only changes in prices but also changes in disposable income caused by changes in direct taxes. Changes in prices, as measured by the RPI, are given a weight of three-quarters and changes in direct taxes (income tax and national insurance) are given a weighting of one-quarter.
- *The index of producer prices (IPP).* This measures changes in the price of goods purchased (input)

and manufactured (output) by UK industries. As it represents the price of goods in their earlier stage of production it is taken as an indicator of future changes in inflation.

- *The harmonised index of consumer prices (HICP).* This is the main measure used by EU countries. It has two main differences from the RPI. One is that it is based on a geometric mean rather than an arithmetic mean. The other is in its coverage of items. It includes, e.g., new cars and air travel but excludes council tax and some health and education expenditure.

OTHER INDICATORS

Economists also examine information on a range of other data to examine the performance of an economy. These include:

- educational attainment
- spending on research and development
- productivity
- human development index (HDI)
- investment (level and type).

For example, the Italian Treasury published the information shown in Table 31.1.

TABLE 31.1 IT LEAGUE TABLE

Country	Internet use among total pop. (%)	Web sites '000	Personal computers (m)	Spending on IT (as a prop. of GDP, %)
US	30.7	33 387	113.0	3.6
Japan	11.1	1 719	27.2	2.9
UK	18.0	1 692	15.2	2.4
Germany	10.0	1 375	17.6	2.4
France	5.2	571	11.0	2.3
Italy	4.0	371	6.6	1.5

Source: Financial Times, 20/7/99.

QUESTIONS

SHORT QUESTIONS

1. What is meant by the underlying rate of inflation?
2. Why may unemployment fall without any corresponding rise in employment?
3. What may a deficit on the current account of the balance of payments indicate?
4. What is the HICP?

MULTIPLE CHOICE

1. What do the weights in the Retail Price Index indicate?

   A Changes in the price of each good.

   B Relative expenditures on different goods.

   C Changes in the rate of taxation on goods.

   D The extent of seasonal fluctuations in prices.

2. Which of the following is likely to indicate that an economy is experiencing an economic recession?

   A A fall in national income.

   B A fall in unemployment.

   C A rise in the inflation rate.

   D A rise in government tax revenue.

3. In which circumstances would a rise in productivity cause a rise in unemployment?

   A When aggregate demand is falling.

   B When there is considerable spare capacity in the economy.

   C When the country has a balance of payments deficit.

   D When the rate of inflation is decelerating.

4. Which of the following would indicate an increase in material living standards?

   A Real GDP increasing by 5% and population increasing by 7%.

   B Money GDP increasing by 4% and an inflation rate of 6%.

   C Money GDP falling more slowly than real GDP.

   D Real GDP falling by 2% and population falling by 5%.

DATA RESPONSE

Country	Position according to Human Development Index	Real GDP per capita $
Canada	1	21 916
France	2	21 716
Norway	3	22 427
USA	4	26 977
Iceland	5	21 064
Finland	6	18 547
Netherlands	7	19 876
Japan	8	21 930
New Zealand	9	17 267
Sweden	10	19 297
Spain	11	14 789
Belgium	12	21 548
Austria	13	21 322
United Kingdom	14	19 302
Australia	15	19 632
Switzerland	16	24 881
Ireland	17	17 590
Denmark	18	21 983
Germany	19	20 370
Greece	20	11 636

Source: Human Development report 1998, United Nations, OUP, 1998.

a] Explain what is meant by real GDP per capita. **(3)**

b] Compare the ranking order generated by the two measures. **(6)**

c] Explain why a country could appear in a high position in terms of real GDP per capita and a low position in terms of the HDI. **(5)**

d] Why might the real GDP figures per capita not reflect the true income level of the countries shown? **(5)**

e] Discuss one other indicator of a country's performance. **(6)**

CASE STUDY

Ask the director of Taiwan's science park who are the country's strongest competitors in computer chips and he will tell you there aren't any, without qualification.

In sight from Kung Wang's office in Hsinchu are the plants of the world's two top chipmakers. The third, in Singapore, hardly rates as competition and lost money even in the good times with a mix of American management and mainland Chinese workforce. 'Teamwork,' they tell you at Winbond, the world's number two chipmaker, 'is the secret in making integrated circuits and that's what Taiwanese are good at.' For Winbond, which licenses Toshiba chip technology, times are good again after a difficult two years, And what's good for the chip business is good for Taiwan, the world's ultimate niche economy.

Being suppliers to the world for almost everything from microprocessors to Christmas hats with pulsating lights is one explanation for Taiwan's escaping the worst of the Asian economic downturn. But deft government manoeuvring to help the private sector to alleviate the worst effects of the bubble economy in real estate and ease the strain on banks also played a role. Four million grannies playing the market every day and a vibrant venture capital sector are evidence too, that Taiwan has the economic nimbleness of a flyweight economy that punches well above its weight.

Source: 'Flexible structure helps school minnows to survive crisis' by David Watts, The Times, 27/8/99.

a] What is meant by 'strong competitors'? **(4)**

b] Explain what enabled the Taiwanese economy to escape the effects of the global financial crisis. **(8)**

c] What data should be examined to assess the extent to which the Taiwanese economy escaped the effects of the global financial crisis. **(10)**

d] What are the advantages of having a diversified industrial structure? **(6)**

e] Explain what is meant by 'a flyweight economy that punches well above its weight'. **(6)**

f] Explain how the success of key industries has a knock on effect on the rest of the economy. **(6)**

g] Discuss the indicators of an economic downturn. **(10)**

STRUCTURED ESSAY

a] Explain how inflation is measured. **(10)**

b] Discuss other indicators of a country's economic performance. **(15)**

32 FISCAL POLICY: PUBLIC EXPENDITURE

DEFINITION

Fiscal policy is deliberate changes in government (public) expenditure and income so as to achieve desired economic and social objectives. The instruments of fiscal policy are government spending and taxation. Changes in the level, timing and composition of government spending and taxation can have a significant impact on the economy.

CATEGORIES OF GOVERNMENT EXPENDITURE

Government expenditure is spending by the public sector, i.e. expenditure by the central and local government and any loans or grants to the nationalised industries.

Government expenditure can be divided into four main categories as follows.

1. *Current expenditure.* This is spending on the day-to-day running of the public services e.g. spending on teachers' pay, the purchase of textbooks, doctors' and nurses' pay, the purchase of medicines, the pay of those in the armed services and the purchase of uniforms.
2. *Capital expenditure.* This is spending on the social infrastructure and includes e.g. spending on new hospitals, new schools and roads. Capital expenditure adds to the country's capital assets.
3. *Transfer payments.* These are payments to, e.g., pensioners, the unemployed and subsidies to producers. They are designed to provide income or increase the income of vulnerable groups and, in the latter case, may also be used to increase the output of particular goods and services.
4. *Debt interest.* This is payment to the holders of government debt, e.g. National Savings Certificates, government bonds.

Categories 1 and 2 involve the direct use of resources by the government. The government decides what is to be produced and employs the resources of land, labour and capital to provide the goods and services. As these forms of spending make use of resources they are sometimes referred to as exhaustive expenditure. In contrast categories 3 and 4 may be referred to as non-exhaustive expenditure. They involve the transfer of economic purchasing power from taxpayers to recipients of welfare payments, some producers and holders of national debt. In the case of non-exhaustive expenditure it is those who receive the transferred income who decide what goods and services are produced.

FUNCTIONS OF GOVERNMENT EXPENDITURE

To a certain extent both the total and pattern of government expenditure will depend upon the political philosophy of the government. Nevertheless it is possible to identify the major functions of government spending.

THE PROVISION OF PUBLIC AND MERIT GOODS AND SERVICES

Public goods, for example defence, have to be paid for by the government. This is because it would not be possible to exclude non-payers from enjoying them. At least some people would act as free riders.

Most governments also subsidise some merit goods and provide others free at the point of use, the intention is to increase their consumption.

The provision of public and merit goods and services is likely to redistribute income from the rich to the poor. This is because the cost is met out of taxation and if the tax system is progressive the benefits received by the lower income groups will be greater than the financial contributions they make to the state.

THE PROVISION OF SOCIAL SECURITY

Social security is the largest single item of public spending in the UK and in a number of other countries. This is shown in the pie chart below.

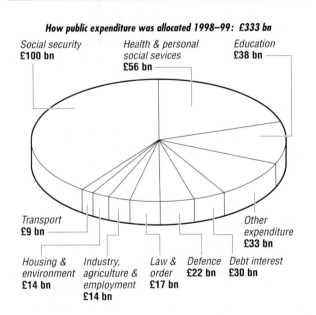

How public expenditure was allocated 1998–99: £333 bn

Social security £100 bn

Health & personal social sevices £56 bn

Education £38 bn

Transport £9 bn

Other expenditure £33 bn

Housing & environment £14 bn

Industry, agriculture & employment £14 bn

Law & order £17 bn

Defence £22 bn

Debt interest £30 bn

FIG. 32.1

Social security covers a wide range of benefits in the form of money grants. These transfers include state retirement pensions, child benefit, income support, family credit and sickness benefit. The government also provides a range of personal social services to assist the elderly and the disabled.

The broad objectives of the system of social security are to ensure that everyone is guaranteed some adequate minimum level of income and to prevent families from suffering undue hardship when their incomes fall due to some misfortune.

THE REGULATION OF ECONOMIC ACTIVITY

The government intervenes in the economic activities of private sector firms to ensure that the firms act in the public interest. For example the Health and Clean Food Acts control standards of hygiene in public and private premises. Town and County Planning Acts regulate trading practices in the business world. There are also numerous road traffic regulations. The government has to spend money to enforce these Acts and regulations.

IMPROVING THE EFFICIENCY OF THE ALLOCATION OF RESOURCES

The government provides grants and subsidies to influence the structure, performance and location of private sector companies. In the UK it also still operates some enterprises itself, for example, the Bank of England. However, privatisation has substantially reduced the number of industries owned by the state.

INFLUENCING THE LEVEL OF ECONOMIC ACTIVITY

Changes in government spending may be introduced to influence output, employment, prices and the balance of payments. Government spending is one of the components of aggregate demand. Keynesian economists argue that if output and employment are low, the government should increase its own spending to raise aggregate demand and output by a multiple amount. New classical economists believe that a government should ensure that its spending does not cause inflation.

INFLUENCES ON THE LEVEL OF GOVERNMENT SPENDING

These influences include the following.

- *Cyclical influences.* Government spending on social security is influenced significantly by changes in the level of economic activity. When output rises more slowly or, even more seriously, falls, unemployment is likely to rise and so expenditure on job seekers' allowance and other benefits, such as housing benefit, is likely to increase. During a recession, which is defined as a fall in national output over a period of at least six months, there will be significant upward pressure on government spending. Whereas during an economic boom spending on benefits will fall as the number of people claiming them will decline.
- *Demographic influences.* Increases in the average age of the population will increase spending on state pensions and health care provision. The ageing population of a number of industrialised countries, including the UK and Japan, is placing upward pressure on government spending.
- *Social changes.* Here, an increase in one parent families and a decline in the number of people willing and able to care for elderly relatives, for example, will increase government expenditure on social security and health care. Rising crime levels will also increase expenditure on law and order.
- *Demand for government financed public goods and merit goods.* Demand for the merit goods of health and education are particularly income elastic. As a society gets richer its inhabitants

demand better and more extensive health and education provision.

- *Demand for private goods.* When demand for a range of private goods increases, demand for complementary government financed goods and services will rise. For example, the continuing rise in car ownership and use means existing roads have to be repaired more frequently and leads to calls for an increase in road building.
- *Changes in technology.* Improvements in technology have made more expensive operations such as multiple organ transplants possible, thereby increasing health care expenditure. Spending on education has risen with the purchase of computers by schools.
- *Political views.* A government which believes that market failure can be significant and that government policy can be effective is likely to spend more than one which believes in the smooth working of markets and has concerns about the effectiveness of government policy.
- *Political cycles.* Government spending tends to rise just before a general election as increases in spending on e.g. health care and education are likely to prove popular.
- *The rate of interest.* An increase in the rate of interest will raise the amount the government has to pay on its debt.
- *The risk of conflicts.* In a situation of world stability, defence spending may fall. The decline in defence spending which followed the end of the cold war was referred to as the peace dividend. Some of the resources which had been used in the defence industry were transferred into the production of civilian goods and services which add more directly to welfare.
- *Increases in real wages.* Health care, the police and education, for example, are labour intensive. So increases in wages, if not offset by productivity increases, will raise government expenditure.

THE FINANCING OF GOVERNMENT EXPENDITURE

Government expenditure is financed in various ways:

- taxes levied by central government
- taxes levied by local authorities (business rates and council tax)
- national insurance contributions paid by employees, the self employed and employers (these contributions are, in fact, a form of taxation)
- borrowing
- sale of assets.

QUESTIONS

SHORT QUESTIONS

1. Define fiscal policy.

2. Distinguish between exhaustive and non-exhaustive expenditure.

3. What is the largest item of government spending in the UK?

4. Explain what would happen to public expenditure in a recession.

MULTIPLE CHOICE

1. Which of the following is a fiscal policy measure?

   A. Anti-pollution legislation.

   B. Changes in the rate of interest.

   C. Government grants to private sector firms.

   D. Restrictions on bank lending.

2. Which of the following produces an automatic reduction in government expenditure during a period of rising national income?

   A. child benefit

   B. job seekers' allowance

   C. defence spending

   D. state pensions.

3. Which of the following is a transfer payment?

   A. The pay of public sector workers.

   B. The allowance paid to job seekers.

   C. Government expenditure on defence equipment.

   D. The profits earned by foreign companies based in the UK.

4. Which of the following would be likely to raise government expenditure?

   A. An ageing population.

   B. A rise in employment.

   C. A fall in the rate of interest.

   D. A decrease in the school leaving age.

DATA RESPONSE

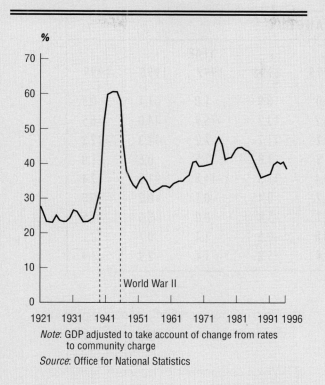

%

70
60
50
40
30
20
10
0

1921 1931 1941 1951 1961 1971 1981 1991 1996

World War II

Note: GDP adjusted to take account of change from rates to community charge

Source: Office for National Statistics

FIG. 32.2

a] Comment on the trend in government expenditure shown in the graph. **(6)**

b] Discuss two reasons why a government may increase its spending. **(4)**

c] Comment on the changes in the pattern of government expenditure shown in the table. **(6)**

d] What factors influence government expenditure in the largest item by function of government expenditure? **(5)**

e] Discuss two benefits government expenditure on higher education provides for university students. **(4)**

TABLE 32.1 GENERAL GOVERNMENT EXPENDITURE IN REAL TERMS: BY FUNCTION

United Kingdom			£ billion at 1996 prices[1]			
	1981	1986	1991	1994	1995	1996
Social security	64	80	85	104	107	107
Health	28	31	36	41	42	43
Education	29	31	34	38	38	39
Defence	26	30	27	25	24	23
Public order and safety	9	11	15	16	16	15
General public services	9	10	13	14	15	13
Housing and community amenities	15	13	10	11	11	10
Transport and communication	9	6	8	7	9	8
Recreational and cultural affairs	3	4	5	5	5	5
Agriculture, forestry and fishing	3	3	3	3	4	5
Other expenditure	46	41	28	38	44	37
All expenditure	241	259	264	302	314	306

NOTE: [1]Adjusted to 1996 prices using the GDP market prices deflator.
Source: Social Trends 28, 1998, Office for National Statistics.

CASE STUDY

% CHANGE					
CATEGORY			YEAR		
	1995	1996	1997	1998	1999
Consumption	2.0	2.9	1.0	−1.1	−0.5
Investment: housing	−6.2	13.2	−15.9	−14.0	−6.5
business	5.2	11.2	7.2	−11.3	−12.3
Government: consumption	3.3	1.8	1.5	0.6	1.0
investment	−0.4	11.3	−11.3	−1.2	12.4
Stockbuilding	0.2	0.4	−0.1	−0.2	0.0
Total domestic demand	2.2	5.8	0.0	−3.5	−1.5
Net exports	−0.8	−0.6	1.4	0.7	0.1
GDP	1.4	5.2	1.4	−2.9	−1.4

Source: Table 7, National Institute Economic Review, April 1999, NIESR.

In 1999 the Japanese economy was experiencing deflation, rising unemployment and a lack of private sector demand. To stimulate economic activity the Japanese government increased its spending significantly. It spent ¥8.1 trillion on social infrastructure projects and ¥3.2 trillion on providing training and employment opportunities for the new unemployed, support for the housing market and providing assistance to other East Asian countries.

The government also spent a considerable amount supporting the Japanese financial system and seeking to raise private sector consumption. One measure it introduced to achieve the latter was the introduction of a shopping voucher scheme. This involved giving families with dependent children and recipients of state pensions coupons which had to be spent within six months.

a] Explain what is meant by:
  i net exports **(3)**
  ii GDP. **(3)**

b] Which components of Japanese aggregate demand were increasing in 1999? **(5)**

c] Which component of Japanese aggregate demand fluctuated the most in the given period? **(5)**

d] Describe the changes in Japanese government spending from 1995 to 1999. **(6)**

e] Why did Japanese government spending rise in 1999? **(6)**

f] Explain in which category of government spending would the shopping vouchers fall. **(4)**

g] Explain which components of aggregate demand might be affected by giving people shopping vouchers? **(8)**

h] For what reasons, other than those mentioned in the passage, might government spending rise. **(10)**

STRUCTURED ESSAY

a] What are the main categories of government expenditure? **(10)**

b] Discuss the main functions of government expenditure. **(15)**

33 FISCAL POLICY: TAXATION AND THE BUDGET

AIMS OF TAXATION

Central and local governments and international organisations (e.g. the EU), impose (levy) taxes for a number of reasons. Taxes are intended to act as follows.

- *To raise revenue and thereby lower private sector spending.* This frees up resources for use by the public sector. The government can finance its expenditure by borrowing. However it would not want to finance much of its spending this way. This is because it could cause inflation. For example, the full employment level of GDP of a country might be £60b. Private sector spending may be £55b and the government may want to spend £8b. If taxation is not used to reduce private sector spending the overall level of spending will exceed the full employment level of output.
- *To reduce demand for demerit goods including alcohol and tobacco.* Taxes imposed for this purpose are sometimes referred to as *sin taxes.*
- *To internalise external costs.* For example pollution taxes transfer the cost of the pollution caused by a factory from the local residents to the company and its customers. These taxes can be called *Pigouvian taxes* as they seek to improve welfare.
- *To discourage imports.* The European Union, for example, imposes tariffs on goods imported from outside the EU.
- *To create a more even distribution of income and wealth.* Progressive taxes make post taxes income and wealth more evenly distributed than pre tax income and wealth.

DIRECT TAXES

In the UK these are collected by the Inland Revenue. They are taxes levied on the income and wealth of individuals and on the profits of companies. The burden of these taxes is borne by the person or the company responsible for paying the taxes.

EXAMPLE

1. *Income tax.* As Figure 33.1 below shows this is the largest source of UK tax revenue.

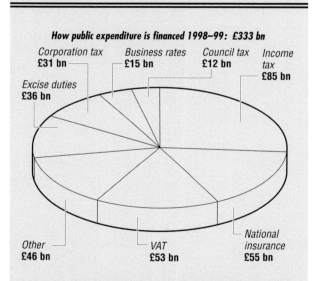

How public expenditure is financed 1998–99: £333 bn

Corporation tax £31 bn
Business rates £15 bn
Council tax £12 bn
Income tax £85 bn
Excise duties £36 bn
Other £46 bn
VAT £53 bn
National insurance £55 bn

FIG. 33.1

A certain amount of a person's income will be tax free. Income over this amount is known as taxable income. It is taxed at higher rates as income increases. Currently in the UK there are three tax rates: a lower rate of 10%, a basic rate of 23% and a higher rate of 40%.

2. *Corporation tax.* This is the tax on the profits of all companies resident in the UK whether the profits are

earned at home or abroad. The tax is charged after allowances for such things as interest on loans and depreciation of capital.

3. *Capital gains tax.* This particular tax is levied on the increase in the value of certain assets, for example shares, between the time of their purchase and the time of their sale. There are important exceptions for such things as personal private residences, private motor cars, winnings from gambling and capital gains on government securities.

4. *Inheritance tax.* This tax applies to transfers of wealth made on death above a certain amount. It is a proportional tax.

INDIRECT TAXES

These can also be called expenditure or outlay taxes. They are taxes on the spending on goods and services. They are collected by the Customs and Excise department.

The term indirect tax comes from the fact that the firm which actually makes the tax payment to the authorities may pass on at least some of the burden to other people. For example, the excise duty on petrol and beer is usually passed on as higher prices to consumers although it is collected from manufacturers and retailers.

EXAMPLE

1. *Value added tax (VAT).* This is a general sales tax which applies to a wide range of goods and services. The standard rate of VAT in the UK is currently 17.5%. Firms add VAT to the value of their outputs, but they deduct from this figure the amount of VAT already paid on their inputs. So they pay VAT only on the value added by their particular activities. There is a lower rate of VAT, currently 5%, imposed on domestic fuel and power.

    Certain goods and services are given special treatment, they are either exempt or zero rated. When goods are exempt the firm does not charge its customer any tax, but he cannot claim back any VAT already paid on its inputs. Exemption from VAT applies to land (including rents), insurance, postage, betting and gaming, finance, education, health services, burial and cremation.

    Zero-rating means complete relief from VAT. A firm does not charge VAT on the goods it sells and it can reclaim any VAT which it has paid on its inputs. Zero-rating applies to exports, food (except meals out), children's clothing, footwear, books, newspapers, construction, passenger transport, drugs, medicines on prescription and certain supplies to charities.

    Since VAT is not levied on exports (i.e. exporters can reclaim any VAT already paid on the goods) it should provide some incentive to exporters.

2. *Excise duties.* These are specific taxes levied mainly on volume. Most of the revenue from these duties comes from three sources: tobacco, alcoholic drinks and hydrocarbon oil.

    The duties on spirits, wines and beer vary according to the alcoholic strength of the liquids. The excise duties on hydrocarbon oil are levied mainly on petrol and diesel oils used in transport.

    In addition to the main sources, excise duty is imposed on most forms of betting and gaming. Matches and mechanical lighters are also subject to the tax.

3. *Tariffs.* Protective duties are levied on imports into the UK from non-EU countries. The rates of duty are those which apply throughout the EU since membership of the EU obliges the UK to apply the common tariffs. Revenues raised by these duties are payable to the EU.

4. *Other indirect taxes.* Car tax is a special tax on motor cars and motor caravans which is levied in addition to VAT. It applies to domestically manufactured and imported vehicles. Motor vehicle excise duty (road tax) is imposed on all motor vehicles in use in the UK. The rates vary according to the type of vehicle, heavier vehicles paying much higher rates. Government revenue is also obtained from the issue of television licences.

LOCAL TAXATION

Local tax revenue comes from firms which pay business rates and from households who pay council tax.

The uniform business rates are levied on firms by the central government which distributes the proceeds to local authorities on the basis of so much per adult. Extra financial assistance is available for those authorities with special problems.

Council tax is based partly on the value, in terms of sale price, of people's houses and partly on how much each council spends. Households in each local authority area are placed in one of eight bands (according to the value of their houses) with those in band A paying the least tax and those in band H, the most. The tax is based on two adults per household. Extra adults do not pay more. Households occupied by just one adult receive a 25% discount.

THE NATURE OF TAXATION

Taxes can be progressive, proportional or regressive.

PROGRESSIVE TAXES

A tax is progressive when it takes a greater percentage of income or wealth from the higher income or wealthier groups than it does from the lower income, poorer groups. As taxable income or wealth increases, it becomes subject to higher rates of taxation. An example of a progressive tax in the UK is income tax.

The table below shows that in the case of a progressive tax, the marginal rate of tax is higher than the average tax rate. In the example there is a tax allowance of £4000. The first £4000 of taxable income is taxed at 25%, the next £12 000 at 50% and any income above that is taxed at 80%.

EXAMPLE

Income (£)	Taxable income (£)	Tax rate	Tax payable	Average tax rate	Marginal tax rate
4 000	0	0	0	0	0.25
8 000	4 000	25%	1000	0.125	0.50
20 000	16 000	50%	7000	0.35	0.80

PROPORTIONAL TAXES

A tax is proportional when all taxpayers pay the same percentage of their income or wealth. In the

UK corporation tax is an example of a proportional tax. In this case the average and marginal tax rates are equal. In the example below income is taxed at 40%.

EXAMPLE

Income (£)	Taxable income (£)	Tax rate	Tax payable	Average tax rate	Marginal tax rate
4 000	4 000	40%	1600	0.4	0.4
8 000	8 000	40%	3200	0.4	0.4
20 000	20 000	40%	8000	0.4	0.4

REGRESSIVE TAXES

Taxes are regressive when they take a greater percentage of income or wealth from the poor. Flat rate taxes, such as the excise duties on tobacco, beer and petrol, act regressively since the amount of tax included in the prices of these goods represents a greater percentage of the incomes of the poorer groups. In this case the average rate of tax will be higher than the marginal rate of tax. In the example below the first £4000 of income is taxed at 60%, the next £4000 at 30%, the next £12 000 at 30% and income above that level at 10%.

EXAMPLE

Income (£)	Taxable income (£)	Tax rate	Tax payable	Average tax rate	Marginal tax rate
4000	4000	60%	2400	0.60	0.30
8000	8000	30%	3600	0.45	0.20
20 000	20 000	20%	5000	0.25	0.10

In deciding whether a tax is progressive, proportional or regressive, it is important to consider the proportion paid rather than the actual amount. As the examples have shown the total amount of tax paid usually rises in the case of all three types of taxes. It is the proportion paid which differs.

QUALITIES OF A GOOD TAX

Adam Smith, the 18th century Scottish economist, identified four principles of taxation. He wrote that a tax should be equitable, certain, convenient and economical. Since his time, two additional qualities have been identified: flexibility and efficiency. The quality of equity has also been developed further.

1. *Equity*. The argument here is that the tax should be fair. Vertical equity occurs when the tax is based on people's ability to pay. Smith thought that proportional taxes would satisfy this criterion. However, most now agree that progressive taxes are the most equitable type of tax. The argument is based on the idea that the principle of diminishing marginal utility applies to income. On this basis it might be argued that taking £90 per week away from a person earning £750 per week only deprives her of the same amount of satisfaction as would the removal of £15 from a person earning £300 per week.

   Economists now also discuss *horizontal equity*. This is achieved when people in the same financial circumstances pay the same amount of tax.

2. *Certainty*. Taxpayers should know how much tax they have to pay, when it must be paid and how much must be paid. They should be able to assess their tax liability from information provided and should not be subject to tax demands made in an arbitrary fashion.

3. *Convenience*. Taxes should be convenient for taxpayers to pay and for the government to collect. Taxes should be easy to pay and the timing of their payment should also be appropriate.

4. *Economy*. The cost of tax collection and administration should be small in relation to the total revenue for both the government and the taxpayer.

5. *Flexibility*. A tax should be capable of being changed to meet changing economic conditions and changing government objectives. The revenue from some taxes, e.g. income tax and VAT, changes automatically with changes in national income. The rates of some taxes can also be adjusted relatively quickly and easily.

6. *Efficiency*. A tax should not reduce economic efficiency and should ideally increase it. A *Pigouvian tax* is one which aims to increase efficiency by eliminating a market failure and ensuring that price reflects marginal social cost.

THE ECONOMIC EFFECTS OF TAXATION

ON THE DISTRIBUTION OF INCOME

Progressive taxes make income more evenly distributed and regressive taxes make income less evenly distributed, whereas proportional taxes leave the distribution of income unchanged.

Income tax, a direct tax, is a progressive tax and its imposition reduces the inequality of incomes.

In contrast most indirect taxes are regressive. The goods which are subject to heavy indirect taxation are widely consumed and have inelastic demand. Since the lower income groups tend to spend a greater proportion of their incomes on some of these commodities the effect of the taxes can be regressive. For example, there is evidence that the tax on tobacco is regressive: it takes a higher proportion of the income of the poor than of the rich. It appears to be getting more regressive because tobacco consumption has fallen among the higher income groups. On the other hand, the tax on some forms of alcohol seems to act progressively. The higher income groups consume relatively more wines and spirits which are subject to higher rates of tax.

ON CONSUMPTION

Direct and indirect taxes will affect both the total and the pattern of consumer spending.

Direct taxes reduce disposable income, but the effect on consumption will depend upon the propensity to consume and the level of saving. If there is very little saving, direct taxes will reduce con-

sumption. If, however, taxpayers are enjoying a relatively high standard of living which enables them to save, an increase in indirect taxes may have relatively little effect on consumption. People may resist any cut in their current living standards by reducing saving rather than spending.

Indirect taxes will also reduce the total demand for goods and services. The higher prices will reduce people's purchasing power. However again the effect will depend on the propensity to consume and the existing levels of saving.

ON INCENTIVES

Direct taxes, particularly income tax and corporation tax are criticised by some for reducing the incentives to work, save, invest and take risks.

It is argued that high and progressive rates of income tax will discourage some people from entering or staying in the labour force, some from working extra hours and some from taking promotion and extra responsibility and some from declaring the income they earn.

This is the thinking behind the *Laffer curve*. This principle, illustrated in Figure 33.2, suggests that a cut in a high rate of income tax from T to T^I can increase tax revenue from R to R^I by encouraging more labour market activity and by reducing the size of the black economy.

There is obviously some level of taxation at which disincentive effects will come into operation, but it is very difficult to determine that level. Indeed at certain levels, a rise in tax rates may increase the number of hours people will work. This is because people become accustomed to a certain standard of living and might react to higher taxes by working longer hours to maintain the same disposable income. In this case the income effect will outweigh the substitution effect.

High and progressive taxation on saving will also reduce the incentive to save. This is reinforced by

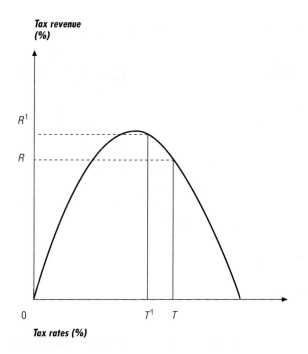

Tax revenue (%)

R^1

R

0 T^1 T

Tax rates (%)

FIG. 33.2

the double taxation which takes place on some saving. This occurs because the income from which savings are made is taxed and then the savings are themselves taxed. However some forms of savings are tax free and there are a number of influences on savings.

High corporation tax will similarly reduce the ability and incentive to invest. This is likely to be particularly true of risky projects.

ON THE GENERAL PRICE LEVEL

Direct taxes fall on income and do not have a direct influence on the general price level. However they could reduce inflationary pressure by lowering aggregate demand. Conversely they could result in cost-push inflation by stimulating workers to press for wage rises to maintain their real incomes.

A rise in indirect taxes will raise the general price level as measured by RPI, RPIX and HICP but not RPIY. Whether this results in inflation (i.e., a sustained rise in the price level) will depend on how people and firms react to the initial rise in price.

TAX HARMONISATION

Tax harmonisation is the standardisation of tax rates and regulations throughout a group of countries. The EU is seeking to promote the harmonisation of taxes within its area. Member countries have already agreed that the standard rate of VAT will not fall below 15%.

The main motive behind tax harmonisation is to allow countries to compete on equal terms. If sales tax rates differ between countries people will be encouraged to purchase goods and services in the countries with the lowest rates. For example, some people in the UK go to France on so-called 'booze cruises' to purchase alcohol which carries a lower rate of tax.

There is also concern about differences in corporate taxation. A number of member countries are worried that some countries are using tax competition (operating lower rates) to attract foreign investment. For example, Ireland has been accused of unfair competition because of the low corporation tax rate it charges.

Austria, Belgium and Germany, which are relatively highly taxed countries, are also concerned about the tax evasion they see when private investors move their savings to lower taxed countries, like Luxembourg.

However, deciding on what are equitable and efficient tax rates is difficult. Some argue that countries should have the freedom to operate different tax rates to take into account their different economic circumstances. Questions of tax policy are still subject to unanimous decision-taking among member countries.

THE BUDGET

The budget is the occasion when the Chancellor of the Exchequer announces expenditure plans and taxation plans. The budget proposals are given legal force when passed in the Finance Act.

A budget deficit arises when government expenditure exceeds government revenue, whereas a budget surplus occurs when the government raises more in tax revenue than it spends.

FISCAL STANCE

A government may deliberately set out to run a budget deficit. In this case the government would be operating a reflationary fiscal policy, seeking to increase aggregate demand and thereby reduce unemployment and raise growth. This is referred to as a structural deficit. However, a budget deficit can also arise as a result of changes in the level of economic activity. This is referred to as a *cyclical deficit*. It occurs when a fall in economic activity lowers tax revenue and raises government expenditure, particularly on job seekers' allowance.

To estimate the nature of the budget position, economists make use of the full employment budget concept. This measures what the budget position would be at full employment. Figure 33.3 shows three budget positions.

Budget *B* shows no structural deficit since when there is full employment there is a budget balance.

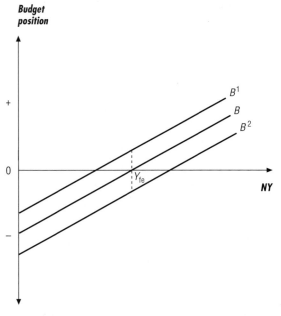

FIG. 33.3

Any deficit or surplus would arise as a result of changes in national income. Budget position B^1 shows a deflationary or contractionary budget position. At the full employment level there will be a structural budget surplus. B^2 represents an expansionary budget position with a structural budget deficit at the full employment level.

TABLE 33.1 BALANCING THE BOOKS 1999–2000

Where the money comes from	£bn	Where the money goes	£bn
Income tax	88	Social security	102
National insurance	56	Health	61
VAT	54	Education	41
Excise duty	36	Debt interest	26
Corporation tax	30	Defence	22
Business rates	16	Law & order	19
Council tax	13	Industry, agriculture & employment	15
Other receipts	56	Housing & environment	13
		Transport	9
		Other expenditure	41
General government receipts	349	General government expenditure	349

PUBLIC SECTOR NET CASH REQUIREMENT (PSNCR)

The public sector net cash requirement (which used to be called the public sector borrowing requirement) arises when the public sector spends more than it raises in revenue. Public sector finances are made up of the central government's budget position, local authorities' budget positions and the net trading surplus or loss of nationalised industries and public corporations. The largest component is the central government's budget position. A PSNCR can be financed by borrowing from the banking sector, from overseas or from the non-bank private sector. It is this last source which is the most widely used with the government selling government securities to, for example, pension funds.

A negative PSNCR or PSDR (public sector debt repayment) occurs when the public sector receives more revenue than it spends. The government instead of having to borrow is able to repay some past debt.

In recent years public expenditure has usually exceeded public revenue. However in the years 1987 to 1990 and 1999 there was a negative borrowing requirement.

FISCAL POLICY RULES

In 1998 the Chancellor of the Exchequer, Gordon Brown, committed himself to meeting two fiscal policy rules.

- *The golden rule* which states that over the economic cycle the government will only borrow to finance investment spending and will not borrow to fund current expenditure. So current spending must balance with revenues over the course of a business cycle. To assess whether the Chancellor is meeting this rule, economists and commentators look at the surplus on the current budget.

- *The public sector debt rule* which states that the ratio of net public sector debt to gross domestic product will be kept at 'a stable and prudent' level over the economic cycle. This level is defined as 40% of GDP. To assess whether this rule is being adhered to, economists and commentators, examine the public sector net borrowing figure. Public sector net borrowing differs from the PSNCR by the value of sales of financial assets and other financial adjustments.

THE NATIONAL DEBT

The national debt is the accumulation of government borrowings over past years. It is not the debt of the whole public sector; it is the debt of the central government. It rises whenever there is a budget deficit.

ADVANTAGES OF FISCAL POLICY

The instruments of fiscal policy (taxation and government spending) act directly on the major economic variables (e.g. output, employment and the price level); they are powerful instruments. A budget surplus will remove purchasing power from the economy and reduce aggregate demand. A budget deficit will inject purchasing power and raise aggregate demand.

Fiscal policy can also be used in a discriminating manner to change the allocation of resources both industrially and regionally. The products of some industries can be taxed while other industries receive subsidies. Some industries may be selected for protection by means of tariffs while others may be allowed to compete with unrestricted imports. Some types of investment may be encouraged with investment grants or preferential tax treatment of profits. If the government wishes to encourage economic growth in particular regions it can apply such measures as investment grants, training grants etc., on a strictly regional basis. It may also deliberately bias its own spending by placing a disproportionate share of its orders with firms in selected regions.

DISADVANTAGES OF FISCAL POLICY

A major disadvantage of fiscal policy is its relative inflexibility. Major changes in taxation and public expenditure cannot be carried out at frequent intervals — there is a great deal of administrative work involved. Changes in income tax, for example, involve the calculation and distribution of millions of new codes. Changes in public spending on goods and services can take some time before they are effective. Much of this expenditure is tied to long term contracts (e.g., the building of roads, power stations, hospitals) which cannot be switched on and off as short term regulators. There is often a serious time lag between the identification of the problem to be dealt with and the time when the fiscal measures begin to take effect.

AUTOMATIC STABILISERS

Most fiscal arrangements have some features built into them which are known as *automatic stabilisers*. For example, as money incomes rise, a progressive system of income tax will automatically remove an increasing proportion of those incomes in taxation. Providing government spending remains unchanged there will be some restraining effects on inflationary tendencies. When incomes are falling the opposite effect occurs, proportionately less is taken in taxation, and if government spending is unchanged total demand will not fall as fast as gross money incomes. VAT and excise revenue also move with the level of economic activity to offset changes in income.

Job seekers' allowance and other social security benefits also act as automatic stabilisers. When unemployment rises and incomes fall, expenditure on job seekers' allowance increases and the opposite effect applies when unemployment is falling. Thus, a reduction in wages due to rising unemployment will not lead to a proportionate fall in aggregate demand.

QUESTIONS

SHORT QUESTIONS

1. Explain what is meant by the incidence of taxation.
2. What is the difference between a progressive and a proportional tax?
3. Why might a reduction in taxation increase employment?
4. What are the aims of taxation?

MULTIPLE CHOICE

1. A tax is regressive when:

   A. marginal tax rates exceed average tax rates

   B. there is a wider range in pre-tax than post-tax incomes

   C. the cost of collecting the tax exceeds the tax revenue raised

   D. low income earners pay a higher proportion of their income in tax than high income earners.

2. Books are zero-rated for VAT in the UK. What does this mean for booksellers?

   A. They do not have to charge their customers any VAT and can reclaim any VAT paid to their suppliers.

   B. They do not have to charge their customers any VAT but cannot reclaim any VAT paid to their suppliers.

   C. They have to charge the same VAT rate as all the other EU member countries.

   D. They have to pay the VAT out of their profits and pass none of it on to their customers.

3. In a country there is a tax allowance of £5000. The tax rates on taxable income are 20% on the first £5000, 50% on the next £10 000 and 80% above that. A person earns £25 000. What is her average rate of taxation?

   A. 0.40   B. 0.50

   C. 0.64   D. 0.80

4. In Figure 33.4, which curve illustrates a proportional tax?

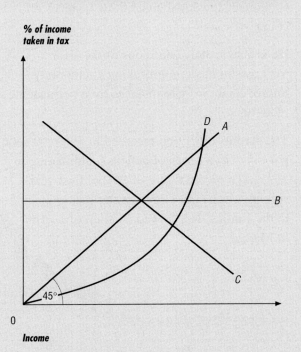

% of income taken in tax

Income

0

45°

D A

B

C

FIG. 33.4

DATA RESPONSE

Gordon Brown yesterday became the first Chancellor this decade to record a budget surplus. Official figures showed that public finances were in the black to the tune of £5.2bn in the financial year just ended.

It was the first time government tax revenue had exceeded expenditure since 1989–90, when the Treasury's coffers were swelled by the Lawson boom.

Francesca Massone, economist at the American investment bank Goldman Sachs, warned, however, that extra money banked by the Treasury could easily be needed to cover the cost of the war in Kosovo.

Rather than celebrating, Mr Brown kept a low profile, however. He is thought to be concerned not to be seen crowing at a time when the economic slowdown could blow finances off course.

He is also acutely conscious of the error Mr Lawson made in mistaking a temporary improvement in state finances for a permanent recovery.

The surplus of £1.9bn recorded in 1989–90 soon gave way to a series of deficits, culminating in 1993–94's record figure of £51bn. Last year's surplus was nearly £2.5bn better than projected in the Budget. It followed a deficit of £4.1bn in March.

Source: 'Brown plays down surplus in budget' by Mark Atkinson, the Guardian, 21/5/99.

a] What is meant by a budget surplus? **(2)**

b] What are the main sources of tax revenue in the UK? **(4)**

c] Explain why an economic boom may result in a budget surplus. **(6)**

d] Why might an economic slowdown 'blow public finances off course'? **(6)**

e] Why might a government seek to run a budget deficit? **(7)**

CASE STUDY

The budget changes will do little to iron out the substantial differences in tax and duty between Britain and other European countries.

Following this budget the ratio of debt to national income will fall below 40% in the next fiscal year and is forecast to stay below 40% for the rest of the Parliament. On the face of it, this puts the UK at the lower end of the European taxation scale.

Closer inspection reveals that this broad picture masks some important variations. In particular, it disguises the fact that — contrary to popular belief — many taxes in the UK are among the highest in Europe.

'Tax harmonisation is seen as forcing a low-tax hard-working UK to match Europe's uncompetitive level of state dominated inflexibility,' said Alison Cottrell, chief international economist at PaineWebber. 'All very entertaining and containing more than an element of truth — which still leaves it some distance from reality.'

The UK's corporate tax burden, for example, is substantially higher than in Germany, Italy or France, on Organisation for Economic Co-operation and Development calculations. Recent OECD data puts the UK effective rate of company tax — which includes factors such as allowances and depreciation rules — at around 45%. This is despite the fact that the UK's 30% top rate of corporation tax is lower than any other major country in Europe.

Sales tax is another field where the UK fails to shine. The OECD puts the effective rate of sales tax — which includes excise taxes — at just under 15%; roughly similar to Germany, above Spain, but below Scandinavia. And as far as particular duties — such as those on alcohol and tobacco — are concerned, UK consumers pay through the nose. The tax on a pack of 20 cigarettes in the UK, for example, is almost £1.50 higher than the average of other EU states, according to recent calculations by the Tobacco Manufacturers' Association. 'We are

one of the most highly taxed for "sin" taxes,' said Bill Robinson, a director of the London Economics consultancy.

One area where the UK's reputation as a low-tax, flexible economy does hold true is labour tax. Relatively, the British economy enjoys low rates of personal income tax. UK workers also tend to be cheaper to employ than abroad. Ms Cottrell said: 'Continental Europe has on the whole taxed capital far more lightly than labour. In the "Anglo" economies the reverse has been true.'

Looking forward, both market forces and greater European integration will smooth out some of the tax differentials, although domestic political and cultural concerns limit how far this can go.

Although some differences will never disappear, budgets in the years to come will increasingly have to take account of the fiscal situation abroad.

Source: 'Still a case of "vive la difference" in EU' by Lea Paterson, The Independent Budget Review, 10/3/99.

a] Does the article suggest that the government would meet the public debt rule it has set itself? **(5)**

b] Explain what is meant by tax harmonisation. **(5)**

c] What is corporation tax? **(3)**

d] What effect may high rates of corporation tax have on investment? **(8)**

e] Explain what is meant by 'sin taxes'. **(5)**

f] What are the arguments for taxing cigarettes at a high rate? **(10)**

g] How do UK tax rates compare to those of other European countries? **(6)**

h] What effect may low rates of personal income tax have on the supply of labour? **(8)**

STRUCTURED ESSAY

a] Discuss the functions of taxation. **(10)**

b] Assess whether the government should raise a larger proportion of tax revenue from indirect taxation than it does currently. **(15)**

34 MONETARY POLICY

DEFINITION

Monetary policy refers to the attempts to manipulate either the rate of interest or the money supply so as to bring about desired changes in the economy. Some economists also include the exchange rate in monetary policy whereas others treat it as a separate type of policy.

RECENT MONETARY POLICY

In the 1980s attention was focused on monetary policy following the monetarist view that the control of the money supply is probably the most important instrument for regulating total demand in an economy. The Conservative government sought to control the growth of the money supply.

In the early 1990s attention switched to the exchange rate. With the UK's entry into the ex-change rate mechanism (ERM) a target value was set for the pound. This was maintained for two years.

After the UK's departure from the ERM a target rate was set for the underlying rate of inflation of between 1–4% and the main monetary tool became the rate of interest.

When the Labour Government was elected in May 1997 one of its first actions was to give the Bank of England independence to set the rate of interest. The Bank has to do this in the context of the target it has been given for the underlying rate of inflation. This is 2.5% (with a margin of 1% point either side). A Monetary Policy Committee (see Chapter 16) consisting of Bank of England represen-tatives and Treasury appointments was set up to take interest rate decisions.

Changes in the rate of interest is now the main government policy measure being used to influence the macroeconomy on a day to day basis.

NAME: Matt Barrett
Banker

BORN: 20 September 1944 in Tralee, County Kerry

NATIONALITY: Irish

EDUCATED: Christian Brothers' School

POSTS HELD: 1962 joined the Bank of Montreal's branch in Waterloo in a junior capacity
1967 sent on a management trainee programme in Montreal
1990 appointed Chairman and Chief Executive of the Bank of Montreal
1999 appointed Group Chief Executive of Barclays Bank

AWARDS: 1995 made Canadian businessman of the year and made officer of the Order of Canada (the country's highest civilian honour)

When young, Matt Barrett had thought about becoming a writer but as he has said: 'I found I couldn't write but I was very good at balancing cheques'.

CONTROL OF THE MONEY SUPPLY

As noted in Chapter 7 the most important form of money is bank deposits; a large part of these deposits come into being as a result of lending by the banking sector (including building societies). Total spending is very much influenced by firms' and households' ability to borrow from the banks either directly through loans and overdrafts, or indirectly through credit schemes. So any attempt to control the money supply must be directed at controlling the banking sector's ability to lend, or to influencing firms' and households' willingness to borrow.

POLICY INSTRUMENTS

A central bank, acting on behalf of a government or group of governments, may seek to influence banks' ability to lend (the supply of money) or customers' demand for loans (the demand for money). If it seeks to control the former it may try to influence the banks' supplies of liquid assets (items they own which can quickly be converted into cash). Liquid assets are important because the amount a bank can lend depends on its ability to meet the demands of its customers for cash. The more liquid assets a bank has, the greater the amount it can potentially lend. If, on the other hand, it seeks to influence demand for loans it may decide to alter the rate of interest.

Relationship between controlling the money supply and changing the rate of interest. A central bank such as the Bank of England can fix either the quantity of money or its price. It cannot fix both simultaneously. If the demand for money (liquidity preference) does not change, any changes in the supply of money will alter the rate of interest (except at very low levels). Figure 34.1 shows a decrease in the money supply from MS to MS^1 causing the rate of interest to rise from R to R^1.

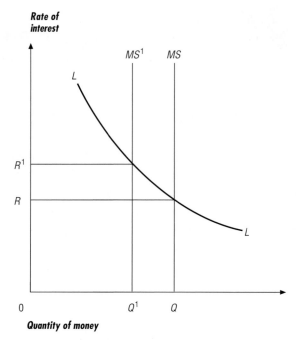

Quantity of money

FIG. 34.1

Alternatively, if the supply of money remains fixed, any change in the demand for money will bring about changes in the rate of interest. Figure 34.2 shows an increase in demand for money causing a rise in the rate of interest.

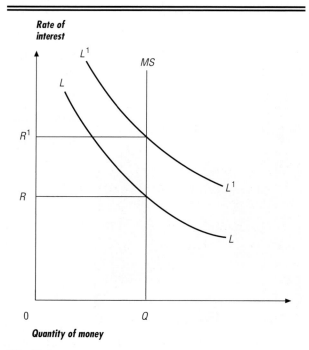

Quantity of money

FIG. 34.2

Since the central bank cannot determine demand it is in the same position as a monopolist it can determine the quantity or the price — not both.

If it chooses to fix a particular rate of interest then it must supply whatever quantity of money will be demanded at that rate. As the demand for money changes, so must the supply; otherwise the rate of interest must change. If the authorities decide to fix the supply of money, the rate of interest will vary as the demand for money varies. The authorities are thus presented with a dilemma — should they try to influence demand by manipulating the rate of interest or control the supply of money by more direct means?

THE MONEY TRANSMISSION MECHANISM

The money transmission mechanism is the link between changes in the money supply and output and the price level. Increases in the money supply will mean that the money supply will be greater than the demand for money. Demand for goods, services and financial assets will rise. The rise in demand for financial assets will raise their price and lower the rate of interest. Consumption and investment will rise which will shift the aggregate demand curve to the right and may cause a rise in the general price level. This process is shown in Figure 34.3.

Monetarists think that changes in the money supply can have a significant effect on the price level. They think that they cause large shifts in aggregate demand and, due to the shape of the long run aggregate supply curve, will leave output unchanged in the long run but will alter the price level.

Keynesians disagree. They believe that financial assets are relatively close substitutes so that the main impact of changes in the money supply occurs via changes in demand for financial assets and hence

the rate of interest. However, they think that consumption and investment are relatively interest inelastic and so that the aggregate demand curve will not move far as a result of changes in the money supply. They also believe that the effect of a change in aggregate demand will depend on what point of the long run aggregate supply curve an economy is operating at. If there is considerable spare capacity in the economy an increase in aggregate demand curve may raise output but leave the price level unaffected.

The money transmission mechanism shows how changes in the money supply affect the economy and also highlights differences in views between Keynesians and monetarists on the effectiveness of monetary policy (discussed below).

POSSIBLE MONETARY POLICY MEASURES

These include the following.

- *The rate of interest.* As already mentioned in recent years the rate of interest is most widely used by the Bank of England. It can operate as a buyer and seller in the money market so as to influence the rate of interest. It can keep the banking system short of money and then lend the required amount at an interest rate which it decides.
- *Open market operations.* In addition to setting the terms on which it is prepared to lend, the central bank can act directly on the supply of financial assets in the banking system by means of its activities in the markets for securities. The Bank of England through its officials buys and sells securities (government bonds and other government securities) in the open market. On a daily basis the Bank of England seeks to avoid sharp fluctuations in interest rates. So if there is a shortage of funds it will purchase government securities to increase them. However, if it wishes

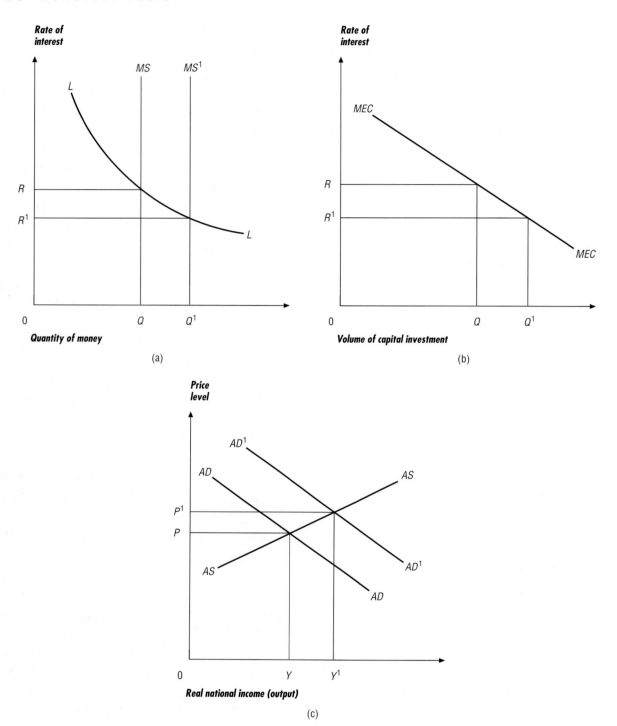

FIG. 34.3

to restrict bank lending it will sell securities. The banks and other buyers will pay for these securities with cheques drawn on their accounts in the retail (commercial) banks. These cheques will be payable to the Bank of England which will then hold claims on the retail banks. The debts will be settled by a reduction of the bankers' deposits at the Bank of England. A fall in these deposits represents a reduction in the banks' liquid assets ratio and they will be obliged to reduce the level of their total deposits in order to restore the required ratio of liquid assets to deposits. However, this measure will only force the banks to reduce their lending if they are operating with the minimum level of liquid assets. If the banks have a surplus of liquid assets, a reduction of their deposits at the central bank might still leave them with an adequate total supply of liquid assets and they will not be obliged to reduce their total deposits.

When the central bank wishes to see an expansion of bank lending it will enter the market and buy securities, making payment for them with cheques drawn on itself. The banks and other sellers of these securities will pay the central banks' cheques into accounts in the retail banks. The banks now hold claims on the central bank which will settle its indebtedness by crediting the outstanding amounts to the bankers' deposits. An increase in bankers' deposits at the central bank amounts to an increase in the liquid assets ratio. The banks will be able to expand their lending.

- *Special deposits*. The central bank can instruct retail banks to place some of their liquid assets with it. This reduction in their liquid assets may mean that they will have to reduce their bank lending. If the central bank wishes to encourage bank lending it can release any special deposits it is holding and thus increase the banks' supply of liquid assets. However the Bank of England has not called for any special deposits for several decades.

- *Funding*. Although open market operations and calls for special deposits may be successful in changing the banks' liquid assets ratio, they will not be effective instruments for restraining bank lending when the banks are holding surplus liquid assets. Funding is a way of reducing the supplies of liquid assets available to the banking system.

The policy requires the Bank of England to change the structure of the national debt by issuing more long-term securities and fewer short-term securities (Treasury bills). This operation would make the banks more vulnerable to open market operations and calls for special deposits because Treasury bills are liquid assets and long-term securities are not.

- *Quantitative and qualitative controls*. A central bank can make use of quantitative controls (limits on bank lending) and qualitative controls (directives on who should receive loans). However, these have not been used in the UK since the 1970s.

- *Moral suasion*. A central bank may seek to persuade banks to lend less.

- *The exchange rate*. The exchange rate is the price of the currency in terms of other currencies. Governments which operate their own currencies have to decide whether to operate fixed, managed or floating exchange rates. A fixed rate is one which is set at a certain price and is kept at that price by government action when necessary. A managed exchange rate is one where the extent to which the value of the exchange rate can change is limited by intervention of the central bank and a floating rate is one determined by market forces.

If a government decides that it does want to fix or influence the value of its currency it has to decide whether it wants a high or a low exchange rate. A high exchange rate will mean that export prices (in terms of foreign currency) will be high whilst import prices will be low (in terms of domestic currency). One advantage of a high exchange rate is that it tends to reduce inflationary pressure by forcing domestic firms to keep prices low in order to remain price competitive.

In October 1990 the UK entered Europe's exchange rate mechanism (ERM) which is a managed exchange rate system. It left in September 1992 after speculative attacks on its value. It is currently operating a floating exchange rate system and is considering whether to enter the single currency (the euro) which is also a floating exchange rate. (See Chapter 51 for more details on the exchange rate.)

MONETARY POLICY STANCE

A restrictionist (or tight) monetary policy is one which seeks to reduce aggregate demand, often in an attempt to reduce inflationary pressures or correct a balance of payments deficit. It involves an increase in the rate of interest and/or a reduction in the growth of the money supply. It may also involve raising the exchange rate. In contrast, an expansionary monetary policy would be implemented to increase aggregate demand, probably to raise output and employment. In this case the rate of interest will be reduced and/or the growth of the money supply stimulated. The exchange rate may also be lowered.

MONETARY POLICY AND THE NATIONAL DEBT

In addition to its responsibility for operating the government's monetary policy the Bank of England has the responsibility for the management of the national debt. These two responsibilities may present the central bank with conflicting objectives. As manager of the national debt the Bank of England has the task of raising large sums of money for the government every year. It must float new issues of securities to repay the loans which are maturing and may have to finance some of the current government spending. The money and capital markets will only take up large issues of government securities if they are attractively priced, the risk of capital losses are not too great and the yield is satisfactory. The current rate of interest is a very important consideration because it influences the rate of interest which must be offered on new issues of securities,

and with such a large national debt, it is desirable to minimise the interest burden.

But the central bank is also obliged to carry out open market operations with a view to controlling the lending activities of the retail banks. It is likely, therefore, that the objectives of debt management will sometimes conflict with those of monetary policy. For example, the central bank may be obliged to conduct open market sales of securities in order to reduce the banks' liquid assets. Heavy sales of securities, however, will depress security prices which will in turn have the effect of raising interest rates. Existing holders of government securities will suffer capital losses and this will not make the market very receptive to any new issue of securities which the central bank may be trying to float in order to finance government expenditure. There may also be occasions when monetary policy calls for a fall in interest rates (to stimulate private spending). If this occurs at the same time as the central bank has the responsibility for putting a large issue of securities on the market, the Bank of England would be frustrating its debt policy objective since increasing the supply of securities would raise interest rates instead of lowering them.

MONETARY POLICY AND FISCAL POLICY

Fiscal policy affects monetary policy and vice versa. For instance if the government spends more than it raises in revenue it will have a net borrowing requirement. If this is financed by borrowing from the banking sector then, other things being equal, there will be an increase in the money supply.

If the government borrows from the non-bank private sector the money supply will not change because bank deposits are transferred from the private sector to the public sector. However the increase in borrowing may have an effect on the rate of interest.

CROWDING OUT

New classical economists argue that an increase in government borrowing can result in crowding out, i.e. an increase in public sector spending replacing private sector spending. The argument is that an increase in government borrowing will increase the demand for loans and bid up the rate of interest. The higher rate of interest will reduce private sector spending by:

- reducing private sector investment
- reducing consumption
- reducing foreign demand for the country's goods and services by pushing up the exchange rate and thereby raising export prices and lowering import prices.

However, Keynesians dispute that crowding out will occur. They claim that if the government spends more than it raises in revenue there will be a net injection in the circular flow of income. This will cause national income to rise and as a result savings will increase. The higher level of savings will create extra funds for investment and do away with the need for the rate of interest to rise.

Indeed Keynesians argue that crowding in can occur — an increase in public sector spending, causing a rise in private sector spending. The idea is that the higher level of national income, arising from net government expenditure, will cause a rise in private sector investment and consumption.

Empirical evidence does not appear to support the crowding out argument. In the United States and the UK the rate of interest does not usually move in line with changes in the government's borrowing requirement.

THE QUANTITY THEORY

The quantity theory is based on an interpretation of the equation $MV = PT$ or, as it is sometimes written, $MV = PY$ where M stands for the money supply, V for the velocity of circulation, P the general price level and T (or Y) the total volume of transactions which can be regarded as output.

THE VELOCITY OF CIRCULATION

This is the term used to describe the rate at which money changes hands. For example if GDP was £20 000m and the money supply was £500m then the velocity of circulation is 4 since each £1 must have changed hands 4 times.

$$V = \frac{GDP}{MS}$$

If the velocity of circulation increased to 5, the same supply of money would now purchase £25 000m worth of goods and services.

THE QUANTITY EQUATION

The value of total expenditure (MV) must be equal to the value of goods and services sold (PT). They are simply two different ways of looking at the same thing — the total spending on goods and services. The quantity equation is not a theory as it does not state anything about the causes of changes in the quantities concerned.

KEYNESIAN VIEWS

Keynesians believe that the equation cannot be used as the basis for a theory. This is because they do not think it is possible to predict what will happen if any of the variables change. For example if initially:

$$MV = PT$$
$$£10\text{bn} \times 6 = £3 \times 20\text{bn}$$

then a change in the money supply to e.g. £15bn may, they argue, cause a change in V, P or T. For instance, if there is spare capacity in the economy, T may increase so that:

$$£15bn \times 6 = £3 \times 30bn$$

So Keynesians do not think that the equation can be used as the basis to make predictions about the effects of changes in the money supply.

MONETARIST VIEW

The monetarists, in contrast, think this equation can be converted into a theory. This is because they believe that V and T are constant in the short run so that changes in M cause a direct and proportionate change in P. For example if initially again:

$$MV = PT$$
$$£10bn \times 6 = £3 \times 20bn$$

and V and T are constant, then a rise in M to £15bn (i.e. by 50%) will cause P to rise to £4.5 (50%).

$$£15bn \times 6 = £4.5 \times 20bn$$

In the 1960s there was a great revival of interest in the quantity theory. This was largely due to the best known monetarist, Professor Milton Friedman of Chicago University. His studies and research showed that fluctuations in the rate of inflation appeared to follow the fluctuations in the growth of the money supply quite closely.

EFFECTIVENESS OF MONETARY POLICY

As monetarists believe that changes in the money supply have a direct and proportionate effect on the general price level, they also believe it is very important for a government to control the money supply — to ensure that it does not grow faster than output. The Conservative government in 1980 set targets for the growth of the money supply and the government's borrowing requirement. In practice the government found it difficult to control the money supply. It was also discovered that there did not appear to be a direct link between changes in the money supply and inflation. The money supply started to grow erratically as predicted by Goodhart's law. This was named after Professor Goodhart, a current member of the monetary policy committee. It states that any measure of the money supply behaves differently when it is targeted as a result of the very act of targeting it.

Controlling the money supply is difficult. The greatest part of the money supply consists of bank deposits and a large part of these deposits are created by bank lending (see Chapter 66). Retail banks' most profitable activity is lending so they are likely to seek to get round any restrictions on their ability to lend. For example, if the central bank placed a limit in the amount a bank could lend, banks may arrange loans for its customers with overseas branches which would not come under the central bank's control.

For a number of years now the main monetary policy tool has been the rate of interest. However, there are again questions about the effectiveness of this measure. In times of boom when entrepreneurs are very optimistic, the rate of interest may have to be very high to have any effect on aggregate demand. Such high interest rates may well conflict with other objectives of government policy. As the largest borrower in the country the government will be seriously affected by the greatly increased burden of the national debt. High interest rates will also be very unpopular in the politically sensitive housing market where interest charges are a major cost item to voters. At the opposite extreme, low interest rates are not likely to be very effective as a stimulant when the economy is depressed. Reducing interest rates to very low levels is not likely to encourage borrowing and spending on capital goods when new investment offers little or no prospect of reasonable profits. When there is heavy unemployment lower interest rates are not likely to lead to any significant increase in borrowing on credit in the markets for consumer goods.

Some economists also argue that changes in interest rates can take time to work through the economy.

A government's independence of action on the money supply and interest rates may also be limited. In the case of members of Europe's economic and monetary union (EMU) it is the European Central Bank which controls the money supply and decides on the rate of interest and not the member governments (although they have representatives on the decision making committee). Whilst the UK currently operates, in theory, an independent monetary policy its autonomy is nevertheless limited. This is because its rate of interest cannot be significantly different from those operating in the euro area or in the United States. This is because, for example, if much higher interest rates could be gained in the USA funds would be transferred from the UK to the USA. This would harm UK financial institutions and lower the exchange rate.

QUESTIONS

SHORT QUESTIONS

1 Why can a central bank not control both the money supply and the rate of interest simultaneously?

2 Explain how funding can reduce the money supply.

3 What is meant by a restrictionist monetary policy?

4 Use the Quantity Theory to explain why an increase in the money supply may result in an increase in output or prices or both.

MULTIPLE CHOICE

1 A central bank sells securities in the open market. What effect is this likely to have on the money supply and the rate of interest?

	Money supply	Rate of interest
A	reduce	reduce
B	reduce	increase
C	increase	increase
D	increase	increase

2 Which of the following policy measures might a government wishing to pursue an expansionary monetary policy adopt?

A An increase in the rate of interest.

B The purchase of government securities.

C A reduction in income tax.

D An increase in government spending.

3 The idea of crowding out suggests that an increase in government borrowing will cause a decrease in:

A the rate of interest

B the money supply

C private sector spending

D the rate of income tax.

4 According to the monetarist interpretation of the quantity theory:

A $M = PV/T$

B the supply of money is determined by the transactions demand for money

C the velocity of circulation varies inversely with the general price level

D the price level varies proportionately with the quantity of money in circulation.

DATA RESPONSE

'The US Federal Reserve may need to raise interest rates before any sign that inflation is returning to the economy,' Alan Greenspan said yesterday.

With speculation still rife that the Fed will raise rates at its next meeting in two weeks time, the Fed chairman appeared to be looking towards a reversal of the interest rate cuts last year which stoked the US recovery.

'It is useful to pre-empt forces of imbalance before they threaten economic stability,' he said. 'When we can be pre-emptive we should be, because modest pre-emptive actions can obviate the need for more drastic actions at a later date that could destabilise the economy.'

Mr Greenspan, in testimony to Congress, said 'developing imbalances' could cause problems for the economy, with the trade deficit widening and personal savings at new lows. The trade gap closed slightly in April to $18.94bn from $18.95bn in March, the Commerce department reported yesterday. The figures showed the first increase in US exports since last October. But the deficit is still heading for another record this year; after last year's revised $164bn.

Source: 'Greenspan hints at pre-emptive rate rise'
by Andrew Marshall, the Independent, 18/6/99.

a] Explain how a rise in interest rates could reduce inflation. **(6)**

b] Why may a cut in interest rates stimulate an economic recovery? **(6)**

c] Explain how a rise in interest rates could reduce a trade deficit (the negative gap between export revenue and import expenditure). **(6)**

d] What are the possible dangers of low personal savings? **(4)**

e] Why was the Federal reserve keen to take action quickly? **(3)**

CASE STUDY

Whatever it was that the Bank of England's monetary policy committee (MPC) took last autumn, I think they should sell the recipe.

Until then, the committee looked slow, excessively cautious and once, on that celebrated occasion last June, spectacularly misguided. Now it is transformed, catching out the market quickly and imaginatively to what is happening in both the real economy and to inflationary pressures. Some observers attribute the change to the bill giving the Bank of England independence becoming law last summer. This gave the MPC the confidence to act independently.

If year zero for British policy was in the autumn of 1992, after the ERM debacle, this easily represents the sharpest movement, in either direction. In the absence of bank independence, rates may not have gone up so much — although knowing this chancellor they may have risen sooner and by more. I doubt, however, whether any chancellor would have had the courage effectively to admit he was wrong and bring rates down so quickly.

Will rates drop next month? This week's inflation report is likely to say rates have reached a level consistent with achieving the 2.5% inflation target, implying they do not need to fall again. This should, however, be treated with a pinch of salt, as has been demonstrated in recent months.

Before its next meeting on March 3–4, the MPC will be briefed on the March 9 budget by Gus O'Donnell, the government's chief economic adviser. The message will be one of fiscal prudence. Although Gordon Brown plans to pave the way for the 10p starting rate of income tax next year, this budget will be mainly concerned with micro measures to improve productivity, particularly among small businesses and high-technology firms. There will be no giveaway.

Brown appears to be pursuing his own version of the 'Clinton-Greenspan' approach now favoured by many of his European colleagues. If you keep fiscal policy tight, the argument goes, you will reap your reward in lower interest rates. Fiscal policy is not, of course, the only consideration, hence the current worry about higher American interest rates.

Source: 'Doing it by the book' by David Smith, the Sunday Times, 7/2/99.

a] What are the advantages of a central bank setting interest rates independently? **(7)**

b] What is the UK's current exchange rate policy? **(5)**

c] What action would the MPC be likely to take if the inflation rate fell below 1.5%? **(6)**

d] What is meant by fiscal prudence? **(4)**

e] What was the 'ERM debacle'? **(4)**

f] Discuss the effect of higher American interest rates in the UK. **(9)**

g] Explain the relationship between fiscal and monetary policy. **(8)**

h] Explain why a tight fiscal policy may permit lower interest rates. **(7)**

STRUCTURED ESSAY

a] Explain what is meant by monetary policy. **(10)**

b] Discuss the monetary policy measures a government and/or central bank may take to stimulate economic activity. **(15)**

35 SUPPLY-SIDE POLICIES

DEFINITION

Supply-side policies are those designed to increase the economy's long term growth potential and thereby, in the long run, improve the economy's performance in terms not only of economic growth but also in terms of employment, inflation and the balance of payments position. They aim to improve the workings of product and factor markets.

It is a microeconomic approach designed to raise the performance of the macroeconomy. If supply-side policies are successful the quantity and/or the quality of resources will increase thereby shifting the long run aggregate supply curve to the right and enabling the country to produce more goods and services.

DIFFERENT APPROACHES

Supply-side policies tend to be associated with new classical economists. However now both new classical economists and Keynesian economists recognise the importance of the supply-side of the economy. They both advocate supply-side policies but due to their different views they advocate mainly different policies.

New classical economists advocate supply-side policies which are designed to improve the efficiency and flexibility of markets by increasing economic incentives and the level of competition and reducing the role of the government.

In contrast Keynesian believe that government intervention can improve the workings of markets. They advocate interventionist supply-side policies which will encourage the private sector to do things which they are either not doing or not doing in sufficient quantity e.g. giving grants to firms to set up in depressed regions and to increase their level of investment.

FREE MARKET SUPPLY-SIDE POLICIES

DEREGULATION

Deregulation involves removing laws and regulations which restrict competition. Although new classical economists believe that some restrictions are justified e.g. limits on the age at which people can start work and health and safety regulations, they favour getting rid of regulations which just protect the interests of existing suppliers. For example in the UK in 1979 the National Bus Corporation had its monopoly of local distance coach travel removed when the Conservative Government allowed private operators to compete. This was followed in 1986 by the deregulation of local bus services and the Stock Exchange.

PRIVATISATION

This involves transferring assets from the public to the private sector, e.g. selling of nationalised industries and putting local authority services such as refuse collection into the private sector. New classical economists believe that firms operate more efficiently in the private sector where they are subject to the discipline of the market — if they do not produce what consumers want they will go out of business.

CUTTING INCOME TAX

It is argued that reducing the marginal rate of income tax will raise the supply of labour in a number of ways:

- it will encourage more people to seek employment, for example mothers and those who have retired early
- it will persuade some people to work longer hours
- it will encourage the unemployed to seek work more actively as the income gap between after-tax wage rates and unemployment benefit will have been increased.

A lower marginal rate of income may also have the benefit of reducing the size of the black economy.

CUTTING CORPORATION TAX

This will increase the funds firms have available to invest and will increase the financial incentive to invest.

SIMPLIFYING THE TAX SYSTEM

This will reduce the time firms have to spend calculating their tax returns and filling out forms. Hence it will reduce their administrative costs. It may also encourage more people to set up their own business. The one type of tax which new classical economists believe does not alter incentives or distort choice is a lump sum tax which is sometimes referred to as a poll tax. This is because the amount paid does not vary with a taxpayers' actions in earning income, investing it or spending it.

WELFARE

New classical economists favour cutting welfare payments and making the criteria for receiving them more rigorous. They believe that this will reduce voluntary unemployment by, as with a cut in income tax, increasing the gap between paid employment and unemployment benefit and by ensuring that those who do receive benefits are genuinely unable to find work. It is thought that if unemployment benefit, called job seekers' allowance in the UK, is at a relatively low level the unemployed will seek work more actively and be less inclined to turn down offers of low paid employment.

REFORM OF TRADE UNIONS

New classical economists believe that trade unions can cause unemployment by pushing wage rates up above the equilibrium level and by reducing productivity through maintaining restrictive practices. The Conservative Governments of the 1980s and early 1990s passed a range of legislation which reduced the power of trade unions.

INTERVENTIONIST SUPPLY-SIDE POLICIES

TRAINING

Keynesian economists believe that the private sector tends not to spend the optimum amount on training. Firms may under-spend on training because they plan to poach trained workers from other firms and/or because they fear that other firms will poach any workers they train. So Keynesians advocate government provision of training schemes and the subsidising of private sector training schemes. A better-trained labour force will be more employable, more productive and more mobile.

EDUCATION

Education, like training, is a merit good and if left to market forces is likely to be under-consumed. Government measures to improve education should raise the quality of the labour force.

INVESTMENT GRANTS

Increases in the quality and quantity of investment are thought to be very important for economic growth (see Chapter 53). It has been claimed that UK firms tend to under-invest and do not always invest in appropriate product ranges.

REGIONAL POLICY

Firms deciding to set up new plants may not always consider all sites and may take into account non-economic factors e.g. proximity to a golf course. Economic theory might suggest that firms would move to depressed regions where labour and land costs are likely to be low and the unemployed would move from depressed regions to more prosperous areas. However in practice this does not always happen. Labour is often immobile, due to e.g. social ties, and firms tend to be attracted by success. So Keynesians argue that the government may have to intervene to provide incentives for firms to set up in depressed regions.

SUPPLY-SIDE POLICIES AND THE MACROECONOMY

Successful supply-side policies as well as increasing potential output can improve the performance of the economy by:

- reducing unemployment by increasing the incentive to work and by improved training and reduced trade union power, making workers more attractive to employers
- reducing inflationary pressure by raising the productivity of labour
- improving the balance of payments position by increasing the price and quality competitiveness of UK goods and services.

SUPPLY-SIDE POLICIES AND UK GOVERNMENTS

The Conservative Governments, and the USA Governments, of the 1980s and 1990s implemented a wide-range of free market supply-side policies. The Labour Government elected in May 1997 has introduced a range of both free market and interventionist supply-side policies to improve the economy's long run performance.

QUESTIONS

SHORT QUESTIONS

1. Explain what is meant by deregulation.

2. What is the advantage claimed for a lump sum tax?

3. How can a government increase the income gap between paid employment and unemployment?

4. Why are supply-side policies so-called?

MULTIPLE CHOICE

1. A government wants to increase output. Which of the following is a supply-side policy designed to promote growth?

   A. privatisation

   B. the imposition of a tariff

   C. an increase in unemployment benefits

   D. the introduction of a prices and incomes policy.

2. Which of the following is a supply-side policy designed to reduce unemployment?

   A. an increase in the money supply

   B. an increase in the exchange rate

   C. a reduction in government expenditure on training

   D. a reduction in the marginal rate of income tax.

3. What is the new classical supply-side argument for a reduction in government spending?

   A. to increase the money supply

   B. to reduce private sector investment

   C. to permit a greater role for free market forces

   D. to encourage a depreciation in a floating exchange rate.

4. Which policy would new classical supply-side supporters oppose?

   A. a cut in job seekers' allowance

   B. an increase in income tax

   C. trade union reform

   D. privatisation.

DATA RESPONSE

…it should be realised that the whole process of privatisation fits well into the supply-side ideology. Successive Conservative governments have felt that companies in the private sector are better at using resources than those in government hands. It is therefore no surprise that those governments sought to place the main utilities into private hands over the last decade. The more 'lenient' attitude towards mergers and acquisitions during the 1980s and 1990s was another by-product of this general view that the private sector can better utilise resources.

The UK has been regarded by many commentators as having had some success in changing the microeconomic environment through supply-side policies, thereby increasing the flexibility of the labour market.

Source: Applied economics, edited by A.Griffiths and S.Wall, 8th edition, Longman, 1999.

a] Explain what is meant by 'supply-side ideology'. **(4)**

b] Discuss one reason why the private sector may not be better at using resources than the government. **(5)**

c] What is meant by a 'more lenient attitude towards mergers and acquisitions'? **(3)**

d] Discuss the effect a 'more lenient attitude towards mergers and acquisitions' may have on competition. **(6)**

e] Discuss how supply-side policies may change the 'microeconomic environment'. **(7)**

CASE STUDY

Moves to introduce compulsory job interviews as a condition of receiving benefit lie at the heart of the Welfare Reform and Pensions Bill, under plans ministers say herald a 'radical change in culture'.

The new 'single gateway' to the benefit system for people of working age will mean that, for the first time, all claimants will be obliged to turn up regularly for information on options available to them, though ministers say there are no plans to force them to accept jobs.

The 75-clause bill, published yesterday, encompasses a raft of other measures, including a new stakeholder pension sharing for divorced couples, reforms to widows' benefit, and its extension to widowers, and changes to benefits for people with disabilities or long-term illnesses.

The principle behind the new 'single work-focused gateway', ministers say, is that the state should no longer pay benefits passively, but should help become more independent. It will be piloted in 12 areas, requiring a total of 145 000 people to come to job centres for interviews on work and training options, usually within three days of making a benefit claim.

It will cover everyone on income support and housing benefit, as well as lone parents and disabled people.

Under the gateway scheme, first-time claimants refusing three calls to interview would effectively forfeit all benefit, since their claims would not be processed. Those already on benefit will also gradually be called in for interview — those who refuse three times would see their benefit docked.

Source: 'Claimants at gateway to new culture' by Lucy Ward, the Guardian, 11/2/99.

a] Why would 'compulsory job advice interviews as a condition of receiving benefit' be regarded as a supply-side policy? **(7)**

b] What effect might the removal of benefits from some people have on aggregate demand? **(5)**

c] Which of the economically inactive groups are not affected by the measure? **(6)**

d] Discuss the effect the measure might have on poverty. **(12)**

e] Why might the measure increase or reduce the size of the black economy? **(12)**

f] Discuss one other supply-side policy to reduce unemployment. **(8)**

STRUCTURED ESSAY

a] Explain what is meant by supply-side policies. **(8)**

b] Compare a supply-side policy approach and a fiscal policy approach to raising output. **(17)**

PART SIX: FIRMS AND THEIR OBJECTIVES

36 FIRMS' OBJECTIVES

Firms may have a range of objectives. At any particular time one or a combination of objectives may be dominant. There are a number of factors which influence which objectives firms pursue and these include:

- number of competitors — market structure
- activities of competitors
- relative power of different groups within the firm
- views of consumers
- legal restraints
- whether the firm is in the private sector or in the public sector.

For instance, taking the fourth influence listed above, recent concern about genetically modified foods has led a number of supermarkets to withdraw all genetically modified foods.

State owned corporations might be instructed to have as their primary objective to provide a public service. Below concentration is focused on the objectives of private sector firms.

OBJECTIVES

PROFIT MAXIMISATION

The traditional objective of firms is profit maximisation. It is usually assumed that firms seek to make as high profits as possible and that this is achieved where marginal cost (the change in cost resulting from producing one more unit) is equal to marginal revenue (the change in revenue from selling one extra unit).

However, some economists challenge this view. They argue that many entrepreneurs are not aware of the concepts of marginal revenue and marginal cost and the ones who are may find it very difficult to obtain any precise measurements of MR and MC. But this does not destroy the profit-maximisation theory. If entrepreneurs try to increase profits by trial and error adjustments of their price and/or output they will be tending towards the output where $MC = MR$, even if they are unaware of the concepts.

PROFIT SATISFICING

Some studies of firms' activities suggest that rather than trying to maximise profits, the managers of some firms aim for a satisfactory level of profits which will keep shareholders happy. They seem content with some acceptable level of profit which might be less than they could earn if they adopted more fiercely competitive policies. Managers may be reluctant to accept the increased risks and pressures which occur with more aggressive and ambitious practices. Or it may be the case that once a satisfactory level of profits has been made, they feel free to pursue other objectives, some of which may conflict with profit maximisation. While profit satisficing as an objective is available to a firm with some degree of market power, in perfectly competitive markets, where no firm has any significant market power, firms must attempt to maximise profits in order to survive.

GROWTH

The fact that large firms are not directly controlled by shareholders (the people most likely to be interested in profit-maximisation) but by professional managers has led some economists to argue that the main motive pursued is likely to be growth. The status, prestige, and remuneration of managers is usually closely linked to the size of the firm and it is likely, therefore, that such people will be more interested in maximising sales rather than maximising profits. They cannot be indifferent to the profit position of the firm, but, having achieved a satisfactory level of profits, managers are more inclined to make sales maximisation their major objective.

In the short run to increase the amount it sells a firm may cuts its prices. This may lower its profit level in the short run but if it does manage to capture more of the market it can then raise its prices again. So that it is possible that growth and long run profit maximisation may be compatible.

LIMIT PRICING

Firms with considerable market power may, at a time when they feel under threat from potential competitors, have as their main short-term objective preventing the entry of new firms into the industry. To achieve this they may set their prices at a level which would make it difficult for new firms to compete with, even if this means that they earn lower profits or even losses. They will do this to increase their chances of attaining their long-term objectives.

PREDATORY PRICING

This is again a short-term objective which may be pursued by a firm with considerable market power. This time the objective will be to drive its competitors out of the industry by lowering price. The firm has to believe that it either has lower costs or more funds than its competitors so that it can survive for longer than its rivals at the lower price.

SURVIVAL

During difficult times this may become the key objective of a firm. If a firm is making a loss it will have to take corrective action to stay in existence. This may include changing its product range, downsizing and seeking new funds.

COST PLUS PRICING

Several investigations into business practices have shown that firms' prices are in practice more stable than would be the case if they tried to change price and output levels in line with every change in cost and demand conditions in order to maintain an output where $MC = MR$. Instead it is suggested that a large number of firms establish their prices on what is described as a *cost plus* basis. Here, estimates are prepared of the firm's average total cost because for a number of firms this is constant over a wide range of outputs. To this average cost figure, management adds an element representing a conventional profit margin (described as the *mark-up*) and this determines the price at which the product is marketed. Sales are determined by what the market will demand at this price. Under this system the critical decision is the extent of the mark-up. In many cases the mark-up is periodically adjusted in the light of changes in demand conditions and the extent of competition from other firms. In effect what firms may be doing by adopting a cost plus pricing policy is to aim for long run profit maximisation. Changing prices too frequently may have a number of disadvantages including the administrative cost of, for example updating catalogues and details in advertisements. These changes may be unpopular with consumers, may be misinterpreted and may cause rivals to act in a way which will harm the firm's position. For example, a price rise during a period of rising demand may be considered to be taking undue advantage of consumers and a reduction in price during falling demand may indicate to consumers that the firm is in difficulties and/or may provoke a price war.

BEHAVIOURAL THEORIES

Behavioural theories argue that groups connected with a firm have a variety of objectives for a firm. At any one time one particular objective may be paramount. Whether this is the case and which objective will depend on the relative strength of the different groups who influence the firm's objectives. The groups who have a direct interest in the success of a firm are sometimes referred to as *stakeholders*. They include not only managers and shareholders but also workers, consumers, the government, the local authority and environmental groups. Each group will have a minimum level of demands. For example consumers are likely to want a minimum level of quality and workers a minimum level of pay and job satisfaction. The power, objectives and activity of these groups can change over time. For instance in the 1980s and early 1990s the power of trade unions declined.

CONFLICTS OF OBJECTIVES

At any one time groups may follow similar or conflicting aims. For instance managers and workers may be interested in growth, whilst shareholders may favour profit maximisation as the main objective and environmental groups see pollution reduction and animal welfare as key objectives.

A number of objectives may appear to conflict in the short run but may actually be compatible in the long run. For instance, showing greater concern for the environment may increase a firm's costs but it may also provide the firm with good publicity. If this attracts more customers then in the long run revenue may rise by more than costs and profit will increase. Similarly raising workers' wages will raise costs in the short run but may reduce average costs in the longer run if they result in a rise in labour productivity and lower staff turnover.

Where conflicts between groups persist, the outcome will depend on which is able to exercise the most power.

Q U E S T I O N S

SHORT QUESTIONS

1. According to traditional theory what is the main objective of firms?

2. Explain what is meant by cost plus pricing.

3. What is meant by profit satisficing?

4. What influences firms' ability to achieve their objectives?

MULTIPLE CHOICE

1. Profits are maximised where:

   A. marginal revenue equals marginal cost

   B. average revenue equals average cost

   C. total revenue is maximised

   D. total cost is minimised.

2. A firm follows a cost plus pricing strategy with a 10% mark up. Its long run average cost is £5. What price will it charge for its product?

   A. £4.50   B. £5.10

   C. £5.50   D. £6

3. The managers of a company decide to aim for a level of profits just sufficient to keep shareholders happy. This is an example of:

   A. profit minimisation

   B. profit maximisation

   C. profit satisficing

   D. profit stability.

4. A firm produces products with high positive income elasticity of demand. What is likely to be its main objective during a recession?

   A. Survival.

   B. Pollution reduction.

   C. Investment in new plant.

   D. Raising the wages of its workers.

DATA RESPONSE

BAA, the privatised airport operator, will this week launch a 'contract with the community' programme designed to transform the business into a stakeholder corporation.

It will put environmental and community issues at the heart of business development with the aim of avoiding the kind of lengthy and expensive battles which have continually delayed approval of a new terminal at Heathrow.

Sir John Egan, BAA chief executive, will tell the group's 150 senior managers at a conference on Thursday that they have to change the way they work if they are to achieve business objectives — including further expansion of airport capacity in the south east of England. In future they will have to adopt the sustainability agenda of the government and environmentalists who have opposed Heathrow's terminal five and new runways at Gatwick and Stansted.

BAA's mission statement previously referred to customer needs including safety, and continuous improvement in financial performance and service quality. After a lengthy debate among management another element was added, which commits the group to grow 'with the support and trust of our neighbours.'

Source: 'Stakeholding BAA seeks neighbourly trust' by Roger Cowe, the Guardian, 17/5/99.

a] Which group, or groups, appear to have influenced the change in BAA's objectives? **(3)**

b] Why might the change in objectives help the company to achieve its business objectives? **(6)**

c] What consumer objectives are mentioned in the extract? **(4)**

d] Discuss how the consumer objectives might conflict with the objectives of another group. **(7)**

e] If BAA is to take 'environmental and community issues' into consideration upon what costs and benefits may its decisions be based? **(5)**

CASE STUDY

Sir Clive Thompson, the combative chief executive of Rentokil Initial and president of the Confederation of British Industry … has been made to feel pretty uncomfortable this week by the sniggering that followed his announcement that Rentokil Initial had abandoned its long-standing target of 20% annual earnings growth.

Suddenly, Mr 20-per-cent has turned into the rather less snappy Mr 'substantially outperform our business sector' — Rentokil's revised target. Hubris has caught up with Sir Clive, whose 17 years as chief executive of the rat-catching to plants group has delivered nothing but success.

Perhaps it is a good thing almost everyone is on holiday. As it is, many of those left holding the August reins in the City and Westminster chuckled over Rentokil's dip in pre-tax profits growth to 10.2% for the six months to the end of June.

The target had become a millstone around the company's neck, says Sir Clive. Getting rid of it was first discussed with institutional investors four years ago, but dropping it then would have meant immediate pain for shareholders. After all, the target has helped transform Rentokil from a British pest controller capitalised at about £100m into an international business services group, which peaked in value this year at £13.6bn.

But the target was based largely on squeezing better margins out of poorly performing acquisitions. Clearly it could not go on indefinitely. 'We would have had to end up with the entire population of Britain working for us. It just wasn't possible,' says Sir Clive.

This makes some sense. Bigger companies than Rentokil Initial have destroyed themselves by sticking to inflexible targets in the face of awkward reality. A notable example was ITT, the US conglomerate, in the 1960s, which imploded under the strain of delivering steadily increasing quarterly earnings.

Source: 'A rat-catcher who bites' by Kevin Brown, Financial Times, 21/8/99.

a] What was the objective which Rentokil Initial dropped? **(3)**

b] Explain how it could be assessed whether a company has substantially outperformed its business sector? **(9)**

c] What may cause a firm's profits growth to decline? **(6)**

d] Why may Rentokil Initial's long-standing objective have benefited shareholders? **(7)**

e] Why was the long-standing objective unrealistic? **(5)**

f] Discuss the dangers of 'sticking to inflexible targets'. **(7)**

g] How might a firm raise its profits margins? **(5)**

h] How may the objectives of a private sector firm and a state run concern differ? **(8)**

STRUCTURED ESSAY

a] Explain three possible objectives of a firm. **(12)**

b] Discuss whether these objectives are compatible. **(13)**

FREE RESPONSE ESSAY

Discuss whether all firms seek to maximise profits. **(25)**

37 COMBINING THE FACTORS OF PRODUCTION

VARYING THE PROPORTIONS

Entrepreneurs usually seek to organise land, labour and capital in such a way that output can be produced at the lowest possible cost. To do this they have to consider both the costs of the factors of production but also the units of output they will produce.

The relationship between the output of a product and the inputs (factors of production) used to produce it is known as the *production function*. For instance it may take two hairdressers, four bottles of shampoo, eight hairdryers, four combs, two pairs of scissors and other equipment to cut, shampoo and style eighty customers in one week. However, in making a product, a firm does not have to use the necessary inputs in fixed proportions. Many farm crops can be grown either by using relatively little labour and relatively large amounts of capital equipment (machinery, fertilisers etc.) or by using relatively large amounts of labour with very little capital equipment. In most cases a firm is able to vary the 'input mix'.

The effect of varying the proportions between factors of production is a subject of great importance because nearly all short-run changes in production involve some changes in these proportions. When a firm wishes to increase (or decrease) its output, it cannot, in the short run, change its fixed factors of production, but it can produce more (or less) by changing the amounts of the variable factors (labour, materials, etc.). When farmers wish to increase their output they are usually obliged to do so by using more labour, more seed or more fertiliser (i.e. variable factors) on a fixed supply of land (the fixed factor).

Manufacturers are in a similar position. In the short run they cannot extend their factories or install more machinery but they can adjust their output by varying the quantities of labour, raw materials, fuel and power. The short run is defined as the period of time during which at least one factor of production is fixed.

DIMINISHING RETURNS

Many years ago economists pondered over the implications of varying the proportions in which the factors of production were combined and came up with a principle which has become known as the *law of diminishing returns* (sometimes also known as the *law of variable proportions*).

They applied this law to agriculture on which the example below is therefore based. However, the law holds true for all kinds of production.

EXAMPLE

A particular crop is grown on a fixed area of land of 20 acres. The amount of capital is also fixed in supply. Labour is the variable factor. Table 37.1 sets out some hypothetical results obtained by varying the amount of labour employed and illustrates some important relationships. Assumptions on which the table is based are as follows.

- Labour is the only variable factor.
- All units of the variable factor are equally efficient.
- There are no changes in the techniques of production.

On these assumptions it can be concluded that any changes in productivity arising from variations in the number of people employed are due entirely to the changes in the proportion in which labour is combined with the other factors.

TABLE 37.1 NON-PROPORTIONAL RETURNS

(1) Number of workers	(2) Total product (tonnes)	(3) Average product (tonnes)	(4) Marginal product (tonnes)
1	8	8	8
2	24	12	16
3	54	18	30
4	82	20.5	28
5	95	19	13
6	100	16.7	5
7	100	14.3	0
8	96	12	−4

Table 37.1 illustrates the law of diminishing returns which states that as successive units of one factor are added to other, fixed, factors, the increments in total output will at first rise and then decline.

The details in Table 37.1 can be used to illustrate this law. Columns 1 and 2 are self-explanatory — they show the total output at different levels of employment. Average product (or output per worker) is shown in column 3 and is obtained by using the formula:

$$\frac{\text{Total product}}{\text{Number of workers}} = \text{average product}$$

Marginal product, shown in column 4, describes the changes in total output brought about by varying employment by one person. The addition of a third person adds 30 tonnes to total output, while significantly the employment of a fourth person increases total output by 28 tonnes.

RETURNS TO THE VARIABLE FACTOR

Since labour is the only variable factor in the example, changes in output are related directly to changes in employment. So it is possible to speak of changes in the productivity of labour or changes in the returns to labour. As the number of people increases from 1 to 6, total output continues to increase, but this is not true of the average product (AP) and the marginal product (MP). As more people are employed, both AP and MP begin to rise, reach a maximum and start to fall. These movements are illustrated in Figure 37.1 which is based on Table 37.1.

As the number of people increases from 1 to 3 the marginal product of labour is increasing. Up to this point the fixed factors are being underutilised — the people are 'too thin on the ground'. When the number of people employed exceeds 3 the marginal product of labour begins to fall — an indication that the proportions between the fixed and variable factors are becoming less favourable. Marginal product begins to fall before average product and the maximum average product of labour occurs when 4 people are employed. To increase output and maintain the same productivity of labour it is necessary to increase the fixed factors along with the variable factors. This would be a change in the scale of production (discussed below and in Chapter 39).

It is this feature of increasing production and falling productivity which is described by the law of diminishing returns. In Table 37.1 diminishing marginal returns set in after employment of the third person and diminishing

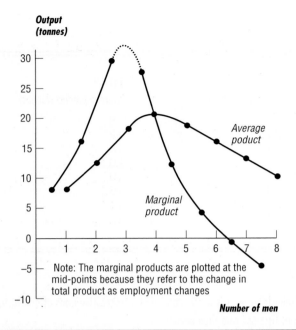

FIG. 37.1

average returns after the employment of the fourth person. When economists discuss diminishing returns they are usually referring to diminishing marginal returns.

The marginal productivity of the seventh person is zero — his employment does not change total output. This may not be so unrealistic as it first appears. In some developing countries with high numbers of people working on the land marginal productivity may be zero.

Using the total product curve, Figure 37.2 provides another view of the relationship between employment and output where the supply of some of the factors is fixed.

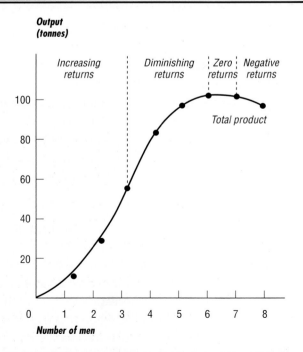

FIG. 37.2

The possible effects of increasing the quantity of variable factors can be summarised as:

- increasing returns — total product increases at an increasing rate (*MP* is increasing)
- constant returns (not illustrated) — total product is increasing at a constant rate (*MP* is constant)
- diminishing returns — total product is increasing at a decreasing rate (*MP* is falling)
- zero returns — total product is constant (*MP* is zero)
- negative returns — total product is falling (*MP* is negative).

APPLICATION OF THE LAW OF DIMINISHING RETURNS

It is important to note that although the illustration used above concentrated on labour as the variable factor, the law of diminishing returns is equally applicable to land and capital and perhaps even to entrepreneurship. The marginal and average productivity of capital will, at some point, start to decline as more and more capital is applied to a fixed supply of land and labour. The same will apply to the productivity of land as more and more land is combined with a fixed amount of labour and capital.

Experiments in which increased amounts of feed were given to a fixed number of cows, and others where increased amounts of fertiliser were applied to a given area of land have clearly demonstrated the applicability of non-proportional returns. Increments in the yields at first increased more than proportionally but eventually there came a point where the law of diminishing returns asserted itself.

ASSUMPTIONS OF THE LAW OF DIMINISHING RETURNS

The law of diminishing returns applies only when 'other things remain equal'. The efficiency of the other factors and the techniques of production are assumed to be constant. In practice improvements in technology have tended to offset the effects of the law of diminishing returns. Improved methods of production increase the productivity of the factors of production and move the *AP* and *MP* curves upwards. But this does not mean that the law no longer applies. It is still true that in the short run (when other things can change very little) increments in the variable factors will at some point yield increments in output which are less than proportionate. Also in countries which are not able to take significant advantage of improvements in technology the law may also apply.

THE LEAST COST COMBINATION

The preceding explanation of the law of diminishing returns should not be taken as an indication that the ratio of labour to land and capital which gives the maximum output per worker is the ratio which the firm should adopt. All that has been done is to show the tendency of output per unit of the variable factor to change when the proportions between the factors are varied. The most profitable way of combining the factors of production depends upon their prices as well as their productivity.

The physical productivity of factors enables entrepreneurs to assess technical efficiency but they are more concerned with economic efficiency and for this purpose they measure output and inputs in monetary terms. Their inputs they measure as costs and their output is measured in terms of revenue. They are interested in making profits and their aim will be to maximise the difference between costs and revenue. They will not be very interested in maximising the productivity of labour if labour is very cheap relative to the other factors.

It has already been noted that there will be several different ways of combining the factors of production to produce any given output. Suppose a firm wishes to produce 100 units per week of some particular product. It can be assumed that this output can be produced with any of the combinations shown in Table 37.2.

TABLE 37.2 POSSIBLE FACTOR COMBINATIONS

	Land	Labour	Capital
Method 1	20	10	4
Method 2	20	7	7
Method 3	15	9	9

The question of which is the best method now arises. Given the assumption that entrepreneurs will always try to maximise their profits, it follows that the firm will adopt that method which minimises costs. The cost of the factors of production is as follows.

Land: £20 per unit; labour: £10 per unit; and capital: £15 per unit. So Method 1 will therefore cost £560; Method 2 will cost £575; and Method 3 will cost £525. The entrepreneur will choose Method 3.

The optimum combination of factors occurs where:

$$\frac{\text{Marginal productivity of factor A}}{\text{Price of factor A}} = \frac{\text{MP of factor B}}{\text{P of factor B}} = \frac{\text{MP of factor C}}{\text{P of factor C}}$$

RETURNS TO SCALE

The law of diminishing returns deals with what are essentially short run situations. It is assumed that some of the resources used in production are fixed in supply. In the long run, however, it is possible for a firm to vary the amounts of all the factors of production employed: more land can be acquired, more buildings erected and more machinery installed. In the long run, it is possible for a firm to change the scale of its activities. Strictly speaking, a change of scale takes place when the quantities of all the factors are changed by the same percentage so that the proportions in which they are combined are not changed, as is illustrated in Table 37.3.

TABLE 37.3 RETURNS TO SCALE

Unit of labour	Units of land (acres)	Total output (tonnes)	Increase in size of firm	Increase in total output
4	20	100		
			100%	150%
8	40	250		
			50%	68%
12	60	420		
			$33\frac{1}{3}$%	$33\frac{1}{3}$%
16	80	560		
			25%	20%
20	100	672		
			20%	16%
24	120	780		

It is a feature of production that when the scale of production is changed, output changes are not usually proportionate. For example, when a firm doubles its size, its output will tend to change by more than 100% or less than 100%. The relationships between changes in scale and changes in output are described as returns to scale.

Table 37.3 shows the increase in total output as the scale of production increases. The firm increases its size but the proportion between the factors remains unchanged (e.g. 1 unit of labour per 5 acres of land). As the firm increases its size from 4 people and 20 acres of land to 12 people and 60 acres of land, it experiences increasing returns to scale (output increases more than proportionately). A change of scale from 12 people and 60 acres to 16 people and 80 acres yields constant returns to scale (size and output change by the same percentage). Any further growth in the size of the firm yields decreasing returns to scale because output increases less than proportionately.

THE RELATIONSHIPS BETWEEN RETURNS TO SCALE AND ECONOMIES OF SCALE

Increasing returns to scale are usually associated with falling average (unit) costs which can also be referred to as *economies of scale*. This is because, in the absence of changes in the costs of inputs, if output increases by a greater percentage than inputs, each unit will become cheaper to produce.

In the same way decreasing returns to scale are usually matched by *diseconomies of scale*, with average costs rising as output increases more slowly than the change in the scale of production. Constant returns to scale will result in constant costs i.e., unchanged average costs if, again the cost of inputs remains unchanged.

Table 37.4 shows both the change in total output and the change in total cost as a firm increases its scale of operation. It is assumed that the proportion of inputs remains unchanged and that the cost of each input is constant at £20.

TABLE 37.4 CHANGES IN OUTPUT AND COSTS

Total inputs	Total cost	Total output	Increase in inputs	Increase in output	Average cost
10	200	200			£1
			100%	150%	
20	400	500			80p
			50%	60%	
30	600	800			75p
			$33\frac{1}{3}\%$	$33\frac{1}{3}\%$	
40	800	1067			75p
			25%	25%	
50	1000	1280			

When inputs increase from 10 to 30, output increases by a greater percentage (increasing returns to scale) and average costs fall (economies of scale). Output rises by the same percentage when inputs rise from 30 to 40 (constant returns to scale) and average costs remain unchanged. Finally, as inputs rise from 40 to 50, output rises by a smaller percentage (decreasing returns to scale) and average costs rise (diseconomies of scale). Economics of scale and diseconomies of scale are discussed in more detail in Chapter 39.

QUESTIONS

SHORT QUESTIONS

1. Explain what is meant by marginal product.

2. What is the optimum combination of resources?

3. How would the rate of return on capital be expected to change if the supply of labour is fixed and the quantity of capital increases?

4. What is likely to be happening to long run average costs when increasing returns to scale are being experienced?

MULTIPLE CHOICE

1. What is happening to the total variable cost when the law of diminishing returns begins to operate?

   A. It falls at an increasing rate.

   B. It falls at a decreasing rate.

   C. It rises at a decreasing rate.

   D. It rises at an increasing rate.

2. A firm has access to the information shown in the following table about the productivities of the factors it employs.

No. of workers	Total product	No. of machines	Total product
1	15	1	20
2	40	2	65
3	80	3	115
4	110	4	180
5	130	5	270
6	140	6	400
7	148	7	540
8	152	8	660

Workers are paid £4 per hour and machines cost £45 an hour to run. What is the optimum combination of workers and machines?

A. 4 workers and 3 machines.

B. 5 workers and 7 machines.

C. 5 workers and 5 machines.

D. 7 workers and 5 machines.

3. Why does the law of diminishing returns operate?

A. As employment of a factor of production rises its price increases.

B. As output rises the price of extra units produced falls.

C. Factors of production are not perfect substitutes for each other.

D. The most skilled factors of production are employed first.

4. The following table shows the inputs needed to produce different levels of output.

Inputs	Output
100	400
140	600
180	800
200	1000
240	1200

Over which output range will the firm be operating under constant returns to scale?

A. 400 – 600.

B. 600 – 800.

C. 800 – 1000.

D. 1000 – 1200.

DATA RESPONSE

A restaurant with an initial seating capacity of thirty originally employed one chef, one manager, one person to wash up and three waiters. With this staff the restaurant could serve 14 people in an hour. When it took on an extra waiter the number of people served per hour rose to 20 people. The employment of a further waiter increased served to 28.

As the restaurant continued to be successful and customers had to be turned away, a decision was made to extend the restaurant to a seating capacity of 60 and to double the staff from the original position. The number of customers served per hour increased to 70 and reduced the cost per meal served. The success of the restaurant enabled the owner to charge a higher price per meal.

a] What is the marginal product of the fourth waiter? **(3)**

b] What are the fixed factors of production employed by the restaurant in the short run? **(4)**

c] When the restaurant employs the fifth waiter is it experiencing diminishing returns, increasing returns, decreasing returns to scale or increasing returns to scale? Explain your answer. **(5)**

d] When the restaurant is increased in size is it experiencing diminishing returns, increasing returns, decreasing returns to scale or increasing returns to scale? Explain your answer. **(5)**

e] As a result of expanding the size of the restaurant what is likely to have happened to the firm's:
  i   average costs of production **(3)**
  ii total cost of production **(2)**
  iii total profit? **(3)**

CASE STUDY

Why can we not grow all the world's food in one garden? A silly question perhaps, but it illustrates a very important principle. We can get a greater output from a garden of fixed size by working longer hours or adding more seeds, etc., but the extra output we obtain will rapidly diminish. Indeed, if we just go on dumping more and more seeds in the garden, total output may even go down.

The principle involved here is known as the law of diminishing returns. This law is one of the most important and fundamental principles involved in economics. We may state it thus:

If one factor of production is fixed in supply and successive units of a variable factor are added to it, the extra output derived from the employment of each successive unit of the variable factor must, after a time, decline.

The law of diminishing returns may be offset by improvements in technology, but it cannot be repealed.

At any particular time any business must have at least one of the factors of production in fixed supply. For example, the buildings which a firm uses cannot be expanded overnight, so that if the firm wants to obtain more output it must use more of the variable factor such as labour.

The period of time in which at least one factor is fixed in supply is defined as the short run. Given time, all the factors may be varied, i.e. new buildings can be constructed, more land acquired, etc. The period of time in which all factors may be varied and in which firms may enter or leave the industry is defined as the long run. The length of time involved will vary from business to business. Obviously it will take much longer for an oil refinery to vary its fixed factors by constructing a new refinery than it would, for example, for a farmer to rent more land.

The law of diminishing returns is thus a short run phenomenon because, by definition, it is concerned with a situation in which at least one factor is fixed in supply.

Source: Economics: a student's guide, 4th edition by J. Beardshaw et al, Longman, 1998.

a] What returns are said to be experienced when total output falls? **(3)**

b] In the example given at the start of the extract what is the fixed factor of production? **(3)**

c] Explain what will happen to marginal costs when diminishing returns set in. **(5)**

d] Explain why improvements in technology may offset the law of diminishing returns. **(6)**

e] Discuss what may make it difficult for a firm to hire more of a variable factor of production. **(7)**

f] Explain why, even if it could recruit more labour in the short run, a firm may chose to rely on overtime from its existing labour force to meet higher demand. **(7)**

g] Describe and explain the likely shape of the long run average cost curve of an oil refinery. **(7)**

h] Explain what is likely to happen to a firm's average, marginal and total product as it increases its output in the short run. **(12)**

STRUCTURED ESSAY

a] Explain the difference between diminishing returns and decreasing returns to scale. **(12)**

b] Discuss how realistic are the assumptions which underline the law of diminishing returns. **(13)**

FREE RESPONSE ESSAY

Discuss the significance of the law of diminishing returns for the output and employment decisions of firms. **(25)**

38 REVENUES

Revenue is the payment a firm receives for selling a good or service or the amount the government raises from taxation. In this chapter it is the first meaning which is being concentrated on.

TYPES OF REVENUE

Total revenue (TR) is the amount earned from the total amount sold. Average revenue (AR) is another name for price because it is equal to revenue per unit sold, i.e:

$$AR = \frac{\text{total revenue}}{\text{number of units sold}}$$

The demand curve is often referred to as the average revenue curve.

Marginal revenue (MR) is the additional revenue obtained when sales are increased by one unit or, more precisely, it is the change in total revenue when the quantity sold is varied by one unit. For example, the marginal revenue of the tenth unit is equal to the total revenue from the sale of 10 units minus the total revenue from the sale of 9 units.

REVENUES UNDER CONDITIONS OF PERFECT COMPETITION

Firms operating in a perfectly competitive market are too small to affect the market price by altering their output. In this case MR must always be equal to AR and both are constant. This is because as the quantity sold increases, the price remains unchanged so that each additional unit sold increases total revenue by an amount equal to its price. Table 38.1 shows the revenue position of a perfectly competitive firm.

TABLE 38.1 THE REVENUE POSITION OF A PERFECTLY COMPETITIVE FIRM

Price (AR) (£)	Quantity demanded (units)	Total revenue (£)	Marginal revenue (£)
4	1	4	4
4	2	8	4
4	3	12	4
4	4	16	4
4	5	20	4
4	6	24	4
4	7	28	4
4	8	32	4
4	9	36	4

Figure 38.1 illustrates the average and marginal revenue curve (and demand curve) of a perfectly competitive firm.

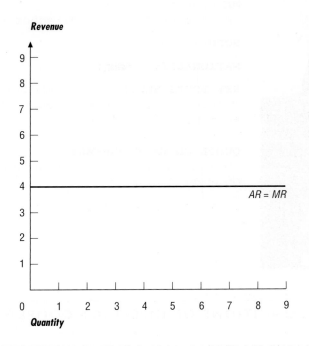

FIG. 38.1

As average revenue is constant, the firm's total revenue curve rises smoothly as shown in Figure 38.2.

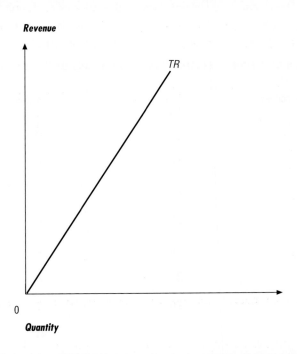

FIG. 38.2

NAME: Kate Barker
Chief economist and director of the CBI

BORN: 1958

NATIONALITY: British

KEY POSTS HELD: On the advisory panel of the former Chancellor of the Exchequer, Kenneth Clarke Chief economist at Ford

QUOTE ON KATE BARKER:
'*One of the top industrial economists of the UK*', The Observer *9/8/98*.

REVENUES UNDER CONDITIONS OF IMPERFECT COMPETITION AND MONOPOLY

In market conditions where firms have some market power marginal revenue will be below average revenue and total revenue will not rise smoothly.

Firms operating under conditions of monopolistic competition, oligopoly or monopoly are price makers — changes in their output influence price. To sell more a firm has to lower price. This means that not only is the price of the last unit lower but so is that of the former units. For example a firm may have the choice of selling 5 units at £12 or 6 units at £11 each. The decision to sell 6 will lower the price of each unit to £11. In this case the marginal revenue of the sixth unit will be £6 (£66–£60) which is below the average revenue of £11. Table 38.2 shows the revenue position of a firm producing under conditions of imperfect competition or monopoly.

TABLE 38.2 THE REVENUE POSITION OF A FIRM OPERATING UNDER CONDITIONS OF IMPERFECT COMPETITION OR MONOPOLY

Price (AR) (£)	Quantity demanded (units)	Total revenue (£)	Marginal revenue (£)	Price elasticity of demand
10	1	10	10	
9	2	18	8	E>1
8	3	24	6	E>1
7	4	28	4	E>1
6	5	30	2	E>1
5	6	30	0	E=1
4	7	28	–2	E<1
3	8	24	–4	E<1
2	9	18	–6	E<1

A number of important features about the relationship between output and revenue in the case of a price maker can be gleaned from this table. Average and marginal revenue start off as equal but thereafter as the firm sells a higher and higher output marginal revenue falls further below average revenue. Both average and marginal revenue fall as more is sold.

When marginal revenue is positive, total revenue is rising and demand is elastic (a fall in price causes a rise in total revenue).

When marginal revenue is zero, total revenue is maximised and there is unit price elasticity of demand.

When marginal revenue is negative, total revenue is falling and demand is inelastic.

Figure 38.3 illustrates the relationship between, and nature of, average and marginal revenue in the case of a price maker.

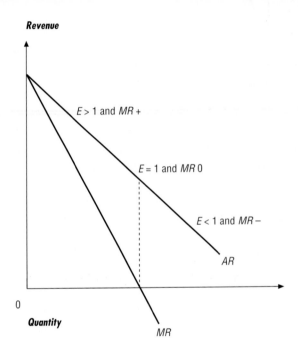

FIG. 38.3

Note that marginal revenue cuts the horizontal axis half way along the point where average revenue would cut it.

A price maker's total revenue curve will have a different shape to that of a perfectly competitive firm. This is illustrated in Figure 38.4.

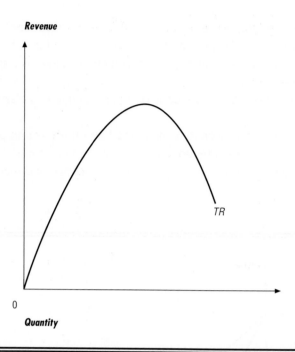

FIG. 38.4

A firm is unlikely to want to sell more if this will mean that its marginal revenue is negative so firms with market power will usually seek to produce where demand is elastic.

QUESTIONS

SHORT QUESTIONS

1. Explain what is meant by marginal revenue.

2. What will be happening to total revenue when marginal revenue is negative?

3. In which market structure is a firm's average revenue constant?

4. When marginal revenue is positive what is the price elasticity of demand for the product?

MULTIPLE CHOICE

1 When is total revenue maximised?

- A When average revenue is maximised.
- B When average cost is minimised.
- C When marginal revenue is zero.
- D When marginal revenue equals marginal cost.

2 A firm increases its sales from 20 units to 21 units and as a result its total revenue rises from £623 to £630. What is the marginal revenue?

- A £7
- B £30
- C £31.15
- D £630

3 Which of the following conditions indicates that a firm has some market power?

- A It is making normal profits.
- B Marginal cost is equal to marginal revenue.
- C Marginal cost is equal to average cost.
- D Average revenue is greater than marginal revenue.

4 When marginal revenue is zero, price elasticity of demand is:

- A unity
- B elastic
- C inelastic
- D perfectly inelastic.

DATA RESPONSE

Price (£)	Demand (units)
6	30
5	46
4	60
3	80
2	90
1	100

a] Calculate average, marginal and total revenue. **(8)**

b] At what price is price elasticity of demand unity? **(3)**

c] Explain what is happening to marginal revenue as price falls. **(3)**

d] Is the firm producing under conditions of perfect or imperfect competition? Explain your answer. **(5)**

e] Explain the relationship between average and marginal revenue. **(6)**

CASE STUDY

Marginal revenue is the change to total revenue from the sale of one more unit of a commodity.

Suppose for example that a firm was selling 4 units a week at £10 each. Then the total revenue would be £40 but, since this is imperfect competition, if it wishes to sell more it must lower its prices. Therefore selling 5 units a week for example, may involve dropping the price to £9, in which case the total revenue will now be £45. Thus, the change to the firm's total revenue as a result of selling one more unit is £5. This is termed the marginal revenue.

In order to sell more the imperfect competitor must, as we have seen, lower the price. If, for example, sales are 50 units per week at a price of £10 and sales are increased to 51 units by lowering the price to £9, then not only does the firm lose money on the 51st unit but also all preceding units now have to be priced at £9. Thus total revenue decreases from £500 to £459, giving a marginal revenue of minus £41. (For the extra £9 sales revenue gained from the 51st unit the firm has sacrificed £1 on the preceding 50 units; thus $MR = (£9 - £50 = -£41)$. Whether or not marginal revenue is positive or negative depends on whether the gain in revenue from extra sales is greater or smaller than the loss on preceding units.)

Source: *Economics: a student's guide by J. Beardshaw et al, 4th edition, Longman, 1998.*

a] Explain what is meant by imperfect competition. **(6)**

b] In what circumstances would a firm not have to lower price in order to sell more? **(8)**

c] Calculate the price elasticity of demand when price is lowered from £10 to £9 in the first example given. **(5)**

d] Explain the shape of the total revenue curve of a firm producing under conditions of imperfect competition. **(6)**

e] At what point on its demand curve is a monopoly firm likely to produce? **(5)**

f] Discuss what may happen to a monopolist's marginal and average cost when it sells more units of a product. **(8)**

g] Which revenue curve is equal to the demand curve? **(4)**

h] What is likely to happen over time to the average and marginal revenue curves of a firm producing a product with positive income elasticity of demand? **(8)**

STRUCTURED ESSAY

a] What is meant by marginal, average and total revenue? **(10)**
b] Explain the relationship between marginal revenue and price elasticity of demand. **(15)**

FREE RESPONSE ESSAY

Discuss the relationship between the shape of a firm's demand curve and its total revenue curve in perfect competition and in monopoly. **(25)**

39 THE SCALE OF PRODUCTION

As noted in Chapters 13 and 37, when an increase in the scale of production results in a more than proportionate increase in output, the firm is said to be experiencing economies of scale. These economies might be defined as those aspects of increasing size which lead to falling long-run average costs. Economies of scale are classified as internal or external economies.

INTERNAL AND EXTERNAL ECONOMIES OF SCALE

Internal economies of scale are those which arise from the growth of the firm independently of what is happening to other firms. They arise simply from an increase in the scale of production in the firm itself. A firm may grow as a result of increasing the number of plants (workplaces) it has or increasing the size of its plants. External economies of scale are those advantages in the form of lower average costs which a firm gains from the growth of the industry. These economies are available to all the firms in the industry independently of changes in the scales of their individual outputs.

INTERNAL ECONOMIES OF SCALE

These can be divided into plant economies of scale and firm economies of scale.

PLANT ECONOMIES OF SCALE

These arise from the growth of individual workplaces e.g. factories and offices and include:

- *Increased specialisation*. The larger the workplace the greater the opportunities for the specialisation of workers and machines. In the larger workplace the process can be broken down into many separate operations, workers can be employed on specialised tasks, and the continuous use of highly specialised equipment becomes possible. For example, in a large college staff can specialise in a wide range of courses for which there may be specialist rooms.
- *Indivisibility*. Some types of capital equipment can only be employed efficiently in units of minimum size, a size which may be too large for a small plant to sustain. There is a lower limit to the size of a blast furnace, a nuclear power station, a car assembly line, and a power press. This lower limit may be a technical limit as where the manufacture of a smaller version of the equipment is impracticable. More generally, however, the lower limit is an economic one: smaller versions of the equipment can be purchased but their usefulness would not justify the cost of buying them. Such indivisibility of plant means that workplaces with small outputs cannot take advantage of some highly specialised equipment. In a small plant, this type of capital equipment would be standing idle for a large part of the time, the heavy fixed costs it incurs would be spread over small outputs, and the average cost per unit of output would be disproportionately high.
- *Increased dimensions*. If you double the length, breadth and height of a cube, its surface area is four times as great and its volume eight times as great as the original. This simple arithmetical principle accounts for the remarkable increase in the dimensions of much large scale capital equipment in recent years. For example, a modern oil tanker of 240 000 tonnes is only twice the size of a 30 000 tonne tanker in terms of length, width

and height and only four times as large in terms of surface area despite having eight times its capacity. It requires very few extra crew and, if any, will certainly not require eight times the power to propel it through the water. Economies of increased dimensions account for the tendency of industries which make use of tanks, vats, furnaces, and transport equipment, etc. to operate larger and larger units.

- *The principle of multiples.* Industrial plants may use a variety of machines, each carrying out a different operation. Each of these machines is likely to have a different capacity. For example, the machine which moulds the blocks of chocolate will operate at a much slower speed than the machine which wraps the blocks in silver paper.

EXAMPLE

Assume that a particular process requires a team of four machines, A, B, C, and D, the productive capacities of which are 50, 60, 20 and 30 units per hour. If the team comprises only one machine of each type, the maximum output per hour will be 20 units and machines A, B and D will be working below full capacity. This would be the kind of problem facing a small plant producing a small output. For small outputs it is not possible to obtain a balanced team of machines such that each machine is being fully utilised.

The lowest common multiple of 50, 60, 20 and 30 is 300. This is the smallest output per hour which will enable a sequence of machines of this type to work at full capacity. Such a balanced team of machines would be:

Machine A	Machine B	Machine C	Machine D
6	5	15	10

This assembly of machines would provide an output of 300 units per hour and all machines would be working at full capacity. If output is to be increased it will only be possible to maintain 100 per cent utilisation if production is increased by multiples of 300 units (i.e., 600, 900, 1200, etc.).

- *By-product economies.* A large plant may be able to sell or convert its by-products. For instance, a large stable may be able to sell the manure from its horses on a commercial basis. A large petroleum refinery plant may process chemicals extracted from oil and sell them. One of the most famous by-products is Tupperware which has become a very profitable concern.
- *Economies of linked processes.* A large plant may have the capacity to produce more than one product or service. For instance, iron and steel may both be produced in one large factory. A large bank branch, in addition to carrying out the standard banking services, may also operate an estate agency department.
- *Stock economies.* A large plant can operate with smaller stocks in proportion to its sales than a smaller firm can. This is because variations in orders from individual customers and unexpected changes in customers' demands will tend to offset each other when total sales are very large.

FIRM ECONOMIES OF SCALE

There are a number of advantages which can be gained if a firm, such as a building society, grows in size. These advantages can be gained if the building society opens more branches or if it increases the size of individual branches.

Examples of firm economies of scale include the following.

- *Marketing economies.* A large firm is able to buy its material requirements in large quantities. Bulk buying enables the large firm to obtain preferential terms from the supplier. It will be able to obtain goods and services at lower prices and be able to dictate its requirements with regard to quality and delivery much more effectively than the smaller firm. By placing large orders for particular lines bulk buyers enable suppliers to take advantage of the lower cost of 'long runs' — a much more economical proposition than trying to meet a large number of small orders from small firms each requiring a different colour, or quality, or design.

The large firm will be able to employ specialised buyers, whereas in the small firm, buying will usually be the responsibility of an employee who will have several other responsibilities. Specialist buyers are likely to have better knowledge and skill which enables them to buy the right materials, at the right time and at the right price more easily.

The selling costs of the larger firm will be much greater than those of the small firm, but the selling costs per unit will generally be much lower because the number of units is also greater. The selling costs of a large firm might be £100 000 per annum while those of a small firm might be as low as £5000 per annum. But if the large firm is selling 1 000 000 units while the small firm only sells 20 000 per annum, the selling cost per unit in the large firm (10p) is very much less than that of the small firm (25p). In selling, as in buying, the larger firm can afford to employ experts whose specialised skills can give it economic advantages.

Packaging costs per unit will be lower. A package containing 100 articles is much easier to pack than 10 separate packages each containing 10 articles. The clerical and administrative costs of dealing with an order for 1000 articles involves no more work than that involved in an order for 100, neither do transport costs increase proportionately with volume. Although many large firms spend huge sums on advertising, their advertising costs per unit sold may well be less than those of a small firm.

- *Financial economies.* A large firm has several financial advantages. The fact that it is large and well known makes it a more credit-worthy borrower. Its greater selling potential and larger assets provides the lenders with greater security and encourages them to provide bigger loans at lower rates of interest than would be charged to a smaller firm.

  A large firm has access to more sources of finance. In addition to borrowing from the banks, it may approach a wide variety of financial institutions as well as taking advantage of the highly developed market in the issuing of new shares and debentures.

  The terms on which funds can be borrowed are more favourable to a large-scale borrower because the lending of money, in large amounts, like the bulk supply of materials, yields economies of scale.

- *Research and development economies.* A research department must be of a certain size in order to work effectively. To a small firm this minimum efficient size may represent a level of expenditure too large to justify any possible returns. To a large firm, however, the expenditure may be relatively small because the cost is spread over a large output.

- *Managerial economies.* Large firms can employ specialist accountants, lawyers, personnel officers, etc. In these large firms specialists can be fully utilised, but it is doubtful if a smaller firm could find enough specialised work to keep them fully occupied. Small firms, however, can overcome this problem to some extent by 'buying in' such expertise as they require from specialised agencies when it is needed.

- *Risk-bearing economies.* Large firms are usually better equipped than small firms to cope with the risk of trading. Total demand over time will be more stable and more predictable than will be the case with small firms where variations in individual orders will tend to have a relatively large impact on the total business. An example of this is the operation of a national grid to which many generating stations are connected. If each electricity-generating station supplied only its own locality, every station would have to maintain enough capacity to meet any possible level of demand, however exceptional. With a national grid, however, many of these exceptional variations in demand are 'balanced' because they occur at different times or in different places so that the total capacity required of the system to meet the national demand will be much less than if there were many separate generating stations each supplying its own area.

  Many large firms choose to reduce the risks of trading by means of a policy of diversification. They produce either a variety of models of a particular product or a variety of products so that they do not put all their eggs in one basket. A fall in the demand for any one of its products may not mean serious trouble for the firm if demand for one or more of the other products increases. A small firm, on the other hand, usually has to specialise in producing a much narrower range of products, any fall in the demand for which may have much more serious consequences. A larger firm is also likely to have a diversified market structure. In the national market, demand fluctuations between regions may offset one another: a fall in the demand in the home market might be balanced by a rise in the demand abroad. A small firm with a restricted market is much more vulnerable to changes in market conditions.

- *Plant specialisation economies.* A firm may be large enough for its individual plants to specialise. For instance, a large motor vehicle company may have different plants producing buses, cars and lorries.
- *Staff facilities economies.* A large firm may be able to offer, among other things, staff canteens, sports grounds and medical care. With a large number of staff the cost of providing these facilities may be relatively low. The large retailer Marks and Spencer provides a range of facilities for its staff.

The main internal economies of scale are shown in Figure 39.1.

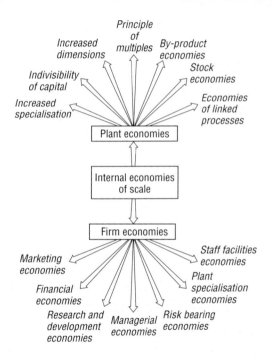

FIG. 39.1

INTERNAL DISECONOMIES OF SCALE

Increasing size brings many advantages, but it can also bring disadvantages.

For each particular industry there will be some optimum size of firm in which average cost reaches a minimum. This optimum size will vary over time as technological progress changes the techniques of production. As firms grow beyond this optimum size, efficiency declines and average costs begin to rise. The main problems which arise when a firm grows too large are thought to be mainly attributable to management difficulties.

MANAGEMENT PROBLEMS

As the size of the firm increases, management becomes more complex. It becomes increasingly difficult to carry out the management functions of co-ordination, control, communication and to maintain good industrial relations.

- *Co-ordination.* Large firms are likely to be divided into many specialised departments (production, planning, sales, purchasing, personnel, accounts etc.). As these departments multiply and grow in size, the task of co-ordinating their activities becomes more and more difficult. Consulting a team of managers takes time and decision taking in a large firm may be slower than in a small firm. If this is the case a large firm will respond less quickly to changes in market conditions than a small firm.
- *Control.* Essentially, management consists of two basic activities: the taking of decisions and seeing that those decisions are carried out. This latter function is that of control. The large firm usually has several tiers of management (managing director, director, head of department etc.) but, in practice, the problem of overseeing what is going on can be difficult.
- *Communication.* Keeping everyone informed and feeling involved in a large firm can be a difficult and time-consuming process. Much time may have to be spent in meetings and ensuring that everyone knows what is going on and why.
- *Industrial relations.* Large plants tend to have worse industrial relations than small ones. It is thought that this is because when there is a large number of people working in one place it takes longer to sort out any problems which people have and because there are more people to have conflicts with. In large firms employing thousands of workers it can be difficult to make any individual worker feel they are an important part of the firm and people low down the pyramid of control may lack an identification of interest with the firm.

PRICES OF INPUTS

A further reason why growth in the size of the firm may lead to rising average costs may be an increase in the prices of the factors of production. As the scale of production increases, the firm will increase its demands for materials, labour, energy, transport and so on. It may, however, be difficult to obtain increased supplies of some of these factors such as skilled labour, for example, or minerals from mines which are already working at full capacity. In such cases a firm attempting to increase the scale of production may find itself bidding up the prices of some of its inputs.

EXTERNAL ECONOMIES OF SCALE

External economies of scale are the advantages which accrue to a firm from the growth in the size of the industry. These advantages may be gained by firms of any size. Indeed, a collection of relatively small independent firms in a large industry can take advantage of external economies of scale.

External economies are especially significant when industries are heavily localised in industrial clusters. In this particular case they are often referred to as economies of concentration.

Examples of external economies of scale include:

- *Labour.* The concentration of similar firms in any one area leads to the creation of a local labour force skilled in the various techniques used in the industry. Local colleges develop special courses of training geared to the particular needs of the local industry. The further education colleges in Cornwall and Devon have important travel and tourism departments while the further education college in Witney has a stud and stable husbandry course attracting students from throughout the UK and abroad.

- *Ancillary services.* In areas where there is a high degree of concentration of a particular industry, ancillary industries catering for the needs of the dominant industry establish themselves. For example, many of the participants of the horse racing industry are based in Newmarket which means that many firms which support it, specialising in the provision of horse feed, vets specialising in the treatment of horses and black-smiths to shoe horses, etc. are also located in the area.

  Even when an industry is dispersed, if it is large enough, ancillary industries will develop. For example, the fertiliser industry supplies farmers throughout the country.

- *Disintegration.* Where an industry is heavily localised there is a tendency for individual firms to specialise in a single process or in the manufacture of a single component. For example, in Lancashire the production of cloth is broken down into many processes, each carried out by a specialist firm including spinning, weaving, dyeing, finishing, etc. This development produces among the firms the same sort of advantages which result from the economies of scale in the single large firm. It means, for example, that each individual firm may obtain its components and other requirements at relatively low cost because they are mass produced for the industry.

- *Co-operation.* Regional specialisation encourages co-operation among the firms. A good example is provided by the research centres established as joint ventures by the firms in heavily localised industries. The pottery firms in Stoke-on-Trent, the footwear firms in the East Midlands, and the cotton firms in Lancashire have all set up research centres for their particular industries. The opportunities for formal and informal contacts between members of the firms are much greater when the firms themselves are all in one locality. The formation of trade societies, the publication of a trade journal and other such co-operative ventures are more easily stimulated in a localised industry.

- *Commercial facilities.* External economies also arise from the fact that the service industries in the area develop a special knowledge of the needs of the industry and this often leads to the provision of specialised facilities. Banking and insurance firms become acquainted with the particular requirements of the relevant industry and find it worthwhile to provide special facilities. Transport firms may find it economical to develop special equipment (e.g. containers and vehicles) to meet the industry's requirements. Improved infrastructure in the form of better roads and airports may be provided. Again, each firm is a beneficiary, not because the firm itself is large, but because the industry as a whole provides a large demand for these services.

- *Specialised markets.* When an industry is large enough specialised places and facilities to bring buyers and sellers into contact may be developed. An example is Lloyds of London which serves the insurance industry.

EXTERNAL DISECONOMIES OF SCALE

A firm may also experience disadvantages as a result of the industry to which it belongs becoming too large. These are referred to as *diseconomies of scale*. For example, a shortage of labour with the appropriate skills may develop so that firms in the industry may find themselves bidding up wages as they try to attract more labour (or hold on to their existing supplies). Increasing demands for raw materials may also bid up prices and cause costs to rise. If the industry is heavily localised, land for expansion will become increasingly scarce and hence more expensive both to purchase and to rent. Transport costs may also rise because of increased congestion. All firms in the industry, whether they are seeking to expand or not, may suffer rising costs as a result of the industry getting too large too quickly.

ECONOMIES OF SCALE AND THE LONG-RUN AVERAGE COST CURVE

A change in output will cause a movement along the long-run average cost curve. It will fall whilst the firm is experiencing internal economies of scale and rise when it is experiencing internal diseconomies of scale.

There are a number of factors which can cause it to change its position. These include changes in technology, taxation on an industry (e.g. national insurance contributions and corporation tax). Improvements in technology will cause the average cost curve to fall whilst increases in taxation will raise average costs. Another significant influence on the position of the average cost curve is external economies and diseconomies of scale. If external economies of scale are experienced, the long-run average cost curve will shift down — since any level of output will now be cheaper to produce. Whereas if external diseconomies of scale are encountered, the long-run average cost curve will move up.

QUESTIONS

SHORT QUESTIONS

1. What is meant by plant economies of scale?

2. Identify three types of internal economies of scale which are not dependent on a firm making a narrow range of products.

3. Describe two economies of scale which could be gained by a car manufacturer as it grows in size.

4. What are the main management problems a firm may encounter if it grows too large in size?

MULTIPLE CHOICE

1. What is meant by financial economies of scale?

   A. The ability of a firm to raise finance more easily and more cheaply as it grows in size.

   B. The ability of a firm to buy raw materials at a discount as it grows in size.

   C. The fall in unit costs experienced by firms working in the financial sector as they grow in size.

   D. The fall in unit costs experienced by larger firms arising from more efficient handling of revenue.

2. The table shows a firm's short run and long run costs.

Output	1	2	3	4	5
Short run total cost	10	18	24	28	30
Long run total cost	10	22	36	52	70

From this information, what conclusions can be drawn about the characteristics of production in the short run and long run?

	Short run	Long run
A	increasing average costs	economies of scale
B	increasing average costs	diseconomies of scale
C	decreasing average costs	diseconomies of scale
D	decreasing average costs	economies of scale

3. Which of the following is most likely to result in a firm being able to benefit from external economies of scale?

   A. An increase in its output.

   B. A diversification into a wider range of products.

   C. Location in the same area as other firms in the industry.

   D. Introduction of new, more capital-intensive methods of production.

4. Which of the following would indicate that a firm is experiencing internal diseconomies of scale?

   A. Average costs are falling as the scale of production increases.

   B. Long run marginal costs are greater than long run average costs.

   C. The percentage increase in output is greater than the percentage increase in inputs.

   D. Fixed costs of production are rising at a more rapid rate than variable costs.

DATA RESPONSE

Figure 39.2 shows the long run average and marginal cost curves of a firm.

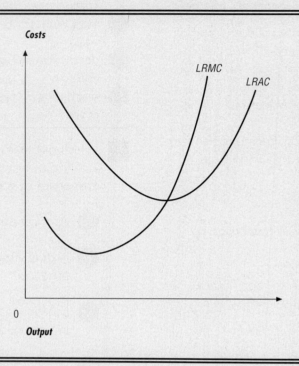

FIG. 39.2

a] Explain the shape of the long run average cost curve. **(4)**

b] Do all firms have this shaped long run average cost curve? **(5)**

c] Discuss the relationship between the long run marginal cost curve and the long run average total cost curve. **(5)**

d] Discuss the effect an increase in the external economies of scale available to a firm would have on its long run average cost curve. **(5)**

e] Explain the difference between diminishing returns and diseconomies of scale. **(6)**

CASE STUDY

In 'old style' production industries, economies of scale often exist. A bigger factory can often produce at lower unit cost than a small plant — an example of supply-side economies of scale. But generally there are limits to this. As size gets too big to manage easily, inefficiencies grow, so that at some point economies become diseconomies of scale. The natural market structure is then often one of oligopoly, a small number of large producers.

In information industries, the first copy of a product (say software, or a video) may be very expensive to produce, but subsequent copies have negligible cost by comparison; the natural market structure in such industries is monopoly, a single producer able to turn out limitless numbers of additional copies at effectively zero cost once investment has been sunk in creating the original. Because they ensure production at the lowest possible cost, such monopolies are not necessarily against the public interest. And they may be short-lived, lasting only so long as it takes a new entrant to devise a better product.

Unlike the markets of basic economics textbooks, many markets for information products enjoy demand-side economies of scale — the more consumers, the greater the benefit to each consumer. The fax machine is a classic example. If only one person owns a fax machine, it has no value. Once a second person buys a machine, the value to the first person increases. The more owners of fax machines, the greater the value of each machine to its owner. Equally, the more people with e-mail addresses, the greater the value of e-mail capability to each user. The more owners of VHS video machines, the greater the value to each because wider ownership encourages increased production, supply and rental of VHS videos.

These are all examples of positive 'externalities' — one person's consumption benefits other consumers. They are sometimes called network externalities, because they often arise through use of a network. But such network externalities can exist without a physical network, VHS videos are one example. The Windows and Apple operating systems are other examples. Users of each operating system benefit from its use by others, since this encourages the development of new applications, books, training courses, and widens the applicability of their skills in using such systems.

Network externalities, especially when combined with supply-side economies, often makes it sensible for suppliers to price new products at low, or even zero, cost in the hope of establishing a sufficiently large group of users to attract others. It encourages co-operation or agreement with other producers, even if they are rivals, to establish common standards. Note this is not new. Examples from history include railways, telephones and television.

Source: 'A new (micro) economy' by Patrick Foley, Lloyds Bank Economic Bulletin, No.24, December 1998.

a] What may cause diseconomies of scale? **(8)**

b] Explain two reasons why a 'bigger factory can often produce at lower unit cost than a smaller plant'. **(6)**

c] Why might a monopoly market structure in an IT industry benefit consumers? **(6)**

d] Discuss how easy it is for a firm, producing an improved product, to enter an IT industry. **(8)**

e] Explain what is meant by demand side economies of scale. **(4)**

f] Explain why a video machine enjoys demand side economies of scale. **(5)**

g] What is meant by network externalities? **(5)**

h] Why do many IT firms give away free copies of software? **(8)**

STRUCTURED ESSAY

a] Distinguish, with examples, between internal economies and diseconomies of scale. **(10)**

b] Discuss the external economies and diseconomies of scale which computer firms may experience. **(15)**

FREE RESPONSE ESSAY

Discuss the plant and firm economies of scale which a chemical company may enjoy. **(25)**

MOTIVES BEHIND GROWTH

The motives which cause a firm to grow in size are many and complex, but there are at least three which can be clearly distinguished:

- the desire to achieve economies of scale
- the desire to obtain a greater share of the market and hence greater market power
- the wish to achieve greater security by extending the range of products and markets.

METHODS OF ACHIEVING GROWTH

There are two methods by which growth may be achieved. The first of these is *internal growth*, or organic growth, where a firm increases its size by making more of its existing product or by extending the range of its products. It grows within the framework of its existing management and control structure. Dyson is an example of a firm which is growing in size on the basis of its original product (vacuum cleaners) and by using the same approach to extend its range of products.

The second and more common method nowadays is *external growth*. This is achieved by merger or takeover. A merger usually implies consent, with two or more firms agreeing to combine to create a new firm whereas a takeover is sometimes taken to mean that the firm taken over loses its identity and is absorbed into the firm carrying out the takeover. However, in practice, the terms are often used interchangeably. Sometimes a new firm is created for the sole purpose of acquiring the assets of a number of separate firms. Such a firm is known as a holding company. Hanson Trust controls firms producing bricks, tobacco, batteries, engineering products and frozen food.

Growth by merger (or takeover) may be referred to as *integration* which, in turn, may be vertical, horizontal, or conglomerate, although this is not a watertight classification.

VERTICAL INTEGRATION

Vertical integration is when a merger takes place between firms engaged in different stages of the productive process. It is 'vertical' in the sense that the merger is a movement up or down the productive process which runs from extraction to distribution. For example, a large manufacturer of tea (in the secondary sector) may take over tea plantations (in the primary sector).

BACKWARD VERTICAL INTEGRATION

Vertical integration backwardness is when the merger impetus is towards the source of supplies such as the example of the tea manufacturer above. It is often carried out so that a firm may exercise a much greater control over the quantity and quality of its supplies and be in a position of greater financial security with regard to their delivery to the market. It may also have the aim of restricting the availability of such supplies to a competitor. An additional motive might be the absorption of the intermediate profit margins.

FORWARD VERTICAL INTEGRATION

Where the movement is towards the market outlets, the process is described as forward vertical integration. For example, the large oil companies now control most of the world's petrol stations.

MOTIVES FOR VERTICAL INTEGRATION

Important motives for this type of combination are the desire to secure an adequate number of market outlets and the wish to raise the standard of these outlets. Since manufacturers carry the main burden of advertising costs it is only natural that they should be concerned that their products reach the public in a form and in an environment which lives up to the image created by their advertising. Firms may be forced to take over some market outlets when a major competitor has already made a move in this direction — they must react or face the prospect of being squeezed out of the market.

OTHER MOTIVES FOR VERTICAL INTEGRATION

Apart from providing greater security and control of supplies or markets, vertical integration may also give rise to economies of scale. This is most noticeable when a series of production processes are brought together in one large plant. In iron and steel making, for example, the hot pig iron from blast furnaces can be converted into steel with minimum loss of heat and by-product gases from the coke ovens can be used to heat furnaces in the finishing department. Some industries have remained integrated from an early stage in their development because it was the only way in which balanced growth at different stages of production process could have been achieved. The companies which found crude oil were obliged to build the necessary oil refineries and to develop the means of transporting oil from oilfields to distant markets.

Vertical integration is sometimes adopted as a means of accelerating the development of new discoveries. The production and adoption of a new fibre, new microchip or new plastic material may be speeded up if the producer of the new material takes over the facilities for turning it into marketable products.

PROBLEMS

There are also some problems associated with vertical integration. A manufacturer moving backwards to acquire the source of its raw materials may find itself with a rapidly depreciating asset if technology develops a superior substitute material. A rubber plantation may quickly lose its value if synthetic rubber proves a superior product in the manufacture of tyres. During a world recession raw material prices fall very sharply. The independent manufacturer will obtain very low-priced supplies — the burden of losses being borne by the supplier. The integrated firm, however, cannot avoid the losses during the slump in raw material prices.

The optimum size of plants at different stages of production may be very different. The integration of firms with very different capacities will create the problem of finding enough 'outside work' to keep the plant with the larger capacity fully operational.

HORIZONTAL INTEGRATION

The merger of firms engaged in producing the same kind of good or service and at the same stage of production merge is described as *horizontal integration*, or a horizontal merger. This is the most common form of merger. In recent years there have been a number of high profile mergers in the banking, communications, pharmaceuticals and motor industries.

MOTIVES FOR HORIZONTAL INTEGRATION

Market domination is undoubtedly one of the motives leading to horizontal integration. When a number of firms producing the same or similar products form a single firm there is clearly a reduction in competition allowing the new firm to exert more market power as it controls a much greater share of the total market.

Firms may be encouraged to integrate horizontally in order to carry out a rationalisation of the industry's capacity, particularly if demand is falling. If there are, say, three firms, each operating one plant making similar products and each firm is working at only two-thirds capacity, a merger will enable the new firm to close down the least efficient plant and work the two remaining at full capacity.

Horizontal integration also enables the joint capacity of the merged firms to be operated with a greater degree of specialisation. Suppose there are three independent firms each making a vacuum cleaner, a washing machine and an electric heater. In this case, a merger would enable the group to concentrate the production of each product in one factory allowing larger scale production of each.

In many cases a horizontal merger is carried out with a view to obtaining economies of scale. The larger unit, as indicated above, will be able to achieve greater specialisation; it will also be in a position to take advantage of many of the other economies described in Chapter 39. By increasing the range of products (or models), horizontal integration provides greater security in the form of risk-bearing economies of scale. Ford's wide range of vehicles provides it with a more stable pattern of demand than would be the case if it were dependent on the demand for one type of vehicle.

PROBLEMS

The major criticism of horizontal mergers derives from the obvious tendency towards monopoly as the number of firms in an industry is reduced.

There is also the possibility of management diseconomies of scale as the size of the firm increases. Integration may present particularly difficult management problems where a number of different firms with different markets or using different technologies are brought together, or where firms are geographically dispersed.

Problems also arise where it becomes necessary to bring together managers from firms with different histories, traditions and outlooks to form one management team.

CONGLOMERATE INTEGRATION

Conglomerate mergers are mergers between firms which produce goods or services that are not directly related to one another. For example, a firm producing cigarettes may take over a firm producing potato crisps, or a firm producing fertilisers may merge with a manufacturer of paint.

MOTIVES FOR CONGLOMERATE INTEGRATION

The main aim of a conglomerate merger is to obtain a diversification of output so as to reduce the risks of trading. Conglomerate mergers may also arise where a firm believes that there is little scope for any further growth in the markets for its existing products. It may then satisfy a desire for further growth by merging with a firm in a different industry.

Although the output of a large conglomerate may appear to comprise a range of very different products, the diversification of output is rarely completely random. There may be some connection between the products in terms of the use of common raw materials, a common technology or common markets.

Nevertheless there are several conglomerates where the only common links seem to be those of managerial and financial services. The justification for such mergers appears to be the promised injection of better management techniques and a more efficient use of the available resources.

PROBLEMS

A conglomerate which consists of an amalgam of several sub-optimal firms operating in different industries may not achieve any worthwhile economies of scale. Co-ordinating a range of products is likely to prove challenging and will require good management.

MULTINATIONAL FIRMS

A multinational firm is a company which produces products in more than one country. Multinational companies (MNCs) are sometimes referred to as multinational corporations or transnational corporations (TNCs). UK based MNCs include British Petroleum, ICI, British Telecom, British Gas and British Aerospace. Foreign MNCs with branches in the UK include Esso, Ford, Nestlé, IBM, Mitsubishi and Nissan.

Most MNCs come from industrialised countries, particularly the USA. They are very significant with the combined output of the largest two hundred MNCs being equivalent to approximately one-third of the entire output of the world. Indeed the output of General Motors exceeds the output of many countries including Denmark, Norway and Poland.

ADVANTAGES OF OPERATING ABROAD

Producing and selling in a major market abroad will reduce a firm's transport costs, enable it to keep in close contact with that market and may enable it to overcome any resistance to buying products made outside the host country. Firms also set up plants abroad to order to avoid import restrictions, take advantage of regional assistance or to obtain new materials. In some cases MNCs set up plants where wages are lower and health and safety and other employment legislation is more lax than in the home country.

THE EFFECTS OF MNCS ON THEIR HOST COUNTRIES

MNCs can bring a number of benefits to their host countries. They may provide employment although some of the top management jobs may be given to people from the MNCs' countries. They may bring in new methods of technology and a new approach to management. The production and management techniques in Japanese plants in the UK have been copied by a number of UK firms. They also contribute to economic growth and exports. They are likely to assist regional policy since they are more often willing to set up in development areas than host firms.

Consumers in host countries may benefit from the increased competition that MNCs bring in the form of more choice, higher quality and lower prices. However, not all the effects of MNCs are beneficial. MNCs may eliminate domestic producers so that consumers will not receive the advantages of increased competition. They may exhaust natural resources at a rapid rate and may not follow as high health and safety standards as in their own home countries. They may engage in transfer pricing — essentially shifting profit from high-tax countries to low-tax countries — causing high-tax countries to lose revenues. As already noted MNCs may be larger producers than their host countries. MNCs also have the potential to shift production around the world. This gives them considerable bargaining power in wage negotiations and in discussions with governments. They may even use the threat of closing down plants in order to win concessions on e.g. health and safety standards.

THE SURVIVAL OF SMALL FIRMS

The preceding discussion seems to indicate that there are substantial advantages to be obtained from increasing the size of a firm. There is, indeed, evidence to show that the number of large firms is increasing and that they are getting larger. Nevertheless, the fact remains that about one-half of the manufacturing output of the West comes from firms employing fewer than 500 workers and most UK firms employ between 1 and 50 workers.

There are hundreds of thousands of successful small firms in the UK (and in other countries) operating in all kinds of industries. Despite the many advantages of large-scale operation there are a number of reasons why small firms continue to survive including the size of the market, objectives of entrepreneurs, management problems and lack of finance.

MARKET LIMITATIONS ON MASS PRODUCTION

The ability to take advantage of large scale production is limited by the size of the market. Where the market is small it is not possible to obtain significant economies of scale, most of which are dependent upon the existence of a large market for a standardised product. The size of the market may be restricted by a number of factors including the following.

- *A demand for variety.* Some industries are faced with the problem that consumers demand a wide variety of styles, patterns and designs. The market for any one style or model may be very small indeed. Obvious examples are the clothing, millinery, furniture, footwear and jewellery trades. Firms in industries catering for such variety are confronted with the problem of 'short runs' and 'one-off' types of production — they cannot set up their capital and labour for specialised production. In such cases firms are likely to be small.
- *Geographical limitations.* If a product has great bulk in relation to value, transport costs will be high relative to production costs. In such cases the market for the product is likely to be local rather than national. Bread, bricks and coal may be cited as examples of products where markets have been confined to fairly small regions, although improvements in transport have tended to weaken this particular restriction on the size of the firm. Transport costs, however, still provide the village or suburban shop with some protection against the out-of-town superstore.
- *Personal services.* Industries which provide services rather than manufactured goods are usually characterised by a large number of small firms. Where the element of personal attention required by the purchase is an important part of the service, then it is not possible to introduce standardisation and mass production methods. As a result a large number of small firms are found in professions such as law, accountancy, architecture, and medicine where personal attention to individual problems is required. For similar reasons most firms specialising in repair work are relatively small. Hairdressing and bespoke tailoring provide other examples of the demand for personal attention seriously limiting the size of the firm.
- *Luxury items.* The market may be limited by income and wealth. Expensive sports cars, luxury yachts, high-quality jewellery and fur coats are examples of goods produced by small firms for very restricted prestige markets.

- *Disintegration*. As already noted there is a tendency for mass production industries to disintegrate into a large number of specialist firms each supplying some standardised part to a large assembly plant. This has been a structural change which has operated very much to the benefit of the firm. It is possible for the industry's total requirements of some particular component to be supplied by one relatively small firm.
- *Joint ventures*. Co-operation between smaller firms may lead to the setting of jointly owned enterprises which enable them to enjoy many of the economies of scale obtained by larger firms. Farmers have, for a long time, operated schemes (farmers' co-operatives) that allow them to obtain the benefits of bulk buying in feedstuffs, seeds, fertilisers and so on. The collective ownership of large units of capital (combine harvesters) makes such resources available to small farmers on an economic basis. Small manufacturing firms in some industries (e.g. footwear and pottery) operate jointly owned research establishments.

ENTREPRENEURS

Many firms remain small because of the reluctance of the person who has started the firm to accept the increased risks associated with growth — s/he may prefer a reasonable income and a 'quiet life'.

MANAGEMENT PROBLEMS

Management problems may be a barrier to growth. A large firm can be difficult to manage whereas in a small firm it is often possible to adjust quickly to changes in demand especially in those industries where fashions and tastes are subject to frequent changes.

FINANCE

Some firms remain small because they encounter difficulties in raising, on reasonable terms, the necessary finance for further expansion. Whereas large and medium-sized firms have a wide variety of sources of external finance available to them, internally generated funds and bank overdrafts tend to be the principal sources of finance for small firms. Smaller firms tend to be at a disadvantage compared with larger firms when seeking finance from external sources. In particular they usually have to pay more for any money they borrow than large firms due to the greater element of risk and the fact that administrative costs of small loans are proportionately greater than those for large loans.

THE FINANCE OF FIRMS

As referred to above the sources of funds for firms may be external or internal, that is, firms may borrow from different types of lender, or they may generate funds for investment purposes by allocating some of their profits for use within the firm.

INTERNAL FINANCE

By far the most important source of finance for firms is internal finance. Nearly 70% of investment finance is obtained from retained profits. These are profits which are kept back to invest in the firm rather than distributed to shareholders in the form of dividends. The significance of retained profits is not surprising. Firms are likely to want to expand and to buy new equipment when prospects are good and profit levels are high.

EXTERNAL FINANCE

The main sources of external finance are:

- issuing new shares
- borrowing
- other sources
- obtaining grants.

SHARES

Shareholders are owners of public and private limited companies and receive a share of profits called dividends. The principal type of share is known as an *ordinary share* (or equity). The dividend on ordinary shares is not fixed and varies with the profitability of the business and the policy of the directors with regard to the amount of profit to be retained in the company. The dividend may be high or it may be zero. The ordinary shareholder is entitled to the residue of profits after all other claims have been met. Ordinary shares, therefore, are the riskiest type of investment and dividends on them may fluctuate from year to year. Since they bear the major risks, ordinary shareholders have the greatest say in the management and control of the enterprise, and most ordinary shares carry voting rights.

Issuing shares provides a useful source of finance for private and public limited companies and has the advantage that if the business is not doing well payments do not have to be made to shareholders. However, issuing new shares carries the possible disadvantage of reducing the price of existing shares (due to the increase in their supply) and causes the ownership of the business to be more widely dispersed.

BORROWING

Firms can borrow in a number of different ways and from a number of different sources.

- *Debentures*. Debentures are loans and the purchasers of debentures are creditors of the company and not owners. A debenture is a kind of IOU. The rate of interest on debentures is fixed and debenture holders rank before all classes of shares for payments out of profits. The holders of these securities have the right to sell their debentures to third parties.
- *Bank loans and overdrafts*. By tradition British banks are providers of relatively short-term loans. For most firms they are the main source of short-term external finance. A typical bank loan is often described as a 'self-liquidating' loan, because it finances the purchase of raw materials which are transformed into saleable products in a matter of weeks or months. In other words, the means of repaying the loan is generated in a fairly short period of time. Apart from the provision of this type of working capital, banks also provide 'bridging' finance. A firm may experience cash-flow problems with its income and outgoings not being in balance week by week. Temporary deficits will arise during periods when expenditures exceed receipts and these may be covered by 'bridging' loans from banks. Medium and long-term loans are also given for longer-term projects although UK banks have been criticised for not lending enough to UK industry. Whilst bank loans are usually for a specific purpose, bank overdrafts are used, in the main, to meet short-term unexpected cash flow problems.

  Using bank loans as a source of finance has the disadvantage that interest has to be paid on a regular basis, whatever the state of the business.

OTHER SOURCES OF FINANCE

These include the following.

- *Leasing.* Instead of using a medium-term loan to buy new assets, a firm may lease them. Under a leasing arrangement, the leasing company buys the plant, equipment or vehicles to the firm's requirements and then leases them to the firm for an agreed rental. The leasing company sometimes provides servicing and maintenance facilities as well. The assets remain the property of the leasing company.
- *Trade credit.* Trade credit is an important source of finance for the smaller firm. When a firm supplies on credit terms which allow the purchaser 3 or 6 months in which to make payment, it is, in effect, providing the buyer with a short-term loan.
- *Hire purchase.* After making an initial down-payment, and paying regular fixed amounts over an agreed period (covering interest and the balance of capital cost), a firm acquires the ownership of the goods. When a firm buys goods on hire purchase it is, in effect, obtaining a loan from the finance firm which supplies the funds to support the hire purchase scheme.
- *Factoring.* This involves a company selling its debts, usually to a finance company. This enables it to receive immediate payment less a charge for the service. It also saves the company time in vetting customers and passes the risk of collecting bad debts to the finance companies. This service is used mainly by small and medium sized firms.

LOAN AND RISK CAPITAL

Loan capital consists of those funds advanced by creditors at fixed or variable rates of interest, whereas risk capital is raised by the sale of shares.

As already noted interest charges on loan capital must be paid each year whereas dividends on risk capital need not be paid in those years when the firm has not prospered. Firms which operate in industries where the market for the product is subject to continuous fluctuation would not take the risk of having a high proportion of loan capital. Loan capital is more appropriate to firms operating in stable markets and which have a large part of their assets in the form of land and buildings which are good subjects for mortgages (e.g. brewery companies).

GEARING

The ratio of loan capital to risk capital (shares) is known as gearing. The greater the proportion of risk capital to loan capital the lower the gearing. So, if profits are rising, the dividends on the ordinary shares will rise much faster in those firms with high gearing than in those with low gearing. The opposite will apply when profits are falling. It will be found that the dividends on ordinary shares are much more variable when the gearing is greater.

OBTAINING GRANTS

Firms may receive investment grants from government or (in Europe) from the European Union to set up in regional development areas, to introduce new technology and to continue in production if they are facing difficulties and are perceived to be crucial for the smooth running of the economy. The amount of money available from this source will be influenced by views on the effectiveness of state intervention. In Europe, agriculture has been a main beneficiary of individual government and European Union grants.

Q U E S T I O N S

SHORT QUESTIONS

1. What are the main motives behind horizontal mergers?
2. Briefly discuss two advantages a firm may gain from setting up a branch abroad.
3. Give, and briefly explain, three reasons for the survival of small firms.
4. What are the main three sources of finance for firms?

MULTIPLE CHOICE

1. A tobacco company purchases an insurance company. This is an example of:

   A. a horizontal merger

   B. a conglomerate merger

   C. a vertical backwards merger

   D. a vertical forwards merger.

2. A vertical merger is one which occurs between two firms:

   A. making different types of products

   B. producing in the same geographical area

   C. producing at the same stage of production of the same product

   D. at different stages of production of the same end product.

3. Why may the optimum size of a firm be small?

   A. Raw materials costs are high.

   B. The machinery used is expensive.

   C. The market for the product is limited in size.

   D. Diseconomies of scale set in at a high level of output.

4. What is the most important source of investment finance?

   A. Shares.

   B. Bank loans.

   C. Retained profits.

   D. Government investment grants.

DATA RESPONSE

Top takeovers: takeovers over £20bn during last 18 months		
Companies	Business	Value of deal (£bn)
Exxon/Mobil	oils	48
Travellers/Citicorp	financial services	43
SBC Comms/Ameritech	telecoms	38
Vodafone/Airtouch	phones	38
NationsBank/BankAmerica	banking	37
Bell Atlantic/GTE	communication	32
BP/Amoco	oils	29
WorldCom/MCI	telecoms	25
Daimler-Benz/Chrysler	motor	25
Monsanto/American Home Products	life sciences	21
Astra/Zeneca	drugs	21
Norwest/Wells Fargo	financials	21

Fuelled by the hunger of financial architects and driven by growing competition, the appetite for takeovers and mergers appears unstoppable. No deal is regarded as too big to be contemplated.

Yet evidence shows mergers fail to achieve what they set out: recent research suggests only one in every three takeovers gets anywhere near achieving its goals.

While directors' egos push them relentlessly towards bigger and bigger deals, the price is paid lower down the corporate scale. It is almost unknown for a takeover or merger not to be predicated on saving costs, largely by sacking staff.

The wave of activity in the 1960s was mainly about diversification — ICI wanted to move away from chemicals and become more involved in textiles — seen as a growth business at the time.

In the 1980s, however, diversification was out of fashion. Suddenly it was all the rave to buy another business in order to cut costs.

Now business thinks it needs to be global. Many industries such as oil, drinks and banking are regarded as 'mature', with their best growth years behind them, so the only way to continue to drive profits forward is to reduce the costs.

Source: 'Merger mania — coming to a company near you' by Lisa Buckingham and Roger Cowe, the Guardian, 23/1/99.

a] What type of merger were most of the top takeovers in the table? Explain your answer. **(4)**

b] Discuss two possible goals of a merger. **(4)**

c] Explain why mergers often result in redundancies. **(5)**

d] If firms want to diversify what type of merger are they most likely to engage in and why? **(4)**

e] Explain why a merger may actually raise a firm's unit costs. **(8)**

CASE STUDY

Why do firms grow? It is an important question. Yet economists, management gurus and business-school boffins have so far failed to answer it convincingly.

There are three main competing theories. The traditional explanation is that firms grow to reap economies of scale, and to increase their market power. They stop growing once they reach an optimum size, when they run out of profitable investment opportunities or become too big and bureaucratic to manage.

Life-cycle theories, which became popular in the 1970s and 1980s, identify several stages in the growth of firms, including an entrepreneurial phase, maturity and finally a period of decline. A third view, currently fashionable, attributes firms' growth to their 'core competencies'. Admittedly, this is a somewhat nebulous concept. But in essence, it means that a firm's performance is determined by building on a set of key skills that distinguish it from its rivals. These might include better technology, a trusted brand name, or the experience of its employers.

All three theories seem plausible. Yet none of them squares with the evidence. That at least is the conclusion of a new paper about corporate growth by Paul Geroski, an economist at London Business School. The most important empirical finding, confirmed by study after study of companies big and small, is that a firm's growth largely follows a 'random walk' — an erratic and unpredictable course. That is not quite the same as saying that it is driven purely by chance or good luck. But it does undermine theories that purport to explain, and hence predict, corporate growth.

But it is not a total mystery. There is in fact some evidence that smaller firms grow faster than bigger ones. In particular, very small, very new firms tend to grow much faster than established ones. But company sizes do not appear to converge, either within particular industries, or across them.

More surprisingly, firms' growth rates are only weakly correlated with that of the economy as a whole or, indeed, with that of their own industry. Recessions seem to hit only a few firms badly; most are largely unaffected, while some actually prosper.

Two other findings complement the observation that corporate growth is erratic. The first is that firms typically restructure their operations in big, infrequent bursts, rather than with small, continuous adjustments. This tends to make it hard to predict the timing of companies' growth. The second is that most firms are sporadic innovators. Although most big companies frequently spend money on research, few make a habit of producing big innovations or patents. Typically, firms innovate every once in a while, then go a long time before doing it again. This is also likely to make firms' growth spurts unpredictable.

Source: 'The corporate-growth puzzle', The Economist, 17/7/99.

a] Explain what is meant by the optimum size of a firm. **(6)**

b] Compare the three growth theories discussed in the extract. **(8)**

c] Why might small firms grow more rapidly than large ones? **(6)**

d] Which type of firms may prosper during a recession? **(5)**

e] Why might a small firm not grow? **(8)**

f] Explain what is meant by innovation. **(4)**

g] Discuss the factors which are likely to encourage firms to innovate. **(8)**

h] Discuss the effect that the growth of firms is likely to have on market structure. **(5)**

STRUCTURED ESSAY

a] Distinguish between horizontal, vertical and horizontal mergers. **(10)**

b] Discuss whether horizontal mergers benefit consumers. **(15)**

FREE RESPONSE ESSAY

Discuss why, despite the advantages of large scale production, so many small firms survive. **(25)**

PART SEVEN: MARKET PERFORMANCE

41 PERFECT COMPETITION

DEFINITION

The economist's model of perfect competition is largely theoretical but it does provide a useful tool for economic analysis. The market structure is used as a means of assessing the degree of competition in real world markets. Economists set out the conditions for a perfectly competitive market and then contrast these with the situations found in the markets for goods and services.

CHARACTERISTICS

A perfectly competitive market has a number of key characteristics.

- All units of the product are *homogeneous* (i.e. one product is exactly the same as another). So buyers have no preference for the products of any particular seller.
- There are many buyers and sellers so that the behaviour of any one buyer, or any one seller, has no influence on the market price. Each individual buyer comprises such a small part of total demand and each seller is responsible for such a small part of total supply that any change in their plans will have no influence on the market price.
- Buyers are assumed to have perfect knowledge of market conditions; they know what prices are being asked for the product in every part of the market. Equally sellers are fully aware of the activities of buyers and other sellers.
- There must be no barriers to the movement of buyers from one seller to another. Since all units of the product are identical, buyers will always approach the seller quoting the lowest price. There is no attachment between buyers and sellers.
- There are no restrictions on the entry of firms into the market or on their exit from it.
- There is perfect mobility of resources so that firms wishing to expand their output can attract more resources.
- There is no advertising.

These characteristics mean that in a perfect market there will be one and only one market price which is beyond the control of any one buyer or any one seller. Firms cannot charge different prices because they are selling identical products, each of them is responsible for a tiny part of the total supply, and buyers are fully aware of what is happening in the market.

THE INDIVIDUAL FIRM

Under conditions of perfect competition the firm is powerless to exert any influence on price. It sees the market price as 'given', that is, established by market forces beyond its control. For example, in most countries, the individual farmer has no influence on the price he sells his wheat, or beef, or milk, or vegetables. Any changes in the amounts of these products which he brings to market will have negligible effects on their prices. The firm, under perfect competition is a 'price-taker'.

The demand curve for the output of the single firm, therefore, must be a horizontal line at the ruling price; in other words, a perfectly elastic demand curve. No matter how many units the firm sells it cannot change the price. It can sell its entire output at the ruling market price. If it tries to sell at higher prices its demand will drop to zero, and there is obviously no incentive to sell at lower prices.

THE FIRM AND THE INDUSTRY

Whilst the demand curve for the product of an individual firm is perfectly elastic, the market demand curve for the output of the industry will be of the normal shape (i.e. sloping downwards from left to right). Market price for the industry is determined by the total demand and supply curves as shown in Figure 41.1 (a).

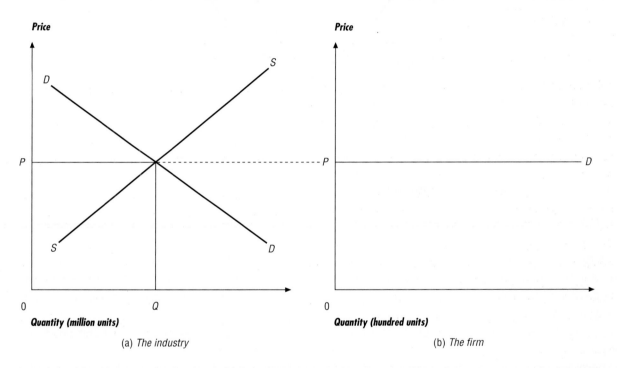

(a) *The industry* (b) *The firm*

FIG. 41.1

DD is the demand curve facing the industry and SS is the total supply provided by all the firms in that industry.
Figure 41.1 (b) shows the situation facing the individual firm. Market price (P) is externally determined and the firm sees the demand for its product as being perfectly elastic. In the two diagrams, the scales on the price axes will be the same, but the scales on the quantity axes will be very different, because the firm supplies a negligibly small part of the total output of the product.

THE OUTPUT OF THE FIRM

It is assumed that firms producing under conditions of perfect competition are profit maximisers. As long as the price (AR) it receives for each unit exceeds the average costs of production, a firm will be making supernormal profits. Figure 41.2 shows when price is P, the firm will be making supernormal profits in the range of output Q to Q^3, because at all outputs in this range, AR is greater than AC.

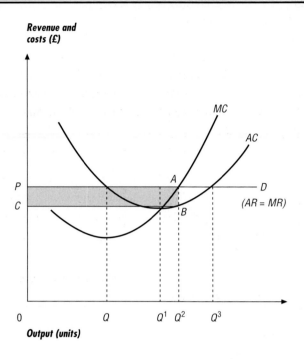

Revenue and costs (£)

Output (units)

FIG. 41.2

Output Q yields the maximum profit per unit. However firms seek to maximise total profit and not profit per unit. As output increases from Q to Q^2, the firm's total profit will be increasing because for each additional unit produced, the increase in total revenue (i.e. marginal revenue) is greater than the increase in total cost (i.e. marginal cost).

As output is expanded beyond Q^2, total profit will decrease because for each additional unit produced, the increase in total revenue (i.e. MR) is less than the increase in total cost (i.e. MC).

Therefore since total profit is increasing up to Q^2 and falling beyond Q^2, profits must be maximised when output is at Q^2, that is, when marginal revenue = marginal cost. Under conditions of perfect competition this is also where $AR = MR = MC$.

NORMAL AND SUPERNORMAL PROFIT

Normal profit is the minimum level of profit which will persuade an entrepreneur to stay in business. It will vary from industry to industry depending upon the degree of risk involved. Since production will not continue unless this minimum level of profit is forthcoming, normal profit may be legitimately regarded as a cost of production. Normal profits, therefore, are included in the calculations which produce the AC curve. Therefore, when price exceeds average cost, the firm is said to be earning *supernormal* (or abnormal) profits. Supernormal profit is illustrated by the shaded area in Figure 41.2. When output is Q^2, the cost per unit is equal to BQ^2, but the price is equal to AQ^2. Supernormal profit per unit, therefore is AB. Total supernormal profit is equal to the area *CPAB* (i.e. the shaded area). Supernormal profits arise when either costs fall or demand for the industry's product increases.

THE ELIMINATION OF SUPERNORMAL PROFITS

Although the firm in Figure 41.2 is in equilibrium, the industry is not in equilibrium. There will be forces at work tending to change the size of the industry. The situation depicted in Figure 41.2 will not persist in the long run, because the supernormal profits being earned by the existing firms will attract other firms into this industry. As new firms come in, total supply will increase, market price will fall, and the process will continue until the supernormal profits have been 'competed away'. Figure 41.3 shows that the entry of new firms moves the industry's supply curve to the right and lowers market price. This will cause firms to move into a position of long-run equilibrium.

The long-run equilibrium of the firm is shown in Figure 41.4. The market price has fallen to P^1 and the most profitable output is now Q^1, where $AR = MR = MC$. The price, or average revenue, is now equal to average cost so that the firm is making only normal profits. There is no incentive for firms to enter or leave the industry so that both the firm and the industry are in equilibrium. The long-run equilibrium of the firm, therefore, is to be found where: $P = AR = AC = MC = MR$.

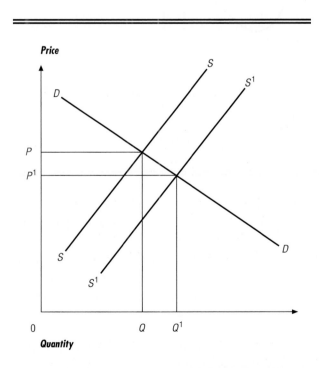

FIG. 41.3

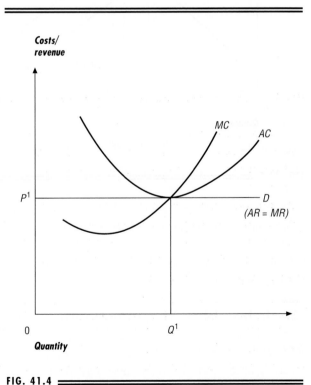

FIG. 41.4

In theory, the system of perfect competition produces a long-run equilibrium where all firms earn only normal profits and produce at minimum average cost.

LOSSES

In the short run firms may experience losses. This means that firms will operate under conditions where average cost exceeds average revenue. Losses occur if either costs rise or demand falls. Figure 41.5 shows losses arising due to a decrease in demand for the industry's product. (a) shows the effect on the industry and (b) the effect on an individual firm.

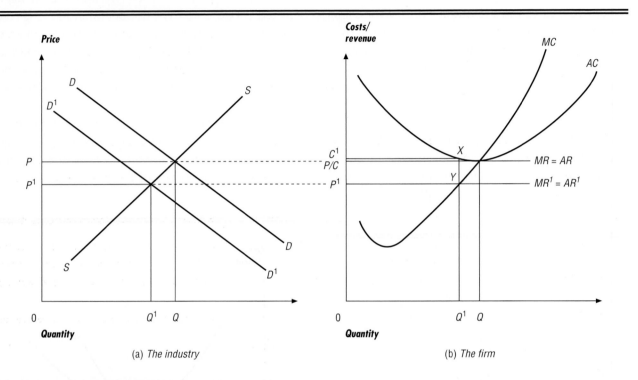

(a) *The industry* (b) *The firm*

FIG. 41.5

   The area C^1XYP^1 in Figure 41.5(b) represents the area of loss that the firm is incurring. It is costing the firm C^1 per unit to produce the product but the firm is receiving a price of only P^1 so it is not covering all of its costs.

   In this situation some firms will leave the industry but some will remain. Those that stay will be those that believe that they will be able to return to earning at least normal profits and that can currently cover their variable costs of production. If the price a firm is receiving is covering its average variable costs it will be covering the direct cost of production and may be making some contribution to average fixed costs. Whereas if the firm shut down it would not be able to cover any of the fixed costs that it would still have to meet. Figure 41.6 shows two firms experiencing losses. Firm A is covering its average variable cost and will stay in the industry, at least in the short run, whilst firm B is not and will leave the industry.

   Firms in perfect competition are often assumed to have identical cost curves. However, this is not a very realistic assumption. This is because even if all units of land, labour, and capital were equally efficient and available to all firms on identical terms, it is most unlikely that all entrepreneurs will have the same outlook, the same ability, and the same energy. It is the marginal firms (i.e. those with the highest costs) which will be the first to leave the industry when losses are being made and the last to enter when supernormal profits are experienced.

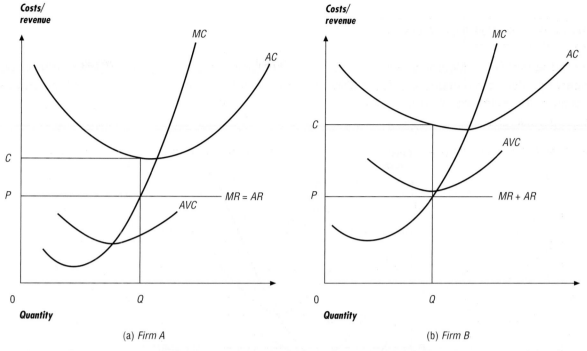

(a) Firm A   (b) Firm B

FIG. 41.6

The existence of losses will cause some firms to leave the industry. This will move the industry's supply curve to the left, raise price and return profits to the normal profit level. Figure 41.7 shows the industry and a firm returning to long-run equilibrium where there is no incentive for firms to enter or leave the industry and where firms are earning normal profit.

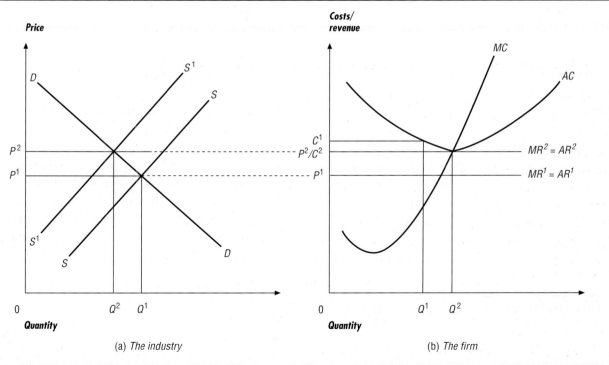

(a) The industry   (b) The firm

FIG. 41.7

THE FIRM'S SUPPLY CURVE

As noted above firms attempt to set their outputs at the point where $MC = MR$. For the firm in perfect competition, MR is always equal to AR (i.e. price) so that the individual firm will try to adjust its output so as to equate price and marginal cost.

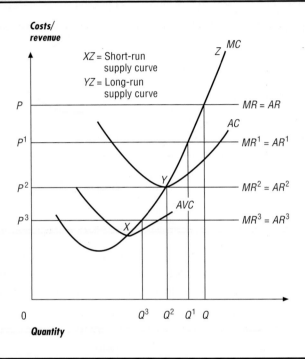

FIG. 41.8

In the conditions shown in Figure 41.8 when the market price is P the firm will produce output Q. If the market price falls to P^1, the firm, in trying to maximise profit, will reduce output to Q^1. The MC curve, therefore, is acting as the firm's supply curve, because it is determining the quantity supplied at any given price. If the market price falls to P^2, the firm will adjust its output to Q^2 (where price equals marginal cost). At this point, however price $= MC = MR$ so that the firm will be making no more than normal profits.

If market price falls below P^2, the firm will be making losses because, at all outputs price will be less than average cost. So when price is P^3 the firm will be making losses, but at this price, Q^3 still represents the 'most profitable' output in the sense that it represents the output at which losses are minimised. In the short run, the firm may still produce even when price is less than average total cost provided it is above average variable cost. So the short-run supply curve is that part of the MC curve which lies above the AVC curve. In the long run all costs have to be covered so the long-run supply curve is that part of the MC curve which lies above the AC curve. It slopes upwards from left to right because increasing output gives rise to increasing marginal cost.

THE INDUSTRY'S SUPPLY CURVE

The total or market supply curve for a product is obtained by adding together the supply curves of all the firms producing that product. This total supply curve is described as the industry supply curve. It is affected by the movement of firms into and out of the industry. If market price rises, not only will existing firms produce more, there will also be new firms moving into the industry. Similarly, falling prices will cause existing firms to reduce output and some of the higher cost firms will be driven out of the industry.

If, when new firms enter the industry, greater advantage can be taken of external economies of scale, the industry will be referred to as a decreasing cost industry and its long-run supply curve will slope downwards, as illustrated in Figure 41.9.

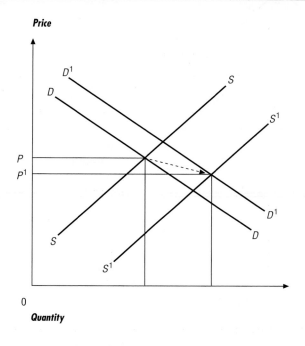

FIG. 41.9

If, however, the entry of new firms bids up the price of factors of production and creates external diseconomies of scale the long-run supply curve will slope upwards as shown in Figure 41.10.

The last possibility is a constant cost industry where the entry of new firms does not result in any change in firms' average costs. This is shown in Figure 41.11.

REALISM OF THE MARKET STRUCTURE

Perfect competition is not found in the real world, although it is possible to point to some markets where there is some rough approximation to this model. There are hundreds of thousands of wheat producers all over the world and no one of them is large enough to influence the world price of wheat. The world markets for a number of agricultural products contain many of the features of a perfect market. There are many producers and many buyers; modern methods of communication make knowledge of market conditions almost perfect, and the standardised grading of commodities means that the products in any one grade are regarded as homogeneous. Another, often quoted, example of a market which bears some resemblance to a perfect market is the market in foreign exchange.

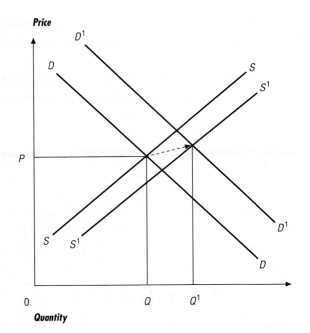

FIG. 41.10

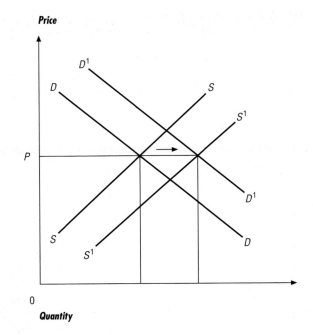

FIG. 41.11

Q U E S T I O N S

SHORT QUESTIONS

1. Do consumers have choice in a perfectly competitive market?

2. If a perfectly competitive firm is earning supernormal profits is its average cost rising, at its lowest point or falling?

3. Which cost curve is the short-run supply curve of a perfectly competitive firm based on?

4. What are the conditions needed for a perfectly competitive industry to be in long-run equilibrium?

MULTIPLE CHOICE

1. A perfectly competitive firm is faced with the following total revenue and total cost schedules.

Output (£)	Total revenue (£)	Total cost (£)
1	8	10
2	16	16
3	24	23
4	32	31
5	40	40
6	48	50

Within which of the following ranges of output will profits be maximised?

A   1–2 units.   B   2–3 units.

C   3–4 units.   D   4–5 units.

2. Which of the following may be found under conditions of perfect competition?

A   Advertising.

B   Differentiated products.

C   Investment in new plant.

D   Different prices charged to different groups of consumers.

3. A perfectly competitive firm is producing where marginal revenue exceeds marginal cost. To maximise profit what should it do?

	Price	Output
A	increase	reduce
B	reduce	keep unchanged
C	keep unchanged	increase
D	reduce	increase

4. Figure 41.12 shows the cost and revenue conditions faced by a profit maximising firm producing under conditions of perfect competition.

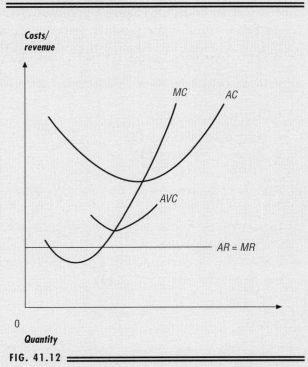

FIG. 41.12

The firm is making a loss. What will the firm do?

A   Lower price to increase demand for its product.

B   Raise price in order to cover its average cost of production.

C   Leave the industry in search of higher profits elsewhere.

D   Continue in production in the short run in the hope that demand and price will rise in the future.

DATA RESPONSE

It is argued that in a perfectly competitive market firms are forced to be efficient. If firms fail to produce what consumers want or if they fail to keep their costs low they will lose customers to their rivals and will be driven out of the industry.

Firms, collectively as an industry, also respond quickly to changes in consumer demand. If, for example, demand increases more firms will enter the industry thereby increasing the quantity of resources devoted to the production of the product and meeting the higher consumer demand.

However whilst perfectly competitive firms may be productively efficient in the long run and allocatively efficient in terms of private costs and benefits, the conditions of perfect competition do not ensure that they are allocatively efficient in terms of social costs and benefits.

The assumption is that perfectly competitive firms are profit maximisers, producing where $MC = MR \, (= AR)$. In the absence of government intervention, in deciding their output private sector firms take into account only private costs and benefits. If the output they produce generates more external costs, for example pollution, than external benefits more resources will be devoted to the production of the product than the socially optimum output requires. A pareto improvement would be achieved by reducing the output of the product.

a] Why do new firms enter a perfectly competitive market when demand increases? **(5)**

b] Explain the meaning of:
   i productive efficiency **(2)**
   ii allocative efficiency. **(3)**

c] Are perfectly competitive firms always productively efficient?

d] Explain the difference between external costs and private costs. **(4)**

e] Explain in what circumstances a perfectly competitive market will fail to allocate sufficient resources to the production of a product. **(5)**

CASE STUDY

Many countries now operate floating exchange rates. This means that the value of their currency is determined by demand and supply. Demand for the pound sterling, for example, comes from foreigners wishing to buy UK goods and services, from UK citizens who have received payment in foreign currency, from foreigners wishing to place money in UK financial institutions or in sterling deposits in overseas banks and from speculators. Indeed speculation is now the main reason for the purchase of many currencies. The supply of pounds comes from foreigners who have received payment in terms of pounds, from UK citizens who wish to buy imports, from UK citizens who want to place money in foreign currency deposits and again from speculators.

Speculators buy and sell currencies in order to make a profit from changes in price. If speculators believe the price of a currency will rise they will buy it and sell it on at a higher price. If it is thought that the price of a currency will rise significantly speculators and dealers who had previously concentrated on other currencies may switch to the purchase of this one.

Dealers and speculators are well informed about the prices of currencies in different parts of the world. They use up to date technology to keep an eye on prices and they study news stories and leaks from influential people and bodies to gain an insight into future prices. If they notice a price difference, of e.g. pounds in Bermuda and Tokyo, they will buy in the cheaper market and sell in the more expensive market. This quick action tends to equate the price of a currency in all the markets.

a] Are pounds homogeneous or differentiated products? **(4)**

b] Why would one dealer in a currency be unable to charge a higher price than other dealers in the same currency? **(5)**

c] What may cause an increase in demand for pounds? **(7)**

d] What effect will an increased demand for pounds have on the price of pounds? **(5)**

e] Why is the price of a currency usually the same in all foreign currency markets throughout the world? **(5)**

f] Explain two ways in which advances in technology are making the market for foreign currency approach perfect competition more closely. **(6)**

g] What characteristics of perfect competition does the foreign exchange market exhibit? **(10)**

h] Discuss the advantages for consumers of the high level of competition in the foreign exchange market. **(8)**

STRUCTURED ESSAY

a] Under what conditions would a market be perfectly competitive? **(5)**

b] Discuss the effects of an increase in demand for the product of a perfectly competitive industry in the short run and in the long run. **(20)**

FREE RESPONSE ESSAY

Discuss whether perfectly competitive firms always earn normal profits. **(25)**

42 MONOPOLISTIC COMPETITION

DEFINITION

Monopolistic competition is a market structure in which there are a large number of firms making similar products. It derives its name from the fact that it contains elements of both perfect competition and monopoly. This form of market structure is common in the service sector, for example, public houses, car repair firms, hairdressers and retailers.

CHARACTERISTICS

There are a number of characteristics of monopolistic competition. As already mentioned, there are a large number of firms. Also as previously stated the products are similar. They are, but nevertheless each firm's product is differentiated from those of its competitors and so is unique. For instance, one public house may have a games room, one may specialise in vegetarian food and another may organise a local pub quiz. This means that there can be some consumer loyalty to a particular seller (in this case to a particular public house).

There are no or very low barriers to entry. Firms contemplating market entry do not require large-scale capital investment and use equipment which can be sold on (so there are few sunk costs). Indeed the firms in monopolistic competition tend to operate on a relatively small scale. They may be able to take advantage of economies of scale but not to any great extent.

There is said to be excess capacity in the industry. This means that the firms produce an output below the optimum (productively efficient level).

Firms may seek to gain extra customers by advertising, which will be on a relatively small and local scale, and by improving the good or service they provide, for example by, in the case of a car repair firm, staying open late.

As there are a large number of firms in the industry, each with an insignificant share of the market, each one will act independently. When deciding on their pricing and output strategy they will not be concerned about how their rivals will react. It is assumed that the firms are profit maximisers and so produce where $MC = MR$.

AVERAGE AND MARGINAL REVENUE

Although there are many firms in a monopolistically competitive industry, as each one is selling a differentiated product, each has some limited control over price. These firms are price makers: they can raise prices without losing all of their customers and they must lower their prices if they want to sell more. This means that a firm's average and marginal revenue will fall with output as shown in Figure 42.1.

The firm's demand curve is the average revenue curve. It is relatively elastic as the products or services of its competitors will be relatively close substitutes.

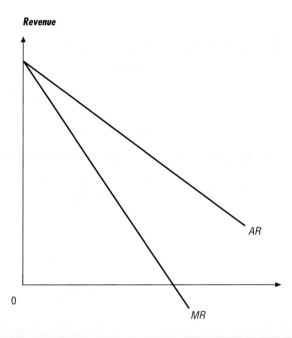

FIG. 42.1

TOTAL REVENUE

The firm's total revenue will rise at first when marginal revenue is positive and demand is elastic and reach a peak when marginal revenue is zero and elasticity of demand is unity. After a certain level of output is reached, marginal revenue will become negative and demand becomes inelastic. This is shown in Figure 42.2.

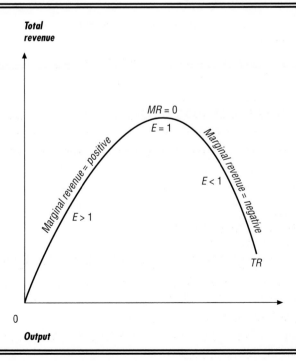

FIG. 42.2

SHORT-RUN OUTPUT AND PROFIT LEVELS

In the short run, firms may experience supernormal or normal profits or losses. As with perfect competition, supernormal profits will arise if there is a fall in costs or an increase in demand. Figure 42.3 shows a firm making supernormal profits. It is producing where MC = MR and where AR > AC.

Losses arise when costs rise or demand decreases. Figure 42.4 shows this situation.

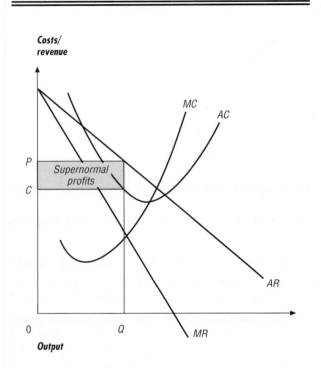

FIG. 42.3

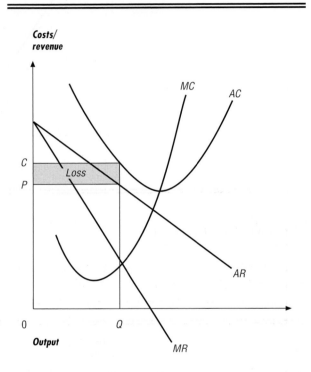

FIG. 42.4

THE LONG-RUN EQUILIBRIUM POSITION

As there are no or low barriers to entry and exit, i.e. nothing or virtually nothing to stop firms entering or leaving the industry, normal profits will be earned in the long run. If, for example, supernormal profits are experienced new firms will be attracted into the industry. This will cause supply to increase, price to fall and profits to return to the normal profit level. Figure 42.5 shows the long-run equilibrium position where MC = MR, AC = AR and AC = AR > MC = MR.

MONOPOLISTIC COMPETITION AND PERFECT COMPETITION COMPARED

Monopolistic competition is similar to perfect competition in a number of ways. Both market structures contain many buyers and sellers, although the number is less in monopolistic competition.

In both cases the firms are profit maximisers and, because of the absence of barriers to entry and exit, will earn normal profits in the long run.

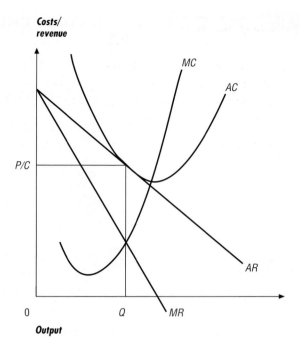

Costs/revenue

Output

FIG. 42.5

However, there are a number of key differences. Firms in monopolistic competition are price makers with each firm's output affecting the price charged whereas firms in perfect competition are price takers.

Firms in monopolistic competition face elastic demand for their goods or services whereas in perfect competition the demand for a firm's product is perfectly elastic. There can be advertising, albeit on a small scale, in monopolistic competition and firms operating in this market structure offer consumers a diversity of products. Consumers can prefer the product of one producer since its differentiated nature may meet the requirements or tastes of the particular consumers more than the products of the other firms. This feature may be seen to be an advantage of monopolistic competition.

However, whereas firms producing under conditions of perfect competition produce at the bottom of the average cost curve in the long run, firms operating under conditions of monopolistic competition produce where average costs are falling and there is spare capacity. They also do not achieve allocative efficiency. (See Chapter 45 for more similarities and differences.)

QUESTIONS

SHORT QUESTIONS

1. Explain two similarities and two differences between perfect competition and monopolistic competition.

2. What type of profits are earned in the long run in monopolistically competitive industries and why?

3. Give four examples of industries which operate under conditions of monopolistic competition.

4. Explain two ways in which a monopolistically competitive industry may benefit consumers more than a perfectly competitive one.

MULTIPLE CHOICE

1. Monopolistic competition is best described as a market structure where:

   A. the firms are price takers

   B. there are barriers to entry and exit

   C. the firms produce differentiated products

   D. most of the firms make supernormal profits in the long run.

2. Which one of the following diagrams in Figure 42.6 shows the long run total revenue curve of a firm operating in monopolistic competition?

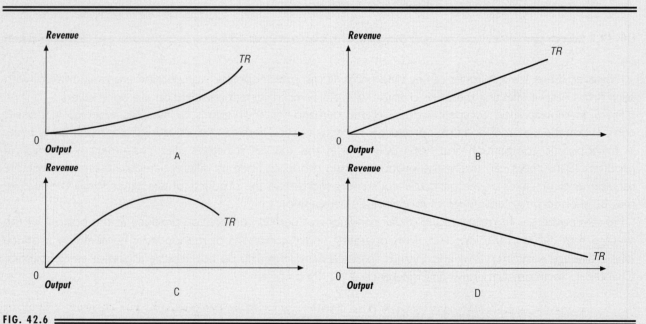

FIG. 42.6

3 Which of the following may occur if firms are in long run equilibrium under conditions of monopolistic competition?

- **A** Average revenue exceeding marginal revenue.

- **B** Average revenue exceeding average cost.

- **C** Marginal revenue exceeding marginal cost.

- **D** Marginal cost exceeding marginal revenue.

4 Figure 42.7 shows the cost and revenue position of a firm operating in monopolistic competition. Which one of the following rectangles represents the total costs of the equilibrium level of output?

- **A** 0AHJ
- **B** 0CFJ
- **C** 0DEJ
- **D** 0BGK

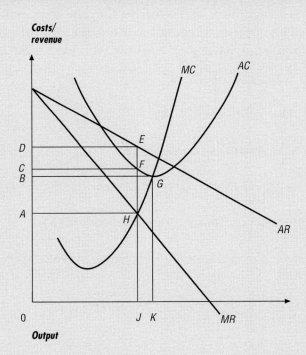

FIG. 42.7

DATA RESPONSE

When there are a large number of sellers producing a similar but differentiated product, then a state of monopolistic competition is said to exist. Thus seller concentration is quite low and the products tend to be fairly close substitutes. Such a market is characterised by the frequent entry and exit of firms. It is called monopolistic competition because, owing to imperfections in the market, each organisation has a small degree of monopoly power.

Examples of monopolistically competitive markets are more likely to be found in the service sector; estate agents, dry cleaners, restaurants and various forms of retailing. However, as noted previously, in a small town one or two individual sellers may possess considerable market power.

It is paradoxical that under perfect competition very little competition is visible since there is no advertising and promotion of products, whereas under all types of imperfect competition rivalry between firms is only too obvious. Even firms with a significant market power advertise. Tate and Lyle, for example, which has a large share of the market for cane sugar production, not only promotes its product but extols the virtues of free competition. It is a case, as Professor Galbraith wrote in *The Affluent Society*, of competition being advocated 'by those who have most successfully eliminated it'.

Source: 'Economics: a student guide', 4th edition, John Beardshaw et al, Longman, 1998.

a] Explain what is meant by 'seller concentration'. **(4)**

b] What would cause firms to enter and exit a market? **(6)**

c] What imperfections in competition exist in a monopolistically competitive market? **(6)**

d] How do firms compete in a monopolistically competitive market? **(5)**

e] Does Tate and Lyle operate in a monopolistically competitive market? Explain your answer. **(4)**

CASE STUDY

A taxi company, HiCabs, operates in the centre of Birmingham. It employs seven drivers and operates six cabs. There are thirty one other taxi companies operating in the city.

HiCabs' taxis have a distinctive red and yellow livery. To attract more customers the company has recently run an advertising campaign in local Birmingham newspapers. It is considering cutting its fares to attract more customers and has paid a company to carry out market research into the local taxi market. A summary of its findings about consumers' demand for taxi travel is given below.

Elasticities of demand for local taxi travel

Price	Cross	Income
1.2	0.7	2.8

a] To what extent does HiCabs appear to be operating in a monopolistically competitive market? **(7)**

b] Does the cross elasticity of demand figure suggest travel in other taxi firm companies is a close or distant substitute? **(5)**

c] What are the other substitutes for taxi travel? **(6)**

d] Using the information given, comment on the pricing policy HiCabs should use if it wants to increase the revenue of the firm. **(6)**

e] Comment on the significance of the income elasticity of demand figure. **(6)**

f] How could a firm assess whether an advertising campaign has been successful or not? **(6)**

g] What effect will an advertising campaign be likely to have on a firm's costs in the short and long run. **(8)**

h] Discuss two measures, other than advertising and price changes, which HiCabs could take to attract more customers. **(6)**

STRUCTURED ESSAY

a] Explain why firms operating under conditions of monopolistic competition are price makers. **(5)**

b] Distinguish between perfect competition and monopolistic competition. **(20)**

FREE RESPONSE ESSAY

Discuss the significance of an absence of barriers to entry and exit for perfect competition and monopolistic competition. **(25)**

43 OLIGOPOLY

DEFINITION

In many industries, especially the science-based, and technologically advanced industries, a market situation known as *oligopoly* is found. As the term implies, this is where the market is dominated by a few large producers. In other words, a small number of very large firms account for practically the whole output of the industry. Good examples of oligopoly are to be found in the industries producing oil, detergents, tyres, motor cars, synthetic fibres, and cigarettes.

Where there are important technical economies of scale to be gained, the process of merger has drastically reduced the number of firms in an industry and brought into being some very large business units. In several industries in the UK more than 90% of the market is supplied by no more than three or four firms.

CHARACTERISTICS

As noted above, this market structure is characterised by a high degree of industrial concentration. The good or service produced may be very similar and indeed may be homogeneous. Examples include cement and sugar. In this case the market structure may be referred to as perfect oligopoly. More commonly the products are differentiated (e.g. cars, newspapers) and this can be referred to as imperfect oligopoly.

There are barriers to entry. One of the most significant of them is the large scale on which the dominant firms are producing and the resulting economies of scale which they are able to enjoy. Indeed the industry is likely to be a high-technology industry with significant indivisible costs and with the long-run average cost curve falling over a large range of output.

The firms in this market structure are capable of earning supernormal profits in the long run. However, in practice, profits may not always be as high as possible. Firms may engage in limit pricing, i.e. setting prices below the maximum profit level in order to discourage the entry of new firms into the industry or predatory pricing which is setting prices very low in order to drive competitors out of the market.

Prices are likely to be *sticky*, meaning that, in theory at least, they are unlikely to change very often, sometimes even when demand and costs change.

Although the industry may contain hundreds of firms, as has been stated, it will be dominated by a few large firms. These firms will be interdependent. They will know a considerable amount about each other and will be influenced by expectations about how the other firms will react. Indeed firms may engage in open or tacit collusion.

Economists have found it difficult to predict the behaviour of firms in oligopolistic markets. What is reasonably certain is that there will be a considerable amount of non-price competition.

NON-PRICE COMPETITION

Firms may use non-price competition either because they have agreed not to compete by means of price (collusion) or because they are afraid they will lose out in a price war.

Non-price competition can take many forms. These include the use of brand names, distinctive packaging, free gifts, special features to the products, and competitions. In perfect oligopoly competition based on research

NAME: DeAnne Julius
Member of the Monetary Policy Committee

BORN: 1949

NATIONALITY: American

EDUCATED: Iowa State University, University of California

KEY POSTS HELD: CIA analyst
Economist at the World Bank
Director of the international economics programme at the Royal Institute of International Affairs
Chief economist at Royal Dutch Shell
Chief economist at British Airways and deputy strategy director and chairman of the company's pension fund

QUOTE ON DEANNE JULIUS:
'… *one of her chief skills is the ability to make technical economic data and theories relevant to business, and easily understandable by all audiences.*' The Guardian 7/6/97

and development, free delivery, after-sales services and guarantees are common. Whereas in imperfect oligopoly the most important form of non-price competition is usually advertising.

COLLUSION

Firms may engage in open collusion in order to maximise their joint profits and to reduce uncertainty. Collusion may take the form of agreeing on the price to charge, the market share the firms are going to have and/or the advertising expenditure each firm is going to undertake.

Firms are more likely to agree not to compete on price where the product is fairly standardised. The agreed price is normally well above the average costs of the more efficient firms since, in order to persuade enough firms to join the scheme to make it operational, the price must be high enough to provide profits for the less efficient. In order to make the price effective, a price agreement is usually supported by a complementary agreement to limit output (e.g. firms agree to accept output quotas).

One form of open collusion is the cartel. This includes firms producing separately but acting as one firm in determining output and price. Figure 43.1 shows the position of the industry in which firms are operating as a cartel.

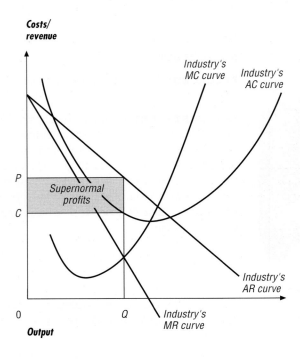

FIG. 43.1

TACIT COLLUSION

Firms may also reduce price competition and thereby increase price stability by:

- following a dominant firm's price lead, i.e. moving their prices in line with that firm's prices
- following a barometric firm's price lead. A barometric firm is a firm which seems to be sensitive to changing market conditions.
- using average cost pricing. This involves mark-up pricing, i.e., estimating long-run average costs and then adding a percentage for profits to find price. Firms producing under conditions of oligopoly, may set this price fairly low in order to ensure that they can sell a large output and thereby spread the costs of using their indivisible capital equipment over a high number of units.

FACTORS FAVOURING COLLUSION

There are a number of circumstances which would make collusion more likely to be successful. These include a stable market with firms having similar production methods, costs and objectives. Firms should know a lot about each other, be able to estimate their own costs and revenue reasonably accurately and be willing to share information. The number of dominant firms should be small, for instance, four rather than nine. There should also be significant barriers to entry so that firms would not be afraid that their arrangements would be disrupted by the entry of new firms.

REASONS FOR COLLUSION BREAKING DOWN

In most cases collusion does not last. There are a number of reasons for this. Firms are likely to have different costs and so each will want to set a price that is more beneficial to them than to others. Overtime market conditions will change, meaning that agreements will have to be renegotiated, which may not prove to be easy. Collusion agreements are also difficult to monitor and if known about, are likely to prove unpopular with consumers. Collusion is also likely to be illegal and if it is, the firms will risk investigation and possible penalties. However, the most common reason for collusion breaking down is that some firms try to capture a larger share of the market by cheating on the agreement.

NON-COLLUSIVE BEHAVIOUR

Firms which do not collude will have to consider carefully other firms' reactions before changing their price, product range or advertising strategy. They may be reluctant to change their price, in particular, for fear of how rival firms will react. The kinked demand curve as shown in Figure 43.2 seeks to describe these circumstances.

The price is P and output Q. The demand curve is kinked at G. At prices higher than P, demand is very elastic. The explanation is that the oligopolist fears that if his prices are raised, competitors will not follow suit and a large part of his market will be lost. At prices lower than P, demand is more inelastic because the oligopolist believes that if he cuts his price his rivals will follow suit and he will gain relatively little in the way of additional sales.

It is widely thought that oligopolists are not very keen to indulge in severe price competition. They know that any move on the part of one firm to reduce its price will provoke similar action from the other firms. The final

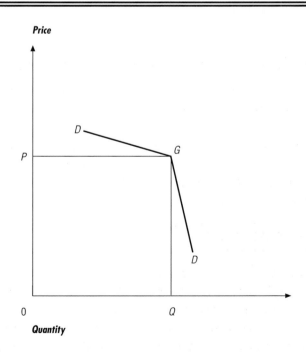

FIG. 43.2

result is likely to be that all the firms will finish up selling at lower prices while their market shares remain much the same as before the price war.

However a firm may be prepared to undertake this potentially high risk strategy if it believes that its costs are lower than its rivals, if it has reserves it can draw on or if it can subsidy this company from profits being earned from other companies it owns.

A price war broke out in the newspaper industry in the UK in 1993–94. *The Times* and the *Sun* both succeeded in increasing their market shares by lowering their prices.

GAME THEORY

In seeking to explain the behaviour of oligopolistic firms' behaviour economists often make use of game theory. This suggests that firms, concerned about how their rivals will react, often opt for the second-best strategy. So, as mentioned above, firms may be reluctant to change their prices.

This tendency to opt for the second-best, but relatively safe strategy, is frequently illustrated by means of the 'prisoner's dilemma'. Two people are arrested for robbery and held separately. Each is told that if he confesses and implicates his partner he will receive a sentence of three years. However, if the prisoner does not confess but is found guilty on the evidence of his partner he will receive a sentence of ten years. The best outcome for each prisoner is for neither to confess and both to be released. However, each is likely to be afraid to take the risk that the other one will not confess. So the second-best option of confessing is likely to be taken.

QUESTIONS

SHORT QUESTIONS

1 Distinguish between perfect and imperfect oligopoly.

2 Explain the significance of game theory in analysing the behaviour of oligopolistic firms.

3 Giving examples, describe four forms of non-price competition in which firms may engage.

4 Explain what is meant by a price war.

MULTIPLE CHOICE

1 Which of the following may be found in oligopoly but not monopolistic competition?

A Advertising.

B Collusion.

C Excess capacity.

D Product differentiation.

2 The kinked demand curve suggests that firms operating in oligopolistic markets will:

A sell their products in more than one market

B follow price cuts initiated by rival firms but not price rises

C have a downward sloping average revenue curve but a horizontal marginal revenue curve

D face inelastic demand above and elastic demand below the current market price.

3 What is a cartel?

A A group of producers who agree to fix common prices and output quotas in an oligopolistic market.

B A market structure in which there are a few very dominant producers but many buyers.

C A group of firms in the same industry and located in the same area.

D A firm which has plants in more than one country.

4 Why may an oligopolistic firm be reluctant to reduce its price on its own initiative?

A It may encourage the entry of new firms into the industry.

B Other firms in the industry may decide to leave their prices unchanged.

C It may lead to price reductions on the part of rival firms.

D Its demand curve is perfectly inelastic below the current price.

DATA RESPONSE

There are three main companies selling cars in the UK market. These are Ford, with 19% of total car sales, Vauxhall with some 14% and BMW (including Rover) with 13%.

These companies compete in a number of ways. One is by spending large amounts on advertisements which appear on television and in newspapers. Other methods include interest free credit, special features such as air bags, and guarantees.

The industry has come in for much criticism for what are perceived to be the high prices the firms charge UK consumers for new cars. It has been estimated that people in the UK pay 60% more for new cars than in other European Union countries.

One reason for the price differential is that demand for new cars in the UK is more inelastic than in the rest of the EU. A higher proportion of new cars in the UK are sold to companies as company cars (the fleet market) and public transport is not perceived as close a substitute as it is in the rest of the EU.

However things may change in the future as the industry comes under closer investigation by the Monopolies and Mergers Commission and as the limit on the sale of Japanese cars in the UK market is lifted.

a] What evidence is there in the passage that the UK car industry operates under conditions of oligopoly? **(6)**

b] Why may companies' demand for cars be more inelastic than individuals' demand? **(6)**

c] What does the passage suggest about the nature of the cross elasticity of demand between changes in the price of cars and demand for public transport in the UK? Illustrate your answer with a diagram. **(5)**

d] What effect may the lifting of the limit on Japanese cars coming into the UK have on the structure of the UK car market? **(5)**

e] Discuss two forms of non-price competition used by car manufacturers not mentioned in the passage. **(4)**

CASE STUDY

The UK newspaper industry is an example of an oligopolistic market. It has seven publishers who produce ten daily and nine Sunday titles. Even with this small number, the four largest publishers, News International, the Mirror Group, Express Newspapers and Associated Newspapers sell nearly 90% of all daily papers. The publishers differentiate their products in a number of ways, including large scale advertising, competitions, content and style. There are significant barriers to entry particularly in the form of economies of scale.

The newspaper market can be divided into the daily and Sunday paper markets or more commonly into the broadsheet (quality) and tabloid (popular) markets. Some analysts identify a third group by separating out from the tabloid market the *Daily Mail* and the *Daily Express* to form a mid market.

Newspapers have two sources of income, the revenue gained by selling papers and advertising revenue. The broadsheets receive approximately 58% of their total revenue from advertising revenue whereas the tabloids receive 36% from advertising revenue.

If a publisher reduces the price of a newspaper its circulation revenue is likely to fall as demand for newspapers is inelastic. However, its advertising revenue may rise as a larger circulation may attract more advertising.

In August 1993 News International cut the price of the Sun by 20% from 25p to 20p. A month later it cut the price of *The Times* by 33% from 45p to 30p. The rival titles responded by increasing non-price competition and in 1994 the *Telegraph* and the *Independent* cut their prices. In response *The Times* cut its price further.

Before 1993 newspaper readership had been falling. However it was thought that News International (publishers of the *Sun* and *The Times* among other titles) was pursuing an aggressive rather than a defensive policy. With the financial support of its parent company, the global media empire News Corporation, News International was able to bear a cut in its profits in the short run in the hope of longer run increases.

a] Identify:
   i two forms of non-price competition not mentioned in the passage **(2)**
   ii two other oligopolistic industries, explaining why you consider them to be so. **(6)**

b] Why do you think broadsheet newspapers are more able to attract advertising revenue than tabloid newspapers? **(6)**

c] What effect may a rise in the price of a newspaper have on its publisher's revenue? **(5)**

d] Why is demand inelastic for:
   i newspapers in general? **(3)**
   ii a particular newspaper? **(3)**

e] Which would have the more inelastic demand — newspapers in general or a particular newspaper? Explain your answer. **(3)**

f] What could cause a fall in demand for newspapers? **(6)**

g] Why might cutting price in an oligopolistic market be considered to be a high risk strategy for publishers? **(8)**

h] Discuss whether consumers are likely to benefit from a publisher cutting its prices? **(8)**

STRUCTURED ESSAY

a] Explain what is meant by oligopoly. **(5)**

b] Discuss the strategies an oligopolistic firm might take:
   i to maintain its market share **(10)**
   ii to increase its market share. **(10)**

FREE RESPONSE ESSAY

Discuss whether competition in oligopolistic markets benefits consumers. **(25)**

44 MONOPOLY

DEFINITION

There are two definitions of monopoly. A pure monopoly exists when there is a sole supplier. In this case the firm will be the industry. An example is the Bank of England which is the only supplier of bank notes in England and Wales.

The government definition is a firm which has a 25% or greater share of the market. For example in 1999 Cadbury's controlled 32% of the UK chocolate market and the *Sun* newspaper 30% of the national daily papers market and 56.2% of the UK tabloid paper market.

However, market share alone is not always a good guide to monopoly power. A firm supplying a quarter of the total market may have greater market power if the rest of the market is shared by numerous firms. Whereas it may face very fierce competition if the rest of the market is supplied by three firms of almost equal size.

Reference is also often made to natural monopolies. A natural monopoly occurs when there is room for only one firm in the industry producing at the minimum efficient scale. The situation can arise when there is just one source of supply of a raw material. However more commonly it occurs when economies of scale are very significant and so permit only one firm to supply the entire market at a lower price than any other number of firms.

MONOPOLY POWER

A monopolist has the power to determine either:

• the price at which s/he will sell the product or
• the quantity s/he wishes to sell.

S/he cannot determine both price and quantity, because s/he cannot control demand. If s/he decides on the price at which s/he is prepared to sell, the demand curve will determine the quantity s/he can sell at the chosen price. Whereas if s/he wishes to sell a given quantity per month, then the demand curve will determine the price at which this quantity may be sold.

The monopolist's power to influence price and to earn supernormal profit (which in this case can be referred to as monopoly profits) depends upon two crucial factors:

• the availability of close substitutes
• the power to restrict the entry of new firms.

These two features are closely related because the greater a monopolist's ability to prevent the entry of new firms, the fewer direct substitutes it will have.

In the case of a pure monopoly there will be no direct substitutes. However in the case of the government's definition there will be substitutes. If their prices and qualities compare favourably with that of the monopolist, his/her market power will be very limited.

The ability to earn long-run supernormal profits will only be possible if there are effective barriers to the entry and exit of new firms into and out of the industry. The more effective the restrictions, the greater will be the power of the monopolist to charge consumers a price above average variable cost.

BARRIERS TO ENTRY

There are a number of possible restrictions on the entry of new firms. These are also referred to as the sources of monopoly power. This is because they explain why a firm can have a dominant or sole position in the industry.

OWNERSHIP OF NATURAL RESOURCES

Some natural resources are concentrated into small regions. For example, a large proportion of the total world supply of gold and diamonds comes from South Africa. Peculiarities of soil and climatic conditions can also provide certain regions with monopoly powers. For example, the wines of champagne, burgundy and moselle are associated with the areas where they are produced.

OWNERSHIP OF OUTLETS

If a firm owns the retail outlets for a product it can enjoy monopoly power. For example in some areas, certain petrol companies own a significant proportion of the garages selling petrol.

ECONOMIES OF SCALE

Economies of scale are an important and common barrier to entry. Indeed in the case of a natural monopoly, for example the provision of rail track, technical economies of scale are so significant that the industry can only support one firm. In industries where economies of scale are significant there may be little prospect of a firm being able to enter the market. The firm could not compete with the existing firm or firms because its average cost of production would be so much greater. Only by starting on a scale comparable to that employed by the existing firm or firms would a new entrant be able to compete effectively. However even this would be risky unless the market had a very large growth potential, because the large increase in supply would reduce market prices.

LEGAL BARRIERS

Acts of Parliament can grant monopoly power to nationalised industries and public corporations. As mentioned already, the Bank of England has been granted the sole right to issue bank notes in England and Wales.

Patents also limit competition. The firm holding the patent is protected from the threat of competition from new (or existing) firms making identical products for the life of the patent, which is usually sixteen years.

TRANSPORT COSTS

High transport costs can create local and national monopolies. For example shops in villages and suburbs are sometimes able to charge a little more than the larger shops in city centres because they have some degree of protection in the form of transport costs (e.g. bus fares).

High transport costs may also provide a domestic firm with protection from foreign rivals.

TARIFFS

Tariffs protect domestic producers from foreign competition. They have the same effect as transport costs, for they raise the price in the home market above the foreign producers' costs of production.

RESTRICTIVE PRACTICES

Although in most countries most restrictive practices are illegal, agreements between firms to restrict competition in an industry have been an important means of establishing monopoly situations.

There are many ways in which the existing firms in an industry can combine to prevent the entry of new firms. These include forming cartels and withholding supplies from any wholesaler or retailer who stocks the goods of any new producer.

MERGERS

Mergers increase the size of firms. This directly reduces competition, increases the market share of the new company, may increase economies of scale and may make it more difficult for new firms to enter the market.

BARRIERS TO EXIT

Firms will also be discouraged from entering an industry if they believe that, should market conditions change, it would be difficult to leave it.

The two key barriers to exit are probably *sunk costs* and *long term contracts*. Sunk costs involve expenditure which cannot be recouped should the firm leave the industry. For example, if a firm decides to leave the coal mining industry it may not be able to get back the money it has spent on drilling and excavation if they are not able to sell the company when they need to. Indeed most of its capital equipment is specific to the needs of the industry and cannot be used in other industries which will make it difficult or impossible to sell if the industry is declining. Money spent on advertising campaigns also cannot be recouped.

The existence of long term contracts to supply a product may also discourage firms from seeking to enter an industry.

COST AND REVENUE CURVES

Since a pure monopolist is a sole supplier the demand curve for its product is the total demand curve. The cost and revenue curves are illustrated in Figure 44.1.

The monopolist is producing at its maximum profit output (*MC* = *MR*) and is enjoying supernormal profits of *PABC*. Supernormal profits earned under conditions of monopoly may also be referred to as monopoly profits. These supernormal profits or monopoly profits can continue in the long run because of the existence of barriers to entry and exit.

OTHER POSSIBLE OUTPUT POSITIONS

In addition to profit maximisation there are a number of other possible objectives a monopolist may follow.

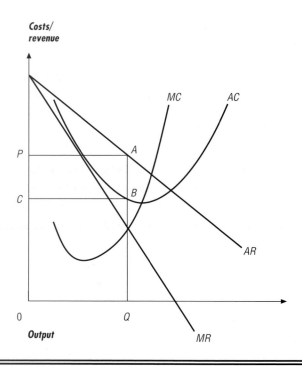

FIG. 44.1

SALES REVENUE MAXIMISATION

The directors of a firm may seek to maximise sales revenue. Their motives may be to increase their salaries and to make it more difficult for another firm to take over the company.

Sales revenue maximisation is achieved where marginal revenue is zero since this is where total revenue is at its peak. Figure 44.2 illustrates the sales revenue maximisation output.

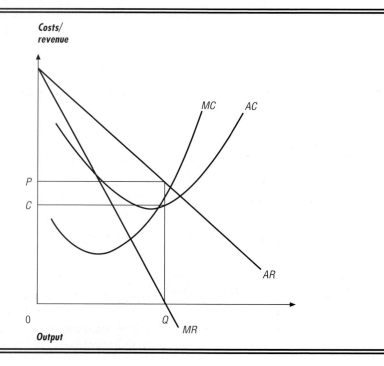

FIG. 44.2

NORMAL PROFIT OUTPUT

State monopolies may be instructed to break even (i.e. to make only normal profits). This is achieved where average cost equals average revenue. It is illustrated in Figure 44.3.

PRODUCTIVELY EFFICIENT OUTPUT

This can also be called optimum output. Again a state owned monopoly may be told to produce at the minimum average cost output. This is achieved where marginal cost equals average cost and is illustrated in Figure 44.4.

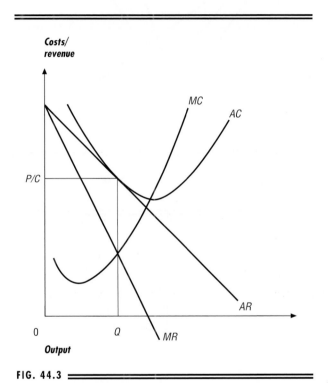

FIG. 44.3

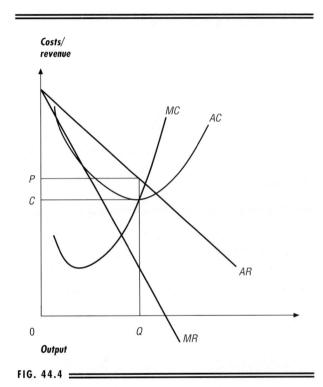

FIG. 44.4

ALLOCATIVELY EFFICIENT OUTPUT

This can also be referred to as the socially optimum output. It occurs where price (average revenue) is equal to marginal cost and is shown in Figure 44.5.

PREDATORY PRICING AND LIMIT PRICING OUTPUTS

A monopolist may, in the short run, set price not with the aim of earning maximum profit but with the aim of reducing competition. In the case of an oligopolist or a monopolist with 25% or more share of the market this may be actual competition. The firm may set price relatively low in order to drive out competitors. This is called predatory pricing. In the cases of pure monopoly, a monopoly without a 100% share and an oligopolist, price may be set with the aim of discouraging potential rivals from entering the market. This is called limit pricing.

Figure 44.6 shows a firm setting the price above the normal profit level but below the maximum profit level.

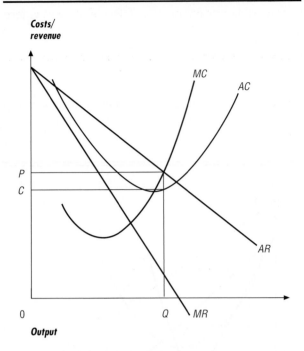

FIG. 44.5

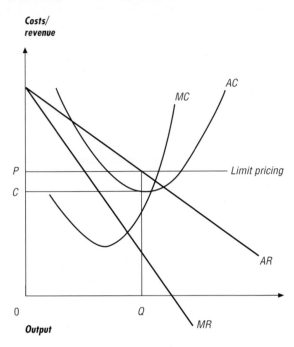

FIG. 44.6

PRICE DISCRIMINATION

Price discrimination occurs when a firm charges different prices to different consumers for the same good. The motive is to increase profit by reducing consumer surplus. If the same price is charged to all consumers, some potential revenue is lost since some of the consumers would have been prepared to pay more.

DEGREES OF PRICE DISCRIMINATION

The highest degree of price discrimination occurs when a firm charges each consumer the maximum price he/she is prepared to pay. Second degree price discrimination is when a different price is charged per unit according to how many units are purchased. For example, three bars of chocolate in one packet may be sold at a price which is lower than the price of three individual bars.

However it is third degree price discrimination which is the most common. This involves charging different prices to different groups of consumers who are separated into different markets.

CONDITIONS NECESSARY FOR PRICE DISCRIMINATION

There are three conditions needed for a firm to be able to charge different prices for the same good:

● the firm must be a price maker
● the elasticity of demand must be different in the different markets. If it was the same in all the markets the profit maximising price would also be the same and there would be no incentive to engage in price

discrimination. Where the elasticity does differ, the higher prices will be charged in the markets where demand is less elastic.

The firm will produce where the *MR* values in the individual markets are equal to the *MC* of producing the output as shown in Figure 44.7(a) and (b).

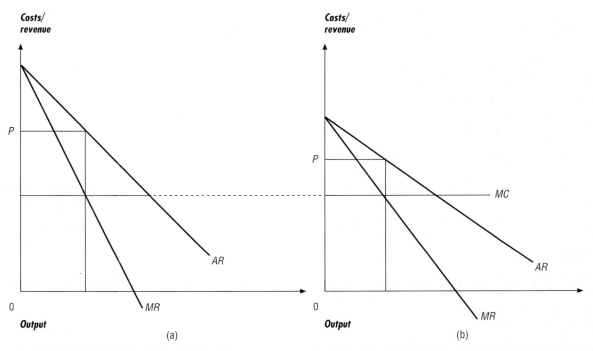

FIG. 44.7

- the markets must be clearly separated so that those paying lower prices cannot resell to those paying higher prices.

SEPARATION OF MARKETS

There are a number of ways in which markets can be separated. One is by a time barrier. Most passenger transport firms charge cheaper rates for off-peak journeys.

Markets can also be separated by geographical distance. Transport costs and, in the case of foreign markets, perhaps also tariffs may keep them apart. The price differential, of course, cannot exceed the cost of transporting the good back to the home market plus any tariff imposed.

It is also possible to separate buyers on the basis of age, gender, income and type. For example electricity may be sold at a lower price to industrial and commercial users than to domestic households.

EFFECTS OF PRICE DISCRIMINATION

Price discrimination means that some groups are charged higher prices than others. This may be regarded as an 'unfair' practice. It may also be used to drive out competitors by charging a low price in the markets where it faces more competition.

However, there are some possible benefits which may be gained from price discrimination. It may enable those who are charged the lower prices, to buy goods they could not otherwise afford. In addition, where price discrimination results in an expansion of sales and output and a fall in average costs of production, even those in the higher priced market may be obtaining goods at lower prices than they would be charged in a single market. For example, a large export market (gained by selling at prices lower than the home price) may lead to economies of scale which benefit home consumers even though the home price is higher than the export price.

ADVANTAGES AND DISADVANTAGES OF MONOPOLY

Monopoly has come in for some considerable criticism. The case against it is based on the assumptions that it results in higher prices, supernormal profits, inefficiency and a slower rate of technical progress.

However there are defenders of monopoly who argue that it can result in lower costs, lower prices and a more rapid rate of technical progress.

ADVANTAGES OF MONOPOLY

In the case of a natural monopoly where large-scale capital is required, average and marginal costs can fall significantly if the output is produced by one firm. Even in the case of monopolies which are not natural monopolies significant advantage may still be taken of economies of scale. The lower average costs may result in price being lower than under other forms of market structure. This may give the firms a competitive advantage in overseas markets and increase exports.

Having the whole or a large share of the market may encourage firms to undertake large-scale investment and research and investment. This is because they are likely to have the finance to do so and the ability to protect the gains derived from any ideas/projects developed.

Some economists argue that innovations are more likely to occur under conditions of monopoly. This is because existing firms may bring new techniques and products into use to strengthen their barriers to entry and because firms outside the industry will try to innovate to get round the barriers to entry. An Austrian economist, Schumpeter, developed the creative destruction theory. This argues that one monopoly will replace another one by developing a better product in order to overcome the barriers to entry.

Another argument sometimes advanced in favour of monopoly is that it provides some stability of output and prices. The monopolist will know the market well and should be capable of estimating the market trends and have the confidence to make long term plans.

DISADVANTAGES OF MONOPOLY

Critics say that monopolists will use their market power to restrict supply and thereby drive price above cost. Consumers may suffer from prices being higher and output lower than the allocatively efficient levels.

The lack of competition may also mean that monopolies may not feel the need to seek to lower costs, innovate and improve the quality of the product. Market power is likely to lead to supernormal profits, with or without innovation.

Monopolies are also accused of delaying technical progress by restricting the entry of new firms. Entrepreneurs with fresh ideas may be excluded from the market.

In addition, under conditions of monopoly, whilst there may be a range of products on offer there will be a lack of, or restricted, choice of producers.

The producers will be in a stronger position than consumers with consumer surplus likely to be low. Indeed consumer surplus is likely to be less under monopoly than under any other market structure.

QUESTIONS

SHORT QUESTIONS

1. A discriminating monopolist may separate markets on the basis of, for example, age. Explain two other bases for separating markets.

2. Who gains and who loses from price discrimination?

3. How, and why, do the total revenue curves of firms producing under monopoly and perfect competition differ?

4. Under what conditions will firms produce at minimum average cost?

MULTIPLE CHOICE

1. A monopolist firm decides to maximise profits by engaging in price discrimination. It sells its output in two separate markets, Y and Z. Figure 44.8 below shows the average revenue and marginal revenue curves for the good in the two separate markets.

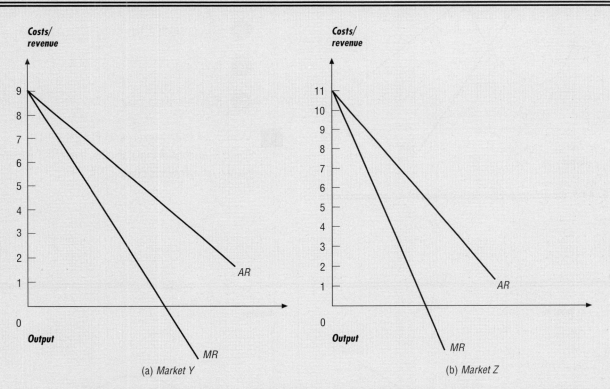

FIG. 44.8

(a) Market Y

(b) Market Z

The marginal cost of production is £5. Which set of prices would maximise the monopolist's profits?

	Price in market Y (£)	Price in market Z (£)
A	4	3
B	5	4
C	6	6
D	7	8

2 Figure 44.9 below shows the cost and revenue curves of a monopolist.

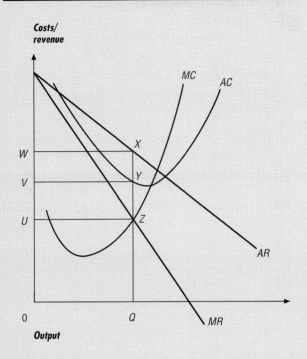

Costs/revenue

MC
AC

W
V
U

X
Y
Z

0
Q
Output

AR
MR

FIG. 44.9

To maximise profits the firm produces an output of Q. Which area includes the normal profit earned by the firm.

A 0UZQ

B UVYZ

C VWXY

D 0VYQ

3 A monopolist's marginal revenue is negative. What does this indicate about its price elasticity of demand?

A It is infinity.

B It is greater than one.

C It is one.

D It is less than one.

4 Which of the diagrams in Figure 44.10 (below and overleaf) shows the total revenue curve of a monopolist?

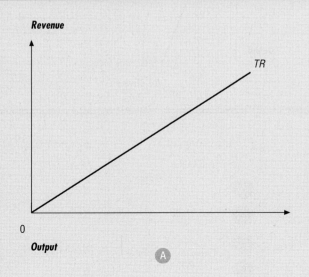

Revenue

TR

0
Output

A

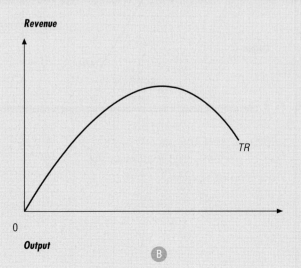

Revenue

TR

0
Output

B

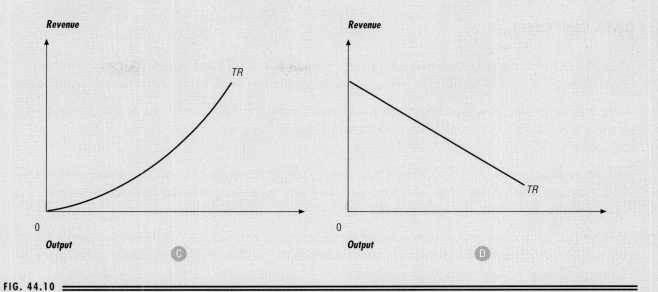

FIG. 44.10

DATA RESPONSE

The Post Office yesterday warned the government that it would put at risk Britain's universal mail delivery service at a uniform price if it ordered further costs in the corporation's monopoly.

The warning came as senior Post Office executives voiced growing concern at the threats to the corporation's business posed by last week's white paper, designed to give it greater commercial freedom.

Ministers plan to cut the Post Office's monopoly over letters from £1, or 350 grammes, to 50p or 150 grammes, from April 2000 and have said they will urge the proposed new regulator to consider a further reduction as a priority task.

Post Office executives and unions lobbied fiercely against the reduced monopoly, arguing that a universal system allowing letters from, say, Lewisham in London to be sent for the same price to Lambeth, Leeds and Lerwick depended on it.

Yesterday, unveiling an 8.4% cut in pre-tax profits last year to £608m because of increased competition, Post Office Chief Executive John Roberts urged the government to stay its hand over deeper cuts in the monopoly until the new European Commission came up with fresh proposals to liberalise the European Union market.

The white paper proposal will, according to the Post Office, reduce its annual earnings by about £100m.

Source: 'Post Office delivers prices warning' by David Gow, the Guardian, 15/7/99.

a] What is the source of the Post Office's monopoly? **(4)**

b] Discuss two advantages consumers may gain from a state run monopoly. **(6)**

c] What effect did increased competition have on the Post Office's profits? **(2)**

d] Why do monopolies tend to earn high profits? **(6)**

e] What benefits may consumers gain from more competition in the mail delivery service? **(7)**

CASE STUDY

'Always Coca-Cola' is the advertising slogan for the drink that symbolises the American way of life — and it seems to be a message with its own meaning for the European Union's competition authorities.

Ten times in the last decade, they have clashed with the Atlanta-based company that makes the world's favourite soft drink over its marketing practices in individual member states. Now the European Commission, the EU's Brussels-based executive, has launched an investigation covering three EU countries that looks likely to raise some fundamental questions about Coke's business tactics.

With about half the EU soft drinks market for brands such as Sprite and Fanta as well as its trademark cola, Coke is a natural target for regulators. But the relish with which some exercise their prerogatives seems to reflect a desire to cut the owner of the world's favourite brand down to size.

Karel Van Miert, the EU competition watchdog, caught the flavour in May when he warned the US group it faced fines for not seeking clearance from Brussels for its proposed acquisition of the Cadbury Schweppes soft drinks business.

Much of Coca-Cola's phenomenal growth in the last two decades has come from placing its products within 'an arm's length of desire', with Coke chill-cabinets in convenience stores, vending machines in public places, premium positioning in supermarkets and drink dispensers, or 'fountains' in fast-food outlets.

Many of these are practices regulators instinctively dislike because they have the effect of excluding competitors from prime marketing positions. The authorities in many European countries and in Brussels, for example, have attacked the provision of exclusive ice-cream freezer cabinets in convenience stores as anti-competitive since most of the shops are too small for more than one.

In 1989, The European Commission extracted undertakings from Coca-Cola after an investigation into its alleged abuse of its dominant position in Italy.

Despite these undertakings, other regulators have since raised similar issues in connection with Coke's activities in France, Denmark and the UK. And the Italian authorities opened a new case against Coca-Cola last year after complaints from PepsiCo, the world's second largest soft drinks maker, and Esselunga, an Italian supermarket chain.

According to the country's competition authority, Pepsi alleged that Coca-Cola had signed contracts with wholesalers and retailers that discouraged them from stocking other cola products by means of end-of-year bonuses and loyalty agreements.

The complaint made by Esselunga alleged that Coca-Cola required contracts which required them to display the group's products prominently on shelves.

CARBONATED SOFT DRINK MARKET SHARE			
COUNTRY		% SHARE	
	COCA-COLA	PEPSICO	CADBURY SCHWEPPES
Denmark	42.8	9.0	2.2
France	55.0	6.8	5.3
Greece	72.7	25.9	0.1
Ireland	36.8	20.0	1.8
Italy	44.9	6.2	1.0
Portugal	24.3	16.8	0.7
UK	33.7	12.5	7.5

Source: 'Coca-Cola's style offends European regulators' taste' by John Willman and James Blitz, Financial Times, 22/7/99.

a] In what sense is Coca-Cola a monopoly in the EU? **(4)**

b] In which country, shown in the table, is Coca-Cola not a monopoly? **(4)**

c] Discuss the possible advantages and disadvantages to consumers of Coca-Cola purchasing Cadbury Schweppes. **(10)**

d] According to the article what has been the main cause of Coca-Cola's growth in recent years? **(8)**

e] Explain what makes it difficult for new firms to enter the carbonated soft drinks market. **(6)**

f] How might PepsiCo gain a larger market share? **(6)**

g] Why does Coca-Cola produce a variety of soft drinks? **(6)**

h] Discuss two 'abuses' of monopoly power not mentioned in the article. **(6)**

STRUCTURED ESSAY

a] Explain what is meant by barriers to entry into an industry. **(8)**

b] Discuss, given the existence of barriers of entry, monopolists are likely to seek to improve the quality of the products they produce. **(17)**

FREE RESPONSE ESSAY

Assess whether perfectly competitive markets are always more efficient than monopoly markets. **(25)**

There are differences in the characteristics of different market structures and the ways in which firms behave and perform in these different market structures.

CHARACTERISTICS

LEVEL OF COMPETITION

This is the key defining characteristic from which the others follow. The highest level of competition exists in perfectly competitive industries where there are many firms competing. The lowest is in pure monopoly where one firm has no direct competitors.

NUMBER OF FIRMS

There are many firms operating in a perfectly competitive market. There are not so many firms in monopolistic competition but the number will still be large and the firms will be of a similar size. In oligopoly there may be any number from a few to a relatively large number. What distinguishes oligopoly is that the market is dominated by a few firms. The UK government defines a monopoly as up to four firms. However, in the case of a pure monopoly there can, of course, only be one firm. The industrial concentration ratio measures the extent to which an industry is dominated by a few firms. It shows the percentage of total sales, output or employment accounted for by the largest firm or firms. For example, in an oligopolistic industry there may be a three firm concentration ratio of 85% in terms of sales. It is obviously very high in monopoly (100% in a pure monopoly) and low in perfect competition.

TYPES OF PRODUCTS

Under conditions of perfect competition the product is homogeneous. It is differentiated under conditions of monopolistic competition. In the case of oligopoly and monopoly, in terms of the government definition, the product may be homogeneous (e.g. salt, cement and sugar) or, more commonly, differentiated (e.g. airlines, newspapers, TV companies and banks). In a pure monopoly the product is exclusive to that market.

AN INDIVIDUAL FIRM'S INFLUENCE ON PRICE

Firms in perfect competition are price takers ($AR = MR$). The change in the output of one firm is too insignificant to affect price. In all other market structures, firms are price makers ($AR > MR$). The output of the individual firms influences price. To sell more a firm has to lower its price.

ELASTICITY OF DEMAND FOR THE PRODUCT

The demand for the product becomes more inelastic the more market power a producer has. Demand for the product of a perfectly competitive firm will be perfectly elastic since the consumer will be willing and able to switch to rival producers should the price rise. Whilst a pure monopolist will be likely to be able to raise the price of the product and retain a high proportion of consumers.

BARRIERS TO ENTRY AND EXIT

There are no barriers to entry and exit in perfect competition and no, or in practice low, barriers to entry and exit in monopolistic competition. In these two market structures capital expenditure is low and firms wishing to enter the industry can set up easily. These firms may have previously been producing another product or they may be newly established firms. Entrepreneurs will be encouraged to enter the industry by the knowledge that there are no barriers to exit in the form of, for example, heavy advertising expenditure, and other sunk costs.

In contrast there are usually barriers to entry and exit in both oligopoly and monopoly. The most common barrier is the high cost of capital expenditure required to compete with the dominant firms who will be operating on a large scale. There may also be barriers to exit. For instance, government regulation requires the Post Office to deliver mail to remote rural areas and the sunk costs involved in coal-mining may make it difficult for a private sector firm to leave the industry.

CONSUMER SOVEREIGNTY

In perfect competition consumers are assumed to be fully informed and have considerable power (*consumer sovereignty*). If they want more of a product, existing and new producers will respond quickly and allocate a sufficient quantity of resources to the output of the product to satisfy consumers' needs. The fewer the number of dominant firms in the market the less power and influence consumers have and the more power and influence the producers have.

CHOICE

In perfect competition consumers have a choice of producers but the product produced is homogeneous. In monopolistic competition and oligopoly there is a choice of producers and differentiated products. In a pure monopoly there is no choice of producer but the firm may produce a range of differentiated products.

BEHAVIOUR

TYPE OF COMPETITION

In conditions of perfect competition, firms are constantly seeking to gain a competitive advantage over their rivals. However, as competition is fierce the best most firms can usually hope for is to match their rivals' quality and production methods. This high level of competition between equally matched firms has sometimes been compared with top quality athletes all trying to inch ahead of their fellow competitors.

Firms in monopolistic competition and oligopoly engage in non-price competition as well as, on occasions, price competition. Non-price competition, including advertising, free gifts, building up the strength of brand names, competitions and packaging, is a particular feature of oligopoly. Oligopolistic firms may seek to avoid price competition for fear of provoking a price war, although price wars do break out every so often.

INNOVATION

As previously mentioned there is a debate about which form of market structure is most likely to innovate, that is to introduce new products and new production techniques. The monopolist, it is argued, has little incentive to innovate. If s/he does not innovate, his/her control of the market means that s/he can still make profits. The competitive firm, however, may fear that if it does not innovate it will lose its market share to its competitors who will take advantage of new developments.

On the other hand, there is support for the view that the existence of monopoly can encourage technological progress. Firms in monopolistic (and oligopolistic) markets are more likely to have the resources required for research and development than a small firm in a competitive market. In addition the monopolist has more incentive to innovate since his/her secure market ensures that s/he obtains all the gains from any successful new technique or product. S/he can, moreover, retain these gains over the long run. Under conditions of perfect competition any innovation will soon be copied and the gains to the innovator will be short-lived. The existence of a monopoly may also encourage outside firms to develop new methods and new products in order to overcome barriers to enter into the industry.

COLLUSION

Collusion is a particular feature of an oligopolistic market. Oligopolistic firms may collude in order to reduce uncertainty and increase profits. In monopolistic competition there are too many firms to collude, in pure monopoly there are no other firms to collude with and in perfect competition firms act independently.

LIMIT PRICING

Limit pricing is setting price with the aim of discouraging the entry of new firms into the market. This strategy can occur under conditions of oligopoly or monopoly.

PREDATORY PRICING

This is a more aggressive strategy as it involves setting price at a level designed to drive rivals out of the market. Oligopolistic firms and firms producing under conditions of monopoly, as defined by the government, may engage in predatory pricing.

PROFIT SATISFICING

Profit satisficing involves firms aiming for a satisfactory level, one which will keep shareholders happy, rather than maximum profits. This may enable the firms to follow other objectives. Profit satisficing may occur in circumstances where firms are price makers, i.e. in monopolistic competition, oligopoly and monopoly.

OTHER OBJECTIVES

In addition to profit satisficing, limit and predatory pricing, oligopolies and monopolies may pursue other objectives. These include sales revenue maximisation, growth, survival and, according to behavioural theories, multiple objectives.

PERFORMANCE

PRICE LEVELS

Price levels may be low under conditions of perfect competition because of the force of competition. It might be expected that prices will be higher under oligopoly and monopoly because of the lower level of competition. This may indeed be the case since firms will be able to set price above average cost. However, if economies of scale are significant, the firms' average costs will be lower and, even with a gap between average revenue and average cost prices, may be lower. This is particularly likely to be so in the case of a natural monopoly.

PROFIT LEVELS

The existence of barriers to entry means that firms producing under conditions of oligopoly and monopoly can earn supernormal profits in the long run. Figure 45.1 shows a monopoly producing where $MC = MR$ and $AR > AC$.

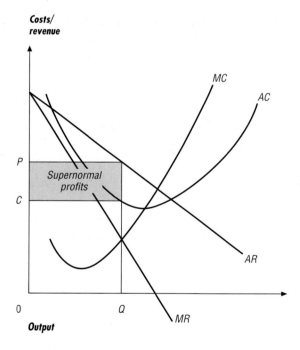

FIG. 45.1

The absence of barriers to entry, in contrast, means that firms producing under conditions of perfect competition and monopolistic competition, can earn supernormal profits only in the short run. The existence of supernormal profits will, in both cases, encourage new firms to enter the industry. The increase in supply will compete away the supernormal profits and return the industry to the long-run position of normal profit. Figure 45.2 (a) shows the long-run position of a firm operating under conditions of perfect competition and (b) a firm operating under conditions of monopolistic competition.

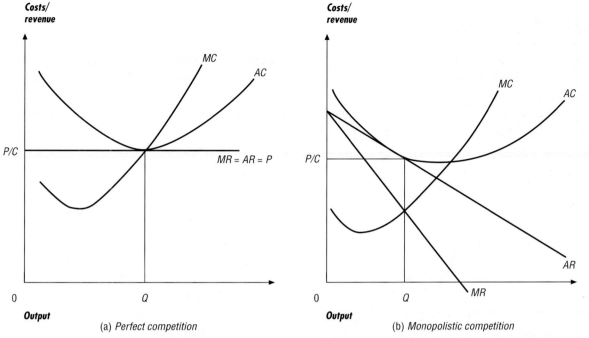

FIG. 45.2

(a) *Perfect competition* (b) *Monopolistic competition*

There are no barriers to exit under conditions of perfect competition and monopolistic competition so losses will exist only in the short run. Firms will leave the industry, causing supply to decrease, price to rise and normal profits to be earned again. It is not often mentioned that barriers to exit may mean that firms producing under conditions of oligopoly and monopoly may experience losses in the long run. Figure 45.3 shows a monopoly firm producing where $MC = MR$, thereby minimising losses, and where $AC > AR$. For some years, whilst under state ownership, British Airways made substantial losses but stayed in production.

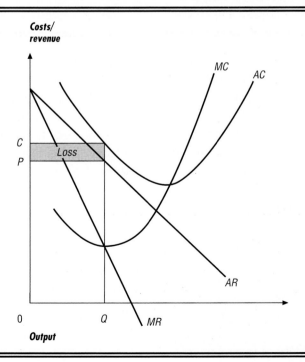

FIG. 45.3

CONSUMER SURPLUS

A comparison often made is between the consumer surplus which is earned under conditions of monopoly/ oligopoly and perfect competition. Monopolists usually deliberately restrict output. Consumers lose out by having less of the product and paying more for it than under conditions of perfect competition. A simplified diagram is often used to highlight this. Figure 45.4 assumes a constant MC curve and shows monopoly and perfect competition on the same diagram.

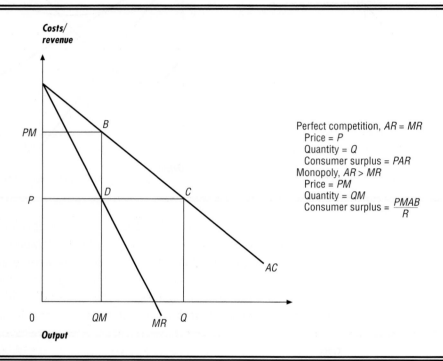

FIG. 45.4

According to this diagram if an industry moves from perfect competition to monopoly, price would rise, output would fall and consumer surplus would decline by PPMBC. Of this decline in consumer surplus, PPMBD converts to the monopolist and becomes producer surplus (a payment above what producers are willing to accept to supply the product). BDC is lost to consumers and producers and is referred to as a deadweight welfare loss. However, if a monopolist's costs are lower than those of firms operating under conditions of perfect competition, due to economies of scale, price and output may be lower and may offset the deadweight welfare loss. In Figure 45.5 the cost savings of PXZY exceed the deadweight loss of SXT.

PRODUCTIVE EFFICIENCY

This occurs when output is produced at the lowest possible cost and occurs where MC = AC. This is achieved in perfect competition in the long run as shown in Figure 45.6.

Private sector firms producing under conditions of monopolistic competition, oligopoly and monopoly do not produce at the bottom of the average cost curve and so do not achieve productive efficiency. Indeed, one of the main criticisms of monopolistic competition is that firms produce with spare capacity. A higher output would lower their costs. Most state sector monopolies are also unlikely to achieve productive efficiency unless specifically instructed to produce at minimum cost.

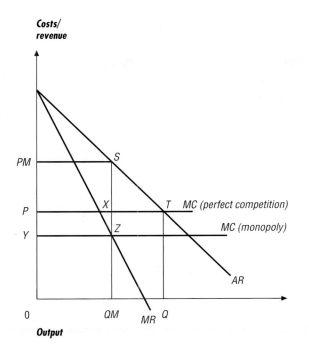

FIG. 45.5

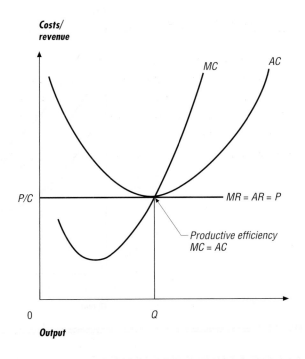

FIG. 45.6

ECONOMIES OF SCALE

Economies of scale are most likely to occur under conditions of monopoly or oligopoly. So whilst these firms may not be producing at the bottom of their average cost curves, their average cost curves may fall over a greater range of output than those of firms producing under conditions of monopolistic competition and perfect competition. Some monopolies and oligopolies will have *AC* curves which are continuing to slope down.

X EFFICIENCY

This is achieved when average and marginal costs are as low as possible. It is usually thought that this will occur under conditions of perfect competition where the force of competition will drive down costs. It is expected that X inefficiency may occur under conditions of oligopoly and, even more likely, under conditions of monopoly. This means that average cost and marginal cost curves are higher than they could be as shown in Figure 45.7.

X inefficiency occurs, in part, from complacency. Lack of competition may mean that production methods become inefficient. There may be overstaffing, failure to develop new products while out-of-date machinery and methods may be commonplace. There may also be deliberately created organisational slack to enable entrepreneurs to respond more easily with these extra resources to changing market conditions. All these features will push up the *AC* curve. However, monopolists and oligopolists may lower their costs by innovation while as noted above it is not only the position of the *AC* curve that matters but also its shape.

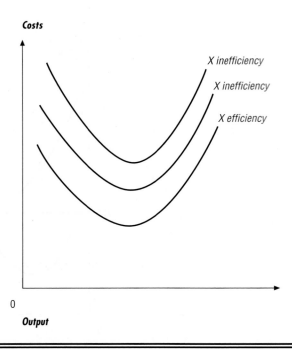

Costs

X inefficiency

X inefficiency

X efficiency

0

Output

FIG. 45.7

ALLOCATIVE EFFICIENCY

Productive and allocative efficiencies are concerned with how products are produced, whilst allocative efficiency is concerned with the quantity produced. Allocative efficiency is achieved where price (AR) = MC. At this point the cost of producing the extra unit (MC) matches the value that people place on the product. The resources devoted to the production of the product are sufficient to meet the demand of consumers at a price which matches the marginal utility they receive from the product. Perfectly competitive firms always produce at the allocatively efficient output in terms of private costs and benefits, irrespective of what type of profits they are earning. Figure 45.8 shows a perfectly competitive firm producing where $P = MC$ when making (a) supernormal profit, (b) normal profit and (c) a loss.

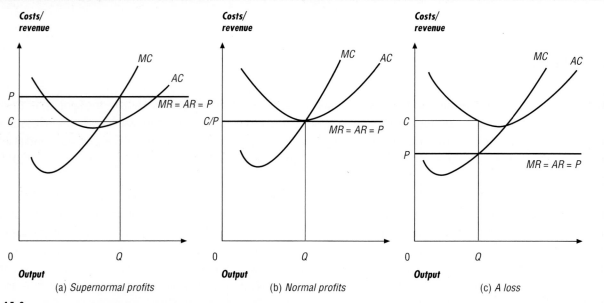

(a) Supernormal profits

(b) Normal profits

(c) A loss

FIG. 45.8

Firms producing under conditions of imperfect competition do not achieve allocative efficiency. If they are profit maximisers they will produce where $MC = MR$ but also where $P > MC$. This means that they could produce more of the product at a cost below the value that consumers place on it. However, firms deliberately restrict output in order to keep price and profits high. So there are insufficient resources devoted to making the product. Figure 45.9 compares the profit maximising output and the allocatively efficient output of a monopolist. Here, $0P$ = profit maximising price, $0Q$ = profit maximising output, $0PX$ = allocatively efficient price and $0QX$ = allocatively efficient output.

There is one exception to the above discussion. A state run monopoly may be instructed to produce at the allocatively efficient output. This is sometimes referred to as *marginal cost pricing*. One problem with marginal cost pricing is that firms which have large scale economies of scale may experience a loss. This is because if average costs fall over a large range, the firm is likely to be producing where AC is above MC and so price will be below average cost. This is illustrated in Figure 45.10.

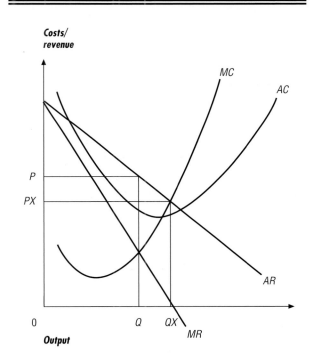

FIG. 45.9 ══════════════════════════

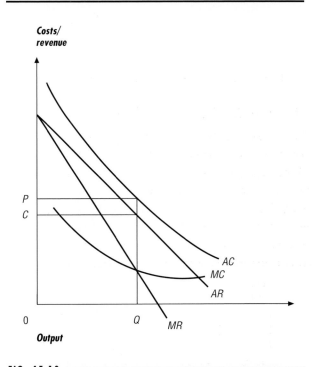

FIG. 45.10 ═════════════════════

Firms producing under conditions of both perfect and imperfect competition may not achieve allocative efficiency if there are external costs and benefits. Private sector firms take into account only private costs and benefits when deciding on their output. If, for example, there are external costs firms may devote too many resources to the production of the product. State concerns may be instructed to take external costs and benefits into account.

CONTESTABLE MARKETS

Another way of comparing markets is to examine not the degree of actual competition but the degree of potential competition.

A market is defined as *contestable* when there are no significant barriers to entry, new entrants would face similar costs to existing firms and exit costs are zero. Entry costs will either be low or will be recoverable on exit. In this case, the capital which is used will be non-specific — it will be capable of being transferred to other uses — and there will be no sunk costs. For example, a coach company may be willing to operate on a particular route if it knows that if it proves to be unprofitable it can use its coaches on alternative routes.

In the knowledge that new firms would be encouraged and would be able to enter the market if supernormal profits are earned, it is argued that costs and prices will be kept low in contestable markets. So the threat of competition has a similar effect to actual competition.

In theory, monopolists and oligopolists operating in contestable markets may benefit consumers more than firms operating under conditions of perfect competition. This is because not only may the firms be able to achieve low costs through economies of scale, but also the potential competition will ensure the firms act in a competitive way, keeping profits and prices low.

QUESTIONS

SHORT QUESTIONS

1 Explain two similarities and two differences between perfect competition and monopolistic competition.

2 How, and why, do the total revenue curves of firms producing under monopoly and perfect competition differ?

3 In which types of market structure may differentiated products be found?

4 Explain under which market structures the following UK operate:

    A commercial banks

    B civil airlines

    C public houses.

MULTIPLE CHOICE

1 Figure 45.11 shows the total revenue and total costs of a firm.

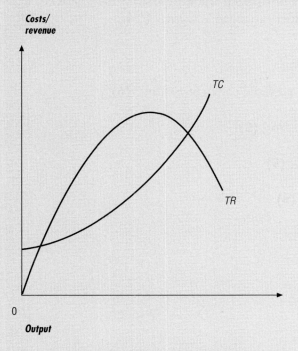

Costs/revenue

TC

TR

0

Output

FIG. 45.11

Does the diagram represent:

A monopoly in the short run

B monopoly in the long run

C perfect competition in the short run

D perfect competition in the long run?

2 What is the essential difference between a firm operating under conditions of perfect competition and a monopoly firm?

A The monopolist will maximise growth whilst the perfectly competitive firm will seek to maximise profits.

B Demand for a monopolist firm's product is more elastic than demand for the perfectly competitive firm.

C The perfectly competitive firm can sell any quantity at the going market price whilst the monopolist can only increase sales by reducing price.

D The perfectly competitive firm always produces at minimum average cost whilst the monopolist usually produces where average cost is still falling.

3 In which market structures can supernormal profits be earned in the long run?

A Perfect competition and monopolistic competition.

B Monopolistic competition and oligopoly.

C Oligopoly and monopoly.

D Monopoly and monopolistic competition.

4 Which of the following is an essential characteristic of a contestable market?

- (A) There are many buyers and sellers.

- (B) No one firm can influence price.

- (C) There is no advertising of the industry's product.

- (D) There are no significant barriers to entry into and exit from the industry.

DATA RESPONSE

Monopolies can become complacent. They dominate a market and may come to believe that their dominance will last because of the strength of their products and through their underestimation of the threat of competition.

International Business Machines (IBM) had a head start in the computer market. Its products overwhelmed all their competitors. However, it stuck with its original product line for too long. It was reluctant to change its methods and product range because its factories were always busy, demand was high and its costs were low. When the competition emerged in the form of new computing systems and software, IBM was ill-prepared.

Now Microsoft may face the same danger. It currently dominates the market for PC operating systems and basic office software systems. However, if it sits back thinking that this dominance is the natural order of events, dismissing the prospects of its competitors and seeks to preserve compatibility with previous products, its position could be threatened.

Some economists argue that monopoly contains the seed of its own destruction. A monopoly position can bring considerable benefits for a firm but to keep these benefits a firm is likely to have to update its methods of production and product range on a regular basis.

a] How is monopoly being defined in this passage? **(3)**

b] Why may monopolies be less likely to innovate than perfectly competitive firms? **(6)**

c] What benefits may a monopoly position confer on a firm? **(5)**

d] How may new firms break into a monopoly industry? **(5)**

e] Explain Schumpeter's theory of creative destruction. **(6)**

CASE STUDY

The theory of contestable markets is relatively new and is based on the assumption that there is freedom of entry into an industry and that exit is costless. Free entry means that potential entrants to a market are at no disadvantage in terms of higher costs than firms already in the market or from consumers preferring the products of existing firms. Costless exit means that firms are able to leave the market without financial penalty. The result of a contestable market is that potential entrants are not deterred from entering an industry by the possibility of existing firms reducing their prices since they can always leave the market given the absence of unrecoverable or sunk costs.

Unlike the traditional theory of price and output determination, most notably perfect competition and monopoly, the theory of contestable markets states that the structure of a market, and how firms behave within that market, cannot be determined simply by the number of firms which operate in the industry. Thus, in contestable markets, the number of firms operating is not important, what is important is the threat of entry. The threat of entry is sufficient to make existing firms, whether large or small, behave competitively. Contestable markets experience hit and run entry since the existence of supernormal profits encourages new firms to enter the market obtaining a share of the profits and leaving the industry when profits are creamed off. If there are unrecoverable or sunk costs involved then these are a cost of entry and as such therefore a barrier to entry. In a contestable market there are no such sunk costs to inhibit entry.

Although first impressions would appear to support the idea of the local bus service market being a contestable market, in that entry costs are low, given the active second-hand bus market, and sunk costs are small, given that the vehicles can be resold, there are in fact certain barriers to entry. For example, new entrants may find it difficult to obtain access to certain bus stations and there may be passenger loyalty to existing operators.

Source: 'The structure of the British Bus Industry' by Stephen Ison, The British Economy Survey, Vol. 25, No. 1, Autumn 1995.

a] Explain what is meant by 'sunk costs'. **(4)**

b] How does the theory of contestable markets differ from 'the traditional theory of price and output'? **(6)**

c] What is meant by 'hit and run entry'? **(4)**

d] Discuss whether a monopoly market can also be a contestable market. **(6)**

e] Discuss two barriers to entry not mentioned in the extract. **(6)**

f] What effect does the existence of supernormal profits have in a perfectly contestable market? **(8)**

g] How could a new bus company seek to break down passenger loyalty to existing bus companies? **(5)**

h] Discuss whether the UK telecommunications industry operates in a contestable market. **(11)**

STRUCTURED ESSAY

a] Compare and contrast perfect competition, monopolistic competition and oligopoly. **(12)**

b] Explain why prices in an oligopolistic market structure may be higher or lower than those in a perfectly competitive one. **(13)**

FREE RESPONSE ESSAY

Assess whether a perfectly competitive market structure is more likely to benefit consumers than a monopoly market structure. **(25)**

46 COMPETITION POLICY

Competition policy in the UK aims to promote efficiency and to protect the interests of the consumer. It is based on the assumption that the possession of market power by monopolies and oligopolies is not, in itself, against the public interest. What has to be considered is how market power is used and the behaviour of firms is considered on a case-by-case basis. Three main aspects of market power are targeted and these are how existing monopolies and oligopolies behave, the growth of market power through mergers and oligopolistic collusion. This policy is operated by three government created agencies: the Office of Fair Trading (OFT), the Competition Commission (which used to be called the Monopolies and Mergers Commission) and the Restrictive Practices Court.

THE OFFICE OF FAIR TRADING

This important office was created by the Fair Trading Act of 1973. The Director General of Fair Trading (DGFT) collects information on trading practices and is, in effect, a kind of official watchdog in the market place. The OFT operates in three main areas:

- competition policy: monopolies, restrictive trade practices, mergers
- consumer credit
- consumer affairs.

THE COMPETITION COMMISSION

The functions of the Competition Commission are to investigate monopolies and proposed mergers referred to it and to report on whether it considers the existing situation or the proposed changes to be in the public interest. It also makes recommendations to the government on any actions it thinks are necessary to protect the public interest.

The Competition Commission does not have the power to initiate investigations; it can take action only when a case is referred to it by the DGFT or by the Trade and Industry Secretary. Whether or not any action is taken on the findings of the Competition Commission rests upon a decision by the Trade and Industry Secretary. The duties of the Competition Commission are to conduct enquiries into:

- monopolies in the supply of goods and services
- merger proposals
- local (or geographical) monopolies
- the general effects of monopolistic practices (e.g. price discrimination)
- the efficiency, costs and quality of services provided by public enterprises
- anti-competitive practices pursued by an individual firm whether or not it is a monopoly.

MONOPOLIES

The Competition Commission can only carry out an investigation where a firm has a 25% or greater market share or where two or more firms together having a 25% or greater market share are acting together so as to restrict competition. The DGFT has the duty to keep the market under continuous review and to ascertain the existence of monopoly situations. It is the DGFT who decides the priority for references to the Competition Commission. The Competition Commission looks into the supply of particular goods and services and not into the activities of large firms as such. This means that a large multi-product firm may be the subject of more than one Competition Commission investigation.

The Trade and Industry Secretary has the power to make orders giving legal effect to any recommendations of the Competition Commission, but this power has rarely been used. Even so the reports of the Competition Commission have led to substantial changes in business practices. Adverse comments have usually led to voluntary agreements by the firms concerned (in negotiation with the Trade and Industry Secretary) to modify or abandon the offending practice. The fear of investigation and unwelcome publicity may also have had some beneficial effects on business behaviour.

Over the years the Competition Commission has made a variety of recommendations for the control or modification of firms' policies. These have included proposals for price reductions; government supervision of prices, costs and profits; the lowering of tariffs on competing imports; substantial reductions in advertising and other selling costs, and the prohibition of any further take-overs of competitors.

MERGERS

A proposed merger may be referred to the Competition Commission for investigation where it would involve the transfer of gross assets of at least £70m or where the merger would lead to a monopoly situation (i.e. the control of at least 25% of the market). The DGFT has the responsibility of keeping a watch on all merger situations qualifying for possible reference to the Competition Commission. The DGFT carries out preliminary investigations and then advises the Trade and Industry Secretary on whether the proposed merger should be referred to the Competition Commission; only the Trade and Industry Secretary can refer a proposed merger to the Competition Commission although s/he usually endorses the recommendations of the Competition Commission. Only a small percentage of proposed mergers are referred. However, the restraining effects of merger control are greater than the official statistics indicate because some merger proposals are dropped after informal consultations with the DGFT.

Decisions on merger references are taken on a case-by-case basis. The key considerations are whether there is a threat to competition and whether the merger is being undertaken openly and legally, that is, without insider dealing and fraud.

Obviously the number of mergers which are investigated is, in part, a function of the number of mergers proposed. Mergers tend to come in cycles. There was, for instance, a merger boom between 1992 and 1997.

A number of economists have suggested that the government should take a more critical approach to mergers. This is because studies of the effects of mergers have shown that a high proportion have proved unprofitable or much less successful than anticipated. One explanation for this may be the fact that the planned gains from mergers often depend upon substantial reorganisation of production facilities which may include the closure of some plants with inevitable redundancies. Such changes are likely to meet with strong resistance especially from organised labour and so may take a long time to carry out. There is also concern that many mergers appear to have been motivated by a desire to increase market power (by reducing competition) rather than a desire to increase efficiency.

THE RESTRICTIVE PRACTICES COURT

The legal regulation of restrictive trade practices began with the Restrictive Practices Act of 1956, the provisions of which have been extended and modified by the Restrictives Practice Acts of 1976 and 1977.

There is an obligation on the parties to certain types of restrictive agreement to place those agreements on a public register which is maintained by the DGFT. An agreement is registrable if the parties to it include two or more people (whether individuals or firms) who are engaged in business in the UK in the manufacture or supply of goods or in the supply of services. Typical examples of the types of practice which are registrable are cartels, pooling of patents and collusive tendering.

It is the job of the DGFT to select practices on the register for reference to the Restrictive Practices Court which then has the task of deciding whether or not the practices are operating in the public interest. The Restrictive Practices Court has the status of a High Court and its judgements become legally binding. All registered agreements are presumed to be against the public interest and the onus is on the parties to the agreements to prove to the satisfaction of the court that they are not harmful to the public interest.

The firms or trade associations which choose to defend their agreements must select a form of defence from a restricted list set out in the Restrictive Practices Act. There are eight approved grounds for defence, generally referred to as the eight 'gateways'.

THE EIGHT GATEWAYS

The respondents must show that the agreement confers benefits in one or more of the following ways:

- by protecting the public against injury in connection with the installation, use or consumption of goods
- by making available other specific and substantial benefits
- by counteracting restrictive measures taken by any one person who is not party to the agreement
- by permitting negotiation of fair terms for the purchase or sale of goods and services with buyers and sellers who represent a preponderant part of the trade
- by preventing the occurrence of serious and persistent unemployment in an area heavily dependent upon the particular trade
- in maintaining the volume or earnings of the export trade in the commodity or service where this is substantial in relation to the export trade of the UK as a whole, or in relation to the whole business of the particular trade
- in maintaining some other restriction which the Court holds to be justified on its own merits
- the restriction does not directly or indirectly restrict or discourage competition.

The defendants must, in addition, show that any gain from the operation of the practice is not outweighed by any detrimental effects on persons not party to the agreement.

The number of cases considered by the court has not been very great, but by carefully selecting the agreements to be judged by the court it has been possible to make each reference a test case for a large number of similar agreements. If a particular case is lost then similar agreements are likely to be abandoned by other firms.

RESALE PRICE MAINTENANCE

One particular restrictive practice has been the subject of its own legislation. The Resale Prices Acts of 1964 and 1976 prohibited resale price maintenance but made provision for suppliers to claim exemption.

Resale price maintenance is the practice whereby the manufacturer fixes the price of the product at each stage of distribution. Although the products are being distributed by independent wholesalers and retailers they are obliged to charge prices which are laid down by the manufacturers. It means, of course, that the profit margins at these subsequent stages are being fixed by the manufacturers. The main motive behind resale price maintenance is to maintain a range of outlets for manufacturers. This gives manufacturers more power than wholesalers and retailers in setting the price that the distributors are to pay. The practice can be enforced by manufacturers threatening to withhold supplies if the distributor breaks the price agreement. The one remaining example of resale price maintenance, pharmaceuticals, is currently under investigation.

EUROPEAN LEGISLATION

Mergers and restrictive practices are also subject to regulation by the European Commission. Articles 85 and 86 of the Treaty of Rome lay out the main provisions of European competition law. Article 85 relates to collusive behaviour and prohibits agreements and restrictive practices which reduce competition in the EU and which affect trade between member states, e.g. price fixing and restriction of technical development. Such agreements are not permitted under European law unless it can be shown that the agreement will help to improve production, distribution or technical progress and that consumers will receive a fair share of the benefits.

Article 86 bans the abuse of a dominant position within the EU, for example charging 'unfair prices'. The European Commission can impose fines, up to 10% of a firm's turnover if the firm is found to have abused a dominant position or to have operated anti-competitive agreements.

In 1990 a Merger Control Regulation was introduced. This set out the three criteria by which it is judged whether a merger should be referred to the European Commission:

- the merging firms, together, have a world turnover greater than £3.6b
- the merging firms have a turnover in the European Union of at least £180m
- less than two-thirds of the combined turnover comes from one member state.

The European Commission can decide to prevent the merger, allow it to occur or permit it subject to various conditions.

PRIVATISATION

One way a government can seek to increase competition is privatisation. This involves transferring assets from the public to the private sector. The most well-known form of privatisation is denationalisation — the selling-off of nationalised industries. However, the term also includes the sale of government-owned shares in private sector companies, the sale of council houses to sitting tenants and the contracting out of services by government and local authority departments, as with catering and laundry services in hospitals, for example. The Conservative Governments and many other governments in the 1980s and 1990s followed large-scale privatisation programmes. Among the major firms and industries which were transferred to the private sector in this period are those shown in Table 46.1.

TABLE 46.1 EXAMPLES OF PRIVATISED CONCERNS

Associated British Ports	Cable and Wireless
British Airports Authority	Electricity distribution companies
British Aerospace	Electricity generating companies
British Airways	Jaguar
British Gas	Rolls-Royce
British Petroleum	Sealink
British Steel	Water companies
British Telecom	Britoil

ARGUMENTS FOR PRIVATISATION

These include:

- *Raising revenue for the government.* The revenue gained from the sale makes it possible for the government to reduce its need to borrow and to cut tax rates without reducing its own spending. Extra government revenue may also arise in the form of higher corporation tax receipts if the privatised concerns become more profitable.
- *Increased competition.* It is argued that the private sector has the spur of competition since inefficiency is punished with bankruptcy. A failed firm will go out of business and resources will be reallocated in line with consumer demand whereas state enterprises cannot go bankrupt because the government guarantees their borrowings.

     A private sector firm may have to compete in financial markets for funds and has to persuade banks, and other financial institutions or its shareholders that its plans are viable.

     Greater competition may also be created in the product market if an industry, which was run as a monopoly under state ownership, is split into competing parts, for example, separate telecommunication firms operating in competition with each other.
- *Increased efficiency.* Managers of privatised firms will be freed from political control and interference — they will be able to charge the prices they regard as commercially appropriate and to make the investments they think will produce the right return. The stock market may also put pressure on private sector firms to be more efficient. If they are not performing well their share price will fall and they will run the risk of being taken over by another firm.
- *Wider share ownership.* The broadening of share ownership may be another aim of privatisation. The idea is to shift ownership away from the state and large institutions towards individuals.
- Cost push inflation may be reduced. Private sector managers may be more reluctant to concede wage rises not matched by higher productivity and may be less willing to accept inefficient working practices.

ARGUMENTS AGAINST PRIVATISATION

These include:

- *Long term loss of revenue.* Whilst selling off profitable assets raises revenue for the government in the short term, it loses the future profits from these industries. Indeed privatisation has been likened to 'selling off the family silver'. If the loss of profits is greater than any rise in corporation tax resulting from the privatisation, future government borrowing requirements may be larger.
- *Competition in product markets may not be increased.* If a public sector monopoly is replaced by a private sector monopoly then, other things being equal, competition will not increase. In cases of a natural monopoly it is difficult to provide competition.
- *Market forces may not ensure greater efficiency.* Privatised firms, if they have a high degree of monopoly power, are likely to be able to earn supernormal profits even if they are inefficient. The stock market may also fail to put pressure on the firms to become efficient. Monopolies and oligopolies are likely to be able to rely heavily on retained profits for their investment finance and their large size is likely to prevent other firms from being able to take them over.
- *Loss of potential revenue from the sale of privatised concerns.* It is thought that in the past some state concerns were sold off too cheaply. Evidence for this was provided by the sharp rise in price of shares which occurred

the day after shares were sold in many former state concerns. Whilst this provided a speculative gain for the purchasers there was a corresponding sacrifice in revenue for the state and taxpayers. In practice it is difficult to set the price of shares in privatised industries at the appropriate level.

- *Private sector firms may not act in the public interest.* Private sector firms do not take into account externalities. They are also unlikely to base their output and pricing decisions on considerations of equity.
- *Loss of government control over the economy.* The government's ability to influence pay, prices and output decisions directly will be reduced.

REGULATION OF PRIVATISED INDUSTRIES

To counter the risk that privatised utilities with natural monopoly power would abuse their monopoly power the UK government has set up a number of regulatory agencies including OFGEM (Office for Gas and Electricity Regulation), OFTEL (Office of Telecommunications), OFWAT (Office of Water Supplies) and ORR (Office of the Rail Regulator). These agencies seek to apply the competitive pressures that these utilities would experience in a more competitive market structure by, for example, setting limits on price rises (and in some cases instructing the firms to make price cuts) and targets for improvements in quality. They also seek, in the longer run to make it easier for new firms to enter the industry.

One criticism made of the regulatory agencies is that they can fall prey to 'regulatory capture'. This refers to the danger that because the agencies usually have more contact with the managers of the firms than with the customers and because the managers are likely to have a high level of technical knowledge they may be unduly influenced by the arguments put forward by the firms and as a result will be too easy on them.

NATIONALISATION

Where it is felt that the risk of market failure is too great a government may decide to take an industry into state ownership. Under state ownership, industries can be run in the public interest and attempts can be made to avoid the creation of negative externalities, allocative inefficiency and lack of provision of basic necessities which may occur in the private sector.

ARGUMENTS FOR NATIONALISATION

- *Natural monopolies.* In the case of industries where there is only room for one firm to operate efficiently there is a risk that a private sector monopoly would abuse its market power. Whereas a state monopoly can be run in the national interest and not with a view to private profit.
- *Adjustment to changing market conditions.* One of the main arguments used in presenting the case for public ownership when basic industries such as steel, coal and the railways were nationalised was that only the state could and would provide the very large injections of capital which were needed to restructure and modernise these capital intensive industries.
- *Helping to manage the economy.* A further argument for having a large sector of the economy directly under government control is that it can be used as a powerful lever to control the economy. During a recession, for example, the investment programmes of the nationalised industries can be increased and, via multiplier effects, will help to stimulate an increase in income and employment.

Governments can also use their powers to restrict price increases by nationalised industries as a means of reducing the rate of inflation. This use of government power, however, makes it very difficult for the nationalised industries to carry out long-term planning.

- *Social costs and benefits.* Private sector firms usually only undertake production if private benefits (revenue) are greater than private costs; they will not take into account externalities. Nationalised industries, charged with operating in the public interest, will be under strong political and social pressures to give much more attention to externalities. They may be obliged to operate some loss-making activities where social benefits are clearly greater than social costs — for example, rural postal and transport services. The government, recognising these social obligations, may provide subsidies for such non-commercial operations.

The arguments against privatisation are essentially the mirror image of the arguments for privatisation, including lack of competition, lack of incentive and inefficiency.

QUESTIONS

SHORT QUESTIONS

1 What is the aim of competition policy?

2 What are the functions of the Competition Commission?

3 Explain what is meant by resale price maintenance.

4 What effect may privatisation have on government revenue?

MULTIPLE CHOICE

1 What is meant by regulatory capture?

A A regulatory agency protecting the interests of the producers.

B A regulatory agency being closed down after complaints from producers.

C The government introducing new regulations on the activities of private sector firms.

D A referral by the Director General of Fair Trading to the Monopolies and Mergers Commission of a firm's pricing strategy.

2 Which of the following is the aim of the agencies which the UK government has established to regulate privatised utilities?

A To protect profit levels.

B To maintain price levels.

C To prevent the abuse of monopoly power.

D To ensure shareholders have more say in the running of firms than managers.

3 Which of the following is an argument for nationalisation?

A To increase competition.

B To increase government revenue.

C To raise the profitability of the firm.

D To ensure the firm's decisions are based on social costs and benefits.

4 Which of the following restrictive practices may be considered to be in the public interest?

A The use by all pharmaceutical companies of 'child proof' containers.

B The creation of barriers to entry into an expanding industry.

C An agreement by car producers to delay the introduction of rust proof cars.

D Supermarkets agreeing to charge the same price for a range of items.

DATA RESPONSE

The cosy cartel is about to feel the chill wind of competition. It and its fellow travellers, such as price fixing and abuse of market dominance, will soon be dangerous territory for business.

Under plans for the Competition Act, which comes into force next March, anti-competitive behaviour in the UK will face some of the toughest actions outside the US, Stephen Byers, the Trade and Industry Secretary, yesterday upped the stakes in the Government's attempts to end the reign of unscrupulous companies in 'rip-off Britain' by declaring that they could be fined up to 30% of their UK sales.

The fight against 'rip-off Britain' is a perfect populist campaign. No one except advocates of an unaccountable free market at any price would disagree with it. But a toughening of competition policy will not only benefit the vulnerable shopper, it will also be a powerful help to business. It will assist smaller companies that are squeezed out of an arena by the iron grip of a few businesses setting the rules among themselves. And it will help larger ones wishing to break into new markets. Everyone should gain.

Business believes — perhaps optimistically — that it may often be difficult to prove charges against companies that merit fines.

The OFT is not so worried. It believes that charges of anti-competitive behaviour are clear cut.

Source: 'Byers targets cosy cartels in clean-up of "rip-off Britain"' by Christine Buckley, The Times, 10/8/99.

a] What is a cartel? **(3)**

b] Discuss the motives behind anti-competitive behaviour. **(6)**

c] What is meant by 'an unaccountable free market'? **(4)**

d] What is the role of the OFT? **(4)**

e] Discuss whether everyone will gain from a 'toughening of competition policy'. **(8)**

CASE STUDY

Allegations of market rigging and anti-competitive behaviour in the multi-billion pound health insurance industry are being investigated by the Office of Fair Trading, it emerged yesterday.

The inquiry was prompted by complaints suggesting big health insurers are channelling patients into their own hospitals and abusing their muscle to force independent hospitals to lower charges.

The OFT has been looking at complaints since the middle of 1997, but, a spokeswoman said, it had 'never been able to find sufficient evidence for … a reference to the Monopolies and Mergers Commission'. Now the inquiry has been given added urgency by a detailed complaint from former Northern Ireland minister Sir Richard Needham, chairman of the Heart Hospital, in Harley Street, London.

Sir Richard, who served in the Province as health minister, alleged that the powerful PPP health insurance group had 'frozen out' the Heart Hospital and was pushing PPP patients into its own institutions, principally the nearby Harley Street Clinic. Sir Richard accused PPP of engaging in a 'blatant abuse of market power to retain its grip on the private health sector.'

Last night PPP said: 'We choose hospitals … by competitive market tender based on a full range of criteria, including the quality, value and comprehensiveness of services and facilities offered.' It added it was not using the Heart Hospital 'because we believe that, at the current time, it offers a relatively restricted range of treatments which are catered for in other, nearby multi-speciality facilities.'

PPP, 51% owned by insurer Guardian Royal Exchange, which is being taken over by France's Axa group, is thought to have about 40% of the British private health insurance market.

In 1994, the Monopolies and Mergers Commission ruled that private medical services must work within a competitive environment.

Source: 'OFT inquiry into health insurers' by Dan Atkinson, the Guardian, 12/2/99.

a] What anti-competitive behaviour was the private health insurance industry accused of? **(5)**

b] What is the Monopolies and Mergers Commission now called? **(2)**

c] How could the case against PPP be assessed? **(8)**

d] How much market power does PPP have? **(3)**

e] Explain what is meant by a competitive environment. **(6)**

f] Does competition always benefit consumers? **(9)**

g] Discuss three causes, apart from abuse of market power, of market failure which may occur in the private health care market. **(9)**

h] Explain the relationship between the market for private health care and the macroeconomy. **(8)**

STRUCTURED ESSAY

a] Discuss the benefits of competition. **(10)**

b] Assess three methods a government may employ to promote competition. **(15)**

FREE RESPONSE ESSAY

Discuss whether government action to curb the power of monopolies will benefit consumers. **(25)**

PART EIGHT: INTERNATIONAL TRADE

47 THE NATURE OF INTERNATIONAL TRADE

UNIQUE FEATURES OF INTERNATIONAL TRADE

International trade involves the exchange of goods and services across international boundaries. It differs from internal trade in a number of ways. There may be restrictions imposed by governments and international organisations on the movement of products into, and sometimes out of, countries. Communication may be difficult during the trading process. Higher costs may be involved including possibly greater transport costs. There may be the need to translate advertising messages and related literature into other languages. It is necessary to keep up with changes in tastes in foreign markets. In some cases cash flows may have to be converted into different currencies while firms may have to deal with differences in technical and legal requirements in overseas markets. There are also extra risks involved in international trade including wars and changes in government policies.

However, the increased development of a global market (globalisation) with improved communication links throughout the world, increased global competition and increased similarity of tastes is reducing the differences between internal and international trade.

BENEFITS OF INTERNATIONAL TRADE

As well as the costs and uncertainty involved in international trade there are benefits. Indeed firms engage in international trade because they believe that the benefits outweigh the costs. Engaging in international trade gives firms access to larger markets enabling them to take greater advantage of economies of scale. They may also be able to purchase raw materials and component parts more easily and more cheaply.

Consumers can also gain from international trade. They are able to purchase goods not made in their own countries, have access to a greater variety of products and can benefit from increased competition in the form of lower-priced and better-quality products.

The overriding benefit claimed for international trade is that, by enabling the principle of division of labour to be extended to the international arena, it increases world output and hence raises the material standard of living.

THE PATTERN OF UK TRADE

The UK exports and imports mainly finished manufactured goods. It trades mainly with countries possessing similar markets and its main export markets tend to coincide with its main sources of imports. Table 47.1 and Figure 47.1 show that most of the UK's trade is with other members of the European Union.

THE BASIS OF INTERNATIONAL TRADE

International trade arises because the production of different kinds of goods and services requires different kinds of resources used in different proportions and because the various types of economic resources are unevenly distributed throughout the world. The international mobility of resources is limited. Land is obviously immobile in the geographical sense. The international mobility of labour is restricted by barriers of language

TABLE 47.1 THE UK'S MAIN TRADING PARTNERS 1998

	Most important providers of imports to the UK	*Most important recipients of exports from the UK*
1	USA	USA
2	Germany	Germany
3	France	France
4	Netherlands	Netherlands
5	Italy	Irish Republic
6	Japan	Italy
7	Belgium & Luxembourg	Belgium & Luxembourg
8	Irish Republic	Spain
9	Spain	Japan
10	Switzerland	Switzerland

Source: Monthly Digest of Statistics, April 1999, Office for National Statistics

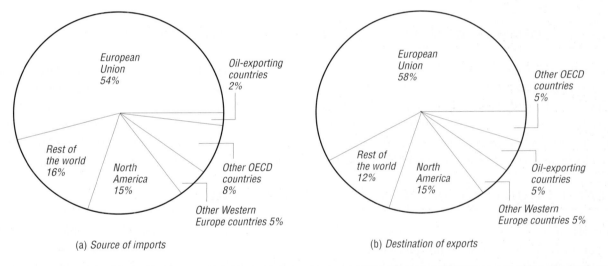

(a) *Source of imports*   (b) *Destination of exports*

FIG. 47.1

and custom and restrictions on immigration. Capital is more mobile geographically but it only crosses international boundaries when favourable conditions exist (e.g. political stability, no threats of confiscation, no barriers to taking profits out of the country, etc.).

Since it is very difficult to move resources between nations, the goods and services which represent the resources must move. Nations which have an abundance of land relative to labour will tend to concentrate on 'land-intensive' commodities such as wheat and meat. They will exchange these goods for 'labour-intensive' products such as manufactured goods made by countries which have an abundance of labour and capital relative to land.

Just as individual abilities and aptitudes fit people for different occupations, so the different resources and the historical development equip them for the production of different products. Unlike individuals, nations do not specialise completely in one process or in one product. They tend to concentrate on certain types of activity, but even the greatest importers of food, for example, grow some of their own food requirements, while net importers of manufactured goods also carry out some manufacturing.

THE GAINS FROM INTERNATIONAL TRADE

In the real world international trade is carried on by a large number of countries in a vast range of goods and services. This is a complex situation but it is possible to gain an understanding of the principles which underlie international trade by using a simplified model. In this model we consider two countries, Country A and Country B. It is assumed that only two commodities are produced: tractors and wool; that there are no barriers to trade and no transport costs; that resources within each country can easily transfer from one industry to another and there are constant opportunity costs as resources are moved from one use to another.

Within these limits three possibilities can be considered:

- each country can produce only one of the commodities
- each country can produce both commodities, but tractors can be produced more efficiently in one country and wool more efficiently in the other
- each country can produce both commodities, but one of the countries can produce both commodities more efficiently than the other.

EACH COUNTRY CAN PRODUCE ONLY ONE COMMODITY

Here the gains from international trade are self-evident. It increases the variety of goods available to each country. There are certain goods and services a country may not be able to produce or may experience difficulty producing. The UK, for example, must rely on foreign trade for some of its raw materials and part of its food supply. It does not, however, explain much of international trade, because this takes place between countries which could well produce for themselves the goods and services which they import. For example, the greatest producer of cars in the world, the USA, is also the greatest importer of cars.

EACH COUNTRY HAS AN ABSOLUTE ADVANTAGE

We also assume that each country is more efficient than the other in the production of one of the commodities. Country B produces wool more efficiently than Country A, while Country A has the advantage in producing tractors. An arithmetic example can be used to illustrate the potential gains from trade.

EXAMPLE

Suppose each country has 10 resources. Country A can produce 20 tractors with one resource and 100 bales of wool with one resource. Country B can produce 10 tractors with one resource and 150 bales of wool. Initially the countries do not specialise and devote half their resources to the production of each good. They do not engage in international trade.

| | Output of | |
	tractors	wool
Country A	100	500
Country B	50	750
Total output	150	1250

Then the countries specialise completely and output changes to:

	Output of	
	tractors	wool
Country A	200	0
Country B	0	1500
Total output	200	1500

Total output increases. In order to obtain the benefits of specialisation these countries must exchange some part of their individual outputs, but the rate at which they exchange the goods must be beneficial to both countries. This will occur if the exchange rate lies between the domestic opportunity cost ratios of the two countries.

In Country A the 'cost' of 1 tractor is 5 bales of wool since this is the output of wool which must be forgone in order to produce 1 tractor. Country A, therefore, will not accept less than 5 bales of wool for each tractor since she can obtain wool on these terms by transferring resources at home. Similarly, Country B will not offer more than 15 bales of wool for 1 tractor since she can obtain tractors at this 'price' by using her own resources. The domestic opportunity cost ratios are:

	tractors		wool
In Country A	1	:	5
In Country B	1	:	15

Suppose the exchange rate settles at 1 tractor for 10 bales of wool and 70 tractors are exchanged for 700 bales of wool, the position after trade is:

	tractors	wool
Country A has	130	700
Country B has	70	800
Total output	200	1500

Both countries are better off than when they were operating on a basis of self-sufficiency. Country A has 30 more tractors and 200 more bales of wool. Country B now has more tractors and 50 more bales of wool. In Figure 47.2 the information used in the above example is used to provide a diagrammatic representation of the situation in Country B before and after specialisation and trade. Country B can produce any combination of tractors (T) and wool (W) on the line joining 100 tractors and 1500 bales of wool. It chooses the combination represented by (50T + 750W) when trading possibilities are not available. When trading opportunities arise, Country B specialises in wool which exchanges internationally at the rate of 10W for 1T. It now chooses position Y.

EACH COUNTRY HAS A COMPARATIVE ADVANTAGE

In this case one country is more efficient than the other in the production of both commodities. It is assumed that Country A is the more efficient country; it has an absolute advantage over Country B in both industries. Even in this situation, which is thought to explain a large part of international trade, both countries can benefit from specialisation and trade providing each country has a comparative cost advantage and providing the exchange rate lies between the countries' domestic opportunity cost ratios.

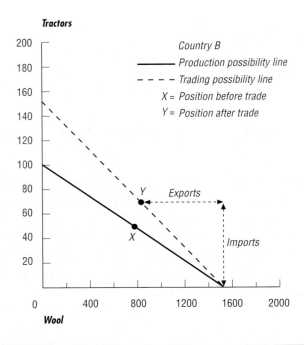

Tractors

Country B
Production possibility line
Trading possibility line
X = Position before trade
Y = Position after trade

Wool

FIG. 47.2

Comparative cost relates to the opportunity cost of producing the commodities and not the absolute costs.

EXAMPLE

Again it is assumed that each country has 10 resources, does not trade initially and devotes half of its resources to the production of each good.

	tractors	wool
Country A	100	1000
Country B	50	750

Country A is better at producing both products. It has the absolute advantage in the production of both tractors and wool. However it is even better at producing tractors. It can make twice as many tractors and only 1.25 more wool. Country B is not so bad at making wool. It can produce three-quarters as much wool as Country A but only half as many tractors. This can also be discerned by examining the domestic opportunity cost ratios. In Country A the 'cost' of 1 tractor is 10 bales of wool (1000/100), while in Country B it is 15 bales of wool (750/50). Country A has a comparative advantage in tractors. In Country A the cost of a bale of wool is one-tenth of a tractor, while in Country B the cost is one-fifteenth of a tractor. In terms of the output of tractors forgone, wool is cheaper in Country B than in Country A. Country B has a comparative advantage in wool.

If trading possibilities arise, each country will tend to specialise, but in this case if they specialise completely the total output of tractors would rise but the output of wool would fall. Each country will specialise in that industry in which it has a comparative advantage so that complete specialisation would give 200 tractors and 1500 bales of wool. It is possible to show that the increase in the output of tractors, in value terms, more than offsets the fall in the output of wool, but this is not really necessary because by partially specialising the more efficient country can have more of both goods. Thus if Country A devotes 2 resources to wool and 8 resources to tractors while Country B specialises completely in wool:

	tractors	wool
Country A	160	400
Country B	0	1500
Total output	160	1900

Output has increased and if trade does take place based on an exchange rate lying between the domestic opportunity cost ratios both countries will be able to consume more of both goods.

THE EXTENT TO WHICH COMPARATIVE ADVANTAGE EXPLAINS INTERNATIONAL TRADE

Most countries specialise in the production of those goods and services in which they have a comparative advantage. Over time comparative advantage changes. For example, the UK has in recent decades become less competitive in manufacturing industries and more competitive in service industries. Reflecting this change in comparative advantage resources have moved from the secondary to the tertiary sector.

Among the industries the UK is currently thought to have a comparative advantage in are computer software, pharmaceuticals and business services. These industries are knowledge based and are good industries to be competitive in. This is because they possess positive income elasticity of demand and so have good prospects for long-term growth. The industries in which the UK is least competitive are those which are dependent on heavy capital investment or cheap labour. In a number of these industries world demand is growing slowly and there is increasing competition from developing countries.

QUALIFICATIONS TO THE LAW OF COMPARATIVE ADVANTAGE

Although comparative advantage explains much of the pattern of international trade it does not explain all of it. This is because there are limitations to the theory and practice of specialisation. These include the following.

- The gains from trade are modified by the existence of transport costs and tariffs. The economic effects of these are similar since in both cases the cost of moving the goods is increased. In the case of transport costs the increase in price is unavoidable, whereas in the case of tariffs the cost increase is 'artificial' because it is the result of a policy decision and, therefore, reversible.
- The theory outlined above is based on the unrealistic assumption that the opportunity cost ratios remain constant as resources are moved from one industry to another. This is not very likely since some resources will be more efficient in one industry than in others and some may be immobile.
- It is possible that increasing specialisation will yield advantages in the form of economies of scale, particularly in manufacturing industries.
- There are risks in specialisation. A country which concentrates most of its resources on a narrow range of industries is vulnerable to sudden and unpredictable changes in demand and supply conditions.
- In practice the exchange rate may not lie within the opportunity cost ratios and may benefit developed countries at the expense of developing countries.
- The existence of imperfect competition in product and factor markets may mean that some prices do not reflect domestic opportunity cost ratios.

QUESTIONS

SHORT QUESTIONS

1. What are the differences between internal and international trade?

2. Distinguish between absolute and comparative advantage.

3. What is the significance of opportunity cost in determining the pattern of specialisation and trade?

4. Why might countries not benefit from specialisation and trade?

MULTIPLE CHOICE

1. The basis of international trade is that countries have:

   A. similar patterns of demand

   B. different economic systems

   C. similar balance of payments positions

   D. different endowments of factors of production.

2. The table shows the output per worker in two countries X and Y when each country divides its resources equally between two products.

	Units of output	
	Country X	Country Y
TVs	50	32
Cars	10	4

Which of the following exchange rates will benefit both countries?

A. 1 car for 2 TVs   B. 1 car for 5 TVs

C. 1 car for 7 TVs   D. 1 car for 8 TVs.

3. Figure 47.3 shows the production possibility curves of two countries each producing only two types of commodities.

What can be concluded from the diagram?

A. Country Z has a comparative advantage in the production of agricultural goods.

B. Country Y will export agricultural goods and import manufactured goods.

C. Country Z has an absolute advantage in the production of both agricultural and manufactured goods.

D. It is not possible for Country Y to benefit from trading with Country Z.

4. Figure 47.4 shows a country's pre-trade (RS) and post-trade (RT) consumption possibilities of goods X and Y.

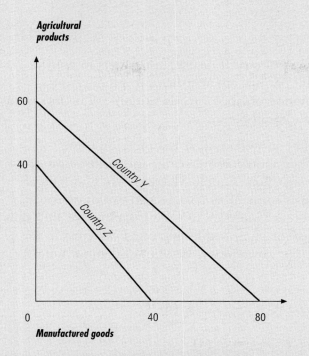

FIG. 47.3

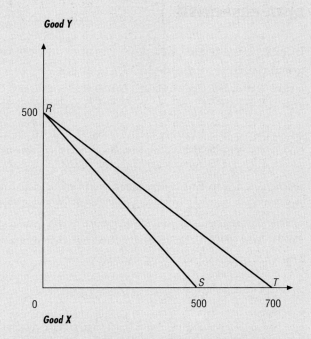

FIG. 47.4

Which of the following statements could explain the diagram?

A The country has a comparative advantage in the production of good Y.

B The country is unable to produce as much of X and Y as its trading partner.

C The country's consumers prefer X to Y.

D The country exports good X.

DATA RESPONSE

International trade provides a number of benefits for a country. It enables consumers to enjoy a greater variety of products, some at a lower price, and permits efficient firms to produce on a larger scale. By permitting countries to engage in division of labour, world output can be increased and the living standards of people throughout the world can be raised.

To achieve this higher world output countries should concentrate their resources on those products which they can produce most efficiently. They should also facilitate the reallocation of resources in line with changes in comparative advantage. For example Malaysia is rich in natural resources, including petroleum, rubber and tin and uses some of its resources to exploit these. In the 1970s some of its resources were diverted from other industries, including agriculture, into the textile industry as Malaysia's productivity and cost advantage in textiles increased. Whereas in the 1980s and 1990s the fastest growing industries were the car industry, the semi-conductor industry and the financial services industry.

a] Discuss two advantages of international trade not discussed in the passage. **(4)**

b] Discuss two benefits a firm can gain from operating on a larger scale **(4)**

c] Explain why if countries 'engage in division of labour world output can be increased'. **(6)**

d] How can countries determine in which products they have a comparative advantage? **(5)**

e] Why might it be argued that it is better for a country to have a comparative advantage in a manufactured product than a primary product? **(6)**

CASE STUDY

For a thumbnail portrait of the changing face of British industry, you could do no better than yesterday's figures for the past year showing textiles output down 9%, metals (including steel) down 6%, but production of mobile phones and pagers rocketing 45%.

The once proud textiles industry has been in decline for thirty years. It has not enjoyed any recovery in output since the trough of the recession in 1992. Competition on cost from emerging economies in a labour-intensive business has proved too stiff at any level of the exchange rate, and certainly with today's strong pound.

So we have gone from cloth caps and steel-capped clogs to mobiles within a generation. The lesson is that the future of British manufacturing lies in industries that can compete on more than cost alone. Pharmaceuticals is one example — including biotechnology, if the green lobby does not strangle its development in the UK.

Mobile phone production is another. So much do Britons love their mobiles that we account for nearly 15% of the European market; and a thriving domestic market is important for any industry. Plants in the UK also produce for export, with buoyant demand helping them overcome the effects of sterling.

Perhaps unfortunately, the manufacturers of these devices are virtually all foreign-owned companies, as in many other technologically-sophisticated parts of British industry. But never mind: they create jobs, source from local companies, and generate export revenues.

The transformation carries two messages for both government and industry. One is the importance of the science and technology base for the future of the economy. The other is not to get too carried away by any sentimental attachment to the older industries: textiles and steel still resonate but they account for only a small share of the British industry's output. For public policy purposes, they scarcely deserve a look in.

Source: 'A mobile future in manufacturing', Outlook, the Independent, 10/6/99.

a] According to the article which are Britain's expanding and contracting industries? **(3)**

b] What evidence is there that Britain has lost her comparative advantage in textiles? **(6)**

c] Explain how 'companies can compete on more than cost'. **(8)**

d] Why is 'a thriving domestic market important for any industry'? **(6)**

e] What are the benefits of having foreign based firms based in Britain? **(5)**

f] According to the article how should resources be reallocated in Britain? **(4)**

g] How easy is it to assess where a country's comparative advantage lies? **(8)**

h] Explain the difference between absolute and comparative advantage. **(10)**

STRUCTURED ESSAY

a] Discuss the difficulties and benefits of international trade. **(10)**

b] Explain the theory of comparative advantage. **(15)**

FREE RESPONSE ESSAY

Discuss the extent to which the theory of comparative advantage explains the pattern of trade of international trade. **(25)**

48 PROTECTIONISM

Protectionism is the restriction of international trade. It prevents consumers and producers reaching the equilibrium price and quantity that would prevail in a free market. Every country operates some form of restriction on its trade with the rest of the world.

METHODS OF PROTECTION

TARIFFS

These can also be called customs duties and are the most well-known barrier to trade. They act in exactly the same way as a tax by artificially raising the price of foreign products as they enter the country. Tariffs may be *ad valorem*, that is, a percentage of the price of the imports, or specific, that is, a tax per unit of weight or physical quantity.

   Figure 48.1 shows the effect of a specific tariff. Domestic demand is shown by the domestic demand curve (*DD*) and domestic supply curve (*DS*). When the country engages in free trade the price is set where domestic demand equals the world supply (*WS*). In this situation domestic consumers purchase *M* amount at a price of *P*. Quantity *J* is supplied by domestic producers and *JM* quantity is imported.

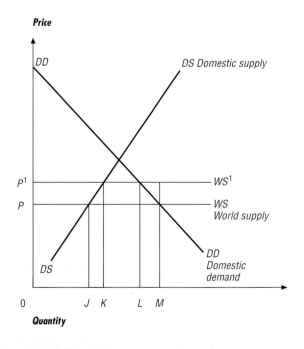

FIG. 48.1

The imposition of a tariff shifts the world supply to WS¹. This raises the price to P¹ and reduces the quantity bought and sold to L. However, domestic production rises by JK to K, and imports fall to KL.

TRADITIONAL NON-TARIFF BARRIERS

These include the following.

- *Quotas.* A quota takes the form of a physical limitation on the quantity of a commodity which is allowed to enter the country in a given year. It may be set on the value or volume of imports. Quotas do not bring in revenue to the state unless they are operated by means of import licences. The effect of the imposition of a volume quota is shown in Figure 48.2. The government sets an import quota of Q¹. This makes the supply curve vertical at Q¹ and raises price to P¹.

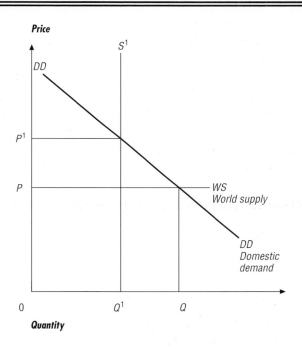

FIG. 48.2

- *Embargoes.* This is the most extreme form of quota since it places a physical limit on imports of zero. In other words it is a complete ban. It may be placed on imports from particular countries (e.g. Iraq during and after the Gulf War and Serbia during the Kosovan crisis) or on imports of certain goods (e.g. weapons and hard drugs).
- *Exchange control.* Importers need foreign currencies to buy goods and services from abroad. American firms will require payment in dollars, German firms in euros, and so on. A country obtains its supplies of foreign currencies by means of the efforts of its exporters. A system of exchange control will require the foreign currencies earned by exporters to be surrendered to the central bank which will pay for them in the home currency. Importers wanting foreign currency must apply to the central bank which can thus control the variety and volume of imports by controlling the issue of foreign currency.

- *Import deposit schemes*. A government can seek to limit imports by requiring importers to place, in advance, a deposit usually with the central bank before they can buy goods and services from abroad. This makes importing more time consuming and more expensive as it reduces the importing firms' liquidity.

NEWER NON-TARIFF MEASURES

The late 20th century witnessed the growth of a number of new methods of trade restriction.

- *Voluntary Export Restraint (VERs)*. A voluntary export restraint is an agreement between two countries where the government of the exporting country agrees to restrict the volume of its exports of a certain good or services. It may do this to prevent tariffs or quotas being imposed on its product. Japan has entered into a number of VERs with EU members and with the USA in the export of its cars.
- *Product standard regulations*. A country can use health and safety regulations to limit imports. Harsh health and safety standards which differ from those operating in the exporting countries can raise exporters' costs and can be used to limit imports on the grounds that they have not reached adequate quality standards.
- *Complex customs procedures*. Imposing the need for laborious and difficult paperwork for goods to enter a country and creating frontier delays, increases the difficulty and cost of exporting.
- *Government contract policy*. A government may have a policy of placing orders with domestic producers in preference to importers even if their goods and services are cheaper or of a better quality. In this case the demand for imports is likely to fall but their price may remain unchanged as shown in Figure 48.3.

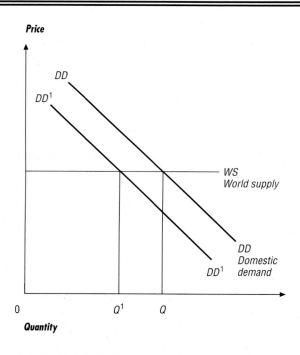

FIG. 48.3

INDIRECT MEASURES

The measures discussed above seek to limit imports directly. Protection from competition from overseas can also come from making domestic products more attractive relative to imports.

- *Subsidies.* A country may decide to subsidise certain domestic industries as a means of protecting them from the competition of lower-priced foreign goods and services. The subsidy will reduce the price of the domestic product and hence make it more difficult for the foreign producer to sell a similar product in the home market. There will be a redistribution of income towards the producers and consumers of the subsidised good or service because the cost of the subsidy will fall on taxpayers.
- *Campaigns.* Governments can seek to switch consumption from imports to domestic products by running campaigns extolling the virtues of buying home produced goods and services and emphasising their quality.

ARGUMENTS ADVANCED FOR PROTECTION

A number of arguments are advanced for limiting free trade.

REVENUE RAISING

Tariffs have been used throughout history to provide the state with revenue. This is one of the motives, albeit not the main one, of the EU common external tariff.

PROTECTING EMPLOYMENT AND COUNTERING THE EFFECT OF A GENERAL DEPRESSION

During the Great Depression of the 1930s, most countries resorted to increased protection of home industries in an attempt to maintain employment at home by diverting expenditure from foreign to domestic products. The idea is that money spent on home produced goods and services creates employment at home while that spent on imports does not. But the imports of one country are the exports of another and restrictions on imports creates unemployment in other countries. They are very likely to retaliate by protecting their own industries. There is the risk of a trade war occurring with barriers to trade becoming higher and higher and more widespread. As world exports decline all trading nations must, to some extent, be worse off.

PROTECTING PARTICULAR INDUSTRIES

- *The infant, or sunrise, industry argument.* This is probably the best-known argument. A nation may be relatively late in developing a particular industry and yet be favourably endowed with the basic economic requirements for the effective operation of such an industry. If the industry were to be established on a small scale in conditions of free trade, it would not survive the competition from fully developed large-scale producers who would be enjoying economies of scale and so would be operating at much lower costs. It may therefore be necessary to protect the infant industry until it reaches a scale of production large enough to allow its costs to fall to a level which is competitive with its foreign rivals. Unfortunately, once imposed, there is the danger that the industries become reliant on them and do not very actively seek to reduce their average costs.
- *The declining, or sunset, industry argument.* The comparative advantages enjoyed by different countries in the production of different goods and services are always changing. These changes in the comparative costs of

production will mean that particular industries will be declining in some countries and expanding in others. Ideally, a country should be moving its resources from those industries where it is losing its cost advantages, but resources are usually not sufficiently mobile for this transfer to take place without some hardship. Capital and labour cannot be moved quickly and easily from say the cotton industry to the computer industry; specialised labour and capital are very immobile. When industries come under pressure from the lower-priced goods and services of the more efficient foreign competitors there is usually a strong political demand for some measure of protection while some adjustment to the new situation takes place. The industries may be allowed to scale down or decline gradually through natural wastage. This should prevent a sudden and possibly significant rise in unemployment.

- *Prevention of dumping argument.* A strong argument can be advanced to protect industries against dumping. Foreign producers may be selling their products at less than cost in order to get rid of surplus stock and to gain a monopoly position in the export market by driving out domestic producers.
- *Protection of strategic industries.* Some industries such as agriculture and armaments are regarded as strategic industries which are important to a nation in a war situation. It is considered that such industries should be maintained so as to reduce a nation's dependence on foreign supplies of strategic materials. Where they have not been competitive in world markets these industries have normally protected by means of tariffs or quotas.
- *Avoiding the risks of overspecialisation.* A number of industries may be protected to ensure a diversified industrial structure.

SAFEGUARDING THE INTERESTS OF WORKERS

The basis of this particular argument is that imports from countries where wages are relatively low represent 'unfair' competition and threaten the living of the more highly paid workers in the home industries.

In recent years concern has been expressed about the UK's ability to compete against, e.g., China and India. However a policy of restricting imports from low-wage countries will simply reduce the demand for these products, increase unemployment in these countries and drive wages there even lower. It will also increase the cost of living at home and lessen the incentives to move resources out of the industries which have lost their comparative advantages. It is an argument which could well be used against the country imposing the restrictions. For example, the USA might use such an argument to restrict the entry of UK goods, since, relative to the USA, the UK is a low-wage country.

PREVENTING OR ELIMINATING A BALANCE OF PAYMENTS DEFICIT

A country may find that it is persistently spending more on foreign goods and services than it is earning from the sale of its exports. It may, after attempting to eliminate this deficit by increasing its exports and substituting home products for imported goods resort to import restrictions. However, if the cause of the deficit is poor quality goods and services or lack of price competitiveness the problem may return.

The Cambridge Economic Policy Group has advocated a general system of import controls to protect the UK economy whilst the UK economy is restructured by building up infant industries and allowing some industries to decline gradually. They argue that in the past the UK governments have reduced imports by deflationary policy which has had an adverse effect on UK and foreign employment. They believe that by controlling the value of imports which enter the UK, the UK economy can grow and with growth will come an increased ability to afford to purchase imports.

PROTECTIONISM VERSUS FREE TRADE

There are strong arguments against the restriction of international trade. Tariffs, for example, distort true cost relationships and reduce the differences in comparative costs. The extent of international specialisation is reduced and so is the potential level of world output. Consumers in the home country are obliged to pay higher prices for the protected home-produced goods and services and for imports. The erection of trade barriers also invites retaliation and increases the probability of a general reduction in world trade. Industries operating behind a tariff wall are protected from foreign competition and this could lead to a lower level of efficiency.

On the other hand there are arguments which can be advanced for the protection of particular industries or for a general system of protection in particular circumstances. Some of these may apply particularly in the case of developing countries which are trying to build up infant industries and industries producing substitutes for imports.

THE WORLD TRADE ORGANISATION

The World Trade Organisation (WTO), which is based in Geneva, came into existence on 1 January 1995. It replaced the General Agreement on Tariffs and Trade (GATT). The WTO is a multilateral trade organisation covering goods, services and intellectual property rights. It seeks to encourage the lowering of trade restrictions and to settle trade disputes with a common disputes procedure. Member countries meet at regular intervals to negotiate agreements to reduce quotas, tariffs and other restrictions.

Q U E S T I O N S

SHORT QUESTIONS

1. Explain the difference between a tariff and a quota.

2. What are the main motives behind dumping?

3. What is the main argument for free trade?

4. Explain what is meant by strategic industries.

MULTIPLE CHOICE

1. What effect will the imposition of a tariff have on prices and production in the country imposing the tariff?

	Prices	Production
A	raise	raise
B	raise	lower
C	lower	lower
D	lower	raise

2. Figure 48.4 shows the domestic market for a good. With free international trade the price is P. The country then imposes a tariff on imports of the good causing domestic price to rise to P^1.

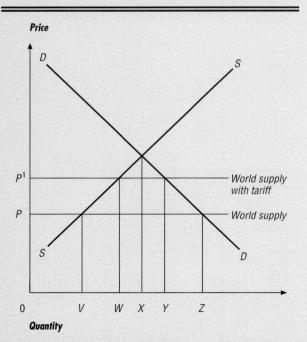

FIG. 48.4

What will be the change in the quantity of goods imported as a result of the tariff? A fall from:

A. Z to Y

B. Z to X

C. VZ to VY

D. VZ to WY.

3. What is an *ad valorem* tariff?

A. A tax imposed on the price of imports.

B. A tax imposed on the volume of imports.

C. A limit on the volume of imports.

D. A limit on the value of imports.

4. Which of the following would reduce the level of protection enjoyed by a domestic industry?

A. An increase in the level of an import quota on the product.

B. An increase in the rate of import duty on the product.

C. The imposition of an embargo on the import of the product.

D. The granting of a subsidy to domestic producers of the product.

DATA RESPONSE

Trade relations between America and Europe have rarely been so bad. They are embroiled in a battle over hormone-treated beef. They are at loggerheads over genetically modified crops. They have fallen out over noisy aircraft, mobile telephones and data privacy. They are coming to blows over aerospace subsidies and champagne. And they have yet to patch up their split over bananas.

True, transatlantic trade tiffs are nothing new. Indeed, some friction is perhaps inevitable between the world's top two trading entities, which do trade of around $400b a year with each other. The mood in both Washington and Brussels is resentful and uncompromising. Events could easily get out of hand. The current conflict is about more than just hormones in beef or aircraft noise. It is a battle about how far countries are willing to accept constraints on domestic policy in sensitive areas such as food safety or environmental protection for the sake of free trade.

The battle is putting huge strains on the World Trade Organisation. The body that polices world trade cannot function properly unless America and Europe accept its writ.

The timing of the recent clashes is partly chance. Long-standing wrangles over bananas and beef have finally worked their way through the WTO's dispute-settlement mechanism. On 6 April the WTO ruled for the third time that the European Union must amend its banana-import rules, which discriminate unfairly against American fruit distributors. On 19 April the WTO gave America the go-ahead to slap retaliatory sanctions against $191m of European imports — the first time it has sanctioned such a move.

The WTO has also ruled that the EU must lift its ban on hormone-treated beef by 13 May, because there is no scientific evidence that the hormones are dangerous. America is planning to impose sanctions on around $300m of European imports, mainly foodstuffs and motorcycles, if the EU shows no signs of complying with the WTO's ruling by then. Last week the EU hit back with a new report claiming that the hormones could cause cancer. It also raised the stakes after hormones were found in imports of supposedly hormone-free American beef. It is threatening to ban all American beef on 15 June unless America can provide watertight guarantees that it is hormone-free.

Last week the Europeans also issued new restrictions on noisy aeroplanes that will hit American companies particularly hard, although the new rules will not take effect until next year. America in turn launched two new WTO cases against the EU. One is about subsidies to Airbus, Boeing's rival in aerospace. The other is over EU rules on geographical labels, which prevent, for instance, sparkling Californian wines being called champagne.

America and Europe (like most countries) tend to see trade as a zero-sum game. They aim to pry open markets for their exporters while protecting their domestic industries. Access to their markets is granted only in exchange for access to others. Such policies are wrong-headed, since a country as a whole gains by opening its markets unilaterally. But they are pervasive, since industries that fear foreign competitors tend to lobby governments harder than the disparate millions of consumers who benefit from cheaper imports.

The EU has never been particularly keen on free trade. Over half its budget goes on the explicitly protectionist Common Agricultural Policy (CAP). Trade barriers between EU member states have been removed less out of a liberal belief in free trade than with the aim of creating a large, protected market for European firms.

Source: 'At daggers drawn', The Economist, 8/5/99.

a] Explain why the Common Agricultural Policy is protectionist. **(5)**

b] What is the role of the World Trade Organisation in international trade? **(4)**

c] Discuss two non-tariff protectionist measures mentioned in the extract. **(4)**

d] What benefits may consumers and producers gain from their country 'opening its markets unilaterally'? **(6)**

e] Discuss the possible costs and benefits of the EU banning American beef. **(6)**

CASE STUDY

At a meeting of American and European business leaders in North Carolina last weekend, senior US officials, led by vice-president Al Gore, harshly criticised the EU for not doing enough to increase demand and open its market to Asian imports.

US steelmakers have filed anti-dumping complaints against Brazil, Japan and Russia. But it is uncertain whether the US International Trade Commission, an independent federal agency which decides dumping cases, will find in the industry's favour. That has prompted Mr Clinton's advisers to consider other, unspecified types of retaliation.

The outcome is shaping up as a watershed. If US steelmakers win protection, that risks setting off a round of similar demands from others. The European steel industry recently decided to file complaints against competitors in Africa, Asia and eastern Europe.

US chipmakers have already brought dumping complaints against Taiwan while US apple growers, who have been devastated by a slump in world market prices, are considering similar action against China.

It has long been clear that pressures for protection would focus on anti-dumping policy, because it is one of the few forms of trade restriction permitted under WTO rules. Although it is governed by some WTO-imposed constraints, its practice has been widely criticised as arbitrary and elastic.

Recently, the critics seemed to be gaining ground in the EU, where a slim majority of member governments has repeatedly rebuffed European Commission attempts to impose dumping duties on cotton fabric from Asia and the Middle East.

However, it is unclear how firmly resistance will hold up if European economic recovery falters, and the US begins to close its markets. Much may also depend on whether the new German government's taste for intervention leads it to question its country's traditional role as a champion of free trade.

Source: 'Slipping on a banana skin' by Guy de Jonquieres, Financial Times, 13/11/98.

a] How could a government 'open its market' to imports? **(5)**

b] Explain what is meant by dumping. **(5)**

c] How might the American government restrict imports of steel? **(6)**

d] Discuss the effect of the imposition of import restrictions on the operation of the law of comparative advantage. **(6)**

e] What are the risks of a country specialising in a limited range of goods and services? **(6)**

f] Explain the effect of imposing dumping duties on imports on the market for a product. Illustrate your answer with a diagram. **(7)**

g] Why may an economic recession make a country or a group of countries be more inclined to impose import restrictions? **(7)**

h] Discuss the arguments for not placing import restrictions on steel imports from Africa, Asia and eastern Europe. **(8)**

STRUCTURED ESSAY

a] Discuss the forms that import restrictions may take. **(10)**

b] Evaluate the arguments for and against protectionism. **(15)**

FREE RESPONSE ESSAY

Assess the advantages and disadvantages consumers may experience as a result of import restrictions. **(25)**

49 THE TERMS OF TRADE

DEFINITION

The terms of trade is the rate at which one country's products exchange against those of other countries. The terms of trade can be expressed as the quantity of goods and services which one country exchanges for a given quantity of goods and services from other countries. However, it is more common to express the terms of trade as a ratio between the index of export prices and the index of import prices:

$$\frac{\text{Index of export prices}}{\text{Index of import prices}} \times 100$$

MEASUREMENT

The index of export prices and the index of import prices are weighted price indexes. They are constructed from a sample of prices of more than 200 export and import commodities respectively.

In the base year each of the two index numbers will be 100 so the terms of trade will be 100. If export prices rise relative to import prices the terms of trade will rise. The terms of trade index will fall if import prices rise relative to export prices. There are a number of ways in which such changes might come about. Export prices and import prices could be moving in opposite directions, one set of prices could be stable while the other is changing or export prices and import prices could be moving in the same direction but one could be rising or falling faster than the other.

MOVEMENTS IN THE TERMS OF TRADE

A rise in the terms of trade is described as a favourable movement or an improvement in the terms of trade. This is because it indicates that any given volume of exports will exchange for a greater volume of imports. Similarly a fall in the terms of trade is described as unfavourable, adverse or a deterioration as any given volume of exports will exchange for a smaller volume of imports. However, the terms can be misleading. For example, a so-called favourable movement in the terms of trade may have an unfavourable effect on the country's trade position. This is because export revenue and import expenditure depend not only on price changes but also on quantity changes.

TABLE 49.1 THE UK TERMS OF TRADE (1995 = 100)

Year	Index of export prices	Index of import prices	Terms of trade
1993	95.0	91.2	104.2
1994	96.9	94.3	102.8
1995	100.0	100.0	100.0
1996	100.8	100.1	100.7
1997	95.2	93.8	101.5
1998	90.2	88.3	102.2

Source: ONS, Monthly Digest of Statistics, April 1999.

CAUSES OF MOVEMENTS IN THE TERMS OF TRADE

Changes in demand and supply conditions, inflation rates and the external value of the currency can alter the terms of trade. For example an unfavourable movement in a country's terms of trade could be caused by:

- a decrease in foreign demand for the country's exports and hence the price of exports
- an increase in the supply of major exports which results in a fall in their price
- a rise in other countries' inflation rates relative to the country's inflation rate which raises import prices
- a fall in the value of the country's currency. This leads to a fall in the price of exports relative to imports. Devaluation is sometimes referred to as a deliberate worsening of the terms of trade.

PROFILE

NAME: Alan Greenspan
Chairman of the Federal Reserve of the United States

BORN: 1926

NATIONALITY: American

EDUCATED: George Washington High School, Juilliard School of Music, New York University

KEY POSTS HELD: Chief economic adviser to Presidents Nixon, Ford and Reagan

QUOTES ON GREENSPAN:
'... *he is the most powerful man in the world*' The Observer *29/8/99*.

THE EFFECTS OF CHANGES IN THE TERMS OF TRADE

The effects of changes in the terms of trade are influenced by their cause, the income effect and by the time period under review.

CAUSE

An increase in export prices arising from an increase in demand will have a more beneficial effect on the balance of payments position than an increase arising from inflation.

TIME PERIOD

In the short run demand for exports and imports is likely to be relatively inelastic. This is because it will take some time for purchasers to notice price changes and to find alternative suppliers. When demand is inelastic a fall in export prices will result in a smaller percentage increase in demand for exports and so export revenue will fall. Whereas if imports are in inelastic demand and their price rises, demand will fall by a smaller percentage resulting in a rise in import expenditure. The rise in import expenditure and fall in export revenue will worsen the country's current account position on the balance of payments.

However, in the longer run demand for exports and imports is likely to be more elastic as people have time to adjust to the price changes. If demand for exports is elastic, demand will rise by more than the fall in price and export revenue will rise. And if demand for imports is inelastic a rise in their price will result in a greater percentage fall in demand and a fall in import expenditure. So in the longer run an 'unfavourable' movement in the terms of trade could lead to an improvement in the country's current account position.

THE INCOME EFFECT

Higher prices for imports could mean that foreign countries are earning more from their exports. As a result their abilities to buy from other countries will be correspondingly increased. So the country may find that it is selling more abroad because the price of its imports have risen.

THE SIGNIFICANCE OF THE TERMS OF TRADE

For countries which engage in world trade on a large scale, as e.g. the UK and Singapore do, movements in the terms of trade are important. When the volumes of imports and exports are very large, quite small changes in the terms of trade can make a large impact on the balance of payments. For example in the UK in 1998 imports were £184 302m. So even a 1% fall in import prices would have meant a saving of £1843m in foreign currency, or alternatively the existing level of exports could have bought additional imports of £1843m.

QUESTIONS

SHORT QUESTIONS

1. What effect would a fall in export prices and a rise in import prices have on the terms of trade?
2. What is meant by a favourable movement in the terms of trade?
3. What effect would a decrease in the supply of a major export have on a country's terms of trade?
4. What effect would a rise in a country's exchange rate have on its terms of trade?

MULTIPLE CHOICE

1. What is an adverse movement in the terms of trade?

    A. The movement of the balance of trade from a surplus to a deficit.

    B. A fall in the volume of exports relative to the volume of imports.

    C. A fall in the total value of exports relative to the total value of imports.

    D. A fall in the average price of exports relative to the average price of imports.

2. The following figures show a country's export and import prices and volumes for two years.

	Exports	
	Price index	Volume index
2000	105	110
2001	110	108
	Imports	
2000	120	100
2001	120	120

What happened to the country's terms of trade from 2000 to 2001?

A. There was a favourable movement from 87.5 to 91.7.

B. There was an unfavourable movement from 114.3 to 109.1.

C. There was a favourable movement from 90.9 to 111.1.

D. There was an unfavourable movement from 110 to 90.

3. Which of the following could cause a deterioration in a country's terms of trade?

    A. A rise in the price of imports the country buys.

    B. A rise in the value of the country's currency.

    C. A fall in export revenue.

    D. A fall in the country's trade in goods balance.

4. The figures in the table show the terms of trade for a country:

Year	Terms of trade
2000	102
2001	108
2002	120
2003	125

What could have caused the movement in the terms of trade for the period shown?

A. Import prices rising more than export prices.

B. Import prices rising and export prices falling.

C. Import prices remaining unchanged and export prices falling.

D. Import prices falling more than export prices.

DATA RESPONSE

The data below relate to a hypothetical country which exports and imports mainly manufactured goods. The country increased the quality of its exports in 1995 and its export market was also helped by rising incomes abroad in the same year. However in 1996 the country experienced a rise in inflation. Its current account position began to worsen and at the end of 1998 the value of its currency fell.

Year	Index of export prices	Index of import prices
1994	96	98
1995	100	100
1996	105	101
1997	107	102
1998	104	96
1999	103	98

a] Calculate the terms of trade for the period shown. **(4)**

b] Describe the movement in the terms of trade from 1994 to 1995. **(4)**

c] Which is the base year? Explain your answer. **(3)**

d] Explain the effect that the events in 1995 and 1996 were likely to have had on:
   i   the terms of trade **(4)**
   ii the country's current account position. **(5)**

e] Discuss what may have caused the movement in the terms of trade which occurred in 1999. **(5)**

CASE STUDY

In March 1999 the pound sterling rose to a six month high despite the UK earning less from exports and spending more on imports (causing a negative gap between revenue from exports and expenditure on imports — a deficit on trade in goods). The surplus on trade in services was also falling. Demand for pounds was rising not due to trade in goods and services but because investors were considering that the pound was a safe currency. This higher demand caused the sterling effective exchange rate (the price of the pound in terms of a trade weighted basket of currencies) to rise above the level of 1998.

UK exporters expressed concern about the strength of the pound. Throughout the first part of 1999 exports continued to fall in both value and volume. The lost export business had a lagged effect on unemployment. Whilst manufacturing output, which is particularly exposed to foreign competition, fell in early 1999 by 1.2% relative to 1998, manufacturing employment fell by 2.9% several months later.

The rise in the pound did, however, produce an increase of more than 20% in UK citizens' international purchasing power relative to their European neighbours.

YEAR	STERLING EFFECTIVE EXCHANGE RATE
1994	100.0
1995	95.1
1996	96.7
1997	112.7
1998	116.5

a] What effect will a rise in the value of the pound have on the UK's terms of trade? **(6)**

b] Explain why a rise in the value of the pound may be accompanied by a deterioration in its balance of payments position. **(6)**

c] Discuss what effect a fall in export revenue will have on national income. **(6)**

d] Why may there be a time lag between changes in output and unemployment? **(5)**

e] Discuss two reasons, other than a change in the currency, for a rise in expenditure on imports. **(6)**

f] Explain what effect the movement in the sterling effective exchange rate from 1994 to 1995 would have had on the UK's terms of trade. **(6)**

g] Discuss what, apart from a rise in the currency, could cause a change in the terms of trade. **(7)**

h] Explain how the terms of trade are measured. **(8)**

STRUCTURED ESSAY

a] Discuss the meaning and causes of a favourable movement in the terms of trade. **(10)**

b] Assess the effect of a favourable movement in the terms of trade on a country's current account on the balance of payments position. **(15)**

FREE RESPONSE ESSAY

Discuss the possible effects on the living standards of a country's inhabitants of a change in the country's terms of trade. **(25)**

50 THE BALANCE OF PAYMENTS

DEFINITION

A country engaging in foreign trade will be making payments to foreign countries and receiving payments. Each nation keeps an account of its transactions with the rest of the world, which it presents in the form of a balance sheet described as the balance of payments.

SECTIONS OF THE UK BALANCE OF PAYMENTS

In 1998 the presentation of the UK balance of payments was changed to fit in with the new European System of Accounts. It now consists of four main sections. These are the current account, the capital account, the financial account and the international investment position.

THE CURRENT ACCOUNT

This section concerns income and expenditure and is divided into four categories as follows.

Trade in goods

This covers the exports and imports of goods. For example, the export of oil from the UK appears as a credit item as it involves money coming into the country, whereas the import of cars from Germany appears as a debit item. The UK's trade in goods is usually in deficit. Figure 50.1 shows the UK's trade in goods balance from 1976 to 1997. The surplus in the early 1980s was largely the result of exports of North Sea oil.

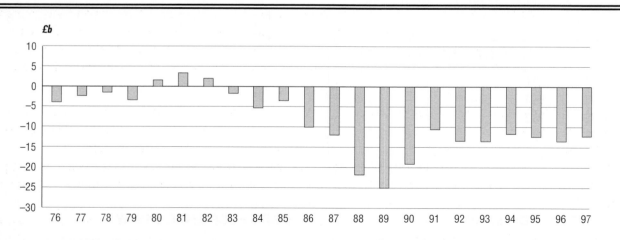

FIG. 50.1

Trade in services

In contrast to the trade in goods, the UK's trade in services is usually in surplus. Indeed it has been in surplus from 1966. Figure 50.2 shows the UK trade in services balance from 1976 to 1997.

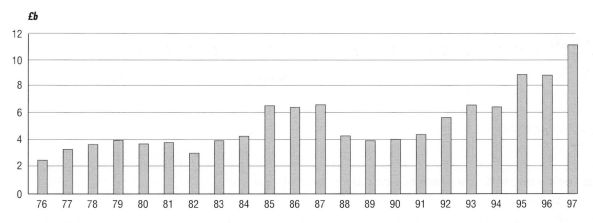

FIG. 50.2

By definition, trade in services covers exports and imports of services. For example, foreign tourist expenditure in the UK is recorded as a credit item and the purchase by UK residents of financial services from abroad appears as a debit item. There are eleven main product groupings in this category: transportation (sea, air, rail, road and pipeline); travel (tourism, educated and health related travel); communications services (postal, courier and telecommunications services); construction services; insurance services; financial services; computer and information services; royalties and licence fees; other business services (e.g., legal and management consultancy and advertising); personal; cultural and recreational services, and government services (e.g. spending by embassies, military units and agencies).

Income

This covers compensation of employees' earnings arising from employment abroad and investment income. The former consists of employment income from cross-border and seasonal workers. This is not very significant in the UK. Indeed it is investment income which dominates this section accounting for more than 95% of total income credits and debits. Investment income, in the form of profits, dividends and interest payments and receipts, arises from foreign investment and the holdings of financial assets and liabilities. For example, earnings on foreign shares held by UK residents and financial institutions are recorded as credit items whereas interest paid by UK companies on loans from foreign banks are recorded as debit items. Investment income is broken down into the following four categories.

- *Direct investment income.* This covers, as credit items, profits earned by UK companies from their overseas branches, subsidiaries and associated companies and rent on foreign property held by UK residents. Debit items include earnings by foreign companies and citizens on their corresponding assets held in the UK.
- *Portfolio investment income.* This comprises interest earned on foreign bonds and dividends earned on foreign shares held by UK companies and residents minus earnings enjoyed by foreigners on UK bonds and shares.
- *Other investment income.* This includes earnings on loans and deposits.
- *Reserve assets.* This covers the interest received on the official reserves the UK holds, e.g. on foreign exchange reserves and special drawing rights (SDRs).

Current transfers

Current transfers consist of payments and receipts where there is no corresponding exchange of a good or service. This section is broken down into two categories as follows.

- *Central government transfers.* The items in this category include taxes and payments to and receipts from the European Union, bilateral aid, social security payments abroad, military grants and miscellaneous (e.g. cost of involvement in the Kosovan crisis).
- *Other sector transfers.* These include, e.g., receipts from the EU social fund which the UK passes on to the final beneficiaries, taxes on income and wealth paid by UK workers and businesses to foreign governments, insurance premiums and claims, workers' remittances and private gifts. The current transfers account is usually in deficit.

The recent UK current account position

The current account balance fluctuates but is usually in deficit. In the early 1980s it was in surplus, in the late 1980s it moved into a significant deficit. From 1990 the deficit started to decline and in 1997 it moved into surplus as shown in Figure 50.3. This improvement was largely the result of increasing surpluses in investment income. In 1999 a deficit reappeared.

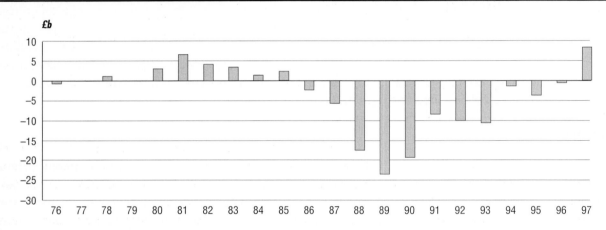

FIG. 50.3

THE CAPITAL ACCOUNT

The new capital account came into existence in 1998. It is a relatively small section which is usually in surplus. It includes two categories as follows:

Capital transfers

These include government investment grants and a new item, debt forgiveness which is the forgiveness of a debt by a creditor by mutual agreement.

Acquisition/disposal of non-produced, non-financial assets

This category is concerned with the purchase or sale of particular assets e.g. land purchased or sold by a foreign embassy, purchases and sales of patents, copyrights, trademarks, franchises and leases.

THE FINANCIAL ACCOUNT

This section corresponds to the old capital account which was also known as transactions in assets and liabilities. It concerns investments by residents in the UK abroad and investment by non-residents in the UK. Foreign investment in the UK involves money entering the country and is recorded as a credit item whereas UK investment abroad, which involves money leaving the country, is recorded as a debit item.

It is these investments which generate the income and payments which appear in the investment income category in the income account. As with investment income it is divided into four categories as follows.

- *Direct investment.* This involves the transfer of ownership of UK and foreign businesses e.g. the setting up of a branch of a UK company abroad and the expansion of a foreign-owned firm in the UK.
- *Portfolio investment.* This covers the purchase of foreign government bonds, treasury bills and shares by UK residents and the purchase of UK stocks and shares by foreign residents.
- *Other investment.* This includes deposits with banks held by UK residents abroad and those held by foreign residents in the UK and loans between UK banks and the government and foreign banks and governments.
- *Reserve assets.* This involves changes in government reserve assets of foreign exchange, reserve position in the IMF, SDRs and gold.

In recent years investment transactions have increased significantly and now involve large sums.

NET ERRORS AND OMISSIONS

As noted above the balance of payments is a balance sheet. As with all balance sheets it must balance. The total outflow of money, debit items, must equal the total inflow of money, credit items. So when added together, the current, capital and net transactions balances should add up to zero. However, in practice, because of mistakes and failure to record all items, often due to a time delay, there is always a discrepancy.

The net errors and omissions figure (which used to be known as the balancing item) is the amount which is required to bring the recorded balance of payments into balance. The inclusion of net errors and omissions makes the sum of the credit and debit items equal zero. A positive balancing item means there has been an unrecorded net inflow of foreign currency.

Summary of the UK balance of payments in 1998

	£m	£m
Current account		
Trade in goods and services	−7920	
Income	15782	
Current transfers	−6388	
Current balance		1474
Capital balance		438
Net financial transactions		−9094
Net errors and omissions		7182

Sources: Monthly Digest of Statistics, April 1999, Office for National Statistics

THE INTERNATIONAL INVESTMENT POSITION

This shows the levels of external assets and liabilities. In contrast to the financial account, which shows the flows (purchases and sales) of external assets and liabilities, this section shows the stock of these items which has been built up over time.

The structure of this account is essentially the same as the financial account and the investment income account. It is again subdivided into direct investment, portfolio investment, other investment and reserve assets.

Table 50.1 summarises the position.

TABLE 50.1 SUMMARY OF BALANCE OF PAYMENTS IN 1997: CURRENT, CAPITAL AND FINANCIAL ACCOUNTS

£ million

	Credits	Debits	Balances
CURRENT ACCOUNT	**354 179**	**346 173**	**8 006**
Goods and services	228 702	229 334	−632
Goods	171 798	183 590	−11 792
Services	56 904	45 744	11 160
Income	109 427	97 259	12 168
Compensation of employees	1 007	924	83
Investment income	108 420	96 335	12 085
Direct investment	32 715	18 365	14 350
Portfolio investment	26 002	23 454	2 548
Other investment (including earnings on reserve assets)	49 703	54 516	−4 813
Current transfers	16 050	19 580	−3 530
Central government	6 358	5 071	1 287
Other sectors	9 692	14 509	−4 817
CAPITAL AND FINANCIAL ACCOUNTS	**249 187**	**257 037**	**−7 850**
Capital account	1 052	790	262
Capital transfers	982	686	296
Acquisition/disposal of non-produced, non-financial assets	70	104	−34
Financial account	248 135	256 247	−8 112
Direct investment	23 257	36 344	−13 087
Portfolio investment	29 621	51 989	−22 368
Other investment	195 257	170 271	24 986
Reserve assets		−2 357	2 357
TOTAL	**603 366**	**603 210**	**156**
Net errors and omissions	−156		−156

United Kingdom Balance of Payments 1998, Office for National Statistics

DEFICITS AND SURPLUSES

Although the overall balance of payments must balance, the different sections need not balance. For example a country may spend more on imports of goods and services than it earns from the export of goods and services. To finance this the country may borrow from abroad or sell assets.

CAUSES OF DEFICITS ON THE TRADE IN GOODS AND SERVICES BALANCE

A deficit may arise from high income levels in the domestic economy. This is because when incomes are high people will usually buy more goods and services. Some of these will come from abroad, thereby increasing imports, and some from domestic producers, thereby reducing exports. In addition to increasing the imports of finished manufactured goods, high incomes may also increase expenditure on imported raw materials as domestic firms expand output to meet higher domestic demand. In contrast, it is when income levels abroad are low that a deficit may arise. This is because overseas countries are likely to import less and to compete more vigorously in export markets.

Another possible cause of a deficit is an overvalued exchange rate. This will make exports expensive in terms of foreign currencies, and imports cheap in terms of the domestic currency. If demand for exports and imports is elastic, export revenue will fall and import expenditure will rise.

There are, however, more serious problems which can cause a deficit. The country may be producing goods and services of a low quality, its costs of production may be higher and it may be producing goods and services in low world demand.

EFFECTS OF DEFICITS AND SURPLUSES ON THE TRADE IN GOODS AND SERVICES BALANCE

The effects will depend on the size, cause and duration of the deficit or surplus. In the short term a deficit will increase living standards. This is because the country will be consuming more goods and services than it produces. However, if the deficit is not covered by investment income or an inflow of overseas investment, it will have to be financed by drawing on reserves or borrowing. Reserves are not finite and it may be difficult to find willing lenders. In addition, borrowing and attracting overseas investment will later involve an outflow of interest, profits and dividends in the future, thereby weakening the investment income account.

A deficit will reduce the money supply if it is not offset by the monetary authorities or another section of the balance of payments. It will reduce inflationary pressure as it involves a net leakage of demand but will also reduce employment and economic growth.

In contrast, a surplus involves a net injection of extra demand in the economy. It is often taken to be a sign of economic strength. However, it is not completely beneficial. It involves an opportunity cost since the country is forgoing the opportunity to consume more goods and services. It may also add to inflationary pressure as it involves a net inflow of money and a net outflow of goods and services.

QUESTIONS

SHORT QUESTIONS

1. What is meant by investment income?

2. In what sense must the balance of payments always balance?

3. What is the difference between direct and portfolio investment?

4. What does the net errors and omissions section of the balance of payments cover?

MULTIPLE CHOICE

1. Which of the following items would appear as a credit item in the financial account of the UK balance of payments?

   A. The investment by a UK company in a foreign subsidiary.

   B. A South Korean firm building a motor assembly plant in the UK.

   C. The purchase of a US television series by a UK television company.

   D. The payment of interest by a UK company on a loan from a French bank.

2. The following table shows data relating to the 1996 UK balance of payments.

	£m
trade in goods	−13086
trade in services	8897
net income	8111
net current transfers	−4522
capital account balance	736
financial account balance	1781

   Source: United Kingdom Balance of Payments, 1998, Office for National Statistics

   What can be deduced from these data?

   A. The balance of trade in goods and services was £21983m.

   B. The current account balance was £136m.

   C. Transactions in assets exceeded transactions in liabilities.

   D. Net errors and omissions amounted to −£1917m.

3. What is meant by a surplus on the current account of the balance of payments?

   A. An excess of export goods over import goods.

   B. An excess of exported services over imported services.

   C. An excess of total receipts from goods and services over total payment for goods and services.

   D. An excess of total receipts from goods, services, investment income and current transfers over total payments for goods and services, investment income and current transfers.

4. Which of the following would appear as debit item in the French current account of the balance of payments?

   A. Expenditure of foreign tourists in France.

   B. Expenditure of French embassies abroad.

   C. Sales of shares in German companies to French citizens.

   D. Sales of French manufactured goods to Thailand.

DATA RESPONSE

Since 1980 the Chinese economy has become much more open, in terms of international trade. Its international trade volume has grown very rapidly and has attracted billions of direct foreign investment. Exports and imports, as a proportion of GDP, have more than tripled.

China currently has a comparative advantage in labour-intensive activities and its exports include textiles and light manufactured goods. Its main imports consist of machinery and other capital equipment.

Despite its good trade record in the 1980s and most of the 1990s the economy started to experience difficulties in the late 1990s mainly as a result of the East Asian crisis. In May 1999 its trade surplus fell by 48.6% after a significant rise in imports. The Chinese economy was experiencing a fall in demand but the government did not want firms to make workers redundant. As a result manufacturing firms sought to increase their efficiency and restore corporate profit margins by importing high technology equipment. In the first five months of 1999 imports of machinery and electronic equipment, which are purchased mainly by state enterprises, grew by 27.7%. The largest increase was accounted for by electronic equipment. In the same period Chinese exports rose by 4.2%.

a] What may cause a trade surplus to fall? **(5)**

b] Explain what is meant by:
   i   an open economy **(2)**
   ii comparative advantage. **(4)**

c] Explain two advantages Chinese consumers may have gained from their economy becoming more open. **(4)**

d] What effect does inward direct foreign investment have on a country's balance of payments in the short run? **(5)**

e] Explain why the importing of high technology equipment may result in an improvement in China's trade position in the future. **(5)**

CASE STUDY

Once upon a time the balance of payments was the key indicator for the British economy. Forget about inflation, growth, or even unemployment — the thing that people really honed in on was the trade gap.

The British 'obsession' reached its peak in the 1970s, that nadir for the British economy. Four successive, and big, annual current-account deficits over the period 1973–76 meant, along with the accompanying loss of control over both fiscal and monetary policy, that Britain had to turn to the International Monetary Fund for help.

In the 1980s all this changed. The arrival of North Sea oil meant that a £3b current-account deficit in 1974 (about £18b in today's prices), was converted into a £6.5b surplus by 1981. The obsession was over. The only residual worry about the balance of payments was that, thanks to oil, it was so healthy that it pushed the pound to uncompetitive levels.

In the late 1980s, when the boom sucked in imports to produce a record £23.5b current-account deficit, nobody was too bothered.

Nigel Lawson, the then chancellor, said the only important thing about the current-account deficit was whether it could be easily financed. Britain's could be easily financed, so there was no need to worry.

The early 1990s recession and sterling's subsequent sharp fall provided the basis for a sustained current-account improvement. In 1997, an election year, the current account was in surplus by £6.3b.

All this is now changing. Last week it was reported that the trade deficit in goods in the first three months of the year was £7.1b, the worst on record. Despite better-than-expected figures for the non-EU trade deficit in April, the trend is worrying, particularly with exports to Europe down by more than 4% in the first quarter.

Britain's deteriorating external position is also having a clear impact on growth. The downward revision of the first-quarter gross domestic figures offered a crumb of comfort to those of us who had predicted recession, and was explained by the weakness of net exports.

It is one thing, of course, to have a deteriorating trade position, but surely, as happened last year, other bits of the current account will come to the rescue. Last year, Britain's net investment income from abroad jumped from £11b in the previous year to £15.7b. The strength of investment income is something of a mystery.

Britain, which in the 1980s had net external assets second only to Japan, now has net liabilities (liabilities exceeding assets) of £58b. Despite having fewer assets abroad than foreigners have here, Britain manages to achieve substantial, and expanding, net investment income.

This is either a tribute to the City of London's financial management capabilities, or it is unsustainable. The evidence is that there is a bit of the former, but quite a lot of the latter. Last year's improvement, for example, owes much to the fact that the London operations of foreign-owned banks made big losses during last autumn's financial crisis. Instead of repatriating profits, as they normally would do, they repatriated losses.

As these factors drop out, which they surely will, and as the deteriorating trade position kicks in, the current account will worsen sharply.

Source: 'Mind the ballooning trade gap' by David Smith, The Sunday Times, 30/5/99.

a] Explain what is meant by:
i a trade gap **(2)**
ii a current account deficit **(3)**
iii uncompetitive level of the pound. **(3)**

b] In which sector of the UK balance of payments would revenue from the sale of North Sea oil appear? **(2)**

c] Explain why:

i an economic boom may result in a current account deficit **(6)**

ii a recession may result in an improvement in the current account position. **(6)**

d] What may cause a decrease in exports? **(6)**

e] Discuss the effect a current account deficit is likely to have on employment and growth. **(8)**

f] Explain what is meant by investment income. **(4)**

g] What is the difference between net external assets and net external liabilities. **(4)**

h] Explain why David Smith believed the current account position would worsen in 1999. **(6)**

STRUCTURED ESSAY

a] Distinguish between the current account and the financial account on a country's balance of payments. **(10)**

b] Explain the effects that an American multinational company setting up a branch in the UK would have on the UK's balance of payments in the short and long run. **(15)**

FREE RESPONSE ESSAY

Discuss whether a deficit on a country's trade in goods and services balance is necessarily a cause for concern. **(25)**

51 EXCHANGE RATES

The exchange rate is the price of a currency in terms of another currency or currencies. Countries can operate a floating, managed or fixed exchange rate. They may also have the choice of operating their own currency or using the same currency as the other members of a trade bloc.

FLOATING EXCHANGE RATES

DEFINITION

A floating exchange rate can also be referred to as freely floating or freely fluctuating exchange rate. It is one where the price of one currency in terms of another, or others, is determined by the forces of demand and supply operating without any official interference.

   For example, in this type of market the price of the pound in terms of the dollar would depend on the demand for pounds from holders of dollars and the supply of pounds from holders of sterling who are wanting to buy dollars. UK residents trying to buy foreign goods and services will be supplying pounds to the foreign exchange market (and demanding foreign currencies) while overseas residents wishing to buy UK goods and services will be demanding pounds (and supplying foreign currencies). There will be some equilibrium price (i.e. exchange rate) which equates these two forces. The price of pounds will be expressed in terms of foreign currencies. Figure 51.1 shows the equilibrium price of pounds in terms of dollars.

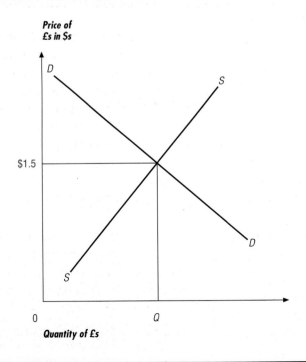

FIG. 51.1

If the demand for pounds increases, as a result, for example, of an improvement in the quality of UK goods and services and hence their popularity, its price will rise. This in turn will cause supply to extend as foreign exchange dealers will become more willing to sell the currency at a higher price. This is illustrated in Figure 51.2.

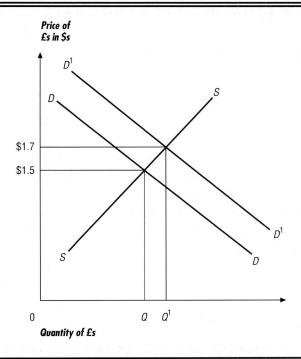

FIG. 51.2

Thus, the foreign exchange value of a national currency will be influenced by that country's balance between exports and imports. It will also be affected by the capital transactions between that country and the rest of the world. In addition to the normal commercial transactions, however, there are the activities of speculators. These buy and sell foreign currencies with a view to making a capital gain. They buy when the value of a currency is expected to rise and sell when it is expected to fall. If the exchange rate of the pound is expected to rise and in fact does rise say, from £1 = $1.5 to £1 = $2, then someone who transfers $15 000 into pounds at the lower rate and moves back into dollars at the higher rate will make a profit of £5000. These transactions, when carried out on a large scale, can have a significant influence on exchange rates.

ADVANTAGES OF FLOATING EXCHANGE RATES

The great attraction of a floating exchange rate is that in theory it provides a kind of automatic mechanism for keeping the balance of payments in equilibrium. If a country is importing goods and services of a greater value than it is exporting, the supply of its currency will exceed the demand for it. As a result its currency will depreciate, thereby making its exports cheaper in terms of foreign currencies and its imports will become more expensive in terms of its own currency. The changes in the exchange rate will alter the terms of trade but whether these relative price changes can bring about the necessary changes in the volumes and values of exports and imports depends on the elasticities of the demand for and supply of exports and imports. If they are elastic export revenue should rise and import expenditure fall.

If a government is confident a floating exchange rate system will ensure a balance of payments equilibrium it will not have to hold reserves of foreign currency. Another advantage of operating a floating exchange rate is that it stops the exchange rate being a target. The government will not have to introduce measures to protect the value of the currency at a fixed rate which might threaten its other objective.

DISADVANTAGES OF A FLOATING EXCHANGE RATE

A major possible disadvantage of a floating exchange rate is that they add a further element of uncertainty to international trading. The world prices of many commodities are not stable and traders have to accept a high degree of risk on this account. A system of floating rates, however, injects another variable element into the cost structure of firms buying goods and services from abroad. Buyers now have two price levels to watch — the foreign price of the commodity, and the price of the foreign currency. For example, it would be possible for the dollar price of cotton to be falling while the price of cotton to the Lancashire importer is rising. This would be the case where the value of the pound falls proportionately more than the dollar price of cotton. This added element of uncertainty may discourage international trade and the use of long-term contracts.

To offset this uncertainty some traders make use of the forward market. On this market fixed prices for foreign currencies are quoted for future delivery. Importers buying raw materials from abroad, for which payment is due several months hence, can be certain of the prices they must pay in e.g. euros by agreeing now a price for the euros they will buy in the future.

Critics of floating rates say that the external prices of domestically-produced goods will be subject to constant change and this will lead to a very unstable pattern of demand. This makes production planning very difficult.

Under a system of floating exchange rates, a balance of payments surplus or deficit is, in theory, automatically adjusted by movements in the exchange rate. This is very attractive to governments who are relieved of the unpleasant task of dealing with a deficit by using tariffs or quotas, or by taking measures to restrict home demand. But there are dangers in this greater freedom. If a country is suffering from inflation, a floating rate may remove some of the pressure on the government to deal with the problem, because the higher prices of home produced goods will not prejudice exports (the rate of exchange will fall and the foreign prices of exports will not rise). But the depreciation of the currency in the foreign exchange market will make imports dearer and this could well lead to cost-push inflation. So a floating exchange rate cannot insulate the home economy from external forces.

MANAGED EXCHANGE RATES

Although market forces are the main determinant of floating exchange rates, in practice there are times when the central banks try to influence the market rates. They can do this by adjusting interest rates (to influence the flows of funds into and out of the country), for example, or by intervening directly in the foreign exchange market by buying or selling the currency.

A central bank may attempt to manage the exchange rate in order to smooth out fluctuations around what is believed to be the equilibrium exchange rate.

Freely floating exchange rates have not always proved capable of moving easily and quickly to levels which would correct payments imbalances. They have shown a tendency to 'overshoot' their equilibrium values and then, after some time, to 'undershoot'. Large changes in exchange rates can be very disturbing to international trade; it is estimated that profit margins on exports can be halved or doubled if exchange rates change by 10%.

THE EXCHANGE RATE MECHANISM (ERM)

The ERM is an example of a managed exchange rate. It was created in 1979 and is an adjustable peg system operated by the EU. Member countries have to maintain the value of their currencies within a set band. If a currency begins to move outside this band the country is expected to take action to bring it back into line. For instance, if the exchange rate is falling near to its lower limit a country would be expected to buy its currency, and if this failed, to raise its domestic interest rate. Figure 51.3 shows how an increase in the supply of the currency, arising for instance from an increase in demand for imports, would lower the price of the currency and place it outside the set band. To avoid this the government of the country concerned, possibly with the support of other member governments, steps in and buys the currency. This shifts the demand curve to $D^1 D^1$ and keeps the value of the exchange rate within the set band.

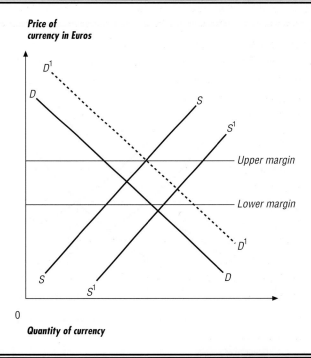

FIG. 51.3

If there are serious pressures on the currency, either up or down, its value will have to be adjusted or the currency will have to leave the system. The ERM does allow for realignment of the members' currencies with the agreement of the other member countries, although the aim is to avoid realignments if possible. The currencies of the member countries are allowed to float against non-members.

The UK joined the ERM in October 1990 with a central parity of 2.95 deutschmarks. During most of its two years of membership its value was relatively stable. However, it was forced to leave on 16 September 1992 when sales of pounds rose to high levels due to the high interest rate in Germany, concern that French would vote no on the Maastricht Treaty, the statement by the Bundesbank president that the value of the pound was too high and the resulting speculation.

FIXED EXCHANGE RATES

DEFINITION

A fixed exchange rate is one which is pegged (fixed) against the value of another currency or currencies and its rate is guaranteed by the government. In order to maintain a currency at a fixed value, the central bank must stand ready to buy and sell the currency at the fixed price. To do this it would have to have supplies of foreign currencies in order to buy the currency when necessary.

Figure 51.4 helps to explain this situation. It is assumed that the UK authorities have agreed to maintain a fixed exchange rate of £1 = $2. Initially the market is in equilibrium at this price. Imports now increase and the supply curve moves from SS to S^1S^1. In the absence of any intervention by the central bank the price would fall to £1 = $1.5. The central bank, however, enters the market and buys pounds raising demand from DD to D^1D^1 and maintaining the exchange rate at £1 = $2.

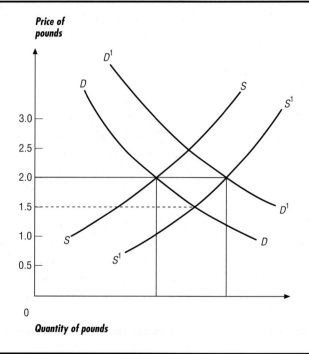

FIG. 51.4

When the central bank buys its own currency it uses its reserves of foreign currencies. Whereas when the demand for the currency exceeds its supply at the fixed price, the central bank will be selling the domestic currency on the foreign exchange market and adding to its reserves of foreign currency.

ADVANTAGES OF A FIXED EXCHANGE RATE

The great advantage of a fixed exchange rate is that it removes the uncertainty associated with floating rates. The negotiation of long-term contracts, the granting of long-term credits, and the undertaking of long-term investment overseas are less risky when there is some confidence in the stability of the exchange rate.

A fixed exchange rate is also said to impose discipline on a country to avoid inflation. This is because it will not be able to rely on a fall in the exchange rate to regain competitiveness lost through inflation — it will have to tackle the cause of the inflation.

DISADVANTAGES OF A FIXED EXCHANGE RATE

The main disadvantage of fixed exchange rates is that while with floating rates the burden of adjusting a balance of payments disequilibrium falls on the exchange rate itself, under a fixed rate system this burden tends to fall on the domestic economy. A country with a persistent deficit would soon exhaust its foreign currency reserves and indeed any temporary borrowing facilities in trying to hold up the exchange value of its currency. It must take steps to remove the cause of the deficit. The necessary measures to reduce imports and stimulate exports are likely to have some adverse effects on the domestic economy. The use of tariffs and quotas will probably raise prices on the domestic market and deflationary measures will harm domestic employment and growth.

There may be circumstances when the exchange rate cannot be held and when, if an adjustment has had to be made, it may not have been of the correct magnitude.

REVALUATION AND DEVALUATION

Situations arise when the exchange rate cannot be maintained at the current value. A persistent surplus or deficit indicates that the fixed rate is being held at well below or well above its true market rate of exchange. A persistent surplus might be dealt with by measures which increase home demand so as to encourage more imports and, perhaps, raise home prices making exports less competitive. A reduction in the restrictions on imports would also help to reduce the surplus. A persistent deficit might be eliminated by measures to reduce home demand and/or increase the restrictions on imports.

When these measures prove ineffective, or more likely, when governments are not prepared to impose them on the domestic economy, the only solution is to change the rate of exchange. Countries with surpluses would revalue by moving the exchange values of their currencies to higher parities. Countries with deficits would devalue by lowering the exchange value of their currencies in terms of other currencies.

Revaluation makes exports relatively dearer (in terms of foreign currencies) and imports relatively cheaper (in terms of the home currency).

EFFECTIVE EXCHANGE RATES

For any given currency there is a large number of exchange rates. The external value of the pound, for example, may be expressed in terms of dollars, euros, yen, and so on. Effective exchange rates are a way of measuring a currency's external value in terms of other currencies, in much the same way as a price index measures its internal value.

An effective, or trade-weighted, exchange rate is a weighted average of the individual exchange rates. The weight given to each country's currency reflects the importance of that country both as a trading partner and as a trading competitor.

Year	Exchange rates (annual averages)	
	US dollars per £	Sterling exchange rate index (1990 = 100)
1988	1.78	105.3
1989	1.64	102.3
1990	1.79	100.0
1991	1.77	100.7
1992	1.77	96.9
1993	1.50	88.9
1994	1.53	89.2
1995	1.58	84.8
1996	1.56	86.3
1997	1.64	100.6

Sources: United Kingdom Balance of Payments, 1998, Office for National Statistics

EQUILIBRIUM EXCHANGE RATE

The purchasing power parity theory argues that exchange rates will be in equilibrium when people are able to buy the same basket of products in any country with a given amount of money. For example if a basket of products costs £200 in the UK and $300 in the USA the equilibrium exchange rate would be £1 = $1.5.

If, e.g., the UK has a higher inflation rate than its competitors and a floating exchange rate it will experience a trade deficit and as a consequence its exchange rate will fall. This will equalise out prices between countries.

So according to the purchasing power parity theory, if initially a floating exchange rate is too high or low, it will in theory adjust until prices are equalised in domestic and foreign currency terms. Whereas if a currency is fixed and not at the equilibrium level internal prices will adjust.

However the purchasing power parity theory has come in for a number of criticisms, including:

- Many products, e.g. housing, hairdressing and bus travel are not traded internationally.
- Exchange rates are affected by factors other than the price of traded products. In practice the equilibrium exchange rate will be influenced by capital flows, non-price competitiveness, speculation, interest rates and confidence.

EFFECTS OF THE VALUE OF THE EXCHANGE RATE

ADVANTAGES OF A HIGH EXCHANGE RATE

These include the following.

- *Downward pressure on inflation.* Prices of finished imported products will be relatively low. These count in the measure of a country's inflation rate. The lower price of imported finished products will also put pressure on domestic firms to keep their prices low in order to remain competitive. Wage claims may be modified if the prices of some consumer products fall. The low price of imported raw materials will also keep costs of production down.

- *Improvement in the terms of trade and living standards.* More imports can be purchased for a given quantity of exports the higher the exchange rate rises. For example if the exchange rate is initially £1 = $1.5, a £10 export could be exchanged for three imports costing £5 each. If the exchange rate were then to rise to £1 = $2 it could now exchange for four imports costing $5.
- *May encourage foreign direct investment.* When foreign firms send back profits they will be worth more in their domestic currency.

ADVANTAGES OF A LOW EXCHANGE RATE

- Domestic goods and services will be price competitive in the domestic and foreign markets.
- Balance of trade in goods and services should be in equilibrium or in surplus given that export prices will be low in terms of foreign currency and import prices high in terms of domestic currency.
- Demand for domestic goods and services is likely to be high and so employment and growth are also likely to be high.

THE EUROPEAN SINGLE CURRENCY

The European single currency, the euro, came into existence on 1 January 1999. Eleven EU members joined — Austria, Belgium, Finland, France, Germany, Ireland, Italy, Luxembourg, the Netherlands, Portugal and Spain. Greece had wanted to join but did not meet the criteria. Denmark, Sweden and the UK chose not to join.

MAASTRICHT CRITERIA

To join the single currency a country has to met certain criteria. These are as follows.

- The government budget deficit must not exceed 3% of GDP.
- Government debt must not be more than 40% of GDP.
- A stable inflation rate and one which for at least a year before membership is no more than 1.5% points above the average of the three member countries with the lowest inflation rates.
- A long term interest rate, which for at least a year before membership does not exceed 2% points above the average of those countries with the lowest inflation.
- A stable exchange rate which for at least two years before membership has stayed within the margins of the ERM.

POSSIBLE BENEFITS OF JOINING THE SINGLE CURRENCY

- *Reduced transaction costs.* Firms and individuals save money as they do not have to pay to change currencies as they move themselves or goods and services from one EU country to another.
- *Reduced exchange rate uncertainty.* Firms do not have to worry about the amount they will have to pay European suppliers or the amount they will earn from European countries changing as a result of currency values changing.
- *Increased transparency.* As prices are expressed in one currency it is easier to compare prices throughout Europe. This reduces the scope for price discrimination between national markets within the EU. It also increases competitive pressure to keep prices low.

- *Lower interest rates.* Prior to the formation of the single currency most EU countries had to keep their interest rates above that of Germany's to prevent funds flowing to Germany. In addition a group of countries with a firm and credible commitment to low inflation can operate with lower interest rates.
- *Lower inflation.* The European Central Bank (ECB) takes a firm line against inflation, initiating changes in monetary policy if inflation rises above its target rate of 2%.
- *Increased foreign investment.* Direct inward investment is likely to be attracted by the reduced uncertainty, reduced transaction costs and large market size.

POSSIBLE COSTS OF JOINING THE SINGLE CURRENCY

- *Transitional costs.* These include psychological costs, e.g. resistance to change, which may be experienced more by the elderly, and financial costs including the costs of changing tills and staff training.
- *Loss of independent monetary policy.* Members of the single currency cannot operate an independent interest rate policy and lose independent control of the money supply. It is the European Central Bank which determines monetary policy.
- *Reduced independence of fiscal policy.* Euro members still have some independent control of fiscal policy. However, their scope for fiscal policy changes is restricted by the need to ensure that budget deficits do not exceed 3% of the country's GDP.
- *Inability to devalue independently.* A member of the single currency cannot increase the price competitiveness of its goods and services and its employment by devaluing. Individual governments lose this policy instrument.
- *Misalignment.* An exchange rate and an interest rate which benefits most EU members may not benefit all. Some economists claim that the UK economy has significant differences from the rest of the EU — it has an important oil industry, it is the second most importer exporter of services in the world and it trades more than most EU members with countries outside the EU.
- *Asymmetric policy sensitivity.* In most EU countries most borrowing is at fixed rates whereas in the UK most borrowing is at variable rates. This means that a rise in interest rates will have a greater impact on UK borrowers.
- *Regional problems.* There is a risk that regional differences will increase as firms, more aware of cost differences, will increasingly move to the prosperous areas.

UK'S CONDITIONS

The UK Labour government has set out five conditions which have to be met before the UK will consider membership. These are as follows.

- Membership must be expected to create better conditions for companies to invest in the UK.
- The effect on the UK's financial services industry would have to be beneficial.
- There must be a convergence of European business cycles and economic structures.
- There must be sufficient flexibility for the system to cope with economic change and shocks.
- Membership must be good for jobs and economic growth.

QUESTIONS

SHORT QUESTIONS

1. Explain what is meant by the term 'the effective exchange rate'.
2. What is the difference between devaluation and depreciation?
3. Would the UK currently meet the Maastricht criteria?
4. Why might a governmental body set the value of its exchange rate above its current market rate?

MULTIPLE CHOICE

Figure 51.5 shows the demand and supply of pounds in international money markets.

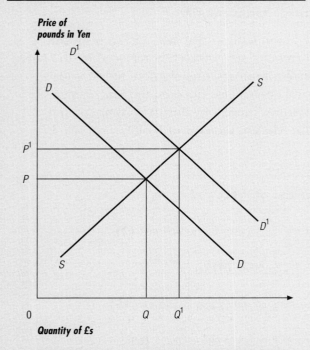

FIG. 51.5

1. What could have caused the rise in the value of the pound?

   A An increase in the quality of Japanese goods.

   B A rise in the marginal propensity to consume in the UK.

   C A higher rate of inflation in the UK than in Germany.

   D A rise in UK interest rates relative to Japanese interest rates.

2. What will be the effect of the value of the pound sterling changing from £1 = $1.72 to £1 = $1.98?

   A The pound will be overvalued.

   B UK exports to the USA will become cheaper.

   C American exports to the UK will become dearer.

   D The American dollar will be cheaper in terms of the pound.

3. An appreciation of the exchange rate of the euro against the dollar from 1 euro = $1 to 1 euro = $1.5 must mean that:

   A the euro will be overvalued

   B US imports from the Euro area will become cheaper

   C the euro's trade in goods and services has moved into surplus

   D dollars will become cheaper in terms of euros.

4. The Federal Reserve Bank of the United States raises the American rate of interest. If its currency is floating freely what effect is the higher interest rate likely to have on the exchange rate of the dollar?

   A Raise it as exporters will experience a fall in their costs of production.

   B Raise it as foreigners buy dollars in order to acquire assets with a higher yield.

   C Lower it as domestic investment is discouraged by the higher interest rate.

   D Lower it as a rise in the rate of interest will be accompanied by a fall in credit creation and the money supply.

DATA RESPONSE

EMU initially takes the form of an irrevocable locking of exchange rates. For the next three years, the D-Mark, French franc, Dutch guilder, Italian lire and the other national currencies of the participating European Union countries will continue to be legal tender. Only in 2002 will they be replaced by euro notes and coins.

But it is difficult to exaggerate the importance of the new single currency. Over time, the euro is sure to affect the lives of everyone in the EU.

In essence, the participants have agreed that regions as varied as eastern Germany and the Paris basin, northern Finland and the south of Spain, can and should operate with a single short-term interest rate determined by an independent central bank in Frankfurt.

The euro is an important step towards completing a vast single market in Europe. Exchange rate costs and risks, until now a bug bear for exporters throughout the EU, will be of as little significance as for businesses in the US.

Among large companies, the prospect of greater competition in a bigger market devoid of fluctuating exchange rates has unleashed an urge to merge across frontiers.

Consumers should be clear winners from the increased competition that will accrue from the greater transparency of prices, even before national currencies are completely replaced by the euro. A survey, published last month by BEUC, the European consumers' organisation, found wide variations in prices of consumer goods, such as electrical appliances, video equipment, cameras, clothes and sports shoes. The euro will make such variations more 'obvious to consumers' and 'should help reduce price differences', according to Jim Murray, director of BEUC.

Source: 'The experiment goes live' by Peter Norman, Financial Times, 2/1/99.

a] Which EU countries have not joined the single currency and why? **(2)**

b] i   In setting interest rates what is the main objective of the European Central Bank? **(2)**

   ii Explain how interest rates can be used to achieve that objective. **(4)**

c] Discuss the ways in which the euro is likely to affect the 'lives of everyone in the EU'. **(5)**

d] Explain the advantages of the European single currency mentioned in the extract. **(6)**

e] Discuss three disadvantages an EU member may experience from joining the European single currency. **(6)**

CASE STUDY

In 1994 the Brazilian government introduced a new currency, the real. The Brazilian government was determined to maintain a strong currency in order to keep inflation low. So to promote monetary stabilisation it pegged the external value of the real against the American dollar. Initially the value of the real was relatively constant against the dollar and this did help to reduce inflation.

However, in 1995 inflationary pressure began to appear again. Brazil did not initially change the value of its currency. As a result it became overvalued. Whilst the country benefited from cheap consumer goods and high real wages in urban areas, the exchange rate was not sustainable. The government was forced to allow the currency to fall within its narrow band. However even then its value was too high. When the East Asian crisis occurred speculators started to sell the real in large quantities. To protect the value of the real, in October 1997 the Brazilian government raised interest rates to 50%. This very high interest rate reduced economic activity and raised unemployment.

The weak state of the Brazilian economy caused speculation to continue. In January 1999 the Brazilian central bank was forced to devalue the real. It abandoned the narrow band within which the real could move and allowed it to drop to R1.32 to the dollar within an existing wider band. The new arrangement also permitted a further devaluation of 3% over the course of the year. This followed a crisis of confidence after a state governor announced a ninety day freeze on debt repayment to the central government and a growing recession.

The real fell quickly by 8% to its newly permitted floor. As a result of the devaluation, Gustavo Franco, the governor of the Brazilian Central Bank, and a former economics professor, resigned.

The government announced that it would use its reserves and, if necessary, higher interest rates to prevent the exchange rate falling too low. The new governor of Brazil's central bank, Francisco Lopes, said that Brazil wanted to avoid further large devaluations since these would only produce inflation.

He also said that the new exchange rate policy would discourage 'hot money' inflows of short-term capital: 'We do not want large amounts of speculative capital. We do not want a repeat of 1998, when a large amount of capital entered the country at the beginning of the year and left rapidly in recent days.'

a] How may a government maintain a fixed exchange rate? **(4)**

b] Why might a fixed exchange rate reduce inflationary pressure? **(5)**

c] What is meant by a currency being overvalued? **(5)**

d] What are the advantages a country may gain from a high exchange rate? **(5)**

e] Explain why a rise in interest rates is likely to:
i protect the value of the currency **(5)**
ii reduce economic activity. **(5)**

f] Why may a government be forced to devalue its currency by:
i speculation
ii a recession?

g] Why do countries want to discourage 'hot money inflows'? **(5)**

h] Explain why devaluation may cause inflation. **(6)**

STRUCTURED ESSAY

a] Distinguish between a fixed and a floating exchange rate. **(10)**

b] Discuss whether a country should operate a fixed or a floating exchange rate. **(15)**

FREE RESPONSE ESSAY

Assess whether the UK should join the single currency. **(25)**

PART NINE: MACROECONOMIC PROBLEMS AND POLICIES

52 CHANGES IN OUTPUT, EMPLOYMENT AND THE PRICE LEVEL

DISEQUILIBRIUM NATIONAL INCOME

Disequilibrium national income (for example as measured by GDP) occurs when national income is changing. National income will change if total planned expenditure is not equal to output and hence aggregate demand is not equal to aggregate supply and planned leakages are not equal to planned injections. If leakages exceed injections, aggregate supply is greater than aggregate demand and output is higher than planned total expenditure, national income, output and employment will fall.

SAVINGS AND INVESTMENT

To illustrate why and how national income changes when leakages do not equal injections, a simple two sector economy (households and firms) can be used. In this model the injection is investment and the leakage is savings. In any time period the amount which people plan to save is not likely to match the amount which firms plan to invest. By and large the decisions to save and invest are taken by different groups of people who have different objectives. There will be some limited amount of overlapping because firms both save (i.e. they retain some profits) and invest. When people plan to save more than firms plan to invest, total expenditure on goods and services will be less than the value of firms' current output. Firms' payments for factor services (wages, rent, interest and profits) are equal in value to their total output. These incomes are either consumed or saved. Thus:

$$\text{Income } (= \text{value of output}) = \text{consumption} + \text{saving}$$

Firms receive revenue from the consumption spending of households and the spending of other firms on investment goods. Thus:

$$\text{Total expenditure} = \text{consumption} + \text{investment}$$

When planned saving is greater than planned investment, therefore, total planned expenditure will be less than the value of output. Firms will have unsold products. These are regarded as stocks and hence as investment. Actual investment (planned investment plus changes in stocks) always equals actual saving in a two sector model. However, when, as in this case, planned saving exceeds planned investment firms will be receiving less in revenue than they are paying out in incomes to the factors of production. They will reduce output, and income and employment will fall.

In contrast when firms plan to spend more on investment than people plan to save, the opposite will happen: total planned spending will exceed the value of the national output. Stocks will be run down and firms will increase production, and employment and income will rise.

Only when the amount which people plan to save is equal to planned investment will the economy be in equilibrium and planned expenditure be just sufficient to purchase the planned output of firms. There will be no tendency for income and employment to rise or fall. In summary:

When planned I > planned S, income will rise
When planned I < planned S, income will fall
When planned I = planned S, income will not change.

THE PARADOX OF THRIFT

Keynes argued that what people plan to save and what in fact they do save are different things. An increased desire to save does not necessarily result in a higher level of saving. It could, indeed cause the total level of saving to fall! The immediate effect of an increased desire to save is a fall in consumption. A fall in consumption spending reduces the incomes of those who produce and sell consumer goods and services. This fall in consumption spending, as explained in the next section, develops into a cumulative process. This fall in the propensity to consume will lead to an eventual fall in total income much greater than the initial fall in consumption spending. It could be so great in fact that although people are trying to save more, the ability to save is reduced to such an extent that total savings actually fall. This effect is known as the paradox of thrift.

THE FULL MODEL

Using all injections and leakages, national income will rise when:

$$I + G + X > S + T + M$$

and hence when:

$$Y < C + I + G + (X - M)$$

National income will fall when:

$$I + G + X > S + T + M$$

and hence when:

$$Y > C + I + G + (X - M).$$

THE MULTIPLIER

As has been noted, discrepancies between the rate of leakage and the rate of injection cause movements in income but these upward and downward movements will not continue for ever. The expansions or contractions of income will gradually peter out because there are forces at work which tend to bring the economy into equilibrium. Changes in income bring about changes in saving and investment until the plans to save and the plans to invest are made compatible. This adjustment is explained by the process of the multiplier.

EXAMPLE

Assume an economy is initially in equilibrium when $Y = £10\,000m$, $S = £4000m$ and $I = £4000m$. Now suppose that investment increases to £5000m due to an increase in housebuilding, The income received by those engaged in the building industry will rise by £1000m, but this is not the end of the matter. If the saving habits of the community remain unchanged (i.e. they continue to save 0.4 of their income), then £600m of this additional income will be spent and £400m will be saved. The recipients of this extra spending will have additional income equal to £600m. They will spend £360m of this income and save £240m, and so it will go on. The increase in the rate of investment will set up a series of rounds of spending and saving. The total income and total saving will gradually increase, and at each stage the increments are getting smaller and smaller until they become immeasurably small. The series looks like this:

Increase in income = £1000m + £600m + £360m + £216m + + + +
Increase in saving =   + £400m + £240m + £144m + + + +

The increase in investment causes income to rise until the level of saving is once again equal to the level of investment. In this case income will change until it rises to £12 500m. At this level the economy will be in equilibrium again with saving = £5000m and investment = £5000m.

The value of the multiplier can be calculated after the change in income which occurs as a result of a change in an injection. It is found by dividing the change in income by the change in the injection, which in this case is investment, i.e. $\Delta Y / \Delta J$.

In the example the multiplier is $2\frac{1}{2}$, as national income rises by £2500m as a result of a rise in investment of £1000m.

THE DOWNWARD MULTIPLIER

The multiplier works in both ways. A fall in investment has downward multiplier effects and income falls until saving is equal to the new and lower level of investment. The same formula and series can be used to calculate the effects of a fall in investment (or any other injection). The only difference will be the signs in the spending and saving series; they will now be minus signs.

CALCULATING THE MULTIPLIER BEFORE THE CHANGE IN INCOME

As well as calculating the multiplier by using $\Delta Y / \Delta J$ it is also possible to calculate the multiplier by using the formula

$$\frac{1}{\text{Marginal propensity to leak (or withdraw)}}.$$

The size of the multiplier depends upon the proportion of any increase in income which is spent (i.e. passed on within the circular flow). In the example used earlier, 0.6 of each addition to income was spent and 0.4 was saved. Clearly if 0.8 of an additional income had been spent, the final increase in income would have been much larger. Another way of looking at it is to say that the size of the multiplier depends upon the proportion of any increase in income which leaks out of the system. Thus, the smaller the fraction saved, the larger the multiplier.

THE MARGINAL PROPENSITY TO CONSUME (MPC)

The marginal propensity to consume is the proportion of any small increase in income which is spent on consumer goods and services. If an extra £10 of income leads to an increase of spending of £7, the mpc is 0.7. Empirical evidence indicates that the mpc declines as income increases. In other words, although consumption rises as income increases, the rate of increase of consumption tends to decline. As an economy becomes more affluent people spend more on consumer goods and services, but spend a smaller proportion of their income.

THE MARGINAL PROPENSITY TO SAVE (MPS)

The mps is the proportion of any small increase in income which is saved. In the two sector model of the economy income can only be disposed of in two ways — it can be consumed or saved. So, if of every extra £10 of income, £7 is spent and £3 is saved, the mpc will be 0.7 and the mps will be 0.3. In a two sector model, $mpc + mps = 1$, and $1 - mpc = mps$. So the formula for the multiplier in a two sector economy can be expressed as either:

$$\frac{1}{mps} \text{ or } \frac{1}{1 - mpc}$$

EXAMPLE

In a two sector economy, $mps = 0.2$, $I = £5000m$ and $Y = £25\,000m$.

Questions
1. Assuming investment remains constant, what is the equilibrium level of saving and what is the value of the multiplier?
2. If investment were to increase by £100m what would be the new equilibrium level of income?

Answers
1. In equilibrium $S = I$, so that if investment remains constant at £5000m, the economy will settle in equilibrium where $S = £5000m$. If mps = 0.2, then mpc = 0.8.

$$\text{The multiplier} = \frac{1}{1 - mpc} \text{ or } \frac{1}{mps} = \frac{1}{1 - 0.8} \text{ or } \frac{1}{0.2} = 5.$$

2. Increase in income $=$ increase in investment $\times$ the multiplier
$$= £1000m \times 5$$
$$= £5000m.$$
New level of income $= £25\,000m + £5000m = £30\,000m$.

THE MULTIPLIER IN A FOUR SECTOR ECONOMY

The multiplier is still governed by the proportion of any marginal change in income which consumers spend on domestic output. The formula:

$$\frac{1}{1 - mpc}$$

still gives the value of the multiplier, but the proportion of additional income which is 'passed on' within the system is now reduced by three leakages, i.e. saving, imports and taxation. This means that $1 - mpc$ is no longer equal to mps. In fact $1 - mpc$ is equal to that proportion of any increase in income which leaks out of the circular flow. As a proportion of additional income this leakage is equal to $mps + mrt + mpm$ where $mpm =$ the marginal propensity to import and $mrt =$ the marginal rate of taxation. So the formula for the multiplier in a four sector economy is:

$$\frac{1}{1 - mpc} \text{ or } \frac{1}{mps + mrt + mpm}$$

The multiplier takes effect whenever there is a change in the planned rate of spending. Thus a change in I, or G, or X will have multiplier effects on income. There will also be multiplier effects when there is a change in spending which is independent of changes in income.

A rise in any of the leakages will reduce the size of the multiplier and thereby reduce the impact that changes in planned expenditure will have on income.

EXAMPLE

Out of every extra £10 of income, a community saves £2, spends £1.50 on foreign goods and services, and the government takes £1.50 in taxation. What is the value of the multiplier?

Out of every extra £10 of income, consumption spending on domestic output accounts for £10 $-$ (£2 + £1.50 + £1.50) = £5. Therefore $mpc = 0.5$, $mps = 0.2$, $mrt = 0.15$ and $mpm = 0.15$.

$$\text{The multiplier} = \frac{1}{1 - mpc} \text{ or } \frac{1}{mps + mrt + mpm}$$

$$= \frac{1}{1 - 0.5} \text{ or } \frac{1}{0.2 + 0.15 + 0.15}$$

$$= 2$$

The workings of the multiplier can be shown on a diagram. Figure 52.1 shows the effect on national income of a rise in exports.

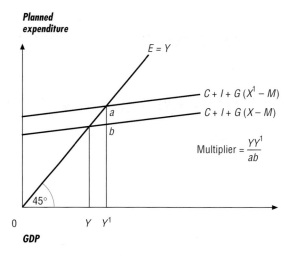

FIG. 52.1

CHANGES IN AGGREGATE DEMAND

The preceding analysis has shown how changes in planned spending brings about changes in national income which are much greater than the initial changes in the rate of spending. The effect of an increase in aggregate demand can also be analysed by using aggregate demand and supply diagrams. Figure 52.2 also shows the effect of an increase in exports. The higher level of demand for domestic goods and services shifts the aggregate demand curve to the right. Real national income rises and the higher output is likely to cause employment to rise.

Of course if the economy is operating at the full employment level of national income, a rise in expenditure will have no impact on employment and output. It will merely cause the general price level to rise.

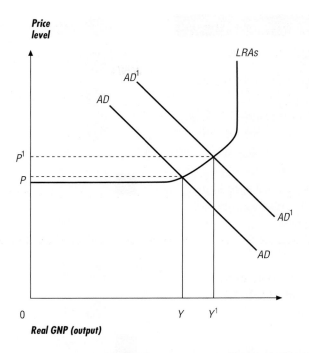

FIG. 52.2

QUESTIONS

SHORT QUESTIONS

1. Explain what is meant by disequilibrium level of national income.
2. If planned injections exceed planned leakages what will happen to national income?
3. Explain what is meant by the marginal propensity to save.
4. What are the injections and leakages in a three sector, closed economy (households, firms and the government)?

MULTIPLE CHOICE

1. Which of the following concepts explains how changes in investment may bring about changes in national income?

   A The accelerator.

   B The consumption function.

   C The multiplier.

   D The speculative demand for money.

2. An economy is operating below full employment. What will be the effect on national income of a decision by consumers to spend a higher proportion of their income?

   A Lower it.

   B Leave it unchanged.

   C Increase it by a multiple amount.

   D Increase it by the amount of the rise in consumption.

3. A country has a marginal propensity to save of 0.1, a marginal rate of tax of 0.1 and a marginal propensity to import of 0.2. What is the value of the multiplier?

   A 0.4

   B 0.6

   C 1.67

   D 2.5

4. The paradox of thrift refers to:

   A the inverse relationship between saving and consumption

   B the greater the propensity to save, the smaller the multiplier

   C the tendency for an increase in the propensity to save to reduce the level of total saving

   D the tendency for a fall in the propensity to save to discourage investment and cause national income to fall.

DATA RESPONSE

Just as we can project a schedule showing the relationship between consumption and income so it is possible to project the relationship between imports and income. If we relate movements in imports to movements in income we obtain the propensity to import or the import function. The average propensity to import will give us the level of imports associated with any given level of income and may be represented by M/Y. The marginal propensity to import (mpm or m) will tell us what proportion of any increase in income will be spent on foreign goods and services and may be represented by: $\dfrac{\Delta M}{\Delta Y}$

For example, if, when Y increases by 100, M increases by 10, the marginal propensity to import is 0.1. This mpm is an important concept since it indicates how much of a change in our national income will be transmitted to other countries through variation in our purchases of their goods and services. Similarly exports will be dependent upon the rest of the world's propensity to import.

The marginal propensity to import is a part of the marginal rate of leakage and, as such, will influence the size of the multiplier. Moving from a closed economy to an open economy has introduced a further leakage (imports) and hence reduced the size of the multiplier. The import leakage means that a smaller proportion of any increase in income is now passed on, within the circular flow, to generate further increases in income.

Source: 'Macro economics: an introduction', 4th edition by G.F. Stanlake, Longman.

a] If £30 out of a disposable income of £200 is spent on imports, what is the average propensity to import? Explain your answer. **(4)**

b] Explain what is meant by the marginal propensity to import. **(3)**

c] What are the other leakages? **(2)**

d] Explain why a rise in the marginal propensity to import will reduce the size of the multiplier. **(6)**

e] Discuss the factors which could cause a rise in the marginal propensity to import. **(10)**

CASE STUDY

Last year saw the introduction of self-assessment for income tax, a system devised by the last Conservative government. This led to a massive jump in income tax payments, far larger than anyone (including the Treasury) expected. In first quarter 1998, around £28.7bn was paid in income tax, a rise of almost 40% on the previous year. Some of this was improved compliance, as people who had not previously filled in tax returns owned up to undeclared income. Yet it was generally believed that most of the extra tax receipts resulted from speeding up tax collection from those who paid income tax outside the PAYE system, including Britain's 3 million self-employed; many people paid tax for two years at once. Distinguishing between these two explanations is important because the latter would be a one-off implying that tax receipts would fall to normal levels this year.

As a result of last year's surge in income tax, household real disposable income fell by 1.4% in first quarter 1998, despite rising wages and employment. It is very unusual for real household income to decline by this amount. Previous declines of this magnitude have only occurred in the midst of severe recessions and oil price hikes. For 1998 as a whole, real household income was unchanged, the worst performance since 1982 and only the seventh year in the past 50 when real incomes have not risen. Given the data on tax payments for January and February, another big decline in real household disposable income looks likely in the first three months of this year.

So what was the overall impact of self-assessment on the consumer last year, and what are the implications for 1999? Income tax is, of course, just one of many influences on consumer spending. When a consumer's income changes the impact on their spending depends on whether the change was anticipated and whether it is believed to be temporary or permanent. It would seem that self-assessment was largely unanticipated, initially believed to be temporary but now likely to be seen as permanent. If this is true, it fits the stylised facts of the consumer slowdown well. Because it was unanticipated the impact was delayed, with increased credit demand and lower saving taking up part of the slack. As the tax hit turned out to be larger and more enduring than first expected, it has taken time for the impact to build. Indeed it will probably take most of the rest of this year before the full effect on growth in consumer spending has worked through.

Source: 'Why spending is a taxing question' by Steven Bell, the Independent, 29/3/99.

a] What effect did the introduction of self-assessment for income tax appear to have had on the size of the black economy? **(5)**

b] What effect does a rise in tax payments have on real disposable income? **(4)**

c] Discuss three influences on consumer spending, other than income tax. **(6)**

d] What effect will a fall in real household disposable income have on people's standard of living? **(10)**

e] Explain the effects of an unanticipated rise in consumers' income on spending. **(5)**

f] What effect would a rise in the marginal rate of tax have on national income? **(6)**

g] What is meant by the downward multiplier? **(6)**

h] Explain why a change in taxation will take some time before its full effect is experienced. **(8)**

STRUCTURED ESSAY

a] Explain what is meant by the multiplier process. **(10)**

b] Discuss the effects on the multiplier of:
  i   a rise in the marginal propensity to save
  ii a fall in the marginal propensity to import
  iii a rise in government spending. **(15)**

FREE RESPONSE ESSAY

Analyse the effect of an increase in export revenue on national income, employment and the price level. **(25)**

53 ECONOMIC GROWTH

Insistent demands for higher standards of living have put pressures on governments throughout the world to achieve faster rates of economic growth. One of the most publicised aspects of economic activity in recent years has been the 'league table' showing the economic growth rates achieved by different countries. Table 53.1 is an example of a league table.

TABLE 53.1 A COMPARISON OF DIFFERENT COUNTRIES' GROWTH RATES

Country	% change in GDP on previous year
China	6.9
Colombia	−4.8
France	2.3
Germany	0.7
The Netherlands	3.2
Italy	0.9
Japan	0.1
Malaysia	4.1
Philippines	3.6
Russia	−3.9
Singapore	6.7
South Korea	9.8
South Africa	0.0
UK	1.2
USA	3.9
Euro-11	1.8

Source: The Economist, 4/9/99.

ACTUAL AND POTENTIAL GROWTH

Actual economic growth is increases in real GDP. An increase in real GDP can occur as a result of using previously unemployed resources, reallocating existing resources into more productive areas or using new or improved resources.

Potential economic growth is increases in the productive capacity of the economy i.e. in the ability of the economy to produce goods and services. This occurs as a result of an increase in the quantity and/or quality of resources. Potential economic growth is illustrated by a shift outwards of the production possibility curve or of the long run aggregate supply curve.

Figure 53.1 shows a country's productive capacity increasing and actual growth occurring as the economy moves from point Y to point Z as a result of employing unemployed resources and as a result of using new or improved resources.

It is thought that the productive capacity of an economy will usually increase each year largely as a result of improvements in technology and education. This expected potential economic growth is referred to as trend growth. In practice an economy's output may rise by less than this trend growth, if for example aggregate

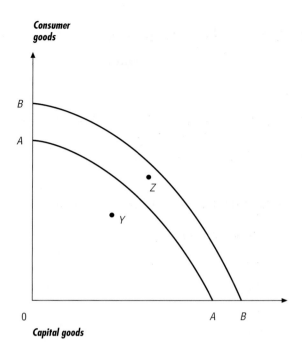

FIG. 53.1

demand is rising very slowly or even falling, and may rise by more if demand is rising rapidly and unemployed resources are being brought into use.

THE CAUSES OF ECONOMIC GROWTH

In the short run, if an economy has spare capacity (and so is operating inside its production possibility curve) economic growth can occur as a result of an increase in aggregate demand. However for an economy to continue to produce more goods and services aggregate supply must also increase.

SHORT-RUN CAUSES

A steady increase in aggregate demand will encourage producers to expand their output. Aggregate demand will increase if any of the components of aggregate demand rise i.e. $C + I + G + X - M$.

Consumption may increase as a result of, e.g., increases in consumer confidence, fall in interest rates and an increase in wealth. Investment will also increase if entrepreneurs become more confident, there is a fall in interest rates or if e.g. there are new capital goods on sale which embody improved technology. Government spending may rise in order to stimulate a rise in output. Net exports will increase if the price or quality competitiveness of domestic goods and services rise or if, e.g. incomes rise abroad.

Steady increases in aggregate demand are more effective in encouraging firms to produce more than fluctuations in aggregate demand. This is because the latter will create uncertainty. Firms will be reluctant to expand their capacity if they are uncertain that any higher level of aggregate demand will persist into the next year.

In the short-run economic growth can also occur as a result of a re-allocation of resources from low-productivity to high-productivity activities. The economist Nicholas Kaldor argued that economic growth is most rapid when countries shift resources from low productivity agriculture into higher productivity manufacturing.

LONG-RUN CAUSES

As noted above for economic growth to continue the productive capacity of the economy has to increase. This occurs when the quantity and/or quality of resources increases as a result of e.g.:

- *Investment in human capital.* Increases in the availability and improvements in education, training and health care raises the productivity of the labour force.
- *Increases in net investment.* There are two ways in which the stock of capital may increase. When the labour force is increasing, an equivalent amount of investment may be made otherwise the amount of capital per worker would be falling. This process is known as *capital widening* and need not necessarily lead to a rise in productivity — although new capital often embodies more advanced technology. Increasing the amount of capital per worker is known as *capital deepening* and this process should lead to increasing labour productivity.

  The type of investment undertaken is important. The construction of schools, houses, hospitals and other forms of social capital takes longer to influence labour productivity than manufacturing, commercial and agricultural investment. The extent to which new capital is used efficiently is important. Having improved machinery is no good if workers are not skilled enough to use it. The average age of the capital stock is also important. If one country replaces its capital more frequently than another, it will have better and more efficient equipment even though the net investment figures may be the same for both countries.
- *New technology.* This includes new inventions, new methods of production, improvements in the design and performance of machinery, better organisation of factors of production and more efficient systems of transport and communication. Technological progress and investment are very closely linked. Much new technology tends to be 'embodied' in new kinds of equipment.

THE DESIRABILITY OF ECONOMIC GROWTH

Economic growth is an important objective of government policy because it is the key to higher material standards of living. It is economic growth which has made it possible for millions of people to escape from the miseries of long hours of back-breaking work, deplorable living conditions, a low expectancy of life and other features of low income societies. Furthermore, people have come to expect economic growth — they expect their children to have a better life (in the material sense) than they had.

From the government's point of view, economic growth is desirable because it brings in increasing revenues from a given structure of tax rates. It means that more and better schools, hospitals and other social services can be provided without resorting to the politically unpopular measure of raising the rates of taxation. Economic growth also makes it easier (politically) to help the poor. If real income per head is rising, a more than proportionate share can be allocated to low income groups.

Of great importance is the cumulative nature of economic growth. For example, a country which maintains a growth rate of 3% per annum will achieve a doubling of real income in 24 years. It is this aspect of economic growth which explains why relatively small differences in national economic growth rates can, in a matter of 10 or 15 years, lead to large absolute differences in living standards. It also explains why the differences in real income between a rich country and a poor country can widen even when they are both experiencing the same rate of economic growth. A 3% increase on e.g. £30bn is a much greater increase in absolute terms than 3% on £30m.

THE BENEFITS AND COSTS OF ECONOMIC GROWTH

There are a variety of ways in which the benefits of economic growth may be enjoyed. By maintaining the same labour force working the same number of hours, the society may enjoy the gains from its increased ability to produce in the form of higher levels of consumption. Alternatively, since any given output can now be produced with a smaller labour input, workers may decide to take part of their improved living standards in the form of increased leisure. It would also be possible to maintain consumption levels and reduce the proportion of the population at work by extending the provisions for full-time education and/or reducing the age of retirement. Economic growth, as pointed out earlier, also makes it possible to devote more resources to the social services without having to cut private consumption.

Nevertheless, in whatever form society chooses to take the future benefits, economic growth may impose a sacrifice in terms of current living standards. In a fully employed economy, a higher rate of investment can only be carried out by allocating more resources to the production of capital goods; the current output of consumption goods and services, therefore, will be less than it might otherwise be. However, a greater output of consumer goods and services will be available in the future.

Economic growth also gives rise to a variety of external costs. Rising incomes make it possible for more people to own cars, but this could lead to problems of pollution and traffic congestion. Natural resources, including the rainforests, may be depleted at a rapid rate.

Modern industries may be very efficient on the basis of private costs but they may impose external costs by destroying natural beauty and other amenities. Modern methods of agriculture may greatly increase yields per acre, but they could have damaging effects on wildlife. On the other hand, economic growth makes it possible to devote more resources to the search for safer and cleaner methods of production.

Economic growth is often associated with a rapid pace of economic change. The technical progress will require workers to learn new skills, adopt new methods of working and possibly accept more frequent changes of occupation.

QUESTIONS

SHORT QUESTIONS

1. Distinguish between actual and potential growth.
2. What is the principle cause of economic growth in the short-run?
3. What is the main benefit of economic growth?
4. What is meant by capital deepening?

MULTIPLE CHOICE

1. Economic growth is an increase in:

   A. money GDP

   B. real GDP

   C. the PSNCR

   D. the government's budget surplus.

2. Which of the following is most likely to promote economic growth?

   A. A lowering of the retirement age.

   B. Net emigration.

   C. Net investment.

   D. Capital consumption.

3. Which of the following is a possible cost of economic growth?

   A. Increased tax revenue.

   B. The alleviation of poverty.

   C. Forgone consumer products in the short run.

   D. An increase in the spare capacity in the economy.

4. If there is full employment in the economy what could cause economic growth?

   A. An increase in the rate of interest.

   B. A rise in labour productivity.

   C. A reallocation of resources from manufacturing to agriculture.

   D. A fall in the exchange rate.

DATA RESPONSE

Investment has a dual role to play within any economy. In the short run, investment may be seen mainly as a component of aggregate demand which, if increased, will have the effect of stimulating the economy and, through the multiplier, substantially raising the level of national income. Fixed investment made up some 13% of total expenditure in 1997.

In the long run, investment will also affect the supply side of the economy, raising its productive potential and thereby pushing outwards the production frontier.

There have been a number of studies into the importance of investment as a generator of growth, though the results have not been conclusive. For example, in 1961 Kuznets, using time-series data for a number of countries, found little relationship between the share of investment in GDP, and the growth in output over time. Similarly, a 1970 OECD survey based on cross-sectional data found no clear well-defined relationship between investment shares and growth in output.... It could, of course be argued that the growth in output is the cause, rather than the effect, of the growth in investment. To expand production may require additional capacity, giving rise to extra investment.

Source: 'Applied economics', 8th edition, edited by Alan Griffiths and Stuart Wall, Longman, 1999.

a] Identify the three other components of aggregate demand. **(3)**

b] Explain, with the use of a diagram, why an increase in investment will increase national income. **(6)**

c] Distinguish between the two meanings of economic growth discussed in the extract. **(6)**

d] Discuss two causes of an increase in a country's productive potential other than investment. **(4)**

e] Discuss why, in practice, it is difficult to establish a relationship between growth in investment and growth in output. **(6)**

CASE STUDY

One of the big disappointments in the performance of the UK economy, both recently and over the longer term, has been the slow growth and relatively low level of productivity. If there is to be hope of a 'new paradigm' that will allow the economy to return to full employment with low inflation, as David Blunkett, the Secretary of State for Education called for last week, it will depend on a burst of faster growth in the amount of output the economy can produce per unit of input.

The reason is that long run improvements in living standards have to keep pace with underlying gains in productivity; any more, and pay rises will ultimately just trigger higher inflation.

France, Germany and Japan have experienced significantly faster post-war productivity growth than the UK, and the US has lagged behind all the others in terms of growth. Therefore, France and Germany have closed the gap on American total productivity levels, overtaking the UK by around 1970. Japan, which started with the lowest level, has caught up towards the UK thanks to high levels of investment, but has continued to use both capital and labour inefficiently.

The British deficit is far less pronounced in the market sector than in the economy as a whole, suggesting the relative productivity performance of the public sector is particularly weak.

Picking apart the reasons for differences in performance suggests that variations in investment and therefore the amount of capital available per worker per hour explain about 40–50% of productivity growth. Improvements in other factors such as the skills of the labour force, in production innovations, in organisational improvements and so on must explain the rest.

In short, the British problem is a lack of investment year after year in both human and physical capital, especially in the public sector.

Source: 'UK slips down the productivity league' by Diane Coyle, the Independent, 16/8/99.

a] What is meant by productivity? **(3)**

b] Explain why if improvements in living standards do not keep pace with productivity, inflation may occur. **(7)**

c] In what sense may Japan be using 'both capital and labour inefficiently'? **(7)**

d] Discuss what could cause an increase in UK productivity. **(9)**

e] Distinguish between human and physical capital. **(4)**

f] Discuss the relationship between productivity and economic growth. **(6)**

g] Why might productivity be lower in the public than in the private sector? **(6)**

h] Discuss two factors, other than increases in productivity, which could cause economic growth. **(8)**

STRUCTURED ESSAY

a] What could cause economic growth in a country with unemployed resources? **(12)**

b] Discuss the causes of an increase in a country's productive potential. **(13)**

FREE RESPONSE ESSAY

Assess the costs and benefits of economic growth. **(25)**

54 BUSINESS CYCLES

DEFINITION

The business (or trade cycle) is a periodic fluctuation in economic activity and it occurs as the economy moves away from its trend growth path. The general tendency is for output to rise but actual increases in GDP can deviate, sometimes quite significantly from trend GDP. For example, the UK experienced serious recessions in 1980–81 and 1990–92.

The business cycle was first identified in 1862 by the French economist, Clement Juglar. Some economists, taking into account the new economic paradigm (see Chapter 59) question whether business cycles are a phenomenon of the past. However the global financial crisis which occurred at the end of the 20th century has shown how countries are still vulnerable to significant fluctuations in economic activity.

THE PHASES OF THE BUSINESS CYCLE

THE DOWNTURN (OR CONTRACTION)

This is when economic activity slows down. Consumption starts to decline and entrepreneurs become more cautious, cancelling expansion plans and not undertaking net investment. Marginal firms will close, causing unemployment to rise. The lower consumption and rising unemployment are likely to reduce inflationary pressure, lower government tax revenue and raise government expenditure on unemployment related benefits.

THE TROUGH

This is characterised by a high level of pessimism amongst entrepreneurs, negative net investment (firms not replacing worn out machines), falling demand for consumer goods and services as well as capital goods, high unemployment and usually a low level of imports.

A recession can occur. This is defined as a fall in GDP over two or more successive quarters. Even more serious is a deep trough which is called a slump or depression — output falling over a period of several years.

The trough is demand-constrained. Demand cannot fall to zero. A point will come where households will resist any further falls in their consumption, even if this means using up their savings, and where they will have to replace certain consumer durables, e.g. beds and washing machines. Firms also have to replace at least a proportion of their worn-out machines. Where the trough bottoms out and the economy begins to expand is referred to as the lower turning point.

THE UPTURN (OR EXPANSION OR RECOVERY)

In this period consumption increases, production expands, profits rise and net investment becomes positive. Entrepreneurs and workers become more confident. Unemployment falls which further stimulates demand for consumer and capital goods. Inflationary pressures may begin to develop.

THE PEAK (OR BOOM)

During a peak or boom period employment is high as are expectations, profits and imports. There is a high level of demand for capital goods and consumer goods and services. Risky investments may be undertaken and some inefficient firms may be able to survive. The high level of demand results in a shortage of some of the factors of production, inflation accelerates and the economy becomes supply-constrained. The upper turning point is reached where a peak turns into a downturn.

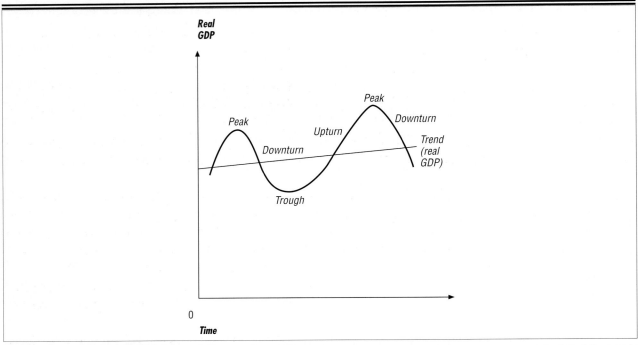

FIG. 54.1

DURATION OF CYCLES

A number of cycles may be identified, distinguishable by their different durations and sometimes by their causes.

- *The Kitchin inventory cycle.* This lasts approximately three to five years from peak to peak and is associated with changes in stock levels.
- *The Juglar, or investment, cycle.* This lasts approximately seven to eleven years and as its name suggests relates to changes in net investment over time.
- *The Kuznets cycle.* This is thought to last between fifteen and twenty five years and is caused by fluctuations in activity in the construction and allied industries.
- *The Kondratieff cycle.* These cycles are also referred to as long waves as they describe long-run fluctuations in economic activity — lasting from forty-five to sixty years. Kondratieff, a Russian economist writing in the 1920s, argued that short waves, or cycles, occur within long cycles. The long cycles, he suggested, are caused by technological innovations, wars, revolutions and discoveries of gold. All of these events will have impacts on economies which can take decades to work through. For example, the introduction of the microchip is still resulting in the creation of new products, new industries, new skills and new work methods and patterns of employment.

EXPLANATIONS OF BUSINESS CYCLES

These can be divided into two broad categories. One category is called *internal* or *endogenous* and these arise from changes within the economy itself, for instance, changes in stocks.

The other category is called *external* or *exogenous*. This includes causes arising from factors outside the particular economy, such as the supply-side shocks which can arise from rises in the price of oil and from war situations, for example.

Examples of explanations include the following.

- *Fluctuations in the money supply*. Monetarists, who believe that changes in the money supply are the most important determinant of nominal national income, argue that when the money supply increases faster than output and the rate of interest is low spending rises. The economy expands and moves into a boom. However, the higher level of demand increases demand for money, both by firms and consumers, for transaction purposes. This raises the rate of interest which in turn reduces investment and consumption and leads to a downturn.

- *Bursts of technological innovation*. As already noted, technological innovation, such as the development of the motor car and the computer, increases the range of products, number of industries and demand and can raise productivity.

- *Stop-go cycles*. To stimulate growth and employment a government may increase aggregate demand. This reflationary action will increase activity but as the economy expands the government may become concerned about inflationary pressures and balance of payments difficulties developing. As a result the government may adopt deflationary policies. These may cause a downturn which will continue until the government again becomes concerned about low levels of output and employment.

- *Political cycles*. These are linked to stop-go cycles. A government is more likely to take harsh deflationary measures after a general election and may seek to boost the economy before a general election in order to win political popularity.

- *Keynesian cycles*. Keynesians emphasise the cumulative nature of business cycles and the role of the multiplier and accelerator. They argue that if there is, e.g., a rise in exports, national income will rise by a multiple amount. This (the *accelerator*) in turn will cause investment to rise which will generate a further multiple rise in national income. A ceiling will be reached as shortages in labour and other resources are experienced (the supply constraint) and when income grows more slowly investment will fall. This will set in motion a downward movement in national income.

- *The inventory cycle*. This is linked to the accelerator theory. Inventories are stocks of raw materials and finished products held by producers and finished products held by retailers. If there is a rise in demand for consumer goods, retailers will initially run down their stocks. They will then order more goods from producers who in turn will order more raw materials. When retailers and producers are again content with their stock levels they will reduce their orders which will slow down the economy. This fall in economic activity will continue until firms have reduced their stocks to such an extent that they have to replenish them.

- *Demand and supply-side shocks*. New classical economists emphasise the role of unanticipated shocks. For example in 1998 El Niño, a hurricane which damaged crops and infrastructure in parts of Latin America, Asia and Africa, led to a downturn in economic activity while the global financial crisis which started in 1997 led to a reduction in demand for products throughout the world.

PROFILE

NAME: Gavyn Davies
City Economist, journalist and government adviser

BORN: 1951 in Rhodesia (now Zimbabwe)

NATIONALITY: British

EDUCATED: University of Cambridge and University of Oxford

KEY POSTS HELD: Member of Downing Street Policy Unit
One of Treasury's 'Wise Men' advising the Conservative Chancellors of the Exchequer
Unofficial adviser to Tony Blair
Economic journalist on the *Independent*
Head of Global Economics and Partner in Goldman Sachs
In 1999 he was assessed to be the City's highest paid and wealthiest economist. His partnership was worth £30m and he had bonuses and other assets of £10m.

QUOTE ON DAVIES:
One of his rivals was quoted in the Guardian *as saying: 'Gavyn is the most successful UK economist in terms of influence and wealth since Keynes'.*

FORECASTING BUSINESS CYCLES

Firms and the government seek to forecast business cycles by using surveys, such as the regular CBI survey, and by examining historical economic statistics. There are three types of indicator.

- *Leading indicators*. These react ahead of the cycle and so indicate changes in activity in advance. They include new car registrations, housing starts and surveys of consumer and business confidence.
- *Coincident indicators*. These occur with the cycle, and provide evidence that the cycle is occurring. The most important is obviously changes in real GDP. However, others include the index of the volume of retail sales and levels of business capacity.
- *Lagging indicators*. These react after the changes in economic activity and confirm the turning points in the cycle. The best two known are unemployment and investment. For instance, it may be a year or more before a rise in economic activity is reflected in employment and investment. This is because firms will want to see that e.g. a rise in demand will last before they increase the number of workers and machines they employ.

QUESTIONS

SHORT QUESTIONS

1. What is a business cycle?

2. Explain the Kondratieff cycle.

3. How do economists forecast business cycles?

4. Explain what is meant by a recession.

MULTIPLE CHOICE

1. An economy is experiencing a recession. Why does income not fall to zero?

   A. There is a demand constraint.

   B. There is a supply constraint.

   C. Confidence will rise.

   D. Other countries will provide aid.

2. Profits and consumption are rising. New enterprises are set up. Inflationary pressures begin to appear. Which phase of the business cycle does this describe?

   A. The downturn.

   B. The peak.

   C. The trough.

   D. The upturn.

3. What are inventories?

   A. Shares.

   B. Stocks.

   C. The invention of new products.

   D. The introduction of new methods of production.

4. Which of the following concepts explains how changes in the level of aggregate demand may bring about changes in new capital formation?

   A. The accelerator.

   B. The business cycle.

   C. The multiplier.

   D. The production function.

DATA RESPONSE

Despite a few flutters, the emerging markets recovery continues. The success of these economies matters to us because they are the most dynamic part of the world economy, worth more than a fifth of world output at market prices (and a third in real terms, once allowance is made for their lower prices). They are also disproportionately important in British exports.

The good news is that some have been growing like a rocket. Most impressively, South Korea posted industrial production up 21.8% over the year to May and Thai industrial production was up 7.2%.

Even Indonesian and Russian production is edging up, despite their respective political uncertainties, while the first glimmers of recovery are now visible in Brazil.

The bad news is that this growth is following unusually sharp falls in output; the recessions in the three Asian crisis economies were greater than the falls in the Western economies during the Great Depression of 1929–31. Indonesian national output dropped 14% last year, putting the world's third most populous country under enormous social stress.

Even as the recovery begins, it is worth trying to ensure that this never happens again. That, however, may prove difficult.

The 1997–99 crisis may be the first of many in the same mould. We are back to the capital markets crises which were such a feature of the classical business cycle up until the great crash in 1929.

Source: 'Do not forget the lessons of Asia' by Christopher Huhne, the Independent, 9/8/99.

a] Why is the economic well being of the emerging markets important for the UK? **(5)**

b] How serious was the East Asian crisis? **(4)**

c] Distinguish between a recession and a recovery. **(6)**

d] What is meant by a capital market crisis? **(4)**

e] Why may it be difficult to avoid business cycles? **(6)**

CASE STUDY

In an article on 13 May I rejected the rationalisations used to justify the Wall Street surge ('Nonsense on stilts'). It was accompanied by a chart showing an uncanny resemblance to the upturn leading to the 1929 crash.

Nothing has happened to make me repent, even though the Dow Jones Average reached a new peak last week — Wall Street indices are 50% higher than when Alan Greenspan, chairman of the US Federal Reserve, first referred to signs of irrational exuberance. Indeed Stephen King of HSBC has presented a perceptive analysis, not only suggesting that the US stock market boom is indeed a bubble but venturing a view on how and when it might burst ('Bubble trouble', *HSBC Economics*, July 1999).

Strong growth in the money supply, a rising investment share within GDP, a widening current account deficit and a personal sector plunging into deficit are all classic indicators of a bubble.

'Virtually all the indicators on the bubbles checklist are flashing red for the US.... When such bubbles burst soft landings never seem to be within reach.'

Mr King argues that the US high-technology breakthrough is far from unprecedented and reminiscent of the breakthroughs of the 1920s. These were genuine enough but became the pretext for excessive equity valuations, fuelling an economic boom.

Some commentators and policymakers are being misled by the absence of inflationary pressures in the goods and services markets. But this is a deceptive sign frequently seen in past bubbles. 'Most bubbles develop during a period of above-average growth and below-average inflation. The inflationary pressure is often disguised by declines in global commodity prices or strong exchange rates that suppress inflationary symptoms for a while.... Moreover, during a boom, rapid money growth feeds directly into higher output or higher asset prices, and the link between money and inflation is temporarily broken.'

Source: 'Bubbles do burst' by Samuel Brittan, Financial Times, 22/7/99.

a] What is meant by a stockmarket boom? **(5)**

b] Why may a boom be accompanied by a widening current account deficit? **(8)**

c] Describe the features of an economic boom. **(6)**

d] Which phase follows a boom? **(2)**

e] Why might an economic boom not be accompanied by inflation? **(7)**

f] Explain what is likely to bring an economic boom to an end. **(8)**

g] Does Mr King appear to support the new economic paradigm? Explain your answer. **(6)**

h] Explain how strong exchange rates suppress inflationary symptoms. **(8)**

STRUCTURED ESSAY

a] Describe the phases of the business cycle. **(10)**

b] Discuss three explanations of business cycles. **(15)**

FREE RESPONSE ESSAY

Discuss whether business cycles are 'dead'. **(25)**

55 POLICIES TO PROMOTE ECONOMIC GROWTH

DEMAND-SIDE POLICIES

Demand-side policies, largely associated with Keynesian economists, seek to promote economic growth by ensuring that aggregate demand rises at a smooth rate. The policies involve active (also called discretionary) demand management, i.e. the government manipulates aggregate demand by means of fiscal policy. The government acts counter-cyclically — reflating the economy by raising government spending and/or cutting taxes when private sector demand is too low and deflating the economy by cutting government spending and/or raising taxes when private sector demand is too high. Keynesians tend to favour changing government spending rather than taxation as they believe that changes in government spending have a greater multiplier effect as the recipients of government spending have a higher marginal propensity to consume than taxpayers.

Attempts to achieve a fairly precise level of real GDP are referred to as fine tuning whereas the less ambitious, but probably more realistic, aim of coarse tuning refers to moving the economy in the desired objective.

In designing demand-side policies governments make use of the concepts of the multiplier, accelerator and other concepts including the consumption and saving functions.

THE CONSUMPTION AND SAVING FUNCTIONS

The consumption function shows how much will be spent at different income levels. It is represented by the equation $C = a + bY$, where a is autonomous consumption (i.e. spending which is independent of changes income — the amount which will be spent even if income is zero), b is the marginal propensity to consume and Y is income. So that if the consumption function is $C = £100bn + 0.8Y$ and national income is £1000bn, consumption will be $£100bn + 0.8 × £1000bn = £900bn$.

The saving function shows how much will be saved at different income levels. If the consumption function is known the saving function can be calculated and vice versa.

The saving function is represented by the equation $S = -a + sY$, where s is the marginal propensity to save. Using the example above, if mpc is 0.8, mps is $1 - 0.8 = 0.2$ and the saving function is $S = -£100bn + 0.2Y$. If national income is £5000bn, saving will be $-£100bn + 0.2 × £5000bn = £900bn$.

SUPPLY-SIDE POLICIES

Supply-side policies seek to promote economic growth by increasing the productive capacity of the economy via raising the quantity and quality of factors of production. New classical economists favour free market supply-side policies including trade union reform, privatisation, deregulation, direct tax cuts and benefit cuts. Whereas Keynesians favour interventionist supply-side policies including increased government spending on education, training and investment grants.

POLICY CONFLICTS

If economic growth was the only policy objective it would be much easier to achieve. However, it is only one of the four major macroeconomic objectives. Higher economic growth is compatible with the objective of high employment. However a government seeking to raise economic growth by increasing aggregate demand may run into conflicts with its objectives of price stability and a balance of payments of equilibrium. Higher demand may push up prices and is likely to result in increased expenditure on imports and may cause goods and services to be diverted from the export to the home market. It is because of these risks that most economists now favour a combination of demand-side and supply-side policies to promote economic growth. Higher demand stimulates producers to seek to raise output but there has to be an adequate supply of skilled resources within the economy to meet the higher demand.

OTHER PROBLEMS

If the economy is fully employed, any attempt to raise the rate of economic growth must entail some sacrifice in terms of present living standards, otherwise measures designed to increase investment will simply give rise to inflation. The government may find it difficult to persuade people to accept the rise in interest rate or taxation which may be needed to encourage them to forgo current consumption.

STOP-GO CYCLES

The use of demand management techniques to achieve government macroeconomic objectives has in the past resulted in a series of stop-go cycles. Deflationary measures were applied to slow down the rate of inflation or to reduce the level of imports and they were relaxed when unemployment rose to politically unacceptable levels. These stop-go policies did not encourage the attitudes and expectations which are conducive to economic growth. If entrepreneurs become convinced that any expansionary phase will be short-lived, they will not undertake the longer term investment projects which would increase the country's productive capacity. When there is a lack of confidence in the ability of the government to carry out a sustained programme of expansion, any increase in aggregate demand is likely to increase short-term speculation in shares and property rather than industrial investment.

PRESENT UK GOVERNMENT POLICY APPROACH

The Labour government is seeking to raise the UK's economic growth rate by using a mixture of free market and interventionist supply-side policies and by creating a greater stability of government policy. It believes that the latter will increase entrepreneurs' confidence and encourage them to undertake long term investment projects. To achieve this greater stability it has e.g. passed the responsibility for determining the rate of interest to the Bank of England and introduced 'rules' for government spending and public sector debt.

QUESTIONS

SHORT QUESTIONS

1 Explain what is meant by demand management.

2 Distinguish between fine and coarse tuning.

3 What is the consumption function?

4 Discuss two supply-side policies to promote economic growth.

MULTIPLE CHOICE

1 In an economy with unemployed resources, which of the following would cause an increase in output in the short run?

A a rise in the rate of interest

B the introduction of price controls

C the government budgeting for a deficit

D the government reducing investment incentives.

2 What is the stop-go cycle?

A The tendency for private sector investment to fluctuate with changes in business optimism.

B The tendency of governments to alternate deflationary and reflationary policies.

C Swings in the balance of payments position resulting from changes in the rate of economic growth.

D Swings in the rate of inflation which result from changes in employment levels.

3 An economy is operating at full employment. Which of the following could increase output in the long run?

A Raising income tax.

B Reducing the exchange rate.

C Increasing the money supply.

D Switching some resources from producing consumer goods and services to producing capital goods.

4 An economy has a consumption function of $C = £200bn + 0.75Y$. If national income is £4000bn, what is the average propensity to consume?

A 0.2

B 0.5

C 0.75

D 0.8

DATA RESPONSE

Moreover 'rapid output growth per se need not signal concern given Ireland's low inflation rate and current account surplus'. Certainly, Ireland is growing at a fearsome rate — 8.9% last year — having handsomely outstripped British output per head in 1997.

This is the 'Celtic tiger', an economic success built on a commitment to education and therefore to a skilled workforce, and on a business-friendly set of policies which has attracted direct foreign investment. In the past five years, the average annual growth rate of output in Ireland was a staggering 8.5%, the best performance of any developed country in the world and some five times the rate achieved by Britain.

The risk of demand outpacing supply — overheating — is difficult to judge because most people do not believe that Ireland can go on growing at its recent rates. After all, Ireland's GDP per head is 5% above the EU average (and above the UK average) and it becomes more difficult to grow when you are no longer just catching up with the leaders.

But there is a debate about how much Ireland's potential or trend growth will slow. The Government thinks long-run growth should be 4 to 5% a year, while the International Monetary Fund is more optimistic at 6 to 6.5% a year. It could even be higher.

Source: 'Ireland shows UK the way to euroland' by Christopher Huhne, the Independent, 23/8/99.

a] In what circumstances would a high economic growth rate cause concern and why? **(7)**

b] Why was Ireland being described as the 'Celtic tiger'? **(3)**

c] What were the causes of Ireland's high growth rate? **(6)**

d] Explain why 'it becomes more difficult to grow when you are no longer just catching up with the leaders'. **(6)**

e] What is trend growth? **(3)**

CASE STUDY

So what can the Japanese Government do to get the economy moving? As far as corporate restructuring, or the supply side, is concerned, it needs to embrace cultural change and put its weight behind promoting rationalisation. In the case of the consumer sector, or the demand side, the approach so far has been to combine ultra easy monetary policy — interest rates are virtually zero in Japan — with generous spending packages. If, as looks likely, this fails to do the trick, more will need to be done.

In 1996, the Japanese economy experienced a leap in growth, supported by temporary tax cuts and government spending. But in 1997, when the tax cuts were reversed, growth collapsed. The risk now is that history will repeat itself. If government support for the economy dries up before corporate restructuring is complete then there will be nothing to offset the detrimental mix of rising unemployment, overcapacity and tumbling profitability. Wages will continue to fall, and consumer spending will dry up once again.

Given that the scope for further cuts in Japanese interest rates is negligible, the Government will have to rely on fiscal measures.

Source: 'A false dawn breaks over the land of the Rising Sun' by Lea Paterson, The Times, 27/7/99.

a] Explain what is meant by 'rationalisation'. **(4)**

b] What problems was the Japanese economy facing at the time the extract was written? **(5)**

c] Distinguish between the demand and supply side. **(6)**

d] What effect would 'virtually zero' interest rates be expected to have on consumption and investment and why? **(8)**

e] Explain why tax rates and increased government spending would be expected to raise output? **(6)**

f] Discuss the effect that frequent changes in government spending are likely to have on economic growth. **(7)**

g] What is meant by fiscal measures and why was the Japanese government going to have to rely on them? **(6)**

h] Discuss two policy measures, other than those mentioned in the extract, which a government could implement to promote economic growth. **(8)**

STRUCTURED ESSAY

a] Explain why economic growth as a government policy objective may conflict with the objective of a balance of payments equilibrium. **(10)**

b] Discuss how monetary policy could be used to promote economic growth. **(15)**

FREE RESPONSE ESSAY

Compare the effectiveness of increasing government expenditure and cutting the rate of income tax as policy measures to stimulate economic growth. **(25)**

56 UNEMPLOYMENT

MEASURING UNEMPLOYMENT

THE CLAIMANT COUNT

Unemployment can be measured in a number of different ways. The traditional measure in the UK is the claimant count. This includes as unemployed anyone between the ages of 18 and 60 receiving an unemployment benefit such as job-seekers' allowance. However, the accuracy of this measure has been questioned. There are some people in the claimant count who are working in the black economy, and some who, whilst claiming and receiving benefits are not actively looking for work. However, there are others who might be considered as unemployed but who do not appear in the official claimant count. These include those who are looking for a job but who are aged under 18 or over 60, or who are not entitled to benefits or who do not claim benefits. If this group is larger than those working in the black economy or those not looking for work but claiming benefits, the official figures will understate the level of unemployment.

THE LABOUR FORCE SURVEY

The measure which the UK government is now giving most attention to is the Labour Force Survey measure. This is also known as the ILO measure as it uses the International Labour's Organisation's definition of unemployment. This counts as unemployed all those who are actively seeking and available to start work, whether or not they are claiming benefit. Each measure has its advantages and disadvantages. These are outlined in Table 56.1.

TABLE 56.1 SURVEY-BASED ILO UNEMPLOYMENT AND ADMINISTRATIVE CLAIMANT UNEMPLOYMENT COMPARED

ILO unemployment

Advantages
- internationally standardised
- usable for inter-country comparisons
- considerable potential for analysis of other labour market characteristics, or of particular sub-groups
- articulated with data from the same source on employment and the economically inactive

Disadvantages
- relatively costly to compile
- normally less timely
- subject to sampling and response error
- not always suitable for small areas due to sampling limitations

Claimant count unemployment

Advantages
- relatively inexpensive
- available quickly (normally monthly)
- available frequently
- 100% count gives figures for small areas

Disadvantages
- not internationally recognised
- coverage changes whenever administrative system changes, although recalculation of consistent series allows meaningful comparisons over time
- coverage depends upon administrative rules; may not be suitable for other purposes
- limited analysis of characteristics of unemployed people

Source: Employment Gazette, July 1994.

STOCKS AND FLOWS

Unemployment is a stock. It is a measure of the number of people unemployed at a particular point of time. However, the stock of unemployment is influenced by the flow of people into unemployment and the flow of people leaving unemployment. New people entering the stock of unemployment will not only be those losing jobs but also previous non-participants in the labour force who are now seeking employment, for example, students finishing degree courses who cannot find employment. People who leave the stock may have found employment, may have given up looking for work, may have retired, may have joined a government training scheme or may have entered higher education.

Unemployment will rise if the number entering the stock exceeds the number of new jobs.

DURATION

In examining unemployment it is important to consider not only the numbers unemployed but also how long they have been unemployed, i.e., how long it is after they enter the stock that they leave it. For example, an unemployment rate of 12% with an average duration of three months unemployed may be considered to be less of a problem than an unemployment rate of 8% if the average duration is three years.

UNEMPLOYMENT RATE

The unemployment rate is the number of people unemployed expressed as a percentage of the labour force:

$$\frac{\text{Unemployed}}{\text{Labour force}} \times 100$$

The labour or work force includes all those who are economically active i.e. willing and able to work. So it consists of those in employment and the unemployed. This contrasts with the working population which is those of working age. Not all of those in the working population are in the labour force. Students, those who have retired early, some disabled and homemakers are in the working population but not in the labour force.

TYPES AND CAUSE OF UNEMPLOYMENT

Unemployment can be categorised in a number of ways. One way is to classify it in accordance with its causes.

RESIDUAL UNEMPLOYMENT

In all societies there is an element of residual unemployment because there will always be some people who are virtually unemployable on a permanent basis. These are people who, for whatever reason, find it difficult or impossible to cope with the demands of modern production methods and the disciplines of organised work.

FRICTIONAL UNEMPLOYMENT

This arises from immobilities in the labour force. Labour is neither perfectly geographically nor occupationally mobile. So people can remain unemployed despite the fact that there are jobs available, either in other parts of the country, or requiring skills they do not have.

SEARCH UNEMPLOYMENT

This is a form of frictional unemployment. It occurs when people who are unemployed do not take the first job on offer but search for better-paid employment.

CASUAL UNEMPLOYMENT

This again is a form of frictional unemployment. There are certain groups of people who are out of work between periods of employment. For instance, opera singers, actors and roof repairers.

SEASONAL UNEMPLOYMENT

This occurs in those industries which experience marked seasonal patterns of demand. Industries such as farming, building and tourism are affected in this way.

STRUCTURAL UNEMPLOYMENT

This is unemployment which arises from a fundamental change in the structure of industry. For example, the decline of mining in the UK has resulted in a large number of former coal-miners becoming unemployed.

REGIONAL UNEMPLOYMENT

This is linked to structural unemployment. It arises when the declining industry is concentrated in one area. The region dependent upon the industry may suffer particularly heavy unemployment because there will be a local multiplier effect arising from the decline in the income generated by the major industry.

TECHNOLOGICAL UNEMPLOYMENT

This is a form of structural unemployment and arises from the introduction of new technology. For instance, the increasing use of cashpoint, telephone banking, switch and other plastic cards has reduced the number of bank clerks.

INTERNATIONAL UNEMPLOYMENT

This, again, is a form of structural unemployment and arises when workers lose their jobs due to a fall in demand for domestically produced goods and services.

CYCLICAL UNEMPLOYMENT

This is also referred to as *demand deficiency unemployment*. It arises due to inadequate demand. Figure 56.1 shows that the level of aggregate expenditure is insufficient to achieve full employment (Yf^e). There is a deflationary gap of *ab*.

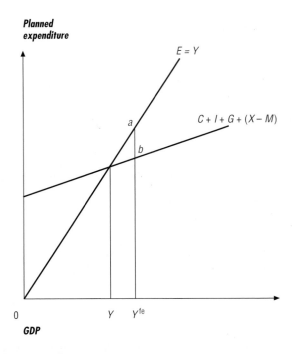

Planned expenditure

$E = Y$

a

$C + I + G + (X - M)$

b

0

Y Y^{fe}

GDP

FIG. 56.1

THE NON-ACCELERATING INFLATION RATE OF UNEMPLOYMENT

In the 1960s and 1970s, attempts to reduce the level of unemployment by increasing aggregate demand led to sharp increases in the rate of inflation and balance of payments problems. This experience led economists, and governments to pay increasing attention to the concept of a natural rate of unemployment. More recently it has come to be known as the *non-accelerating inflation rate of unemployment* (NAIRU), as it can be defined as that rate of unemployment which is consistent with a stable rate of inflation. It can also be defined as the rate of unemployment which exists when an economy is producing its potential output and is associated with an equilibrium situation in the labour market. At this level of unemployment, the demand for labour is equal to the supply of labour at the existing real wage rate.

EQUILIBRIUM UNEMPLOYMENT

Equilibrium unemployment is the unemployment which exists when the aggregate demand for labour is equal to the aggregate supply of labour and vacancies match the number unemployed. Whilst there may be macroeconomic equilibrium at the current wage rate, people may still be unemployed. This may be because they are unaware of the vacancies, unsuitable to take up the vacancies or unwilling to take up the vacancies.

Figure 56.2 shows equilibrium unemployment. The *ADL* curve shows the aggregate demand for labour. The *ASL* curve shows the aggregate supply curve of labour consisting of those workers willing to accept jobs at each wage rate. The curve *ALF* represents the total labour force. The macroeconomic labour market is in equilibrium at a wage rate of *W* but there is unemployment (equilibrium unemployment) of *LL*^X. As the real wage rate rises the gap between the total labour force and those willing and able to work at the wage rate narrows. This is because people are becoming more willing to accept jobs at higher wage rates. The NAIRU is

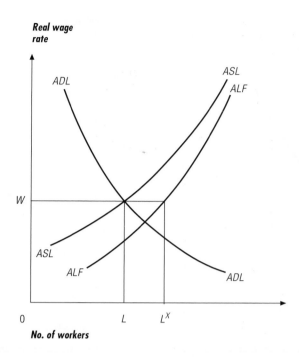

Real wage rate

ADL

ASL
ALF

W

ASL

ALF

ADL

0   L   L^X

No. of workers

FIG. 56.2

not zero and the types of equilibrium unemployment which exist include voluntary (i.e. those who choose to live on benefits rather than work), search, residual, frictional, seasonal, casual, structural and technological.

In all these cases there may be vacancies in some occupations, industries and geographical areas whilst unemployment exists in other occupations, industries and different parts of the country.

DISEQUILIBRIUM UNEMPLOYMENT

This occurs when there is disequilibrium in the labour market, specifically when aggregate supply exceeds aggregate demand at the current wage rate. This is shown in Figure 56.3. At the wage rate W there is disequilibrium unemployment of LL^Z.

If the wage rate were to fall to W^l the disequilibrium unemployment would disappear. So for disequilibrium unemployment to exist two conditions have to hold. One is that the aggregate supply of labour must exceed the aggregate demand for labour. The other is that wages are not flexible downwards. This is often referred to as wages being *sticky downwards*.

CAUSES OF DISEQUILIBRIUM UNEMPLOYMENT

There are a number of reasons why the real wage rate may be higher than the market clearing (equilibrium) rate. One possible reason is the wage rate being driven up above the equilibrium rate either by trade union power or a government-set minimum wage rate. However, the effects are somewhat uncertain. This is because the higher wage earned may stimulate increased expenditure and a rise in demand for labour.

Another possible reason is a growth in the labour supply not matched by a rise in the aggregate demand for labour. Figure 56.4 shows the market initially in equilibrium. When the supply of labour increases from ASL to ASL^l the wage rate, being sticky downwards, remains at W and unemployment of LL^Z arises.

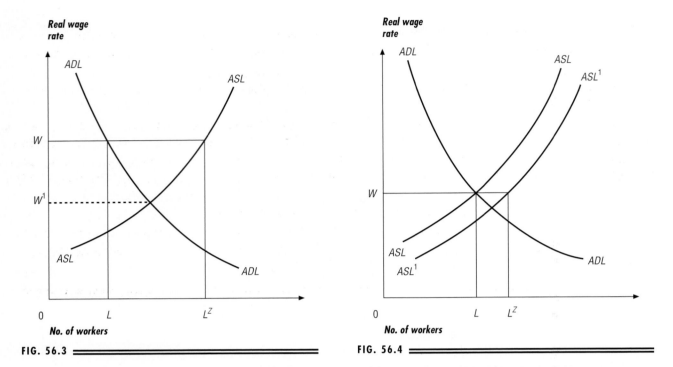

FIG. 56.3

FIG. 56.4

The most significant cause of disequilibrium unemployment is a fall in aggregate demand. As previously mentioned this is cyclical unemployment. Figure 56.5 shows the labour market initially in equilibrium. Then a fall in aggregate demand shifts the aggregate demand curve to the left, i.e. from ADL to ADL^1. The wage rate does not fall and LL^Z unemployment is created.

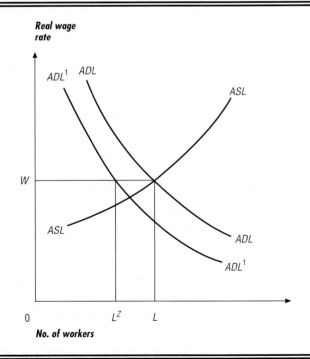

FIG. 56.5

When aggregate demand falls, cyclical unemployment could occur even if the wage falls to the equilibrium level. This is because falling wages will lower demand for consumer goods which, in turn, will lower demand for labour.

EQUILIBRIUM AND DISEQUILIBRIUM UNEMPLOYMENT

New classical economists believe that the real wage adjusts relatively quickly to changes in the supply and demand for labour. Hence they think that the unemployment which exists is of an equilibrium nature. In contrast, Keynesians argue that the labour market is usually in disequilibrium with the demand and supply of labour not being brought into equality with quick adjustments in real wages. They consider the main cause of unemployment to be a fall in aggregate demand.

Some economists take the middle ground and argue that it is possible for equilibrium and disequilibrium unemployment to occur simultaneously. Figure 56.6 shows equilibrium and disequilibrium unemployment occurring at the same time. The total unemployment experienced is LL^X, with LL^Z being disequilibrium unemployment and L^ZL^X being equilibrium unemployment.

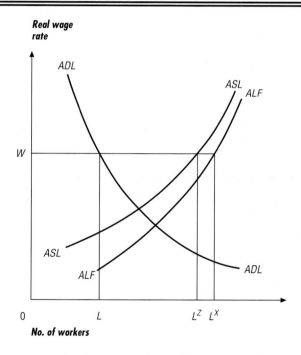

FIG. 56.6

THE EFFECTS OF UNEMPLOYMENT

Unemployment has consequences for the unemployed themselves and for society as a whole.

BENEFITS OF UNEMPLOYMENT TO THOSE UNEMPLOYED

It may seem strange to discuss the benefits of being unemployed. For most people the disadvantages of being unemployed far exceed the benefits. Nevertheless there may be some benefits. One is the time it gives people to explore job opportunities and apply for jobs (frictional and search unemployment). Being unemployed may also provide people with more time to pursue their leisure activities. The unemployed may also be offered training and education by the government which may enable them to gain a more rewarding job.

BENEFITS OF UNEMPLOYMENT TO SOCIETY

Unemployment creates greater flexibility. An economy will be able to expand relatively quickly and easily if there is a pool of suitably qualified unemployed workers. It is also argued that unemployment reduces cost-push inflation by lowering wage claims, making workers more willing to accept new methods of production and more reluctant to take industrial action. Most economists, however, argue that the costs of unemployment exceed any possible benefits.

COSTS OF UNEMPLOYMENT TO THE UNEMPLOYED

Although people may have more time to pursue leisure activities they may be constrained in so doing by a lack of income. This is because most people experience a fall in income, often a significant fall. The unemployed also suffer a loss of status as a certain amount of social stigma is still attached to being unemployed. The unemployed are more likely to experience divorce, nervous breakdowns, bad health and are more likely to attempt suicide than the rest of the adult population. In addition long periods of unemployment reduce the value of human capital. When people are out of work their skills can become rusty, and they miss out on training in new methods. The longer the time a person has been out of work, the harder they are likely to find another job. Economists call this tendency *hysteresis*.

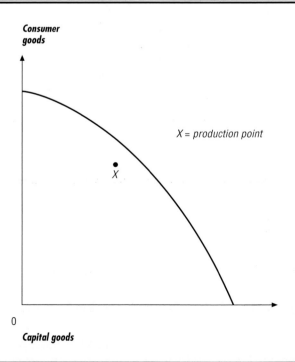

FIG. 56.7

COSTS OF UNEMPLOYMENT TO SOCIETY

The main cost to society is the output which is lost. This is the opportunity cost of unemployment. The output is lost for all time. Even if unemployment later falls, the lost output can never be regained. People will enjoy fewer goods and services than they could have consumed with higher employment. The country will be producing inside its production possibility curve as shown in Figure 56.7.

Unemployment depresses incomes and thereby deprives the government of both direct and indirect tax revenue. Whilst government revenue will fall as unemployment rises, it will have to increase its spending on unemployment related benefits.

The burden of unemployment is not borne evenly by society. The young, people from ethnic minorities and those lacking skills are more likely to experience unemployment.

In recent years there has been increased evidence of a link between crime and unemployment particularly in the case of young unemployed men.

Q U E S T I O N S

SHORT QUESTIONS

1. Why might the claimant count measure understate the true unemployment figure?
2. Are there any benefits of unemployment?
3. Distinguish between structural and cyclical unemployment.
4. Explain what is meant by the unemployment rate.

MULTIPLE CHOICE

1. Coal miners are made redundant as a result of the closure of a number of coal mines. This is an example of:

   A. residual unemployment

   B. seasonal unemployment

   C. structural unemployment

   D. cyclical unemployment.

2. What is the main cost to society of unemployment?

   A. The value of job seekers' allowance and other benefits paid to the unemployed.

   B. The output those unemployed could have produced if they had been in employment.

   C. The reduction in wages resulting from the increase in competition among the labour force.

   D. The increase in the size of the public sector net cash requirement arising from the fall in tax revenue.

3. Figure 56.8 shows the aggregate labour market in which the wage rate is *W*.

What type of unemployment is shown?

   A. Seasonal.

   B. Structural.

   C. Disequilibrium.

   D. The natural rate.

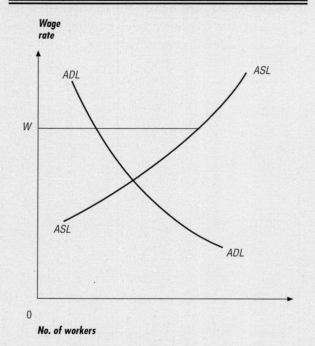

FIG. 56.8

4. What is the non-accelerating inflation rate of unemployment? The level of unemployment which will exist:

   A. when the labour market is in equilibrium

   B. after adjustment for seasonal variations

   C. when the rate of unemployment is falling

   D. when technological and frictional unemployment are excluded.

DATA RESPONSE

Barclays Bank announced plans yesterday to scrap 6000 jobs as part of a fundamental shake-up of its high street and corporate businesses.

The management said the shake-up would cost £400m, but would save £200m year in running costs. It would pave the way for the introduction of new technology, the centralisation of many of the bank's financial processes, but would not involve closure of branches.

Source: 'Troubled Barclays Bank to axe one in ten of 60 000 staff' by Barrie Clement, the Independent, 21/5/99.

A further 40 000 jobs could be in immediate danger in the banking industry because of growing competition from supermarkets and other newcomers to the business, according to industry estimates.

The banking sector has been hit hard by a series of 'restructuring' exercises — some 150 000 jobs have been lost over the past seven years — but there is more to come, analysts believe. Apart from the intervention of companies such as Egg, Tesco, Sainsbury and Virgin, there is also the growing use of new technology.

Increasing numbers of customers are indulging in armchair banking. Telephone call centres, a far cheaper means of conducting transactions for banks, are now the fastest growing sector of the industry. 'Banks are very aware that people are going to be conducting their banking affairs at home,' said Jeremy Batstone of NatWest Stockbrokers. More customers are also using the Internet, while digital television can also be used for a similar purpose.

Mr Batstone said that before the late Eighties a job in banking was seen as a 'job for life' but tougher competition had put paid to that. Banks wanted to replace staff with technology, he said. Unifi, the banking union, fears that the high street could be inundated with completely automated banks in which customers would 'interact' with machines and screens rather than speak to staff.

Source: 'Old-style financial services at risk from new methods' by Barrie Clement, the Independent, 21/5/99.

a] What type of unemployment is the article discussing? **(3)**

b] Why is the loss of 6000 and then possibly 400 000 jobs likely to lead to a greater, faster loss of jobs throughout the economy? **(5)**

c] What has caused employment to fall in the banking sector? **(4)**

d] What effect does a relatively high degree of substitution between labour and capital in a sector have on:
   i   the elasticity of demand for labour **(4)**
   ii the wage rates of workers? **(3)**

e] Discuss whether any groups of workers now have a 'job for life'. **(6)**

CASE STUDY

Some economists are convinced unemployment can be brought down to the levels of the 1950s and 1960s, and that the era of mass joblessness will eventually be seen as the exception, rather than the rule. ... privately policymakers are delighted and surprised that unemployment has continued to fall at a time when the economy has been weak. They believe the outlook for jobs is bound to improve as growth picks up, provided there is no rise in earnings pressure to frighten the Bank of England.

It seems the high water mark of post-war unemployment may have come in the mid-1980s, when the dole queues stretched to almost 3.1m. Unemployment fell sharply in the Lawson boom of the late 1980s then surged in the subsequent recession back to 2.9m. Once Britain's ill-fated membership was terminated on Black Wednesday in September 1992, the downward trend resumed.

Both government measures of unemployment have fallen since the early 1990s. The claimant count, which measures those eligible for certain state benefits, is down to 4.4% while the labour force survey, which measures those looking for work, stands at 6.2%.

Peter Robinson, chief economist of the Institute for Public Policy Research, said that full employment would be a jobless total of 2–2.5% on the claimant count and 4% on the labour force survey.

Some regions have, by Mr Robinson's definition, already made it back to full employment. The south-east, according to claimant count data, has a jobless total of 2.5%, and some of the boom towns are suffering from labour shortages.

By contrast those regions heavily reliant on manufacturing have been hard hit by the strength of sterling. Factory jobs fell by 45 000 in the latest three months, offset by a rise in jobs in services.

Another problem is that many of those excluded from the labour market — single parents, the disabled, over-50s — are not captured either by claimant count or labour force survey. The number described as economically inactive, or not looking for work, rose by 77 000 during the last quarter, reflecting the growth hiatus since the autumn.

Source: 'Jobless facts counter inflation theory' by Larry Elliott, the Guardian, 15/7/99.

a] Why would unemployment be expected to fall when 'growth picks up'? **(5)**

b] What was the main cause of the fall in unemployment in the late 1980s? **(5)**

c] Distinguish between the two main measures of unemployment. **(6)**

d] How did Peter Robinson define full employment? **(4)**

e] Is unemployment evenly spread? **(6)**

f] Why may people be excluded from the labour market? **(7)**

g] Why when unemployment falls to low levels do the 'economically inactive' become particularly significant? **(8)**

h] Discuss the reasons why people cease to be unemployed. **(9)**

STRUCTURED ESSAY

a] Distinguish between equilibrium and disequilibrium unemployment. **(10)**

b] Discuss the causes of equilibrium and disequilibrium unemployment. **(15)**

FREE RESPONSE ESSAY

Assess the costs and benefits of unemployment. **(25)**

57 MEASURES TO REDUCE UNEMPLOYMENT

For some time in the 1980s it was thought the UK would never return to a situation of full employment. However more recently economists have begun to discuss again not only the desirability but also the possibility of achieving full employment.

THE MEANING OF FULL EMPLOYMENT

Full employment cannot mean a situation where everyone wanting and able to work is constantly employed. It is not zero unemployment. This is because there will always be some elements of frictional, structural, seasonal and residual unemployment.

Full employment is sometimes taken to mean a situation where the number of vacancies is at least equal to the numbers out of work.

However it is more common to define full employment in terms of some politically acceptable level of unemployment. This level will vary according to the prevailing conditions and the experience of recent years. Some economists now define UK full employment as less than 3% unemployed.

THE KEYNESIAN APPROACH

Keynesians believe that unemployment is largely involuntary, will not be corrected by free market forces and results largely from a lack of aggregate demand. This analysis indicates that equilibrium GDP (output) at less than the full level of GDP is possible because total planned expenditure consists of spending decisions by households, firms and the government which are not co-ordinated in any way. It is possible, therefore, that the amount which people plan to save plus the amount they plan to spend on imports out of a full employment level of income will be greater than the amounts which firms plan to invest and which other countries plan to spend on domestically produced goods and services. In other words, if at a full employment level of GDP, planned leakages are greater than planned injections, GDP will fall and settle in equilibrium at a level which is below the full employment level.

DEMAND MANAGEMENT

Keynes suggested that the achievement of a full and stable level of employment required the government to play an active part in determining the level of total expenditure. This policy is known as *demand management*.

To manage aggregate demand the government seeks to influence the components of aggregate demand i.e. C, I, G, X and M. Government spending and taxation are important instruments for this purpose. By running budget deficits or surpluses, the government can inject or withdraw purchasing power into or from the economy.

REDUCING UNEMPLOYMENT

As Keynesians believe that unemployment is caused principally by a lack of aggregate demand, they advocate increasing aggregate demand. Figure 57.1 shows that output is initially at Q. This is below the full employment level of QX and there is a deflationary gap. An increase in government expenditure shifts the aggregate demand curve from AD to AD^1, thereby raising output to the full employment level.

It should be noted that the increase in government spending has a magnified effect on GDP. This is because of the multiplier. For example if the deficiency of aggregate demand is estimated to be £10 000m and the multiplier is believed to be 2, then one or more of the components of aggregate demand must be raised in total by £500m. There are a number of policies which can be employed to achieve this objective.

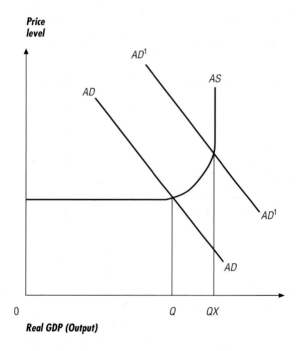

FIG. 57.1

FISCAL POLICY

The government might act in a direct way by increasing its own expenditures on goods and services while leaving taxation unchanged. Alternatively it might decide to stimulate private spending (both C and I) by reducing taxation, but the effects here are more difficult to estimate because some of the increase in disposable income will be saved rather than spent. An increase in social security benefits will be an effective way of bringing about an increase in consumption because the marginal propensities to consume of the recipients will be very large. Private investment might be encouraged by more generous investment grants.

EXAMPLE

Question

In an economy, GDP = £1000m. The injections are, G = £100m, I = £80m, X = £70m. The leakages are M = 0.05 of income, S = 0.1 of income and T = 0.1 of income. These proportions are constant. The government considers that it is necessary to raise GDP to £1200m in order to achieve full employment. It decides to increase its own expenditure and leave the rate of taxation unchanged. By how much must G be raised?

Answer

$$\text{The multiplier is } \frac{1}{mps + mrt + mpm} \text{ i.e. } \frac{1}{0.1 + 0.1 + 0.05} = 4$$

In order to raise GDP by £200m, therefore, government spending must increase by £200m/4 = £50m (i.e. to £150m). Alternatively, in equilibrium, planned injections = planned leakages

$$\text{i.e.} \quad I + G + X \quad = \quad S + T + X$$

When the equilibrium level of GDP is £1200m,

$$I\ (£80m) + G + X\ (£70m) = S\ (£120m) + T\ (£120m) + M\ (£60m)$$

So G = £150m.

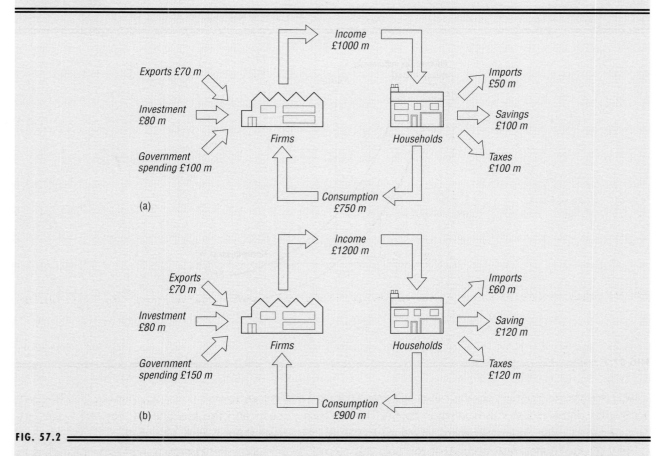

(a)

(b)

FIG. 57.2

The initial and final situations are illustrated in Figure 57.2 where (a) shows the original equilibrium and (b) the equilibrium situation after the effects of the increase in G have worked themselves out.

MONETARY POLICY

In this case, attempts will be made to encourage private investment and consumption spending by relaxing any restrictions on the commercial banks' lending activities and to lower the rate of interest.

EXCHANGE RATE POLICY

To increase aggregate demand a government might decide to lower its exchange rate. This will make its exports cheaper in terms of foreign currency and imports more expensive in terms of the domestic currency. This should switch demand from foreign goods and services to domestic goods and services thereby raising domestic employment.

THE SUPPLY-SIDE APPROACH

New classical economists believe that increasing aggregate demand will not in the long run reduce unemployment but will cause inflation to rise. Figure 57.3 shows that unemployment is initially at *UN* and there is price stability.

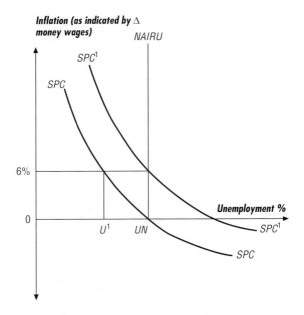

FIG. 57.3

Increasing government spending, raises aggregate demand and initially lowers unemployment to U^1. However, the higher demand also raises inflation to 6%. The increase in costs and the recognition that real wages are being eroded causes unemployment to return to NAIRU. However there is now 6% inflation.

New classical economists argue that the only way to reduce unemployment without increasing inflation is to increase aggregate supply. They advocate policies which are directed towards increasing the quantity and quality of labour and supply. Such policies include measures which aim to reduce the imperfections in the labour market and the use of tax incentives to encourage more investment and improvements in productivity.

These measures include widening the gap between unemployment benefits and low wages so as to increase the incentive to work by reducing job seekers' allowance, tightening the eligibility criteria for the benefit and reducing direct tax to increase the return from working. They support trade union reform to reduce the tendency for trade unions to push up wages above their equilibrium levels and engage in restrictive practices, thereby making labour less attractive to employers. They also oppose minimum wage legislation.

As well as potential workers being unwilling to take up employment, they may be unable to do so because of the lack of suitable skills. So new classical economists advocate education and training as ways of increasing labour productivity and hence making employers more willing to expand their labour force. They also believe that improving labour flexibility, making it easier to 'hire and fire' workers and using less rigid work patterns, including part-time and casual employment, will also encourage employers to recruit more workers.

In addition, new classical economists argue that deregulation and privatisation, by shifting resources from the public to the private sector, improve efficiency and thereby raise output and employment.

All these measures are aimed at increasing the economy's aggregate supply potential and lowering NAIRU. Figure 57.4 shows the long-run aggregate supply curve shifting to the right thereby increasing output.

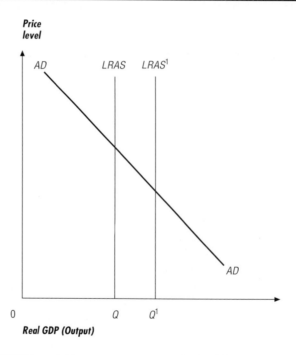

FIG. 57.4

COMMON GROUND

Keynesians and supply-side supporters both favour improving information, promoting labour mobility and training to reduce frictional and structural unemployment. They also agree that raising aggregate demand when the problem is one of regional unemployment is more likely to generate inflationary pressures in the prosperous areas while leaving the depressed regions largely unaffected — although they disagree about what alternative measures should be used.

Most economists now accept that to reduce unemployment both aggregate demand and aggregate supply may need to be raised. Improving the quality of the workforce, and making people more willing to take up employment will not be effective if demand for goods and services is insufficient to create an adequate number of jobs. Similarly, increasing demand without ensuring that the unemployed have the necessary skills and willingness to take up the vacancies created would be likely to cause inflation and a balance of payments deficit rather than a reduction in unemployment.

The Labour Government, elected in May 1997, has used a combination of demand- and supply-side measures to reduce unemployment. Government spending has been increased and its New Deal, whilst offering the unemployed a choice of subsidised jobs, education, training or a place on a government environmental task force, has tightened up the eligibility criteria for job seekers' allowance.

QUESTIONS

SHORT QUESTIONS

1. Distinguish between involuntary and voluntary unemployment.
2. What is meant by demand management?
3. Identify, and explain, one supply-side measure to reduce unemployment.
4. What effect may a devaluation of the currency have on unemployment?

MULTIPLE CHOICE

1. According to new classical economists, which of the following policies would reduce the natural rate of unemployment?

   A. An increase in the supply of money.

   B. An increase in government expenditure.

   C. The introduction of new training initiatives.

   D. The introduction of a statutory incomes policy.

2. Which of the following policies is most likely to reduce the level of frictional unemployment?

   A. Reducing income tax.

   B. Reducing the rate of interest.

   C. Increasing labour mobility.

   D. Increasing job seekers' allowance.

3. A country is experiencing both unemployment and negative growth. Which of the following policy combinations is appropriate to deal with these problems?

   A. A devaluation of the currency and a reduction in interest rates.

   B. A reduction in government spending and an increase in direct taxation.

   C. An increase in investment grants and a revaluation of the currency.

   D. An increase in interest rates and a reduction in indirect taxation.

4. Which of the following policies is likely to reduce cyclical unemployment?

   A. An increase in income tax.

   B. A rise in the exchange rate.

   C. A decrease in the rate of interest.

   D. A decrease in government investment grants.

DATA RESPONSE

The most surprising news last week was the announcement of a 17 400 fall in claimant unemployment in April. True, the rival labour-force survey measure showed a rise of 24 000 in the January–March period, the latest data available. And true, the claimant count is somewhat distorted by the government's New Deal.

But it is hard to avoid the conclusion, backed by the Office for National Statistics, that unemployment is flat rather than rising sharply. Unemployment should be one of the easier indicators for economists to predict. When growth falls significantly below trend, as it has clearly done recently, the jobless total should go up, and vice versa. There are reasons to be optimistic about unemployment. Britain's labour-market flexibility is a factor. So, related to this, is a new 'long-termism' among employers. Manufacturing has been obliged to cut jobs in response to the overvalued pound, employment having fallen by 135 000 in the past year. But other sectors have been either holding on to labour or increasing it. Employment, at 27.4m, stands at a record. That said, there are some pointers suggesting that, beneath the surface, the job market is weakening.

If you work for Barclays, with its announcement last week of 6000 job cuts this year, your confidence in employment prospects is not that high. Retrenchment, it appears, may no longer be confined to industry.

The job figures themselves also point to a cooling labour market. Employment rose by 63 000 in the January–March period, less than in recent quarters. Total hours worked in the economy have not increased over the past 12 months, reflecting the fact that a high proportion of the new jobs have been part-time. Jobcentre vacancies fell for the fifth successive month, the first time this has happened since the 1990–92 recession. The other reason for thinking that all is not as its seems in the job market is the behaviour of retail sales. Record employment and very low mortgage rates should be a recipe for strongly rising spending.

However there was a 0.5% volume in retail sales last month. The Bank of England's regional agents reported to the MPC for its meeting earlier this month that 'retail-sales growth had been subdued'.

There is an underlying fragility to the economy, perhaps because of job worries. This means that following the MPC's 5–4 split vote in favour of leaving base rates on hold earlier this month, there is a strong case for it to cut further on domestic grounds. The case for lower rates, in other words, does not rest entirely on the continued strength of sterling.

The economy is at a fascinating juncture. Suppose a significant rise in unemployment was to be avoided and the economy, with the MPC's help, could gain momentum. The prospects then would be very exciting indeed. The journey from 4.5% claimant unemployment to the 3% rate usually regarded by economists as the practical equivalent of full employment is a short one. Even a few years ago the idea of an imminent return to full employment would have been regarded with incredulity.

Source: Extracts from 'Brown's magic moment' by David Smith, the Sunday Times, 23/5/99.

a] Why would the labour-force survey measure of unemployment be expected to be higher than the claimant count measure? **(2)**

b] Explain what is meant by:
  i   growth falling below its trend growth **(2)**
  ii labour-market flexibility **(2)**
  iii long-termism **(2)**
  iv full employment. **(2)**

c] Discuss whether, according to the article, the UK labour-market was in a healthy state in the period under review. **(7)**

d] Explain what measure the writer was recommending should be implemented to reduce unemployment and why. **(8)**

CASE STUDY

The government yesterday held out the prospect of unemployment falling well below the one million mark after the education and employment secretary, David Blunkett, said he would not be satisfied until dole queues were reduced to levels last seen in the 1940s.

Mr Blunkett's pledge to restore full employment came as official figures showed the number of people out of work and claiming benefit fell by 33 000 last month, the sharpest decline for nearly two years, bringing the total to 1.24m. This is the lowest level since May 1980.

Mr Blunkett said the figures proved that doom and gloom merchants — City economists who had predicted the economic slowdown would boost the dole queues by half a million — had got it wrong. But he wanted to see further reductions in the jobless total.

'Despite falling to a near 20 year low, unemployment remains high by initial postwar standards and there are many inactive people who can still be brought into the world of work,' he said. 'I will not be satisfied until we reach those postwar levels again.' The number of people claiming unemployment benefit ranged between 202 000 and 495 000 in the 10 years after the end of the war, between 1 and 3% of the working-age population. The claimant count rate last month was 4.3%, down from 4.4% in June.

Mr Blunkett's ambitious plans might be derailed if the robust labour market figures prompt the Bank of England to raise interest rates. Economists fear employers will bid up pay rates to attract applicants from the shrinking queue of job hunters, reviving wage inflation.

The government hopes programmes like the New Deal will help to improve the trade-off between inflation and unemployment. 'We have a range of policies in place to help reduce unemployment even further,' Mr Blunkett said. 'With these programmes in place I am confident that we can move ever closer towards our goal of full employment in the new economic environment.'

Economists cast doubts, however, that the government's programme for the long-term unemployed could cause a dramatic fall in the jobless rates.

Source: 'Blunkett vows to bring back full employment' by Charlotte Denny, the Guardian, 12/8/99.

a] Explain what is meant by a trade-off between inflation and employment. **(5)**

b] Why might an economic slowdown not result in unemployment? **(6)**

c] Discuss the benefits of reducing unemployment. **(7)**

d] Explain what is meant by the claimant count rate. **(3)**

e] Why might a rise in interest rates result in unemployment? **(7)**

f] Explain the relationship between unemployment and wage rates. **(6)**

g] Discuss one policy measure to reduce long-term unemployment. **(8)**

h] What effect will a fall in unemployment have on a government's budget position? **(8)**

STRUCTURED ESSAY

a] Explain why a country might experience a significant rise in unemployment. **(12)**

b] Assess two measures a government could take to reduce unemployment. **(13)**

FREE RESPONSE ESSAY

Compare the effectiveness of increasing government spending and reducing job seekers' allowance as methods of reducing unemployment. **(25)**

58 INFLATION

DEGREES OF INFLATION

Inflation is a situation in which the general price level is persistently moving upwards. In an extreme form of inflation, prices rise at a phenomenal rate and terms such as *hyperinflation*, runaway inflation, and galloping inflation have all been used to describe these conditions. Germany experienced this kind of inflation in 1923 and by the end of that year prices were one million million times greater than their pre-war level.

Under conditions of hyperinflation people lose confidence in the currency's ability to carry out its functions. It becomes unacceptable as a medium of exchange and other commodities, such as cigarettes, are used as money. When things have become as bad as this the only possible course of action is to withdraw the currency and issue new monetary units.

Another type of inflation is described as *suppressed inflation*. This occurs where demand exceeds supply, but the effect on prices is minimised by the use of such devices as price controls and rationing.

Creeping inflation is a low level of inflation.

CAUSES OF INFLATION

Traditionally Keynesians have classified the causes of inflation as demand-pull or cost-push.

DEMAND-PULL INFLATION

Demand-pull inflation may be defined as a situation where aggregate demand persistently exceeds aggregate supply at current prices so that the general price level is 'pulled' up.

DEMAND-PULL INFLATION AND FULL EMPLOYMENT

All economists agree that once the country's resources are fully employed, an increase in aggregate demand must lead to an upward movement of prices. This is illustrated in Figure 58.1 which shows that the increase in aggregate demand from AD to AD^1 occurring at the full employment level of real national income results in a rise in the general price level from P to P^1.

Conditions of excess demand when there is full employment can arise in several different ways. Wartime conditions are one example. War brings full employment, a large increase in the number of those at work and a great deal of overtime working. The net result is a large increase in total income and hence in potential demand. On the other hand, the supply of consumer goods and services will fall as resources are diverted to meet military demands. In the markets for consumer goods, demand will be much greater than supply at current price levels. During wartime the excess demand is not allowed to exert its full effect on the price level. The government imposes price controls on essential commodities and supports these price controls with a system of rationing. Large-scale savings campaigns and heavy taxation are also used to remove some of the excess demand.

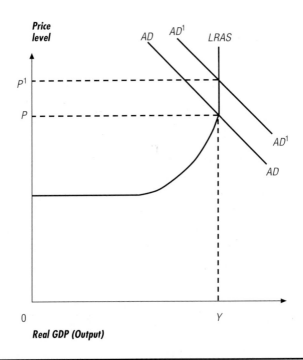

FIG. 58.1

A situation of excess demand may arise when a country is trying to achieve an export surplus, in order, perhaps, to pay off some overseas debt. Exports can be inflationary as they generate income at home, but reduce the supply of goods and services at home. Imports, of course, can make good this deficiency of home supplies, but if exports are greater than imports there will be excess demand in the home market unless taxes and savings are increased to absorb the excess purchasing power.

Demand-pull inflation might develop when, with full employment, a country tries to increase its rate of economic growth. In order to increase the rate of capital accumulation, resources will have to be transferred from the production of consumer goods and services to the production of capital goods. Incomes will not fall since the factors of production are still employed, but the supply of the items on which these incomes may be spent will fall in the short run. Unless taxation and/or savings increase there will be excess demand and a rise in the price level.

Another possible cause of inflation under conditions of full employment is an expansion of government spending financed by borrowing from the banking system. In this case the expenditure is being financed by an increase in the money supply. Even when the additional government spending is financed from taxation the effect may still be inflationary since the additional taxes will reduce spending by a lower amount (some of the extra tax will be paid by reducing saving).

Figure 58.2 shows planned expenditure increasing above the full employment level of income and an inflationary gap of *ab* being created.

LESS THAN FULL EMPLOYMENT

It is possible that increases in aggregate demand can result in a rise in the general price level at less than full employment, if output cannot be adjusted proportionately. Supply constraints can arise due to shortages of skilled labour, skilled entrepreneurs or specialised capital equipment. Figure 58.3 shows an increase in aggregate

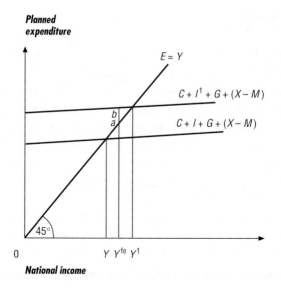

FIG. 58.2

demand, occurring at less than full employment, causing a rise in both output and the general price level as bottlenecks begin to be experienced.

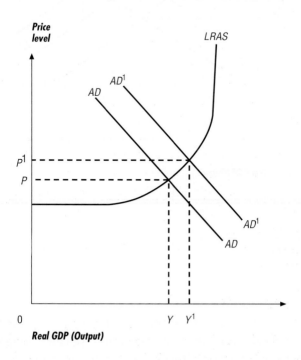

FIG. 58.3

THE INFLATIONARY PROCESS

An increase in aggregate demand can cause a rise in the general price level. However inflation is a sustained, and not just a one off rise in the general price level. So it is necessary to explain not only why such an increase can cause a rise in the general price level but why the rise continues. An inflationary process of the demand-pull induced type is usually explained in terms of the conditions in the markets for the factors of production.

When aggregate demand is rising firms increase their demand for the factors of production. As these become in shorter supply their prices rise. For instance firms competing for workers will raise wage rates. If the rise in wages exceeds any increase in productivity, costs will rise and these will be passed on to consumers in the form of higher prices. The higher wages also increases aggregate demand and the process proceeds with prices in the markets for goods and in the markets for factors of production being pulled upwards. Figure 58.4 shows an increase in aggregate demand resulting in an initial rise in the general price level to P^1. The rise in output to Y^1 causes costs to rise which shifts the short run aggregate supply curve to the left and raises the price level even higher to P^2. The higher wages cause aggregate demand to go up again and this pulls up the price level to P^3 and so on.

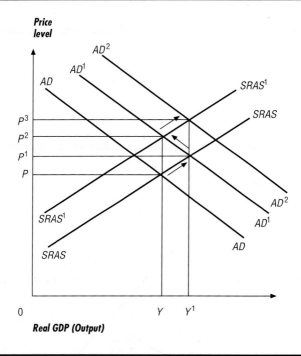

FIG. 58.4

COST-PUSH INFLATION

INITIATING FACTORS

Cost-push inflation describes a situation where the process of rising prices is initiated and sustained by rising costs which push up prices. It should not be confused with a situation where excess demand is causing entrepreneurs, faced with shortages, to bid up the prices of factors of production. In such cases the passing on of the higher costs in the form of higher prices is a feature of demand inflation.

Cost-push inflation occurs when prices are forced upwards by increases in prices of factors of production (i.e., costs) which are not caused by excess demand. There are several ways in which costs may rise independently of the state of demand.

One example of a supply-side shock which will shift the short run supply curve is a rise in price of imported raw materials. Under these circumstances domestic costs, and hence prices, are increased whatever the level of domestic demand.

This is illustrated in Figure 58.5 which shows the rise in costs of production moving the aggregate supply curve to the left and pushing up the general price level.

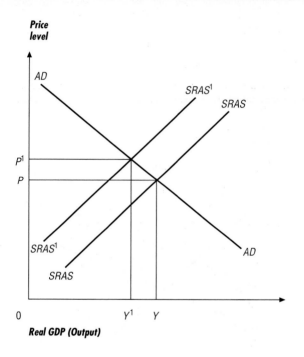

FIG. 58.5

An increase in indirect taxation (i.e., taxes on goods and services) is another way of giving the general price level an inflationary 'push'. Again prices would rise regardless of the state of demand. Possibly the most common cause of cost-push inflation, however, is an increase in wages which exceeds any increase in productivity.

THE INFLATIONARY PROCESS

An increase in indirect taxes will lead to a one off rise in prices. Import prices may rise for several months, but eventually they level out or begin to fall. Cost-push inflation continues because the increases in costs which lead to price increases are also increases in income. Factor prices are incomes to the factors of production, so that although prices increase so does the ability to pay these higher prices. An increase in costs is followed by an increase in demand.

THE MONETARIST EXPLANATION OF INFLATION

Monetarists believe that the main cause of inflation is the growth of the money supply. Many of them think this is the sole cause. They argue that excess demand or rising costs are symptoms of inflation and not the cause. Monetarist theory holds that there is a strong connection between the money supply and output. They argue that if the money supply is allowed to grow at a faster rate than the output of goods and services (real GDP), the inevitable effect will be inflation. Nominal GDP will be increasing at a faster rate than the real GDP.

The monetarist theory is based on the quantity theory $(MV = PT)$. They assume that a change in the money supply has a direct and proportionate effect on the price level as they think V and T are stable.

Monetarists believe a rise in the money supply will increase aggregate demand. In the short run this will increase output (and employment). Figure 58.6 shows the aggregate demand curve shifting to the right (AD^1) and aggregate supply extending. However in the long run, as wages and costs rise, the short run aggregate supply curve will move to the left to $SRAS^1$. There is a move up the vertical long run aggregate supply curve and output returns to its previous level but at a higher price level.

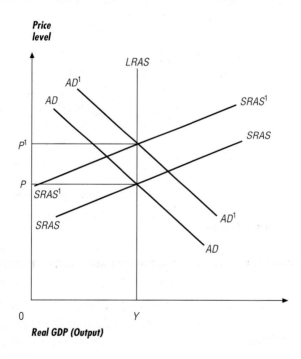

FIG. 58.6

KEYNESIAN VIEWS OF INFLATION AND THE MONEY SUPPLY

Economists agree that inflation is a monetary phenomenon in the sense that it will be combined with an increase in the money supply. However, while monetarists believe that increases in the money supply cause inflation, Keynesians believe that inflation causes an increase in the money supply. If the general price level is rising, firms and individuals will borrow more to meet higher costs and prices, and the resulting higher bank lending will increase the money supply.

THE EFFECTS OF INFLATION

The effects of inflation will depend on its level, whether it is constant or accelerating and whether it is anticipated or unanticipated. Indeed a low, stable and correctly anticipated rate of inflation can be beneficial.

THE EFFECTS ON THE DISTRIBUTION OF INCOME

Inflation leads to an arbitrary redistribution of real income. Although a rise in the general price level produces a corresponding rise in money incomes, all prices do not rise to the same extent and different income groups will be affected in different ways.

There will be some 'gainers' and some 'losers'. The losers are those whose incomes are fixed, or rise by less than the rate of inflation. For example people whose income is derived from fixed interest securities will experience a fall in their real incomes.

When incomes are directly related to prices (index-linked), e.g. state pensions, real income will remain unchanged. However, because wages tend to rise by more than inflation, the gap between the incomes of wage earners and pensioners usually widens during periods of inflation.

The effects on incomes derived from profits depend largely upon the kind of inflation being experienced. During demand-pull inflation, real profits tend to rise. The prices of final goods and services tend to rise by more than many factor prices, some of which are fixed on fairly long-term contracts. The margin between the two price levels tends to widen because of this time lag. When there is cost-push inflation, profits may be squeezed. Since there is no excess demand some firms may find it rather difficult to pass on the full effects of rising costs in the form of higher prices. Wage earners generally more than hold their own when the price level is rising. In the UK and many other countries wages rise faster than prices. However, there tends to be some redistribution effect as those with superior bargaining power gain at the expense of the weaker groups.

Inflation tends to encourage borrowing and discourage lending because debtors 'gain' and creditors 'lose'. This is because the nominal rate of interest usually rises by less than the rate of inflation. So the real rate of interest tends to fall.

There can be a transfer of income from taxpayers to the government if *fiscal drag* occurs. Fiscal drag is when tax payers are dragged into higher tax brackets when their money incomes rise and as a result experience lower real incomes. However, governments now usually adjust tax brackets in line with inflation to prevent this occurring.

EFFECTS ON PRODUCTION

Demand-pull inflation is associated with buoyant trading conditions and sellers' markets where the risks of trading are greatly reduced. These easy market conditions might give rise to complacency and inefficiency since the competitive pressure to improve both product and performance will be greatly weakened. This is not likely to be the case in a cost-push inflation where trading conditions are likely to place a premium on greater efficiency. Where firms cannot absorb some of the higher factor prices by improving productivity they may find it difficult to survive. It is possible that employers seeking to hold down costs will react to rapidly rising wage costs by devising means of economising in their use of labour and hence raise the level of unemployment.

Demand-pull inflation, it is sometimes argued, is conducive to a faster rate of economic growth since the excess demand and favourable market conditions will stimulate investment and expansion.

However inflation can also raise firms' costs. There may be *menu costs* (i.e. costs involved in altering prices), *shoe-leather costs* (costs experienced in moving money around to gain high interest rates and searching out the lowest prices) and *administrative costs* involved in calculating the future prices that will have to be paid for raw materials etc. There may also be inflationary noise (problems involved in reading price signals which are distorted by inflation). For example, a firm witnessing a rise in the price consumers are prepared to pay for its product, may conclude that their product is becoming more popular and so increase their production of it. However the rise may not be an increase in the relative price but merely an increase in line with inflation.

EFFECTS ON THE BALANCE OF PAYMENTS

In economies such as the UK which are dependent upon a high level of exports and imports, inflation often leads to balance of payments difficulties. If other countries are not inflating to the same extent, home-produced goods will become less competitive at home and abroad. Exports will fall in demand and imports will rise. This could result in a deficit, or a larger deficit, on the current account of the balance of payments. The problem will be a particularly difficult one where inflation is of the demand-pull type. This is because in addition to the price effects the excess demand at home will tend to 'suck in' more imports. The problems can also be serious if the country is operating a fixed exchange rate system as a fall in the exchange rate cannot be used to restore price competitiveness. However there are also risks with a floating exchange rate. A vicious circle can develop with inflation lowering the exchange rate, which in turn, raises the price of imported goods and services and thereby further contributes to inflation.

EFFECTS OF ANTI-INFLATIONARY POLICIES

The measures taken against inflation may sometimes cause more harmful effects than inflation itself. For example deflationary monetary and fiscal policy measures are likely to raise unemployment and lower economic growth. Consumers and producers may consider that this is too high a price to pay.

QUESTIONS

SHORT QUESTIONS

1. What might be the costs of zero inflation?

2. Will an increase in aggregate demand always cause inflation?

3. What effect is inflation likely to have on a country's balance of payments?

4. Which is more serious, anticipated or unanticipated inflation?

MULTIPLE CHOICE

1. Which of the following is a possible cause of cost push inflation?

   A. A budget deficit.

   B. A reduction in direct taxes.

   C. An increase in bank lending.

   D. An increase in the price of imported raw materials.

2. Figure 58.7 shows the price level and output operating in an economy.

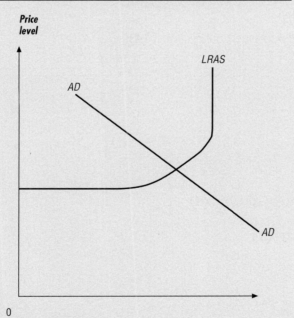

Price level

AD

LRAS

AD

0

Real GDP (Output)

FIG. 58.7

What effect will an increase in consumer expenditure have?

   A. Increase aggregate supply.

   B. Increase the general price level.

   C. Reduce the level of output.

   D. Reduce the level of employment.

3. Which of the following must occur during inflation?

   A. Fiscal drag.

   B. A fall in the value of the country's money.

   C. A reduction in the price competitiveness of the country's products.

   D. A redistribution of income from creditors to debtors.

4. In a fully employed economy which of the following would, by itself, be inflationary?

   A. An increase in savings.

   B. An increase in demand for exports.

   C. An increase in the rate of income tax.

   D. An increase in the productivity of labour.

DATA RESPONSE

For several decades the bogeyman for most rich economies has been inflation. Policymakers began to fight it seriously 20 years ago, when Paul Volcker, chairman of America's Federal Reserve, dramatically tightened monetary policy. Countries from Britain to Brazil then joined the fray. With great success: the average inflation rate in the G7 economies is now a mere 1%, the lowest for half a century. But even as the old enemy seems quiescent, a new and possibly more dangerous one may be rising up: deflation.

This is not a claim that *The Economist* makes lightly. We have long urged central banks on in their determination to resist inflation. And isn't the sign of a good central bank its willingness to turn a deaf ear to calls for monetary expansion, whatever the circumstances? Actually, no. The right target is broadly stable prices, which requires that a central bank should be ready to attack deflation as fiercely as it does inflation. Not only that, but a good central bank also keeps in mind that deflation can be more damaging than inflation, if it creates a downward spiral in which expectation of falling prices reduces demand and pushes prices lower still, as happened in the Great Depression.

In much of the world outside America, the risk of falling consumer prices (i.e. deflation) is at its greatest since the 1930s. Japan is already in the grip of deflation. Prices are falling in China and some other parts of East Asia. Continental Europe's inflation rate, if correctly measured, is close to zero. Prices are coming down partly thanks to the beneficial effects of new technology and deregulation, and partly thanks to cheaper oil and other commodities. Such deflation is generally benign. But alongside it are signs of a more malign deflation, caused by excess capacity and weak demand. On current forecasts, the global 'output gap' between actual and potential production will, by the end of 1999, be at its widest since the 1930s. If the economies of America or Europe were now to take a sudden lurch downwards, the world might easily experience outright depression, with prices and output falling together, just as they did 70 years ago.

Source: 'The new danger', The Economist, 20/2/99.

a] Why has inflation been 'the bogeyman for most rich economies' until recently? **(4)**

b] Explain what is meant by:
   i   deflation **(2)**
   ii   the G7 economies **(2)**
   iii an output gap **(2)**
   iv   depression **(2)**
   v   monetary expansion. **(2)**

c] Discuss one measure a central bank could adopt to 'attack inflation'. **(4)**

d] In what circumstances will deflation prove to be harmful? **(7)**

CASE STUDY

A bread roll costs about 15 cents (6p) at the A Sua Padaria bakery in Ipanema. But not for long.

The yeast wholesaler yesterday upped his prices by 5%. By Monday flour too will cost more as imported goods like wheat are affected by Brazil's currency devaluation.

'In many places bread is already 18 cents. I'm scared to pass on the increased cost to the customer, but I don't think I can wait any longer. Everything will rise,' laments Jean Bruche, the bakery owner.

In 10 days the Brazilian real has lost more than 40% of its value. The effect is already being felt on the street as the consequences work through the economy. Retailers face difficult decisions as they buy new stock. 'These are really difficult times. If I put up prices I won't sell. But if I keep them the same I won't cover my costs,' says Gabriel Habib, who owns a chain of toy shops.

He adds, 'Even though 70% of my goods are Brazilian, many have foreign components. I also pay royalties in dollars. There is no such thing as a purely national product. Markets are globalised.'

The crisis has revised fears that a contagion of price rises could trigger a return to hyperinflation. Before the real was created in 1994, Brazilians were used to prices rising up to 90% a month.

David Fleischer, of the University of Brasilia, says that inflation is a big worry. 'Products like coffee and rice have already gone up in the supermarkets. There is no reason for this because they are national products. It is greed. People are taking advantage of the moment — this is something very old and traditional in Brazil, and it is coming back to haunt us.'

But, he said, the government's controls — which include a team of inspectors who can take legal action against anyone considered to have increased prices unfairly — should be able to contain hyperinflation for the time being.

Source: 'Inflation threat to Brazil's daily bread' by Alex Bellos, the Guardian, 23/1/99.

a] Explain what is meant by hyperinflation. **(4)**

b] What are the dangers of hyperinflation? **(6)**

c] According to the extract what were the causes of the price rises being experienced in Brazil at the start of 1999? **(8)**

d] Explain what is meant by the statement 'Markets are globalised'. **(4)**

e] Explain what is meant by 'a contagion of price rises'. **(6)**

f] Discuss two groups who would suffer from 'prices rising up to 90% a month'. **(8)**

g] What might the team of inspectors consider to be an 'unfair' rise in price? **(6)**

h] Why might inflation become habitual? **(8)**

STRUCTURED ESSAY

a] Distinguish between cost-push and demand-pull inflation. **(10)**

b] Which groups may benefit and which groups may suffer as a result of inflation? **(15)**

FREE RESPONSE ESSAY

Discuss whether the costs of inflation outweigh the costs of deflation. **(25)**

59 THE RELATIONSHIP BETWEEN INFLATION AND UNEMPLOYMENT

For a number of decades now economists and politicians have debated whether a relationship exists between inflation and unemployment and if so what form the relationship takes. They have also debated whether low inflation or high employment should receive the higher priority.

THE TRADITIONAL PHILLIPS CURVE

Work by the economist Bill Phillips at the London School of Economics published in 1958 suggested that a stable relationship existed between unemployment and money wages. He based his findings on figures for unemployment and money wages over the period 1861 to 1957.

This work was developed to suggest a trade-off between unemployment and inflation (as measured by changes in money wages). This relationship is illustrated by the Phillips Curve as shown in Figure 59.1.

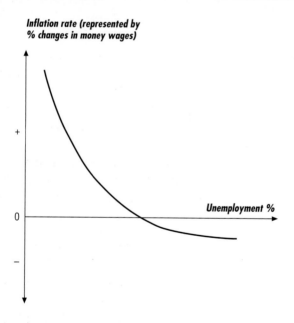

FIG. 59.1

The Phillips Curve shows that when unemployment is low, inflation is high and when unemployment is high inflation is low, i.e. an inverse relationship. When unemployment is low, workers will be in a strong position to press for wage rises. Whereas when unemployment is high more workers compete for each job and wage rises are held down. It also shows that money wages are 'sticky' downwards. Once the curve passes below the horizontal axis it flattens out since even if unemployment rises to high levels workers will resist cuts in their money wages.

The Phillips Curve implies that a government can choose its preferred combination of unemployment and inflation. For example, it can decide to reduce unemployment if it is prepared to 'pay the price' of higher inflation.

REACTION AGAINST THE PHILLIPS CURVE

In the late 1960s and in the 1970s the Phillips Curve came in for considerable criticism. This was based on two grounds, one theoretical and the other empirical.

Milton Friedman, the American monetarist economist, argued that workers are concerned with real and not money wages and that, whilst there may be a short-run trade-off relationship between unemployment and inflation, there is no long-run relationship. He developed the expectations-augmented Phillips Curve to explain this difference between the short- and long-run positions. His analysis led him to conclude that governments cannot reduce unemployment by increasing aggregate demand. This view was taken up by the Labour Government in 1976. In a famous speech the then Prime Minister, James Callaghan, rejected the Phillips Curve relationship and the Keynesian solution to unemployment:

'It used to be thought that a nation could just spend its way out of recession and increase employment by cutting taxes and boosting government spending. I tell you in all candour that, that option no longer exists. In so far as it existed in the past, it had always led to a bigger dose of inflation, followed by a higher level of unemployment.' (Speech to the Labour Party Conference.)

The period of the late 1960s, 1970s and 1980s cast considerable doubt on the inverse relationship by the Phillips Curve. Over this period both inflation and unemployment rose. Keynesians explained this breakdown in the relationship by arguing that the Phillips Curve had moved out to the right. They believed the two key reasons for this were the unexpected external inflationary shocks caused by the OPEC oil price rises in the mid 1970s and early 1980s and by labour market imperfections. They claimed that labour markets had changed with the labour force being divided into two groups, the insiders and the outsiders. The insiders were those in work and those who had recently become unemployed. Whereas the outsiders were the long-term unemployed who lacked skills. This latter group were thought to have little influence on pay so that as their number increased it did not have the effect of moderating wage claims by the insiders.

THE EXPECTATIONS-AUGMENTED PHILLIPS CURVE

Milton Friedman argues that workers and employers will not suffer from money illusion in the long run but that it will take time for people's expectations to adjust to changes in prices and money wages. His view is illustrated in his expectations-augmented Phillips Curve as shown in Figure 59.2.

For example unemployment may initially be at the NAIRU level with inflation stable at 4% per annum. This will be the expected rate of inflation, and wage settlements will be linked to it so that real wage rates will be constant. If the government then tries to reduce the level of unemployment to U^1 by increasing aggregate demand, the effect will be an increase in prices, and production will become more profitable because many costs will not change immediately: wages, for example, are normally adjusted annually.

The increase in demand, therefore, will lead to an increase in prices, an increase in output and an increase in employment. Unemployment may fall to U^1 but now there is a higher rate of inflation, say 9%, and the economy moves on to a higher short-run Phillips Curve, SPC^2 with a worse trade-off relationship.

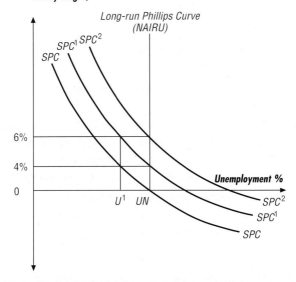

FIG. 59.2

In time 9% will become the expected rate of inflation. In order to restore the level of real wages, workers will negotiate 9% increases in money wages. Other costs will also adjust to the higher rate of inflation. When this happens, firms will have lost all the gains (higher profitability) from the higher level of demand. They will be faced with the same ratio of costs to prices as they experienced before the demand increased. Output will be cut back to its former level and unemployment will return to the NAIRU. The rate of inflation, however, will remain at 9% because wages and other costs have fully adjusted to this annual rate of increase in the price level.

FULLY ANTICIPATED INFLATION

If people fully anticipate that a change in government expenditure (and the money supply) will lead to a rise in prices but not output, then there will be no long-run and no short-run effect on unemployment. Workers will demand a proportionate increase in wages and firms will raise their prices proportionately. So the change in government expenditure will, in this case, leave real wages and real profits unchanged. Figure 59.3 shows the economy operating at 5% inflation. A rise in government spending has no effect, short or long-run, on unemployment and the economy moves up the long-run Phillips Curve, in this case to 11%.

RECENT EXPERIENCE

The 1990s saw a return to the relationship described in the traditional Phillips Curve. As Table 59.1 shows, inflation and unemployment moved in opposite directions, with the exception of 1996.

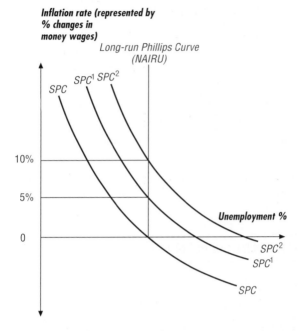

FIG. 59.3

TABLE 59.1 INFLATION AND UNEMPLOYMENT

Year	Inflation % (change in RPI)	Unemployment % (Claimant count)
1989	7.5	6.3
1990	7.7	5.8
1991	5.9	8.1
1992	3.7	9.8
1993	1.6	10.3
1994	2.4	9.3
1995	3.5	8.0
1996	2.4	7.3
1997	3.1	5.5
1998	3.4	4.7

In the consumer boom of the late 1980s increased spending reduced unemployment whilst contributing to inflation. In the early 1990s the effect of the recession and the reduction in expectations of inflation resulted in unemployment rising and inflation falling. Then from 1993 the economy started to pick up. Unemployment fell whilst inflation rose. However the rise in inflation was significantly lower than in previous periods. With the decline in inflation the economy appeared to have moved onto a lower Phillips curve. However at the very end of the 1990s the UK, and a number of other countries, began to experience both falling unemployment and falling inflation and some economists began to question whether economic conditions had changed in such a way that they no longer had to trade off the two objectives.

THE NEW ECONOMIC PARADIGM

At the end of the 1990s the USA, the UK and some European countries experienced rising output, falling unemployment and low inflation. This led some economists to argue that there is a new economic *paradigm* (model) operating. They suggest that advances in technology are causing productivity to rise and thereby allowing output to continue to increase even as economies approach full employment. This shifting of the aggregate supply curve to match rises in aggregate demand and lower expectations of inflation, it is argued, means that the risk of high inflation is eliminated and the trade-off between unemployment and inflation no longer applies.

The new economic paradigm, or new economy, as it is sometimes known, is said to be particularly evident in the USA as this is where the most significant advances in information technology are currently being experienced.

INFLATION VERSUS UNEMPLOYMENT

From the mid 1970s to the end of the 1980s price stability was the prime objective of UK governments. However in the early and mid 1990s, with high unemployment and low inflation many economists and some politicians shifted their focus from reducing inflation to reducing unemployment. The costs of unemployment are very evident, not evenly spread and whilst, in theory, it is possible to cushion the unemployed from the financial costs, it is very difficult to protect them from the psychological effects. Whereas not only may the costs of moderate inflation be relatively low, there may be costs in lowering inflation further.

Zero, or a very low level of, inflation is not necessarily a desirable objective. It may change consumers' attitudes. Instead of buying now before prices rise they may postpone purchases in the hope that prices will fall. Firms which had previously benefited from demand-pull inflation (expanding and innovating in the expectation of rising profits) may now seek to improve their profit margins by cutting costs which may be at the expense of employment and the quality of products.

Firms, and individuals, who had taken out loans in the expectation that inflation would erode their real cost will face higher real debt burdens than they had anticipated.

There may be a reverse money illusion with people thinking that the returns they are receiving on savings are falling as nominal interest rates fall in line with inflation, leaving the real rate unchanged or even raising it if nominal interest rates fall by less than inflation. This misreading of the situation may encourage them to seek higher but riskier returns.

Very low inflation may also make it more difficult for firms to adjust their costs in the face of falling demand. With inflation it may be possible to cut real wages by raising nominal wages by less than inflation. However with zero or very low inflation money wages may have to be cut. This may provoke industrial unrest and if it proves difficult to reduce wage rates, employers may take the alternative option of making some workers redundant.

QUESTIONS

SHORT QUESTIONS

1. Explain what is meant by money wages being 'sticky downwards'.
2. Why might inflation be high when unemployment is low?
3. What would a shift to the left of the Phillips Curve indicate?
4. Explain how inflation may enable firms to cut their costs.

MULTIPLE CHOICE

1. The Phillips Curve shows the relationship between unemployment and:

   A output

   B inflation

   C the balance of payments

   D tax revenue.

2. Figure 59.4 shows a long-run Phillips Curve (*LPC*) and three short-run Phillips Curves (*SPC*). The economy is initially at the NAIRU rate of unemployment (0*X*) with an inflation rate of 5%.

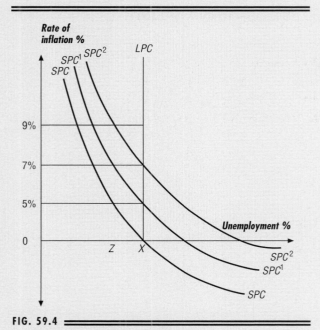

FIG. 59.4

If the government seeks to reduce unemployment to 0Z what will be the effect on the rate of inflation?

A reduce it to 0%

B leave it unchanged at 5%

C raise it to 7%

D raise it to 9%.

3. According to the expectations-augmented Phillips Curve why does an increase in aggregate demand have no effect on unemployment in the long run?

   A Firms respond to higher demand by increasing prices rather than output and employment.

   B Unemployment will return to the natural rate when workers and firms realise that real wages and real costs have returned to their previous levels.

   C Higher aggregate demand increases imports and affects employment levels abroad more than the domestic employment level.

   D In the long run advances in technology and education increase productivity and enable a higher output to be produced with a smaller labour force.

4. Why may a fall in unemployment be associated with a rise in the rate of inflation?

   A The fall in unemployment will cause the government to reduce tax rates.

   B A fall in unemployment will increase aggregate demand and claims for wage rises.

   C If unemployment falls below the natural rate of unemployment the real wages of workers will rise in the long run.

   D A fall in unemployment will reduce government expenditure on job seekers' allowance and other unemployment related benefits.

DATA RESPONSE

Even the most robust defenders of the view that computers are delivering a new American paradigm, under which growth can be sustainably stronger for longer, are beginning to recognise that the imbalances in the US economy just cannot go on. Certainly, US productivity growth may have accelerated to some 2.1% a year in the late-Nineties rather than the 1.1% a year which was the economy's lot in the Seventies, Eighties and early Nineties. And that does justify higher overall growth rates without raising inflation, and also higher profits growth which underpins Wall Street.

But the earnings growth from US corporates is not just due to a change in the productivity trend. If it was, unemployment would not have been falling; the definition of higher productivity is more output for a given amount of labour. Unemployment has in fact been falling quite quickly during the recent US upswing: from a peak of 7.2% in 1992 on the standardised international measures, US unemployment is now down to 4.3%.

This is, of course, good news. The US economy is proving able to operate at a lower level of unemployment without stirring up much in the way of inflationary pay pressures which would then feed through into prices. But it also means that much of the growth in the US economy — and the profits growth which is delighting Wall Street — is the usual one-off upswing due to the business cycle rather than a change in the long-run underlying trend. And that means that it must come to an end at some point, because you cannot have negative unemployment.

Source: 'Superspan faces his toughest test' by Christopher Huhne, the Independent, 26/7/99.

a] What is the new economic paradigm? **(5)**

b] Why does a rise in productivity 'justify higher overall growth rates without raising inflation'? **(6)**

c] Describe the upswing of the business cycle. **(4)**

d] Why must an upswing come to an end? **(5)**

e] Why is the new economic paradigm supposed to apply particularly to the USA? **(5)**

CASE STUDY

Unemployment has fallen to 1.28m. This is the lowest level since 1980, a year that saw inflation of 20%.

Today the underlying rate of inflation is below the 2.5% government target and the headline rate is at a six year low of 1.3%. If it falls below 1.2%, which still requires a bit of luck, we shall have the lowest inflation since July 1963 — when Gerry and the Pacemakers' 'I Like It' was at number one. A 36-year low on inflation; a 19-year low on unemployment; whatever happened to the (Phillips curve) trade-off between the two?

It was not supposed to be this way. In June last year, when the Bank of England's monetary policy committee (MPC) raised rates to 7.5%, its concern was that a tight labour market, as evinced by skill shortages and upward pressure of pay, was threatening the inflation target.

The MPC's June minutes were candid: 'The earnings data suggested that it was more likely that unemployment was below the rate compatible with stable inflation. In that case, it was probable that unemployment would have to rise to hit the inflation target on a sustainable basis.'

The MPC was careful not to say how far unemployment would have to rise, but others were less timid. Leader writers on the *Financial Times* argued that the level of unemployment (then above 1.3m) was incompatible with the inflation target and that 'unemployment must now be allowed to rise — perhaps by 500 000 — to bring the economy back to a non-inflationary path.'

The implication was clear: unless unemployment was pushed back up to nearly 2m, a rate of 7%–8%, inflation would exceed 2.5%.

Since then unemployment and inflation have fallen. This is interesting. Where a year ago many were arguing that only a large increase in unemployment could stabilise inflation, today a lower level of unemployment seems to carry little or no inflationary threat. What is going on?

To answer that we need to understand the policy debate of a year ago. The framework was the trade-off between inflation and the real economy as embodied in the Phillips curve and the concept of the natural rate of unemployment or the NAIRU (the non-accelerating inflation rate of unemployment). The theory says falling unemployment is typically associated with an increase in wage pressure and that there comes a point where any attempts to expand demand result not in permanently lower unemployment but in accelerating inflation.

Source: 'Unemployed need not pay for low inflation' by Geoffrey Dicks, the Sunday Times, 1/8/99.

a] What is meant by the underlying rate of inflation. **(4)**

b] Explain what is meant by a 'tight labour market'. **(5)**

c] Why might a rise in unemployment reduce inflation? **(7)**

d] Explain the trade-off relationship shown by the Phillips Curve. **(7)**

e] What is NAIRU? **(4)**

f] Why might a fall in unemployment not be accompanied by a rise in inflation? **(7)**

g] Is a low level of inflation necessarily desirable? **(7)**

h] Discuss two costs of an increase in unemployment. **(8)**

STRUCTURED ESSAY

a] What is meant by inflation and unemployment and how are they measured? **(10)**

b] Compare the relative costs of inflation and unemployment. **(15)**

FREE RESPONSE ESSAY

Discuss whether it is possible to reduce unemployment without increasing the rate of inflation. **(25)**

60 ANTI-INFLATIONARY POLICIES

THE NEED FOR ANTI-INFLATIONARY POLICIES

Although opinion is divided on whether a low and stable rate of inflation is undesirable, there is little disagreement on the undesirability of high and accelerating rates of inflation.

In Chapter 58 it was seen that inflation can cause serious tensions because it tends to redistribute income in favour of those with stronger bargaining powers and debtors and penalises those with weaker bargaining power and creditors. It may also lead to a deterioration in the balance of payments.

The problem of inflation can become particularly serious when inflation escalates. This creates expectation of further increases in the rate of inflation. These expectations lead workers and firms to raise wages and prices by amounts which take into account not only past and present, but also of future price increases. Once inflation becomes firmly established, the most important and difficult objective of any policy to cure inflation is to change those expectations.

Whether policy measures are implemented will depend on the rate of inflation, whether it is stable or increasing and the relative costs and benefits of the inflation being experienced.

If it is decided to implement anti-inflationary policies, the policies selected will be influenced by what is thought to have caused the inflation, the state of the economy and the effectiveness of the policies.

FISCAL POLICY

Fiscal policy measures may be implemented to reduce inflation arising from a variety of causes and at different levels of economic activity.

DEMAND-PULL INFLATION

To combat demand-pull inflation occurring at full employment a government can employ deflationary fiscal policy. This will involve raising taxation and/or cutting government expenditure. Increasing income tax will be likely to lower consumer spending, raising corporation tax will tend to lower investment and reducing government spending will directly lower aggregate demand. A reduction in any or all of these components of aggregate demand will have a downward multiplier effect and may succeed in removing an inflationary gap. Figure 60.1 shows that a fall in government spending from G to G^1 removes the inflationary gap of AB.

All these measures have their limitations. Increasing income tax may cause prices to rise if it stimulates workers to press for wage rises to maintain their real disposable income. It may prove difficult to cut government spending and reducing public and private sector investment will lower future potential output.

It may, alternatively, seek to correct the imbalance in aggregate demand and aggregate supply by increasing aggregate supply. Fiscal policy measures which may be used include government grants for firms setting up in development areas, cuts in corporation tax, increased government expenditure on education and training and subsidies to sunrise industries.

To achieve an increase in aggregate supply new classical economists recommend cutting direct taxes. They believe that reducing income tax and corporation tax will increase the willingness of people to enter the

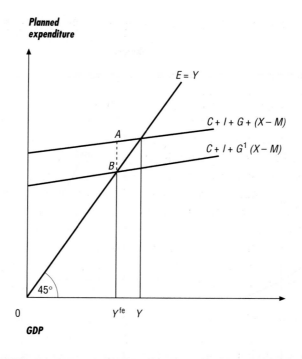

FIG. 60.1

workforce and entrepreneurs to expand their output. Some new classical economists also favour cutting unemployment-related benefits to encourage the unemployed to seek work more actively.

COST-PUSH INFLATION

Some of the fiscal policy measures outlined above could also be employed to combat cost-push inflation. For instance, reducing corporation tax will lower firms' costs. Other possible fiscal policy measures include reducing indirect tax, cutting income tax in an attempt to lower wage claims, reducing the prices charged by government concerns, subsidising production costs and lowering wage rises in the public sector. If the government lowers its expenditure by more than it lowers tax, it may be able to reduce firms' costs without adding to aggregate demand.

MONETARY INFLATION

Lowering expenditure by more than tax revenue is a fiscal policy approach which might also be adopted if the cause of inflation is thought to be the money supply growing faster than output because of government borrowing. Reducing a public sector net cash requirement will reduce a government's need to borrow. However in practice most of the public sector net cash requirement is normally financed by borrowing from the non-bank private sector and hence does not add to the money supply.

MONETARY POLICY

As has been noted, monetarists argue that the cause of inflation is the money supply growing faster than output. To combat this they argue that the growth of the money supply should be reduced to match the growth of output. Figure 60.2 shows the money transmission mechanism. A fall in the money supply raises the rate of interest, the higher interest rate reduces investment and this in turn lowers aggregate demand.

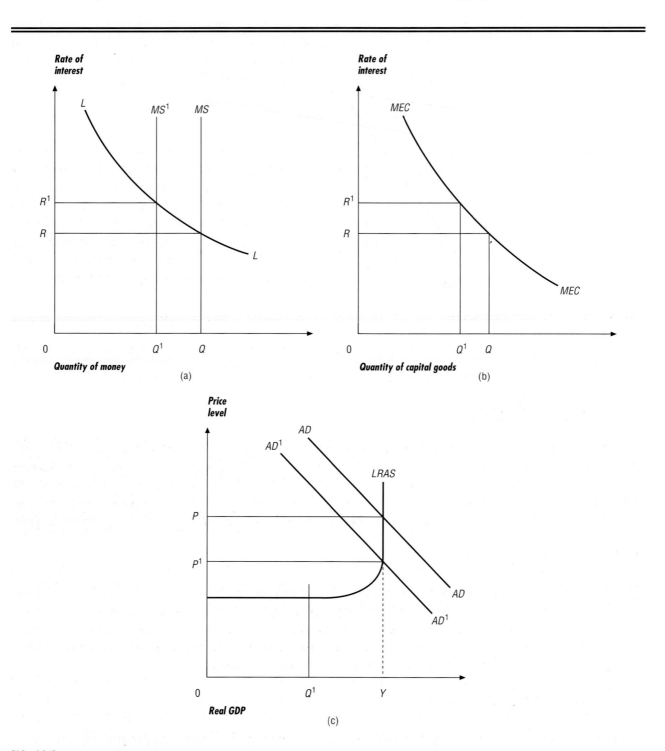

FIG. 60.2

Some monetarists also argue that if aggregate demand is rising and putting inflationary pressure on the economy, a government can prevent this from developing into inflation by refusing to validate the increase in demand by increasing the money supply.

Keynesians make use of the money transmission mechanism in their studies. However they question whether inflation is caused by excessive growth of the money supply. Indeed they argue that inflation causes an increase in the money supply and not the other way round. They maintain that increasing economic activity creates a demand for money and the money supply is increased to meet the growing demand for it.

DEMAND-PULL INFLATION

Deflationary monetary policy may also be employed against demand-pull inflation. Raising interest rates and reducing bank lending will be likely to lower investment and reduce consumer spending, particularly on housing and other items brought on credit. However, the effectiveness of an increase in interest rates depends very much on the state of business and consumer expectations. If firms and consumers are optimistic that incomes will rise in the future they may be willing to borrow at high interest rates. In addition, with a high rate of inflation, high interest rates may not be a serious deterrent to borrowers because the real rate of interest may be quite low; indeed, it may even be negative. The alternative measure, controlling bank lending, has been found difficult to implement in practice with, for example, firms getting round limits by lending directly to each other.

COST-PUSH INFLATION

A government might adopt an expansionary rather than a restrictionary monetary policy in the case of cost-push inflation. In particular, it could reduce firms' costs by lowering interest rates.

EXCHANGE RATE POLICY

A government or, for example, the European Central Bank may seek to reduce inflation by encouraging a rise in the exchange rate. A higher exchange rate can reduce inflation in three main ways. It lowers the price of imported finished goods which count in the RPI and it reduces the cost of imported raw materials. In addition it puts pressure on domestic firms to lower their costs and prices to remain competitive against cheaper foreign imports in their home market and to offset the rise in price of their goods in foreign markets resulting from the higher exchange rate. However, a high exchange rate can have an adverse effect on employment and growth.

A fixed exchange rate can also be used as an anti-inflationary measure. As the value of the currency is fixed, a competitive advantage lost by higher domestic costs, cannot be regained by a fall in the value of the currency. This will put pressure on domestic firms to keep their costs and prices low.

INCOMES POLICIES

The main aim of an incomes policy, introduced to reduce inflation, is to link the growth of incomes to the growth of productivity so as to prevent the excessive rises in factor incomes which raise costs and hence prices. Although an incomes policy may embrace all forms of income — wages, interest, rent and profits — it will tend to concentrate largely on wages because these account for about two thirds of total costs.

DIFFICULTIES WITH INCOMES POLICIES

A government will have to decide whether to set a percentage, e.g. 5%, or flat rate, e.g. £10, limit to pay rises. A percentage limit maintains wage differentials and benefits mainly the high paid. Whereas a flat rate limit reduces differentials and benefits mainly the low paid.

There is also the problem of whether exceptions should be allowed. If the government is anxious to encourage labour mobility it will have to allow industries which are short of labour to offer something higher than the limit while industries trying to shed labour will pay something less than the limit or nothing. There will also be demands from other groups for 'exceptional' treatment. Workers who feel that they have been left behind in previous wage-price spirals will press for special treatment. It might also be necessary to allow some exceptions in order to encourage greater efficiency by permitting increases above the limit where workers have made a substantial contribution to increased productivity.

It is very difficult to introduce flexibility into an incomes policy without causing resentment among those who do not qualify for special treatment. It is also difficult to enforce and supervise an incomes policy. There are many thousands of separate wage settlements and the effective policing of these agreements to make sure that they conform with the general principles of the incomes policy is a formidable administrative task.

Statutory rent control on privately owned houses can be imposed. Landlords can be required to satisfy a public rent tribunal before being allowed to raise rents. However, when this policy has been used to keep rents below the market price a number of disadvantages have arisen. In particular, supply has decreased with houses being sold rather than rented.

EFFECTIVENESS OF INCOMES POLICIES

Incomes policies have sometimes taken the form of a complete freeze on wages and prices. It is difficult to maintain a wage and price standstill for more than a few months, because demand and supply conditions will continue to change and hence relative prices must be allowed to change if the price mechanism is to perform any useful function. In addition, trade unions will strongly oppose any protracted wage freeze. While they are in force, wage and price freezes are likely to slow down the pace of inflation. However their effect may be like that of a temporary dam. Once the policy is relaxed, there may be a flood of wage claims and price increases which will soon bring wages and prices back on their former trend.

It is difficult to assess the effectiveness of incomes policies which have been tried in a variety of countries. It is not sufficient to conclude that the measures are a failure if it is found that wages and prices have risen faster in periods of controls than in periods without them. Incomes policies are normally applied when inflationary pressures have become very intense. The effects of the policies should be judged by the difference between what actually happened and what might otherwise have happened in the absence of any controls.

Incomes policies, unlike deflationary fiscal and monetary policies, do not cause unemployment. However new classical economists criticise them. They argue that they do not address the real causes of inflation and they interfere with free market forces, for instance, making it difficult for firms which wish to expand to recruit labour.

PRICE CONTROLS

To many people, the obvious way to stop prices rising is to apply price controls. Such controls, however, attack the symptoms of inflation rather than the causes. Where the cause of inflation is excess demand, price controls will only lead to shortages and create a demand for a system of rationing. Another problem is that the size of the administrative task means that price controls and rationing can only be applied to a limited range of key commodities. Price controls, if maintained for any extended period, will distort the allocation of resources because price movements are the indicators which inform suppliers and purchasers of the extent and direction of the changes in supply and demand which are always taking place. Nevertheless, price controls, combined with incomes policies, may have a role to play in dealing with the problem of cost-push inflation.

TARGETS

A number of economists believe that expectations play a key role in creating and reducing inflation. If workers and firms become convinced that the government is committed to and able to reduce inflation, they will moderate their wage claims and rises in the prices of their products, thereby reducing inflation.

It is thought by some that setting targets will increase people's and firms' conviction that the government is taking a firm line against inflation. A number of targets have been used in recent years including a target growth of the money supply and a target value for the exchange rate. The current target in the UK is the inflation rate itself. The government has instructed the Bank of England to ensure that the underlying rate of inflation (RPIX) averages 2.5%, with a margin of 1% point either side.

QUESTIONS

SHORT QUESTIONS

1 Explain what is meant by deflationary fiscal policy.

2 What are the possible disadvantages of raising the exchange rate to reduce inflation?

3 What are the difficulties of designing an incomes policy?

4 In what circumstances might a government decide to take no action to reduce inflation?

MULTIPLE CHOICE

1 If the prime aim of the government is to reduce inflation and it believes the cause of inflation is cost-push, which of the following would it be likely to introduce?

A A revaluation of the exchange rate.

B A reduction in government spending.

C An increase in the rate of interest.

D An increase in the general level of taxation.

2 An incomes policy will make the distribution of income more equal if:

A it freezes the growth of all incomes

B it ensures that everyone receives the same percentage increase in income

C it requires that everyone receives the same absolute increase in income

D it links the growth of all incomes to the rate of growth of productivity.

3 What is the main aim behind a government setting a target for the rate of inflation?

A To limit government spending.

B To influence expectations.

C To reduce the risk of fiscal drag occurring.

D To ensure that inflation falls below the target level.

4 If a government considers that the cause of inflation is excess demand occurring at the full employment level of national income, which action is it likely to take?

A Increase taxation.

B Impose import controls.

C Reduce the rate of interest.

D Increase government spending on the health service.

DATA RESPONSE

Year	UK claimant unemployment %	Retail prices (annual % change)	Exchange rate (sterling-DM)
1990	5.8	9.5	2.9
1991	8.0	5.9	2.9
1992	9.7	3.7	2.7
1993	10.3	1.6	2.5
1994	9.3	2.5	2.5
1995	8.2	3.4	2.2
1996	7.4	2.4	2.4
1997	5.6	3.1	2.8

Sources: Tables 5, 6 and 10, National Institute Economic Review, No. 166, October 1998, National Institute of Economic and Social Research.

a] Explain what is meant by 'claimant unemployment'. **(1)**

b] Analyse the relationship between changes in unemployment and in the rate of inflation for the period shown. **(5)**

c] Do your findings in (b) accord with what you would expect from economic theory? **(5)**

d] Analyse the relationship between changes in the sterling-DM exchange rate and changes in the rate of inflation for the period shown. **(5)**

e] Do your findings in (d) accord with what you would expect from economic theory? **(5)**

f] Identify and briefly comment on any two factors, other than unemployment and the exchange rate, which may influence changes in the rate of inflation. **(4)**

CASE STUDY

As Japan's economy gets sicker, so the calls for a radical approach to resuscitation get louder. A chorus of senior politicians, bureaucrats and economists has suggested that a dose of inflation might be just what the country needs.

The idea that it might has been gaining ground thanks to two economists. One is Kazuro Ueda, who sits on the Bank of Japan's policy board. The other is Paul Krugman, professor of economics at the Massachusetts Institute of Technology.

To be fair, all Mr. Ueda really wants is to avoid a deflationary spiral. Wholesale prices are already falling in Japan, as in most other rich industrial economies: but the same is not yet true for consumer prices. He and others at the Bank are worried that they might fall too.

His answer to this is to suggest that the central bank should have an explicit inflation target — say between zero and 2%. At the moment its guidelines eschew such targets. Introducing one should actually increase inflationary expectations and, hence, demand. If they think prices are likely to rise a bit, people may buy today rather than tomorrow.

Mr. Krugman's approach is more radical than Mr. Ueda's. He wants outright inflation. In recent papers he has argued that most analyses of the cause of Japan's plight — too much corporate debt, unwillingness of banks to lend, over-regulation — are, at best, unproven. Japan, he argues, is in a classic liquidity trap. Overall demand consistently falls short of the economy's productive capacity, and saving consistently exceeds investment — despite near zero interest rates. That means that monetary policy has become ineffective in boosting demand. Yet interest rates cannot fall any further, as it is impossible to have nominal rates below zero.

How to solve this dilemma? A Keynesian spending spree? Tax cuts? Neither, thinks Mr. Krugman, is sufficient, though he believes they might help. He considers monetary policy a better tool. And since nominal interest rates are low, that means bringing real interest rates down by generating inflation of, say 4% a year. Moreover it has to be done on a long term basis — for 15 years, say — in order to raise inflationary expectations.

Although they have different aims in mind, the two economists agree that the central bank should target inflation. But how would it get prices up — and would the economy really benefit?

a] From the table describe the changes which occurred in the Japanese inflation rate for the period shown. **(4)**

b] On what evidence may economists draw in making forecasts of future inflation? **(6)**

JAPAN			
YEAR	% CHANGE IN CONSUMER PRICES	YEAR	% CHANGE IN CONSUMER PRICES
1990	2.5	1995	− 0.5
1991	2.0	1996	0.1
1992	2.0	1997	1.6
1993	1.1	1998	0.5
1994	− 0.5	1999	− 0.2[1]

[1]forecast rate

Sources: 'Messing with money', The Economist, 25/7/98, Table 15, National Institute Economic Review, No.165, July 1998, National Institute of Economic and Social Research.

c] Explain the following terms used in the extract:
  i corporate debt **(2)**
  ii classical liquidity trap **(2)**
  iii productive capacity **(2)**
  iv monetary policy **(2)**
  v real interest rates. **(2)**
d] Discuss the possible dangers of a deflationary spiral. **(6)**

e] Compare and contrast the two methods suggested to create inflation. **(10)**

f] Analyse whether, given the conditions outlined in the extract, the Japanese economy would benefit from inflation. **(14)**

STRUCTURED ESSAY

a] Assess the causes of changes in the rate of inflation in your country over the last five years. **(10)**

b] Discuss the measures which can be taken to reduce the rate of inflation. **(15)**

FREE RESPONSE ESSAY

Analyse whether the advantages of a reduction in the rate of inflation always outweigh the costs involved in achieving that reduction. **(25)**

61 BALANCE OF PAYMENTS POLICIES

Whether a government decides to take action to correct a balance of payments disequilibrium will depend on its size, whether or not it will be self correcting, its cause and the government's priorities. If it does decide to act its choice of policies will depend again on the cause but also on the type of exchange rate system being operated, the level of economic activity, the effects of the policies on other objectives and external constraints.

POLICY CHOICES

There is a range of policy measures a government may be able to adopt. These include changing the value of the exchange rate, imposing or increasing import controls, deflating the economy or taking longer term measures to improve the competitiveness of the country's goods and services.

DEVALUATION

If a country is operating a fixed exchange rate and is experiencing a current account deficit it may decide to lower the value of its currency.

The immediate effect of devaluation is to change the relative prices of imports and exports. Exports become cheaper in terms of foreign currency, while imports become dearer in terms of the home currency.

EXAMPLE

Before devaluation: £1 = $2.
A UK car, price £20 000, costs $40 000 in the USA.
An American machine, price $30 000 costs £15 000 in the UK.
After devaluation £1 = $1.5.
A UK car, price £20 000, costs $30 000 in the USA.
An American machine, price $30 000, costs £20 000 in the UK.

Similarly if a country is operating a managed floating exchange rate system a decision to encourage a fall in the value of the currency will make the country's goods and services more price competitive.

However before there is time for demand and supply to adjust fully, a fall in the exchange rate may cause a deterioration in the balance of payments position. This is known as the *J curve effect* and is illustrated in Figure 61.1.

For a fall in the value of the currency to improve the balance of payments position, the combined price elasticities of demand for exports and imports must be greater than one. This is referred to as the *Marshall-Lerner condition*. Export volume will increase and the volume of imports will fall. But export earnings will only increase if the demand for exports is elastic, that is, if the volume of exports increases by a greater percentage than the percentage fall in their external prices. Since the foreign prices of imports do not change, any fall in the volume of imports, caused by the rise in their prices in terms of the domestic currency, must lead to a reduction in foreign currency expenditures.

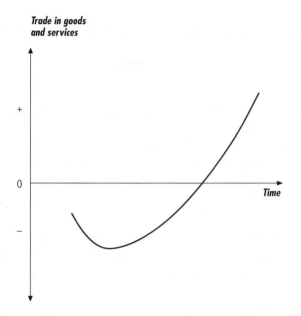

FIG. 61.1

There are several other factors which influence the effectiveness of devaluation as a remedy for a balance of payments deficit. It can only lead to favourable price movements if major trading rivals do not devalue their own currencies. Supply of exports also needs to be elastic so that the increased foreign demand can be met. If the devaluing country is operating at full employment, more goods can only be supplied to export markets by reducing supplies to the home market. It may be necessary, therefore, to increase taxation to reduce demand in order to free supplies for the foreign market.

A fall in the exchange rate, by stimulating demand for domestic goods both by domestic and foreign consumers, will benefit domestic employment and economic growth. However it may contribute to inflationary pressures. The rise in import prices will directly raise the price of some of the goods and services purchased in the UK. It will also raise the price of imported raw materials and thereby increase costs of production and reduce pressure on domestic firms to remain price competitive. There may also be adverse income effects. If devaluation causes a significant fall in imports, other countries will suffer a fall in income. This will reduce their ability to buy foreign goods and services.

IMPORT CONTROLS

There are a variety of methods, including for example tariffs and quotas, which can be used to limit imports and direct demand to home-produced goods and services. However a country's freedom to employ this policy measure can be constrained by membership of the World Trade Organisation (WTO) or a trade bloc such as the European Union.

Import controls also have the potential to increase domestic inflation. Tariffs directly raise the price of imports on the domestic market and quotas, by limiting the supply of imports, are likely to push up their price. In addition, firms which use imported raw materials will experience a rise in their costs of production which they are likely to pass on to their customers in the form of higher prices. Domestic firms, seeing rival goods and services from abroad rising in price, may raise their own price knowing they will be able to remain competitive.

DEFLATION

Deflationary measures seek to reduce imports and increase exports by reducing aggregate demand. This fall in demand may be achieved by a rise in taxation, a fall in government expenditure or a combination of both. A rise in the rate of interest is unlikely to be used as this might result in a rise in the exchange rate which, in turn, would push up the price of exports and lower the price of imports.

Deflationary policy may be adopted when high income levels are sucking in imports, diverting goods and services from the export to the home market and creating inflationary pressures. Lower aggregate demand should lead to a fall in expenditure on imports. It might also lead to an increase in exports as domestic firms find it more difficult to sell in the home market and make greater efforts to sell in foreign markets. However there might be, as with devaluation, adverse income effects with lower incomes abroad resulting in a fall in the country's exports.

The major problem though with deflation is its tendency to increase unemployment. If a current account deficit is large, deflation would be an unpopular policy option as it would require a relatively significant reduction in aggregate demand in order to achieve the required cut in import expenditures. In other words, the 'cost' in terms of unemployment would be politically unacceptable.

EXPENDITURE-SWITCHING AND EXPENDITURE-REDUCING METHODS

Devaluation and import controls can be classified as expenditure-switching measures. An expenditure-switching measure is any measure which seeks to redirect spending from foreign goods and services towards domestically produced goods and services. In contrast expenditure-reducing measures are those which aim to reduce aggregate demand. So by definition deflationary measures are expenditure reducing as they lower demand.

LONGER RUN MEASURES

Devaluation, import controls and deflation may improve a country's balance of payments position only in the short run if there are inherent problems in the economy which mean that foreign goods and services are more attractive than domestically produced ones.

For example firms may be poor at marketing. In order to rectify this a government may promote trade fairs, give awards to top exporters and encourage university and other courses in marketing.

There may also be low productivity and low quality of goods and services produced. In this case measures may be taken to improve education, training, research and development. The country may also be producing products which are not in high world demand. In this case a government may give financial assistance to sunrise industries.

BALANCE OF PAYMENTS SURPLUS

As well as a balance of payments deficit causing problems, there can be disadvantages to a balance of payments surplus.

To remove a surplus a government can use expenditure-switching measures, which this time switch expenditure from domestically produced to foreign produced goods and services. In a fixed exchange rate system it can revalue its currency by moving the exchange value of its currency to higher parity. This will make exports relatively more expensive (in terms of foreign currencies) and imports relatively cheaper (in terms of the home currency). Another expenditure-switching measure to reduce a surplus would be to reduce or remove import controls.

Expenditure-increasing measures may also be employed. These could include, for example, cuts in income tax and increases in state benefits.

QUESTIONS

SHORT QUESTIONS

1 What effect does a revaluation have on export and import prices?

2 Explain the Marshall-Lerner condition.

3 Is the granting of subsidies to exporters an expenditure switching or an expenditure reducing measure?

4 What measures can a government take to reduce a balance of payments surplus?

MULTIPLE CHOICE

1 Which of the following measures to improve a country's balance of payments position is an expenditure-switching one?

A A rise in VAT.

B The opening of a trade fair in another country.

C The reduction in government spending on state pensions.

D The spread of excise duty on to a wider range of products.

2 Which combination of price elasticities of demand for exports and imports would result in a devaluation improving a country's balance of payments' position?

	Price elasticities of demand	
	exports	imports
A	0.1	0.2
B	0.5	0.5
C	0.8	0.6
D	1.0	0.0

3 Which of the following conditions would contribute most towards a devaluation causing an improvement in a country's balance in trade in goods and services?

A Elastic supply of exports.

B Inelastic demand for imports.

C Falling incomes abroad.

D Increasing trade restrictions imposed by foreign countries.

4 What is the J curve effect?

A The tendency for a country's floating exchange rate to fluctuate.

B The effect that a rise in a country's income tends to have on the amount spent on imports.

C The tendency for a devaluation to worsen a country's balance of payments position before it improves it.

D The retaliation which tends to happen when a country imposes import restrictions.

DATA RESPONSE

In the 1990s the Thai currency, the baht, was fixed in value against a dollar-denominated basket of currencies. Its value was above the market rate. The Thai government favoured this high value as it believed that it was putting downward pressure on inflation in the country. To maintain the currency's value the government kept interest rates high.

However the high exchange rate made export prices high in terms of foreign currency and imports cheap in terms of the baht. This resulted in deficits on the country's current account of the balance of payments. In 1996 the deficit reached 8% of GDP. For a number of years the IMF advised the Thai government to stop pegging its exchange rate and to allow it to fall. Thailand resisted this advice.

However in 1997, with East Asian crisis, Thailand's trade position worsened and the economy experienced a recession. Confidence in the economy fell. Speculators, believing that the baht was overvalued, sold it in large quantities. The Thai government tried to protect the value of the baht by buying bahts. However, this caused a significant decline in its foreign exchange reserves and the Thai government was forced to unpeg the exchange rate. The baht floated down sharply. This helped Thailand's drive to increase economic activity in the economy and improve its balance of payments position. However whilst the current account position moved into surplus in mid 1998 Thailand's output continued to fall.

a] What effect is a high exchange rate likely to have on a country's current account position? **(5)**

b] What effect does a fall in a country's exchange rate have on its export and import prices? **(4)**

c] As a result of a fall in the value of the baht the Thai current account did not immediately move into surplus. What might have explained this? **(5)**

d] A country may adopt a range of policy measures to improve its balance of payments. Why would deflation have been an inappropriate measure for the Thai government to adopt in 1997? **(5)**

e] i   What would the elasticity of supply of exports have been like in Thailand in 1997? **(3)**

   ii   What is the significance of this for the effectiveness of allowing the exchange rate to fall in a bid to improve the current account position? **(3)**

CASE STUDY

There has, for several years, been a recurring nightmare that has disturbed the financial markets. It is that for some reason or other, Japan would stop financing the US current account deficit (and by the same token, the fiscal deficit) and repatriate its funds.

Up to now nothing like that has happened. The US has been able to fund its current account deficit because other countries, in particular Japan, have been prepared to carry on investing in the States. Inflows on capital account have matched, or frequently, exceeded, the outflow on current account.

As a result the US has been transformed from being the world's largest creditor nation to the world's largest debtor. However, the inward flow of capital postponed any day of reckoning: those of us who believed that the current account deficit would eventually result in a dollar collapse have so far been proved wrong.

Meanwhile, the long US boom, now in its eighth year, has ended the other US deficit, the fiscal deficit. Rising tax revenues and falling welfare payments have succeeded where Congress failed.

Or so it seemed. The fiscal outlook remains benign but the external deficit has suddenly become a serious concern. One of the reasons for the sharp falls of the dollar in the last few days has apparently been a worry about the sustainability of the current account deficit.

Why has the problem that has been simmering for years suddenly blown up? There seem to be at least three reasons for this change of mood. First, the sudden further deterioration of the current account last year as East Asian exports to the US soared and exports fell. Second, the launch of the euro. And third, the surge in bond yields in Japan.

Last year the current account deficit was running at an annual rate more than $200bn — we don't have final figures, but the third quarter was a deficit of $61bn. That is very large, of course, but no worse as a percentage of GDP than it was in the 1980s. There was, however, a qualitative difference from the 1980s deficit. Quite aside from the trade deficit there was, for the first time, also a deficit on investment income. The interest on all those debts was now being added to the principal.

In other words, America is now borrowing to pay the interest on its borrowings. You do not need a degree in international economics to appreciate that this is not a sustainable position. Yesterday Goldman Sachs drew attention to this phenomenon, and used that word 'unsustainable' — which is interesting, because up to now US commentators have tended to be relatively relaxed about the mounting US indebtedness. They have seen the inflow of capital as a statement of faith in US competitiveness and stability (which of course it is), rather than a reflection that Americans live above their means.

Source: 'What if Japan pulls the plug on the US deficit?' by Hamish McRae, the Independent, 7/1/99.

a] Distinguish between a current account deficit and a fiscal deficit. **(6)**

b] The article refers to the capital account. What is this account now called? **(3)**

c] What is meant by a creditor nation? **(3)**

d] Explain why a boom is likely to have opposite effects on a current account deficit and a fiscal deficit. **(8)**

e] Why might a balance of payments not be sustainable? **(8)**

f] How did a decline in economic activity in East Asia harm the US current account position? **(8)**

g] Explain in what sense Americans were living beyond their means. **(6)**

h] Discuss the possible effects of a sharp fall in the dollar on the current account position. **(8)**

STRUCTURED ESSAY

a] Explain the difference between expenditure switching and expenditure reducing policies to improve a country's balance of payments position. **(8)**

b] Compare the effects of deflation and devaluation on a country's employment and price level. **(17)**

FREE RESPONSE ESSAY

Discuss three measures a government could adopt to reduce a balance of payments deficit. **(25)**

62 LIMITATIONS OF GOVERNMENT POLICY

In practice there are a number of difficulties that governments face in choosing and implementing policy measures and in achieving their objectives. Indeed government failure can occur. Government failure is defined as a situation when government intervention fails to improve economic welfare or even reduces it. This clearly is not the aim of a government. It arises for a number of reasons.

CONFLICTS IN GOVERNMENT POLICY

Objectives may be incompatible. In order to achieve one goal governments have sometimes been obliged to sacrifice another. Policies designed to bring about full-employment have sometimes generated unacceptably high levels of inflation; policies aimed at eradicating a balance of payments deficit have restricted the rate of economic growth, and so on. Some economists argue that a government should have at least one instrument to achieve each objective. This is known as *Tinbergen's rule*.

CONFLICTS IN ECONOMIC THEORY

In deciding which policy instruments to use a government will be making use of economic theory. There are conflicts of opinion in economic theory. For instance, monetarists argue that rises in the money supply cause inflation whereas Keynesians argue that it is changes in inflation which cause changes in the money supply.

LIMITATIONS OF ECONOMIC FORECASTS

Governments make use of economic forecasts in deciding whether to take action and the type of policies to employ. In the last three decades there has been a significant increase in the number of forecasting groups and the sophistication of the economic models they use. Nevertheless the strength of their forecasts still depends on the assumptions their models make and the accuracy and relevance of the information they feed in.

TIME LAGS

There are a number of delays involved in government policy. There is the time taken to recognise that there is a problem, the time taken to formulate policy measures, the time to introduce policies and the time for consumers, workers and firms to respond to the policies.

From the time the problem is identified to the time the policy is implemented, economic circumstances may have changed. For instance, a government may decide that a rise in unemployment after the Christmas period is not just a seasonal rise but the start of an upward trend. As a result it may decide to stimulate economic activity by cutting tax rates. However, by the time this measure is introduced, aggregate demand may have been picking up anyway and the measure may instead add to inflationary pressures. Indeed instead of acting counter-cyclically government policies may re-enforce the trade cycle.

Consumers, workers and firms may also not react in the way the government expects. For instance, a reduction in tax rates may not cause consumers to spend more and firms to expand, if there is a lack of confidence.

POLICY CONSTRAINTS

There are also practical problems and international constraints. It is difficult to change much of government expenditure, particularly capital expenditure, taxation and legislation quickly. As a member of the European Union, the UK government, for example, cannot introduce import restrictions against fellow members. It has also committed itself to keeping its standard rate of VAT above 15%.

POLITICAL INFLUENCES

Governments tend to introduce harsh measures just after an election and more popular ones near an election. For example, economic advisers may recommend a rise in taxation but if this is just before a general election a government may choose to ignore the advice. There can be political cycles with aggregate demand and economic activity increasing before a general election and declining after it.

COMPLEXITY

The real world is a complex and constantly changing place. For instance with increasing mobility of financial capital around the world, it is becoming more difficult for governments to monitor and influence private sector investment.

CIVIL SERVANTS' AND POLITICIANS' SELF-INTEREST

Civil servants and politicians may promote the growth of their own department to pursue their own advancement. Entrepreneurs' salaries and status are closely linked to the size of the companies they run. Similarly a civil servant's pay, promotion chances and status and a politician's status and promotion chances may be influenced by the growth of their department even if it is not in the country's interest.

INFLEXIBILITY OF SOME POLICY MEASURES

As noted in Chapter 33 some forms of government expenditure and taxation are difficult to change in the short run. For example it is difficult, if not impossible, to stop building a road half way through the project.

Some other measures are also not very flexible. For example the retirement age can be changed but not on a regular basis as this would involve too many institutional changes.

QUESTIONS

SHORT QUESTIONS

1. Explain what is meant by Tinbergen's rule.

2. Identify two limitations on the freedom of action faced by the UK government.

3. What is meant by a counter cyclical policy?

4. Explain what is meant by a political cycle.

MULTIPLE CHOICE

1. Why might a rise in government spending designed to reduce unemployment, cause a rise in the inflation rate?

   A. it stimulates a rise in labour productivity

   B. its introduction coincides with an upturn in economy activity

   C. it is accompanied by a revaluation of the currency

   D. it is introduced at a time when there is spare capacity in the economy.

2. Which of the following policy measures is likely to produce effects that are inconsistent with the effects of the other three measures?

   A. An increase in interest rates.

   B. An increase in investment allowances.

   C. A decrease in the exchange rate.

   D. A decrease in income tax.

3. Which of the following would be an inappropriate measure to reduce demand-pull inflation?

   A. An increase in the exchange rate.

   B. An increase in the rate of income tax.

   C. A decrease in the rate of interest.

   D. A decrease in the growth of the money supply.

4. To increase employment a government cuts the rate of income tax. What may stop this measure having the intended effect?

   A. Consumers have a low marginal propensity to import.

   B. Consumers save all the extra disposable income.

   C. There is a high degree of mobility of resources.

   D. The economy is operating inside its production possibility curve.

DATA RESPONSE

Britain's public finances swung into the black by £5.4bn last month, putting the chancellor on course to record his second consecutive budget surplus, according to official figures published yesterday.

Gordon Brown predicted a small deficit in 1999–2000. But with tax revenues rising more rapidly than expected this year and social security spending set to undershoot because of lower than expected unemployment, City analysts say he could have an extra £10bn at his disposal by spring.

The savings to the public purse are likely to escalate as cautious treasury accounting assumptions about lengthening dole queues in subsequent years fail to materialise. At the time of the March budget, when it still looked as though the UK economy could go into recession, the chancellor set aside $1bn to pay for a projected rise in unemployment from 1.305m — the average of the first three months of this year — to 1.55m by the end of 1999.

A cushion of a further £4.5bn was built into social security spending for the next two financial years, by the end of which unemployment was expected to have risen to £1.73m. But with economic growth now accelerating and the jobless total having fallen to 1.280m and unlikely to rise much in the months ahead, spending on social security will be much lower than expected. Official figures published yesterday by the office for national statistics showed central government spending up by just 4.7% so far this year versus the treasury's forecast of 6.3% for the full year.

Source: 'Rising tax revenues and lower social security spending point to £10bn surplus' by Mark Atkinson, the Guardian, 18/8/99.

a] Why did Gordon Brown make an incorrect prediction for the 1999–2000 budget position? **(6)**

b] What is meant by a budget deficit? **(2)**

c] What active fiscal policy measures might a government take to eliminate a recession? **(6)**

d] How accurate do you think the unemployment figure was? **(5)**

e] Discuss the implications for government policy of a government underestimating the level of unemployment. **(6)**

CASE STUDY

I am wondering how much longer I shall be on speaking terms with my various friends, colleagues and ex-pupils who have influence on new Labour's macroeconomic policy. Whether in the Bank of England, the Treasury or other august institutions such as Goldman Sachs, with the heroic exception of DeAnne Julius they all seem to have one idea in their heads. That is that the real economy is performing too well and must be stopped. Production is too high, unemployment is too low, there are too many job vacancies and the earnings of ordinary workers, although falling hugely behind those of top people, are growing too fast.

The flavour of the attitude is well caught by an extraordinary passage in the May minutes of the Monetary Policy Committee which led to the symbolically historic decision to raise the base rate.

'The Committee discussed how best to interpret long-term unemployment. One possibility is that current and earlier structural reforms were increasing the employability of the long-term unemployed, which would be helping to relieve labour market pressures. It might also be signalling a very tight market with short-term unemployment having fallen as far as it could, forcing firms to recruit from the long-term unemployed.'

A person from Mars could be forgiven from inferring that the writer of that, who went on to raise interest rates, saw long-term unemployment as a Good Thing. But no, it is OK for long-term unemployment to decline if it is caused by a growth in the demand for labour! Was ever supply-sideism carried to such extremes? Surely everyone knows that the most powerful way of making people 'employable' is to get them into jobs.

But there is increasing evidence that the entire cast of mind we see here and elsewhere is based on a false reading of statistics. In a beautifully professional piece of work published a few days ago,
Neil Blake and Paul Robson show that the rate of growth of productivity in manufacturing has been underestimated by a large amount. The reason is a statistical discontinuity caused by improvements in the official methods of measuring employment.

Source: 'Poor could now count the cost of a chronic mis-reading of the figures' by Robin Marris, The Times, 31/7/98.

a] What is meant by an economy 'performing too well'? **(5)**

b] What is the Monetary Policy Committee? **(4)**

c] Explain how structural reforms might increase the 'employability of the long-term unemployed'? **(9)**

d] What effect is a rise in interest rates likely to have on unemployment? **(10)**

e] What is meant by supply-sideism? **(6)**

f] If productivity is rising more than estimated what implications does this have for predictions about inflationary pressure? **(6)**

g] Explain why it is important for the design of government policy to have accurate information not only on the current but also on the future performance of the economy. **(10)**

STRUCTURED ESSAY

a] Explain what is meant by government failure. **(10)**

b] What measures could a government take to reduce government failure? **(15)**

FREE RESPONSE ESSAY

Discuss the difficulties a government may encounter in simultaneously tackling a high rate of inflation and a deficit on the current account of the balance of payments. **(25)**

PART TEN: TOPICS IN ECONOMICS

63 KEY MARKETS

In this chapter some of the issues facing three important markets, the tourist market, the transport market and the labour market are touched on.

TOURISM

Tourism is the fastest growing industry in the world. For a number of countries income from tourism is a major source of export revenue. This acts as an injection into the circular flow of income causing national income to rise by a multiple amount. This effect is sometimes referred to as the tourism multiplier.

Demand for tourism is income elastic but demand for particular holiday destinations can change very quickly — a resort can be very fashionable one year and then go out of favour the next. If an area is popular with tourists jobs will be created. However these jobs may not be high skilled and high paid jobs. Many people in the tourist industry are actually low paid.

Tourism can also create a number of external costs. The development of resorts can destroy the natural environment and e.g. reduce the amount of land available for farming.

Tourism also brings with it social change. The tourists who enter the country bring e.g. their music, food and taste for particular forms of entertainment with them. The hotels and other holiday accommodation will cater to the tastes of tourists and so introduce new forms of entertainment, e.g. gambling that the local people may feel uneasy about.

There is also the risk that tourism can create congestion in terms of the volume of traffic and people at popular spots and this can make life difficult and unpleasant for the people who live there.

Whilst tourism will bring income into the country it may not bring in as much income as might be anticipated. This is because the firms running the tourist attractions and accommodation may bring in some of their own staff and may import food and other items from the countries that most of the tourists come from.

What a number of countries are now seeking to achieve is ethical and sustainable tourism i.e. tourism which respects the traditions and customs of the area, seeks to plough back some of its earnings into the local community, does not inflict environmental damage and is conducted in such a way as to protect the area as an attractive tourist resort. In the past there have been examples where firms have exploited the short-term potential of an area by bringing in more and more tourists to the detriment not only of the local community but also to the long term ability of the area to attract tourists. Economists talk about the carrying capacity of a tourist area. This refers to the maximum number of tourists the area can cope with in a way that does not destroy the very features which attracted the tourists in the first place.

TRANSPORT

Transport is the movement of people (passenger transport) and goods (freight transport). The output of transport is measured in terms of passenger kilometres (passengers) or tonne kilometres (freight).

DERIVED DEMAND

Although some people enjoy driving or travelling on e.g. an aeroplane, most people undertake journeys for a specific purpose, for example, visiting friends and relatives, travelling to and from work, visiting places of entertainment and leisure and going on holiday. Goods are moved in the production process and finally to the point of sale. So the demand for most transport is a derived demand. It is not wanted for its own sake but for what it will enable people and firms to do.

Demand for transport may increase as a result of an increase in, for example:

- economic activity. A rise in output will result in more freight being transported, more people in employment and so more people travelling to and from work, and people spending more and so visiting more places of entertainment and leisure and going on more holidays and going further afield.
- the distance people travel to work.
- the number of out of town shopping centres.
- the dispersion of families around the country.

MODES OF TRANSPORT

Transport takes a number of different forms i.e. rail, road, inland waterways, air, sea and pipelines. Passenger road transport can be further broken down into private car, taxi, coach, bus, motor cycle, pedal cycle and walking. Nearly 94% of demand for transport is demand for road transport.

Table 63.1 compares the advantages and disadvantages of passenger private car, bus and rail transport.

TABLE 63.1 COMPARISON OF PASSENGER PRIVATE CAR, BUS AND RAIL TRANSPORT

Private car	bus	rail
Advantages		
flexible	efficient use of road space	energy efficient
comfortable	relatively cheap	relatively good safety
convenient	access to city centres	record
door to door service	can be energy efficient	high speeds over long
access to remote rural		journeys
areas		provides the opportunity
		to work on the journey
Disadvantages		
high external costs	low quality of comfort	can be crowded
may be slow during	timetable restrictions	timetable restrictions
peak times	may be unreliable	may be unreliable
relatively high risk of	not door to door service	not door to door service
accidents		

The high and increasing use of road vehicles is causing a number of governments throughout the world considerable concern. This is because the demand for road space is exceeding the supply of road space and because of the high external costs that the use of private cars and lorries causes.

THE EXTERNAL COSTS OF ROAD TRAFFIC

These include:

- Noise pollution. Lorries in particular cause high levels of noise which can cause stress.
- Air pollution. Cars and, again particularly, lorries omit gases which contribute to the greenhouse effect and global warming.
- Visual pollution. Traffic can spoil the attractiveness of an area. Large volumes of traffic have made visiting a number of historic cities a less pleasurable experience.
- Community severance. Motorways and major roads can divide communities. They can make it difficult for people living on one side to visit schools, shops and facilities on the other side.
- Blight. The building and granting of permission to build new roads can create urban blight – reducing the attractiveness of areas for residents and firms.
- Vibrations. The vibrations caused by cars and again lorries undermine and damage buildings.
- Accidents. Road accidents impose a variety of significant costs on the country. These include loss of workers and hence potential output through deaths and serious injuries, distress caused to relatives and loss of potential output resulting from the time they take off to get over their distress and in the longer term the time they have to take off work to look after the injured and the dependents of the dead and injured, costs to the health service and costs to the emergency services.
- Damage to the environment. Cars kill a range of wildlife and the construction of new roads destroys natural habitats.
- Congestion. This occurs when the actual journey time taken is greater than the normal expected time. This in turn imposes a variety of costs including increased fuel and other running costs, reduced vehicle productivity (lorries take longer to make their journeys and so more have to be used to transport a given quantity), stress and frustration.

The negative externalities which the use of road space causes results in an inefficient allocation of resources. Figure 63.1 shows that once the number of journeys reaches a certain level congestion occurs and marginal social cost starts to diverge from marginal private cost.

The number of journeys undertaken is Q at a price of P. However the allocatively efficient number of journeys is QX at a price of PX.

MEASURES A GOVERNMENT CAN EMPLOY TO REDUCE THE USE OF PRIVATE CARS

These include:

- Road pricing to ensure that drivers pay the true costs of their journeys. Technological developments now make it possible to charge individual drivers according to where they drive and when they drive. So a driver who chooses to drive into a city centre at peak time would pay more than a driver who drives on an uncongested road. Road pricing is currently used in Singapore, Norway and Hong Kong. However it may be difficult to estimate the external costs, the payment will take a higher proportion of the income of the poor and as demand for road space is relatively price inelastic, demand may not fall significantly.
- Motorway tolls. This is a form of road pricing and potentially increases the cost of driving. However there is the danger that motorway tolls will just cause drivers to switch to other routes thereby merely changing the location of pollution and congestion rather than their respective levels.

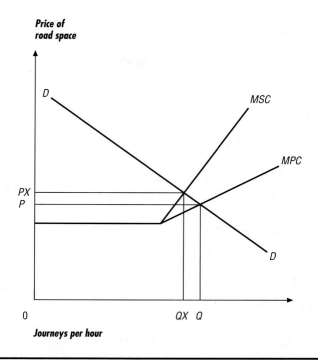

FIG. 63.1

- Increasing taxes on petrol. This should reduce the use of cars but as with road pricing the main burden will fall on the poor (including in the form of higher food prices etc. because of the increase in the cost of freight transport) and demand for road transport is relatively price inelastic.
- Increasing other costs connected with car use e.g. parking charges. This may discourage some people driving their cars to work and into city centres for shopping.
- Subsidising bus, coach and rail transport. This method has the benefits of helping the poor, improving the efficiency of the passenger transport system and helping to promote urban regeneration. However subsidies do not discriminate between those who need them and those who do not and they may encourage inefficiency on the part of operators. Perhaps even more significantly they may not have much impact on demand as the main deterrent to using 'public' transport is thought not to be price but quality and timetable constraints.
- More integrated transport system. If it was easier to link up different forms of transport e.g. buses and trains, and lorries and trains, people might use their cars less frequently and goods might be transported by road over shorter differences.
- Other schemes. For example more cycle and bus lanes and more park and ride schemes.

TRANSPORT POLICIES IN THE 1980S AND 1990S

The Conservative administrations of the 1980s and 1990s sought to improve the performance of a variety of modes of transport by means of deregulation and privatisation. For example the National Freight Company was privatised in 1982, Sealink in 1984, the National Bus Company and its subsidiaries between 1986–88 and British Rail 1994–96. Deregulation, in the form of removing licences which restricted who could operate, occurred in road haulage, coach, domestic air and bus markets.

BUS DEREGULATION

For many years the bus market has been in decline. Fares have risen relative to the cost of using a car and bus travel has increasingly been perceived as an inferior good. It was hoped that bus deregulation and the privatisation of local bus services in 1985 would reverse this trend by increasing consumer choice and stimulating innovation via increased competition. There has been some innovation e.g. the introduction of mini-bus services. However deregulation has also brought some problems. There have been 'bus wars' with bus companies competing over the same routes whilst withdrawing from other routes and some confusion over service patterns. There has also been a trend towards increased concentration of ownership with the large companies buying out many of the small companies and with those companies engaging in restrictive practices.

RAIL PRIVATISATION

British Rail was privatised under the Railways Act 1993. Passenger trains were divided into 25 operating companies which were franchised for a period of between five and twenty years. A new track authority, Railtrack, came into being in 1996. Again it was hoped that privatisation would increase competition efficiency, investment and quality of service. However there appears to have been a deterioration in punctuality and reliability of rail services and concern about the lack of investment in safety improvements.

FUTURE TRANSPORT APPROACH

In the future the approach to transport policy is likely to be influenced by the need for a sustainable transport policy i.e. one which will ensure that in future decades there will be a transport network which will meet the needs of users. This is likely to involve a more determined approach to switch demand from cars and lorries to more sustainable forms of transport.

LABOUR

A number of issues facing the labour market have already been discussed in earlier chapters. Other ones which can be discussed here are the effect on the labour market of the increase in the average age of many countries' populations, how the productivity of the labour force can be increased and the influence of marginal revenue productivity on the demand for labour. People in industrialised countries are living longer and forming a higher proportion of the workforce. This has the potential to increase the burden on the working population. It is also already changing the pattern of demand. Among the implications for the labour force are the following.

- Greater demand for workers in the health care and related sectors.
- The possibility that the retirement age will be raised.
- Increased pressure on workers to take out private pensions.
- Firms having to make more attempts to recruit older workers as young workers will be in relatively short supply.
- The need for retraining of older workers whose skills may be out of date.
- Firms may also seek to recruit a greater proportion of older workers given that their client base will be ageing.
- The possibility that legislation will be brought in outlawing age discrimination.

Productivity is output per worker hour. There are a number of ways in which, it is thought, productivity could be raised. These include:

- increases in the capital/labour ratio. Recently the productivity of American workers has been rising at an above average rate largely due the technologically more advanced equipment they have been working with
- increases and improvements in training
- improvements in health care
- increases and improvements in education
- improvements in industrial relations.

MARGINAL REVENUE PRODUCTIVITY THEORY

Marginal revenue productivity theory seeks to explain the determinants of demand for factors of production, including labour. The demand for factors of production is a derived demand. The factors are not wanted for their own sake but for what they can produce. The more the factors can produce and the more that output can be sold for, the more they will be in demand.

MARGINAL PRODUCT

Marginal product is the change in total output resulting from the employment of one more unit of a variable factor, e.g. one more worker.

Marginal product is often referred to as marginal physical product since it is measured in physical units: tonnes of wheat, number of cars, metres of silk.

MARGINAL REVENUE PRODUCT

Although entrepreneurs are interested in the physical productivity of a factor of production, they are even more concerned with the revenue yielded by the input's efforts. The amount added to the firm's revenue resulting from employing, for instance, one more worker is called marginal revenue product.

$$MPP \times MR = MRP.$$

THE DEMAND CURVE FOR LABOUR

The profit-maximising firm will employ additional workers as long as those workers are adding more to the firm's revenues than to the firm's costs. In other words, labour will be employed up to the point where its marginal revenue product is equal to the wage rate.

CAUSES OF CHANGE IN MARGINAL REVENUE PRODUCTIVITY

The marginal revenue productivity of a factor of production is determined by its marginal physical productivity and by the price of the product produced (changes in price cause changes in marginal revenue in both perfect and imperfect competition). A change in either or both of these variables will change demand for the factor. For instance, an increase in the productivity of labour (due perhaps to improvements in training) or an increase in the price of the product will shift the curve upwards. More workers will now be demanded at any given wage rate. Similarly, a fall in productivity or a fall in the price of the product will reduce the demand for labour at any given wage rate.

THE EFFECTS OF CHANGES IN MRP

If the marginal revenue productivity of a factor of production increases, its price will rise and its supply extend. Figure 63.1 shows an increase in the MRP of lorry drivers. A fall in marginal revenue productivity will have the opposite effect, lowering the price of the factor of production and reducing its supply.

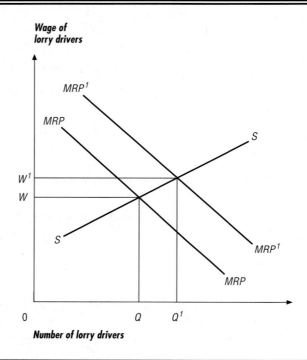

FIG. 63.2

QUESTIONS

SHORT QUESTIONS

1 What is meant by carrying capacity?

2 What type of income elasticity of demand does tourism have?

3 What external costs does the use of private cars create?

4 Why might the retirement age be raised in the future?

MULTIPLE CHOICE

1 To ensure that drivers pay the full cost of using their cars a tax on road use should be based on the:

A marginal external cost of driving

B marginal external benefit of driving.

C marginal social cost of driving.

D marginal social benefit of driving..

2 The tourism multiplier refers to:

A the tendency for the number of tourists visiting an area to build up over time

B the economies of scale which can be achieved by large travel companies

C the eventual change in national income which results from an initial change in tourism revenue

D the rise in the number of travel companies in the industry.

3 Which of the following would reduce demand for car travel?

A The removal of subsidies to rail operators.

B The reduction in car parking spaces in city centres.

C An increase in the road building programme.

D A reduction in excise duty.

4 Which of the following would be a possible disadvantage of an ageing workforce?

A A reduction in labour mobility.

B A reduction in labour turnover.

C An increase in experience.

D An increase in productivity.

DATA RESPONSE

When Walt Disney bought a patch of wetland in Orlando, Florida, it was as barren as the dustbowls created by an earlier generation in the prairies of the mid-West. Florida was a prime example of the destruction of the natural landscape by the excesses of twentieth-century agriculture. The jobs had gone, the wildlife had disappeared and pollution was rife. Two-thirds of this area is now a nature reserve, perhaps a little manicured, but still a haven for the wildlife of the Everglades. On the other third, the Disney magic has created 45 000 well-paid jobs servicing the demands of millions of tourists.

You might be surprised, but I believe that Walt Disney World in Florida is an example of good practice in responsible tourism. It represents an example of sustainability as ethical as all those messages of good triumphing over evil which lie at the core of every classic Disney movie. If these messages were adopted more widely the world would indeed be a better place and the dream of sustainable tourism could come true.

The 1993 award winner the Coral Cay Conservation, Belize, however, proved that retaining the money within a community isn't enough. It must be used to create local jobs and to provide training so that those jobs are not all at the bottom of the market. Education is vital — of the local people, the workforce and the tourists themselves, who must be taught the importance of the environment, of wildlife, local customs and traditional methods of land management.

Both the people and the wildlife (endangered and otherwise) need to be preserved, and a way of achieving this is by not building new resorts in areas of natural vegetation or pristine coastlines and landscapes.

Source: 'Travel needn't cost the earth' by David Bellamy, the Guardian, 27/6/99.

a] What is meant by ethical tourism? **(5)**

b] Why does David Bellamy believe that Walt Disney World in Florida is an example of responsible tourism? **(5)**

c] Discuss whether the money earned in holiday resorts is always retained within the community. **(5)**

d] What conditions are necessary for sustainable tourism to exist? **(6)**

e] Discuss whether jobs in tourism are 'at the bottom of the market.' **(5)**

CASE STUDY

Britain has one of the worst records in Europe for everything from investment to congestion along with a reliance on the motor car that borders on obsession, according to new figures released by the Organisation for Economic Co-operation and Development.

The OECD research reveals that Britain spends less on roads, railways, bus and train networks and canals per head than most of its northern European neighbours, including France, Germany, the Netherlands, Belgium, Switzerland and most of Scandinavia.

Source: 'UK loves to drive but hates to pay the cost' by Joanna Walters, the Observer, 27/6/99.

Oxford, the first city in Britain to develop a park and ride system, will next spring ban cars from its centre streets in return for a promise of £6.5m of investment from Go-Ahead Group.

Go-Ahead's Oxford Bus Company group, which runs the trains and buses around Oxford, is to provide at least 30 new buses with environmentally friendly low-emission diesel engines. It has agreed to spend an extra £850 000 on ten low-floor buses.

In return, the council will erect large 'cassel' kerbs at 20 bus stops, allowing prams and wheelchairs to ride on without any bumps.

Go-Ahead claims that it is the 'only success story of deregulation' because it has, by working with the council, increased passenger levels by 50%.

Source: 'Heading in the right direction' by Fraser Nelson, The Times, 22/7/98.

a] Discuss why the UK has a reliance on the motor car 'that borders on obsession'. **(5)**

b] Why might privatisation have been expected to raise investment in transport? **(5)**

c] Discuss the main costs of traffic congestion. **(8)**

d] What is the prime aim behind 'park and ride schemes'? **(5)**

e] What means was Oxford and its major bus company planning to implement to encourage bus use? **(6)**

f] Discuss the external benefits of bus travel. **(7)**

g] Explain what is meant by deregulation and how it has affected the transport market. **(6)**

h] Discuss two measures not discussed in the extracts which could encourage people to switch from private car to public transport. **(8)**

STRUCTURED ESSAY

a] Explain in what sense demand for travel is a derived demand. **(8)**

b] Assess the measures a government could implement to encourage use of rail travel by firms and individuals. **(17)**

FREE RESPONSE ESSAY

Assess the costs and benefits a country may experience as a result of its domestic tourism industry expanding. **(25)**

64 THE EUROPEAN UNION

TRADE BLOCS

Since the Second World War there have been many examples of groups of countries joining together for the purpose of stimulating trade between themselves and to obtain other benefits of economic co-operation. Economic integration between countries can take several forms.

FREE TRADE AREAS

These consist of groups of countries which have abolished tariffs and quotas on trade between themselves. Each of the member countries, however, maintains its own independent (and different) restrictions on imports from non-member countries. The best known example is the North American Free Trade Area (NAFTA) consisting of the USA, Canada and Mexico.

CUSTOMS UNIONS

Customs unions are a closer form of economic integration. There is free trade between member countries, but all members are obliged to operate a common external tariff on imports from non-member countries. An example is Mercosur of South America which consists of Argentina, Brazil, Paraguay and Uruguay.

COMMON MARKETS

These are customs unions which, in addition to free trade in goods and services, also allow the free movement of factors of production (labour and capital) between member states.

ECONOMIC UNIONS

These organisations include all the features of a common market, but also require member states to adopt common economic policies on matters such as agriculture, transport and taxation. The European Union is moving some way towards economic union.

THE AIMS OF THE EUROPEAN UNION

As set out in the Treaty of Rome the basic aims of the EU are as follows.

- The elimination of customs duties and quotas on the import and export of goods between member states.
- The establishment of a common customs tariff and a common commercial policy towards non-member countries.
- The abolition of obstacles to the free movement of persons, services and capital between member states.
- The establishment of common policies for agriculture and transport.

- The prohibition of business practices which restrict or distort competition within the common market in ways which are considered to be harmful.
- The association of overseas countries and territories in order to increase trade and development. The 1992 Maastricht Treaty on European Union added to this list of aims to include the following.
- The creation of economic and monetary union.
- The development of a common foreign, security and defence policy.

MEMBERSHIP

The European Union came into existence in January 1958, with a membership of six countries — West Germany, France, Italy, Belgium, The Netherlands and Luxembourg. The membership was enlarged to include Denmark, Ireland and the UK (in 1973), Greece (in 1981), Spain and Portugal (in 1986) and Austria, Finland and Sweden (in 1995). There are currently thirteen countries waiting to join the European Union: Bulgaria, Cyprus, Czech Republic, Estonia, Hungary, Latvia, Lithuania, Malta, Poland, Romania, Slovakia, Slovenia and Turkey.

The future enlargement is likely to cause a number of problems as there are some major differences in living standards and the economic cycles of the prospective and existing members.

THE INSTITUTIONS

The key institutions include the following.

THE COMMISSION

The European Commission is based in Brussels. The Commissioners are independent; they are not in Brussels to represent the interests of their own national governments, but are committed to European policies. The role of the Commission is to draft policies and present them to the Council of Ministers for decision. It also has the important tasks of implementing and administering the Union's policies, and for this purpose it has considerable executive powers.

THE COUNCIL OF MINISTERS

This is the body which takes policy decisions. It is the only European institution whose members directly represent their national governments. Different ministers attend; most frequently they are foreign ministers, but agricultural ministers might attend when farm policies are being decided, and finance ministers when financial matters are being considered. Unanimity is required for 'essential' or major decisions, but there is provision for majority decisions on other matters.

THE COURT OF JUSTICE

The Court sits in Luxembourg. Its function is to settle any disputes about the interpretation and application of the Treaty of Rome and Maastricht Treaty. Individuals, institutions and member governments may appeal to the Court. Its decisions become binding on member states.

THE EUROPEAN PARLIAMENT

The European Parliament is based in Strasbourg. The Commission and the Council are answerable to it and it has the power to veto the Union's budget.

THE EUROPEAN CENTRAL BANK (ECB) AND THE EUROPEAN SYSTEM OF CENTRAL BANKS (ESCB)

The ECB is based in Frankfurt. It has been given the main policy aim of price stability. Together with the ESCB it decides on and implements monetary policy including exchange rate policy. It is the responsibility of the national central banks to operate the monetary policies.

THE COMMON AGRICULTURAL POLICY (CAP)

The aims of the CAP, are, briefly:

- to increase agricultural productivity
- to ensure a fair standard of living for the agricultural community
- to stabilise the markets in farm products
- to provide adequate supplies of foodstuffs
- to ensure supplies to consumers at reasonable prices.

For the main agricultural products the system works in the following way. Each year the Council of Ministers sets a target price for the product for the next agricultural year (April to March). This is the price which is considered to be the most appropriate to meet the CAP objectives set out above.

An intervention price is then set a few percentage points below the target price. If the market price falls below this intervention price, farmers can sell their output to EU agencies at the interventionist price; these purchases will be placed in store. In theory, such periods should be offset by others when demand exceeds supply and in which the shortage can be met by selling supplies held by the intervention centres. In fact, in many cases, supply has continued to exceed demand at the intervention prices, which has given rise to the so-called 'food mountains'.

A threshold price is also set. This applies to imports of food entering the EU and ensures that the price of imports is equal to or greater than the target price. Since the world prices of foodstuffs tend to be lower than those in the EU, this means a levy is placed on imports equal to the difference between world prices and threshold prices. The system works as a form of protection for EU farmers.

If world prices are below the intervention prices, then farmers will clearly prefer to sell to the EU authorities rather than export their products. In this case, in order to encourage farmers to export their surpluses. On the other hand, if there is a shortage of foodstuffs in the EU it can be relieved by reducing the threshold price and by reducing the subsidies on exports.

Increasing productivity in agriculture and the fairly stable demand for foodstuffs have led to the accumulation of large surpluses of certain farm products (e.g. cereals and dairy products). These surpluses are costly to store and export. If they are sold abroad at relatively low prices, they tend to reduce world prices and hence reduce the incomes of producers in other countries. The problem with the EU system of guaranteed prices for agricultural products is that it makes farmers' incomes dependent upon their outputs, i.e. there is an incentive to increase output — hence the surpluses. In more recent years, the EU has attempted to reduce these surpluses by slowing down the rate of increase of intervention prices, fixing output quotas for certain products (e.g. milk) and introducing a set-aside scheme whereby farmers are paid a subsidy for not using a proportion of their land.

Assessment of CAP

There is no doubt that the CAP has ensured adequate supplies of good quality foodstuffs, but it has proved to be a costly system. Indeed spending on the CAP is the largest expenditure item in the EU's budget. However, it must be borne in mind that all the EU governments are committed to supporting agriculture. Dismantling the CAP would not mean the creation of free markets in farm products — member governments would then be obliged to spend large sums of money protecting their agricultural industries. Before the UK entered the EU, for example, UK citizens enjoyed relatively cheap food because it was sold in the UK market at world prices. These prices, however, were lower than the costs of production on UK farms. The government, therefore, supplemented farm incomes with subsidies which covered the difference between UK costs of production and market prices.

THE EU BUDGET

The EU's budget is financed by revenue from a number of sources.

- Customs duties on imports from non-EU countries. These are the proceeds of the Common External Tariff (CET) and are paid over to the EU by all member states.
- Agricultural duties on the import of foodstuffs.
- An amount equivalent to 1.27% of each country's GDP, as an annual transfer.
- A VAT contribution equal to 1% of its domestic tax base.

The main items of expenditure are on:

- CAP
- the regional development fund which seeks to reduce regional differences in income and employment
- the European Social Fund (ESF) which promotes improvements in labour market conditions and employment opportunities
- the Community Fund which encourages co-operation between member states on areas of common interest
- the Cohesion Fund which helps the poorer member states prepare for greater integration
- EU foreign aid
- administration.

The UK is a net contributor to the EU budget but since 1984 it has received a rebate on its payments.

THE EFFECTS OF MEMBERSHIP OF THE EU

When a country joins the EU or another trade bloc it may experience trade creation or trade diversion. Trade creation occurs when the removal of trade barriers results in greater specialisation according to comparative advantage and hence a shift in production from higher cost to lower cost production.

Trade diversion results in consumption shifting from lower cost producers outside the trade bloc to higher cost producers inside the trade bloc. Trade creation is obviously advantageous whereas trade diversion is not. These are static effects. They occur once but there are other possible advantages and disadvantages which occur over a period of time.

POSSIBLE DYNAMIC GAINS OF EU MEMBERSHIP

These include the following.

- *Greater specialisation and economies of scale.* Supporters of the EU argue that the creation of a greatly enlarged 'home' market enables the more efficient producers to achieve a much larger scale of production and hence produce at lower costs. Within the EU, industries can operate on a Union rather than on a national scale. It is also pointed out by the supporters of the EU that the spending on and exploitation of the results of technological development and research in areas such as nuclear energy, space, aviation and computers is extremely costly and probably beyond the resources of any single European country. If such industries are to be efficient and capable of competing with the USA countries with smaller economies will have to collaborate, pool their research facilities and operate joint development programmes. Economic integration makes it much easier to operate joint industrial programmes of this sort.
- *Greater competition.* The removal of trade barriers allows more scope for the application of the principle of comparative advantage. Regional cost differences will reveal themselves as differences in market prices and these differences will enable the more efficient firms to expand at the expense of the less efficient who will no longer enjoy the protection afforded by tariffs and quotas. The allocation of resources will be determined by the relative efficiencies of producers within the EU as a whole. This argument assumes, of course, that competition within the EU will not be distorted by the formation of monopolies and cartels.
- *Increased exports.* The increased efficiency of producers within the EU brought about by more competition and larger scale production will, it is believed, enable them to compete more effectively in world markets.
- *More financial assistance.* If the formation of a trade bloc does generate a faster rate of economic growth then the rising prosperity of the group as a whole will make it possible to provide more funds to help the poorer parts of the EU and to provide more aid to developing countries in other parts of the world.
- *Raised expectations.* Knowledge that they are operating in a significant and powerful market may make entrepreneurs more optimistic and may encourage them to undertake more investment both for purposes of modernisation and expansion.

POSSIBLE DYNAMIC LOSSES

These include the following.

- *Diseconomies of scale.* Access to a large market may cause firms to expand too far and experience rising unit costs.
- *Unemployment.* A less efficient country may suffer as firms move out to the more prosperous parts of the trade bloc. This departure can lead to a downward multiplier effect.
- *Administrative costs.* Running a trade bloc can involve high costs. There is a danger that the organisation can become too bureaucratic and too slow to respond to changing economic and political events.

THE MAASTRICHT TREATY

This was signed on 7 February 1992 and represented a move towards economic and monetary union and political union. It set out a common foreign and security policy, a common interior and justice policy and a common social policy. It also outlined a detailed programme and timetable for monetary union.

THE SOCIAL CHAPTER

This is an agreement on social policy. The stated objectives are to promote employment, improve living and working conditions, implement proper social protection, improve dialogue between management and labour, combat social exclusion and develop human resources with a view to lasting high employment. The social provisions include a minimum wage, equal pay for male and female workers for equal work, minimum standards for health and safety at work and the setting up of workers' councils.

ECONOMIC AND MONETARY UNION (EMU)

The first part of this is monetary union. The 1989 Delors Committee Report recommended a three stage route to monetary union. The first stage involved freeing movements of capital, strengthening competition policy and increasing policy co-ordination. Stage 2 was a transition period in which countries were urged to work towards greater monetary convergence by avoiding excessive budget deficits, keeping inflation rates and interest rates in line with each other and maintaining stable exchange rates. The ESCB was also set up.

The third stage came into force on 1 January 1999 with the introduction of the single currency. Eleven countries joined the single currency — Austria, Belgium, Finland, France, Germany, Ireland, Italy, Luxembourg, The Netherlands, Portugal and Spain. Collectively these countries are known as the euro area or euroland. Greece had wanted to join but had not met the convergence criteria and Denmark, Sweden and the UK chose not to join immediately (see Chapter 51 for details on the single currency). The ESCB and ECB operates monetary policy including determining exchange policy, managing foreign exchange reserves, controlling the money supply and taking decisions on interest rates.

QUESTIONS

SHORT QUESTIONS

1 Distinguish between a customs union and a free trade area.

2 What are the aims of CAP?

3 What is meant by EMU?

4 Why might membership of a trade bloc enable a country to take greater advantage of economies of scale?

MULTIPLE CHOICE

1 What is the difference between a customs union and a common market?

A Only the customs union imposes a common external tariff.

B Only the common market requires member countries to adopt common fiscal and monetary policies.

C Only the common market permits free movement of labour between member countries.

D Only the customs union abolishes tariffs on trade between member countries.

2 What is the Common Agricultural Policy of the European Union based on?

A Prices determined by world trends in demand and supply.

B Minimum guaranteed prices to farmers with interventionist purchase of unsold products.

C Subsidies paid to farmers with prices being determined by free market forces.

D Maximum guaranteed prices set to benefit consumers in the European Union.

3 What is the trade diversion effect of membership of a trade bloc?

A A switch from manufacturing production to the production of services.

B A switch from buying cheaper products outside the area to buying more expensive products in the area.

C A greater concentration on the products the countries have a comparative advantage in.

D A greater concentration on products produced by capital intensive methods.

4 What is the aim of the EU's social chapter?

A To promote health care provision in the EU.

B To limit member governments' expenditure on social security.

C To improve workers' conditions and workers' rights in the EU.

D To encourage member governments to spend more on social capital.

DATA RESPONSE

Average per capita net receipts/contributions to the EU budget 1995–97

Net gainers	Euros	Net contributors	Euros
Luxembourg	1769	Italy	− 11
Ireland	635	France	− 14
Greece	382	UK	− 48
Portugal	271	Austria	− 74
Spain	164	Sweden	− 101
Belgium	138	Netherlands	− 140
Denmark	42	Germany	− 141
Finland	1		

The UK receives an annual £2bn rebate on its contribution to the EU budget. However it is coming under pressure to give up this rebate. This is because the costs of the EU will increase with the proposed enlargement into Eastern Europe.

British officials claim that even after the rebate, nearly every person in Britain pays nearly a pound a week for Europe. Each Irish citizen, by contrast, receives over £10 a week from the EU budget, each Greek gets £6 a week, and each Spaniard £2 a week. Each Belgian gets £2 a week, although Belgium is the third richest EU state in terms of GDP per capita. Even after the rebate, the EU spends less per capita in Britain than in any other EU state.

Source: adapted from 'Brown fights to save EU rebate' by Martin Walker, the Guardian, 8/2/99.

a] Compare the countries who are net gainers from and net contributors to the EU budget. **(7)**

b] How does the UK's position compare to the other member countries? **(5)**

c] What is the largest single item of expenditure of the EU? **(2)**

d] Discuss two sources of revenue for the EU. **(4)**

e] Why is it predicted that enlargement will increase the EU's net expenditure? **(7)**

CASE STUDY

In all the arguments over European monetary union, opponents of Emu find nothing more appealing than the unemployment statistics.

Never mind that the French have a higher gross domestic product (GDP) per head and a better health service; just look at the unemployment. It is not a mere debating point. It is a serious matter for euroland.

The 15 years of high unemployment suffered by Britain after 1980 have left social damage that will be with us for some years yet. If euroland cannot get out of its bind by 2000 the same will happen there.

Like all statistics, unemployment numbers need interpretation.

For euroland the lesson is obvious: a sharp, early fall in unemployment must be the priority for policy. European governments, especially Germany's, understand this, but they have a problem with the European Central Bank bosses, who are still pretending the Maastricht treaty gives them no responsibility for anything but money. That conflict may soon generate a political crisis, and if it does not it ought to.

Source: 'Europe is not working' by Robin Marris, the Sunday Times, 21/2/99.

a] What does European monetary union involve? **(5)**

b] How could a country have a higher unemployment rate but also a higher GDP per head than another country? **(6)**

c] What social damage does unemployment cause? **(6)**

d] What is meant by the term 'euroland'? **(4)**

e] How is unemployment measured? **(6)**

f] Why do unemployment figures need interpretation? **(6)**

g] Explain how the European Central Bank would seek to reduce the rate of inflation and why this might conflict with the objective of high employment. **(12)**

h] What other objectives might it be argued that the European Central Bank should pursue? **(5)**

STRUCTURED ESSAY

a] Explain how the Common Agricultural Policy operates. **(10)**

b] Discuss the implications of monetary union for EU member countries. **(15)**

FREE RESPONSE ESSAY

Assess the costs and gains a country may experience as a result of belonging to a trade bloc. **(25)**

65 DEVELOPMENT ECONOMICS

Development economics is concerned with how developing economies can improve their economic welfare. Development is not necessarily the same thing as economic growth since a country may produce more goods and services but the majority of its population may not benefit if income is very unevenly distributed. However, economic growth has the potential of improving people's living standards.

MEASURES OF DEVELOPMENT

Countries can be classified in a number of ways. The IMF divides them into three main categories — industrial countries, developing countries and transitional economies. The World Bank and the United Nations use these categories and divide them further into high income, middle income and low income. In addition, the United Nations classifies countries as high human development, medium human development and low human development countries. It also separates out least developed countries from developing countries. Most of these categories are based on income per head measurement. However the United Nations' human development categorisation is based on the Human Development Index (HDI) — discussed in Chapter 26. The HDI comes close to the approach adopted by some economists who argue that a country can only claim to be developed when certain basic needs are fulfilled. These include availability and access for all to education, health and employment, an adequate supply of food and shelter and sufficient free time.

In 1997 the United Nations started to publish a new measure: the Human Poverty Index. The HPI is based on the percentage of people in a country who do not reach certain minimum standards e.g. percentage of people without access to health services, not expected to live to 40 and adults who are illiterate.

However development is measured there are differences within each category. For example the developing countries category includes the newly industrialising countries (NICs) including Singapore, South Korea and Taiwan, as well as very poor countries including Bangladesh, Eritrea and Mali. Comparing the industrial (sometimes called the developed) countries and the poorer developing countries there is very marked difference between living standards. As most of the industrial countries are in the northern hemisphere and most of the poorer developing countries are in the southern hemisphere, this gap is often referred to as the north-south divide.

SOME COMMON CHARACTERISTICS OF LEAST DEVELOPED COUNTRIES

Every country has its special problems and rates of progress vary widely between different countries but there are some features which are common to the majority of the least developed countries. These include the following.

- *High birth rates, relatively high death rates and a low expectancy of life.* For example in 1995 whereas someone born in Canada had a life expectancy of 79, someone born in Malawi only had a life expectancy of 41. Most of the least developed countries are experiencing a high rate of population growth and a high dependency rate (i.e. a high proportion of children dependent on a small proportion of workers).
- *Concentration on agriculture.* In some countries more than 70% of the labour force is engaged in agriculture, but, in spite of this high degree of 'specialisation', productivity is low. This is due to e.g. the lack of capital equipment and hidden unemployment.

- *A poor natural resource endowment.* Many of the least developed countries are in tropical and sub-tropical regions where soils are fragile and climatic conditions unfavourable to many agricultural activities. Massive investment in programmes for soil conservation, irrigation, the control of pests and the use of fertilisers are needed in order to raise the productivity of the land.
- *Underemployment.* Most people do some work but most are underemployed. Holdings of land are small and the system of land tenure often means that all the members of the family work on the family plot. Under these conditions the marginal productivity of labour may even be zero. There is often little activity between planting and harvesting.
- *Social, religious and cultural patterns.* These often act as serious barriers to change and development. Where people are strongly attached to customary ways of doing things, it is extremely difficult to improve mobility of labour and introduce new techniques.
- *Low levels of investment in human capital.* Workers are lacking in education and technical skills and the relatively low standards of health often mean a low level of physical performance.
- *A heavy dependency on a narrow range of export products (usually primary products).* Foreign currency earnings will be subject to large variations because the world prices of primary products are notoriously unstable.
- *An inadequate industrial and social infrastructure.* Rapid economic development needs a basis in the form of e.g. good communications, adequate power and water supplies, an educated and trained labour force.

CONDITIONS FOR DEVELOPMENT

To achieve a sustained growth in income per head and advancement in economic welfare the quality and quantity of factors of production will have to be improved.

- *Human resources.* The quality of human resources can be increased by improvements in education, training and health.
- *Capital resources.* Output per head will increase with capital deepening and with improved technology.
- *Natural resources.* Fertile land, a favourable climate and a good supply of minerals and fuels are obviously beneficial. However, a number of industrial countries, for example Israel, do not possess a good supply of natural resources.
- *Allocation of resources.* To increase income per head, resources should be moved from low productivity industries to high productivity industries.
- *Innovation.* Economic development will be stimulated by the adoption of new methods, improved technology, better communications and advanced management techniques.

UNDERDEVELOPMENT TRAP

As some developing countries often lack the conditions necessary for development they can become caught in what is known as 'the vicious circle of poverty'. To increase productivity the rate of capital accumulation needs to increase. However investment can only be increased if there is an increase in the rate of saving, but an increase in saving requires an increase in income and an increase in income requires an increase in productivity which in turn requires an increase in investment. The current levels of income cannot provide the necessary savings. One alternative is to raise the necessary funds by means of taxation (forced savings) but taxes are difficult to collect in most developing countries and, in any case, the tax base is narrow. There is a temptation for governments to finance investment by expanding the money supply but this runs the risk of causing inflation and destabilising the economy.

DEVELOPMENT STRATEGIES

There is a debate about the most effective way for developing countries to develop. Among the strategies considered are the following.

- *Increasing primary production.* If the developing countries concentrate on increasing their productivity in primary production, they face the problem that most of these products have very inelastic demand. A large increase in world supplies might well reduce the incomes of the poorer countries. The prices of primary products also tend to fluctuate quite considerably because they can be subject to significant shifts in supply (e.g. due to changes in weather) and because both demand and supply are usually inelastic. There is a risk that demand may decrease dramatically if substitutes are developed.
- *Industrialising through import substitution.* The aim here would be to allow infant industries to grow and establish a comparative advantage behind a protective wall of import controls. Imports would be replaced by domestic goods and services and the industrial structure would become more diversified. However there is a risk with this method that the domestic industries may come to rely on protection and not improve their efficiency.
- *Promoting export-led growth.* As an economy develops, its exports are likely to change from primary products to labour-intensive, low-quality manufactured goods. Competing in world markets holds out the promise of higher income and a stimulation to increase efficiency and competitiveness. However this approach relies on the firms being able to compete against foreign firms which have already achieved low costs and in markets which may have high levels of protection imposed by industrial countries.
- *Tourism.* Tourism has a high income elasticity of demand and is the fastest growing industry in the world. However, it tends to result in low income jobs and runs the risk of damaging the natural environment.
- *Borrowing from abroad.* Funds borrowed from foreign countries can be used to invest in physical and human capital thereby raising productivity. However, developing countries have often run into difficulties following this approach. For instance, in the 1980s a number of countries got into serious debt problems for a variety of reasons including a fall in the price of primary products and a rise in interest rates. In 1997 a number of NICs and the industrial country of Japan and the transitional economy of Russia experienced problems of debt default and the collapse of banks.
- *Relying on foreign aid.* Assistance from other countries can enable developing countries to improve their infrastructure, their capital stock and their education, training and health systems. However, aid has not always been appropriate and has not always improved living standards. For instance, providing capital for high-technology equipment to a very poor and over-populated agricultural country may not be very useful as it will need an educated and trained labour force to operate it and it is not going to generate a large demand for labour. The issue of aid is discussed in more detail below.

DEVELOPMENT THEORIES

There are a number of theories which may be considered in seeking to gain an understanding of the rate at which countries develop.

THE HARROD-DOMAR MODEL

This suggests that the key determinants of economic growth and economic development are the savings ratio, investment and technological change. To increase development countries need to raise their levels of saving or make use of other countries' savings and to stimulate technological change.

PROFILE

NAME: Mahbub ul Haq

BORN.: 22/2/34   **DIED:** 16/7/98

NATIONALITY: Pakistani

EDUCATED: Government College, Lahore, King's College, Cambridge, Yale University

KEY POSTS HELD: Chief economist of Pakistan's planning commission
Director of World Bank's policy planning department
Finance Minister of Pakistan
Commerce Minister of Pakistan
Planning Minister of Pakistan
Special advisor to the United Nations Development Programme
Set up the Human Development Centre for South Asia

MAIN AREA OF WORK: Development economics

SIGNIFICANT CONTRIBUTION: In 1990 he started the Human Development Report. This includes the Human Development Index (HDI) which he also devised. The HDI ranks countries not just on the basis of their GDP but also on the basis of their literacy rates and life expectancies.

QUOTES ABOUT MAHBUB UL HAQ:
'Haq argued that development was about enlarging people's choices and that income, health, education and security were all important dimensions of this process. Even governments with inadequate resources could provide their citizens with sufficient capabilities as long as they gave priority to basic needs.'
    The Times Obituary 10/8/98.

'Mr. Haq became accepted as one of the visionaries of international development.'
    The Economist Obituary 25/7/98.

ROSTOW'S STAGES OF ECONOMIC GROWTH

The American economist, Walt Rostow, argued that countries go through five stages of economic development. These are traditional, transitional, take-off, drive to maturity and age of mass consumption. The key stage is the take-off stage as this is where growth becomes self-sustaining. A virtuous circle of development occurs. High levels of saving enable investment to take place which in turn generates rises in productivity which raise income and in turn raise savings. At this stage the social, political and commercial infrastructure develop which facilitate more rapid economic growth.

THE LEWIS MODEL

This model is named after the West Indian economist, W. Arthur Lewis. It is also sometimes referred to as the dual economy model as it envisages two types of economy co-existing in developing economies. One is a traditional, largely self-sustaining subsistence agricultural sector and the other is a sector in which goods and services are produced for sale and in which more modern methods of production are employed. The model suggests that economies which have a large number of under-employed workers in agriculture can grow more rapidly by transferring workers from agriculture into manufacturing and services. The latter two sectors, he argued, employ more up to date technology and have a higher rate of productivity.

THE BALANCED GROWTH THEORY

This argues that to achieve development government should seek to encourage its industries to grow at a similar rate in order to achieve markets for the goods and services produced and to co-ordinate inputs and outputs.

THE UNBALANCED GROWTH THEORY

In contrast to the balanced growth theory, this suggests that governments should seek to promote the growth of key industries. The thinking is that if these grow they will stimulate other industries by creating a demand for inputs and by creating new markets. The key industries will 'drag up' the other industries.

THE BACKWARD HYPOTHESIS

This suggests that developing countries can increase their growth rates by copying the methods and ideas of industrial countries. In the past some countries, for example Japan, managed to grow very rapidly by copying the technology and skills of industrial countries and attracting direct foreign investment.

DEPENDENCY THEORY

This argues that developing economies have been forced to be dependent on industrial economies and institutions dominated by industrial economies e.g. the International Monetary Fund (IMF) and the World Bank. It is claimed that the development of the developing economies has been held back by unfair trade restrictions imposed by, e.g., the European Union and by inappropriate foreign investment and aid. To achieve more rapid and sustainable development, it is argued, there needs to be a more even distribution of economic and political power.

FOREIGN AID

There are three main motives for providing economic aid to the developing world.

- *Altruism.* A humanitarian desire to help people living in poverty.
- *Political motives.* One of the motives behind government aid is to win the political allegiance of the recipient governments. This was particularly the case during the 'cold war'.
- *Commercial motives.* Bi-lateral aid (which is aid from one government to another) is often in the form of tied aid. This requires the recipient to spend the money on particular items, often products sold by the donor countries.

MULTILATERAL AID

Multilateral aid channels money from groups of countries through agencies to developing countries. The main multilateral agencies are the World Bank and its two affiliates, the IDA and the IFC, the IMF, the United Nations, EU institutions and a range of charities.

FORMS OF AID

These include the following.

- *Grants and loans*. These may be allocated to specific projects. Grants will not require repayment and loans given for aid purposes will be charged at less than the market rate of interest.
- *Technical and direct assistance*. Donor countries and agencies provide technical experts to advise and assist developing countries in operating projects. They also provide technical training programmes for students from developing countries.
- *Education*. Industrial countries provide a number of scholarships for foreign students and send teachers and instructors abroad.
- *Specialist services*. The World Bank, the IMF and the United Nations as well as individual countries carry out economic surveys for, and offer a variety of financial, technical and advisory services to developing countries.

THE WORLD BANK

The International Bank for Reconstruction and Development (IBRD) is better known as the World Bank. It was set up in 1944 to help countries recover from the war. In its early years the major part of its lending was to European countries for purposes of reconstruction. However, its loans now go mainly to developing countries. It is the world's largest multilateral source of development funds.

Initially its loans were mainly for infrastructure projects such as road systems, electric plants, railways, irrigation, water supply, and industrial undertakings. However more recently fewer loans have been given for infrastructure and more for education, health and institutional change. Loans are made to member governments, government agencies, or to private sector firms providing the latter can obtain a government guarantee.

The borrower's application for a loan is carefully examined by World Bank experts who must be satisfied that the loan will be used to strengthen the economy and promote sound economic development. The Bank also provides advice to member countries from its teams of experts who research into the problems of economic development.

THE INTERNATIONAL DEVELOPMENT ASSOCIATION (IDA)

The IDA is an affiliate of the World Bank. The World Bank and the IDA operate with the same staff and the same standards but the IDA makes funds available to the poorer countries free of interest but with a service charge. However, the IDA has much more limited funds than the World Bank.

THE INTERNATIONAL FINANCE CORPORATION (IFC)

This is another member of the World Bank Group. It operates on more commercial lines and has as its main objective the encouragement of the flow of domestic and foreign funds into productive private investment in developing countries. It can supply capital in any form — long-term loans, equity subscriptions, or both, and it can invest without government guarantee of repayment.

THE INTERNATIONAL MONETARY FUND (IMF)

The IMF was set up, along with the World Bank, in 1944. Its aims include the encouragement of the growth of world trade and the provision of assistance to countries in balance of payments difficulties. From the early 1980s, it provided financial assistance, including the rescheduling of debts, to developing countries when they got into debt problems. However, the IMF has been criticised for the conditions it imposes on countries seeking its help. These have included tight fiscal and monetary policies and devaluation. It has been claimed that these measures are not always appropriate to the needs of developing economies and that the IMF's assistance is often too short-term and expensive.

QUESTIONS

SHORT QUESTIONS

1. Explain what is meant by Rostow's stages of growth.
2. What are the disadvantages of relying on the primary sector as a means of promoting economic development?
3. What is meant by the under-development trap?
4. What are three motives for giving foreign aid?

MULTIPLE CHOICE

1. Which of the following is a common characteristic of a developing country?

   A. Low death rate.

   B. Low literacy rate.

   C. A high level of labour productivity.

   D. A high proportion of the population employed in the tertiary sector.

2. What according to the Harrod-Domar model is a key determinant of economic growth?

   A. Health care provision.

   B. Government expenditure.

   C. The savings ratio.

   D. The stage of economic development.

3. In Rostow's model at which stage does growth become self-sustaining?

   A. Age of mass consumption.

   B. Drive to maturity.

   C. Take-off.

   D. Transitional.

4. What is the main role of the World Bank?

   A. To act as a bank for developing countries.

   B. To provide finance for development.

   C. To assist countries with balance of payments difficulties.

   D. To encourage investment in the private sector in developing countries.

DATA RESPONSE

Developing countries are important for innovation and leapfrogging. There is potential for leapfrogging in both processes and products, and often a synergy, between the two. For example, lighting in isolated villages is predominantly kerosene lanterns and candles. Switching to a compact fluorescent lightbulb (CFL), which is four times as efficient as a conventional incandescent bulb, would make it economical to supply power from a solar photovoltaic (PV) panel. Connecting to an electric grid — probably required if inefficient bulbs are used — would be unnecessary, allowing vast savings in capital equipment. These savings could be reflected in improved education, health and livelihoods. The PV-CLF solution leapfrogs over its alternative: a large, expensive electricity generating system.

A second dividend from leapfrog technologies derives from the avoided cost of long-term environmental clean-up, such as mopping up old toxic sites and scrubbing coal power plants. Using leapfrog technologies minimises clean-up costs, as well as health care costs linked to environmental pollution and degradation.

Leapfrog technologies are not only ideas — they are a reality. And they are being used in many developing as well as industrial countries.

But technology alone is not the solution. It must be supplemented with policy reforms, institutional arrangements and changes in collective responsibility.

Source: 'Human Development Report 1998', United Nations Development Programme, OUP.

a] What is meant by leapfrogging in the context of the article? **(3)**

b] Explain why developing countries 'are important areas for innovation'. **(6)**

c] What are the benefits of leapfrogging? **(5)**

d] Distinguish between developing and industrial countries. **(4)**

e] Why is technology alone not a sufficient condition for economic development? **(7)**

CASE STUDY

One world, two fates. Of children who die before their fifth birthday, 98% are in the developing world. Of people who are HIV positive, some 95% are in poor countries. Of the millions who die prematurely of tuberculosis, malaria, measles, tetanus and whooping cough, all but a few thousand live in the poor world. Indeed, tuberculosis alone kills more people each year than lung cancer, the most prevalent cancer and the terror of the West. The gap is widening between rich and poor countries, especially between the very richest and the very poorest. Although that has happened for a century or more, the continued early deaths of the poor and their children are a reproach to us all. What is to be done to save these millions of young lives?

The good news is that there is some new thinking about ways to respond to this challenge. Aid agencies and drug companies are talking to each other in more constructive ways than they once did. For donor countries, this is not mere altruism; as international travel grows, rich-world governments acquire a direct interest in halting diseases such as tuberculosis, which may otherwise infect their own citizens. But affordable drugs are only part of the cure. Developing-country governments can do more to improve the health of their people than simply getting hold of western money and ingenuity.

Part of the new thinking lies in the application of economics to what has often been a purely emotional pitch for aid. Since it published an influential paper on health in 1993, the World Bank has consistently advanced the argument that unhealthy countries are condemned to slow growth. The idea that ill health reinforces poverty is less familiar than the view that poverty causes ill health, but equally true. However, one of the main virtues of the World Bank's argument is that it allows multinational aid donors to talk straight to developing-country finance ministers, who typically have more clout in the allocation of resources than do their colleagues in the health ministry.

Now, economists are tackling — or struggling with — another aspect of the health of the poor; their lack of access to drugs. Jeffrey Sachs, a Harvard economist, has drawn attention to the scale of the problem: poor countries cannot afford expensive medicines, and drug companies naturally tend to focus their research on finding cures for the ills of the rich rather than the afflictions of the poor. Americans and Europeans rarely suffer from schistosomiasis, which afflicts 200m people worldwide, or lymphatic filariasis, which makes life miserable for another 120m. So the market is said to be too small to attract research. Gone are the days when Jonas Salk refused to patent polio vaccine, saying that to so would be 'like patenting the sun'. When a drug company spends millions to develop a vaccine, it wants an economic return.

Source: 'Helping the poorest', The Economist, 14/8/99.

a] How do health care standards of the poor and rich countries compare? **(4)**

b] What are the motives behind donor countries helping to improve health conditions in developing countries? **(5**)

c] Discuss two ways developing country governments can improve the health of their people other 'than simply getting hold of western money and ingenuity'. **(8)**

d] In what sense might it be claimed that there is an ill health vicious circle? **(6)**

e] How significant are economies of scale in the pharmaceutical industry? **(5)**

f] What is meant by 'economic return'? **(4)**

g] Discuss the role of the World Bank in promoting economic development. **(8)**

h] What evidence is there in the extract of market failure in the pharmaceutical industry? **(10)**

STRUCTURED ESSAY

a] What are the characteristics of developing
countries? **(10)**

b] Discuss three strategies a country could adopt
to promote economic development. **(15)**

FREE RESPONSE ESSAY

Assess the main theories of economic
development. **(25)**

66 FINANCIAL MARKETS

FINANCIAL INTERMEDIARIES

The main functions of financial institutions are to collect deposits from those with surplus cash resources and to lend the funds to those with an immediate need for them. This is the function of a financial intermediary. There are many advantages of the funds being channelled through a financial institution rather than being loaned directly by savers to borrowers.

Many savers want to save relatively small sums. They will also want liquidity — the ability to withdraw their money when they want it. Most borrowers want to borrow for definite periods of time — often for quite long periods. Financial intermediaries can aggregate many small sums of savings and make relatively large loans. They can offer savers liquidity by borrowing for short periods of time and lending for long periods. Depositors can be allowed to withdraw funds because such withdrawals are likely to be matched by new deposits. If such an institution retains the confidence of its depositors there is no reason why the funds available for lending should fall significantly.

Savers will tend to look for security — they want to feel that their money is 'safe'. By spreading its loans over many different types of borrower, a financial intermediary greatly reduces the risk of losses. It can take account of likely losses in the rate of interest it charges to borrowers. Financial intermediaries can use their size and expertise to offer savers a wide range of savings schemes and to offer borrowers several different types of loan.

BUILDING SOCIETIES

The most important functions of building societies are still those of collecting retail deposits and providing mortgage loans. However, they now carry out a wide range of activities similar to those provided by retail banks. As with retail banks they are now regulated by the Financial Services Authority (FSA).

RETAIL BANKS

These are also called high street banks. Most are also clearing banks which means they participate in a clearing system. This enables cheques, direct debits, standing orders and other methods of payment to be cleared i.e. exchanged so that money is moved out of the deposit of the person making the payment into the deposit of the person receiving the payment.

The strength of a large bank with many outlets, with branches or indeed internet links, derives from its ability to obtain economies of scale, which have become more significant with the application of advanced technology. In addition, with a large number of depositors, no single depositor can embarrass the bank by withdrawing their funds. With many branches, the bank has a geographical spread of risks which enables it to withstand losses due to a slump in any industry or region.

THE FUNCTIONS OF RETAIL BANKS

These are as follows.

- *Attracting deposits.* The banks attract current accounts (sight accounts), deposit accounts (time deposits) and large-fixed term deposits. The banks offer higher rates of interest on large sums of money deposited for fixed periods of time. In order to attract such deposits, the banks offer certificates of deposit which are marketable securities.
- *Lending.* Retail banks are profit-seeking firms and their main source of income is the interest they charge on their loans. These banks lend to all types of industry, as well as to the government and other public authorities. They also have a large market in personal loans. The banks have traditionally concentrated on short-term loans for the provision of working capital. However, they are becoming more flexible in the length and purpose of their lending.
- *Money transmission services.* Banks provide a range of ways in which people can make and receive payments e.g. cheques, standing orders, direct debits and credit cards.
- *Other services.* The banks provide a wide range of other financial services, such as the provision of foreign currency, investment advice, management of funds, executor and trustee services, insurance services, and unit trusts.

THE BANKER'S DILEMMA — LIQUIDITY OR PROFITABILITY?

As banks are private sector firms with shareholders, they have an obligation to their owners to operate as profitably as they can. They also have an obligation to their depositors which requires them to meet all the depositors' demand for cash. This latter obligation means that the banks' assets must contain an adequate proportion (reserve) of cash and additionally some liquid assets to deal with unexpectedly heavy demands for cash.

These different obligations present the banks with a dilemma because the need for liquidity conflicts with the objective of profitability. The more liquid an asset, the lower its earning power. Cash, the most liquid of assets, earns no income. Bank loans (advances) are the most profitable asset but also the most illiquid asset.

Since cash earns no income, banks will try to keep their cash reserves to a minimum. Just how small this cash reserve can be depends upon the people's demand for cash and the banks' ability to obtain income-earning assets which are very liquid. The existence of the money market (which is the market in short-term loans) enables UK banks to acquire a variety of such income-earning assets.

LIQUID ASSETS

These include the following.

- *Cash.* This is the most liquid asset of all.
- *Operational balances at the Bank of England.* These are the current accounts which the banks hold in accounts at the Bank of England and which can be withdrawn on demand.
- *Money at call.* This is money lent to the discount houses which can be called back in at very short notice.
- *Treasury bills.* These are short-term government securities and so represent short-term loans to the government.
- *Commercial bills.* These are issued by firms and are a way of financing trade. Again they are short-term loans.

LESS LIQUID ASSETS

The more profitable, but less liquid, assets held by the banks are as follows.

- *Investments*. These consist largely of long-term government securities although the banks normally buy such securities when they have five years or less to run to maturity.
- *Advances*. These are the banks' loans to individuals, firms and the public authorities. They are the most profitable of the banks' assets, and the ones which banks seek to maximise. Indeed they account for the largest proportion of banks' assets. Interest rates on advances vary according to the duration of the loan and the creditworthiness of the borrower.

Customers' deposits are overwhelmingly the largest of banks' liabilities. These deposits are liabilities as banks are obliged to pay them back at some future time.

CREDIT CREATION

Banks play a very important role in the economy as they are able to create credit (money) in the form of the deposits which are given to borrowers. Banks have this power because only a small proportion of bank deposits are taken out in the form of cash. Every day a large number of people may withdraw cash from the banks, but it is likely that this amount will be more than matched by other people depositing cash. So the net withdraw of cash is usually very small — often less than 2% of total deposits.

As banks know this they use their cash reserves to form the basis for loans of a much greater value than those reserves. In determining the maximum they can lend they make use of the *credit creation multiplier*. For example, suppose the banks decide that a maximum of 4% of total deposits is likely to be cashed they may decide to keep a 5% liquidity asset ratio (proportion of liquid assets to total liabilities) to be safe. This means that they can have deposits 20 times the value of their liquid assets since, e.g., £5 in cash would meet the cash needs of £100 deposits. If someone puts an extra £40 into the banking system the banks will be able to increase their deposits by 20 × £40 = £800 and to create an extra £760 worth of advances (£800–£40 deposit opened for the depositor).

So the credit creation multiplier is calculated as 100/liquidity ratio; the change in bank deposits as the credit creation multiplier × the change in cash holdings; and the change in advances as the change in bank deposits − the change in cash holdings.

The smaller the liquidity ratio held, the greater the credit creation multiplier and hence the greater the banks' ability to create money. For instance, a liquidity ratio of $2\frac{1}{2}$% gives a credit creation multiplier of $100/2\frac{1}{2} = 40$, whereas a liquidity ratio of 25% will give a credit creation multiplier of $100/25 = 4$.

LIMITS ON THE BANKS' ABILITY TO CREATE CREDIT

In addition to the liquidity ratio which they have to keep to there are a number of other limits on banks' ability to create loans by making advances. These include government policy, as implemented by the Bank of England, and the demand for loans.

THE BANK OF ENGLAND

The Bank of England, founded in 1694 and nationalised in 1946, is the UK's central bank. Some of its responsibilities are outlined below.

- *It is the government's bank.* It handles the income and expenditure of the Exchequer and other government departments.
- *It is the bankers' bank.* As mentioned earlier the retail banks maintain accounts at the Bank of England. The Bank is also a banker for a number of foreign central banks and international institutions.
- *Note issuing.* It is the central note-issuing authority for the UK and the sole note-issuing authority for England and Wales.
- *It manages the national debt.* This involves making repayments on government securities when they mature, undertaking new issues of long-term securities, making regular payments of interest to holders of existing government securities, and handling the weekly issues of Treasury bills.
- *It is the lender of last resort.* The Bank of England stands ready to come to the assistance of the banking system in times when it is threatened by a shortage of cash.
- *Price stability.* It has been given the responsibility for price stability in the form of meeting the government's inflation target.
- *System stability.* It is responsible for maintaining the overall stability of the financial system. It does this by monitoring developments in the financial system at home and abroad and by working closely with the Financial Services Authority and with other central banks including the European Central Bank.
- *Effectiveness of UK financial markets.* It seeks to ensure the effectiveness of the UK's financial services by promoting improvements in the structures in the UK financial markets.
- *Monetary union.* It is helping in the move towards monetary union in order to be able to exert as much influence as possible on the design of the system and in order to ensure that the financial sector is prepared should the UK decide to enter the single currency.

THE INDEPENDENCE OF THE BANK OF ENGLAND

In May 1997 the Bank of England was given responsibility for setting the rate of interest in pursuit of achieving the target for inflation set for it by the government. So independence in this case does not mean being removed from government ownership and overall control. It has a more limited meaning.

Interest rates are now set by the Monetary Policy Committee (MPC) which operates within the Bank of England. Once the MPC decides on the rate of interest officials of the Bank of England operate in the money markets to direct short term interest rates to that level. This is achieved by providing liquidity or cash to the banking system at the rate set by the MPC and by buying government securities at prices consistent with the interest rate set by the MPC.

The advantages of allowing the Bank of England to decide on interest rate changes is that the Bank is more likely to take a longer term prospective, is less likely to change the rate of interest to gain political popularity, has considerable experience and may carry greater credibility with the financial markets than the government of the day. However, there is the risk that it may sacrifice the objective of employment in pursuit of price stability.

MERCHANT (INVESTMENT) BANKS

Several merchant, or investment banks, date back to the nineteenth century, when they were simply merchant houses trading in the various parts of the world. Some of them grew in reputation and turned to the finance of trade as a specialised business. The finance of international trade remains an important function but other activities have tended to become more important. The main activities of the merchant banks are summarised below.

- *Accepting, i.e. adding their names to 'promises to pay' issued by traders.* By accepting an IOU, the merchant bank guarantees payment if the person or firm promising payment defaults.
- *Financial advisors to companies.* The best known activity of the merchant banks is the handling of mergers and take-overs, in which they advise and act for the parties concerned in the negotiations. They will, however, advise on any aspect of a company's financial affairs.
- *Share issue.* The merchant banks also act as issuing houses. As well as advising firms on methods of raising finance, and the government on privatisation they will usually carry out all the work involved in floating a new issue of shares or debentures.
- *Investment management.* In addition to their advisory role, merchant banks will take on the active management of investment on behalf of other institutions. They operate investment and unit trusts.
- *Wholesale banking.* The merchant bank's main deposit-taking activity is the acceptance of wholesale deposits (i.e. deposits of very large sums) for periods ranging from one day to a year. They are active in the money market, lending mainly to banks and other financial institutions. In the capital market they provide finance for firms.

THE DISCOUNT HOUSES

The discount market is an important part of the UK banking system. It is mainly concerned with short and very short-term loans. The main institutions operating in the market are the eight discount houses although some banks run money-trading departments which operate in ways similar to discount houses.

The discount houses borrow money on a very short-term basis from various banks in the City of London. Much of this money is borrowed at call (i.e. is repayable on demand) or overnight. The discount houses use these funds to discount (i.e. buying a security for less than its face or redeemable value) a variety of securities including commercial bills and Treasury bills and make profits (or losses) on the difference between the rates of interest they pay on the money they borrow and the rate they charge for discounting securities.

THE LONDON STOCK EXCHANGE (LSE)

The LSE has a physical location but much trading is now done by means of telephone and new technology. The LSE is part of the capital market, i.e. the market in long term loans. It is a second hand market in the sense that it is concerned with the trading of existing shares and securities.

In order to finance long-term projects, both firms and the government need to borrow money for long periods of time. Company shares represent permanent loans — there is no right to repayment. Many government securities and firms' debentures are not redeemable for many years after the date of issue.

In the absence of some kind of stock exchange, securities such as these would be very illiquid assets. It would be difficult to find buyers for them. The existence of a stock exchange solves this problem because it provides a market where holders of shares and long-term securities can always sell them. This means that firms and the government can have the use of funds for long periods, but the providers of these funds can, at any time, convert their securities back into cash. Since the prices of shares and government securities change from day to day, a seller might receive more or less than he or she paid for them.

THE INVESTORS

Broadly speaking there are two classes of investors, those who buy shares because they are seeking income in the form of dividends and those who buy shares because they hope to make a capital gain from the resale of the shares. This latter group are known as *speculators* and they are usually described as bulls and bears. Speculators who buy in the expectation that share prices are about to rise are known as *bulls*. *Bears* sell shares, expecting their price to fall. The terms 'bullish' and 'bearish' are more generally applied to describe markets where share prices are tending to rise or fall. Pension funds and insurance companies are some of the main investors.

SHARE PRICES

Share prices are determined by demand and supply and the willingness to buy and sell is subject to many influences. The following is a brief list of some of them.

- The recent profit record of the firm and especially the recent rates of dividend paid to shareholders.
- The growth prospects of the industry in which the firm operates.
- The economic policy of the government. Changes (or proposed changes) in the system of taxation, in government spending, in monetary policy (e.g. changes in interest rates) and privatisation can have important effects on people's willingness to buy or sell shares. For example a rise in the rate of interest is likely to make saving and the purchase of government securities more attractive and buying shares less attractive.
- Rumours, and announcements, of mergers and takeover bids. Since takeover bids usually offer generous terms to the shareholders of the firm approached, the shares in that firm tend to rise in price.
- The views of advisors and commentators can persuade people to buy or sell certain shares.

FINANCING THE PUBLIC SECTOR NET CASH REQUIREMENT (PSNCR)

The government is a major borrower. If it spends more than it raises in revenue it has four possible sources of finance.

- *It can borrow from the non-bank private sector.* It can do this by, e.g., selling e.g. government securities and national saving certificates. This makes use of existing money and so does not increase the money supply. However, it is likely to add to aggregate demand as the buyers of government securities are likely to have a lower mpc than the recipients of government spending. This is the main source of finance.
- *It can borrow from the retail banks.* This adds to the money supply by increasing banks liquid assets and adds to the money supply.
- *It can borrow from the Bank of England.* This is often referred to as resorting to the printing press and again adds to the money supply and aggregate demand.
- *It can borrow from abroad.* This is the least common source of finance. It is likely to add to the money supply and aggregate demand.

INVESTMENT APPRAISAL

In deciding whether to purchase capital goods firms take into account the costs and the expected yield. In assessing the latter there are a number of methods which can be used.

- *The pay back method.* This takes into account the time it will take to repay the original investment and values more highly investment projects which pay back the original sum quickly.
- *The average rate of return.* This estimates the expected proceeds from an investment project and divides that figure by the number of years of the project to obtain an average annual rate of return.

- *Discounted cash flow.* This is a relatively common method. It is based on the idea that money received now is worth more than money obtained in the future since the money received now can be placed into a financial institution and earn interest. So in this method estimated earnings from a project are converted into present earnings by using the rate of interest. This method of discounting means that the higher the rate of interest the less valuable is a sum of money available in the future.
- *The internal rate of return.* This method works out the rate of interest needed to discount the earnings from the project to the original cost. If this internal rate of return is higher than the rate of interest which would have to be paid on borrowed money it suggests that the investment project is viable.

INTERNATIONAL FINANCIAL FLOWS

International financial flows come in two forms. One is foreign direct investment e.g. a firm opening a plant abroad and the other is foreign portfolio investment e.g. the purchase of a foreign share or placing money in a foreign bank.

INFLUENCES ON THE LEVEL OF INTERNATIONAL FINANCIAL FLOWS

These include:

- actual and expected real rates of interest at home and abroad (the real rate of interest is the nominal rate minus the rate of inflation)
- actual and expected exchange rates
- views on the risks of holding foreign assets
- government policies.

International financial flows are now very significant and countries face the risk of a capital flight which is a large and sudden withdraw of funds from a country. Some countries still have controls on the amount of money which can enter and leave the country. However, these controls tend to discourage inward investment.

QUESTIONS

SHORT QUESTIONS

1. What is meant by the real rate of interest?

2. Why are profitability and liquidity conflicting objectives for a banker?

3. Explain what is meant by money at call.

4. What is meant by the payback criteria for investment appraisal?

MULTIPLE CHOICE

1. Which of the following items, extracted from a bank's balance sheet, is the most profitable asset?

   A. Advances.

   B. Money at call.

   C. Customers' deposits.

   D. Banks' balances at the Bank of England.

2. A banking system is obliged to maintain 10% of its deposits in the form of cash and always lends out the remainder in the form of advances. If a deposit of £10m cash is made into the banking system and the public's demand for cash remains unchanged, what will be the value of the additional deposits created by bank lending?

   A. £9m
   B. £10m
   C. £90m
   D. £100m

3. A government increases its expenditure and finances this by borrowing from the non-bank private sector. What effect will this have on the money supply?

   A. Reduce it.

   B. Leave it unchanged.

   C. Raise it by an amount equal to the rise in government expenditure.

   D. Raise it by an amount greater than the rise in government expenditure.

4. Most merchant banks act as accepting houses. In doing so, what function are they carrying out?

   A. Agreeing to lend to retail banks when they are short of liquidity.

   B. Guaranteeing commercial bills.

   C. Accepting large sum deposits from the private sector.

   D. Issuing shares on behalf of existing private sector firms and newly privatised firms.

DATA RESPONSE

It is starting to look as though some people can buck the market after all. When Mahathir Mohamad, Prime Minister of Malaysia, imposed capital controls last year, he faced almost universal derision in financial markets as pundit after pundit predicted the country would slide inexorably into financial crisis.

Ridicule greeted Dr Mahathir's argument that capital controls were needed to protect Malaysia from the evil and anarchic speculators who had undermined its currency and wiped out the wealth residing in its stock market. This was the wrong way to deal with the Asian crisis, the experts said, a folly that could only have been dreamt up by a leader who had outrageously tried to blame financier George Soros and a conspiracy for his country's woes.

Nearly a year later, however, the critics are having to review their arguments. Malyasia's economy is doing well, and there is mounting evidence to suggest that the controls — involving restrictions on the repatriation of profits made by foreigners from trading shares, an end to offshore trading of the ringgit and a fixed exchange rate — have been far from the disaster they appeared. Instead of the predicted crash, foreign investment has increased, Malaysia has been able to return to borrowing through the international bond markets and forecasts put economic growth at about 2.5% this year.

Malaysian officials say that capital controls had clear and quantifiable benefits. Zeti Akhtar Aziz, deputy governor of Bank Negara, the central bank, argues that they allowed Malaysia a period of calm so that it could deal with its economic problems before it was caught up in the social dislocation and unemployment that traumatised other Asian countries.

But the costs cannot be ignored. Though its stock market has kept pace with others in the region and even outperformed some this year, Malaysia has missed the large inflows of portfolio funds that have sustained markets in the rest of Asia. The net foreign inflow of M$3.9bn (3636m) from February 1 this year to the end of June was only 2.4% of the Malaysian companies over the period.

Source: 'Shelter from the storm' by Peter Montagnon and Shelia McNulty, Financial Times, 4/8/99.

a] Explain what is meant by capital controls. **(5)**

b] Why did Malaysia impose capital controls? **(4)**

c] What effect did the imposition of capital controls have on the Malaysian economy? **(6)**

d] What is meant by portfolio funds? **(3)**

e] Discuss the factors which influence the amount of foreign investment which a country attracts. **(7)**

CASE STUDY

… many studies show that countries with independent central banks are better at keeping inflation low. The mixture of theory and evidence has been influential. *The Economist*, for instance, has long been convinced. And, more important, so have most governments — witness moves in many countries (including Britain) to make their central banks more independent, not to mention the Maastricht design of the ECB itself.

Part of the trouble is that it is genuinely difficult to define 'independence' objectively; it tends to be in the eye of the beholder, and beholders are liable to be influenced by what they know about inflation in the country concerned. At the same time, though, a variety of other, unconnected studies, do also find a correlation. It may turn out to be true after all — but Mr Forder has certainly cast doubt on the point.

What then of the underlying rationale? Here, the findings seem clearer; the orthodox story, which says that (a) independence increases credibility and (b) credibility reduces the cost of getting inflation down, is wrong. To begin with, independence does not seem to increase credibility. If it did, you would expect to see greater rigidity in the setting of nominal wages — reflecting the fact that the bank's promise to keep inflation low had been believed. Likewise, you would also expect to see greater rigidity in the setting of nominal prices. According to research on 17 OECD countries using data from 1950 to 1989, by Adam Posen of the Institute of International Economics, you see neither. Moreover turning from (a) by itself to (a) and (b) taken together, independence not merely fails to reduce the cost of disinflation, it actually seems to increase it. On average, getting inflation down takes as long and calls for a bigger 'sacrifice' of output and jobs in countries with relatively independent central banks.

As before, the problem may lie in getting the definition of independence right. But suppose, for now, that central bank independence is correlated with low inflation and that credibility is not the reason why. The question would then be: how does independence come to have this inflation reducing effect? There are several possibilities. One is correlation without causation; perhaps independence and low inflation are jointly the result of some third factor, such as society's willingness to tolerate high inflation. Or the causation could be genuine after all. Perhaps central bankers are more far-sighted than politicians — or (whisper it softly) less concerned about unemployment. Independence might then lead to lower inflation, even if central bankers' promises were no better believed than politicians.

Source: 'Born Free', The Economist, 27/2/99.

a] What is the ECB? **(2)**

b] Discuss three functions of a central bank. **(6)**

c] Explain how giving the Bank of England greater independence has 'changed the way monetary policy is conducted'. **(5)**

d] How independent is the Bank of England? **(6)**

e] Explain why independence may increase credibility? **(6)**

f] Why might credibility reduce the cost of getting inflation down? **(7)**

g] Discuss why central banks might be more far sighted than politicians and less concerned about unemployment? **(9)**

h] Discuss the relationship between retails banks and inflation. **(9)**

STRUCTURED ESSAY

a] Explain how retail banks can create money. **(12)**

b] Discuss the factors that influence the amount of money they can create. **(13)**

FREE RESPONSE ESSAY

Discuss the functions of the Bank of England and two other financial intermediaries that operate in the UK. **(25)**

GLOSSARY

absolute advantage ability to produce a product with fewer resources than another country, region, firm or person

accelerator theory the principle that a change in the rate of growth will cause a greater percentage change in net investment

ad valorem subsidy a subsidy granted as a percentage of price

ad valorem tax tax levied as a percentage of price

aggregate demand total planned spending at a given price level

aggregate supply total output all firms are willing and able to supply at a given price level

allocative efficiency devoting the appropriate quantity of resources to producing a product, achieved where MC = AR

average cost total cost divided by output, also called unit cost

average product output per factor of production

average propensity to consume proportion of disposable income which is spent

average propensity to save proportion of disposable income which is saved

average revenue total revenue divided by output

automatic stabilisers forms of government spending and taxation that move in the opposite direction to the business cycle

balance of payments a record of a country's trade and financial transactions with other countries

barriers to entry and exit restrictions on the entry and exit of new firms into a market

behavioural theories the view that groups connected with a firm have a variety of objectives for a firm

bilateral monopoly a monopoly facing a monopsonist

black economy undeclared economic activity

business cycles fluctuations in economic activity

capital goods products which produce other goods and services

cartel a group of countries or firms which collude to fix output and price in order to increase profits

circular flow of income the flow of income and expenditure between households, firms and the government

collusion firms agreeing to restrict competition

comparative advantage ability to produce a product at a lower opportunity cost than other countries, regions, firms or people

Competition Commission a government body which investigates existing and potential monopoly situations

complements products which are bought to be used together

composite demand products which are bought for a variety of uses

conglomerate integration a merger between two firms making different products

consumer goods products which satisfy people's wants directly

consumer sovereignty consumers' ability to determine what is produced by means of their purchases

consumer surplus the extra amount that consumers would be prepared to pay for a product over what they actually pay

contestable market a market with no barriers to entry or exit

cost benefit analysis a method of assessing investment projects which takes into account social costs and benefits

cost push inflation rises in the general price level resulting from increases in the costs of production

credit creation the process whereby banks increase the money supply by making loans

cross elasticity of demand a measure of the responsiveness of demand for one product to changes in the price of another product

cyclical unemployment unemployment resulting from a lack of aggregate demand

demand ability and willingness to buy a product

demand pull inflation increases in the general price level resulting from increases in aggregate demand

demand-side policies government policies designed to influence aggregate demand

demerit goods products which the government regards as harmful and which will be over-consumed if left to market forces

deregulation the removal of laws and regulations which restrict competition

diminishing returns additions of a variable factor of production result in a fall in marginal product

direct taxes taxes on income or wealth

diseconomies of scale the disadvantages, in the form of higher average costs of production, of producing on a larger scale

disequilibrium unemployment unemployment arising from aggregate supply of labour exceeding aggregate demand at the going wage rate

disposable income income after the deduction of direct taxes and the addition of state benefits

division of labour the specialisation of workers on particular tasks in the production process

economic development improvements in the quality of life of a country's population

economic goods products which use resources to produce them

economies of scale the advantages of producing on a large scale in the form of lower average costs

economic rent payment above that necessary to keep a factor of production in its current use

elasticity of demand a measure of the responsiveness of demand to a change in a key influence on demand

equilibrium a situation of balance where there is no tendency for change

equilibrium unemployment unemployment which arises when the aggregate demand and aggregate supply of labour are equal. It consists of frictional and structural unemployment and is equivalent to NAIRU

external benefits beneficial effects on third parties for which they do not pay

external costs harmful effects on third parties for which they do not get compensated

factors of production the economic resources of land, labour, capital and the entrepreneur used to produce goods and services

fiscal drag a reduction in disposable income which results from inflation dragging people's income into higher tax brackets

fiscal policy government policy on spending and taxation

fixed costs costs which do not change when output changes

fixed exchange rate an exchange rate which is pegged at a given rate and maintained by government intervention

floating exchange rate an exchange rate determined by market forces

free goods products that do not require resources to produce them

frictional unemployment unemployment which arises when workers are in between jobs

game theory the theory that the behaviour of oligopolists is influenced by assumptions about the reactions of their rivals

Giffen goods low quality products that have negative income elasticity of demand and positive price elasticity of demand

globalisation the increased integration of economies throughout the world

Goodhart's law the view that any measure of the money supply the government targets will start to behave differently as a result of being targeted

gross domestic product total output produced in a country

gross investment total investment including extra and replacement capital goods

HDI human development index – a composite index based on GDP per head, life expectancy and educational attainment

HICP harmonised index of consumer prices – a weighted price index used in the EU

horizontal integration the merger of firms producing the same product and at the stage of production

HPI human poverty index – a composite index of poverty which reflects the distribution of progress and measures the backlog of deprivation that still exists

human capital education, training and skills which increase the productivity of labour

hysteresis unemployment generating unemployment by reducing the confidence and up-to-dateness of the skills of the unemployed

immobility barriers to the mobility of factors of production

income elasticity of demand a measure of the responsiveness of demand to a change in income

indirect taxes taxes on spending

inferior goods products with negative income elasticity of demand

inflation a persistent rise in the general price level

injections spending on domestic output which occurs outside the circular flow of income

interest the price for borrowing and the reward for lending

J curve effect the tendency for a devaluation to worsen the current account of the balance of payments before it improves it

Keynesians a group of economists who follow the ideas of John Maynard Keynes. They believe that market failure is a significant problem and that government intervention can improve the situation

kinked demand curve a diagram which suggests that oligopolists will be reluctant to change price since competitors will not usually follow price rises but will follow price cuts

labour market failure imperfections in labour markets resulting in a misallocation of labour resources and wage rates being above or below equilibrium

Laffer curve a diagram which suggests that cuts in high tax rates can increase tax revenue

limit pricing setting price with the intention of discouraging the entry of new firms

liquidity the ease with which an asset can be changed into cash quickly and without loss

liquidity preference theory the theory that the rate of interest is determined by the demand and supply of money

managed exchange rate an exchange rate system in which a government or pan-government organisation allows the exchange rate to move within margins

marginal cost change in total cost when one more unit is produced

marginal efficiency of capital expected yield from investment

marginal product change in total output resulting from the employment of one more unit of a variable product

marginal propensity to consume proportion of extra income that is spent

marginal propensity to import proportion of extra income that is spent on imports

marginal propensity to save proportion of extra income that is saved

marginal rate of tax proportion of extra income that is taxed

marginal revenue change in total revenue resulting from selling one more unit

marginal revenue product the increase in revenue a firm gains from selling the output of an extra unit of a factor of production

marginal utility change in total utility resulting from the consumption of one more unit

market economy an economy in which consumers determine what is produced and resources are owned by individuals and groups of individuals

market failure the failure of market forces to achieve an efficient allocation of resources

marketable wealth items of wealth which can be transferred to another person

Marshall-Lerner condition the requirement for the price elasticity of demand for exports and imports to be greater than one for devaluation to improve the current account position

menu costs costs involved in having to change prices as a result of inflation

merit goods products which the government regards as beneficial and which will be under-consumed if left to market forces

mixed economy an economy with a private and public sector

monetarists a group of economists who believe that changes in the money supply have a significant impact on an economy and that excessive growth of the money supply causes inflation

monetary policy changes in the rate of interest, money supply and the exchange rate

Monetary Policy Committee a committee of the Bank of England that determines the rate of interest

money items which are generally acceptable in exchange for goods and services

monopolistic competition a market structure in which there are a large number of firms producing a slightly differentiated product

monopoly a single supplier of a product, or according to the government's definition a firm with 25% or more share of the market

monopsony sole buyer

multiplier the ratio of a change in income resulting from a change in an injection

MNCs multinational companies which are firms with plants in more than one country

NAIRU the non-accelerating inflation rate of unemployment. The rate of unemployment that exists when the labour market is in equilibrium and at which the rate of inflation is stable. Also called the natural rate

nationalisation taking private sector firms into state ownership

natural monopoly a market in which there is room for only one firm to produce at minimum efficient scale

negative externalities equivalent to external costs

net exports exports minus imports

net investment gross investment minus depreciation

new classical economists a group of economists who believe that markets usually work efficiently

normal goods goods with positive income elasticity of demand

normal profit minimum level of profit needed to keep a firm in the industry in the long run

oligopoly a market structure dominated by a few large firms

oligopsony a market with a few dominant buyers

open market operations the purchase and sale of government securities by a central bank to influence the money supply

opportunity cost cost in terms of the best alternative forgone

paradox of thrift a situation where the decision to save more, by reducing income, results in a fall in saving

Pareto efficiency where it is not possible to change the existing allocation of resources in such a way that someone is made better off without making someone else worse off

perfect competition a market structure with no barriers to entry and exit, consisting of many firms producing an homogeneous product

Phillips curve a diagram showing the relationship between unemployment and inflation and which suggests a trade off between the two

planned economy an economy where the government makes the decisions on what to produce

positive externalities equivalent to external benefits

predatory pricing setting price low enough to drive competitors out of the market

price discrimination charging different prices to different groups of consumers for the same product

price elasticity of demand a measure of the responsiveness of demand to a change in the price of the product

price elasticity of supply a measure of the responsiveness of supply to a change in the price of the product

private benefits benefits received by those who produce or consume a product

private costs costs incurred by those who produce or consume a product

privatisation transfer of assets from the public to the private sector

production possibility curve a diagram showing the maximum combination of the output of two types of products with a given level of resources and technology

productive efficiency when it is not possible to produce more of one product without producing one less of another product; where output is produced at lowest average cost

productivity output per factor of production

profit maximisation achieving the highest level of profit possible by producing where MC = MR

profit satisficing aiming for a satisfactory level of profits which will keep shareholders happy

progressive taxes taxes that take a greater percentage of the income of the rich

proportional taxes taxes that take the same percentage of the income of all income groups

protectionism restriction of international trade

public goods products that are non-rival and non-excludable and have to be financed by taxation

public sector net cash requirement the amount the government has to borrow to cover the gap between government expenditure and tax revenue

Quantity theory the view that changes in the money supply will cause equal percentage changes in the price level

regressive taxes taxes that take a greater percentage of the income of the poor

regulatory capture a regulator acting in the interest of the industry rather than in the interest of the consumers

relative price price of a product in comparison to the price of another product

restrictive practices anti-competitive behaviour of a firm or groups of firms

Retail Price Index a weighted measure of changes in consumer prices

returns to scale changes in output resulting from increases in the quantity of factors of production employed

RPIX underlying rate of inflation (RPI minus mortgage interest payments)

RPIY core rate of inflation (RPIX minus indirect taxes)

sales revenue maximisation achieving the highest level of revenue by producing where MR = 0

saving income minus consumption

scarcity resources being insufficient to satisfy all of people's wants

Schumpeter's theory of creative destruction the idea that monopolies encourage innovation. To enter and gain control of a monopoly market, a firm has to develop a superior product

social benefit the total benefit to society of the production or consumption of a product – it is equal to private plus external benefit

social cost the total cost to society of the production or consumption of a product – it is equal to private plus external cost

socially optimum output an output where MSC = MSB

specialisation concentration on particular tasks or products

structural unemployment unemployment that results from changes in the structure of industry due to changes in demand and supply conditions

subsidies payments to encourage production or consumption

substitutes products which are seen as alternatives to each other. They are in competitive demand

supernormal profit profit above the normal profit level. It is earned where AR exceeds AC

supply willingness and ability to sell a product

supply-side policies policies designed to increase the economy's long term growth potential

sustainable economic growth economic growth achieved in a way that does not endanger the country's ability to achieve economic growth in the future

tariffs taxes on imports

terms of trade ratio of export prices to import prices

Tinbergen's rule the view that a government should have at least one instrument for each of its objectives

trade blocs groupings of countries with preferential trading arrangements

transfer earnings minimum payment required to keep a factor of production in its current use

transfer payments money transferred from one group to another not in return for providing a good or service

utility satisfaction gained from the consumption of a product

variable costs costs that change with output

Veblen goods products with positive price elasticity of demand purchased to show how wealthy the buyers are

velocity of circulation the number of times money changes hands

vertical integration the merger of firms at different stages of production

welfare loss output where MSC is not equal to MSB

withdrawals parts of income which are not passed on in the circular flow of income (also known as leakages)

X-efficiency output where marginal and average cost are as low as possible

INDEX

ACKNOWLEDGEMENTS

We are grateful to the following for permission to reproduce copyright material:

the author, Greg Dyke, for an extract from his article 'Centre for best practice could straighten twisted economics' in THE TIMES 16.2.99; The Economist Newspaper Limited for extracts from the articles 'Messing with money' in THE ECONOMIST 25.7.98, 'State and market schools brief' in THE ECONOMIST 12.9.98, 'The new danger' in THE ECONOMIST 20.2.99, 'Born free' in THE ECONOMIST 27.2.99, 'The corporate-growth puzzle' in THE ECONOMIST 17.7.99 and 'Helping the poorest' in THE ECONOMIST 14.8.99 and for figures 'Statistics for North and South Korea' in THE ECONOMIST 10.7.99, 'The economies of south-east Asia, November 1998', in THE ECONOMIST 19.12.98, and 'A comparison of different countries' growth rates' in THE ECONOMIST 4.9.99 © The Economist, London 1998, 1999; European Economic Research Ltd for an extract from a job advertisement placed in THE ECONOMIST 12.6.99; Financial Times Ltd for extracts from the articles 'Business wakes up to the end of working nine to five' by Christopher Adams in FINANCIAL TIMES 26.3.99, 'From cowboy to hero' by Kevin Brown in FINANCIAL TIMES 21.5.99 and 'Employees lack adequate training' by John Williams in FINANCIAL TIMES 16.6.99; Guardian News Service Ltd for extracts from the articles 'Age is no bar to success' by John Dunn in THE GUARDIAN 27.4.99 © John Dunn, 'Who recycles the most waste?' by Divya Kohli in THE GUARDIAN 20.5.99 © Divya Kholi, 'Car trouble' by Sue Flook in THE GUARDIAN 21.5.99 © Sue Flook, 'Economists fail to meet demand' by Stephen Machin and Andrew Oswald in THE GUARDIAN 5.7.99 © Stephen Machin & Andrew Oswald, 'The new poor' by Neil McIntosh in THE GUARDIAN 22.7.99 ©Neil McIntosh, 'Organic food outgrows its image with huge rise in demand' by John Vidal and Martin Wainwright in THE GUARDIAN 8.1.99, 'Superspan faces his toughest test' by Christopher Muhne in THE GUARDIAN 23.1.99, 'Claimants at gateway to new culture' by Lucy Ward in THE GUARDIAN 11.2.99, 'OFT inquiry into health insurers' by Don Atkinson in THE GUARDIAN 12.2.99, 'Firms fight ageism' by Laurie Laird in THE GUARDIAN 4.5.99, 'Stakeholding BAA seeks neighbourly trust' by Roger Cowe in THE GUARDIAN 17.5.99, 'Brown plays down surplus in budget' by Mark Atkinson in THE GUARDIAN 21.5.99, 'Economy grinds to a halt' by Charlotte Denny in THE GUARDIAN 25.5.99, 'Trance needn't cost the earth' by David Bellamy in THE GUARDIAN 27.6.99, 'One in 4 QCs earn over 1/4m' by Clare Dyer, 'Black economy booms as crooks eye a nice little earner' by Peter Hetherington and 'Average full-time pay passes £20,000 mark' by Seumas Milne in THE GUARDIAN 5.7.99, 'Post office delivers prices warning' by David Gow in THE GUARDIAN 15.7.99, 'Jobless facts counter inflation theory' by Larry Elliott in THE GUARDIAN 15.7.99, 'Top pay rises by 26%' by Lisa Buckingham and Julia Finch in THE GUARDIAN 19.7.99, 'Blunkett vows to bring back full employment' by Charlotte Denny in THE GUARDIAN 12.8.99, 'Rising tax revenues and lower social security spending point to £10bn surplus' by Mark Atkinson in THE GUARDIAN 18.8.99 and 'The big spenders who make all of us poorer' by Robert Frank in THE OBSERVER 16.5.99, © The Guardian 1999; Controller of Her Majesty's Stationery Office for an extract from the leaflet 'Flexibility of Employment'; Independent Newspapers (UK) Ltd for extracts from the articles 'What if Japan pulls the plug on the US deficit?' by Hamish McRae in THE INDEPENDENT 7.1.99, 'Today, two million will be better paid' by Barrie Clement in THE INDEPENDENT 1.3.99,

'Still a case of vive la difference in EU' by Len Pateson in THE INDEPENDENT BUDGET REVIEW 10.3.99, 'Children learn lack of ambition as inequality triples in 30 years' by Cherry Norton in THE INDEPENDENT 29.3.99, 'Old-style financial services at risk from new methods' by Barrie Clement in THE INDEPENDENT 21.5.99, 'Greenspan hints at pre-emptive rate rise' by Andrew Marshall in THE INDEPENDENT 18.6.99, 'Named: the factories that pollute rivers' by Charles Arthur and 'Job fears keep retail spending under control' by Philys Thornton in THE INDEPENDENT 22.6.99, 'End of guns-to-buns group sounds the last post for the big conglomerates' by Nigel Cope in THE INDEPENDENT 13.7.99, 'UK slips down the productivity league' by Diane Coyle in THE INDEPENDENT 16.8.99 and 'United all over the World' by Nigel Cope in THE INDEPENDENT 28.7.99; Mirror Group Newspapers Ltd for an extract from the article 'Chunkaholics' by Robert Hutton in the DAILY MIRROR 1.6.99; News International Syndication Ltd for extracts from the articles 'Doing it by the book' by David Smith in the SUNDAY TIMES 7.2.99, 'Brown's magic moment' by David Smith in the SUNDAY TIMES 23.5.99, 'Mind the ballooning trade gaps' by David Smith in the SUNDAY TIMES 30.5.99 and 'Euro counterfeiters will forge ahead' by Jon Ashworth in THE TIMES 15.7.99; Solo Syndication for an extract from the article 'House prices: is this the 80s again?' by Sean Poulter in DAILY MAIL 4.8.99; the National Institute for Economic and Social Research for figures 'Real household disposable income 1995-2001' in NATIONAL INSTITUTE ECONOMIC REVIEW July 1999, 'Unemployment figures 1991-7' in NATIONAL INSTITUTE ECONOMIC REVIEW October 1998 and 'Japanese economy 1995-9' in NATIONAL INSTITUTE ECONOMIC REVIEW April 1999; Office for National Statistics for figures 'Highest and lowest paid occupations, Great Britain April 1998' in NEW EARNINGS SURVEY 1998, 'Trade Union membership, working days lost in stoppages and UK unemployment' from LABOUR MARKET TRENDS May 1996 and April 1999 and ANNUAL ABSTRACT OF STATISTICS 1998, 'Average gross weekly earnings per occupation' in NEW EARNINGS SURVEY 1995, 'Time use by economic activity status and gender', 'UK distribution of wealth', 'Income distribution in the UK' and 'Redistribution of UK income through taxes and benefits' in SOCIAL TRENDS 28 1998, 'UK's main trading partners' and 'UK balance of payments' in MONTHLY DIGEST OF STATISTICS April 1999, 'UK balance of payments in 1996', 'Summary of balance of payments in 1997' and 'Sterling and dollar exchange rates' in UNITED KINGDOM BALANCE OF PAYMENTS 1998 © Crown Copyright 1996, 1998, 1999.

We have been unable to trace the copyright holder of the article 'Why spending is a taxing question' by Stephen Bell and would appreciate any information which would enable us to do so.

We are grateful to the following for permission to reproduce copyright photographs:

Katz Pictures/S Henry/SABA for page 6; Camera Press London/Sue Adler for page 69; Rex Features Ltd for page 135; Popperfoto Ltd/AFP/Henry Ray Abrams for page 221; Rex Features/Justin Williams for page 317; Camera Press/David Sillitoe for page 354; Rex Features for page 405; Rex Features/Consolidated News for page 473; Popperfoto/Stewart Kendall for page 522; UNDP for page 618.